EXPERIENCES

in

MATH

for Young Children

EXPERIENCES

in

MATH

for Young Children

Sixth Edition

Rosalind Charlesworth

Weber State University

WADSWORTH
CENGAGE Learning·

Australia • Brazil • Japan • Korea • Mexico • Singapore • Spain • United Kingdom • United States

WADSWORTH
CENGAGE Learning™

Experiences in Math for Young Children, Sixth Edition
Rosalind Charlesworth

Publisher/Executive Editor: Linda
　Schreiber-Ganster

Acquisitions Editor: Mark Kerr

Assistant Editor: Caitlin Cox

Marketing Manager: Kara Kindstrom Parsons

Marketing Communications Manager:
　Martha Pfeiffer

Content Project Management: PreMediaGlobal

Art Director: Jennifer Wahi

Senior Print Buyer: Paula Vang

Rights Acquisition Specialist: Don Schlotman

Production House/Compositor:
　PreMediaGlobal

Cover Designer: Natalie Hill

For product information and technology assistance, contact us at
Cengage Learning Customer & Sales Support, 1-800-354-9706

For permission to use material from this text or product,
submit all requests online at **www.cengage.com/permissions**
Further permissions questions can be emailed to
permissionrequest@cengage.com

International Edition:

ISBN-13: 978-1-111-35579-1

ISBN-10: 1-111-35579-7

Cengage Learning International Offices

Asia
www.cengageasia.com
tel: (65) 6410 1200

India
www.cengage.co.in
tel: (91) 11 4364 1111

Australia/New Zealand
www.cengage.com.au
tel: (61) 3 9685 4111

Latin America
www.cengage.com.mx
tel: (52) 55 1500 6000

Brazil
www.cengage.com.br
tel: (55) 11 3665 9900

UK/Europe/Middle East/Africa
www.cengage.co.uk
tel: (44) 0 1264 332 424

Represented in Canada by
Nelson Education, Ltd.
tel: (416) 752 9100 / (800) 668 0671
www.nelson.com

Cengage Learning is a leading provider of customized learning solutions with office locations around the globe, including Singapore, the United Kingdom, Australia, Mexico, Brazil, and Japan. Locate your local office at: **www.cengage.com/global**

For product information: **www.cengage.com/international**
Visit your local office: **www.cengage.com/global**
Visit our corporate website: **www.cengage.com**

AVAILABILITY OF RESOURCES MAY DIFFER BY REGION. Check with your local Cengage Learning representative for details.

Printed in the United States of America
1 2 3 4 5 6 7 14 13 12 11 10

DEDICATION

This book is dedicated to:
the memory of a dear friend
ADA DAWSON STEPHENS

—R. Charlesworth

Contents

APPENDICES

Preface

Experiences in Math for Young Children, Sixth Edition, is designed to be used by students in training and teachers in service in early childhood education. To the student, it introduces the excitement and extensiveness of math experiences in programs for young children. For teachers in the field, it presents an organized, sequential approach to creating a developmentally appropriate math curriculum for preschool and primary school children. Further, it is designed in line with the guidelines and standards of the major professional organizations: NAEYC and NCTM.

Activities are presented in a developmental sequence designed to support young children's construction of concepts and skills essential to a basic understanding of mathematics. A developmentally appropriate approach to assessment is stressed in order to have an individualized program in which each child is presented at each level with tasks that can be accomplished successfully before moving on to the next level.

A further emphasis is placed on three types of learning: naturalistic, informal, and adult guided. Much learning can take place through the child's natural exploratory activities if the environment is designed to promote such activity. The adult can reinforce and enrich this naturalistic learning by careful introduction of information through developmentally appropriate learning experiences.

The test-driven practices currently reemerging produce a widespread use of inappropriate instructional practices with young children. Mathematics for preschoolers has been taught as "pre-math," apparently under the assumption that math learning begins only with addition and subtraction in the primary grades. It also has been taught in both preschool and primary school as rote memory material using abstract paper and pencil activities. This revision emphasizes the recognition by NCTM of the inclusion of the pre-K level in the revised mathematics principles and standards (NCTM, 2000). This text is designed to bring to the attention of early childhood educators the necessity of providing young children with opportunities to explore concretely this domain of early concept learning. Integration is stressed with language arts, science, social studies, art, and music with the goal of providing a totally integrated program.

New to this Edition

- Expansion of theoretical foundation with addition of the views of Bruner and Dienes.
- Added a description of Polya's contributions to mathematics instruction.
- Expanded discussion of traditional vs. reform instruction.
- Included reference to the National Research Council early childhood mathematics report and the NCTM Focal Points.
- Included a technology box in each concept unit.
- Added new references — including Marshal's 2006 article on number sense and

Fosnot and Cameron — and updated Further Reading sections.

- Included material on instruction for special needs students, including learning disabilities, ELL, and more.
- Special needs material: learning disabilities, ELL, etc. added in each unit
- Enhanced with photos and children's work samples.
- Changed "structured" lessons to "adult guided"

Major Unit-Specific Changes

Unit 1

- Added coverage of Bruner and Dienes, play, new DAP revision
- Introduced Discrete Mathematics
- Expanded traditional vs. reform discussion
- Included research report by NRC

Unit 2

- Updated equity coverage

Unit 3

- Added coverage of Intentional Teacher, Polya's contributions to mathematics instruction, Sudoku
- Increased coverage of analysis of problem solving process

Unit 4

- Added NAEYC position statement and cultural aspects of assessment

Unit 7

- Placed caution on *Baby Einstein* materials and the controversy over their value

Unit 9

- Added examples of children with unit blocks, LEGO, pattern blocks, and puzzles.

Unit 11

- Added culture and food

Unit 20

- Added student work samples and design technology examples

Unit 21

- Added three student work samples and relation of addition and subtraction

Unit 22

- 0-99 chart was replaced with 1–100
- Noted that sequences of patterns need to not be broken up

Unit 23

- Increased geoboard material

Unit 25

- Added STEM and child's graph examples
- Expanded Algebra

Unit 26

- Increased information on analog clocks
- Added child's list of chores

Unit 27

- added material on concete materials
- updated technology section

Unit 29

- added material to Family Math section
- edited and added to childrens'/parents' activities

Online Instructor's Manual

The Online instructor's manual provides suggestions for course organization, introductory activities, multiple choice questions, and answers to Unit Reviews.

References

NCTM. (2000). *Principles and standards for school mathematics*. Reston, VA: National Council of Teachers of Mathematics.

NCTM. (2007). *Curriculum Focal Points*. Reston, VA: National Council of Teachers of Mathematics.

The authors and Cengage Learning make every effort to ensure that all internet resources are accurate at the time of printing. However, due to the fluid, time-sensitive nature of the internet, we cannot guarantee that all URLs and website addresses will remain current for the duration of this edition.

Acknowledgments

The author wishes to express her appreciation to the following individuals and Early Childhood Development Centers:

- Dee Radeloff, for her collaboration in the writing of the first edition of *Experiences in Math for Young Children,* which served as the starting point for this book.
- Kate Charlesworth, for her tolerance of her mother's writing endeavors and Summer Sky Potter for her contributions of anecdotes and work samples.
- Gaile Clement, for sharing her knowledge and expertise in the area of portfolio assessment with Dr. Charlesworth.
- The 30 East Baton Rouge Parish, Louisiana, K-3 teachers who participated in a six-week summer Mathematics/Child Development in-service workshop and to the other workshop faculty, Thelamese Porter, Robert Perlis, and Colonel Johnson, all of whom provided enrichment to Dr. Charlesworth's view of mathematics for young children.
- The following teachers who provided a place for observation and/or cooperated with our efforts to obtain photographs:

  Lois Rector, Kathy Tonore, Lynn Morrison, and Nancy Crom (LSU Laboratory Elementary School), Joan Benedict (LSU Laboratory Preschool), Nancy Miller, and Candy Jones, (East Baton Rouge Parish Public Schools) and 30 East Baton Rouge Parish School System K-3 teachers and their students, and Jill Gibson and Jill Carver (kindergarten teachers, Ogden, Utah Public Schools).

- The staff of Wadsworth/Cengage Learning for their patience and understanding throughout this project.

The following reviewers who provided valuable ideas:

Barbara Cozza,
University of Scranton

Frank D'Angelo,
Bloomsburg University

Mary Fitzgerald,
University of Tennessee – Knoxville

Jeff Gelfer,
University of Nevada – Las Vegas

Wanda Gilbert,
Stanly Community College

Debra Pierce,
Ivy Tech Community College

About the Author

Rosalind Charlesworth is professor emerita and retired department chair in the Department of Child and Family Studies at Weber State University in Ogden, Utah. During her tenure at Weber State University, she worked with the faculty of the Department of Teacher Education to develop continuity from preprimary to primary school in the program for students in the early childhood education licensure program. She also contributed to the Elementary Mathematics Methods class.

Dr. Charlesworth's career in early childhood education has included experiences with both typical and atypical young children in laboratory schools, public schools, and day care and through research in social and cognitive development and behavior. She is also known for her contributions to research on early childhood teachers' beliefs and practices. She taught courses in early education and child development at other universities before joining the faculty at Weber State University. In 1995 she was named the Outstanding Graduate of the University of Toledo College of Education and Allied Professions. In 1999, she was the co-recipient of the NAECTE/Allyn & Bacon Outstanding Early Childhood Teacher Educator award. She is the author of the popular Delmar text *Understanding Child Development,* has published many articles in professional journals, and gives presentations regularly at major professional meetings. Dr. Charlesworth has provided service to the field through active involvement in professional organizations. She has been a member of the NAEYC Early Childhood Teacher Education Panel, a consulting editor for *Early Childhood Research Quarterly,* and a member of the NAECTE (National Association of Early Childhood Teacher Educators) Public Policy and Long-Range Planning Committees. She served two terms on the NAECTE board as regional representative and one as vice-president for membership. She was twice elected treasurer and was also elected as newsletter editor of the Early Childhood/Child Development Special Interest Group of the American Educational Research Association (AERA), is past president of the Louisiana Early Childhood Association, and was a member of the editorial board of the Southern Early Childhood Association journal *Dimensions.* She is currently on the editorial board of the *Early Childhood Education Journal.*

Concept Development in Mathematics

How Concepts Develop in Mathematics

After reading this unit, you should be able to:

- Define concept development.
- List the major elements of early childhood mathematics.
- Explain the purpose of the principles for school mathematics.
- Understand the importance of professional standards for mathematics.
- Describe the purpose of focal points.
- Label examples of Piaget's developmental stages of thought.
- Compare Piaget's and Vygotsky's theories of mental development.
- Identify conserving and nonconserving behaviors, and state why conservation is an important developmental task.
- Explain how concepts develop.
- Describe the relationship between reform and constructivist mathematics instruction.

Early childhood is a period when children actively engage in acquiring fundamental concepts and learning fundamental **process skills**. **Concepts** are the building blocks of knowledge; they allow people to organize and categorize information. Concepts can be applied to the solution of new problems that are met in everyday experience. As we watch children in their everyday activities, we can observe them constructing and using concepts. Some examples are the following:

- *One-to-one correspondence.* Passing apples, one to each child at a table; putting pegs in pegboard holes; putting a car in each garage built from blocks.
- *Counting.* Counting the pennies from a penny bank, the number of straws needed

for the children at a table, or the number of rocks in a rock collection.

- *Classifying.* Placing square shapes in one pile and round shapes in another; putting cars in one garage and trucks in another.
- *Measuring.* Pouring sand, water, rice, or other materials from one container to another.

As you proceed through this text, you will learn how young children begin to construct many concepts during the **preprimary** period (the years before children enter first grade). They also develop processes that enable them to apply their newly acquired concepts and to enlarge current concepts and develop new ones.

During the preprimary period, children learn and begin to apply concepts basic to mathematics. As children enter the **primary** period (grades 1–3), they apply these early basic concepts to explore and help them understand the operations of addition, subtraction, multiplication, and division as well as mathematical concepts such as measurement, geometry, and algebra.

As young children grow and develop physically, socially, and mentally, their concepts also grow and develop. **Development** refers to changes that take place due to growth and experience. It follows an individual timetable for each child. Development is a series or sequence of steps that each child reaches one at a time. Different children of the same age may be weeks, months, or even a year or two apart in reaching certain stages and still be within the normal range of development. This text examines how children develop concepts in math from birth through the primary grades. For an overview of this development sequence, see Figure 1–1.

Period	Section II Fundamental	Section III Applied	Section IV Higher Level	Section V Primary
Sensorimotor (Birth to age 2)	Observation Problem solving One-to-one correspondence Number Shape Spatial sense			
Preoperational (2 to 7 years)	Sets and classifying Comparing Counting Parts and wholes Language	Ordering, seriation, patterning Informal measurement: Weight Length Temperature Volume Time Sequence Graphing	Number symbols Sets and symbols Concrete addition and subtraction	
Transitional (5 to 7 years) Concrete operations (7 to 11 years)				Whole number operations Fractions Number facts Place value Geometry Measurement with standard units

Concepts and Skills: Beginning Points for Understanding

FIGURE 1–1 The development of math concepts and process skills.

Concept growth and development begins in infancy. Babies explore the world with their **senses**. They look, touch, smell, hear, and taste. Children are born curious; they want to know all about their environment. Babies begin to learn ideas of size, weight, shape, time, and space. As they look about, they sense their relative smallness. They grasp things and find that some fit in their tiny hands and others do not. Infants learn about weight when items of the same size cannot always be lifted. They learn about shape when some things stay where they put them, whereas others roll away. Children learn time sequence. When they wake up, they feel wet and hungry and they cry. The caretaker comes and changes and then feeds them. Next they play, get tired, and go to bed to sleep. As infants begin to move, they develop spatial sense. They are placed in a crib, in a playpen, or on the floor in the center of the living room. As babies first look and then move, they discover space. Some spaces are big, some are small.

As infants crawl and creep to explore their environment, they develop a concept of space.

As children learn to crawl, stand, and walk, they are free to discover more on their own and learn to think for themselves. They hold and examine more things. They go over, under, and inside large objects and discover their size relative to them. Toddlers sort things. They put things in piles—of the same color, the same size, the same shape, or with the same use. Young children pour sand and water into containers of different sizes. They pile blocks into tall structures and see them fall and become small parts again. They buy food at a play store and pay with play money. As children cook imaginary food, they measure imaginary flour, salt, and milk. They set the table in their play kitchen, putting one of everything at each place just as is done at home. Their free exploring and experimentation in the first two years provide opportunity for the development of muscle coordination and the senses of taste, smell, sight, and hearing. Children need these skills as a basis for their future learning.

As young children leave toddlerhood and enter the preschool and kindergarten levels of the preprimary period, exploration continues to be the first step in dealing with new situations; at this time, however, they also begin to apply basic concepts to collecting and organizing data to answer a question. Collecting data requires skills in observation, counting, recording, and organizing. For example, for a science investigation, kindergartners might be interested in the process of plant growth. Supplied with lima bean seeds, wet paper towels, and glass jars, the children place the seeds in the jars where they are held against the sides with wet paper towels. Each day they add water as needed and observe the seeds. They dictate their observations to their teacher, who records them on a chart. Each child also plants some beans in dirt in a small container such as a paper or plastic cup. The teacher supplies each child with a chart for his bean garden. The children check off each day on their charts until they see a sprout (Figure 1–2). Then they count how many days it took for a sprout to appear; they compare this number with those of the other class members and also with the time it takes for the seeds in the glass jars to sprout. Thus, the children have used the concepts of number and counting, one-to-one correspondence, time, and

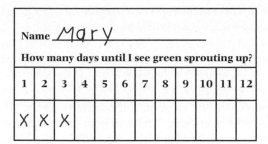

FIGURE 1–2 Mary records each day that passes until her bean seed sprouts.

comparison of the number of items in two groups. Primary children might attack the same problem but can operate more independently and record more information, use standard measuring tools (i.e., rulers), and do background reading on their own. References that provide development guidelines charts for mathematics instruction include Clements and Sarama (2003, 2004), Geist (2001), and "Learning PATHS" (2003).

Children learn through hands-on experience.

Principles and Standards for School Mathematics

In 1987, the National Association for the Education of Young Children (NAEYC) published *Developmentally Appropriate Practice in Early Childhood Programs Serving Children from Birth through Age Eight* (Bredekamp, 1987) as a guide

for early childhood instruction. In 1997, NAEYC published a revised set of guidelines (Bredekamp & Copple, 1997). In 2009 it published a further revision of the *Developmentally Appropriate Practice guidelines* (Copple & Bredekamp, 2009). In 1989, the National Council of Teachers of Mathematics (NCTM) published standards for kindergarten through grade 12 mathematics curriculum, evaluation, and teaching. Two others followed this publication: *Professional Standards for Teaching Mathematics* (1991) and *Assessment Standards for School Mathematics* (1995). In 2000, based on an evaluation and review of the previous standards' publications, NCTM published *Principles and Standards for School Mathematics*. A major change in the age and grade category levels is the inclusion of preschool. The first level is now prekindergarten (pre-K) through grade 2. It is important to recognize that preschoolers have an informal knowledge of mathematics that can be built on and reinforced. However, one must keep in mind that, as with older children, not all preschoolers will enter school with equivalent knowledge and capabilities. During the preschool years, young children's natural curiosity and eagerness to learn can be exploited to develop a joy and excitement in learning and applying mathematics concepts and skills. As in the previous standards, the recommendations in the current publication are based on the belief that "students learn important mathematical skills and processes with **understanding**" (NCTM, 2000, p. ix). In other words, rather than simply memorizing, children should acquire a true knowledge of concepts and processes. Understanding does not develop when children learn mathematics as isolated skills and procedures. It develops through interaction with materials, peers, and supportive adults in settings where students have opportunities to construct their own relationships when they first meet a new topic. Exactly how this takes place will be explained further in the text.

In 2002, the NAEYC and NCTM issued a joint position statement on early childhood mathematics (NCTM & NAEYC, 2002). This statement focuses on math for 3–6-year-olds, elaborating on the NCTM (2000) pre-K–2 standards. The highlights for instruction are summarized in "Math

Experiences That Count!" (2002). In 2009 the National Research Council published a review of research and recommendations for instruction for pre-K and kindergarten mathematics (Cross, Woods, & Schweingruber, 2009), which will be described later in this unit.

Principles of School Mathematics

The Principles of School Mathematics are statements reflecting basic rules that guide high-quality mathematics education. The following six **principles** describe the overarching themes of mathematics instruction (NCTM, 2000, p. 11).

Equity. High expectations and strong support for all students.

Curriculum. Curriculum, which is more than a collection of activities, must be coherent, focused on important mathematics, and well articulated across the grades.

Teaching. Effective mathematics teaching requires understanding of what students know and need to learn and then challenging and supporting them to learn it well.

Learning. Students must learn mathematics with understanding, actively building new knowledge from experience and prior knowledge.

Assessment. Assessment should support the learning of important mathematics and furnish useful information to both teachers and students.

Technology. Technology is essential in teaching and learning mathematics; it influences the mathematics that is taught and enhances student learning. (See Appendix B for a list of suggested software for children and software resources.)

These principles should be used as a guide for instruction in all subjects, not just in mathematics.

Standards for School Mathematics

Standards provide guidance as to what children should know and be able to do at different ages and stages. The ten standards describe the expectations for prekindergarten through grade 12, with

TECHNOLOGY AND EARLY CHILDHOOD MATHEMATICS

Many young children enter school with some technology knowledge. Even preschoolers have had experiences with technology such as *Game Boy, Nintendo,* Video Games, Interactive websites, and electronic media systems such as *Leapfrog*. Preschool teachers need to become acquainted with the popular technology and develop a plan for incorporating technology in their classrooms. How much technology knowledge does the average preschooler bring to the classroom? Nancy S. Maladonaldo, (2009–2010). Technology in the classroom. *Childhood Education*, 86(2), 124–126.)

examples outlined for each standard. The first five standards are content goals for operations, algebra, geometry, measurement, and data analysis and probability. The next five standards include the processes of problem solving, reasoning and proof, connections, communication, and representation. These two sets of standards are linked together as the process standards are applied to learning the content. The standards and principles are integrated within the units that follow.

In 2006, NCTM published *Curriculum Focal Points*. The **focal points** break the standards areas down by grade levels. Table 1–1 outlines the focal points for pre-K through grade 3. Note that there are three focal points at each level with suggested connections to the NCTM Standards in other curriculum areas. The focal points will be discussed further in each relevant unit. In 2009 NCTM decided that *Discrete Mathematics*, previously a high school subject, should be distributed through all the standards (DeBellis, Rosenstein, Hart, & Kenney, 2009). **Discrete Mathematics** includes the major concepts and skills applied in business and industry. These concepts apply in early childhood to repeated patterns, counting and number concepts, geometry, and sorting and organizing groups. Discrete Mathematics will be included in the relevant units.

TABLE 1–1   Curriculum Focal Points by Age/Grade

Age/Grade	Focal Points	Connections	Units
Prekindergarten	• Number and operations • Geometry • Measurement	• Data analysis • Number and operations • Algebra	Focal points: 5, 6, 8, 9, 10, 14, 15 Connections: 3, 7, 13, 16
Kindergarten	• Number and operations • Geometry • Measurement	• Data analysis • Geometry • Algebra	Focal points: 5, 6, 9, 10, 16, 18, 19 Connections: 3, 9, 10, 13, 14, 16, 20
First Grade	• Number and operations and algebra • Number and operations • Geometry	• Number and operations and algebra • Measurement and data analysis • Algebra	Focal points: 3, 21, 25 Connections: 24, 25, 26
Second Grade	• Number and operations • Number and operations and algebra • Measurement	• Number and operations • Geometry and measurement • Algebra	Focal points: 3, 24, 26 Connections: 22, 24, 25
Third Grade	• Number and operations • Number and operations and algebra • Geometry	• Algebra • Measurement • Data analysis • Number and operations	Focal points: 3, 21, 23, 25 Connections: 21, 25, 26

Piagetian Periods of Concept Development and Thought

Jean Piaget contributed enormously to understanding the development of children's thought. Piaget identified four periods of cognitive, or mental, growth and development. Early childhood educators are concerned with the first two periods and the first half of the third.

The first period identified by Piaget, called the **sensorimotor period** (from birth to about age 2), is described in the first part of this unit. It is the time when children begin to learn about the world. They use all their sensory abilities—touch, taste, sight, hearing, and smell—and muscular abilities. They also use growing motor abilities to grasp, crawl, stand, and eventually walk. Children in this first period are explorers, and they need opportunities to use their sensory and motor abilities to learn basic skills and concepts. Through these activities, the young child *assimilates* (takes into the mind and comprehends) a great deal of information. By the end of this period, children have developed the concept of **object permanence**; that is, they realize that objects exist even when they are out of sight. They also develop the ability of **object recognition**, learning to identify objects using the information they have acquired about features such as color, shape, and size. As children near the end of the sensorimotor period, they reach a stage at which they can engage in **representational thought**; that is, instead of acting impetuously, they can think through a solution before attacking a problem. They also enter into a time of rapid language development.

The second period, called the **preoperational period**, extends from about ages 2–7. During this period, children begin to develop concepts that are more like those of adults, but these concepts, often referred to as **preconcepts**, are still incomplete in comparison to what they will be like at maturity. During the early part of the preoperational period, language continues to undergo rapid growth and speech is used increasingly to express concept knowledge. Children begin to use concept terms such as *big and small* (size), *light and heavy* (weight), *square and round* (shape), *late and early* (time), *long and short* (length), and so on. This ability to use language is one of the **symbolic behaviors** that emerges during this period. Children also use symbolic behavior in their representational play, where they may use sand to represent food, a stick to represent a spoon, or another child to represent father, mother, or baby. Play is a major arena in which children develop an understanding of the symbolic functions that underlie later understanding of abstract symbols such as numerals, letters, and written words.

An important characteristic of preoperational children is **centration**. When materials are changed in form or arrangement in space, children may see them as changed in amount as well. This is because preoperational children tend to *center* on the most obvious aspects of what is seen. For instance, if the same amount of liquid is put in both a tall, thin glass and a short, fat glass, preoperational children say that there is more in the tall glass "because it is taller." If clay is changed in shape from a ball to a snake, they say that there is less clay "because it is thinner." If a pile of coins is placed close together, preoperational children say that there are fewer coins than they would say if the coins were spread out. When the physical arrangement of material is changed, preoperational children seem unable to hold the original picture of its shape in mind. They lack **reversibility**; that is, they cannot reverse the process of change mentally. The ability to hold or save the original picture in the mind and to reverse physical change mentally is referred to as **conservation**. The inability to conserve is a critical characteristic of preoperational children.

During the preoperational period, children work with the precursors of conservation such as counting, one-to-one correspondence, shape, space, and comparing. They also work on **seriation** (putting items in a logical sequence, such as fat to thin or dark to light) and **classification** (putting things in logical groups according to some common criteria such as color, shape, size, or use).

During the third period, called **concrete operations** (usually from ages 7–11), children are becoming *conservers*. In other words, they are becoming more and more skilled at retaining the original picture in mind and making a mental reversal when appearances are changed. The time between ages 5 and 7 is one of transition to concrete operations. Each child's thought processes are changing at his own rate. Therefore, during this time of transition, a normal expectation is that some children are already conservers and others are not. This is a critical consideration for kindergarten and primary teachers because the ability to conserve number (the pennies problem) is a good indication that children are ready to deal with **abstract symbolic activities**; that is, they will be able to mentally manipulate groups that are presented by number symbols with a real understanding of what the mathematical operations mean. Section 2 of this text covers the basic concepts that children must understand and integrate to conserve. (See Figure 1–3 for examples of conservation problems.)

Piaget's final period is called **formal operations** (ages 11 through adulthood). During this period, children can learn to use the scientific method independently; that is, they learn to solve problems in a logical and systematic manner. They begin to understand abstract concepts and to attack abstract problems. They can imagine solutions before trying them out. For example, suppose a person who has reached the formal operations level is given samples of several colorless liquids and is told that some combination of these liquids will result in a yellow liquid. A person at the formal operations level would plan out how to systematically test to find the solution; a person still at the concrete operational level might start to combine

Original	Physical Change	Question	Nonconserving Answer	Conserving Answer
Same amount of drink 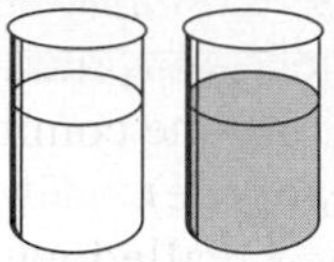	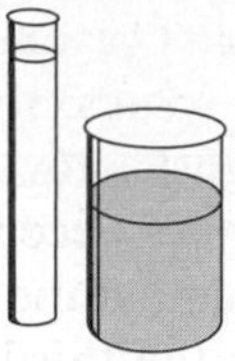	Is there still the same amount of drink?	No, there is more in the tall glass.	Yes, you just put the drink in different size glasses.
Same amount of clay 	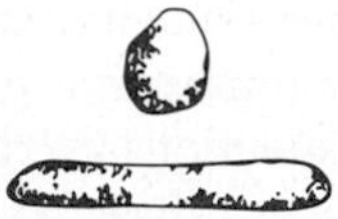	Is there still the same amount of clay?	No, there is more clay in the snake because it is longer.	Yes, you just rolled it out into a different shape.
Same amount of pennies 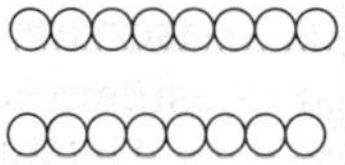	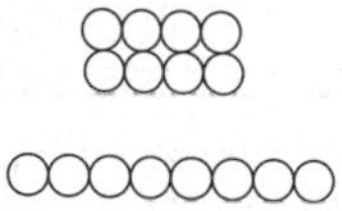	Are there still the same number of pennies?	No, there are more in the bottom row because it is longer.	Yes, you just moved the pennies closer together (points to top row).

FIGURE 1–3 Physical changes in conservation tasks.

the liquids without considering a logical approach to the problem, such as labeling each liquid and keeping a record of which combinations have been tried. Note that this period may be reached as early as age 11; however, it may not be reached at all by many adults.

Piaget's View of How Children Acquire Knowledge

According to Piaget's view, children acquire knowledge by constructing it through their interaction with the environment. Children do not wait to be instructed to do this; they are continually trying to make sense out of everything they encounter. Piaget divides knowledge into three areas.

- **Physical knowledge** is the type that includes learning about objects in the environment and their characteristics (color,

weight, size, texture, and other features that can be determined through observation and are physically within the object).
- **Logico-mathematical knowledge** is the type that includes the relationships (same and different, more and less, number, classification, etc.) that each individual constructs to make sense out of the world and to organize information.
- **Social** (or conventional) **knowledge** is the type that is created by people (such as rules for behavior in various social situations).

Physical and logico-mathematical knowledge depend on each other and are learned simultaneously. In other words, as children learn the physical characteristics of objects, they construct logico-mathematical categories to organize information. In the popular story *Goldilocks and the Three Bears*, for example, papa bear is big, mama bear is middle sized, and baby bear is the smallest (seriation), but all three (number) are bears because they are covered with fur and have a certain body shape with a certain combination of features common only to bears (classification).

Constance Kamii, a student of Piaget, has actively translated Piaget's theory into practical applications for the instruction of young children. Kamii emphasizes that, according to Piaget, **autonomy** (independence) is the aim of education. Intellectual autonomy develops in an atmosphere where children feel secure in their relationships with adults; where they have an opportunity to share their ideas with other children; and where they are encouraged to be alert and curious, to come up with interesting ideas, problems, and questions, to use initiative in finding the answers to problems, to have confidence in their abilities to figure out things for themselves, and to speak their minds. Young children need to be presented with problems that can be solved through games and other activities that challenge their minds. They must work with concrete materials and real problems such as the examples provided earlier in this unit.

In line with the NCTM focus on math for understanding, Duckworth (2006) explains how Piaget's view of understanding focuses on the adult attending to the child's point of view. In other words, we should not view "understanding" from our own perspective but should rather try to find out what the child is thinking. When the child provides a response that seems illogical from an adult point of view, the adult should consider and explore the child's logic. For example, if a child (when presented with a conservation problem) says there are more objects in a spread-out row of ten objects than in a tightly packed row of ten objects, it is important to ask the child for a reason.

Vygotsky's View of How Children Learn and Develop

Like Piaget, Lev Vygotsky was also a cognitive development theorist. He was a contemporary of Piaget, but Vygotsky died at the age of 38 before his work was fully completed. Vygotsky contributed a view of cognitive development that recognizes both developmental and environmental forces. He believed that just as people developed tools such as knives, spears, shovels, and tractors to aid their mastery of the environment, they also developed mental tools. People develop ways of cooperating and communicating as well as new capacities to plan and think ahead. These mental tools, Vygotsky referred to as **signs**, help people to master their own behavior. He believed that speech was the most important sign system because it freed us from distractions and allowed us to work on problems in our minds. Speech both enables the child to interact socially and facilitates his thinking. In Vygotsky's view, *writing and numbering* were also important sign systems.

Whereas Piaget looked at development as if it came mainly from the child alone, from the child's inner maturation and spontaneous discoveries, Vygotsky believed this was true only until about the age of 2. At that point, culture and the cultural signs become necessary to expand thought. He believed that the internal and external factors interacted to produce new thoughts and an expanded menu of signs. Thus, Vygotsky put more emphasis than Piaget on the role of the adult or more mature peer as an influence on children's mental development.

Whereas Piaget placed an emphasis on children as intellectual explorers making their own discoveries and *constructing* knowledge independently, Vygotsky developed an alternative concept known as the **zone of proximal development (ZPD)**. The ZPD is the area between where the child is now operating independently in mental development and where she might go with assistance from an adult or more mature child. The child acquires cultural knowledge with the assistance or **scaffolding** provided by more mature learners. According to Vygotsky, good teaching involves presenting material that is a little ahead of development. Children might not fully understand it at first, but in time they can understand it given appropriate scaffolding. Rather than pressuring development, instruction should support development as it moves ahead. Concepts that children constructed independently and spontaneously lay the foundation for the more scientific concepts that are part of the culture. Teachers must identify each student's ZPD and provide developmentally appropriate instruction. Teachers will know when they have hit upon the right zone because children will respond with enthusiasm, curiosity, and active involvement.

Piagetian constructivists tend to be concerned about the tradition of pressuring children and not allowing them freedom to construct knowledge independently. Vygotskian constructivists are concerned with children being challenged to reach their full potential. Today, many educators find that a combination of the views of Piaget and Vygotsky provides a foundation for instruction that follows the child's interests and enthusiasms while providing an intellectual challenge. The *learning cycle* view (which will be described) provides such a framework.

Bruner and Dienes

Jerome Bruner (Clabaugh, 2009) and Zoltan Dienes (Sriraman & Lesh, 2007) also contributed to theory and instruction in early childhood concept development. Bruner's interest in cognitive development was influenced by Piaget and Vygotsky. He also believed that learning was an active process during which children construct new knowledge based on their previous knowledge. He used math as an example of a context for learning. Bruner identified three stages of learning: enactive, iconic, and symbolic. The enactive stage is a period of manipulation and exploration. Learning activity centers on play. In the iconic stage students can visualize the concrete. In the symbolic stage students can move into abstract thinking. The adult role is to scaffold the students through these stages. Bruner emphasized discovery learning or guided discovery. Learning takes place in problem-solving situations. Instruction involves supporting the students' efforts to discover the problem solution rather than forcing memorization.

Dienes' focus was on how children learn mathematics. He focused on materials and believed the initial stage of mathematics learning should center on free play. During free play children enter a second stage in which they see regularities that provide rules for mathematics games. In the third stage they begin to compare the different games. In the fourth stage they enter a period of abstraction in which they use representations such as tables, coordinate systems, drawings, or other vehicles that can aid memory. During the fifth stage they discover the use of symbols and at the sixth stage students use formalized mathematical rules. Dienes is best known for the invention of multibase blocks, which are used to teach place value. He taught mathematics in a number of cultures using manipulatives, games, stories, and dance. He supported the use of small groups working together in collaboration to solve problems.

The Learning Cycle

Bredekamp and Rosegrant (1992) adapted the learning cycle approach to early childhood education developed by Charles Barman (1989) (Figure 1–4). The **learning cycle** for young children encompasses the following four repeating processes:

- *Awareness.* A broad recognition of objects, people, events, or concepts that develops from experience.
- *Exploration.* The construction of personal meaning through sensory experiences with objects, people, events, or concepts.
- *Inquiry.* Learners compare their constructions with those of the culture, commonalities are recognized, and generalizations are made that are more like those of adults.
- *Utilization.* At this point in the cycle, learners can apply and use their understandings in new settings and situations.

Each time a new situation is encountered, learning begins with awareness and moves on through the other levels. The cycle also relates to development. For example, infants and toddlers will be at the awareness level, gradually moving into exploration. Children who are 3–5 years old may move

CYCLE OF LEARNING AND TEACHING

WHAT CHILDREN DO	WHAT TEACHERS DO
Awareness	
Experience	Create the environment
Acquire an interest	Provide opportunities by introducing new objects, events and people
Recognize broad parameters	Invite interest by posing problem or question
Attend	Respond to child's interest or shared experience
Perceive	Show interest and enthusiasm
Exploration	
Observe	Facilitate
Explore materials	Support and enhance exploration
Collect information	Provide opportunities for active exploration
Discover	Extend play
Create	Describe child's activity
Figure out components	Ask open-ended questions—"What else could you do?"
Construct own understanding	Respect child's thinking and rule systems
Apply own rules	Allow for constructive error
Create personal meaning	
Represent own meaning	
Inquiry	
Examine	Help children refine understanding
Investigate	Guide children and focus attention
Propose explanations	Ask more focused questions—"What else works like this?" "What happens if ___?"
Focus	
Compare own thinking with that of others	Provide information when requested—"How do you spell ___?"
	Help children make connections
Generalize	
Relate to prior learning	
Adjust to conventional rule systems	
Utilization	
Use the learning in many ways; learning becomes functional	Create vehicles for application in real world
	Help children apply learning to new situations
Represent learning in various ways	Provide meaningful situations in which to use learning
Apply learning to new situations	
Formulate new hypotheses and repeat cycle	

FIGURE 1–4 Cycle of learning and teaching. From *Reaching Potentials: Appropriate Curriculum and Assessment for Young Children* (Vol. 1, p. 33), by S. Bredekamp and T. Rosegrant (Eds.), 1992, Washington, DC: National Association for the Education of Young Children. Reprinted with permission.

up to inquiry, whereas those who are 6–8 years old can move through all four levels when meeting new situations or concepts. Bredekamp and Rosegrant (1992) provide an example in the area of measurement:

- Three- and four-year-olds are aware of and explore comparative sizes.

- Four- through six-year-olds explore with nonstandard units, such as how many of their own feet wide is the rug.

- Seven- and eight-year-olds begin to understand standard units of measurement and use rulers, thermometers, and other standard measuring tools.

The authors caution that the cycle is not hierarchical; that is, utilization is not necessarily more valued than awareness or exploration. Young children may be aware of concepts that they cannot fully utilize in the technical sense. For example, they may be aware that rain falls from the sky without understanding the intricacies of meteorology. Using the learning cycle as a framework for curriculum and instruction has an important aspect: The cycle reminds us that children may not have had experiences that provide for awareness and exploration. To be truly individually appropriate in planning, we need to provide for these experiences in school.

The learning cycle fits nicely with the theories of Piaget and Vygotsky. For both, learning begins with awareness and exploration. Both value inquiry and application. The format for each concept provided in the text is from naturalistic to informal to adult guided learning experiences. These experiences are consistent with providing opportunities for children to move through the learning cycle as they meet new objects, people, events, or concepts.

Traditional versus Reform Instruction

A current thrust in mathematics instruction is the reform of classroom instruction, changing from the traditional approach of drill and practice memorization to adoption of the constructivist approach. A great deal of tension exists between the traditional and reform approaches. *Telling* has been the traditional method of ensuring that student learning takes place. When a teacher's role changes to that of guide and facilitator, the teacher may feel a lack of control. The reform or constructivist approach is compatible with early childhood practice but may be inappropriate for older children (Constructivist Versus Traditional Math, 2005). In the elementary grades, efficiency and accuracy are emphasized in the traditional program. Evidence suggests that children from constructivist programs are not prepared for algebra and other higher level mathematics. On the other hand, the traditional "drill and kill" can deaden interest in math. Traditional math programs also

tend to follow a one-size-fits-all approach in contrast to the constructivist differentiated curriculum. Many teachers have developed a mix of the two approaches. Finally, problems are presented when it comes to standardized testing. The required test may favor one method or the other. There should be a balance between teaching for understanding and teaching for accuracy and efficiency. Van de Walle (1999) believes the dilemma can be solved using a problem-solving approach. In this text we have tried to achieve a balance between the traditional and reform approaches by providing a guide to ensuring students have the opportunity to explore and construct their own knowledge while also providing examples of developmentally appropriate direct instruction.

Research on Early Mathematics Instruction

The National Research Council Committee on Early Childhood Mathematics (Cross, Woods, & Schweingruber, 2009) carried out a review of early childhood mathematics learning and instruction. The research supports that all young children are capable of learning mathematics. Children enjoy their early informal experiences. Unfortunately many young children do not have the opportunity to engage in the appropriate early childhood math experiences. Based on their review of research, the committee laid out the critical areas that should be the focus of young children's early mathematics education, described the extent to which math instruction is included in early childhood programs, and suggested changes that could improve the quality of early childhood math instruction. They found that two areas are important for children to learn:

1. Number (whole number, operations, and relations).
2. Geometry, spatial thinking, and measurement.

The committee developed learning paths in each area. The first of nine committee recommendations is that a coordinated national early childhood mathematics initiative be put in place to improve mathematics teaching and learning for all children ages 3 to 6.

Organization of the Text

This text is divided into six sections. The sequence is both integrative and developmental. Section 1 is an integrative section that sets the stage for instruction. The development, acquisition, and promotion of math concepts are described, and a plan is provided for assessing developmental levels.

Sections 2 through 4 encompass the developmental mathematics program for sensorimotor-level and preoperational-level children. Section 2 includes descriptions of the fundamental concepts that are basic to math along with suggestions for instruction and materials. Section 3 focuses on applying these fundamental concepts, attitudes, and skills at a more advanced level. Section 4 deals with higher-level concepts and activities.

Standard	Units
Number and operations	5, 6, 8, 11, 18, 19, 20, 21, 23, 24, 29, 30
Patterns, functions, and algebra	7, 13, 20, 22, 25, 31
Geometry	9, 10, 20, 25
Measurement	8, 14, 15, 26
Data analysis and probability	16, 20, 25
Problem solving	3, 17
Reasoning	12, 17
Connections	12, 17
Communication	12, 17
Representation	12, 17

This chart shows the text units that focus most directly on the mathematics standards, although the process standards apply to all the content goal areas.

Section 5 encompasses the acquisition of concepts and skills for children at the concrete operations level. Section 6 provides suggestions of materials and resources—and descriptions of math in action—in the classroom and in the home. Finally, the appendices include additional concept assessment tasks, lists of children's books that contain math concepts, and list of technology publishers.

As Figure 1–1 illustrates, concepts are not acquired in a series of quick, short-term lessons; development begins in infancy and continues throughout early childhood and beyond. As you read each unit, keep referring back to Figure 1–1; it can help you relate each section to periods of development.

Summary

Concept development begins in infancy and grows through four periods throughout a lifetime. The exploratory activities of the infant and toddler during the sensorimotor period are the basis of later success. As they use their senses and muscles, children learn about the world. During the preoperational period, concepts grow rapidly and children develop the basic concepts and skills of mathematics, moving toward intellectual autonomy through independent activity, which serves as a vehicle for the construction of knowledge. Between the ages of 5 and 7, children enter the concrete operations period and learn to apply abstract ideas and activities to their concrete knowledge of the physical and mathematical world. The learning cycle lesson is an example of a developmentally inspired teaching strategy. Mathematics instruction should be guided by principles and standards developed by NCTM. Mathematics is also guided by curriculum focal points. The recommendations of the National Research Council report are also important. The instructional program should balance traditional and reform elements. The text presents the major concepts, skills, processes, and attitudes that are fundamental to mathematics for young children as their learning is guided in light of these principles and standards and focal points.

KEY TERMS

abstract symbolic activities	inquiry	reversibility
autonomy	learning cycle	scaffolding
awareness	logico-mathematical knowledge	senses
centration	object permanence	sensorimotor period
classification	object recognition	seriation
concepts	physical knowledge	signs
concrete operations	preconcepts	standards
conservation	preoperational period	symbolic behaviors
development	preprimary	understanding
discrete mathematics	primary	utilization
exploration	principles	zone of proximal
focal points	process skills	development (ZPD)
formal operations	representational thought	

SUGGESTED ACTIVITIES

1. Using the descriptions in this unit, prepare a list of behaviors that would indicate that a young child at each of Piaget's first three periods of development is engaged in behavior exemplifying the acquisition of math concepts. Using your list, observe four young children at home or at school. One child should be 6–18 months old, one 18 months to 2½ years old, one of age 3–5, and one of age 6–7. Record everything each child does that is on your list. Note any similarities and differences observed among the four children.

2. Interview three mothers of children ages 2–8. Using your list from Activity 1 as a guide, ask them which of the activities each of their children does. Ask the mothers if they realize that these activities are basic to the construction of math concepts, and note their responses. Did you find that they appreciate the value of their children's play activities in math concept development?

3. Interview two or three young children. Present the conservation of number problem illustrated in Figure 1–3 (see Appendix A for detailed instructions). Audiotape or videotape their responses. Listen to the tape, and describe what you learn. Describe the similarities and differences in the children's responses.

4. You should begin to record on 5½″ × 8″ file cards each math activity you learn about. Buy a package of cards, some dividers, and a file box. Label your dividers with the titles of Units 5 through 29. Figure 1–5 illustrates how your file should look.

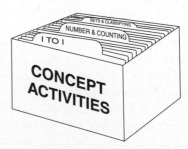

FIGURE 1–5 Start a math activity file now so you can keep it up to date.

REVIEW

A. Define the term *concept development*.
B. List the major elements of early childhood mathematics.
C. Explain the importance of Piaget's and Vygotsky's theories of cognitive development and the contributions of Bruner and Dienes.
D. Decide which of the following describes a child in the sensorimotor (SM), preoperational (P), or concrete operational (CO) Piagetian stages:
   1. Mary watches as her teacher makes two balls of clay of the same size. The teacher then rolls one ball into a snake shape and asks, "Mary, do both balls still have the same amount, or does one ball have more clay?" Mary laughs, "They are still the same amount. You just rolled that one out into a snake."
   2. Michael shakes his rattle and then puts it in his mouth and tries to suck on it.
   3. John's mother shows him two groups of pennies. One group is spread out, and one group is stacked up. Each group contains 10 pennies. "Which bunch of pennies would you like to have, John?" John looks carefully and then says as he picks up the pennies that are spread out, "I'll take these because there are more."

E. In review question D, which child (Mary or John) is a conserver? How do you know? Why is it important to know whether or not a child is a conserver?
F. Explain how young children acquire knowledge. Include the place of the learning cycle in knowledge acquisition. Provide examples from your observations.
G. Explain the purpose and value of having principles and standards for mathematics instruction.
H. Describe the purpose of the focal points.
I. Explain the relationship between reform and traditional mathematics instruction.

REFERENCES

Barman, C. R. (1989). *An expanded view of the learning cycle: New ideas about an effective teaching strategy* (Council of Elementary Science International Monograph No. 4). Indianapolis, IN: Indiana University Press.

Bredekamp, S. (Ed.). (1987). *Developmentally appropriate practice in early childhood programs serving children from birth through age eight*. Washington, DC: National Association for the Education of Young Children.

Bredekamp, S., & Copple, C. (Eds.). (1997). *Developmentally appropriate practice in early childhood programs* (Rev. ed.). Washington, DC: National Association for the Education of Young Children.

Bredekamp, S., & Rosegrant, T. (1992). *Reaching potentials: Appropriate curriculum and assessment for young children* (Vol. 1). Washington, DC: National Association for the Education of Young Children.

Clabaugh, G. K. (Ed.). (2009). *Jerome Bruner's Educational Theory*. Retrieved 1/4/10 from http://www.newfoundations.com

Clements, D. H., & Sarama, J. (2003, January/February). Creative pathways to math. *Early Childhood Education Today*, 37–45.

Clements, D. H., & Sarama, J. (2004, March). Building abstract thinking through math. *Early Childhood Education Today*, 34–41.

Copple, C., & Bredekamp, S. (Eds.). (2009). *Developmentally appropriate practice in early childhood programs serving children birth through age eight* (3rd ed.). Washington, DC: National Association for the Education of Young Children.

Constructivist Versus Traditional Math. (2005). Retrieved 1/10/10 from readingtoparents.org

Cross, C. T., Woods, T. A., & Schweingruber, H. (Eds.). (2009). *Mathematics learning in early childhood.* Washington, DC: National Academies Press.

Curriculum focal points for prekindergarten through grade 8 mathematics. (2006). Retrieved May 24, 2007, from http://www.nctm.org

Debellis, V. A., Rosenstein, J. G., Hart, E. W., & Kenney, M. J. (2009). Navigating with discrete mathematics in prekindergaten—grade 5. Reston, VA: National Council of Teachers of Mathematics.

Duckworth, E. (2006). *The having of wonderful ideas* (3rd ed.). New York: Teachers College Press.

Geist, E. (2001). Children are born mathematicians: Promoting the construction of early mathematical concepts in children under five. *Young Children,* 56(4), 12–19.

Learning PATHS and teaching STRATEGIES in early mathematics. (2003). In D. Koralek (Ed.), *Spotlight on young children and math* (pp. 29–31). Washington, DC: National Association for the Education of Young Children.

Math experiences that count! (2002). *Young Children,* 57(4), 60–61.

National Council of Teachers of Mathematics. (1989). *Curriculum and evaluation standards for school mathematics.* Reston, VA: Author.

National Council of Teachers of Mathematics. (1991). *Professional standards for teaching mathematics. Reston,* VA: Author.

National Council of Teachers of Mathematics. (1995). *Assessment standards for school mathematics.* Reston, VA: Author.

National Council of Teachers of Mathematics. (2000). *Principles and standards for school mathematics.* Reston, VA: Author.

National Council of Teachers of Mathematics & National Association for the Education of Young Children. (2002). NCTM position statement: Early childhood mathematics: Promoting good beginnings. *Teaching Children Mathematics,* 9(1), 24.

Sriraman, B., & Lesh, R. (2007). A conversation with Zoltan P. Dienes. The *Montana Mathematics Enthusiast,* Monograph 2, pp. 151–167. Retrieved 1/04/10 from http://www.math.umt.edu/

Van de Walle, J. A. (1999). *Reform Mathematics vs. the Basics: Understanding the Conflict and Dealing With It.* Presentation at the 77th Annual Meeting of NCTM. Retrieved 1/4/10 from http://mathematicallysane.com

FURTHER READING AND RESOURCES

Baroody, A. J. (2000). Research in review. Does mathematics instruction for three- to five-year-olds really make sense? *Young Children, 55,* 61–67.

Berk, L. E., & Winsler, A. (1995). *Scaffolding children's learning: Vygotsky and early childhood education.* Washington, DC: National Association for the Education of Young Children.

Bodrova, E., & Leong, D. J. (2007). *Tools of the mind: The Vygotskian approach to early childhood education* (2nd ed.). Upper Saddle River, NJ: Pearson-Merrill/Prentice-Hall.

Charlesworth, R. (2005). Prekindergarten mathematics: Connecting with national standards. *Early Childhood Education Journal,* 32(4), 229–236.

Charlesworth, R. (2011). *Understanding child development* (8th ed.). Belmont, CA: Wadsworth Cengage Learning.

Clements, D. H., & Sarama, J. (2008). Curriculum focal points: Pre-K to kindergarten. *Teaching Children Mathematics,* 14(6), 361–365.

Copley, J. V. (2000). *The young child and mathematics.* Washington, DC: National Association for the Education of Young Children.

de Melendez, W. R., & Beck, V. (2007). *Teaching young children in multicultural classrooms* (2nd ed.). Clifton Park, NY: Thomson Delmar Learning.

Epstein, A. S. (2007). *The intentional teacher*. Washington, DC: National Association for the Education of Young Children.

Ginsburg, H. P., Lee, J. S., & Boyd, J. S. (2008). Mathematics education for young children: What it is and how to promote it. *SRCD Social Policy Report*, 22(1).

Golbeck, S. L., & Ginsburg, H. P. (Eds.). (2004). Early learning in mathematics and science [Special Issue]. *Early Childhood Research Quarterly*, 19.

Inhelder, B., & Piaget, J. (1969). *The early growth of logic in the child*. New York: Norton.

Kamii, C. K., & Housman, L. B. (1999). Y*oung children reinvent arithmetic: Implications of Piaget's theory* (2nd ed.). New York: Teachers College Press.

Kilpatrick, J., Martin, W. G., & Schifter, D. (2003). *A research companion to principles and standards for school mathematics*. Reston, VA: National Council of Teachers of Mathematics.

Mathematics education [Special section]. (2007). *Phi Delta Kappan*, 88(9), 664–697.

Mirra, A. (2009). *Focus in prekindergarten—Grade 2: Teaching with curriculum focal points*. Reston, VA: National Council of Teachers of Mathematics.

National Research Council. (2005). *How students learn: History, mathematics, and science in the classroom*. Committee on How People Learn, a targeted report for teachers (M. S. Donovan & J. D. Bransford, Eds.). Washington, DC: National Academies Press.

Piaget, J. (1965). T*he child's conception of number*. New York: Norton.

Sarama, J., & Clements, D. H. (2008). Focal points—grades 1 and 2. *Teaching Children Mathematics, 14*(7), 396–401.

Zambo, R., & Zambo, D. (2008). Mathematics and the learning cycle: How the brain works as it learns mathematics. *Teaching Children Mathematics, 14*(5), 260–264.

How Concepts Are Acquired

OBJECTIVES

After reading this unit, you should be able to:

- List and define the three types of learning experiences described in the unit.
- Recognize examples of each of the three types of learning experiences.
- State possible responses to specific opportunities for the child to learn concepts.
- Be aware of variations in individual and cultural learning styles and capabilities and the need for curriculum integration.
- Know that children learn through interaction with peers as well as adults.
- Recognize the value of technology for young children's math and science learning.

Children learn with understanding when the learning takes place in meaningful and familiar situations. As children explore their familiar environments, they encounter experiences through which they actively construct knowledge and discover new relationships. The adult's role is to build upon this knowledge and support children as they move to higher levels of understanding. These initial child-controlled learning experiences can be characterized as **naturalistic learning**. Two other types of experiences are those characterized as **informal learning** and **adult guided learning**.

Naturalistic experiences are those in which the child controls his choice and action; *informal* is where the child chooses the activity and action, but with adult intervention at some point; and *adult guided* is where the adult chooses the experience for the child and gives some direction to the child's action (Figure 2–1). Naturalistic experiences relate closely to the Piagetian view, whereas the informal and adult guided relate to the Vygotskian view.

Referring back to the learning cycle as described in Unit 1, it can be seen that these three types of experiences fit into the cycle. The learning cycle is basically a way to structure lessons so that children

TYPES OF ACTIVITY	INTERACTION EMPHASIZED
Naturalistic	Child/environment
Informal	Child/environment/adult
Adult Guided	Adult/child/environment

FIGURE 2–1 Concepts are learned through three types of activity.

experience all three ways of learning. Naturalistic experiences are encouraged at the awareness and exploration levels. Informal experiences are added at the exploration, inquiry, and utilization levels. Adult guided experiences are more likely to appear at the inquiry and utilization levels.

In providing settings for learning and types of instruction, keep in mind that there are variations in learning styles among groups of children and among different cultural and ethnic groups. Some of these types of variations will be described later in this unit.

Children's naturalistic learning experiences involve the exploration of the environment.

Naturalistic Learning Experiences

Naturalistic experiences are those children initiate spontaneously as they go about their daily activities. These experiences are the major mode of learning for children during the sensorimotor period. Naturalistic experiences can be a valuable mode of learning for older children as well.

The adult's role is to provide an interesting and rich environment, that is, many things for the child to look at, touch, taste, smell, and hear. The adult should observe the child's activity; note how it is progressing; and then respond with a glance, nod, smile, verbal description of the child's actions or elaboration of the child's comments, or word of praise to encourage the child. The child needs to know when he is doing the appropriate thing.

Some examples of naturalistic experiences are as follows:

- Kurt hands Dad two pennies saying, "Here's your two dollars!"
- Isabel takes a spoon from the drawer— "This is big." Mom says, "Yes, that is a big spoon."
- Tito is eating orange segments. "I got three." (Holds up three fingers.)
- Nancy says, "Big girls are up to here," as she stands straight and points to her chin.
- Aika (age 4) sits on the rug and sorts colored rings into plastic cups.
- Tanya and Javier (both age 4) are having a tea party. Javier says, "The tea is hot."
- Sam (age 5) is painting. He makes a dab of yellow and then dabs some blue on top. "Hey! I've got green now."
- Trang Fung (age 6) is cutting her clay into many small pieces. Then she squashes it together into one big piece.
- Pilar (age 6) is restless during the after-lunch rest period. As she sits quietly with her head on her desk, her eyes rove around the room. Each day she notices the clock. One day she realizes that, when the teacher says, "One-fifteen, time to get up," the short

hand is always on the 1 and the long hand is always on the 3. After that, Pilar knows how to watch the clock for the end of rest time.

- Theresa (age 7) is drawing with markers. They are in a container that has a hole to hold each one. Theresa notices that there is one extra hole. "There must be a lost marker," she comments.
- Mei (age 8) is experimenting with cup measures and containers. She notices that each cup measure holds the same amount even though each is a different shape. She also notices that you cannot always predict how many cups of liquid a container holds just by looking at it; the shape can fool you.

Informal learning experiences involve an adult or more advanced peer who provides comments or asks questions.

Informal Learning Experiences

Informal learning experiences are initiated by the adult as the child is engaged in a naturalistic experience. These experiences are not preplanned for a specific time. They occur when the adult's experience and/or intuition indicates it is time to scaffold. This might happen for various reasons—for example, the child might need help or he is on the right track in solving a problem but needs a cue or encouragement. It might also happen because the adult has in mind some concepts that should be reinforced and takes advantage of a **teachable moment**. Informal learning experiences occur when an opportunity for instruction presents itself by chance. Some examples follow:

- "I'm six years old," says 3-year-old Kate while holding up three fingers. Dad says, "Let's count those fingers. One, two, three fingers. How old are you?"
- José (age 4) is setting the table. He gets frustrated because he does not seem to have enough cups. "Let's check," says his teacher. "There is one place mat for each chair. Let's see if there is one cup on each mat." They move around the table checking and come to a mat with two cups. "Two cups," says José. "Hurrah!" says his teacher.
- With arms outstretched at various distances, Tim (age 4) asks, "Is this big? Is this big?" Mr. Brown says, "What do you think? What is 'this' big?" Tim looks at the distance between his hands with his arms stretched to the fullest. "This is a big person." He puts his hands about 18 inches apart. "This is a baby." He places his thumb and index finger about half of an inch apart. "This is a blackberry." Mr. Brown watches with a big smile on his face.
- Juanita (age 4) has a bag of cookies. Mrs. Ramirez asks, "Do you have enough for everyone?" Juanita replies, "I don't know." Mrs. R. asks, "How can you find out?" Juanita says, "I don't know." Mrs. R. suggests, "How about if we count the cookies?"
- Kindergartners Jorge and Sam are playing with some small rubber figures called Stackrobats. Jorge links some together horizontally, while Sam joins his vertically. The boys are competing to see who can make the longest line. When Jorge's line reaches across the diameter of the table, he encounters a problem. Miss Jones suggests that he might be able to figure out another way to link the figures together. He looks at Sam's line of figures and then at his. He realizes that if he links his figures vertically he can continue with the competition.

- Dean, a first grader, runs into Mrs. Red Fox's classroom on a spring day after a heavy rainstorm. He says, "Mrs. Red Fox! I have a whole bunch of worms." Mrs. Red Fox asks Dean where he found the worms and why there are so many out that morning. She suggests he put the worms on the science table where everyone can see them. Dean follows through and places a sign next to the can: "Wrms fnd by Dean."

- Second grader Liu Pei is working with blocks. She shows her teacher, Mr. Wang, that she has made three stacks of four blocks. She asks, "When I have three stacks of four, is that like when my big brother says 'three times four'?" "Yes," responds Mr. Wang. "When you have three stacks of four, that is three times four." Liu Pei has discovered some initial ideas about multiplication.

- Third grader Jason notices that each time he feeds Fuzzy the hamster, it runs to the food pan before Jason opens the cage. He tells his teacher who uses the opportunity to discuss anticipatory responses, why they develop, and their significance in training animals. The teacher asks Jason to consider why this might happen so consistently and to think about other times he has noticed this type of response in other animals or humans. Several other children join the discussion. They decide to keep individual records of any anticipatory responses they observe for a week, compare observations, and note trends.

Adult guided learning experiences are preplanned by an adult to meet specific learning objectives.

Adult Guided Learning Experiences

Adult guided experiences are preplanned lessons or activities. They can be done with individuals or small or large groups at a special time or an opportune time. They may follow the learning cycle sequence or consist of more focused direct instruction. Examples of some of these adult guided activities follow:

- *With an individual at a specific time with a specific focus.* Cindy is 4 years old. Her teacher decides that she needs some practice counting. She says, "Cindy, I have some blocks here for you to count. How many are in this pile?"

- *A learning cycle example.* Mrs. Red Fox sets up a new activity center in her room. There is a large tub filled with balls of various sizes, colors, and textures. All the children have had some experience with balls and are aware of them in the environment. Mrs. Red Fox points out the tub of balls to the students and tells them that they can explore the balls, looking at what is the same and different. She provides them paper and markers that can be used to record what they learn. Each day the students gather for reporting their daily activities. Those who have explored the balls report on their findings and share what they have recorded. Mrs. Red Fox asks questions and encourages the students to insert their comments and questions. Finally, they discuss other things they might try to find out about the balls and other investigations they might make concerning the balls.

- *With an individual at an opportune time with a specific focus.* Mrs. Flores knows that Tanya needs help with the concept of shape. Tanya is looking for a game to play. Mrs. Flores says, "Try this shape-matching game, Tanya. There are squares, circles, and triangles on the big card. You find the little cards with the shapes that match."

- *With a group at an opportune time.* Mrs. Raymond has been working with the children on the concept of weight. The children ask her to bring some planks to make ramps to attach to the packing boxes and the sawhorses. She brings the planks and explains to the group, "These are the heavy planks. These are the light planks. Which are stronger? Where should they go?"
- *With a large group at a specific time.* The students have had an opportunity to explore a collection of bones that they brought from home. Ms. Hebert realizes classification is an important concept that should be applied throughout the primary grades, since it is extremely important in organizing science data. Ms. Hebert puts out three large sheets of construction paper and has the students explore the different ways bones can be classified (such as chicken, turkey, duck, cow, pig, and deer) or placed in subcategories (such as grouping chicken bones into wings, backs, legs, and so on).

Observe that, throughout the examples in this unit, the adults ask various questions and provide different types of directions for using the materials. It is extremely important to ask many different types of questions. Questions vary as to whether they are *divergent* or *convergent* and also how difficult they are. **Divergent questions and directions** do not have one right answer but provide an opportunity for creativity, guessing, and experimenting. Questions that begin "Tell me about _____," "What do you think _____?" "What have you found out _____?" "What can we do with _____?" "Can you find a way to _____?" "What would happen if _____?" "Why do you think _____?" and directions such as "You can examine these _____" or "You may play with these _____" are divergent.

Convergent questions and directions ask for a specific response or activity. A specific piece of information is called for, such as "How many _____?" "Tell me the names of the parts of a plant," "Find a ball smaller than this one," and so on.

Adults often ask only convergent questions and give convergent directions. Remember that children need time to construct their ideas. Divergent questions and directions encourage them to think and act for themselves. Convergent questions and directions can provide the adult with specific information regarding what the child knows, but too many of these questions tend to make the child think that there might be only one right answer to all problems. This can squelch creativity and the willingness to guess and experiment.

By varying the difficulty of the questions asked, the teacher can reach children of different ability levels. For example, in the office supply store center, pencils are 2¢ and paper is 1¢ per sheet. An easy question might be, "If you want to buy one pencil and two sheets of paper, then how many pennies will you need?" A harder question would be, "If you have 10¢, how many pencils and how much paper could you buy?"

Learning Styles

In planning learning experiences for children, it is essential to consider individual and culturally determined styles of learning. Learning styles may relate to modalities such as auditory, visual, kinesthetic, or multisensory preferences. They may relate to temperamental characteristics such as the easygoing, serious student or the easily frustrated student. They also may relate to strengths in particular areas such as those identified by Howard Gardner in his theory of **multiple intelligences** (Gardner, 1999). Gardner originally identified seven intelligences: *linguistic*, *logical-mathematical*, *bodily-kinesthetic*, *interpersonal*, *intrapersonal*, *musical*, and *spatial*. More recently he added two additional intelligences: *naturalist* and *existential*. Gardner conceptualizes these nine intelligences as combined biological and psychological potentials to process information that can be used in a culture to solve problems or create products that are valuable to the culture. It is important to provide children with opportunities to solve problems using their strongest modalities and areas of intelligence.

Too often, conventional learning experiences focus on the linguistic (language) and logical-mathematical intelligences while ignoring the other areas. Children who may have strength in learning through active movement and concrete activities (bodily-kinesthetic learners) or those who learn best through interacting with peers (interpersonal learners) or one of the other modalities may lose out on being able to develop concepts and skills to the fullest. Incorporating peer tutoring and offering opportunities for group projects expands the chances for success.

The variety of learning styles can be accommodated by integrating the various curriculum areas rather than teaching each particular area such as mathematics, science, social studies, language arts, visual arts, musical arts, etc., as separate subjects. More and more attention has been paid to integrated approaches to instruction (see Unit 17). In this text we focus on mathematics as the major focus with other content areas integrated. However, any one of the content areas can be the hub at different times with different purposes. The section on Further Reading and Resources includes some resources for curriculum integration. Integration is frequently pictured in a weblike structure similar to that constructed by spiders (Figure 2–2). The focus or theme of study is placed in the center, and the other content areas and/or major concepts are attached by the radials.

In planning and instruction, it is important to consider diversity not only in modality-related learning styles but also in race, ethnicity, social class, gender, out-of-school experiences, and special needs. Whereas reform mathematics appears to have positive effects on achievement, research has not looked closely at how reform mathematics affects different groups. The reform classroom itself is a culture different from the traditional classroom. The reform movement is progressing from a linear, formal view of the teacher passing out knowledge to passive students to a setting in which mathematics is constructed, discussed, and questioned by active students. The reform mathematics classroom is an active, productive culture. Unfortunately, developing this type of classroom is not easy

because it requires the teacher to be tuned into each student's learning style and abilities. Reform mathematics is increasingly being criticized as "fuzzy math" (Lewin, 2006), and there is a movement toward again emphasizing basic drills and memorization. However, there is a need to provide balanced instruction that provides for memorization *and* understanding.

Many fundamental concepts in mathematics are learned before the child enters school. Mathematics learned outside of school is referred to as **ethnomathematics** (Nunes, 1992). This type of mathematics is embedded in the out-of-school cultural activities whose primary purpose is not to learn mathematics but rather to accomplish a culturally relevant task. Examples would be activities such as counting out equal shares, setting the table, calculating a recipe, exchanging money, or measuring one's height or weight. Each culture has its own way of doing these tasks. The problem teachers face is how to capitalize on what children learn outside of school while considering that some of these tasks may apply mathematics differently than it is used in the classroom. Teachers must learn about the everyday lives of their students and how mathematics concepts may be applied on a day-to-day basis. To connect out-of-school to in-school experiences, teachers should introduce mathematics in school by providing students with problems based on their everyday experiences. Teachers can then observe as students construct solutions based on their out-of-school life experiences. Once students have developed their own strategies, the conventional strategies or algorithms and formulas can be introduced as an alternative means of solving problems.

Teachers need to be responsive to the diverse cultural values and experiences of their students to identify each individual's ZPD and build from where the children are operating independently to where their capabilities can take them with appropriate scaffolding. Multicultural education is not a topic to be presented in one week or one month and then forgotten; it should permeate the whole curriculum. Practice should be both developmentally

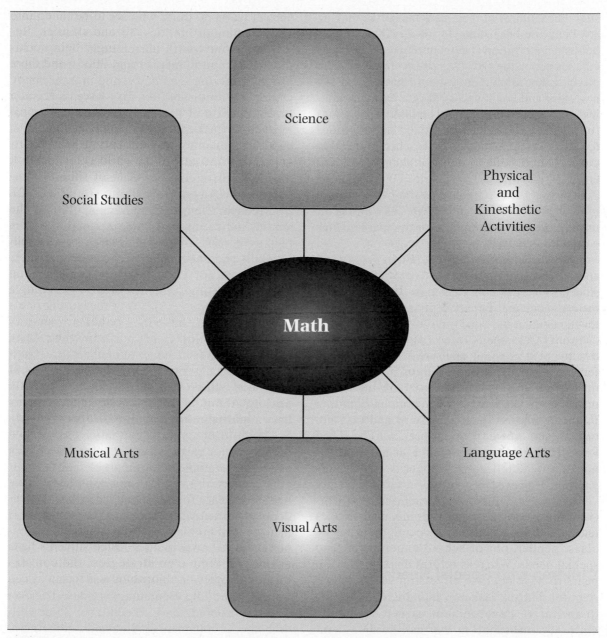

FIGURE 2–2 The basic content area web pattern.

and culturally appropriate (de Melendez & Beck, 2007). Across cultures, children develop in the same sequence physically, socially, and intellectually, but they experience varied cultural experiences within their environments. Child-rearing

practices and environmental variation provide the content of children's knowledge and views of the world. A teacher from another culture may view behavior that is considered normal within a particular culture as unacceptable. Teachers need to study the cultures of their students before making any behavioral decisions. In January 2008 NCTM published a position statement on equity in mathematics education (NCTM, 2008). The statement pledges that all students should have equal opportunity and equal access to quality mathematics instruction. There should be high expectations for all students' achievement and opportunities for challenging mathematics. Teachers should begin with each student's ethnomathematics (Gutierrez, Bay-Williams, & Kanold, 2008). Claudia Zaslavsky (1996) emphasizes the incorporation of math games from many cultures as a means for promoting multiculturalism in the mathematics curriculum.

English language learners (ELLs) also need special consideration (Santa Cruz, 2009). These students have a double challenge: They must learn the language and the concepts and processes of mathematics at the same time.

Equity also needs to be considered in relation to socioeconomic status (SES) (Clements & Sarama, 2002a). Research indicates that children from lower-SES homes lack important mathematics concepts. For example, counting might be limited to small groups and may not be accurate. Lower-SES children who have had very little number experience at home might not be able to tell if one amount is greater than another. However, several researchers have developed early childhood instructional programs that improve lower-SES children's mathematics understanding.

Children with Special Needs

A great deal of research has documented the quantitative development of typical young children—information that can guide our instruction (Mix, Huttenlocher, & Levine, 2002)—but it is also important to consider the mathematical development and instruction of children with special needs. Wilmot and Thornton (1989) describe the importance of identifying appropriate mathematics instruction for special learners: those who are gifted and those with learning disabilities. Teachers can provide gifted students with enrichment experiences that go beyond numeracy and into probability, problem solving, geometry, and measurement. Children with disabilities may have any one or a combination of problems in memory, visual or auditory perception, discrimination deficits, abstract reasoning difficulties, or other difficulties that intrude on their learning. Teachers must take different approaches with each type of learner. Cooperative learning groups can also be effective. Clements and Sarama (2002b) cite studies indicating that computer activities can help to increase all young children's mathematics skills and understanding. Providing positive experiences for young students with special needs can promote confidence as they move through school.

Geary (1996) describes how math anxiety and math disabilities can impede progress. Math anxiety results from a fear of mathematics, but it is hoped that a positive math experience in early childhood will prevent the development of math anxiety. About 6% of school-age children may have a **mathematics learning disorder** (**MLD**). Some children cannot remember basic facts; others cannot carry out basic procedures such as solving a simple addition problem. Math disabilities may also result from brain injury. In his research, Geary found that about half of the students identified with MLD had no perceptual or neurological problem but more likely lacked experience, had poor motivation, or suffered from anxiety. Procedural problems are usually related to slow cognitive development and usually clear up by the middle elementary grades. The fact retrieval problem tends to continue. Some children have problems in reading and writing numbers as well as words and letters. However, these problems are usually developmental and eventually disappear. Some children may have spatial relations problems, which show up when they misalign numbers in columns or reverse numbers. Geary concludes that early experiences that make necessary neural connections in the brain can lessen the chances of MLD.

Geary (1996, p. 285) suggests several ways to help children who have MLD.

- *Memory problems*. Do not expect the child to memorize the basic facts. Provide alternative methods.
- *Procedural problems*. Make sure the child understands the fundamental concepts. For example, be sure that they understand counting before they are taught to count on. Then have the child practice the procedures.
- *Visuospatial problems*. Provide prompts or cues that will help the child organize numbers so they are lined up correctly.
- *Problem-solving difficulties*. First help the child with any basic skill difficulties. Have the child identify different types of word problems and help identify the steps needed to solve the problem.

Young children need to be carefully assessed and provided with extra practice and direct instruction if they do not seem to be developing and acquiring the fundamental concepts. Wright, Martland, Stafford, and Stanger (2002) provide a sequenced assessment and instruction method for teaching numbers to young children. Karp and Howell (2004) emphasize the importance of individualized approaches for children with learning disabilities. They describe four components of individualization:

- *Remove specific barriers*. For example, if a child has motor difficulties that make writing difficult, let the child give his explanations orally and put his responses on tape.
- *Structure the environment*. Children with learning disabilities need a simple environment that is not overstimulating. They also require transitions that are carefully planned and clearly set up.
- *Incorporate more time and practice*. Practice should be for frequent short periods, avoiding "drill and kill."

- *Provide clarity*. Present problems clearly using modeling, questioning, and presenting activities in small steps.

Classroom accommodations for children with physical challenges should include the provision of easily accessible tables and areas. Teachers need to be responsive to each student's special needs and make appropriate accommodations.

Technology

Technology is providing us with an ever-increasing array of learning tools. For example, young children can use interactive websites and software. Teachers can create their own websites. Teacher websites may provide a look into their classrooms, lists of favorite websites, and descriptions of student projects. The Internet provides many opportunities for learning.

Besides collecting information from the Internet, children can enjoy a variety of educational software. More and more preschools and elementary schools are including computers in the classrooms. Douglas H. Clements is a major researcher on the effective use of computers with young children (Clements, 1999, 2001; Clements & Sarama, 2002b). Computer activities can help children bridge the gap from concrete to abstract. Children can learn math concepts from software that presents a task, asks for a response, and provides feedback. However, software should go beyond drill and practice and provide for the expressions of the child's creativity. Creating new shapes from other shapes or using turtles to draw shapes provides children with opportunities for exploration and discovery. Computers also provide social opportunities because children enjoy working together. One or more computers can serve as centers in the classroom. As children explore, the adult can provide suggestions or ask questions. Most important, the adult can observe and learn something about how children think and solve problems. Virtual manipulatives are now

MATH TECHNOLOGY
FOR YOUNG CHILDREN

Douglas Clements (1999) describes the software listed below. See if you can find a classroom that has any one of these items available and observe children using it. Write a description of the children's thinking and problem solving you observe.

- *Shapes* (Lebanon, IN: Dale Seymour Publications)
- *Turtle Geometry* program (Highgate Springs, VT: LCSI)
- *LEGO-Logo* (Enfield, CT: Lego Systems, Inc.)
- *Millie's Math House* (San Francisco: Riverdeep-Edmark)
- *Kid Pix Deluxe 3* (San Francisco: Broderbund)

Try out one of the software evaluation tools found on the Internet.

available online and in CD-ROM format (http://www.mattimath.com).

Calculators can also provide a tool for learning. In Unit 21 we describe some simple activities that young children can explore with calculators. An area for some concern centers on video games and whether children can learn through them (Sherman, 2007). Video games designed to teach basic concepts to young children are now on the market, and more are being designed.

Assistive Technology

Assistive technology supports the learning of children with disabilities (Mulligan, 2003). Technology is available that can help children with developmental challenges "express ideas, play with a toy, or demonstrate understanding of developmental concepts" (Mulligan, 2003, p. 50). High-tech tools such as voice synthesizers, Braille readers, switch-activated toys, and computers and low-tech tools can expand the experiences of children with special needs. Special handles can be put on pans and paintbrushes. Pillows and bolsters can help a child have a place in circle time activities. A board with photos can be used as a means for a child to make choices. Selection of technology must consider the children served and their abilities, the environment, and the cost. Further information can be obtained from the Division of Early Childhood (DEC) of the Council for Exceptional Children.

Summary

We have described and defined three types of learning experiences. Through practice, the teacher and parent learn how to make the best use of naturalistic, informal, and adult guided experiences so that the child has a balance of free exploration and specific planned activities. When planning activities, the children's learning styles and areas of strength should be considered. Culture, socioeconomic status, special needs, and previous experience are all important factors. Technology—in the form of computers and calculators—provides valuable tools for learning math concepts.

KEY TERMS

adult guided learning
convergent questions
  and directions
divergent questions
  and directions

ethnomathematics
informal learning
mathematics learning
  disorder (MLD)
multiple intelligences

naturalistic learning
teachable moment

SUGGESTED ACTIVITIES

1. Observe a prekindergarten, kindergarten, and primary classroom. Keep a record of concept learning experiences that are naturalistic, informal, and adult guided. Compare the differences in the numbers of each type of experience observed in each of the classrooms.
2. Explore the National Library of Virtual Manipulatives materials online at http://nlvm.usu.edu. Evaluate their usefulness. What are the strengths and weaknesses? Have a child try an activity at his developmental level.
3. Evaluate a website that provides mathematics information and activities for children. Write an analysis using the following suggestions from Maria Timmerman (2004).
   - Briefly describe the website.
   - Describe the interactive features of the site.
   - Describe the concept understanding promoted by the site.
   - Describe how one manipulative might be paired with a concept included in the site.
   - Describe a feature of the site that motivates children to continue.
   - Explain how you would assess student learning (such as by journal writing, a recording sheet, observation, or an interview).

REVIEW

A. Write a description of each of the three types of learning experiences described in this unit.
B. Decide if each of the following examples is naturalistic, informal, or adult guided:
   1. "Mother, I'll cut this apple in two parts so you can have some." "Yes, then I can have half of the apple."
   2. John (age 19 months) is lining up small blocks and placing a toy person on each one.
   3. A teacher and six children are sitting at a table. Each child has a pile of Unifix Cubes. "Make a train with the pattern A-B-A-B."
   4. "I think I gave everyone two cookies," says Zang He. "Show me how you can check to be sure," says Mr. Brown.
   5. Four children are pouring sand in the sandbox. They have various containers of assorted sizes and shapes. "I need a bigger cup, please," says one child to another.
   6. The children are learning about recycling. "Everyone sort your trash collection into a pile of things that can be used again and a pile of things that will have to be discarded."
   7. Trang Fung brings her pet mouse to school. Each child observes the mouse and asks Trang Fung questions about its habits. Several children draw pictures and write stories about the mouse.
   8. Mrs. Red Fox introduces her class to LOGO through structured floor games. The children take turns pretending to be a turtle and try to follow commands given by the teacher and the other students.
C. Read each of the following situations and explain how you would react:
   1. George and Dina are setting the table in the home living center. They are placing one complete place setting in front of each chair.
   2. Samantha says, "I have more crayons than you do, Hillary." "No, you don't." "Yes, I do!"
   3. The children in Mr. Wang's class are discussing the show they must put on for the students in the spring. Some children want to do a show with singing and dancing; others do not. Brent suggests that they vote and the others agree. Derrick and Theresa count the votes. They agree that there are 17 in favor of a musical show and 10 against.
D. Explain why it is important to consider individual and cultural learning styles when planning instruction for young children.

E. Match the math learning difficulty on the left with the correct definition on the right.

1. Memory problem
2. Procedural problem
3. Visuospatial problem
4. Difficulty solving problems involving basic number facts

a. Child needs help in basic problem solving and fundamental skills
b. May be evidenced by misaligning numbers
c. Evidenced by student continuing to do finger counting well into the primary grades when engaged with math problems
d. Usually related to slow cognitive development and clears up by the middle elementary grades

F. Decide which of the following statements are true about technology.
1. Computers and calculators are not appropriate tools for young children to use.
2. Kindergartners can learn to use the Internet to gain information.
3. The value of computers as learning tools depends on the developmental appropriateness and quality of the software selected.
4. Drill and practice computer software is the most appropriate software for young children.
5. Assistive technology is available to enhance the learning experiences of children with disabilities.

REFERENCES

Clements, D. H. (1999). The effective use of computers with young children. In J. V. Copely (Ed.), *Mathematics in the early years* (pp. 119–128). Washington, DC: National Association for the Education of Young Children, and Reston, VA: National Council of Teachers of Mathematics.

Clements, D. H. (2001). Mathematics in the preschool. *Teaching Children Mathematics, 7*(5), 270–275.

Clements, D. H., & Sarama, J. (2002a). Mathematics curricula in early childhood. *Teaching Children Mathematics, 9*(3), 163–166.

Clements, D. H., & Sarama, J. (2002b). The role of technology in early childhood learning. *Teaching Children Mathematics, 8*(6), 340–343.

de Melendez, W. R., & Beck, V. (2007). *Teaching young children in multicultural classrooms* (2nd ed.). Albany, NY: Thomson Delmar Learning.

Gardner, H. (1999). *Intelligence reframed*. New York: Basic Books.

Geary, D. C. (1996). *Children's mathematical development*. Washington, DC: American Psychological Association.

Gutierrez, R., Bay-Williams, J., & Kanold, T. D. (2008). Beyond access and achievement: Equity issues for mathematics teachers and leaders. *NCTM News Bulletin, 45*(3), 5.

Karp, K., & Howell, P. (2004). Building responsibility for learning in students with special needs. *Teaching Children Mathematics, 11*(3), 118–126.

Lewin, T. (2006, November 14). As Math Scores Lag, a New Push for the Basics. *New York Times*. Retrieved November 20, 2006, from http://www.newyorktimes.com

Mix, K. S., Huttenlocher, J., & Levine, S. C. (2002). *Quantitative development in infancy and early childhood*. New York: Oxford University Press.

Mulligan, S. A. (2003). Assistive technology: Supporting the participation of children with disabilities. *Young Children, 58*(6), 50–51.

NCTM (National Council of Teachers of Mathematics). (2008, January). *Equity in Mathematics Education, Position Statement*. Retrieved 3/29/09 from NCTM.org

Nunes, T. (1992). Ethnomathematics and everyday cognition. In D. A. Grouws (Ed.), *Handbook of research on mathematics teaching and learning* (pp. 557–574). New York: Macmillan.

Santa Cruz, R.M. (2009, January/February). Giving voice to English language learners in mathematics. *NCTM News Bulletin*. Retrieved 1/16/09 from NCTM.org

Sherman, D. (2007, March 16). *More video games, fewer books at schools?* Retrieved May 25, 2007, from http://uk.reuters.com

Timmerman, M. (2004). Using the Internet: Are prospective elementary teachers prepared to teach with technology? *Teaching Children Mathematics*, *10*(8), 410–415.

Wilmot, B., & Thornton, C. A. (1989). Mathematics teaching and learning: Meeting the needs of special learners. In P. R. Trafton & A. P. Shulte (Eds.), *New directions for elementary school mathematics* (pp. 212–222). Reston, VA: National Council of Teachers of Mathematics.

Wright, R. J., Martland, J., Stafford, A. K., & Stanger, G. (2002). *Teaching number: Advancing children's skills and strategies*. Thousand Oaks, CA: Chapman.

Zaslavsky, C. (1996). *The multicultural math classroom*. Portsmouth, NH: Heinemann.

FURTHER READING AND RESOURCES

Adams, T. L. (2000/2001). Helping children learn mathematics through multiple intelligences and standards for school mathematics. *Childhood Education*, *77*(2), 86–92.

Baker, A., Schirner, K., & Hoffman, J. (2006). Multiage mathematics: Scaffolding young children's mathematical learning. *Teaching Children Mathematics*, *13*(1), 19–21.

Buckleitner, W. (2007, April). Helping young children find and use information. *Scholastic Early Childhood Today*, 33–38.

Clements, D. H., & Sarama, J. (2002). The role of technology in early childhood learning. *Teaching Children Mathematics*, *8*(6), 340–343.

Clements, D. H., & Sarama, J. (2003, January/February). Creative pathways to math. *Early Childhood Today*, 37–45.

Copely, J. V. (Ed.). (1999). *Mathematics in the early years*. Washington, DC: National Association for the Education of Young Children, and Reston, VA: National Council of Teachers of Mathematics.

Derman-Sparks, L, & Edwards, J. O. (2010). *Antibias education for young children and ourselves*. Washington, DC: National Association for the Education of Young Children.

Donovan, M. S., & Bransford, J. D. (Eds.). (2005). *How students learn: History, mathematics, and science in the classroom*. Washington, DC: National Academies Press.

Equity for diverse populations. (2009). *Teaching Children Mathematics* [Focus issue]. 16(3).

Esmonde, I. (2009). Ideas and identities: Supporting equity in cooperative mathematics learning. *Review of Educational Research, 79*(2), 1008–1043.

Geary, D. C., Hoard, M. K., Byrd-Craven, J., Nugent, L., & Numtee, C. (2007). Cognitive mechanisms underlying achievement deficits in children with mathematical learning disability. *Child Development, 78*(4), 1343–1359.

Geist, E. (2001). Children are born mathematicians: Promoting the construction of early mathematical concepts in children under five. *Young Children*, *56*(4), 12–17.

Henderson, A., & Miles, E. (2001). *Basic topics in mathematics for dyslexics*. Florence, KY: Whurr/Taylor & Francis.

Kamii, C. (with Housman, L. B.). (2000). *Young children reinvent arithmetic: Implications of Piaget's theory* (2nd ed.). New York: Teachers College Press.

Kerrigan, J. (2002). Powerful software to enhance the elementary school mathematics program. *Teaching Children Mathematics*, 8(6), 364–370.

Leonard, J., & Guha, S. (2002). Creating cultural relevance in teaching and learning mathematics. *Teaching Children Mathematics*, 9(2), 114–118.

Mathematics and culture [Focus issue]. (2001). *Teaching Children Mathematics*, 7(6).

Moyer, P. S., Bolyard, J. J., & Spikell, M. A. (2002). What are virtual manipulatives? *Teaching Children Mathematics*, 8(6), 372–377.

Silverman, H. J. (2006). Explorations and discovery to a mathematics curriculum for toddlers. *ACEI Focus on Infants & Toddlers*, 19(2), 1–3, 6–7.

Promoting Young Children's Concept Development through Problem Solving

OBJECTIVES

After reading this unit, you should be able to:

- List and describe the six steps in instruction suggested in this unit.
- Identify examples of each of the six steps in instruction.
- Describe the advantages of using the six steps in instruction.
- Evaluate a teacher's instructional approach relative to the six steps.
- Recognize routine and nonroutine problems.
- Explain the term heuristic and its significance for mathematics problem solving.
- List the five NCTM process standards.
- Understand the value of estimation techniques.
- Implement developmentally appropriate problem-solving assessment and instruction.

The focus of instruction in mathematics should be **problem solving**. Not only should teacher-developed problems and investigations be worked on, but child-generated problems and investigations should also be important elements in instruction.

A problem-solving focus emphasizes children working independently and in groups while the teacher serves as a facilitator and guide. For the program to succeed, the teacher must know the students well so that she can support them

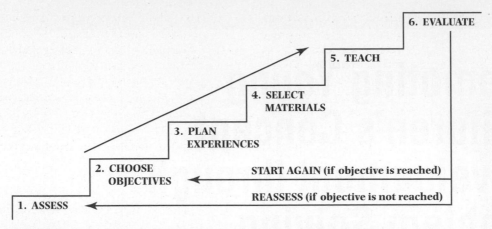

FIGURE 3–1   What should be taught and how?—Follow the Steps.

in reaching their full capacities within the ZPD. This unit outlines the basic instructional process and then describes the problem-solving inquiry approach to instruction as it applies to mathematics.

The steps involved in planning concept experiences are the same as those used for any subject area. Six questions must be answered (Figure 3–1).

- **Assess.** Where is the child now?
- **Choose objectives.** What should the child learn next?
- **Plan experiences.** What should the child do to accomplish these objectives?
- **Select materials.** Which materials should be used to carry through the plan?
- **Teach.** (do the planned experiences with the child): Do the plan and the materials fit?
- **Evaluate.** Has the child learned what was taught (reached objectives)?

Assessing

Each child should be individually *assessed*. Two methods for this are used most frequently. Children can be interviewed individually using specific tasks, and they can be observed during their regular activities. The purpose of assessment is to find out what children know and what they can do

before instruction is planned. The topic of assessment is covered in more detail in Unit 4.

Specific Task Assessment

The following are examples of some specific tasks that can be given to a child:

- Present the child with a pile of 10 counters (buttons, coins, poker chips, or other small things) and say, "Count these for me."
- Show the child two groups of chips: a group of three and a group of six. Ask, "Which group has more chips?"
- Show the child five cardboard dolls, each one a half inch taller than the next. Say: "Which is the tallest?" "Which is the smallest?" "Line them up from the smallest to the tallest."
- Provide a 6-year-old with an assortment of toy cars. Say: "Pretend you have a used car business. A customer wants to buy all your red cars and all your blue cars. Figure out how many of each he would be buying and how many he would be buying altogether. See how many ways you can solve this problem using the toy cars. You may also want to draw a picture or write about what you did."
- Provide a 7-year-old with a container of at least 100 counting chips. Say: "The zoo has a

collection of 17 birds. They buy 12 more birds. Five birds get out of the aviary and fly away. How many birds do they have now? You can use the counters to figure it out. Then draw a picture and even write about what you did."

- Place a pile of 30 counting chips in front of an 8-year-old. Say: "Find out how many different sets of two, three, five, and six you can make from this pile of chips." Record your findings.

Assessment by Observation

The following are examples of observations that can be made as children play and/or work:

- Does the 1-year-old show an interest in experimenting by pouring things in and out of containers of different sizes?

Assessment can be done through observation of children using math materials.

- Does the 2-year-old spend time sorting objects and lining them up in rows?

- Does the 3-year-old show an interest in understanding size, age, and time by asking how big he is, how old he is, and "when will _____" questions?
- Does the 4-year-old set the table correctly? Does he ask for help to write numerals, and does he use numbers in his play activities?
- Can the 5-year-old divide a bag of candy so that each of his friends receives an equal share?
- If there are five children and three chairs, can a 6-year-old figure out how many more chairs are needed so that everyone will have one?
- If a 7-year-old is supposed to feed the hamster two tablespoons of pellets each day, can she decide how much food should be left for the weekend?
- Four 8-year-olds are making booklets. Each booklet requires four pieces of paper. Can the children figure out how many pieces of paper will be needed to make the four booklets?

Through observation, the teacher can find out if the child can apply concepts to real life problems and activities. By keeping a record of these observations, the teacher builds up a more complete picture of the child's strengths and weaknesses. The current trend is to collect samples of student work, photographs, audio tapes, and videotapes and construct a portfolio that represents student accomplishments over time. Assessment will be discussed in more detail in Unit 4.

Choosing Objectives

Once the child's level of knowledge is identified, *objectives can be selected*. That is, a decision can be made as to what the child should be able to learn next. For instance, look at the first task example in the previous section. Suppose a 5-year-old child counts 50 objects correctly. The objective for this child would be different from the one for another 5-year-old who can count only seven objects accurately. The first child does not need any special help with object counting. A child who counts objects at this level at age 5 can probably figure out alone how to go beyond 50. The second child might need some help and specific activities with counting objects beyond groups of seven.

Suppose a teacher observes that a 2-year-old spends very little time sorting objects and lining them up in rows. The teacher knows that this is an important activity for a child of this age, one that most 2-year-olds engage in naturally without any special instruction. The objective selected might be that the child would choose to spend five minutes each day sorting and organizing objects. Once the objective is selected, the teacher then decides how to go about helping the child reach it.

Planning Experiences

Remember that young children construct concepts through naturalistic activities as they explore the environment. As they grow and develop, they feel the need to organize and understand the world around them. Children have a need to label their experiences and the things they observe. They notice how older children and adults count, use color words, label time, and so on. An instinctive knowledge of math concepts develops before an abstract understanding. When planning, it is important for adults to keep the following in mind:

- Naturalistic experiences should be emphasized until the child is into the preoperational period.
- Informal instruction is introduced during the sensorimotor period and increased in frequency during the preoperational period.
- Adult guided experiences are used sparingly during the sensorimotor and early preoperational periods and are brief and sharply focused. The use of adult guided experiences increases in kindergarten and primary grades.
- Follow the learning cycle format.

Abstract experiences can be introduced gradually during the preoperational and transitional periods and increased in frequency as the child

reaches concrete exploratory operations, but they should always be preceded by concrete experiences. Keep these factors in mind when planning for young children. These points are discussed in detail in the following section on selecting materials. In any case, the major focus for instructional planning is the promotion of individual and group problem solving.

Planning involves deciding the best way for each child to accomplish the selected objectives. Will naturalistic, informal, and/or adult guided experiences be best? Will the child acquire the concept best on her own? With a group of children? One-to-one with an adult? In a small group guided by an adult? Once these questions have been answered, the materials can be chosen. Sections 2 through 5 discuss how to plan these experiences for the concepts and skills that are acquired during the early years.

Selecting Materials

Three things must be considered when selecting math materials. First, there are some general characteristics of good materials. They should be sturdy, well made, and constructed so that they are safe for children to use independently. They should also be useful for more than one kind of activity and for teaching more than one concept.

Second, the materials must be designed for acquisition of the selected concepts. In other words, they must fit the objective(s).

Third, the materials must fit the children's levels of development; that is, they must be developmentally appropriate. As stated, acquiring a concept begins with concrete experiences with real things. For each concept included in the curriculum, materials should be sequenced from concrete to abstract and from three-dimensional (real objects), to two-dimensional (cutouts or computer images), to pictorial, to paper and pencil. Too often, however, the first steps are skipped, and children are immersed in paper-and-pencil activities without the prerequisite concrete experiences and before they have developed the perceptual and motor skills necessary to handle a writing implement with ease.

Five steps to be followed from concrete materials to paper and pencil are described as follows. Note that Step 1 is the first and last step during the sensorimotor period; during the preoperational period, the children move from Step 1 through Step 4; and during the transition and concrete operations periods, they move into Step 5.

- *Step 1.* Real objects are used for this first step. Children are given time to explore and manipulate many types of objects such as blocks, chips, stones, and sticks as well as materials such as sand, water, mud, clay, and Play-Doh. Whether instruction is naturalistic, informal, or adult guided, concrete materials are used.
- *Step 2.* Real objects are used along with pictorial representations. For example, blocks can be matched with printed or drawn patterns. When cooking, each implement to be used (measuring spoons and cups, bowls, mixing spoons, etc.) can be depicted on a pictorial sequenced recipe chart. Children can draw pictures each day showing the height of their bean sprouts.
- *Step 3.* Cutouts that can be manipulated by hand are introduced. For example, cardboard cutouts of different sizes, colors, and shapes can be sorted. Cutout dogs can be matched with cutout doghouses. Cutout human body parts can be put together to make a whole body. Although the materials have moved into two dimensions, they can still be manipulated. By manipulating the materials, the child can try a variety of solutions to the problem by trial and error and can engage in self-correction. Virtual manipulatives from online or software sources can provide interesting experiences at this level (see http://nlvm.usu.edu). Many online games are also available.
- *Step 4.* Pictures are next. Commercially available pictorial materials, teacher-created or magazine pictures, and cut-up workbook pages can be used to make card games as well as sequencing, sorting, and matching

activities. For example, pictures of people in various occupations might be matched with pictures of their work tools. Pictures of a person at different ages can be sequenced from baby to old age. Groups of objects drawn on a card can be counted and matched with the appropriate numeral.

Stop Here If the Children Have Not Yet Reached the Transition Stage

- *Step 5.* At this level, paper-and-pencil activities are introduced. When the teacher observes that the children understand the concept with materials at the first four levels, it is time for Step 5. If the materials are available, children usually start experimenting when they feel ready. Now they can draw and write about mathematics.

An example of sequencing materials using the five steps follows. Suppose one of the objectives for children in kindergarten is to compare differences in dimensions. One of the dimensions to be compared is length. Materials can be sequenced as follows:

- *Step 1: Real objects.* Children explore the properties of Unifix Cubes® and Cuisinaire Rods®. They fit Unifix Cubes together into groups of various lengths and compare the lengths of the Cuisinaire Rods®. They do measurement activities such as comparing how many Unifix Cubes® fit across the short side of the table versus the long side.
- *Step 2: Real objects with pictures.* The Unifix Cubes® are used to construct rows that match pictured patterns of various lengths. Sticks are used to measure pictured distances from one place to another.
- *Step 3: Cutouts.* Unifix® and Cuisinaire® cutouts are used to make rows of various lengths. Cutouts of snakes, fences, and so on, are compared.
- *Step 4: Pictures.* Cards with pictures of pencils of different lengths are sorted and matched. A picture is searched for the long

PERIODS OF DEVELOPMENT	HOW CONCEPTS ARE ACQUIRED		
	Naturalistic	Informal	Adult Guided
Sensorimotor	Real objects Objects and pictures Pictures	Real objects Objects and pictures Pictures	
Preoperational	Real objects Objects and pictures Cutouts Pictures	Real objects Objects and pictures Cutouts Pictures Calculators and computers	Real objects Objects and pictures Cutouts Pictures Calculators and computers
Transitional	Real objects Objects and pictures Cutouts Pictures	Real objects Objects and pictures Cutouts Pictures Paper and pencil Calculators and computers	Real objects Objects and pictures Cutouts Pictures Calculators and computers
Concrete Operations	Real objects Objects and pictures Cutouts Pictures	Real objects Objects and pictures Cutouts Pictures Paper and pencil Calculators and computers	Real objects Objects and pictures Cutouts Pictures Paper and pencil Calculators and computers

FIGURE 3–2 Two dimensions of early childhood concept instruction with levels of materials used.

and short paths, the dog with long ears, the dog with short ears, the long hose, the short hose, and so on.

Stop Here If the Children Have Not Yet Reached the Transition Stage

- *Step 5: Paper-and-pencil activities.* For example, students might draw long and short things.

At the early steps, children might be able to make comparisons of materials with real objects or even with cutouts and picture cards, but they might fail if they are given just paper-and-pencil activities. In this case it would be falsely assumed that they do not understand the concept when, in fact, it is the materials that are inappropriate. Calculators and computers can be used at every step. Virtual manipulatives can be supportive of learning.

Figure 3–2 depicts the relationship between the cognitive developmental periods—naturalistic, informal, and adult guided ways of acquiring concepts—and the five levels of materials. Each unit of this text has examples of various types of materials. Section 6 contains lists and descriptions of many materials that are excellent teaching aids.

Intentional Teaching

Once the decision has been made as to what the child should be able to learn next and in what context the concept acquisition will take place, the next stage in the instructional process is teaching. *Teaching* occurs when the planned experiences using the selected materials are put into operation. If the first four questions have been answered with care, the experience should go smoothly. A child will be interested and will learn from the activities because they match his level of development and style of learning. The child might even acquire a new concept or skill or extend and expand one already learned. Epstein (2007) outlines a balanced approach to teaching that she calls *Intentional Teaching*. It balances child guided and adult guided teaching. It is teaching that, as described in this text, is guided by specific goals and objectives.

The time involved in the teaching stage might be a few minutes or several weeks, months, or even years, depending on the particular concept being acquired and the age and ability of the child. For instance, time sequence is initially learned through naturalistic activity. From infancy, children learn that there is a sequence in their daily routines: sleeping; waking up wet and hungry; crying; being picked up, cleaned, fed, and played with; and sleeping again. In preschool, children learn a daily routine such as coming in, greeting the teacher, hanging up coats, eating breakfast, playing indoors, having a group activity time, snacking, playing outdoors, having a quiet activity, lunch, playing outdoors, napping, having a small group activity time, and going home. Time words are acquired informally as children hear terms such as *yesterday, today, tomorrow, o'clock, next, after,* and so on. In kindergarten, special events and times are noted on a calendar. Children learn to name the days of the week and months of the year and to sequence the numerals for each of the days. In first grade, they might be given a blank calendar page to fill in the name of the month, the days of the week, and the number for each day. Acquiring the concept of time is a complex experience and involves many prerequisite concepts that build over several years. Some children will learn at a fast rate, others at a slow pace. One child might learn that there are seven days in a week the first time this idea is introduced; another child might take all year to acquire this information. Some children need a great deal of structured repetition; others learn from naturalistic and informal experiences. Teaching developmentally involves flexible and individualized instruction.

Even with careful planning and preparation, an activity might not work well the first time. When this happens, analyze the situation by asking the following questions:

- Was the child interested?
- Was the task too easy or too hard?

- Did the child understand what she was asked to do?
- Were the materials right for the task?
- Were the materials interesting?
- Is further assessment needed?
- Was the teacher enthusiastic?
- Was it just a "bad day" for the child?

You might try the activity again using the same method and materials or with a change in the method and/or materials. In some cases, the child might have to be reassessed to ensure that the activity is appropriate for her developmental level.

Evaluating

The sixth question concerns *evaluation*. What has the child learned? What does the child know and what can he do after the concept experiences have been presented? The assessment questions are asked again. If the child has reached the objective, a new one can be chosen. The stages of planning, choosing materials, teaching, and evaluating are repeated. If the child has not reached the objective, the same activities can be continued or a new method may be tried. For example, a teacher wants a 5-year-old to count out the correct number of objects for each of the number symbols from 0 to 10. The teacher tries many kinds of objects for the child to count and many kinds of containers in which to place the things the child counts, but the child is just not interested. Finally the teacher gives the child small banks made from baby food jars and real pennies. The child finds these materials exciting and goes on to learn the task quickly and with enthusiasm.

Evaluation may be done using formal, structured questions as well as tasks and specific observations (see Unit 4). Informal questions and observations of naturalistic experiences can also be used for evaluation. For example, when a child sets the table in the wrong way, it can be seen without formal questioning that he has not learned from instruction. He needs some help. Maybe organizing and placing a whole table setting is more than he can do now. Can he place one item at each place? Does he need to go back to working with a smaller number (such as a table for two or three)? Does he need to work with simpler materials that have more structure (such as pegs in a pegboard)? To look at these more specific skills, the teacher would then return to the assessment step. At this point the teacher would assess not only the child but also the types of experiences and materials that she has been using. Sometimes assessment leads the teacher to the right objective, but the experience and/or materials chosen are not (as in the example given) the ones that fit the child.

Frequent and careful evaluation helps both teacher and child avoid frustration. An adult must never take it for granted that any one plan or material is the best choice for a specific child. The adult must keep checking to be sure the child is learning what the experience was planned to teach him.

Problem Solving and the Process Standards

In Unit 1 we outlined the process standards for school mathematics (NCTM, 2000). These five standards include problem solving, reasoning and proof, connections, communication, and representation. *Problem solving* involves application of the other four standards. Although the *reasoning* of preoperational children is different from that of older children and adults, it is logical from their own point of view. Pattern recognition and classification skills provide the focus for much of young children's reasoning. Adults should encourage children to make guesses and explain their reasoning. Language is a critical element in mathematics (see Unit 15). Children can explain how they approach problem solving by *communication* with language. Even the youngest students can talk about mathematics, and, as they grow older, can write and draw about it. The important *connections* for young mathematicians are those made between informal mathematics and the formal mathematics of the school curriculum. The transition can be made through the use of concrete objects and by connecting to everyday activities

such as table setting, finding out how many children are present in the class, and recognizing that when they surround a parachute they are forming a circle. Young children use several kinds of *representations* to explain their ideas: oral language, written language using invented and conventional symbols, physical gestures, and drawings.

Skinner (1990, p. 1) provides the following definition of a problem: "A problem is a question which engages someone in searching for a solution." This means that a problem is some question that is important to the student and thus focuses her attention and enthusiasm on the search for a solution. Problem solving is not a special topic but should be a major focus for every concept and skill in the mathematics programs. Problem solving becomes a type of lesson in which the teacher sets up a situation for children to learn through exploration.

Problems should relate to and include the children's own experiences. From birth onward, children want to learn and naturally seek out problems to solve. Problem solving in school should build on the informal methods learned out of school. Problem solving through the prekindergarten years focuses on naturalistic and informal learning, which promotes exploration and discovery. In kindergarten and primary classes, a more structured approach can be instituted. Every new topic should be introduced with a problem designed to afford children the opportunity to construct their own problem-solving strategies. For an overall look at implementing a problem-solving approach for kindergarten and primary students, read Skinner's book, *What's Your Problem?* (1990). Also refer to the resources listed at the end of this unit.

Overview of Problem Solving in Mathematics

Problem solving is a major focus in the mathematics program today. As students enter the transition into concrete operations, they can engage in more structured problem-solving activities. These activities promote children's abilities to develop their own problems and translate them into a symbolic format (writing and/or drawing). This sequence begins with the teacher providing problems and then gradually pulling back as students develop their own problems. Problem solving became the focus of mathematics through the work of George Polya (O'Connor & Robertson, 2002). For Polya, problem solving was heuristic or providing oneself with a series of self-generated questions. O'Connor and Robertson provide the following quote from Polya:

> The aim of heuristic is to study the methods and rules of discovery and invention…. Hueristic as an adjective, means 'serving to discover'…. its purpose is to discover the solution of the present problem …. What is good education? Systematically giving opportunity to the student to discover things by himself. (p. 4)

Polya is quoted further when speaking of teaching mathematics in the primary grades:

> To understand mathematics is to do mathematics. And what does it mean doing mathematics? In the first place it means to do mathematical problems. (p. 5)

Polya refers to teaching as an art, not a science, because there is no proven best way. Teaching must be active—its main point is to develop the tactics of problem solving. Polya defined four main phases in mathematics problem solving (Hall, 1957): (1) understand the problem, (2) devise a plan, (3) carry out the plan, and (4) look back.

There are two major types of problems in math: **routine** and **nonroutine**. Consider the following descriptions of students working on problems:

- The teacher, Mr. Wang, has given Brent and the other children in his class the following problem. "Derrick has 10 pennies. John has 16 pennies. How many pennies do they have altogether?" Brent notes the key words "How many altogether?" and decides that this is an addition problem. He adds 10 + 16 and finds the answer: 26 pennies.

- Mr. Wang has also given them the following problem to solve. "Juanita and Lai want to buy a candy bar that costs 35¢. Juanita has 15 pennies and Lai has 16 pennies. Altogether, do they have enough pennies to buy the candy bar?" Brent's attention is caught by the word "altogether," and again he adds 15 + 16. He writes down his answer: 31 pennies.

- Brent has five sheets of 8½" × 11" construction paper. He needs to provide paper for himself and six other students. If he gives everyone a whole sheet, two people will be left with no paper. Brent draws a picture of the five sheets of paper, and then he draws a line down the middle of each. If he cuts each sheet in half, there will be ten pieces of paper. Since there are seven children, this would leave three extra pieces. What will he do with the extras? He decides that it would be a good idea to have the three sheets in reserve in case someone makes a mistake.

The first problem is a *routine problem*. It follows a predictable pattern and can be solved correctly without actually reading the whole question carefully. The second is called a *nonroutine problem*. There is more than one step, and the problem must be read carefully. Brent has focused on the word "altogether" and stopped with the addition of the two girls' pennies. He misses the question asked, which is: "Once you know there are 31 pennies, is that enough money to buy a 35¢ candy bar?" The current focus in mathematics problem solving is on providing more opportunities for solving nonroutine problems, including those that occur in naturalistic situations such as the problem in the third example. Note that the third problem is multistepped: subtract five from seven, draw a picture, draw a line down the middle of each sheet, count the halves, decide if there are enough, subtract seven from ten, and decide what to do with the three extras. This last problem really has no single correct answer. For example, Brent could have left two of the children out, or he could have given three children whole sheets and four children halves. Real problem-solving skills go beyond simple one-step problems.

Note that, when dealing with each of the problems, the children went through a process of self-generated questions. This process is referred to as **heuristics**. There are three common types of self-generated questions:

- Consider a similar but simpler problem as a model.
- Use symbols or representations (build concrete representations, draw a picture or diagram, make a chart or graph).
- Use means–ends analysis such as identifying the knowns and unknowns, working backward, and setting up intermediate goals.

We often provide children with a learned idea or heuristic such as a series of problem-solving steps. Unfortunately, if the rules are too specific then they will not transfer (note Brent's focus on the key word). Yet if the rules are too general, how will you know if the idea has been mastered? It is important to recognize that applying a heuristic—such as developing the relevant charts, graphs, diagrams, or pictures or performing needed operations—requires a strong grounding in such basics as counting, whole number operations, geometry, and the like.

Researchers have investigated not only whether heuristics can be taught but also what it is that successful problem solvers do that leads to their success. It has been found that general heuristics cannot be taught. When content is taught with heuristics, content knowledge improves but problem-solving ability does not. The study of successful problem solvers has shown that they know the content and organize it in special ways. Therefore, content and problem solving should be taught together, not first one and then the other. Good problem solvers think in ways that are qualitatively different from poor problem solvers. Children must learn how to think about their thinking and manage it in an organized fashion. Heuristics is this type of learning; it is not simply learning a list of strategies that might not always

work. Children need to learn to apply consciously the following steps as described by Polya:

1. Assess the situation and decide exactly what is being asked.
2. Organize a plan that is directed toward answering the question.
3. Execute the plan using appropriate strategies.
4. Verify the results, that is, evaluate the outcome of a plan.

It is important that children deal with real problems that might not have clearly designated unknowns, that might contain too much or too little information, that can be solved using more than one method, that have no one right answer (or even no answer), that combine processes, that have multiple steps necessitating some trial and error, and that take considerable time to solve. Unfortunately, most textbook problems are of the routine variety: the unknown is obvious, only the necessary information is provided, the solution procedure is obvious, there is only one correct answer, and the solution can be arrived at quickly. It is essential that students have the opportunity to share possible solutions with their peers. If children have the opportunity to explain solutions to others, they will clarify the problem and be better able to explain problems to themselves.

Formal problem solving can be introduced using **contrived problems**, that is, problems teachers devise or select. This procedure provides an opportunity for the teacher to model problem-solving behavior by posing the problem and then acting out the solution. The children can then be asked to think of some variations.

Skinner (1990) presented the first problems to her 5-year-olds in book form to integrate mathematics and reading/language arts. The tiny books were on sturdy cardboard with an illustration and one sentence on a page. They were held together with spiral binding. Skinner encouraged students to use manipulatives such as Unifix Cubes to aid in solving problems or to act out their solutions. Eventually, the students moved into dictating problems and then into writing. By age 7, they were creating most of their own problems. Research indicates that working with concrete materials and drawing and/or writing explanations of solutions for problems are the best experiences for improving problem-solving skills.

Assessment

Assessment of children's problem-solving expertise is not an easy task. It demands that teachers be creative and flexible. Development of problem-solving skills is a long-term activity; it is not learned in one lesson. It must be focused on the process of problem solving, not solely on the answers. Therefore, you must provide children with problem-solving situations and observe how they meet them, interview students, have small groups of children describe how they solved problems, and have students help each other solve problems.

Observe the following as students work on problems:

- Do they attack the problem in an organized fashion; that is, do they appear to have a logical strategy?
- If one strategy does not work, do they try another?
- Are they persistent in sticking with the problem until they arrive at what they believe is a satisfactory solution?
- How well do they concentrate on the problem-solving task?
- Do they use aids such as manipulatives and drawings?
- Do their facial expressions indicate interest, involvement, frustration, or puzzlement?

Behaviors noted can be recorded with anecdotal records or on checklists. Their solutions can be analyzed as to whether they understood or partially understood the problem, whether they planned a solution or had a partial plan, and whether they obtained a correct or partially correct answer.

Interviews will be emphasized as a format for assessment throughout the text. The interview is also an excellent way to look at problem-solving behavior. Present the child with a problem or have the child invent a problem and let her find a solution, describing what she is thinking as she works. Make a tape recording or take notes.

Instruction

Researchers agree that children should experience a variety of problem-solving strategies so that they do not approach every problem in the same stereotyped way. They should be given problems that are at their developmental level. Natural and informal methods of instruction should begin the exploration of problem solving. For example, ask how many children are in the classroom today, how many glasses of juice we will need at Kate's table, and so on.

To be effective problem solvers, children need time to mull over problems, to make mistakes, to try various strategies, and to discuss problems with their friends. When teaching in the kindergarten and primary grades, if you must use a textbook then check the problems carefully. If you find that most of the problems are routine, you will have to obtain some nonroutine problems or devise some yourself. You may use the following criteria:

- Devise problems that contain extra information or that lack necessary information.

  1. George bought two bags of cookies with six cookies in each bag for 10¢ a bag. How many cookies did George buy? (Price is extra information.)
  2. John's big brother is 6 feet tall. How much will John have to grow to be as big as his brother? (We don't know John's height.)

- Devise problems that involve estimation or that do not have clearly right or wrong answers.

  1. Vanessa has $1. She would like to buy a pen that costs 49¢ and a notebook that costs 39¢. Does she have enough money? (Yes/no rather than numerical answer)
  2. How many times can you ride your bike around the block in 10 minutes? In one hour? In a week? In a month? (Estimation)

- Devise problems that apply mathematics in practical situations such as shopping, cooking, or building.
- Base problems on things children are interested in, or make up problems that are about students in the class (giving them a personal flavor).
- Devise problems that require more than one step and provide opportunities for application of logic, reasoning, and testing out ideas.
- Ask questions that will require the children to make up a problem.
- Design problems whose solutions will provide data for decision making.

There are 25 students in the third-grade class. The students are planning a party to celebrate the end of the school year. They need to decide on a menu, estimate the cost, and calculate how much money each of them will have to contribute.

Collect resources that children can use for problem solving. Gather statistics that children can work with (such as the weather information from the daily newspaper). Use children's spontaneous questions (How far is it to the zoo?). Provide children with problems such as those described by Marilyn Burns (1998). Literature (see Unit 12) provides a wealth of information for problem solving. Have children write problems that other children can try to solve. Calculators can be helpful tools for problem solving. Children can try out more strategies because of time saved that might otherwise be spent in tedious hand calculations.

Computers can also be used for problem solving. LOGO programming is a problem-solving activity in itself. Remember, have children work in pairs or small groups. Software is described and referred to in each of the units on mathematics content.

The conventional problem-solving strategies follow Polya's four-step procedure (Reys, Lindquist, Lambdin, Smith, & Suydam, 2001). However, start by letting children develop their own solutions. They will gradually become more direct in their approaches. Through modeling, new strategies can be introduced. Reys and colleagues (2001) suggest several such strategies.

1. Act out the problem. That is, use real objects or representations to set up the problem and go through the steps of finding a solution. This is the type of activity used to introduce whole number operations.
2. Make a drawing or a diagram. The pictures must be extremely simple and should include only the important elements. For example:

George wants to build a building with his blocks that is triangular shaped with seven blocks in the bottom row. How many blocks will he need?

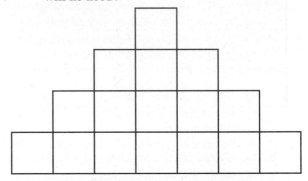

Theresa's mother's van has three rows of seats. One row holds three passengers, the next row holds two, and the back row holds four. Can ten passengers and the driver ride comfortably?

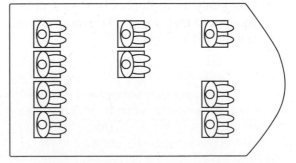

The van holds eight passengers and the driver. Ten passengers and the driver would be crowded.

3. Look for a pattern. (See Unit 28.)
4. Construct a table. (See Unit 31.)
5. Account systematically for all possibilities. In other words, as different strategies are tried or different calculations are made, keep track of what has been used.

A map showing all the roads from Jonesville to Clinton is shown here. Find as many different ways as you can to get from Jonesville to Clinton without ever backtracking.

Jonesville

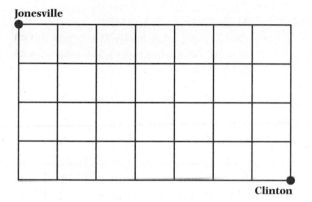

Clinton

6. Guess and check. Make an educated guess based on attention to details of the problem and past experience. Some problems demand trial and error and a "best guess" to solve. Sudoku has become popular with both children and adults. Problems follow the pattern below (Sudoku for Kids, 2008).

Using only the numbers 1 through 9, fill the squares so that the sum in every row and column is 15.

7. Work backward. In some problems, the endpoint is given and the problem solver must work backward to find out how the endpoint

was reached. A maze is a concrete example of this type of problem.

Chan's mother bought some apples. She put half of them in her refrigerator and gave two to each of three neighbors. How many apples did she buy?

8. Identify wanted, given, and needed information. Rather than plunging right into calculations or formulating conclusions, the problem solver should sort out the important and necessary information from the extraneous factors and may need to collect additional data. Taking a poll is a common way of collecting data to make a decision.

Trang Fung says that most of the girls would like to have pepperoni pizza at the slumber party. Sara claims that most of the girls prefer hamburger. To know how much of each to order, they set up a chart, question their friends, and tally their choices.

9. Turn a word problem into an equation or "number sentence."

Mary gives Johnny half of her allowance. With the rest of her money, she uses half to buy an ice cream cone for $2. How much allowance did Mary receive? Number sentence: $2 \times \$2 = \$4 \times 2 = \$8$ allowance.

This process is not easy for students, but is too frequently the only strategy included in a textbook.

10. Solve a simpler or similar problem. Sometimes large numbers or other complications get in the way of seeing how to solve a problem, so making a similar problem may help the child discover the solution. For example, in the following problem, the amounts could be changed to "Derrick has $4 and Brent has $6."

If Derrick has saved $4.59 and Brent has saved $6.37, how much more money has Brent saved?

Sometimes problems have to be broken down into smaller parts. Also, a strategy may be clarified if a problem is put into the child's own words.

11. Change your point of view. Is the strategy being used based on incorrect assumptions? Stop and ask, "What is really being said in this problem?"

All these strategies will not be learned right away. They will be introduced gradually and acquired throughout the elementary grades. Prekindergarten through fourth grade play a crucial role in providing the foundations for problem solving.

Estimation is a challenge for young children.

MATH TECHNOLOGY
FOR YOUNG CHILDREN

Review some problem-solving software such as listed below. Use one of the review procedures suggested in the Tech Box in Unit 2.

- *I SPY Fantasy* (ages 6–10; Scholastic), Windows and MAC.
- *Math Missions: The Race to Spectacle City Arcade* (ages 5–8; Scholastic), Windows and MAC.
- *The Little Raven & Friends* (ages 3–7; Tivola), Windows and MAC.
- *Ollo in the Sunny Valley Fair* (ages 3–5; Hulabee Entertainment), Windows and MAC.

Estimation

Estimation is arriving at an approximation of the answer to a problem. Estimation should be taught as a unique strategy. Estimation is mental and should not be checked to see how accurate it is. Later on, children can apply estimation after computation to help decide if a computed answer is a reasonable one. First, however, the concept must be developed. At the primary level, the most common problems for applying estimation involve length or numerosity and are solved through visual perception. Children might guess how wide the rug is or how many objects are in a container. Computational estimation is usually introduced near the end of the primary period (i.e., in the third grade).

A number of strategies can be used for estimation. At the introductory levels, students work with concrete situations. For example, they might explore by estimating how many trucks could be parked in their classroom or how many shoes will fit in the closet. Children can select some benchmarks for measurement such as a body part; that is, they could estimate how many hands wide the hallway is. Another example would be estimating how many beans would fill a jar using a one-cup measure that holds 100 beans as the benchmark. Keeping the same jar and changing the size or type of objects placed in it will help children build on their prior knowledge and increase their estimation skills.

Two strategies might be used for more advanced estimation. The *front-end* strategy is one that young children can use, which focuses on the first number on the left when developing an estimate. For example:

37 To estimate the sum, focus on the left
43 column first. Note that there are nine
+24 10s, which would be 90. Then look at
the right column. Obviously, the answer is more than 90, and noting that the right column adds up to more than 10, an estimate of 90 + 10 = 100 is reached.

Another strategy, called *clustering,* can be used when numbers are close in value. For example, estimate the total attendance in class for the week.

Class attendance

Monday	27	1. There were about
Tuesday	29	30 students each day.
Wednesday	31	
Thursday	32	
Friday	30	2. 5 × 30 = 150, the estimated total for the week.

Rounding is a strategy that is helpful for mental computation. Suppose you wondered how many primary grade children had eaten lunch at school this week. You found out that there were 43 first graders, 38 second graders, and 52 third graders.

Number of Students

Eating	Lunch	Round	Add
First graders	43	40	40
Second graders	38	40	40
Third graders	52	50	50
			130
			(estimate)

Two additional strategies are much more complex and would be used by more advanced students beyond the elementary grades. *Compatible numbers* strategy involves more complex rounding. *Special numbers* strategy is one that overlaps several strategies. For the most part, primary grade children will be using only the noncomputational and the front-end strategies. The important point is that children begin early to realize that mathematics is not just finding the one right answer but can also involve making good guesses or estimates.

Multicultural Problem Solving

Claudia Zaslavsky (1996) suggests games from many cultures as fun ways to teach mathematics while learning about other cultures. Games offer challenges to children. Problem-solving skills are developed as students think through strategies, think ahead, and evaluate their selections of moves. Older children can teach the games to younger children, and games can be related to the customs of cultures. Games can be played by men or by women, by children or adults, on special occasions or at any time. Young children like to change the rules of the game, which changes the strategies to be used.

Meeting Special Needs

As with other children, instruction for children with special needs must be individualized and related to how children best learn (Bowe, 2007). Children with special needs tend to lose ground and get farther behind in each year of school. Meeting their unique needs and teaching them the required academic skills and knowledge presents an enormous problem. Each type of disability provides a different instructional challenge. Planning is required to be individualized for each child and documented in an Individualized Family Service Plan (**IFSP**) for infants and toddlers and an Individualized Educational Plan (**IEP**) for older children. Children with disabilities require much more individualized instruction than do other children. Approaches to instruction in early childhood special education (**ECSE**) tend to be behaviorist based, in contrast to the constructivist-based approaches used in regular **ECE**. However, there is no evidence that suggests all ECSE students do best with behaviorist instructional approaches. Special education requirements for the youngest children focus on learning in the family and other natural environments that include outdoor activities, experiences with animals, experiences with art materials, and other opportunities recommended for all children. Instruction is embedded in the activities through verbal descriptions, questions, and descriptive statements. Children with disabilities may need ancillary services such as physical therapy, occupational therapy, and/or speech-language therapy. They learn math through the same types of activities as described in this textbook for other children, but with adaptations and accommodations as needed. Teaching needs to be from the concrete to the abstract as described in this unit. Teaching in an inclusive classroom is an enormous challenge due to the wide variety of approaches needed to meet each child's needs.

The needs of English Language Learners (**ELL**) can also be addressed by special instructional approaches. It is important for teachers to maintain a close relationship with the ELL students' families and to learn as much as possible about the students' home countries, language, and customs. Pair language with visual communication using objects, pictures, and gestures. Be sure these students are situated where they can see and hear everything. Vocabulary is critical in math. Bilingual vocabulary, both visual and oral, can be very helpful.

Summary

This unit has described six steps that provide a guide for what to teach and how to teach it.

Following these steps can minimize guesswork. The steps are (1) assess, (2) choose objectives, (3) plan experiences, (4) select materials, (5) teach, and (6) evaluate.

Problem solving is the major process that underlies all instruction in mathematics. George Polya was the major influence on the importance of math problem solving. Problem solving is first on the list of mathematics processes as developed by the NCTM. Problem solving emphasizes the process rather than the final product (or correct answer). The important factor is that, during the early childhood years, children gradually learn a variety of problem-solving strategies as well as when and where to apply them. For young children, problems develop out of their everyday naturalistic activities. It is critical that children have opportunities to solve many nonroutine math problems, that is, problems that are not just simple and straightforward with obvious answers but those that will stretch their minds. Assessment and evaluation should each focus on the process rather than the answers. Both observation and interview techniques may be used.

Problem-solving instruction for young children begins with their natural explorations in the environment. It requires time and careful guidance as teachers move from teacher-initiated to child-initiated problems.

Games can provide a multicultural problem-solving experience. Children with disabilities need more individualized instruction than do other children. ELLs need to work with objects, pictures, and gestures.

KEY TERMS

assess	evaluate	plan experiences
choose objectives	heuristics	problem solving
contrived problems	IEP	routine problems
ECE	IFSP	select materials
ECSE	nonroutine problems	teach
ELLs		

SUGGESTED ACTIVITIES

1. Interview two teachers who teach prekindergarten, kindergarten, and/or primary students. Ask them to describe their mathematics programs. Find out how they address each of the instructional steps described in this unit.
2. Start a section on problem solving in your Activity File. As you progress through the text, look through the units that involve problem solving. If you find some routine problems, rewrite them as nonroutine problems. Look through other resources for additional problem ideas. Write some problems of your own. Look through your favorite science and social studies texts and develop some problems that fit the unit themes in those books.
3. Look through the problem-solving activities in a kindergarten or first-, second-, or third-grade mathematics textbook. Categorize the problems as *routine* or *nonroutine*. Report your findings to the class.

REVIEW

A. List in order the six steps for instruction described in this unit.
B. Define each of the steps listed in A.
C. Read each of the following descriptions and label them with the correct step name:
   1. From her Activity File, the teacher selects two cards from the Classification section.
   2. Mrs. Brown has just interviewed Joey and discovered that he can count accurately through 12. He then continues, "15, 14, 19, 20." She thinks about what the next step in instruction should be for Joey.
   3. The teacher is seated at a table with Fwang. "Fwang, you put three red teddy bears and two blue teddy bears together in one group. Then you wrote 3 1 2 5 5. Explain to me how you figured out how to solve the problem."
   4. During the first month of school, Mrs. Garcia interviews each of her students individually to find out which concepts they know and what skills they have.
   5. Mr. Black has set up a sand table, and the children are pouring and measuring sand using standard measuring cups to learn the relationship between the different size cups.
   6. Katherine needs to work on A-B-A-B type patterns. Her teacher pulls out three cards from the Pattern section of her Activity File.
   7. Mr. Wang looks through the library of computer software for programs that require logical thinking strategies.
D. Describe the advantages of following the instructional steps suggested in this unit.
E. Read the description of Miss Conway's method of selecting objectives and activities. Analyze and evaluate her approach.

   Miss Conway believes that all her students are at about the same level in their mathematics capabilities and knowledge. She has used a math program for 15 years and she believes that it is satisfactory. She assumes that all students enter her class at the same level and leave knowing everything she has taught.

F. Write an *R* for routine problems and an *N* for nonroutine problems.
   ___1. Larry has four pennies, and his dad gave him five more pennies. How many pennies does Larry have now?
   ___2. Nancy's mother has five cookies. She wants to give Nancy and her friend Jody the same number of cookies. How many cookies will each girl receive?

___3. Larry has four small racing cars. He gives one to his friend Fred. How many does he have left?

___4. Nancy has three dolls and Jody has six. How many more dolls does Jody have?

___5. Tom and Tasha each get part of a candy bar. Does one child get more candy? If so, which one?

 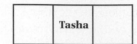

G. Explain what a *heuristic* is. Describe George Polya's contribution to math instruction.

H. Put an *X* by the statements that are correct.

___1. If children have mastered the heuristics, then mastery of the content is not important.

___2. Good and poor problem solvers have about the same heuristic skills.

___3. Expert problem solvers are skilled at thinking about thinking. They can assess the situation, decide what is being asked, organize a plan, carry out the plan, and verify the results in an organized fashion.

___4. Most textbooks today include plenty of nonroutine problems to solve.

___5. Having children work in small groups to solve problems is the most productive instructional approach.

___6. Explaining a problem to someone else will help a child clarify the problem for himself.

I. List three techniques that can be used to assess children's problem-solving skills.

J. Critique the following instructional situation:

"We are going to do some more math problems today. I will pass out the problems to you, and you will have 15 minutes to complete them. Do not talk to your neighbors. Follow the steps on the board." The following steps are listed on the board:

1. Understand   3. Follow the plan
2. Plan   4. Check

There are no manipulatives in evidence, and there is no room on the paper for drawing pictures or diagrams.

K. List the five processes that are included in the NCTM mathematics process standards.

L. In the third-grade math center, two glass jars are filled with marbles. One jar is tall and thin; the other jar is short and fat. Some 3" × 5" cards and a shoebox are beside the jars. There is a sign that reads

---

TODAY'S ESTIMATION EXERCISE

Remember, don't count!

How many marbles are in the TALL jar?

How many marbles are in the SHORT jar?

Does one jar have more, or do they both have the same amount?

On a card write:

1. Your name
2. Number of marbles in the TALL jar
3. Number of marbles in the SHORT jar
4. Put your card in the shoebox

Evaluate this activity. How would you follow up on the information collected?

M. Why are games good for helping children learn math?

N. Explain how children with special needs and disabilities can learn math skills and concepts.

REFERENCES

Bowe, F. G. (2007). *Early childhood special education: Birth to eight.* Albany, NY: Thomson Delmar Learning.

Burns, M. (1998, January/February). Math in action. Raccoon math: A story for numerical reasoning. *Instructor,* 86–88.

Epstein, A. S. (2007). *The intentional teacher.* Washington, DC: National Association for the Education of Young Children.

Hall, A. (1957). *Common-sense Questions-Polya 1957.* Retrieved 1/11/10 from http://mathforum.org

National Council of Teachers of Mathematics. (2000). *Principles and standards for school mathematics.* Reston, VA: Author.

O'Connor, J. J., & Robertson, E. F. (2002). *George Polya.* Retrieved 1/11/10 from http://www-history.mcs.st-and.ac.uk

Reys, R. E., Lindquist, M. M., Lambdin, D. V., Smith, N. L., & Suydam, M. N. (2001). *Helping children learn mathematics.* New York: Wiley.

Skinner, P. (1990). *What's your problem?* Portsmouth, NH: Heinemann.

Sudoku for Kids! (2008). Retrieved 9/4/08 from http://www.activityvillage.co.uk

Zaslavsky, C. (1996). *The multicultural math classroom.* Portsmouth, NH: Heinemann.

FURTHER READING AND RESOURCES

Andrews, A. G. (2004). Adapting manipulatives to foster the thinking of young children. *Teaching Children Mathematics, 11*(1), 15–17.

Baroody, A. J., & Dowker, A. (Eds.). (2003). *The development of arithmetic concepts and skills.* Mahwah, NJ: Erlbaum.

Buschman, L. (2004). Teaching problem solving in mathematics. *Teaching Children Mathematics, 10*(6), 302–309.

Buyea, R. W. (2007). Problem solving in a structured mathematics program. *Teaching Children Mathematics, 13*(6), 300–307.

Clarke, D. M., & Clarke, B. A. (2003). Encouraging perseverance in elementary mathematics: A tale of two problems. *Teaching Children Mathematics, 10*(4), 204–209.

Clements, D. H., Sarama, J., & DiBiase, A. (Eds.). (2004). *Engaging young children in mathematics.* Mahwah, NJ: Erlbaum.

Dougherty, B. J., & Venenciano, L. C. H. (2007). Measure up for understanding. *Teaching Children Mathematics, 13*(9), 452–456.

Findell, C. R., Cavanagh, M., Dacey, L., Greenes, C. E., Sheffield, L. J., & Small, M. (2004). *Navigating through problem solving and reasoning in grade 1.* Reston, VA: National Council of Teachers of Mathematics.

Fiori, N. (2007). Four practices that math classrooms could do without, *Phi Delta Kappan, 88*(9), 695–696.

Green, D. A. (2002). Last one standing: Cooperative problem solving. *Teaching Children Mathematics, 9*(3), 134–139.

Greenes, C. E., Dacey, L., Cavanagh, M., Findell, C. R., Sheffield, L. J., & Small, M. (2003). *Navigating through problem solving and reasoning in prekindergarten–kindergarten.* Reston, VA: National Council of Teachers of Mathematics.

Hartweg, K., & Heisler, M. (2007). No tears here! Third-grade problem solvers. *Teaching Children Mathematics, 13*(7), 362–368.

Hoosain, E., & Chance, R. H. (2004). Problem-solving strategies of first graders. *Teaching Children Mathematics, 10*(9), 474–479.

Kamii, C., & Houseman, L. B. (1999). *Children reinvent arithmetic* (2nd ed.). New York: Teachers College Press.

Lester, F. K., Jr. (Ed.). (2003). *Teaching mathematics through problem solving.* Reston. VA: National Council of Teachers of Mathematics.

Richardson, K. M. (2004). Designing math trails for the elementary school. *Teaching Children Mathematics, 11*(1), 8–14.

Rigelman, N. R. (2007). Fostering mathematical thinking and problem solving: The teacher's role. *Teaching Children Mathematics, 13*(6), 308–319.

Small, M., Sheffield, L. J., Cavanagh, M., Dacey, L., Findell, C. R., & Greenes, C. E. (2004). *Navigating through problem solving and reasoning in grade 2.* Reston, VA: National Council of Teachers of Mathematics.

Whitin, D. J. (2006). Problem posing in the elementary classroom. *Teaching Children Mathematics, 13*(1), 14–18.

Whitin, P., & Whitin, D. J. (2006). Making connections through math-related book pairs. *Teaching Children Mathematics, 13*(4), 196–202.

Williams, C. V., & Kamii, C. (1986). How do children learn by handling objects? *Young Children, 42*(1), 23–26.

Wu, Z., An, S., King, J., Ramirez, M., & Evans, S. (2009). Second grade "Professors." *Teaching Children Mathematics, 16*(1), 34–41.

Young, E., & Marroquin, C. L. (2006). Posing problems from children's literature. *Teaching Children Mathematics, 12*(7), 362–366.

Zaslavsky, C. (1998). *Math games and activities from around the world.* Chicago: Chicago Review Press.

Assessing the Child's Developmental Level

After reading this unit, you should be able to:

- Explain the basic assessment standards of NCTM.
- Explain how to find the child's level of concept development.
- Explain the value of commercial assessment instruments for concept assessment.
- Make a developmental assessment task file.
- Assess the concept development level of young children.
- Understand how to record, report, and evaluate using naturalistic/performance-based assessment.
- Explain the advantages of portfolio assessment.
- Plan how to maintain equity when assessing children's progress.

Children's levels of concept development are determined by observing which concept tasks they are able to perform independently. The first question in teaching is "Where is the child now?" To find the answer to this question, the teacher assesses. The purpose of *assessment* is to gather information and evidence about student knowledge, skills, and attitudes (or dispositions) regarding mathematics. This evidence is then used to *plan* a program of instruction for each child and to *evaluate* each child's progress and the effectiveness of instruction. According to NAEYC (2003), assessment has two major purposes:

1. Supporting learning and instruction.
2. Identifying students who may need additional services.

Assessment should be tied to children's daily activities.

Assessment may be done through observation, through questioning as the child works on a problem or investigation, and/or through interviews in which the child is given a specific task to perform. This information is used to guide the next steps in teaching. The long-term objective for young children is to be sure that they have a strong foundation in basic concepts that will take them through the transition into the concrete operational stage, when they begin to deal seriously with abstract symbols in math. Following the methods and sequence in this text helps reach this goal and at the same time achieves some further objectives as follows:

- Builds a positive feeling in the child toward math.
- Builds confidence in the child that he can do math activities.
- Builds a questioning attitude in response to the child's curiosity regarding math problems.

The NCTM assessment principle (2000, p. 22) states that "**assessment** should support the learning of important mathematics and furnish useful information to both teachers and students." It should be an integral part of instruction, not just something administered at the end of instruction. Assessment should include the following elements:

- Assessment should enhance children's learning by being a part of everyday instruction.
- Assessment tasks that are similar or identical to instructional tasks can indicate to students exactly what they should be able to know and do.
- Student communication skills can be enhanced when assessment involves observations,

conversations, interviews, oral reports, and journals.
- Evaluation guides (or *rubrics*) can clarify for the students exactly what their strengths and weaknesses are and so enable their self-assessment.

Assessment should be integrated into everyday activities so that it is not an interruption but rather a part of the instructional routine. It should provide both teacher and student with valuable information. There should not be overreliance on formal paper-and-pencil tests; instead, information should be gathered from a variety of sources. "Many assessment techniques can be used by mathematics teachers, including open-ended questions, constructed-response tasks, selected response items, performance tasks, observations, conversations, journals and portfolios" (NCTM, 2000, p. 23). In this text the focus is on observations, interviews, and portfolios of children's work, which may include problem solutions, journal entries, results of conversations, photos, and other documentation. It is also important to take heed of the equity principle and diversify assessment approaches to meet the needs of diverse learners such as ELLs, gifted students, and students with learning disabilities.

The NCTM (1995) also advocates decreased attention to a number of traditional assessment elements:

- Assessing what students do not know, comparing them with other students, and/or using assessments to track students relative to apparent capability.
- Simply counting correct answers on tests for the sole purpose of assigning grades.
- Focusing on assessment of students' knowledge of only specific facts and isolated skills.
- Using exercises or word problems requiring only one or two skills.
- Excluding calculators, computers, and manipulatives from the assessment process.
- Evaluating teacher's success only on the basis of test scores.

The NCTM (1989) says this about the assessment of young children: "methods should consider the characteristics of the students themselves.... At this stage, when children's understanding is often closely tied to the use of physical materials, assessment tasks that allow them to use such materials are better indicators of learning" (p. 202).

Assessment Methods

Observations and interviews are assessment methods that teachers use to determine a child's level of development. Examples of both of these methods were included in Unit 3. More are provided in this unit. Assessment is most appropriately done through conversations, observations, and interviews using teacher-developed assessment tasks (Glanfield, Bush, & Stenmark, 2003). Commercial instruments used for initial screening may also supply useful information, but their scope is too limited for the everyday assessment needed for planning. Initial screening instruments usually cover a broad range of areas and provide a profile that indicates the children's overall strengths and weaknesses. These strengths and weaknesses can be looked at in more depth by the classroom teacher to glean information needed for making normal instructional decisions or by a diagnostic specialist (i.e., a school psychologist or speech and language therapist) when an initial screening indicates some serious developmental problem. Individually administered screening instruments should be the only type used with young children. Child responses should require the use of concrete materials and/or pictures, verbal answers, or motoric responses such as pointing or rearranging some objects. Paper and pencil should be used only for assessment of perceptual motor development (i.e., tasks such as name writing, drawing a person, or copying shapes). Booklet-type paper-and-pencil tests administered to groups or individuals are inappropriate until children are well into concrete operations, can deal with abstract symbols, and have well-developed perceptual motor skills.

Assessment information can be obtained through observations of children working with materials to solve problems and inquire into questions.

Observational Assessment

Observation is used to find out how children use concepts during their daily activities. It can be done during naturalistic, informal, and adult guided activities. The teacher has in mind the concepts the children should be using. Whenever she sees a concept reflected in a child's activity, she writes down the incident and places it in the child's record folder. This helps her plan future experiences.

Throughout this book, suggestions are made for behaviors that should be observed. The following are examples of behaviors as the teacher would write them down for the child's folder:

- Brad (18 months old) dumped all the shape blocks on the rug. He picked out all the circles and stacked them up. It shows that he can sort and organize.
- Rosa (4 years old) carefully set the table for lunch all by herself. She remembered everything. Rosa understands one-to-one correspondence.
- Chris (3 years old) and Kai (5 years old) stood back to back and asked Rosa to check who was taller. Good cooperation—it is the first time Chris has shown an interest in comparing heights.
- Mary (5 years old), working on her own, put the right number of sticks in juice

cans marked with the number symbols 0 through 20. She is ready for something more challenging.

- Last week I set out a tub of water and a variety of containers of different sizes in the mathematics and science center. The children spent the week exploring the materials. Trang Fung and Sara seemed especially interested in comparing the amount of liquid that could be held by each container. I gave each of them a standard one-cup measure and asked them to estimate how many cups of water would fill each container. Then I left it up to them to measure and record the actual amounts. They did a beautiful job of setting up a recording sheet and working together to measure the number of cups of water each container would hold. They then lined up the containers from largest to smallest volume, which demonstrated their understanding of ordering or seriation.

- Today I read Chin's (second grader) math journal. Yesterday's entry included a chart showing the names and amounts of each type of baseball card in his collection. He also wrote his conclusions about which players and teams were his favorites as evidenced by the number of cards. Chin is skilled at organizing data and drawing conclusions, and he understands the concepts of more and less.

- Ann and Jason (8-year-olds) argue about which materials will float and sink. They asked their teacher if they could test their theories. They got water, collected some objects, and set up a chart to record their predictions and then the names of the items that sink and those that float. This demonstrates their understanding of how to develop an investigation to solve a problem.

Observational information may also be recorded on a **checklist**. For example, concepts can be listed, and then, each time the child is observed demonstrating one of the behaviors, the date can be put next to that behavior. Soon there will be a profile of the concepts the child demonstrates spontaneously (Figure 4–1).

Assessment through Informal Conversations

As children explore materials, the teacher can informally make comments and ask them questions about their activity to gain insight into their thinking. Glanfield and colleagues (2003, p. 56) suggest several types of questions that can prompt students to share their thinking.

- Tell me more about that.
- Can you show me another way?
- Help me understand.
- Why did you …?
- How did you know what to do next?
- What else do you know about …?
- What were you thinking when you …?

Interview Assessment

The individual interview is used to find out specific information in a direct way. The teacher can present a task to the child and observe and record the way the child works on the task as well as the solution she arrives at for the problem presented by the task. The accuracy of the answers is not as important as how the child arrives at the answers. Often a child starts out on the right track but gets off somewhere in the middle of the problem. For example, Kate (age 3) is asked to match four saucers with four cups. This is an example of one-to-one correspondence. She does this task easily. Next she is asked to match five cups with six saucers: "Here are some cups and saucers. Find out if there is a cup for every saucer." She puts a cup on each saucer. Left with an extra saucer, she places it under one of the pairs and smiles happily. By observing the whole task, the teacher can see that Kate does not feel comfortable with the concept of "one more than." This is normal for a preoperational 3-year-old. She finds a way to "solve" the problem by putting two saucers under one cup. She understands the idea of matching one to one but cannot

CONCEPT ACTIVITY OBSERVATION CHECKLIST

Child's Name _____ Birth Date _____

School Year _____ Grade/Group _____

Concept Activities *(Concepts and activities are described in the text)*	Dates Observed
Selects math center	
Selects cooking center	
Selects math concept book	
Selects sand or water	
Sets the table correctly	
Counts spontaneously	
Sorts play materials into logical groups	
Uses comparison words (i.e., *bigger, fatter,* etc.)	
Builds with blocks	
Works with part/whole materials	
Demonstrates an understanding of order and sequence	
Points out number symbols in the environment	
Demonstrates curiosity by asking questions, exploring the environment, and making observations	
Uses concept words	

FIGURE 4–1   Concept observation checklist.

have things out of balance. Only by observing the whole task can the teacher see the reason for what appears to be a "wrong" answer to the task.

Another example: Tim, age 6, has been given 20 Unifix Cubes®, 10 red and 10 blue. His teacher asks him to count the red cubes and then the blue cubes, which he does with care and accuracy. Next, she asks him to see how many combinations of 10 he can make using the red cubes and the blue cubes. To demonstrate she counts out nine blue cubes and adds one red cube to her group to make 10. She tells him to write and/or draw each combination that he finds. His teacher watches as he counts out eight blue cubes and two red cubes. He then draws on his paper eight blue squares and two red squares.

Finally, in the second-grade class, Theresa's teacher notices that she is not very accurate in her work. The class is working on two-digit addition and subtraction with no regrouping, and the teacher is concerned that Theresa will be totally lost when they move on to regrouping. He decides to assess her process skills by having her show him with Unifix Cubes how she perceives the problems. For 22 + 31 she takes 22 cubes and 31 cubes and makes a pile of 53. For 45 − 24 she takes a pile of 45 and adds 24 more cubes. Her teacher realizes that Theresa is not attentive to the signs for plus and minus. He also decides she needs to work on place value and grouping by 10s and 1s.

An individual interview can provide insight into a child's thinking about math.

If the answers of Kate, Tim, and Theresa were observed only at the endpoint and recorded as right or wrong, the crux of their problems would be missed. Only the individual interview offers the opportunity to observe a child solving a problem from start to finish without distractions or interruptions.

An important factor in the one-to-one interview is that the adult must do it in an accepting manner. The teacher must value and accept the child's answers regardless of whether they are right or wrong from the adult's point of view. If possible, the interview should be done in a quiet place where nothing else might take the child's attention off the task. The adult should be warm, pleasant, and calm. Let the child know that he is doing well with smiles, gestures (nods of approval, a pat on the shoulder), and specific praise ("You are very careful when you count the cubes", "I can see you know how to match shapes", "You work hard until you find an answer"; etc.).

If someone other than a teacher does the assessment interview, the teacher should be sure that the assessor spends time with the children before the interviews. Advise the person doing the interview to sit on a low chair or on the floor next to where the children are playing. Children are usually curious when they see a new person. One may ask, "Who are you? Why are you here?" The children can be told, "I am Ms. X. Someday I am going to give each of you a turn to do some special work with me. It will be a surprise. Today I want to see what you do in school and learn your names." If the interviewer pays attention to the children and shows an interest in them and their activities, they will feel comfortable and free to do their best when the day comes for their assessment interviews.

If the teacher does the assessment herself, she also should stress the special nature of the activity for her and each child: "I'm going to spend some time today doing some special work with each of you. Everyone will get a turn."

Assessment Task File

Each child and each group of children is different. The teacher needs to have on hand questions to fit each age and stage she might meet in individual young children. She also needs to add new tasks as she discovers more about children and their development and should set up a card file or loose-leaf notebook of assessment tasks. Such a file or notebook has three advantages:

1. The teacher has a personal involvement in creating her own assessment tasks and is more likely to use them, understand them, and value them.
2. The file card or loose-leaf notebook format makes it easy to add new tasks and to revise or remove old ones.
3. There is room for the teacher to use her own creativity by adding new questions and making materials.

Use the tasks in each unit and in Appendix A to begin the file. Other tasks can be developed as students proceed through the units in this book and during the teacher's future career with young children. Directions for each task can be put on five-by-eight-inch plain white file cards. Most of the tasks will require the use of concrete materials and/or pictures. Concrete materials can be items found around the home and center. Pictures can be purchased or cut from magazines and readiness-type workbooks and glued on cards.

The basic materials needed are a 5″ × 8″ file card box, 5″ × 8″ unlined file cards, 5″ × 8″ file dividers or a loose-leaf notebook with dividers, a black pen, a set of colored markers, a ruler, scissors, glue, clear Contac or laminating material, and preschool/kindergarten readiness workbooks with artwork.

In Appendix A, each assessment task is set up as it would be on a 5″ × 8″ card. Observe that, on each card, what the adult says to the child is always printed in **bold lower case letters** so that the instructions can be found and read easily. The tasks are set up developmentally from the sensorimotor level (birth to age 2) to the preoperational level (ages 2–7) to early concrete operations (ages 6–8). The ages are flexible relative to the stages and are given only to serve as a guide for selecting the first tasks to present to each child.

Each child is at his own level. If the first tasks are too hard, the interviewer should go to a lower level. If the first tasks are quite easy for the child, the interviewer should go to a higher level. Figure 4–2 is a sample recording sheet format that could be used to keep track of each child's progress. Some teachers prefer an individual sheet for each child; others prefer a master sheet for the whole class. The names and numbers of the tasks to be assessed are entered in the first column. Several columns are provided for entering the date and the level of progress (+, accomplished; √, needs some help; −, needs a lot of help) for children who need repeated periods of instruction. The column on the right is for comments on the process used by the child that might give some clues as to specific instructional needs.

Assessment Tasks

The assessment tasks included in each content unit and in Appendix A address the concepts that young children must acquire from birth through the primary grades. Most of the tasks require an individual interview with the child. Some tasks are observational and require recording of activities during playtime or class time. The infant tasks and observations assess the development of the child's growing sensory and motor skills. As discussed in Unit 1, these sensory and motor skills are basic to all later learning.

The assessment tasks are divided into nine developmental levels. *Levels 1 and 2* are tasks for the child in the sensorimotor stage. *Levels 3–5* include tasks of increasing difficulty for the prekindergarten child. The *Level 6* tasks are those that most children can do upon entering kindergarten between the ages of 5 and 6; this is the level that children are growing toward during the prekindergarten years. Some children will be able to accomplish all these tasks by age 5; others, not until age 6 or over. *Level 7* summarizes the math words that are usually a part of the child's natural speech by age 6. *Level 8* is included as an assessment for advanced prekindergartners and for children enrolled in a

DEVELOPMENTAL TASKS RECORDING SHEET

Child's Name _____ Birth Date _____

School Year _____ School _____ Teacher _____

Grade/Group _____ Person Doing Assessment _____

Levels: +, accomplishes; √, partial; −, cannot do task

Task	Levels			Comments
	Date	Date	Date	

Comments:

Figure 4–2 Recording sheet for developmental tasks.

kindergarten program. The child about to enter first grade should be able to accomplish the tasks at Levels 6 and 8 and should also be using most of the concept words (*Level 7*) correctly. *Level 9* includes tasks to be accomplished during the primary grades.

Example of an Individual Interview

Table 4–1 recounts part of the *Level 5* assessment interview as given to Bob (4½ years old). A corner of the storage room has been made into an

TABLE 4–1   Assessment Interview

Mrs. Ramirez:	Bob's Response:
How old are you?	"I'm four." (He holds up four fingers.)
Count to 10 for me, bob. (Mrs. Ramirez nods her head up and down.)	"One, two, three, four, five, six, seven, eight, nine, ten . . . I can go some more. Eleven, twelve, thirteen, twenty!"
Here are some blocks. How many are there? (She puts out 10 blocks.)	(He points, saying) "One, two, three, four, five, six, seven, eight, nine, ten, eleven, twelve." (He points to some more than once.)
Good, you counted all the blocks, bob. Now count these. (She puts out five blocks.)	(He counts, pushing each one he counts to the left.) "One, two, three, four, five."
(She puts the blocks out of sight and brings up five plastic horses and riders. **Find out if each rider has a horse.**)	(Bob looks over the horses and riders. He lines up the horses in a row and then puts a rider on each.) "Yes, there are enough."
Fine, you found a rider for each horse, bob. (She puts the riders and horses away. She takes out some inch cube blocks. She puts out two piles of blocks: five yellow and two orange.)	
Does one group have more?	"Yes." (He points to the yellow.)
Okay. (She puts out four blue and three green.)	
Does one group have less?	(He points to the green blocks.)
Good thinking.	
(She takes out five cutouts of bears of five different sizes.) **Find the biggest bear.**	"Here it is." (He picks the biggest.)
Find the smallest bear.	(He points to the smallest.)
Put all the bears in a row from biggest to smallest.	(Bob works slowly and carefully.) "All done." (Two of the middle bears are reversed.)
(Mrs. Ramirez smiles.)	
Good for you, bob. You're a hard worker.	

assessment center. Mrs. Ramirez comes in with Bob. "You sit there, and I'll sit here, Bob. We have some important things to do." They both sit down at a low table, and Mrs. Ramirez begins the interview.

An interview need not include any special number of tasks. For the preoperational child, the teacher can begin with matching and proceed through the ideas and skills one at a time, so each interview can be quite short if necessary.

If the interviewer has the time for longer sessions and the children are able to work for a longer period of time, the following can serve as suggested maximum amounts of time:

- Fifteen to twenty minutes for 2-year-olds.
- Thirty minutes for 3-year-olds.
- Forty-five minutes for 4-year-olds.
- Up to an hour for 5-year-olds and older.

Record Keeping and Reporting

The records of each child's progress and activities are kept in a **record folder** and a **portfolio**. The record folder contains anecdotal records and checklists, as already described. The portfolio is a purposeful collection of student work that tells the story of the student's efforts, progress, and achievements. It is a systematic collection of material designed to provide evidence of understanding and to monitor growth. Portfolios provide a vehicle for "authentic" assessment, that is, examples of student work done in many real-world contexts. Students and teacher work together to gather work, reflect on it, and evaluate it.

The physical setup for portfolios is important. A box or file with hanging folders is a convenient place to begin. As work accumulates, it can be placed in the hanging folders. At regular intervals, teacher and child go through the hanging files and select work to place in the portfolio. An expanding legal-size file pocket makes a convenient portfolio container. Each piece of work should be dated so that growth can be tracked. Sticky notes or self-stick mailing labels can be used to write notations on each piece of work. Labels should include the date, the type of activity, and the reason for selecting each sample.

An essential attribute of a portfolio is that items are *selected* through regularly scheduled student/teacher conferences. Teachers have always kept folders of student work, but portfolios are more focused and contain specially selected work that can be used for assessment. A portfolio offers a fuller picture than does traditional assessment because the former provides a vehicle for student reflection and self-evaluation.

Here are some examples of items that might be included in a portfolio:

- Written or dictated descriptions of the results of investigations.
- Pictures—drawings, paintings, photographs of the child engaged in a significant activity; teacher or student sketches of products made with manipulatives or construction materials such as unit blocks, Unifix Cubes, buttons, and so on.
- Dictated (from younger children) or written (from older children) reports of activities, investigations, experiences, ideas, plans, and so on.
- Diagrams, graphs, or other recorded data.
- Excerpts from students' math, science, and/or social studies journals.
- Samples of problem solutions, explanations of solutions, problems created, and so on.
- Videotapes and/or audiotapes.
- Journal entries.

This material is invaluable for evaluation and for reporting progress to parents. When beginning portfolio assessment, it is wise to start small. Pick one focus such as mathematics or science, or focus on one particular area (e.g., problem solving, data from thematic investigations, artwork, writing, etc.). Beginning with a scope that is too broad can make the task overwhelming.

Evaluating a portfolio involves several steps. First, a **rubric** should be developed. A rubric is a list of general statements that define the attributes of the portfolio that should be evaluated, that is, a list of the qualities you believe are important. Rubrics should be developed based on what you are looking for in your class—not on isolated skills but rather on broad criteria that reflect understanding. The statements will vary with the content focus of the portfolio. Figure 4–3 provides a general format and sample statements. Next, a summary providing an overview should be written (Figure 4–4). If grades must be assigned, then there is a final step: the **holistic evaluation** (Figure 4–5). For a holistic evaluation, the portfolios are grouped into piles such as strong, average, and weak (or very strong, strong, high average, low average, somewhat weak, and very weak) based on the rubric and the summary. This comparative analysis can then guide grading. See the reference list for publications that offer additional ideas regarding the development of portfolio assessment practices. Glanfield and colleagues (2003) suggest rubrics for evaluation of K–2 work samples.

SAMPLE PORTFOLIO RUBRIC

	Strong, Well Established	Beginning to Appear	Not Yet Observed
1. Can organize and record data			
2. Explores, analyzes, looks for patterns			
3. Uses concrete materials or drawings to aid in solving problems			
4. Investigations and activities help develop concepts			
5. Persistent, flexible, self-directed			
6. Works cooperatively			
7. Enjoys math			

Figure 4–3 General format for a rubric.

Maintaining Equity

As already mentioned, it is extremely important to maintain equity in assessment. Assessment must be done in an appropriate manner relative to culture, gender, language, and disabilities. Information must be gathered from multiple sources (de Melendez & Beck, 2007). Observations by teachers and family members as well as specialists should be documented. Anecdotal records, photos, videos and audiotapes can be extremely valuable. Conversations with children and parents, home visits, and interviews with family members and with other professionals can provide important information. Portfolios of work products and information from checklists can be compiled. Formal testing, if used at all, should be just one source of information and should never constitute the sole criteria for making high-stakes decisions. De Melendez

and Beck underscore the importance of making modifications and adaptations for children with special needs or with cultural and linguistic differences. Ideally, assessments are done in the child's primary language. Authentic assessment tools such as portfolios are recommended for equitable assessment. Children's pictorial number representations can provide a window into their cultural views of themselves (McCulloch, Marshall, & DeCuir-Gunby, 2009). Completing an assignment to make a sign that would provide visitors with information about their class, some kindergarten and first and second grade students graphed their peers by skin color, observed by McCulloch, Marshall, and DeCuir-Gunby. One student who had many experiences in counting coins depicted twenty-one students as two dimes and one penny.

For young children with special needs, assessment should be "multidisciplinary, multidimensional,

PORTFOLIO SUMMARY ANALYSIS

Child's Name _____ Date _____

Overall Evaluation

Strengths and Weaknesses

Further Recommendations

Figure 4–4   Format for portfolio summary analysis.

---

4 Strong on all the characteristics listed in the rubric.

3 Consistent evidence of the presence of most of the characteristics.

2 Some presence of the characteristics but incomplete communication or presence of ideas, concepts, and/or behaviors.

1 Little or no presence of desired characteristics.

Figure 4–5   Sample of a holistic scoring format.

multimethod, multicontext, proactive and should involve ongoing information exchange" (Gargiulo & Kilgo, 2005, p. 103). Assessment of young children with disabilities is done by a team of professionals and family members. However, day-to-day assessment is the responsibility of the individual teacher. As with other children, the assessment must be authentic. Teachers and parents need to know when to request assessments by specialists such as the physical therapist or the speech-language therapist. Equity requires that appropriate materials are used for instruction to allow for fair assessment. In addition, adequate time must be allowed for students with disabilities to complete tasks. Gargiulo and Kilgo emphasize the importance of regular and systematic collection of assessment information. The goals included in the IFSP or IEP must be checked for progress.

Assessment will result in the identification of a wide variety of achievement levels within a classroom. Instruction should be differentiated to meet the needs of diverse learners (Grimes & Stevens, 2009). Common elements in diverse classrooms include student responsibility, student choice, peer tutoring, flexible grouping, and modified instruction.

Summary

The focus of assessment in mathematics is on assessment integrated with instruction during naturalistic classroom activities and during activities that involve performance of concrete, hands-on problem solving and child-directed problem solving. The major ways to assess the developmental levels of young children are informal conversation and questioning, observation, interview, and the collection of materials in a portfolio. Observation is most useful when looking at how children use concepts in their everyday activities. The interview with one child at a time gives the teacher an opportunity to look at the child's specific ideas and skills.

Guidelines are provided for conducting an interview. A summary of the nine levels of developmental tasks, which are included in Appendix A, is also given. A sample of part of an interview showed how the exchange between interviewer and child might progress.

A system for record keeping, reporting, and evaluation using a record folder and portfolio is described. A holistic approach to evaluation is recommended, and the importance of equitable systems and methods of assessment is emphasized.

KEY TERMS

assessment	holistic evaluation	record folder
checklist	portfolio	rubric

SUGGESTED ACTIVITIES

1. Find out what the expectations are for mathematics concept development for students entering kindergarten and/or first grade in your local school system. Compare the school system list with the tasks suggested at Levels 6 and 7 in the text and in Appendix A. What are the similarities and differences?

2. Obtain permission to help a child develop a math portfolio.
3. Find three articles in professional journals that discuss assessment and evaluation of young children. What are the main ideas presented? Explain how you might apply these ideas in the future.

REVIEW

A. Explain why it is important to make assessment the first step in teaching.
B. Describe the NCTM guidelines for assessment.
C. Describe the advantages of portfolio assessment.
D. Read the following incidents 1 and 2. What is being done in each situation? What should be done?
   1. Ms. Collins is interviewing a child in the school hallway. Other teachers and students are continuously passing by. The child frequently looks away from the materials to watch the people passing by.
   2. Mr. Garcia is interviewing Johnny. Mr. Garcia places five rectangle shapes on the table. All are of the same length, but vary in width. **Mr. Garcia:**
   "**Watch what I do**." (Mr. Garcia lines up the rectangles from widest to thinnest.)

"Now I'll mix them up. You put them in a row from fattest to thinnest." (Mr. Garcia is looking ahead at the next set of instructions. He glances at Johnny with a rather serious expression.)

Johnny's response:
(Johnny picks out the fattest and thinnest rectangles. He places them next to each other. Then he examines the other three rectangles and lines them up in sequence next to the first two. He looks up at Mr. Garcia.)

Mr. Garcia:
"Are you finished?"
Johnny's response:
(Johnny nods his head yes.)
Mr. Garcia:
"Too bad, you mixed them up."

E. Explain how you would plan for math assessment that meets the standards of equity for all types of students.

REFERENCES

de Melendez, W. R., & Beck, V. (2007). *Teaching young children in multicultural classrooms* (2nd ed.). Albany, NY: Thomson Delmar Learning.

Gargiulo, R., & Kilgo, J. (2005). *Young children with special needs* (2nd ed.). Albany, NY: Thomson Delmar Learning.

Glanfield, F., Bush, W. S., & Stenmark, J. K. (Eds.). (2003). *Mathematics assessment: A practical handbook for grades K–2*. Reston, VA: National Council of Teachers of Mathematics.

Grimes, K.J., & Stevens, D. D. (2009). Glass, bug, mud. *Phi Delta Kappan, 90*(9), 677–680.

McCulloch, A. W., Marshall, P. L., & DeCuir-Gunby, J. T. (2009). Cultural capital in children's number representaion. *Teaching Children Mathematics, 16*(3), 184–189.

NAEYC. (2003). Early childhood curiculum, assessment, and program evaluation: Position statement. Retrieved 1/12/10 from www.naeyc.org

National Council of Teachers of Mathematics. (1989). *Curriculum and evaluation standards for school mathematics*. Reston, VA: Author.

National Council of Teachers of Mathematics. (1995). *Assessment standards for school mathematics*. Reston, VA: Author.

National Council of Teachers of Mathematics. (2000). *Principles and standards for school mathematics*. Reston, VA: Author.

National Research Council. (1996). *National science education standards*. Washington, DC: National Academies Press.

National Research Council. (2001). *Classroom assessment and the national science education standards*. Washington, DC: National Academies Press.

FURTHER READING AND RESOURCES

Buschman, L. (2001). Using student interviews to guide classroom instruction: An action research project. *Teaching Children Mathematics, 8*(4), 222–227.

Cooney, T. J., Mewborn, D. S., Sanchez, W. B., & Leatham, K. (2002). *Open-ended assessment in math: Grades 2–12*. Westport, CT: Heinemann.

Copley, J. V. (1999). Assessing the mathematical understanding of the young child. In J. V. Copley (Ed.), *Mathematics in the early years* (pp. 182–188). Reston, VA: National Council of Teachers of Mathematics, and Washington, DC: National Association for the Education of Young Children.

Huniker, D. (Ed.). (2006). *Pre-K–grade 2 mathematics assessment sampler*. Reston, VA: National Council of Teachers of Mathematics.

Kamii, C. (Ed.). (1990). *Achievement testing in the early grades: The games grown-ups play*. Washington, DC: National Association for the Education of Young Children.

Kamii, C., & Lewis, B. A. (1991). Achievement tests in primary mathematics: Perpetuating lower order thinking. *Arithmetic Teacher, 38*(9), 4–9.

Kohn, A. (2001). Fighting the tests: Turning frustration into action. *Young Children, 56*(2), 19–24.

Leatham, K. R., Lawrence, K., & Mewborn, D. S. (2005). Getting started with open-ended assessment. *Teaching Children Mathematics, 11*(8), 413–419.

Shores, E. F., & Grace, C. (1998). *The portfolio book*. Beltsville, MD: Gryphon House.

Snow, C. E., & Van Hemel, S. B. (Eds). (2008). *Early childhood assessment: Why, what and how.* Washington, DC: The National Academies Press.

Wesson, K. A. (2001). The "Volvo effect"— Questioning standardized tests. *Young Children, 56*(2), 16–18.

Fundamental Concepts and Skills

UNIT 5

One-to-One Correspondence

OBJECTIVES

After reading this unit, you should be able to:

- Explain the NCTM expectations for one-to-one correspondence.
- Define one-to-one correspondence.
- Identify naturalistic, informal, and adult guided one-to-one correspondence activities.
- Describe five ways to vary one-to-one correspondence activities.
- Assess and evaluate children's one-to-one correspondence skills.

The NCTM (2000) expectations for **one-to-one correspondence** relate to **rational counting** (attaching a number name to each object counted) as described in Unit 6. Placing items in one-to-one correspondence as described in this unit is a supportive concept and skill for rational counting. One-to-one-correspondence is a focal point for number and operations at the prekindergarten level (NCTM, 2007). It is used in connection with solving such problems as having enough (cups, dolls, cars, etc.) for a whole group.

One-to-one correspondence is the most fundamental component of the concept of number. It is the understanding that one group has the same number of things as another. For example, each child has a cookie, each foot has a shoe, each person wears a hat, and so on. It is preliminary to counting and basic to the understanding of equivalence and to the concept of conservation of number described in Unit 1. As with other mathematics concepts, it can be integrated across the curriculum (Figure 5–1).

Assessment

To obtain information of an informal nature, note the children's behavior during their work, play, and routine activities. Look for one-to-one correspondence that happens naturally. For example, when the child plays train, he may line up a row of chairs so there is one for each child passenger. When he puts his mittens on, he shows that he knows there should be one for each hand; when painting, he checks to be sure he has each paintbrush in the matching color of paint. Tasks for formal assessment are given on page 72 and in Appendix A.

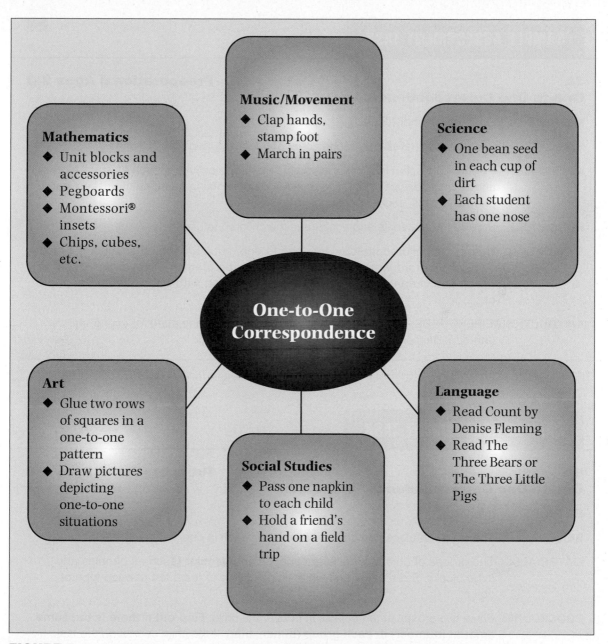

FIGURE 5–1 Integrating one-to-one correspondence across the curriculum.

SAMPLE ASSESSMENT TASK

3A   **Preoperational Ages 2–3**
One-to-One Correspondence: Unit 5

METHOD: Observation, individuals or groups.

SKILL: Child demonstrates one-to-one correspondence during play activities.

MATERIALS: Play materials that lend themselves to one-to-one activities, such as small blocks and animals, dishes and eating utensils, paint containers and paintbrushes, pegs and pegboards, sticks and stones, etc.

PROCEDURE: Provide the materials and encourage the children to use them.

EVALUATION: Note if the children match items one to one, such as putting small peg dolls in each of several margarine containers or on top of each of several blocks that have been lined up in a row. Record on checklist, with anecdote and/or photo or video.

INSTRUCTIONAL RESOURCE: Charlesworth, R. (2011). *Experiences in math for young children* (6th ed.). Belmont, CA: WadsworthCengage Learning.

SAMPLE ASSESSMENT TASK

6A   **Preoperational Ages 5–6**
One-to-One Correspondence: Unit 5

METHOD: Interview.

SKILL: The child can place two groups of ten items each in one-to-one correspondence.

MATERIALS: Two groups of objects of different shapes and/or color (such as pennies and cube blocks or red chips and white chips). Have at least ten of each type of object.

PROCEDURE: Place two groups of ten objects in front of the child. **Find out if there is the same amount (number) in each group (bunch, pile)**. If the child cannot do the task, try it with two groups of five objects.

EVALUATION: The children should arrange each group so as to match the objects one-to-one, or they might count each group to determine equality. Record on checklist.

INSTRUCTIONAL RESOURCE: Charlesworth, R. (2011). *Experiences in math for young children* (6th ed.). Belmont, CA: WadsworthCengage Learning.

Naturalistic Activities

One-to-one correspondence activities develop from the infant's early sensorimotor period. She finds out that she can hold one thing in each hand but can put only one object at a time in her mouth. As a toddler she discovers that five peg dolls will fit one each in the five holes of her toy bus. Quickly she learns that one person fits on each chair, one shoe goes on each foot, and so on. A 2-year-old spends a great deal of his playtime in one-to-one correspondence activities. He lines up containers such as margarine cups, dishes, or boxes and puts a small toy animal in each one. He pretends to set the table for lunch. First he sets one place for himself and one for his bear, with a plate for each. Then he gives each place a spoon and a small cup and saucer. He plays with his large plastic shapes and discovers there is a rod that will fit through the hole in each shape.

Informal Activities

Children have many daily opportunities for informal one-to-one correspondence activities. Oftentimes they must pass things out to a group: food items, scissors, crayons, paper, napkins, paper towels, or notes to go home. Each child should do as many of these things as possible.

Checking on whether everyone has accomplished a task or has what she needs is another chance for informal one-to-one correspondence. Does everyone have a chair to sit on? Does everyone have on two boots or two mittens? Does each person have on his coat? Does each person have a cup of milk or a sandwich? A child can check by matching: "Larry, find out if everyone has a pair of scissors, please."

The infant learns that she can hold one object in each hand.

Young children need many opportunities to practice one-to-one matching.

One-to-one correspondence helps to solve difficulties. For instance, the children are washing rubber dolls in soap suds. Jeanie is crying: "Petey has two dolls and I don't have any." Mrs. Carter comes over. "Petey, more children want to play here now so each one can have only one baby to wash." One-to-one correspondence is often the basis for rules such as, "Only one person on each swing at a time" or "Only one piece of cake for each child today."

Other informal activities occur when children pick out materials made available during free play. These kinds of materials include pegboards, felt shapes on a flannelboard, bead and inch-cube block patterns, shape sorters, formboards, lotto games, and other commercial materials. The teacher can also make materials to serve the same purposes. Most of the materials described in the next section can be made available for informal exploration both before and after they have been used in adult guided activities.

Adult Guided Activities

The extent and variety of materials that can be used for one-to-one correspondence activities is almost endless. Referring to Unit 3, remember the six steps from concrete to abstract materials. These steps are especially relevant when selecting one-to-one correspondence materials. Consider the following five characteristics when selecting materials:

- Perceptual characteristics.
- Number of items to be matched.
- Concreteness.
- Physically joined or not physically joined.
- Groups of the same or different number.

The teacher can vary or change one or more of the five characteristics and can use different materials. In this way, the teacher can design more difficult tasks (Figure 5–2).

Perceptual qualities are critical in matching activities. The way the materials to be matched look is important in determining how hard it will be for the child to match them. Materials can vary a great deal with regard to how much the same or how much different they look. Materials are easier to

match if the groups are different. To match animals with cages or to find a spoon for each bowl is easier than making a match between two groups of blue chips. In choosing objects, make the task more difficult by picking out objects that look more the same.

The number of objects to be matched is also important. The more objects in each group, the more difficult it is to match. Groups with fewer than five things are much easier than those with five or more. In planning activities, start with small groups (fewer than five), and work up step by step to groups of nine. A child who is able to place groups of ten in one-to-one correspondence has a well-developed sense of the concept.

Concreteness refers to the extent to which materials are real (Figure 5–3). Remember from Unit 3 that instruction should always begin with concrete real objects. The easiest and first one-to-one correspondence activities should involve the use of real things such as small toys and other familiar objects. Next, objects that are less familiar and more similar (e.g., cube blocks, chips, popsicle sticks) can be used. The next level would be cutout shapes such as circles and squares, cowboys and horses, or dogs and doghouses, to be followed by pictures of real objects and pictures of shapes. Real objects and pictures could also be employed. Young children who need practice in one-to-one correspondence can use computer software. The following software programs serve this purpose:

- *Coco's Math Project 1* (Singapore: Times Learning Systems Pte. Ltd.)
- *Learning with Leeper* (Coarsegold, CA: Sierra On-Line, Inc.)
- Match-ups for toddlers can be found online at http://www.lil-fingers.com
- *Kids Match* (PBS.org)

Learning to hit the computer keys one at a time with one finger is a one-to-one experience in both the kinesthetic and perceptual as well as the motor skills domains.

When using objects or pictures of objects, it is easier to tell if there is one-to-one correspondence if the objects are joined than if they are not joined. For example, it is easier to tell if there are enough chairs

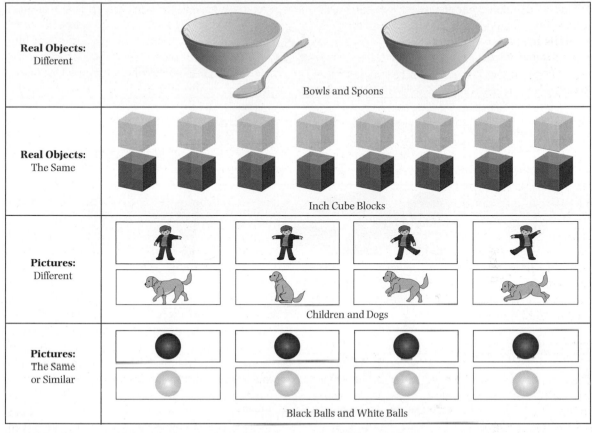

Real Objects: Different	Bowls and Spoons
Real Objects: The Same	Inch Cube Blocks
Pictures: Different	Children and Dogs
Pictures: The Same or Similar	Black Balls and White Balls

FIGURE 5–2   Examples of groups with different perceptual difficulty levels.

for each child if the children are sitting in them than if the chairs are on one side of the room and the children on the other. In beginning activities, the objects can be hooked together with a line or a string so that the children can more clearly see whether or not there is a match. In Figure 5–4, each foot is joined to a shoe and each animal to a bowl; neither the hands and mittens nor the balls and boxes are joined.

Placing unequal groups in one-to-one correspondence is harder than placing equal groups. When the groups have the same number, the child can check to be sure he has used all the items. When one group has more, he does not have this clue (Figure 5–5).

MATH TECHNOLOGY
FOR YOUNG CHILDREN

Try one of the following:
1. If possible, observe a young child interacting with one of the software items listed in this unit. See if the activity appears to support the child's ability to engage in one-to-one correspondence.
2. Select a one-to-one correspondence activity from the Internet. Assemble any materials needed, and use the activity with a small group of pre-K or kindergarten students.

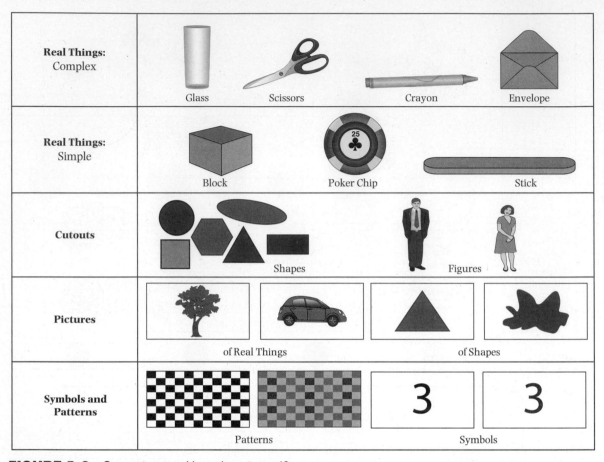

Real Things: Complex	Glass	Scissors	Crayon	Envelope
Real Things: Simple	Block	Poker Chip		Stick
Cutouts	Shapes		Figures	
Pictures	of Real Things		of Shapes	
Symbols and Patterns	Patterns		Symbols	

FIGURE 5–3 Concreteness: How close to real?

The sample lessons presented in Figures 5–6 through 5–11 illustrate some basic types of one-to-one correspondence activities. Note that they also increase the difficulty by varying the characteristics just described. Each activity begins by presenting the students with a problem to solve. The lessons are shown as they would be put on cards for the Idea File.

Ideas for Children with Special Learning Needs

One-to-one correspondence games with objects or picture cards can support the development of perceptual motor skills and the learning of vocabulary. For the child with a language disability or the child who is an ELL, one-to-one correspondence experiences can provide vocabulary support. When playing a matching game the adult can label the examples. For example, when matching toy animals: "**This is a cat, find another cat**." When passing out materials: "**Give each friend some Play-Doh**." When using a pegboard: "**Put a peg in each hole. You put a red peg in the hole**." Or ask questions that encourage speech: "**What should you look for to match this picture?**"

Finger plays can promote one-to-one correspondence. For example, the question "Where is thumbkin?" requires the recognition of one finger

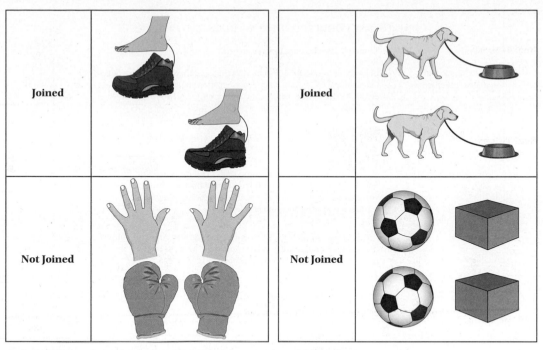

FIGURE 5–4   Joined groups and groups that are not joined.

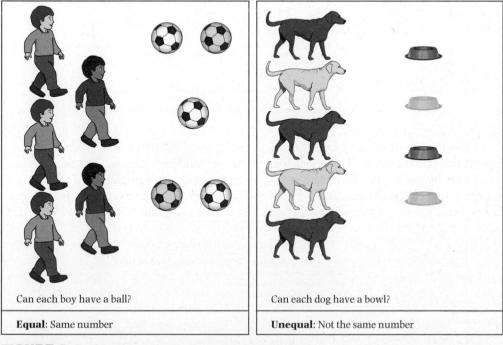

FIGURE 5–5   Matching equal and unequal groups.

ONE-TO-ONE CORRESPONDENCE—DOGS AND PEOPLE

Objective:	To match joined groups of three objects.
Naturalistic and Informal Activity:	In learning centers provide materials that lend themselves to naturalistic and informal one-to-one correspondence experiences: unit blocks and accessories, dishes and tableware, adult and child animals, and so forth. Observe and ask questions and make comments as appropriate.
Materials:	Two sets of three objects that normally would go together. For example, doll people holding toy dogs on leashes.
Structured Activity:	**Here are some people and some dogs. The dogs are on leashes. Does each person have a dog? Show me how you can tell**. Note if the children can show or explain that the leashes connect the dogs and people.
Follow-Up:	Use other groups of objects such as cats and kittens, cups and saucers, houses and roofs, etc. Increase the number of items in each group as the three-to-three task becomes easy.

FIGURE 5–6 One-to-one correspondence activity card—Dogs and people: Matching objects that are perceptually different.

ONE-TO-ONE CORRESPONDENCE—THE THREE PIGS

Objective:	To match joined groups of three items.
Naturalistic and Informal Activity:	Read the story "The Three Little Pigs." In the literacy center place the three pigs, wolf, houses, straw, sticks, and bricks. These might be flannelboard figures or puppets. Observe how the children use the materials. Do they play out the story matching each pig with the appropriate house building material and house? Ask questions or make comments as appropriate.
Materials:	Two sets of cutouts for the bulletin board. Three pieces of yarn. Make three pig cutouts and three house cutouts: straw, sticks, and bricks. Put them on bulletin board and connect each pig to his house with thick yarn.

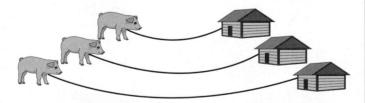

Structured Activity:	**Who are these fellows? (Children answer) Yes, the three little pigs. Is there a house for each pig?** Have one of the children show you how he knows there is by tracing from each pig to his house along the yarn "path." Leave the display up for use by the children during free playtime.
Follow-Up:	Make a set of pigs, houses, and a wolf for the flannelboard. Both teachers and children can use these for storytelling.

FIGURE 5–7 One-to-one correspondence activity card—Matching the three little pigs to cutouts that are perceptually different.

ONE-TO-ONE CORRESPONDENCE—PENNIES FOR TOYS

Objective:	To match groups of two and more objects.
Naturalistic and Informal Activity:	Set up a store center such as toys, groceries, or clothing. Provide play money pennies. Put a price of 1¢ on each item. Discuss with the students what they might do in the store. Observe and note if they exchange one penny for each item. Make comments and ask questions as appropriate.
Materials:	Ten pennies and ten small toys (for example, a ball, a car, a truck, three animals, three peg people, a crayon).
Structured Activity:	**Let's pretend we are playing store. Here are some pennies and some toys.** Show the child(ren) two toys. Place two pennies near the toys. **Do I have enough pennies to buy these toys if each one costs one penny? Show me how you can find out.**
Follow-Up:	Use more toys and more pennies as the children can match larger and larger groups.

FIGURE 5–8   One-to-one correspondence activity card—Pennies for toys: Matching real objects.

ONE-TO-ONE CORRESPONDENCE—PICTURE MATCHING

Objective:	To match groups of pictured things, animals, or people.
Naturalistic and Informal Activity:	Place card sets as described below on a table in one of the classroom learning centers. Observe what the students do with the picture card sets. Do they sort them, match them, and so on? Make comments and ask questions as appropriate.
Materials:	Make or purchase picture cards that show items familiar to young children. Each set should have two groups of ten. Pictures from catalogs, magazines, or readiness workbooks can be cut out, glued on cards, and covered with clear Contac® or laminated. For example, pictures of ten children should be put on ten different cards. Pictures of ten toys could be put on ten other cards.
Structured Activity:	Present two people and two toys. **Does each child have a toy? Show me how you can find out.** Increase the number of items in each group.
	Make some more card sets. Fit them to current science or social studies units. For example, if the class is studying jobs, have pilot with plane, driver with bus, etc.

FIGURE 5–9   One-to-one correspondence activity card—Picture matching.

ONE-TO-ONE CORRESPONDENCE—SIMILAR OR IDENTICAL OBJECTS

Objective:	To match two through ten similar and/or identical objects.
Naturalistic and Informal Activity:	Each day in the math center provide opportunity to explore manipulatives such as inch cube blocks, Unifix® Cubes, Lego®, and so on. Observe what the students do with the materials. Note if they do any one-to-one correspondence as they explore. Make comments and ask questions as appropriate.
Materials:	Twenty objects such as poker chips, inch cube blocks, coins, cardboard circles, etc. There may be 10 of one color and 10 of another or 20 of the same color (more difficult perceptually).
Structured Activity:	Begin with two groups of two, and increase the size of the groups as the children are able to match the small groups. **Here are two groups (bunches, sets) of chips (blocks, sticks, pennies, etc.). Do they have the same number, or does one group have more? Show me how you know.** Have the children take turns using different sizes of groups and different objects.
Follow-Up:	Glue some objects to a piece of heavy cardboard or plywood. Set out a container of the same kinds of objects. Have this available for matching during center time. Also, place baggies with groups of objects of varied amounts in the math center where students can select pairs of objects for matching.

FIGURE 5–10 One-to-one correspondence activity card—Similar or identical objects.

ONE-TO-ONE CORRESPONDENCE—OBJECTS TO DOTS

Objective:	To match zero to nine objects with zero to nine dots.
Naturalistic and Informal Activity:	In the math center provide sets of picture and conventional dominoes and other materials that lend themselves to one-to-one correspondence. Observe what the students do with the materials. Note if they do any one-to-one correspondence as they explore. Make comments and ask questions as appropriate.
Materials:	Ten frozen juice cans or other identical containers, with dots (filled circles) painted in a dark color on each from zero to nine:

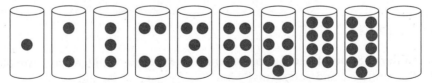

Forty-five tongue depressors or ice cream bar sticks.

Structured Activity:	Give each child a can. Put all the sticks in a container where the children can reach them. **Look at the dots on your can. Put the same number of sticks in your can as there are dots on your can.** Have the children check with each other.
Follow-Up:	Put the can and sticks out during free play. Encourage children who have had a hard time in the group to practice on their own.

FIGURE 5–11 One-to-one correspondence activity card—Matching number of objects to number of dots.

at a time. ELL students whose primary language is Spanish can learn popular Latin American finger-plays in Spanish and English (Orozco & Kleven, 1997).

Evaluation

Informal evaluation can be accomplished by noticing each child's response during adult guided activities. Also observe each child during center play to see whether he can pass out toys or food to other children, giving one at a time. On the shelves in the housekeeping area, place paper shapes of each item (dishes, cups, tableware, purses, etc.) on the shelf where the item belongs. Hang pots and pans on a pegboard with the shapes of each pot drawn on the board. Do the same for blocks and other materials. Notice which children can put materials away by making the right match.

Using the same procedures as in the assessment tasks, make a more formal check regarding what the children have learned. Once children can do one-to-one with ten objects, try more—see how far they can go.

Summary

The most basic number skill is one-to-one correspondence, which children learn about starting in infancy. Sensorimotor and early preoperational children spend much of their playtime in one-to-one correspondence activities.

Many opportunities for informal one-to-one correspondence activities are available during play and daily routines. Materials used for adult guided activities with individuals and/or small groups should also be made available for free exploration.

Materials and activities can be varied in many ways to make one-to-one correspondence fun and interesting. They can also be designed to serve children with special learning needs. Once children have a basic understanding of the one-to-one concept, they can apply the concept to higher-level activities involving equivalence and the concept of *conservation of number*.

The Internet contains a multitude of resources for teaching strategies in mathematics and other content areas. See the Online for examples.

KEY TERMS

concreteness   one-to-one correspondence   rational counting

SUGGESTED ACTIVITIES

1. Present a toddler (18 months to 2 years old) with a plastic container and some small (but safe) objects, such as empty wooden thread spools or plastic lids. Observe how he uses the materials. Note whether anything the child does might indicate the development of the concept of one-to-one correspondence.
2. Develop your own one-to-one correspondence game. Play the game with a young child. Share the game with the class. Are there any improvements you would make?
3. Make copies of the adult guided activities, and add them to your Idea File. Add one or two more activities that you create or find suggested in another resource.

REVIEW

A. Explain how you would define one-to-one correspondence when talking with a parent.

B. Determine which of the following one-to-one correspondence activities is naturalistic, informal, or adult guided. Give a reason for your decision.
1. Mr. Conklin has six cat pictures and six mouse pictures. "Patty, does each cat have a mouse to chase?"
2. Rosa lines up five red blocks in a row. Then she places a smaller yellow block on each red block.
3. Candy puts one bootie on each of her baby doll's feet.
4. Aisha passes one glass of juice to each child at her table.
5. Mrs. Garcia shows 5-year-old José two groups of ten pennies. "Find out if both groups of pennies have the same amount, or if one group has more."

C. Give examples of several ways that one-to-one correspondence activities may be varied.

D. Look at the following pairs of groups of items. Decide which one in each pair would be more difficult to place in one-to-one correspondence.
1. (a) Five red chips and five yellow chips
   (b) Twelve white chips and twelve orange chips
2. (a) Four feet and four shoes
   (b) Four circles and four squares
3. (a) Two groups of seven
   (b) A group of seven and a group of eight
4. (a) Cards with pictures of knives and forks
   (b) Real knives and forks

REFERENCES

National Council of Teachers of Mathematics. (2000). *Principles and standards for school mathematics*. Reston, VA: Author.

National Council of Teachers of Mathematics. (2007). *Curriculum focal points for prekindergarten through grade 8 mathematics*. Retrieved May 24, 2007, from http://www.nctm.org

Orozco, J., & Kleven, E. (1997). *Diez deditos* [Ten little fingers]. New York: Scholastic Books.

FUTHER READING AND RESOURCES

Baratta-Lorton, M. (1972). *Workjobs*. Menlo Park, CA: Addison-Wesley.

Burk, D., Snider, A., & Symonds, P. (1988). *Box it or bag it mathematics: Kindergarten teachers resource guide*. Portland, OR: Math Learning Center.

Clements, D. H., & Sarama, J. (2004). Mathematics everywhere, every time. *Teaching Children Mathematics, 10*(8), 421–426.

Copley, J. V. (2004). The sharing game. In J. V. Copley (Ed.), *Showcasing mathematics for theyoung child*. Reston, VA: National Council of Teachers of Mathematics.

Copley, J. V., Jones, C., & Dighe, J. (2007). *Mathematics: The creative curriculum approach*. Washington, DC: Teaching Strategies.

Newberger, A., & Vaughn, E. (2006). *Teaching numeracy, language, and literacy with blocks*. St. Paul, MN: Redleaf Press.

Richardson, K. (1984). *Developing number concepts using Unifix Cubes*. Menlo Park, CA: Addison-Wesley.

Richardson, K. (1999). *Developing number concepts: Planning guide*. Parsippany, NJ: Seymour.

Number Sense and Counting

After reading this unit, you should be able to:

- Explain the NCTM expectations for number.
- Describe the concept of number sense and its relationship to counting.
- Define rote and rational counting and explain their relationship.
- Identify examples of rote and rational counting.
- Teach counting using naturalistic, informal, and adult guided activities appropriate to each child's age and level of maturity.

The NCTM (2000) expectations for number focus on the ability of children in prekindergarten through second grade to count with understanding and to recognize "how many?" in sets of objects. The children are also expected to develop understanding of the relative position and size of whole numbers, ordinal and cardinal numbers, and their connections to each other. Finally, they are expected to develop a sense of whole numbers and be able to represent and use them in many ways. Children should achieve these expectations through real-world experiences and through using physical materials.

Included in the NCTM standards is the standard that children should develop whole number skills that enable them to "construct number meanings through real-world experiences and the use of physical materials; understand our number system by relating, counting, grouping, and (eventually) place-value concepts; and develop number sense." Number sense and counting can be integrated into other content areas (Figure 6–1).

A major focal point for prekindergarten within the concept of number is developing an understanding of whole numbers (NCTM, 2007). Prekindergartners need to learn to recognize objects in small groups by counting and without counting and to understand that numbers refer to quantities. They begin to use number to solve everyday problems such as how many spoons they will need for a group or how many sides are in a rectangle. They need to be prepared to relate numerals and groups when they enter kindergarten (Units 18 and 19).

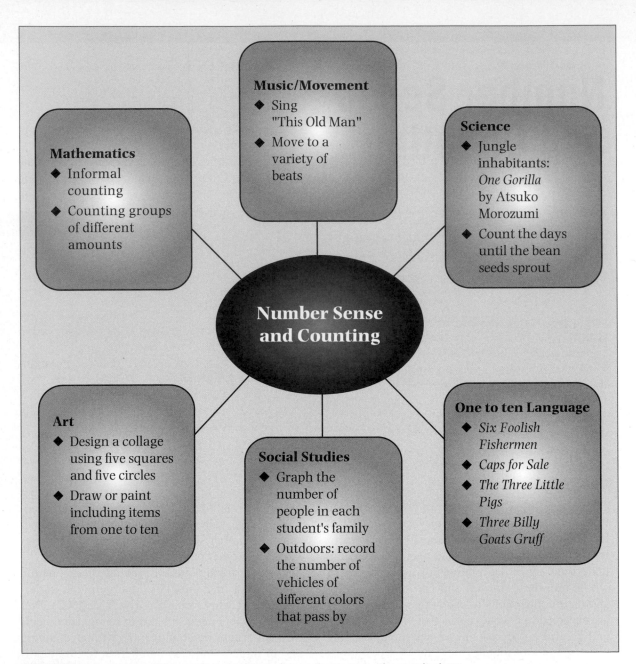

FIGURE 6–1   Integrating number sense and counting across the curriculum.

The concept of number or understanding number is referred to as **number sense**. *Number sense* makes the connection between quantities and counting. It underlies the understanding of more and less, relative amounts, the relationship between space and quantity (i.e., number conservation), and parts and wholes of quantities. Number sense enables children to understand important benchmarks such as five and ten as they relate to other quantities. It also helps children estimate quantities and measurements. Counting assists children in the process of understanding quantity. Understanding that the last number named is the quantity in the group, "oneness" of one, the "twoness" of two, and so on, is a critical fundamental concept (Marshall, 2006).

When shown a group, stating "how many" instantly is called **subitizing**. There are two types of subitizing: perceptual and conceptual. **Perceptual subitizing** is when one can state how many items are in a group without actually counting them. Young children usually learn to subitize up to four items perceptually, that is, when shown a group of four items, they can tell you "four" without counting. **Conceptual subitizing** involves seeing number patterns within a group, such as the larger dot patterns on a domino. The viewer may break the eight-dot pattern down into two groups of four, which makes up the whole. Perceptual subitizing is thought to be the basis for counting and **cardinality** (understanding the last number named is the amount in a group). Conceptual subitizing develops from counting and patterning and helps develop number sense and arithmetic skills. Preschoolers can subitize perceptually. Conceptual subitizing for small quantities usually begins in first grade. Clements (1999) suggests some games for kindergarten play that can bridge into conceptual subitizing. Fosnot and Cameron (2007) provide a means of developing number sense through games. Their games are open-ended, so they provide for the use of more than one strategy. They are also cooperative and noncompetitive.

Children first recognize quantities from one to four or five. Infants can perceive the difference between these small quantities, and children as young as 2½ or 3 years may recognize these small amounts so easily that they seem to do so without counting. The concept of number is constructed bit by bit from infancy through the preschool years, and gradually it becomes a tool that can be used in problem solving.

Number's partner, counting, includes two operations: **rote counting** and **rational counting**. *Rote counting* involves reciting the names of the numerals in order from memory, that is, the child who says "One, two, three, four, five, six, seven, eight, nine, ten" has correctly counted in a rote manner from one to ten. *Rational counting* involves matching each numeral name to an object in a group. It builds on children's understanding of one-to-one correspondence. Reys, Lindquist, Lambdin, Smith, and Suydam (2001) identify four principles of rational counting:

1. Only one number name may be assigned to each of the objects to be counted.
2. There is a correct order in which the number names may be assigned (i.e., one, two, three, etc.).
3. Counting can start with any of the items in the group.
4. The *cardinality rule* states that the last number name used is the number of objects in the group.

As an example, Maria has some pennies in her hand. She takes them out of her hand one at a time and places them on the table. Each time she places one on the table she says the next number name in sequence: "one," places first penny; "two," places another penny; "three," places another penny. She has successfully done rational counting of three objects. Rational counting is a higher level of one-to-one correspondence.

A basic understanding of accurate rote counting and one-to-one correspondence is the foundation of rational counting. The ability of rational counting assists children in understanding the concept of number by enabling them to check their labeling of quantities as being a specific amount. It also helps them compare equal quantities of different things—such as two apples, two children, and two chairs—and realize that the quantity two is *two*, regardless of what makes up a group. Marshall (2006) emphasizes the importance of understanding that numbers are abstractions and that each one refers to its unique amount regardless of what is included in a group. Number, counting, and one-to-one correspondence all serve as the basis for developing the concept of number conservation, which is usually mastered by age 6 or 7. Too often, the preprimary mathematics program centers on counting with repeated teacher-directed drill and practice. Children need repeated and frequent practice to develop counting skills, but this practice should be of short duration and should center on naturalistic and informal instruction. Adult guided activities should include many applications, such as the examples of data collection that follow:

- How many children in the class have brothers? Sisters? Neither?
- How many days will it be until the first seed sprouts? Let's make some guesses, and then we'll keep track and see who comes close.
- How many days did we mark off before the first egg hatched?
- How many carrots do we need so that each rabbit will get one?
- How many of the small blocks will balance the big block on the balance scale?

The normal expectation is that rote counting develops ahead of rational counting. For example, a 2- or 3-year-old who has a good memory might rote count to ten but only be able to rational count one or two or three objects accurately. When given a group of more than three to count, a young child might perform as described in the following example: Six blocks are placed in front of a 2½-year-old, who is asked, "How many blocks do you have?" Using her pointer finger, she "counts" and points.

- "One, two, three, four, five, six, seven, eight" (pointing at some blocks more than once and some not at all).
- "One, two, four, six, three, ten" (pointing to each block only once but losing track of the correct order).

Rational counting is a fairly complex task. To count objects accurately, the child must know the number names in the correct order and be able to coordinate eyes, hands, speech, and memory. This is difficult for a 2- or 3-year-old because she is still in a period of rapid growth in coordination. She is also limited in her ability to stick to a task. The teacher should not push a child to count more things than he can count easily and with success. Most rational counting experiences should be naturalistic and informal.

By age 4 or 5, children's rate of physical growth is slowing. Their coordination of eyes, hands, and memory is maturing. Rational counting skills should begin to catch up with rote counting skills. Adult guided activities can be introduced. At the same time, naturalistic and informal activities should continue.

By age 3 or 4, most children can rational count small groups.

During the kindergarten year, children usually become skilled at rote and rational counting. Many kindergartners are ready to play more complex games with quantities such as counting backward and counting on from a given quantity, which lay the foundation for the whole number operations of addition and subtraction. Estimation activities can begin with prekindergartners playing simple games such as "Guess how many beans are in a small jar" or "How many paper clips wide is the table?"—and checking their guesses by counting the beans and paper clips.

In *Number in Preschool and Kindergarten*, Kamii (1982) particularly emphasizes that it is necessary to be aware of the coordination of one-to-one correspondence and counting in developing the concept of number. Four levels of development in counting have been identified by asking children to place in front of them the same number of items as an adult puts out in groups of sizes four to eight.

1. Children cannot understand what they are supposed to do.
2. They do a rough visual estimation or copy (that is, they attempt to make their group look like the model).
3. They do a methodical one-to-one correspondence. Children seldom reach this stage before age 5½.
4. They count, that is, the child counts the items in the model and then counts out another group with the same amount. Children usually reach this stage at about age 7.

To develop the coordination of the two concepts, it is essential that children count and do one-to-one correspondence using movable objects. It becomes obvious that, among other weaknesses, the use of workbook pages precludes moving the objects to be counted and/or matched. In addition, opportunities should be provided for children to work together, so they can discuss and compare ideas. As the children work individually and/or with others, watch closely and note the thinking process that seems to take place as they solve problems using counting and one-to-one correspondence.

Assessment

The adult should note the child's regular activity. Does she recognize groups of zero to four without counting? "Mary has no cookies," "I have two cookies," "John has four cookies." Does she use rational counting correctly when needed? "Here, Mr. Black, six blocks for you." (Mr. Black has seen her count them out on her own.) For formal assessment, see the tasks on page 88 and those in Appendix A. Be sure to record naturalistic and informal events.

Naturalistic Activities

Young children use a great deal of number sense and the skill of counting in their everyday activities. Once these are in a child's thoughts and activity, he will be observed often engaging in number and counting activities. He practices rote counting often. He may run up to the teacher or parent saying, "I can count—one, two, three." He may be watching a TV program and hear "one, two, three, four …," after which he may repeat "one, two, …." At first he may play with the number names, saying "one, two, five, four, eight, …" to himself in no special order. Listen carefully and note that gradually he gets more of the names in the right order.

Number appears often in the child's activities once she has the idea in mind. A child is eating crackers and says, "Look at all my crackers. I have two crackers." One and two are usually the first amounts used by children ages 2 and 3. They may use one and two for quite a while before they go on to larger groups. Number names are used for an early form of division. For example, a child has three cookies, which he divides equally with his friends: "One for you, one for you, and one for me." Looking at a picture book, the child says, "There is one daddy and two babies." The child wants another toy: "I want one more little car, Dad."

Informal Activities

The alert adult can find a multitude of ways to take advantage of opportunities for informal instruction. For example, the child is watching a children's TV program and the teacher is sitting next to her.

4G   **Preoperational Ages 3–6**
Rote Counting: Unit 6

METHOD: Interview, individual.

SKILL: Child demonstrates her ability to rote count.

MATERIALS: None.

PROCEDURE: Ask "**Count for me. Count as far as you can.**" If the child hesitates or looks puzzled, ask again. If the child still doesn't respond, say, "**One, two, what's next?**"

EVALUATION: Note how far the child counts and the accuracy of the counting. Young children often lose track (i.e., "One, two, three, four, five, six, ten, seven, …") or miss a number name. Children ages 2 and 3 may only be able to count their ages, whereas 4-year-olds can usually count accurately to ten and might try the teens and even beyond. By age 5 or 6, children will usually begin to understand the commonalities in the 20s and beyond and move on toward counting to 100. Young children vary a great deal at each age level, so it is important to find where each individual is and move along from there.

INSTRUCTIONAL RESOURCE: Charlesworth, R. (2011). *Experiences in math for young children* (6th ed.). Belmont, CA: WadsworthCengage Learning.

4H   **Preoperational Ages 3–6**
Rational Counting: Unit 6

METHOD: Interview, individual or small group.

SKILL: Child demonstrates his ability to rational count.

MATERIALS: Thirty or more objects such as cube blocks, chips, or Unifix Cubes®.

PROCEDURE: Place a pile of objects in front of the child (about 10 for a 3-year-old, 20 for a 4-year-old, 30 for a 5-year-old, and as many as 100 for older children). Ask "**Count these for me. How many can you count**?"

EVALUATION: Note how accurately the child counts and how many objects are attempted. In observing the process, note the following:

1. Does the child use just his eyes, or does he actually touch each object as he counts?

2. Is some organizational system used, such as lining the objects up in rows or moving the ones counted to the side?

3. Compare accuracy on rational counting with the child's rote counting ability.

INSTRUCTIONAL RESOURCE: Charlesworth, R. (2011). *Experiences in math for young children* (6th ed.). Belmont, CA: WadsworthCengage Learning.

A voice from the TV rote counts by singing, "One, two, three, four, five, six." The teacher says to the child, "That's fun, let's count too." They then sing together: "One, two, three, four, five, six." Or, the teacher and children are waiting for the school bus to arrive. "Let's count as far as we can while we wait. One, two, three …." Because rote counting is learned through frequent but short periods of practice, use informal activities most for teaching.

Everyday activities offer many opportunities for informal rational counting and number activities. For instance, the teacher is helping a child get dressed after his nap. "Find your shoes and socks. How many shoes do you have? How many socks? How many feet?" Some children are meeting at the door. The teacher says, "We are going to the store. There should be five of us. Let's count and be sure we are all here."

Table setting offers many chances for rational counting. "Put six place mats on each table." "How many more forks do we need?" "Count out four napkins." Play activities also offer times for rational counting. "Mary, please give Tommy two trucks." A child is looking at his hands, which are covered with finger paint: "How many red hands do you have, Joey?"

Present a more challenging problem by asking an open-ended question. For instance: "Get enough napkins for everyone at your table" or "Be sure everyone has the same number of carrot sticks." In these situations, children aren't given a clue to help them decide how many they need or how many each person should get; they must figure out how to solve the problem on their own. Often children will forget to count themselves. This presents an excellent opportunity for group discussion to try to figure out what went wrong. The teacher could follow up such an incident by reading the book *Six Foolish Fishermen* (Elkin, 1968/1971; see Appendix B), in which the fishermen make the same mistake.

Adult Guided Activities

Rote counting is learned mostly through naturalistic and informal activities. However, short, fun things, such as rhymes, songs, and finger plays, can be used to help children learn the number names in the right order. Songs include those such as "This Old Man," "Johnny Works with One Hammer," and "Five Little Ducks."

A favorite old rhyme is as follows:

One, two, buckle your shoe.
Three, four, shut the door.
Five, six, pick up sticks.
Seven, eight, shut the gate.
Nine, ten, a big fat hen.

A finger play can be used, as follows.

"Five Little Birdies"

(Hold up five fingers. As each bird leaves, "fly" your hand away and come back with one less finger standing up.)
Five little birdies sitting by the door,
One flew away and then there were four.
Four little birdies sitting in a tree,
One flew away and then there were three.
Three little birdies sitting just like you,
One flew away and then there were two.
Two little birdies having fun,
One flew away and then there was one.
One little birdie sitting all alone,
He flew away and then there were none.

Tres deditos
Ten Little Fingers (Song)

A counting finger play in Spanish is Diez Deditos (Orozco, 1997).

More direct ways of practicing rote counting are also good. Clapping and counting at the same time teaches number order and gives practice in rhythm and coordination. With a group, everyone can count at the same time, "Let's count together. One, two, three …." Ask individual children, "Count as far as you can."

Groups that have zero to four items are special in developing rational counting skills. Children perceive the number of items in groups of this without counting. For this reason, these groups are easy for children to understand. They should have many experiences and activities with groups of size zero to four before they work with groups of five and more. With adult guided activities it is wise to start with groups of size two because, as mentioned before, so many activities occur naturally. For example, the child has two eyes, two hands, two arms, and two legs. Two pieces of bread are used to make a sandwich, and riding a bike with two wheels is a sign of being big. For this reason, activities using two are presented first in the following examples. The activities are set up so that they can be copied onto activity cards for the file.

Activities

Number: Groups of Two

OBJECTIVE: To learn the idea of two.

MATERIALS: The children's bodies, the environment, a flannelboard and/or a magnetic board, pairs of objects, pictures of pairs of objects.

NATURALISTIC AND INFORMAL ACTIVITIES: As children play with materials in the classroom, note any occasions when they identify two objects. Ask questions such as "How many shoes do you need for your dress-up outfit?" "Can two cups of sand fill the bowl?"

ADULT GUIDED ACTIVITIES:
1. Put several pairs of felt pieces (e.g., hearts, triangles, or bunnies) on the flannelboard (or magnets on the magnet board). Point to each group in turn: **"What are these?" "How many are there?"**
2. Have the children check their bodies and the other children's bodies for groups of two.
3. Have the children, one at a time, find groups of two in the room.
4. Using rummy cards, other purchased picture cards, or cards you have made, make up sets of cards with identical pairs. Give each child a pack with several pairs mixed up. Have them sort the pack and find the groups of two.
5. Fill a container with many objects. Have the children sort out as many groups of two as they can find.

FOLLOW-UP: Have the materials available during center time.

Number: Groups of Three

OBJECTIVE: To learn the idea of three.

MATERIALS: Flannelboard and/or magnet board, objects, picture cards.

NATURALISTIC AND INFORMAL ACTIVITIES: As children play with materials in the classroom, note any occasions when they identify three objects. Ask leading questions: if three children are playing house, "How many cups do you need for your party?" "Can three cups of sand fill the bowl?" To a 3-year-old, "How many candles were on your birthday cake?"

ADULT GUIDED ACTIVITIES: Do the same types of activities as before, now using groups of three instead of two. Emphasize that three is one more than two.

FOLLOW-UP: Have the materials available during center time.

Number: Groups of One

OBJECTIVE: To learn the idea that one is a group.

MATERIALS: Flannelboard and/or magnet board, objects, picture cards.

NATURALISTIC AND INFORMAL ACTIVITIES: As children play with materials in the classroom, note any occasions when they identify a single object. Ask such questions as, "How many cups does each person need for the party?" "How many glasses does each person get for milk at lunch?"

ADULT GUIDED ACTIVITIES: Do the same types of activities using groups of one as were done for groups of two and three.

FOLLOW-UP: Have the materials available during center time.

Number: Zero

OBJECTIVE: To understand the idea that a group with nothing in it is called *zero*.

NATURALISTIC AND INFORMAL ACTIVITIES: Note if children use the term *none* or *zero* during their play activities. Ask questions such as "If all the sand falls on the floor, how much will be left in the sandbox?" "If you eat all of your beans, then you will have how many?"

MATERIALS: Flannelboard, magnet board, objects.

ADULT GUIDED ACTIVITIES:
1. Show the children groups of things on the flannelboard, magnet board, and/or groups of objects. Say "**See all these things?**" Give them a chance to look and respond. "**Now I take them away. What do I have now?**" They should respond with "nothing," "all gone," and/or "no more."
2. Place a group (of flannel pieces, magnet shapes, or objects) of a size the children all know (such as one, two, three, or four). Keep taking one away. Ask "**How many now?**" When none are left, say: "**This amount is called zero.**" Repeat until they can answer "zero" on their own.
3. Play a silly game. Ask "**How many real live tigers do we have in our room?**" (Continue with other things that are obviously not in the room.)

FOLLOW-UP: Work on the concept informally. Ask questions: "How many children are here after everyone goes home?" After snack, if all the food has been eaten: "How many cookies (crackers, pretzels, etc.) do you have now?"

After the children have grasped the ideas of groups of zero, one, two, and three, go on to four. Use the same kinds of activities. Once they have four in mind, go on to activities using groups of all five amounts. Emphasize the idea of *one more than* as you move to each larger group.

When the children have the idea of groups from zero to four, they can go on to groups larger than four. Some children are able to perceive five without counting, just as they perceive zero through four without actually counting. After the children have learned the groups of four and

Activities

Number: Using Groups of Zero through Four

OBJECTIVE: To understand groups of zero through four.

MATERIALS: Concrete objects, magent board with magnets, or felt board with flannel pieces.
1. Show the children several groups of objects of different amounts. Ask them to point to sets of one, two, three, and four.
2. Give the children a container of many objects. Have them find sets of one, two, three, and four.
3. Show the children containers of objects (pennies, buttons, etc.). Ask them to find the ones with groups of zero, one, two, three, and four.
4. Give each child four objects. Ask each one to make as many different groups as she can.
5. Ask the children, "**How many _____ are in the room?**" (Suggest things for which there are fewer than five.)

Activities

Number/Rational Counting: Introducing Five

OBJECTIVE: To understand that five is four with one more item added.

MATERIALS: Flannelboard, magnet board, and/or objects.

NATURALISTIC AND INFORMAL ACTIVITIES: Have a variety of manipulatives in the math center. Note how children group the materials and whether they mention "how many"; for example, "I have five red cubes." "I need three green cubes." Ask questions such as "How many white cubes have you hooked together?"

ADULT GUIDED ACTIVITIES:
1. Show the children a group of four. Ask "**How many in this group?**" Show the children a group of five. Ask "**How many in this group?**" Note how many children already have the idea of five. Tell them "**Yes, this is a group of five.**" Have them make other groups with the same amount by using the first group as a model.
2. Give each child five objects. Ask them to identify how many objects they have.
3. Give each child seven or eight objects. Ask them to make a group of five.

FOLLOW-UP: Have containers of easily counted and perceived objects always available for the children to explore. These would be items such as buttons, poker chips, Unifix Cubes, and inch cubes. Use books that focus on five, such as *Five Little Ducks* (Raffi: Songs to Read Series, Crown) and *Five Little Monkeys Sitting in a Tree* (Christfellow, Clarion).

Number/Rational Counting: Groups Larger than Five

OBJECTIVE: To be able to count groups of amounts greater than five.

MATERIALS: Flannelboard and/or magnet board, objects for counting, pictures of groups on cards, items in the environment.

NATURALISTIC AND INFORMAL ACTIVITIES: Have a variety of manipulatives in the math center. Note how children group the materials and whether they mention "how many," such as "I have seven red cubes." "I need six green cubes." Ask questions such as "How many white cubes have you hooked together?" "If you hooked one more cube to your line, how many would you have?"

ADULT GUIDED ACTIVITIES:

1. One step at a time, present groups on the flannelboard and magnet board or groups made up of objects such as buttons, chips, inch-cube blocks, etc. Have the children take turns counting them—together and individually.
2. Present cards with groups of six or more, showing cats, dogs, houses, or similar figures. Ask the children as a group or individually to tell how many items are pictured on each card.
3. Give the children small containers with items to count.
4. Count things in the room. "**How many tables (chairs, windows, doors, children, teachers)?**" Have the children count all at the same time and individually.

FOLLOW-UP: Have the materials available for use during center time. Watch for opportunities for informal activities.

Number/Rational Counting: Follow-Up With Stories

OBJECTIVE: To be able to apply rational counting to fantasy situations.

MATERIALS: Stories that will reinforce the ideas of groups of numbers and rational counting skills. Some examples are *The Three Little Pigs, The Three Bears, Three Billy Goats Gruff, Snow White and the Seven Dwarfs, Six Foolish Fishermen, The Doorbell Rang*.

ACTIVITIES: As you read these stories to younger children, take time to count the number of characters who are the same animal or same kind of person. Use felt cutouts of the characters for counting activities and one-to-one matching (as suggested in Unit 8). Have older children dramatize the stories. Get them going with questions such as "How many people will we need to be bears?" "**How many porridge bowls (spoons, chairs, beds) do we need?**" Also, "**John, you get the bowls and spoons.**"

FOLLOW-UP: Have the books and other materials available for children to use during center time.

Number/Rational Counting: Follow-Up with Counting Books

OBJECTIVE: To strengthen rational counting skills.

MATERIALS: Counting books (see list in Appendix B).

ACTIVITIES: Go through the books with one child a small group of children. Discuss the pictures as a language development activity, and count the items pictured on each page.

Rational Counting: Follow-Up with One-to-One Correspondence

OBJECTIVE: To combine one-to-one correspondence and counting.

MATERIALS: Flannelboard and/or magnet board and counting objects.

ACTIVITIES: As the children work with the counting activities, have them check their sets that they say are the same number by using one-to-one correspondence. See activities for Unit 8.

FOLLOW-UP: Have materials available during center time.

fewer, teach them five by adding one to groups of four. Once the children understand five as "four with one more" and six as "five with one more," then begin more advanced rational counting. In other words, children can work with groups of objects where they can find the number only by actually counting each object. Before working with a child on counting groups of six or more, the adult must be sure that the child can do the following activities:

- Recognize groups of zero to four without counting.
- Rote count to six or more correctly and quickly.
- Recognize that a group of five is a group of four with one more added.

The following are activities for learning about groups larger than four:

A 100s board provides a challenging way to apply counting skills and explore number sequence.

Children of ages 4 to 6 can play simple group games that require them to apply their counting skills. For example, a bowling game requires them to count the number of pins they knock down. A game in which they try to drop clothespins into a container requires them to count the number of clothespins that land in the container. They can compare the number of pins knocked down or the number of clothespins dropped into the container by each child. By age 6 or 7, children can keep a cumulative score using tick marks (lines) (see Figure 6–2). Not only can they count, they can compare amounts to find out who has the most and if any of them have the same amount. Older children (see Units 18 and 19) will be interested in writing numerals and might realize that, instead of tick marks, they can write down the numeral that represents the amount to be recorded.

Students who are skilled at counting enjoy sorting small objects such as colored macaroni, beads, miniature animals, or buttons. At first they might be given a small amount, for example, ten items, with which to work. They can compare the amounts in each of the groups they construct as well as compare the amounts in their groups with a partner's. Eventually they can move on to larger groups of objects and more complex activities such as recording data with number symbols and constructing graphs (see Unit 16).

Another activity that builds number concepts is the hundred days celebration. Starting the first day of school, the class uses concrete materials to record how many days of school have gone by. Attach two large, clear plastic cups to the bulletin board. Use a supply of drinking straws or tongue depressors as recording devices. Each day, count

Student	Score
Derrick	//////
Liu Pei	////////
Brent	////
Theresa	///////

FIGURE 6–2 By age 6 or 7, children can keep a cumulative score using tally marks.

in unison the number of days of school and add a straw to the cup on the right. Whenever ten straws are collected, bundle them with a rubber band and place them in the left-hand cup. Explain that when there are ten bundles, it will be the 100th day. Ten is used as an informal benchmark. On the 100th day, each child brings a plastic zip-top bag containing 100 items. It is exciting to see what they bring: pieces of dry macaroni, dry beans, pennies, candy, hairpins, and so on. Working in pairs, they can check their collections by counting out groups of ten and counting how many groups they have. To aid their organization, large mats with ten circles on each or ten clear plastic glasses can be supplied. Late 4-year-olds as well as kindergarten and primary grade students enjoy this activity.

Kindergartners can work with simple problem-solving challenges. Schulman and Eston (1998) described a type of problem that kindergartners find intriguing. The children were in the second half of kindergarten and had previously worked in small groups. The basic situation was demonstrated as the "carrot and raisin" problem.

Jackie had carrots and raisins on her plate. She had seven items in all. What did Jackie have on her plate?

The children selected orange rods and small stones to represent carrots and raisins, respectively. They were given paper plates to use as work mats. When they had a solution that worked, they recorded it by drawing a picture. As they worked and shared ideas, they realized that many different groupings were surfacing. They recorded all the solutions. Of course, what they were discovering were the facts that compose seven. This same context led to other problems of varying degrees of difficulty (sea stars and hermit crabs in a tide pool, pineapples and pears in a fruit basket, seeds that germinated and seeds that didn't). Some children continued with random strategies whereas others discovered organized strategies.

Other kinds of problem-solving activities can provide challenges for children learning to count. The activities in "Bears in the House and in the Park" provide simple word problems for pre-K–2 students (Greenes et al., 2003). Using teddy-bear counters or chips, children model problems such as the following:

- *Story Problem 1*
- There are two bears in the kitchen.
- There are three bears in the living room.
- How many bears are downstairs? (Five) (p. 11)

Copley (2004) includes activities such as "Hanny Learns to Count from the Prairie Dogs," "Benny's Pennies," and "How Many Are Hiding?"

Quite a bit of computer software has been designed to reinforce counting skills and the number concept. Five-year-old George sits at the computer,

MATH TECHNOLOGY
FOR YOUNG CHILDREN

Try to obtain some of the computer software and/or CDs, or explore the online resource listed below. Using the criteria suggested in Unit 2, review and evaluate the material:

- *Learn About Numbers and Counting*. Includes counting and other concepts and skills (Elgin, IL: Sunburst Technologies).
- *Reader Rabbit's Math Ages 4–6*. Includes counting and other concepts and skills. (San Francisco: Broderbund at Riverdeep).
- *Destination Math* (San Francisco: Riverdeep).
- *Tenth Planet Number Bundle* (Elgin, IL: Sunburst Technologies).
- *Math Blaster Ages 4–6* (Elgin, IL: Sunburst Technologies).
- *Arthur's Math Games* (http://www.kidsclick.com).
- *Caillou Counting* (http://www.kidsclick.com).
- *How Many Bugs in a Box* (http://www.kidsclick.com).
- *The Count's Countdown* (http://www.shop.com), CD.
- *Numbers* (Sesame Street) (http://www.shop.com), CD.
- *Math* (PBS Kids.org).

deeply involved with *Stickybear Numbers*. Each time he presses the space bar, a group with one fewer appears on the screen. Each time he presses a number, a group with that amount appears. His friend Kate joins him and comments on the pictures. Both of them count the figures in each group and compare the results. The following technology box includes a list of counting resources the reader might wish to review.

Ideas for Children with Special Needs

Most young children learn to count and develop number sense through informal everyday experiences and books and rhymes, but others need additional teacher-directed experiences. Some children will need extra verbalization through finger plays and rhymes. Others will need more multisensory experiences using their motor, tactual, auditory, and visual senses. Examples include the following:

- Jumping up and down on a trampoline saying "one, one, one ..." to get an understanding of the unit.
- Doing other exercises and counting the number of movements.
- Connecting with nursery rhymes, such as by seeing how many times they can jump over a candle stick after reciting "Jack Be Nimble."

Rational counting follows a prescribed sequence that should take on a rhythmical pattern. Help children achieve this goal through the following types of activities:

- Counting objects while putting them into containers provides an auditory, tactile, and verbal experience. Use various types of containers. Cube blocks or large beads can be dropped and counted. Children who have difficulty with motor control may need to take a break between dropping each block or have the adult hand the blocks over one at a time.
- Use self-correcting formboards or pegboards as well as Montessori cylinder boards and pegboards to help develop counting and number sense.

Some children have difficulty organizing their work. They may count a group in a random manner. They may need to be taught to methodically pick up each object for counting and put each in a new place. Start with straight lines and then move to irregular patterns. Gradually move toward asking the child to count out a specific number of objects. Count each object with the child.

Most young children enjoy learning a new language. As ELLs learn to count in English, English-speaking students can learn to count in a second language.

Evaluation

Informal evaluation can be done by noting the answers children give during direct instruction sessions. The teacher should also observe the children during center time and notice whether they apply what they have learned. When children choose to explore materials used in the structured lessons during center time, ask them questions. For instance, Kate is at the flannel-board arranging the felt shapes in rows. As her teacher goes by, he stops and asks "How many bunnies do you have in that row?" If four children are playing house, the teacher can ask, "How many children in this family?" Formal evaluation can be done with one child using tasks such as those in Appendix A.

Place "hundreds" collections and graphs in portfolios. Include photos of children working with materials and use anecdotes and checklists to record milestones in number concept growth and development.

Kathy Richardson (1999, p. 7) provides questions to guide the evaluation of counting and number sense. Some key questions for counting include the following:

- To what amount can children work with (e.g., five, ten, twelve, etc.)?
- What kinds of errors do the children make? Are they consistent or random?
- Do they stick with the idea of one-to-one correspondence as they count?

- Are they accurate? Do they check their results?
- Do they remember the number they counted to and realize that is the amount in the group (cardinal number)?

Key questions to consider when evaluating number sense include the following:

- Can the children subitize perceptually—that is, recognize small groups of four or five without counting?
- Knowing the amount in one group, can they use that information to figure out how many are in another group?
- Can children make reasonable estimates of the amount in a group and revise their estimate after counting some items?
- When items are added to a group that they have already counted, do children count on or start over?

The answers to these questions will help you evaluate whether the children understand the concepts of number and number sense.

Summary

Number sense or the number concept connects counting with quantity. Counting, one-to-one correspondence, arranging and rearranging groups, and comparing quantities (see Unit 11) help children develop number sense, which underlies all mathematical operations. The number concept involves an understanding of *oneness, twoness*, and so on. Perceptual subitizing or recognizing groups of less than four or five without counting usually develops during the preschool/kindergarten period. Counting includes two types of skills: rote counting and rational counting. Rote counting is saying from memory the names of the numbers in order. Rational counting consists of using number sense to attach the number names in order to items in a group to find out how many items are in the group. There are four principles of rational counting: (1) saying the number names in the correct order, (2) achieving one-to-one correspondence between number name and object, (3) understanding that counting can begin with any object, and (4) understanding that the last number named is the total.

Rote counting is mastered before rational counting. Rational counting begins to catch up with rote counting after age 4 or 5. The number concept is learned simultaneously. Quantities greater than four are not identified until the child learns to rational count beyond four. Counting is learned for the most part through naturalistic and informal activities supported by structured lessons. However, some children may need additional multisensory experiences to reinforce their counting skills and understanding of number.

KEY TERMS

cardinality
conceptual subitizing
number sense

perceptual subitizing
rational counting

rote counting
subitizing

SUGGESTED ACTIVITIES

1. Try the sample assessment tasks included in this unit with three or four children of different ages (between 2½ and 6½ years). Record the results and compare the answers received at each age level.

2. Go to the children's section of the library or a local bookstore. Find three number books (such as those listed in Appendix B). Write a review of each one, giving a brief description and explaining why and how you would use each book.

3. With one or more young children, try some of the counting activities suggested in this unit. Evaluate the success of the activity.

4. Add rote counting and rational counting activity cards to your Idea File or Idea Notebook.

REVIEW

A. Discuss the relationship between number sense, counting, and the understanding of quantities and subitizing.

B. Explain the relationship between rote and rational counting.

C. Describe two examples each of rote and rational counting.

D. How should the adult respond in each of the following situations?

1. Rudy (age 3½) looks up at his teacher and proudly recites: "One, two, three, five, seven, ten."

2. Tony, age 2, says, "I have two eyes, you have two eyes."

3. Jada has been asked to get six spoons for the children at her lunch table. She returns with seven spoons.

4. Lan is 4½ years old. He counts a stack of six Unifix Cubes: "One, two, three, four, five, seven—seven cubes."

5. An adult is sitting with some 4- and 5-year-olds who are waiting for the school bus. She decides to do some informal counting activities.

REFERENCES

Clements, D. H. (1999). Subitizing: What is it? Why teach it? *Teaching Children Mathematics, 5*(7), 400–405.

Copley, J. V. (Ed.). (2004). *Showcasing mathematics for the young child*. Reston, VA: National Council of Teachers of Mathematics.

Elkin, B. (1968/1971). *Six foolish fishermen*. New York: Scholastic Books.

Fosnot, C. T., & Cameron, A. (2007). *Games for early number sense*. Portsmouth, NH: Heinemann.

Greenes, C. E., Dacey, L., Cavanagh, M., Findell, C. R., Sheffield, L. J., & Small, M. (2003). *Navigating through problem solving and reasoning in prekindergarten–kindergarten*. Reston, VA: National Council of Teachers of Mathematics.

Kamii, C. (1982). *Number in preschool and kindergarten*. Washington, DC: National Association for the Education of Young Children.

Marshall, J. (2006). Math Wars 2: It's the teaching, stupid! *Phi Delta Kappan, 87*(5), 356–363.

National Council of Teachers of Mathematics. (2000). *Principles and standards for school mathematics*. Reston, VA: Author.

National Council of Teachers of Mathematics. (2007). *Curriculum focal points for prekindergarten through grade 8 mathematics*. Retrieved May 24, 2007, from http://www.nctm.org

Orozco, J. (1997). *Diez deditos and other playround rhymes and action songs from Latin America*. New York: Scholastic.

Reys, R. E., Lindquist, M. M., Lambdin, D. V., Smith, N. L., & Suydam, M. N. (2001). *Helping children learn mathematics*. New York: Wiley.

Richardson, K. (1999). *Developing number concepts: Planning guide*. Parsippany, NJ: Seymour.

Schulman, L., & Eston, R. (1998). A problem worth revisiting. *Teaching Children Mathematics, 5*(2), 73–77.

Further Reading and Resources

Clements, D. H., & Sarama, J. (2004). Mathematics everywhere, every time. *Teaching Children Mathematics, 10*(8), 421–426.

Copley, J. V., Jones, C., & Dighe, J. (2007). *Mathematics: The creative curriculum approach.* Washington, DC: Teaching Strategies.

Cross, C. T., Woods, T. A., & Schweingruber, H. (Eds.). (2009). *Mathematics learning in early childhood.* Washington, DC: National Academies Press.

Epstein, A., & Gainsley, S. (2005). *Math in the preschool classroom.* Ypsilanti, MI: High/Scope.

Equity for diverse populations. (2009). *Teaching Children Mathematics* [Focus issue], *16*(3).

Hands-on standards. (2007). Vernon Hill, IL: Learning Resources.

Hoover, H. M. (2003). The dollar game: A tool for promoting number sense among kindergartners. *Teaching Children Mathematics, 10*(1), 23–25.

McDonald, J. (2007). Selecting counting books: Mathematical perspectives. *Young Children, 62*(3), 38–42.

Richardson, K. (1984). *Developing number concepts using Unifix Cubes.* Menlo Park, CA: Addison-Wesley.

Richardson, K. (1999). *Developing number concepts: Counting, comparing, and pattern.* Parsippany, NJ: Seymour.

Sztajn, P. (2002). Celebrating 100 with number sense. *Teaching Children Mathematics, 9*(4), 212–217.

Logic and Classifying

After reading this unit, you should be able to:

- Explain the NCTM expectations for logic and classifying.
- Describe features of groups.
- Describe the activity of classifying.
- Identify five types of criteria that children can use when classifying.
- Assess, plan, and teach classification activities appropriate for young children.

The NCTM (2000) expectations for logic and classifying focus on the ability of children to sort, classify, and order objects by size, number, and other properties (see also Units 8 and 13), to sort and classify objects according to their attributes, and to organize data about the objects (see also Unit 16).

The focal points for prekindergarten and kindergarten number and operations connect with sorting. By kindergarten, children should be able to use sorting and grouping to solve logical problems. For example, they can collect data to answer such questions as what kinds of pets class members have or how birth dates are distributed over the year. They can also sort and group collections of objects in a variety of ways.

In mathematics and science, an understanding of **logical grouping** and **classifying** is essential. The NCTM standards identify the importance of connecting counting to grouping. Constructing logical groups provides children with valuable logical thinking experiences. As children construct logical groups, they organize materials by classifying them according to some common criteria. A group may contain from zero (an empty group) to an endless number of things. The youngest children may group materials by criteria that are not apparent to adults but make sense to them. As children develop, they gradually begin constructing groups for which the criteria are apparent to adults. Children also note common groupings they observe in their environment: dishes that are alike in pattern go together; and cars have four tires plus a spare, making a total of five in the group. Logical thinking and classification skills are fundamental concepts that apply across the curriculum (Figure 7–1).

To **add** is to put together or join groups. For example, the four tires on the wheels plus the

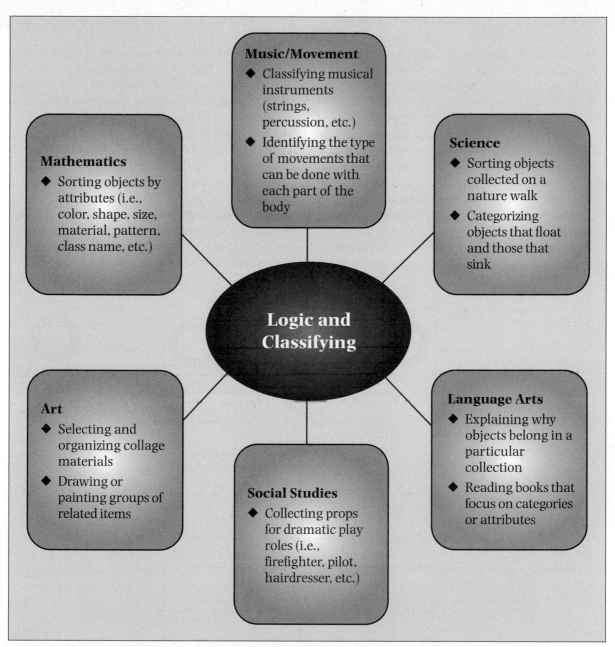

Music/Movement
- ◆ Classifying musical instruments (strings, percussion, etc.)
- ◆ Identifying the type of movements that can be done with each part of the body

Science
- ◆ Sorting objects collected on a nature walk
- ◆ Categorizing objects that float and those that sink

Mathematics
- ◆ Sorting objects by attributes (i.e., color, shape, size, material, pattern, class name, etc.)

Logic and Classifying

Art
- ◆ Selecting and organizing collage materials
- ◆ Drawing or painting groups of related items

Social Studies
- ◆ Collecting props for dramatic play roles (i.e., firefighter, pilot, hairdresser, etc.)

Language Arts
- ◆ Explaining why objects belong in a particular collection
- ◆ Reading books that focus on categories or attributes

FIGURE 7–1 Integrating logic and classification across the curriculum.

spare in the trunk equals five tires. To **subtract** is to separate a group into smaller groups. One tire goes flat and is taken off. It is left for repairs, and the spare is put on. A group of one (the flat tire) has been taken away or subtracted from the group of five. There are now two groups: four good tires on the car and one flat tire being repaired.

Before doing any formal addition and subtraction, the child needs to learn about groups and how he can join and separate them (Figure 7–2). In other words, the child must practice **sorting** (separating) and **grouping** (joining). This type of activity is called *classification*. The child performs tasks in which he separates and groups things because they may belong together: because they are the same color, the same shape, or the same size; do the same work; are always together; and so on. For example, a child may have a box of wooden blocks and a box of toy cars (wood, metal, and plastic). The child has two groups: blocks and cars. He then takes the blocks out of the box and separates them by grouping them into four piles: blue blocks, red blocks, yellow blocks, and green blocks. He now has four groups of blocks. He builds a garage with the red blocks and puts some cars in it. He now has a new group of toys. If he has put only red cars in the garage, he now has a group of red toys. The blocks and toys could be grouped in many other ways using their shape and material (wood, plastic, and metal) as the basis for the groups. Figure 7–3 illustrates some possible groups using the blocks and cars.

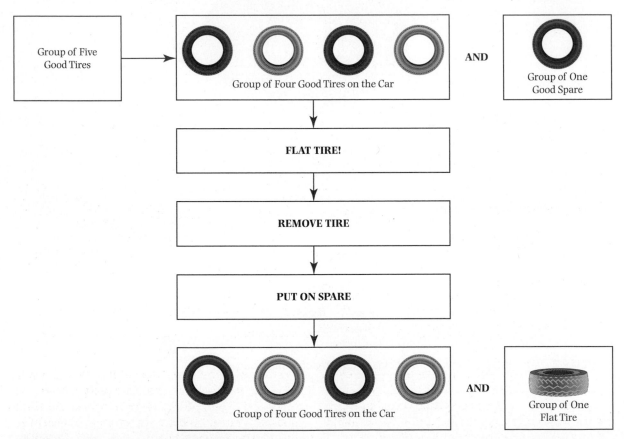

FIGURE 7–2 Groups can be joined and separated.

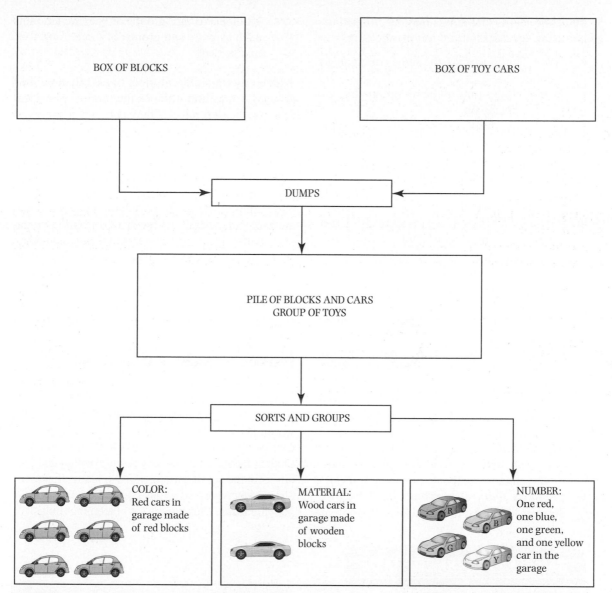

FIGURE 7–3 Classification (forming groups) may be evident in children's play—as with this child, who sorts blocks and cars into several logical groupings.

Young children spend much of their playtime in just such classification activities. As children work busily at these sorting tasks, they simultaneously learn words that label their activity. This happens when another person tells them the names and makes comments: "You have made a big pile of red things." "You have a pile of blue blocks, a pile of green blocks, …." "Those are plastic, and those are wood." As children learn to speak, the adult questions them: "What color are they? Which ones are plastic?" "How many _____?" To count, children must identify a specific group.

The child learns that things may be grouped together using several kinds of common features:

- *Color.* Things that are the same color can go together.
- *Shape.* Things may all be round, square, triangular, and so on.
- *Size.* Some things are big, some are small; some are fat, some are thin; and some are short, some are tall.
- *Material.* Things are made up of different materials such as wood, plastic, glass, paper, cloth, or metal.
- *Pattern.* Things have different visual patterns—such as stripes, dots, or flowers—or they may be plain (no design).
- *Texture.* Things feel different from each other (smooth, rough, soft, hard, wet, or dry).
- *Function.* Some items do the same thing or are used for the same thing (e.g., all in a group are for eating, writing, or playing music).
- *Association.* Some things do a job together (candle and match, milk and glass, shoe and foot), come from the same place (bought at the store or seen at the zoo), or belong to a special person (the hose, truck, and hat belong to the firefighter).
- *Class name.* There are names that may belong to several things (people, animals, food, vehicles, weapons, clothing, homes).
- *Common features.* All have handles, windows, doors, legs, or wheels, for example.

- Number. All are groups of specific amounts such as pairs and groups of three, four, five, and so forth.

Which criteria children select or exactly how they group is not as important as the process of logical thinking they exercise as they sort and group.

Assessment

The adult should note and record the child's play activities. Does she sort and group her play materials? For example, she might play with a pegboard and put each color peg in its own row, or build two garages with big cars in one and small cars in another. When offered several kinds of crackers for snack, she might pick out only triangle shapes. She might say, "Only boys can be daddies—girls are mothers."

More formal assessment can be made using the tasks in Appendix A. Two examples are shown here.

Naturalistic Activities

Sorting and grouping are some of the most basic and natural activities for the young child. Much of his play is organizing and reorganizing the things in his world. The infant learns the group of people who take care of him most of the time (child-care provider, mother, father, and/or relatives and friends) and puts others in the set of "strangers." He learns that some objects when pressed on his gums reduce the pain of growing teeth. They are his set of teething things.

SAMPLE ASSESSMENT TASK

5J
Preoperational Ages 4–6
Logic and Classifying, Clue Sort: Unit 7

METHOD: Interview.

SKILL: Child is able to classify and form sets using verbal and/or object clues.

MATERIALS: Twenty to twenty-five objects or pictures of objects or cutouts that can be grouped into several possible sets by criteria such as color, shape, size, or category (i.e., animals, plants, furniture, clothing, or toys).

PROCEDURE: Set all the objects in front of the child in a random arrangement. Try the following types of clues:

1. Say, "**Find some things that are _____**" (name a specific color, shape, size, material, pattern, function, or class).

2. Hold up one object, picture, or cutout; say, "**Find some things that belong with this.**" After the child makes the choices, ask, "**Why do these things belong together?**"

EVALUATION: Note whether the child makes a conventional logical group and provides a conventional logical reason such as "because they are cars," "they are all green," "you can eat with them," or a "creative" reason that is logical to the child if not to the adult, for example, "My mother would like them," "they all have points," "I like these colors, I don't like those."

INSTRUCTIONAL RESOURCE: Charlesworth, R. (2011). *Experiences in math for young children* (6th ed.). Belmont, CA: WadsworthCengage Learning

---

SAMPLE ASSESSMENT TASK

5K   **Preoperational Ages 4–6**
Logic and Classifying, Free Sort: Unit 7

METHOD: Interview.

SKILL: Child is able to classify and form sets in a free sort.

MATERIALS: Twenty to twenty-five objects or pictures of objects or cutouts that can be grouped into several possible sets by criteria such as color, shape, size, or category (i.e., animals, plants, furniture, clothing, or toys).

PROCEDURE: Set all the objects in front of the child in a random arrangement. Say, "**Put the things together that belong together.**" If the child looks puzzled, backtrack to the previous task, hold up one item, and say, "**Find some things that belong with this.**" When a group is completed, say, "**Now find some other things that belong together.**" Keep on until all the items are grouped. Then point to each group and ask, "**Why do they belong together?**"

EVALUATION: Note the criteria the child uses, as listed in task 5J.

INSTRUCTIONAL RESOURCE: Charlesworth, R. (2011). *Experiences in math for young children* (6th ed.). Belmont, CA: Wadsworth Cengage Learning.

As soon as the child is able to sit up, he finds great fun in putting things in containers and dumping them out. He can never have too many boxes, plastic dishes, and coffee cans along with such items as large plastic beads, table tennis balls, and teething toys (just be sure that the items are too large to swallow). With this type of activity, children have their first experiences making groups.

By age 3, the child sorts and groups things to help organize his play activities. He sorts out from his things those he needs for what he wants to do. He may pick out wild animal toys for his zoo, people dolls for his family play, big blocks for his house, blue paper circles to paste on paper, girls for friends, and so on.

The adult provides the free time, the materials (recycled material is fine as long as it is safe), and the space; the child does the rest.

Informal Activities

Adults can let children know that sorting and grouping activities are of value in informal ways by showing that they approve of what the children are doing. They can do this with a look, smile, nod, or comment.

Adults can also build children's classification vocabulary in informal ways. They can label the child's product and ask questions about what the child has done: "You have used all blue confetti in your picture." "You've used all the square blocks." "You have the pigs in this barn and the cows in that barn." "You painted green and purple stripes today." "Can you put the wild animals here and the farm animals here?" "Separate the spoons from the forks." "See if any of the cleaning rags are dry." "Put the crayons in the can and the pencils in the box." "Show me which things will roll down the ramp." "Which seeds are from your apple? Which are from your orange?" "Put the hamsters in the silver cage and the mice in the brown cage." As the children's vocabularies increase, they will be able to label and describe how and why they are sorting and grouping things. In addition, words give them shortcuts for labeling groups.

Adult Guided Activities

Sorting and grouping, which form the basis of classifying sets of things, lend themselves to many activities with many materials. As discussed in Unit 3, real objects are used first and then representations of objects (e.g., cutouts, pictures). One-to-one correspondence skills go hand in hand with sorting and grouping. For example, given three houses and three pigs, the child may give each pig a house (three groups) or place the pigs in one group and the houses in another (two groups).

The following activities help children develop the process of constructing groups.

Naturalistic classifying and sorting take place during young children's daily play activities.

Informal instruction takes place when an adult provides comments or questions as the children explore objects.

Activities

Logic and Classification: Color

OBJECTIVE: To sort and group by color.

MATERIALS: Several different objects that are the same color and four objects each of a different color. For example: a red toy car, a red block, a red bead, a red ribbon, a red sock; and one yellow car, one green ribbon, one blue ball, and one orange piece of paper.

NATURALISTIC AND INFORMAL ACTIVITIES: Provide students with many opportunities to experiment with color. Provide objects and art materials such as crayons, paint, colored paper, etc. Label the colors: "You have lots of *green* in your picture." "You've used all *red* LEGO blocks." Note when the children label the colors, "Please pass me a piece of *yellow* paper." "I can't find my *orange* crayon." Ask questions: "Which colors will you use for your penguins?"

ADULT GUIDED ACTIVITIES:
1. Hold up one red object, and say, "**Find the things that are the same color as this**." After the children have found all the red things, tell, "**These things are all the same color. Tell me the name of the color**." If there is no correct answer, say, "**The things you picked out are all red things**." Ask, "**What color are the things that you picked out?**"
2. Put all the things together again and say, "Find the things that are *not* red."

FOLLOW-UP: Repeat this activity with different colors and different materials. During center time, place a container of brightly colored materials. Observe whether the children put them into groups by color. If they do, ask, "**Why did you put those together?**" Accept any answer they give, but note whether they give a color answer.

Logic and Classification: Association

OBJECTIVE: To form sets of things that go together by association.

MATERIALS: Buy or make picture card sets. Each set can have one of the following themes:
1. Pictures of people in various jobs and pictures of things that go with their job:

Worker	Things that go with the worker's job
letter carrier	letter, mailbox, stamps, hat, mailbag, mail truck
airplane pilot	airplane, hat, wings
doctor	stethoscope, thermometer, bandages
trash collector	trash can, trash truck
police officer	handcuffs, pistol, hat, badge, police car
firefighter	hat, hose, truck, boots and coat, hydrant, house on fire
grocer	various kinds of foods, bags, shopping cart, cash register

Start with about three groups, and keep adding more.
2. Things that go together for use:

Item	Goes with
glass tumbler	carton of milk, pitcher of juice, can of soda pop
cup and saucer	coffeepot, teapot, steaming teakettle

match   candle, campfire
paper   pencil, crayon, pen
money   purse, wallet, bank
table   four chairs

Start with three groups, and keep adding more.

3. Things that are related, such as animals and their babies.

NATURALISTIC AND INFORMAL ACTIVITIES: During center time, provide groups of items that go together such as those just described. Provide both objects and picture sets. Note what the children do with the items. Do they group related items for play? Ask questions such as "Which things belong together?" "What do you need to eat your cereal?"

ADULT GUIDED ACTIVITIES:

1. One at a time, show the children the pictures of people or things that are the main clue (e.g., the workers) and ask, "WHO (WHAT) IS THIS?" When they have named all the pictures, show the "go with" pictures one at a time and ask, "**Who (what) does this belong to?**"
2. Give each child a clue picture. Hold each "go with" picture up in turn and ask, "**Who has the person (or thing) this belongs with? What do you call this?**"
3. Give a group of pictures to one child and say, "Sort these out. Find all the workers and put the things with them they use. Or: here is a glass, a cup and saucer, and some money. Look through these pictures, and find the ones that go with them."

FOLLOW-UP: Have groups of pictures available for children to use during center time. Note whether they use them individually or make up group games to play. Keep introducing more groups.

Logic and Classification: Simple Sorting

OBJECTIVE: To practice the act of sorting.

MATERIALS: Small containers, such as plastic margarine dishes, filled with small objects: buttons of various sizes, colors, and shapes; or dried beans, peas, corn. Another container with smaller divisions in it, such as an egg carton.

NATURALISTIC AND INFORMAL ACTIVITIES: Notice whether children sort as they play. Do they use pretend food when pretending to cook and eat a meal? Do the children playing adult select adult clothing to wear? When provided with animal figures, do children demonstrate preferences? During center time, place materials such as those just described on a table. Observe how the children sort.

ADULT GUIDED ACTIVITIES:

1. Have the sections of the larger container marked with a model, such as each kind of button or dried bean. The children match each thing from their container with the model until everything is sorted into new groups in the egg carton (or other large container with small sections).
2. Use the same materials, but do not mark the sections of the sorting container. See how the children sort on their own.

FOLLOW-UP: Have these materials available during center time. Make up more groups using different kinds of things for sorting.

Logic and Classification: Class Names, Discussion

OBJECTIVE: To discuss groups of things that can be put in the same class and decide on the class name.

MATERIALS: Things that can be put in the same group on the basis of class name, such as the following:
1. Animals—several toy animals.
2. Vehicles—toy cars, trucks, motorcycles.
3. Clothing—a shoe, a shirt, a belt.
4. Things to write with—pen, pencil, marker, crayon, chalk.

NATURALISTIC AND INFORMAL ACTIVITIES: During center time, note whether children use class names during their play. Give examples of labeling classes: "You like to play with the *horses* when you select from the *animal* collection." Ask questions such as "Which is your favorite *vehicle*?"

ADULT GUIDED ACTIVITIES: The same plan can be followed for any group of things.
1. Bring the things out one at a time until three have been discussed. Ask about each thing.
   a. "**What can you tell me about this?**"
   b. **Five specific questions:**
      "**What do you call this? (what is its name?)**"
      "**What color is it?**"
      "**What do you do with it? Or what does it do? Or who uses this?**"
      "**What is it made out of?**"
      "**Where do you get one?**"
   c. Show the three things discussed and ask, "**What do you call things like this? These are all (animals, vehicles, clothing, things to write with).**"
2. Put two or more groups of things together that have already been discussed. Ask the children to sort them into new groups and to give the class name for each group.

FOLLOW-UP: Put together groups (in the manner described here) that include things from science and social studies.

Classification is one of the most important fundamental skills in science. The following are examples of how classification might be used during science activities.

Logic and Classification: Sorting a Nature Walk Collection

OBJECTIVE: To sort items collected during a nature walk.

MATERIALS: The class has gone for a nature walk. Children have collected leaves, stones, bugs, etc. They have various types of containers (e.g., plastic bags, glass jars, plastic margarine containers).

NATURALISTIC AND INFORMAL ACTIVITIES: Develop collections with items children bring in from home and place them in the science center. Encourage children to observe birds that may be in the area. If the school allows, have them visit animals—for example, children's pets, a person with a guide dog, or a person with a dog trained to do tricks. Have books on nature topics in the library center.

ADULT GUIDED ACTIVITIES:
1. Have the children spread out pieces of newspaper on tables or on the floor.
2. Ask them to dump their plants and rocks on the table. (Live things should remain in their separate containers.)
3. Say, "**Look at the things you have collected. Put things that belong together in groups. Tell me why they belong together.**" Let the children explore the materials and identify leaves, twigs, flowers, weeds, smooth rocks, rough rocks, light and dark rocks, etc. After they have grouped the plant material and the rocks, have them sort the animals and insects into different containers. See if they can label their collections (e.g., earthworms, ants, spiders, beetles, ladybugs).
4. Help them organize their materials on the science table. Encourage them to write labels or signs using their own spellings, or help them with spelling if needed. If they won't attempt to write themselves, let them dictate labels to you.

FOLLOW-UP: Encourage the children to examine all the collections and discuss their attributes. Have some plant, rock, insect, and animal reference books on the science table. Encourage the children to find pictures of items like theirs in the books. Read what the books tell about their discoveries.

Logic and Classification: Sorting Things that Sink and Float

OBJECTIVE: To find out which objects in a collection sink and which float.

MATERIALS: A collection of many objects made from different materials. You might ask each child to bring one thing from home and then add some items from the classroom. Have a large container of water and two empty containers labeled *sink* and *float*. Make a large chart with a picture/name of each item where the results of the explorations can be recorded (Figure 7–4).

NATURALISTIC AND INFORMAL ACTIVITIES: Provide many opportunities for water play. Include items that float and sink. Note the children's comments as they play with the objects. Make comments such as "Those rocks seem to stay on the bottom while the boat stays on top of the water." Ask questions: "What do you think will happen if you put a rock in a boat?"

ADULT GUIDED ACTIVITIES:
1. Place the materials on the science table, and explain to everyone what the activity is for.
2. During center time, let individuals and/or groups of two or three experiment by placing the objects in the water and then in the appropriate container after they float or sink.
3. When the children sort the objects, they can record the objects' names at the top of the next vacant column on the chart and check off which items sank and which floated.
4. After the children have sorted the items several times, have the students compare their lists. Do the items float and/or sink consistently? Why?

FOLLOW-UP: The activity can continue until everyone has had an opportunity to explore it. Add new items. Some children might like to make a boat in the carpentry center.

Sam and Mary are sitting at the computer using the program *Gertrude's Secrets*. This is a game designed to aid in basic classification skills of matching by specific common criteria. Mary hits a key that is the correct response, and both children clap their hands as a tune plays and Gertrude appears on the screen in recognition of their success. A list of resources that help the development of classification is included in the technology box that follows.

MATH TECHNOLOGY FOR
YOUNG CHILDREN

Using the evaluation suggestions in Unit 2, review any of the resources listed next to which you have access:

- *Arthur's Math Games*. Counting and other concepts and skills (San Francisco: Broderbund at Riverdeep).
- *Coco's Math Project 1*. Logical thinking problems (Singapore: Times Information Systems Ptd. Ltd.).
- *Millie's Math House*. Problem solving in a variety of math areas (San Francisco: Riverdeep-Edmark).
- *Thinkin' Things 1*. Logical thinking activities (San Francisco: Riverdeep-Edmark).
- *Baby Einstein Videos* (Glendale, CA: Baby Einstein Company) can provide labels and vocabulary, but baby and adult should view them together.
- *PBS* TeacherSource *for Math (www.pbs .org)*.

	/////	///
	////////	
	////	////
	/////	///
	////////	
		////////

FIGURE 7–4 The students can record the results of their exploration of the floating and sinking properties of various objects.

The teacher provides an adult guided classification experience when she asks, "Which group does this belong with?"

Ideas for Children with Special Needs

Copley, Jones, and Dighe (2007) suggest methods for meeting the needs of ELLs, advanced learners, and children with disabilities. It is suggested that language should be kept simple for ELL students and that rhymes and chants should be repeated. Classification activities provide many opportunities for building English vocabulary. Include culturally relevant materials, and use the children's primary language if possible. Advanced learners may become bored unless they are offered more challenging experiences.

Some prekindergartners may be ready to use number symbols, create charts and graphs, or use more advanced computer programs. Children with disabilities can benefit from accommodations that meet their needs and provide support to their strengths while working with their problem areas. As described in Unit 6, children with disabilities may need more multisensory experiences, may need to have concepts broken down for them into smaller parts, and may benefit from special technology or other accommodations. In Units 27 and 28 these factors will be discussed further.

Evaluation

As the children play, note whether each one sorts and groups as part of his play activities. There should be an increase in such behavior as children grow and have more experiences with sorting and classification activities. Children should use more names of features when they speak during work and play. They should use color, shape, size, material, pattern, texture, function, association words, and class names.

1. Enrique has a handful of colored candies. "First I'll eat the orange ones." He carefully picks out the orange candies and eats them one at a time. "Now, the reds." He goes on in the same way until all the candies are gone.

2. Diana plays with some small wooden animals. "These farm animals go here in the barn. Richard, you build a cage for the wild animals."

3. Mr. Flores tells Bob to pick out, from a box of toys, some plastic ones to use in the water table.

4. Yolanda asks the cook if she can help sort the clean tableware and put it away.

5. George and Sam build with blocks. George tells Sam: "Put the big blocks here, the middle-sized ones here, and the small blocks here."

6. Tito and Ako take turns reaching into a box that contains items that are smooth or rough. When they touch an item, they say whether it is smooth or rough, guess what it is, and then remove and place it on the table in the smooth or the rough pile.

7. Jin-sody is working with some containers that contain substances with pleasant, unpleasant, or neutral odors. On the table are three pictures: a happy face, a sad face, and a neutral face. She puts each of the containers on one of the three faces according to her feelings about each odor.

For more structured evaluation, use the sample assessment tasks and the tasks in Appendix A.

Summary

By sorting objects and pictures into groups based on one or more common criteria, children exercise and build on their logical thinking capabilities. The act of putting things into groups by sorting out things that have one or more common features is called *classification*.

Classifying is a part of children's normal play. They build a sense of logic that will form the basis of their understanding that mathematics makes sense and is not contrived. Children learn that mathematics is natural and flows from their intrinsic curiosity and play. Classifying also adds to their store of ideas and words, and they learn to identify more attributes that can be used as criteria for sorting and grouping.

Naturalistic, informal, and adult guided classification activities can be done following the sequence of materials described in Unit 3. The sequence progresses from objects to objects combined with pictures to cutouts to picture cards. Books are another excellent pictorial mode for learning class names and members. Computer games that reinforce classification skills and concepts are also available. Logical grouping and classification are essential math components. Accommodations need to be made for children with special needs.

KEY TERMS

add	function	shape
association	grouping	size
classifying	logical grouping	sorting
class name	material	subtract
color	number	texture
common features	pattern	

SUGGESTED ACTIVITIES

1. Assemble a collection of objects of various sizes, shapes, colors, classes, textures, and uses. Put them in an open container, for example, a small plastic dishpan. Present the collection to children of different ages from 18 months through age 8. Tell the children that they may play with the objects, and observe and record what each child does with them. Particularly note any classifying and sorting as well as the criteria used.

2. Find some sorting and classifying activities to include in your Activity File.

3. Devise a sorting and classifying game, and ask one or more children to play the game. Explain the game to the class, and describe what happened when you tried it out with a child (or children). Ask the class for any suggestions for modifying the game.

REVIEW

A. Explain what is meant by the terms *logical group* and *classification*. Relate your definitions to the NCTM expectations.

B. Decide which features, as described in this unit, are being used in each of the following incidents:
   1. "Find all the things that are rough."
   2. "Pour the milk into Johnny's glass."
   3. "Put on warm clothes today."
   4. Tina says, "There are leaves on all of the trees. Some are green, some are brown, some are orange, and some are yellow."
   5. "Find all the things that you can use to write and draw."
   6. Carlos makes a train using only the red cube blocks.
   7. Tony is putting the clean silverware away. He carefully places the knives, spoons, and forks in the appropriate sections of the silverware container.
   8. Fong makes a design using square parquetry blocks.
   9. "Please get me six paper napkins."
   10. "I'll use the long blocks, and you use the short blocks."
   11. Mrs. Smith notices that Tom is wearing a striped shirt and checked pants.

REFERENCES

Copley, J. V., Jones, C., & Dighe, J. (2007). *Mathematics: The creative curriculum approach.* Washington, DC: Teaching Strategies.

National Council of Teachers of Mathematics. (2000). *Principles and standards for school mathematics.* Reston, VA: Author.

FURTHER READING AND RESOURCES

Eichinger, J. (2009). Activities linking science with mathematics. Arlington, VA: NSTA Press (Activities 1 & 2).

Epstein, A. S., & Gainsley, S. (2005). *Math in the preschool classroom.* Ypsilanti, MI: High/Scope.

Gallenstein, N. L. (2004). Creative discovery through classification. *Teaching Children Mathematics, 11*(2), 103–108.

Hands-on standards. (2007). Vernon Hills, IL: Learning Resources.

Novakowski, J. (2009). Classifying classification. *Science & Children*, 46(7), 25–29.

Richardson, K. (1999). *Developing number concepts: Planning guide.* Parsippany, NJ: Seymour.

Schwerdtfeger, J. K., & Chan, A. (2007). Counting collections. *Teaching Children Mathematics, 3*(7), 356–361.

Taylor-Cox, J. (2009). Teaching with blocks. *Teaching Children Mathematics*, 15(8), 460–463.

Young, S. L. (1998). *What to wear?* (Harry's Math Books Series). Thousand Oaks, CA: Outside the Box.

Ziemba, E. J., & Hoffman, J. (2006). Sorting and patterning in kindergarten: From activities to assessment. *Teaching Children Mathematics, 12*(5), 236–241.

Comparing

After reading this unit, you should be able to:

- Explain the NCTM expectations for comparison.
- List and define comparison terms.
- Identify the concepts learned from comparing.
- Do informal measurement and quantity comparing activities with children.
- Do adult guided measurement and quantity comparing activities with children.

The NCTM (2000) expectations for comparison include the ability of children to relate physical materials and pictures to mathematical ideas; understand the attributes of length, capacity, weight, area, volume, time, and temperature; and develop the process of measurement. Development of measurement relationships begins with simple comparisons of physical materials and pictures. The expectation is that students will be able to describe qualitative change, such as "Mary is taller than Jenny." Figure 8–1 shows how comparing might be integrated across the content areas.

Comparing is a focal point for measurement in prekindergarten and kindergarten. Prekindergartners identify and compare measurable attributes such as height, weight, and temperature. Kindergartners move into comparing three or more cases by sequencing measurable attributes, as described in Unit 13. Connections are made to data analysis as children compare attributes, such as distribution of hair color in the class, and amounts, such as the number of children with birthdays in each month.

When **comparing**, the child finds a relationship between two things or groups of things on the basis of some specific characteristic or attribute. One type of attribute is an **informal measurement** such as size, length, height, weight, or speed. A second type of attribute involves **quantity comparison**. To compare quantities, the child looks at two groups of objects and decides if they have the same number of items or if one group has more. Comparing is the basis of ordering (see Unit 13) and measurement (see Units 14 and 15).

Examples of measurement comparisons:

- John is taller than Maria.
- This snake is long; that worm is short.
- Father bear is bigger than baby bear.

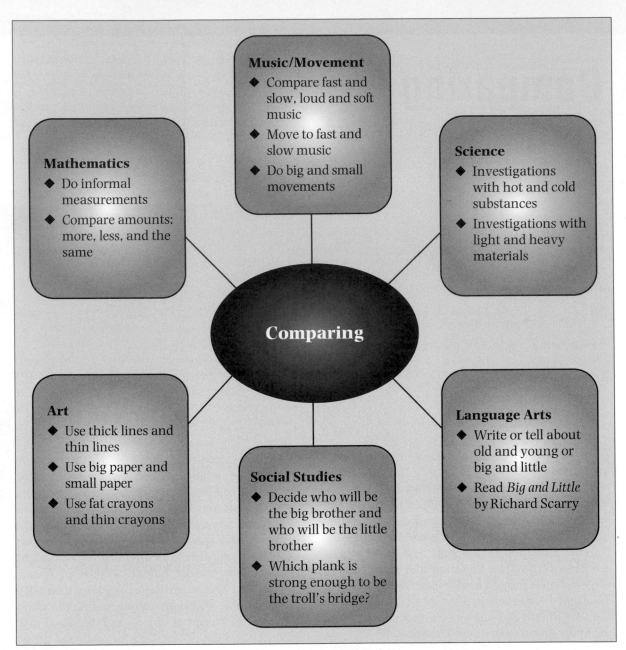

FIGURE 8–1 Integration of comparing across the curriculum.

Examples of number comparisons:

- Does everyone have two gloves?
- I have more cookies than you have.
- We each have two dolls—that's the same.

The Basic Comparisons

To make comparisons and understand them, the child learns the following basic comparisons:

- Informal measurement

large	small
big	little
long	short
tall	short
fat	skinny
heavy	light
fast	slow
cold	hot
thick	thin
wide	narrow
near	far
later	sooner (earlier)
older	younger (newer)
higher	lower
loud	soft (sound)

- Number

more	less/fewer

The child also finds that sometimes there is no difference when he makes a comparison. For instance, the compared items might be the same size or the same age. With regard to quantity, they may discover that there is the same amount (or number) of things in two groups that are compared. The concept of one-to-one correspondence and the skills of counting and classifying assist the child in comparing quantities.

Assessment

During the child's play, the teacher should note whether any of the child's activities show that she is comparing. For example, when a bed is needed for a doll and two shoe boxes are available, does she look the boxes over carefully and try different combinations to find the right size box for each doll? If she has two trucks, one large and one small, does she build a bigger garage for the larger truck? The adult should also note whether children use the words given in the preceding list of basic comparisons.

In individual interview tasks, the teacher should question the child to see if he understands and uses the basic comparison words. Present the child with some objects or pictures of things that differ or are the same regarding some attribute(s) or number and then ask the child to tell if they are the same or different. Two sample tasks are given here; see also Appendix A.

SAMPLE ASSESSMENT TASK

5D   **Preoperational Ages 4–5**
Comparing, Informal Measurement: Unit 8

SKILL: The child will be able to point to big (large) and small objects.

MATERIALS: A big block and a small block (a big truck and a small truck, a big shell and a small shell, etc.).

PROCEDURE: Present two related objects at a time, and say, "**Find (point to) the big block. Find (point to) the small block**." Continue with the rest of the object pairs.

EVALUATION: Note whether the child is able to identify big and small for each pair.

INSTRUCTIONAL RESOURCE: Charlesworth, R. (2011). *Experiences in math for young children* (6th ed.). Belmont, CA: Wadsworth/Cengage Learning.

SAMPLE ASSESSMENT TASK

4D
Comparing, Number: Unit 8   **Preoperational Ages 3–4**

SKILL: The child will compare groups and identify which group has more or less (fewer).

MATERIALS: Two dolls (toy animals or cutout figures) and ten cutout poster board cookies.

PROCEDURE: Place the two dolls (toy animals or cutout figures) in front of the child. Say, "**Watch, I'm going to give each doll some cookies.**" Put two cookies in front of one doll and six in front of the other. Say, "**Show me the doll that has more cookies.**" Now pick up the cookies and put one cookie in front of one doll and three in front of the other. Say, "**Show me the doll that has fewer cookies.**" Repeat with different amounts.

EVALUATION: Note whether the child consistently picks the correct amounts. Some children might understand *more* but not *fewer*. Some might be able to discriminate if there is a large difference between groups, such as two versus six, but not small differences, such as four versus five.

INSTRUCTIONAL RESOURCE: Charlesworth, R. (2011). *Experiences in math for young children* (6th ed.). Belmont, CA: Wadsworth/Cengage Learning.

Before giving the number comparison tasks, the teacher should be sure that the child has begun to match, count, and classify.

Naturalistic Activities

The young child encounters many comparisons in his daily life. At home, mother says, "Get up, it's *late*. Mary was up *early*. Eat *fast*. If you eat slowly, we will have to leave before you are finished. Use a *big* bowl for your cereal; that one is too *small*." At school, the teacher might say: "I'll pick up this *heavy* box; you pick up the *light* one." "Sit on the *small* chair, that one is too *big*." "Remember, the father bear's porridge was too *hot*, and the mother bear's porridge was too *cold*."

As the child uses materials, he notices that things are different. The infant finds that some things can be grabbed and held because they are *small* and *light*, whereas others cannot be held because they are *big* and *heavy*. As he crawls about, he finds that he cannot go behind the couch because the space is too *narrow*. He can go behind the chair because the space between the chair and the wall is *wide*. The young child begins to build with blocks and finds that he has *more small* blocks than *large* ones. He notices that there are people in his environment who are *big* and people who are *small* in relation to him. One of the questions he most often asks is "Am I a big boy?" (or "Am I a big girl?").

Informal Activities

Small children are very concerned about size and number, especially in relation to themselves. They want to be bigger, taller, faster, and older. They want to be sure they have more—not fewer—things than other children have. These needs of young children bring about many situations in which the adult can help in an informal way to aid the child in learning the skills and ideas of comparing.

The toddler learns about "big" through a naturalistic experience.

Informal measurements are made in a concrete way. The things to be compared are looked at, felt, lifted, listened to, and so on, and the attribute is labeled.

- Kato (18 months old) tries to lift a large box of toy cars. Mr. Brown squats down next to him, holding out a smaller box of cars. "Here, Kato, that box is too big for your short arms. Take this small box."
- Kate and Chris (3-year-olds) run up to Mrs. Raymond, "We can run fast. Watch us. We can run faster than you. Watch us." Off they go across the yard while Mrs. Raymond watches and smiles.

- Sam and George (5-year-olds) stand back to back. "Check us, Mr. Flores. Who is taller?" Mr. Flores says, "Stand by the mirror, and check yourselves." The boys stand by the mirror, back to back. "We are the same," they shout. "You are taller than both of us," they tell their teacher.
- After a fresh spring rain, the children are on the playground looking at worms. Various comments are heard: "This worm is longer than that one." "This worm is fatter." Miss Collins comes up. "Show me your worms. It sounds like they are different sizes." "I think this small, skinny one is the baby worm," says Badru.

Comparative numbers are also developed in a concrete way. When comparing sets of things, just a look may be enough if the difference in number is large.

- "Teacher! Juanita has all the spoons and won't give me one!" cries Tanya.

If the difference is small, then the child will have to use his matching skill (one-to-one correspondence). Depending on his level of development, the child may physically match each time or he may count.

- "Teacher! Juanita has more baby dolls than I do." "Let's check," says Mr. Brown. "I already checked," replies Tanya; "She has four, and I have three." Mr. Brown notes that each girl has four dolls. "Better check again," says Mr. Brown. "Here, let's see. Tanya, put each one of your dolls next to one of Juanita's." Tanya matches them up. "I was wrong. We have the same."

A child at a higher level of development could have been asked to count in this situation.

To promote informal learning, the teacher must place materials that the child can use to learn comparisons on his own. The teacher must also be ready to step in and support the child's discovery using comparison words and giving needed help with comparison problems that the child meets in his play and other activities.

Adult Guided Activities

Most children learn the idea of comparison through naturalistic and informal activities. For those who do not, more formal experiences can be planned. There are many commercial materials available individually and in kits that are designed for teaching comparison skills and words. Also, the environment is full of things that can be used. The following are some basic types of activities that can be repeated with different materials.

A preschooler learns how fast his vehicle will move as he experiments with ramps at different angles.

Activities

Comparisons: Informal Measurements

OBJECTIVES: To gain skill in observing differences in size, speed, temperature, age, and loudness; to learn the words associated with these differences.

MATERIALS: Use real objects first. Once the child can do the tasks with real things, introduce pictures and whiteboard drawings.

Comparison	Things to Use
large–small and big–little	buttons, dolls, cups, plates, chairs, books, records, spools, toy animals, trees, boats, cars, houses, jars, boxes, people, pots and pans

long–short	string, ribbon, pencils, ruler, snakes, worms, lines, paper strips
tall–short	people, ladders, brooms, blocks, trees, bookcases, flagpoles, buildings
fat–skinny	people, trees, crayons, animals, pencils, books
heavy–light	containers of the same size but different weight (e.g., shoe boxes or coffee cans filled with items of different weights and taped shut)
fast–slow	toy cars or other vehicles for demonstration, the children themselves and their own movements, cars on the street, music, talking
hot–cold	containers of water, food, ice cubes, boiling water, chocolate milk and hot chocolate, weather
thick–thin	paper, cardboard, books, pieces of wood, slices of food (bologna, cucumber, carrot), cookie dough
wide–narrow	streets, ribbons, paper strips, lines (chalk, crayon, paint), doorways, windows
near–far	children and fixed points in the room, places in the neighborhood, map
later–sooner (earlier)	arrival at school or home, two events
older–younger (newer)	babies, younger and older children, adults of different ages; any items brought in that were not in the environment before
higher–lower	swings, slides, jungle gyms, birds in trees, airplanes flying, windows, stairs, elevators, balconies, shelves
loud–soft	voices singing and talking, claps, piano, drums, records, doors slamming

NATURALISTIC AND INFORMAL ACTIVITIES: Observe children as they use a variety of classroom materials. Take note of their vocabulary—do they use any of the terms listed here? Observe whether they make any informal measurements or comparisons as they interact with materials. Comment on their activities: "You built a *tall* building and a *short* building." "You can pour the *small* cup of water into the *big* bowl." Ask questions such as "Which clay snake is *fat* and which is *skinny*?" "Who is *taller*, you or your sister?"

ADULT GUIDED ACTIVITIES: The basic activity involves the presentation of two items to be compared using opposite terms. The items can be real objects, cutouts, or pictures—whatever is most appropriate. Then ask the comparison question. Some examples follow:

- Place two pieces of paper in front of the children. Each piece is 1 inch wide. One is 6 inches long, and the other is 12 inches long. Say, "**Look carefully at these strips of paper. Tell me what is different about them.**" If there is no response, ask, "**Are they the same length or are they different lengths?**" If no one responds with long(er) or short(er), say, "**Show me which one is longer (shorter).**" From a variety of objects, ask the children to select two and to tell which is longer and which is shorter.
- Place two identical coffee cans on the table. One is filled with sand; the other is empty. They are both taped closed, so the children cannot see inside. Say, "**Pick up each can. Tell me what is different about them.**" If there is no response or an incorrect response, hold each can out in turn to the child. Say, "**Hold this can in one hand and this one in the other**" (point).

"This can is heavy; this can is light. Now, you show me the heavy can and the light can." Children who have a problem with this comparison should do more activities that involve the concept.

An almost endless variety of experience can be offered with many things that give the child practice exploring comparisons.

FOLLOW-UP: On a table, set up two empty containers (so that one is tall, and one is short; one is fat, and one is thin; or one is big, and one is little) and a third container filled with potentially comparable items such as tall and short dolls, large and small balls, fat and thin cats, long and short snakes, big and little pieces of wood, and so on. Have the children sort the objects into the correct empty containers.

Comparisons: Number

OBJECTIVE:

- To enable the child to compare groups that are different in number.
- To enable the child to use the terms *more, less, fewer*, and *same number*.

MATERIALS: Any of the objects and things used for matching, counting, and classifying.

NATURALISTIC AND INFORMAL ACTIVITIES: Notice whether children use any of the comparison vocabulary during their daily activities, "He has *more* red Unifix Cubes than I do." "I have *fewer* jelly beans than Mark." Ask questions: "Does everyone have the *same number* of cookies?" Make comments such as "I think you need *one more* dress for your dolls."

ADULT GUIDED ACTIVITIES: The following basic activities can be done using many different kinds of materials:

1. Set up a flannelboard with many felt shapes or a magnet board with many magnet shapes. Put up two groups of shapes, and ask, "**Are there as many circles as squares? (Red circles as blue circles? Bunnies as chickens?) Which group has more? How many circles are there? How many squares?**" The children can point, tell with words, and/or move the pieces around to show that they understand the idea.
2. Have cups, spoons, napkins, or food for snack or lunch. Say, "**Let's find out if we have enough _____ for everyone.**" Wait for the children to find out. If they have trouble, suggest they match or count.
3. Set up any kind of matching problems in which one group has more things than the other group: cars and garages, firefighters and fire trucks, cups and saucers, fathers and sons, hats and heads, cats and kittens, animals and cages, and so on.

FOLLOW-UP: Place groups of materials the children can use on their own. Go on to cards with pictures of different numbers of things that the children can sort and match. Watch for chances to present informal experiences.

- Are there more boys or girls here today?
- Do you have more thin crayons or more fat crayons?
- Do we have the same number of cupcakes as we have people?

MATH TECHNOLOGY FOR
YOUR CHILDREN

Using the guidelines suggested in Unit 2, evaluate some of the following resources:

- *Coco's Math Project 1* (Singapore: Times Information Systems Ptd. Ltd.).
- *Millie's Math House.* Includes comparing and matching sizes (San Francisco: Riverdeep-Edmark).
- *Learning about Number Meanings and Counting* (Sunburst, 1-800-321-7511).
- *Destination Math* (Riverdeep, http://www. riverdeep.net).
- *PBS Teachers* (www.pbs.org/teachers).

Mr. Flores introduced his class of 4- and 5-year-olds to the concept of comparisons that involve opposites using books, games, and other materials. To support their understanding of the opposed concepts, he has shown the students how to use the computer software *Stickybear*

Opposites Deluxe (English and Spanish, http:// www.stickybear.com). This program is controlled by two keys, making it a natural for two children working together cooperatively. Jorge and Cindy can be observed making the seesaw go up and down, watching the plant grow from *short* to *tall*, and comparing the eight (*many*) bouncing balls with the three (*few*).

Ideas for Children with Special Needs

Comparing groups begins with concrete objects and one-to-one correspondence comparisons. The comparison of pictorial representations is a more advanced step that may require extra time and practice for some children. Begin with card sets that show groups in a variety of configurations (e.g., several groups of three or four). Make up matching lotto games such as those depicted in Unit 19. Have the children compare all kinds of visual configurations such as stripes, shapes,

An adult guided lesson is prepared for children to figure out which corral has more animals.

animals, and so forth. Have them count out loud to experience auditory stimulation. Have them experience tactile stimulation by providing sandpaper shapes or sand glued on card drawings. Use terms such as "the same as," "less than," and "more." Auditory comparisons can also be made with sounds—for instance, one drumbeat compared with three drumbeats.

Evaluation

The teacher should note whether the child can use more comparing skills during her play and routine activities. Without disrupting her activity, the adult asks questions as the child plays and works:

- Do you have more cows or more chickens in your barn?
- (The child has made two clay snakes.) Which snake is longer? Which is fatter?

- (The child is sorting blue chips and red chips into bowls.) Do you have more blue chips or more red chips?
- (The child is talking about her family.) Who is older, you or your brother? Who is taller?

The assessment tasks in Appendix A may be used for formal evaluation interviews.

Summary

Comparing involves finding the relationship between two things or two groups of things. An informal measurement may be made by comparing two things. Comparing two groups of things incorporates the use of one-to-one correspondence, counting, and classifying skills to find out which sets have more, less/fewer, or the same quantities. Naturalistic, informal, and adult guided experiences support the learning of these concepts.

KEY TERMS

comparing   informal measurement   quantity comparison

SUGGESTED ACTIVITIES

1. Prepare the materials needed for the assessment tasks in this unit, and then interview two or more children. Based on their responses, plan comparison activities that fit their level of development. Do the activities with the children. Record their responses, and report the results in class.

2. Find some comparison activities to include in your Activity File or Activity Notebook.
3. On the Web, find an activity like the one suggested in this unit or another activity that provides comparison experiences. Try it out with one or more young children.

REVIEW

A. Explain with examples the two aspects of comparing: informal measurement and number/quantity comparisons. Relate your examples to the NCTM expectations for comparison.
B. Decide which type of comparison (number, speed, weight, length, height, or size) is being made in the following examples:
   1. This block is longer than your block.
   2. My racing car is faster than your racing car.

   3. My doll is bigger than Janie's doll.
   4. Mother gave you one more apple slice than she gave me.
   5. I'll take the heavy box and you take the light box.
   6. My mom is taller than your mom.
C. Give two examples of naturalistic, informal, and adult guided comparison activities.

REFERENCE

National Council of Teachers of Mathematics. (2000). *Principles and standards for school mathematics*. Reston, VA: Author.

FURTHER READING AND RESOURCES

Burk, D., Snider, A., & Symonds, P. (1988). *Box it or bag it mathematics: Kindergarten teachers resource guide*. Salem, OR: Math Learning Center.

Copley, J. V. (Ed.). (2004). *Showcasing mathematics for the young child* (chap. 5, Measurement). Reston, VA: National Council of Teachers of Mathematics.

Copley, J. V., Jones, C., & Dighe, J. (2007). *Mathematics: The creative curriculum approach*. Washington, DC: Teaching Strategies.

Cross, C. T., Woods, T. A., & Scghweingruber, H. (Eds.). *Mathematics learning in early childhood*. Washington, DC: National Academies Press.

Epstein, A., & Gainsley, S. (2005). *Math in the preschool classroom*. Ypsilanti, MI: High/Scope.

Learning Resources. (2007). *Hands-on standards*. Vernon Hills, IL: Author.

National Council of Teachers of Mathematics. (2007). *Curriculum focal points*. Reston, VA: Author.

Porter, J. (1995). Balancing acts: K–2. *Teaching Children Mathematics, 1*(7), 430.

Richardson, K. (1999). *Developing number concepts: Counting, comparing, and pattern*. Parsippany, NJ: Seymour.

Richardson, K. (1999). *Developing number concepts: Planning guide*. Parsippany, NJ: Seymour.

Yusawa, M., Bart, W. M., Yuzawa, M., & Junko, I. (2005). Young children's knowledge and strategies for comparing sizes. *Early Childhood Research Quarterly, 20*(2), 239–253.

Early Geometry: Shape

OBJECTIVES

After reading this unit, you should be able to:

- Explain the NCTM expectations for shape as the foundation of beginning geometry.
- Describe naturalistic, informal, and adult guided shape activities for young children.
- Assess and evaluate a child's knowledge of shape.
- Help children learn shape through haptic, visual, and visual motor experiences.

During the preprimary years, children should be able to reach the first expectation for geometry (NCTM, 2000): recognize, name, build, draw, compare, and sort two- and three-dimensional shapes. This beginning knowledge of geometry can be integrated with other content areas as illustrated in Figure 9–1. Geometry for young children is more than naming shapes; it is understanding the attributes of shape and applying them to problem solving. Geometry also includes spatial sense, which is the focus of Unit 10.

Identifying shapes and describing spatial relationships is a focal point for prekindergarten. This unit examines identification of shapes, and Unit 10 examines spatial relations. The focal point for kindergarten focuses on further shape identification, including three-dimensional shapes and verbalization of shape characteristics.

Each object in the environment has its own shape. Much of the play and activity of the infant during the sensorimotor stage centers on learning about shape. The infant learns the objects through looking and feeling with hands and mouth. Babies learn that some shapes are easier to hold than others, that things of one type of shape will roll and that some things have the same shape as others. Young children see and feel shape differences long before they can describe these differences in words. In the late sensorimotor and early preoperational stages, the child spends a lot of time matching and classifying things. Shape is often used as the basis for these activities.

Children also enjoy experimenting with creating shapes. Three-dimensional shapes grow out of their exploration of malleable substances such as Play-Doh and clay. When they draw and paint, children create many kinds of two-dimensional shapes from

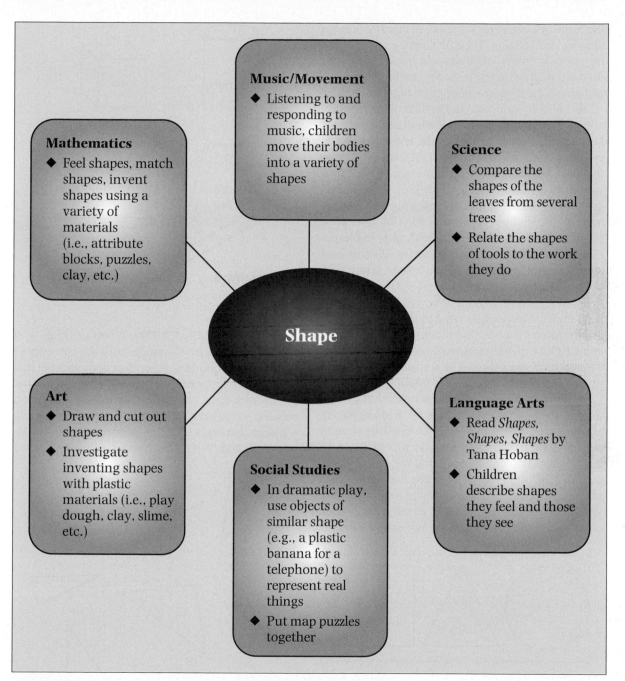

FIGURE 9–1   Integrating shape across the curriculum.

the stage of controlled scribbles to representational drawing and painting. Their first representative drawings usually consist of circles and lines. Young children enjoy drawing blob shapes, cutting them out, and gluing them onto another piece of paper.

As children move into the middle of the preoperational period, they begin to learn that some shapes have specific names such as **circle**, **triangle**, **square**, **cylinder**, and **sphere**. Children first learn to describe the basic characteristics of each shape in their own words, such as "four straight sides" or "curved line" or "it has points." Gradually, the conventional geometry vocabulary is introduced. Children need opportunities to freely explore both two- and three-dimensional shapes. Examples of two-dimensional and three-dimensional (cylinder, sphere, **triangular prism**, and **rectangular prism**) shapes are illustrated in Figures 9–2 and 9–3, respectively. Children need time to freely explore the properties of shapes. Manipulatives such as unit blocks, attribute blocks, and LEGO provide opportunities for exploration. The value of unit blocks is described in more detail in Unit 26. Blocks and LEGOs provide experiences in organizing shapes into structures that can be used as the basis for dramatic play. Kindergartners are observed flying their LEGO airplanes around the classroom. Others are building castles with unit blocks. Two children are making designs with pattern blocks. Three children are examining puzzle pieces looking for places where shapes fit. Preschoolers are just beginning to develop definitions of shapes, which probably are not solidified until

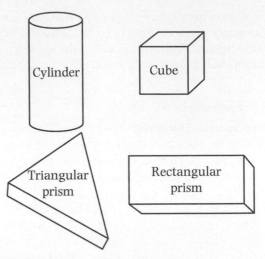

FIGURE 9–3 Examples of three-dimensional geometric figures.

after age 6 (Hannibal, 1999). When working with shapes, use a variety of models of each category of shape so that children generalize and perceive that there is not just one definition. For example, triangles with three equal sides are the most common models, so children frequently do not perceive right triangles, isosceles triangles, and so forth, as real triangles (Figure 9–4). Many preschoolers do not see

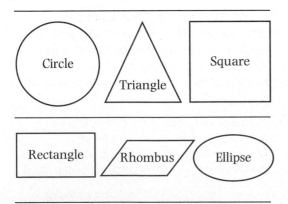

FIGURE 9–2 Geometric shapes.

FIGURE 9–4 Triangles have many varieties.

that squares are a type of rectangle. After experience with many shape examples and discussion of attributes, children begin to see beyond the obvious and can generalize to related shapes.

Assessment

Observational assessment can be done by noticing whether the child uses shape to organize his world. As the child plays with materials, the adult should note whether he groups things together because the shape is the same or similar. For example, a child plays with a set of plastic shape blocks. There are triangles, squares, and circles that are red, blue, green, yellow, or orange. Sometimes he groups them by color, sometimes by shape. A child is playing with pop beads of different colors and shapes.

Sometimes he makes strings of the same shape and sometimes of the same color. The child may use certain shape names in everyday conversation.

The individual interview tasks for shape will center on discrimination, labeling, matching, and sorting. *Discrimination* tasks assess whether the child can see that one form has a different shape from another form. *Labeling* tasks assess whether the child can find a shape when the name is given and whether he can name a shape when a picture is shown to him. At a higher level, he finds shapes in pictures and in his environment. *Matching* would require the child to find a shape like one shown to him. A *sorting* task would be one in which the child must separate a mixed group of shapes into groups having the same shape (see Unit 7). Two sample tasks follow.

SAMPLE ASSESSMENT TASK

4E
Shape, Identification: Unit 9   **Preoperational Ages 3–4**

METHOD: Interview.

SKILL: When provided with shapes of varying types, sizes, and colors, the child will be able to label and describe them using his current knowledge.

MATERIALS: A variety of shapes, both two- and three-dimensional. Select items from small unit blocks, cube block sets, tangrams, and/or attribute blocks; you can also make cardboard cutouts or cover cylindrical containers and small boxes with Contac paper. Have 15–20 different objects.

PROCEDURE: Lay out the materials in front of the child. Ask, "**Tell me about these shapes. Do you have any names for any of these shapes? What makes the shape a (name of shape)? Are any of the shapes the same in any way? Have you seen anything else with this shape?** (Either one the child selected or one you selected.) **At school? Outside? At home? What kind of a picture can you make with these shapes?**"

EVALUATION: Note if the child has labels for any of the shapes, if she makes any connections to familiar items in the environment, if she can make a picture with them that is logical, and, in general, if she appears to have noticed the attributes of shape in the environment. Whether or not she uses conventional labels at this point is not important.

INSTRUCTIONAL RESOURCE: Charlesworth, R. (2011). *Experiences in math for young children* (6th ed.). Belmont, CA: Wadsworth/Cengage Learning.

SAMPLE ASSESSMENT TASK

5E
Preoperational Ages 5–6
Shape, Geometric Shape Recognition: Unit 9

METHOD: Interview.

SKILL: The child can identify shapes in the environment.

MATERIALS: The natural environment.

PROCEDURE: Once a child has had experience with a variety of two- and three-dimensional shapes, use the following question to assess his ability to recognize and generalize. Ask, "**Look around the room. Find as many shapes as you can. Can you find a (square, triangle, rectangle, cylinder, sphere, circle, rectangular prism)?**"

EVALUATION: Note how observant the child is. Does he note the obvious shapes such as windows, doors, and tables? Does he look beyond the obvious? How many shapes and which shapes is the child able to find?

INSTRUCTIONAL RESOURCE: Charlesworth, R. (2011). *Experiences in math for young children* (6th ed.). Belmon, CA: Wadsworth/Cengage Learning.

Children learn about shape as they sort and match pattern blocks in their naturalistic play.

Naturalistic Activities

Naturalistic activities are most important in the learning of shape. The child perceives the idea of shape through sight and touch. The infant needs objects to look at, to grasp, and to touch and taste. The toddler needs different things of many shapes to use as she sorts and matches. She needs many containers (e.g., bowls, boxes, coffee cans) and many objects (e.g., pop beads, table tennis balls, poker chips, empty thread spools). She needs time to fill containers with these objects of different shapes and to dump the objects out and begin again. As she holds each thing, she examines it with her eyes, hands, and mouth.

The older preoperational child enjoys a junk box filled with things such as buttons, checkers, bottle caps, pegs, small boxes, and plastic bottles that she can explore. The teacher can also place a box of *attribute blocks* (wood or plastic blocks in geometric shapes). Geometric shapes and other shapes can also be cut from paper and/or cardboard and placed out for the child to use. Figure 9–5 shows some

FIGURE 9–5   Blob shapes: You can make up your own.

blob shapes that can be put into a box of shapes to sort.

In dramatic play, the child can put to use his ideas about shape. The preoperational child's play is representational. He uses things to represent something else that he does not have at the time. He finds something that is "close to" and thus can represent the real thing. Shape is one of the main characteristics used when the child picks a representational object.

- A stick or a long piece of wood is used for a gun.
- A piece of rope or old garden hose is used to put out a pretend fire.
- The magnet board shapes are pretend candy.
- A square yellow block is a piece of cheese.
- A shoe box is a crib, a bed, or a house—as needed.
- Some rectangular pieces of green paper are dollars, and some round pieces of paper are coins.
- A paper towel roll is a telescope for looking at the moon.
- A blob of Play-Doh is a hamburger or a cookie.

Informal Activities

The teacher can let the child know that he notices her use of shape ideas in activities through comments and attention. He can also supply her with ideas and objects that will fit her needs. He can suggest or give the child a box to be used for a bed or a house, some blocks or other small objects for her pretend food, or green rectangles and gray and brown circles for play money.

Labels can be used during normal activities. The child's knowledge of shape can be used, too.

- "The forks have sharp points; the spoons are round and smooth."
- "Put square place mats on the square tables and rectangular place mats on the rectangular tables."
- "Today we'll have some crackers that are shaped like triangles."
- As a child works on a hard puzzle, the teacher takes her hand and has her feel the empty space with her index finger, "Feel this shape and look at it. Now find the puzzle piece that fits here."
- As the children use clay or Play-Doh, the teacher remarks: "You are making lots of shapes. Kate has made a ball, which is a sphere shape; Jose, a snake, which is a cylinder shape; and Kaho, a pancake, which is a circle shape."
- During cleanup time, the teacher says, "Put the square rectangular prism blocks here and the other rectangular prism blocks over there."

The teacher should respond when the child calls attention to shapes in the environment. The following examples show that children can generalize and that they can use what they know about shape in new situations:

- "Ms. Moore, the door is shaped like a rectangle." Ms. Moore smiles and looks over at George. "Yes, it is. How many rectangles can you find on the door?" "There are big wide rectangles on the sides and thin rectangles on the ends and the top and bottom."

- "The plate and the hamburger look round like circles." "They do, don't they?" agrees Mr. Brown.
- "Where I put the purple paint, it looks like a butterfly." Mr. Flores looks over and nods.
- "The roof is shaped like a witch's hat." Miss Conn smiles.
- Watching a variety show on TV, the child asks: "What are those things that are shaped like bananas?" (Some curtains over the stage are yellow and do look just like big bananas!) Dad comments laughingly, "That is funny. Those curtains look like bananas."

Adult Guided Activities

Adult guided activities are designed to help children see the attributes that are critical to each type of shape. These activities should provide more than learning the names of a limited number of models. Models should vary. For example, not every figure should have a horizontal base. Some examples should be rotated, as in Figure 9–4. Some nonexamples should be provided for comparison. Preoperational children need to learn that orientation, color, and size are irrelevant to the identification of shape. Clements and Sarama (2000, p. 487) suggest that children can be helped to learn what is relevant and what is irrelevant through the following kinds of activities:

Puzzles provide informal shape experiences.

- Identifying shapes in the classroom, school, and community.
- Sorting shapes and describing why they believe a shape belongs to a group.
- Copying and building with shapes using a wide range of materials.

Children need both haptic and visual experiences to learn discrimination and labeling. These experiences can be described as follows.

- *Haptic activities* use the sense of touch to match and identify shapes. These activities involve experiences in which the child cannot see to solve a problem but must use only his sense of touch. The items to be touched are hidden from view. The things may be put in a bag or a box or wrapped in cloth or paper. Sometimes a clue is given. The child can feel one thing and then find another that is the same shape. The child can be shown a shape and then asked to find one that is the same. Finally, the child can be given just a name (or label) as a clue.
- *Visual activities* use the sense of sight. The child may be given a visual or verbal clue and asked to choose, from several things, the one that is the same shape. Real objects or pictures may be used.
- *Visual motor activities* use the sense of sight and motor coordination at the same time. This type of experience includes the use of puzzles, formboards, attribute blocks, flannelboards, magnet boards, Colorforms, and paper cutouts, all of which the child can manipulate by herself. She may sort the things into sets or arrange them into a pattern or picture. Sorting was described in Unit 7; examples of making patterns or pictures are shown in Figure 9–6.

The National Library of Virtual Manipulatives (2010) includes a variety of shape activities. For example, the selection includes activities with attribute blocks, triangles, geoboards, pattern blocks, and tangrams.

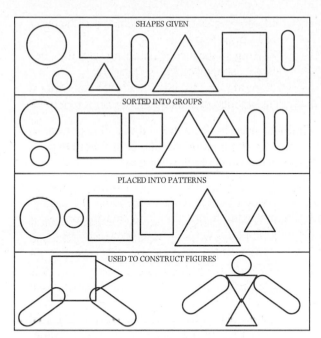

FIGURE 9–6 Shapes can be sorted into groups, placed into a pattern, or made into figures.

MATH TECHNOLOGY
FOR YOUNG CHILDREN

Using one of the guidelines suggested in Unit 2, evaluate one or more of the following computer programs designed to reinforce shape concepts:

- *Millie's Math House.* Includes exploration of shapes (San Francisco: Riverdeep-Edmark).
- *Geometry Bundle* (Tenth Planet). This bundle includes: Spatial Relationships, Combining Shapes, Introduction to Patterns, Creating Patterns from Shapes, Mirror Symmetry, and Shapes within Shapes (Hazelton, PA: K–12 Software).
- *Shape up!* A variety of shape activities (Hazelton, PA: K–12 Software).
- *Baby Einstein Discovering Shapes* (http://www.disneyshopping.go.com), DVD.
- *National Library of Virtual Manipulatives* (http://nlvm.usu.edu).

As the child engages in haptic, visual, and visual motor activities, the teacher can provide him labels (words such as *round, circle, square, triangle, rectangle, shape, corners, points, cone, cylinder, rectangular prism*). The following activities are some examples of basic types of shape experiences for the young child.

Ideas for Children with Special Needs
Addressing Perceptual Motor Challenges

Children who are challenged by perceptual motor tasks can learn to identify shapes by practicing their perceptual motor skills with shape templates. Large shape templates can be used on the chalkboard or whiteboard. Students should start with a circle and then try reproducing the square, the triangle, the rectangle, and the diamond. After

completing the large templates, they can work with desktop templates on paper. Once they have mastered drawing with the templates, they can move on to tracing and then to free drawing.

Bilingual Geometry

Alfinio Flores (1995) provides an approach to geometry for bilingual students in grades K–3. Geometry was taught in Spanish to develop higher-order thinking skills in the children's primary language. Kindergartners did five activities. The students used five templates: one square, one equilateral triangle, and four right triangles. They were given problems that required them to compare the template shapes with shapes on paper in different positions.

Multicultural Geometry

Zaslavsky (1996) presents a focus on comparing the shapes of homes in a variety of cultures. When

Activities

Shape: Feeling Box

OBJECTIVE: To provide children with experiences that will enable them to use their sense of touch to label and discriminate shapes.

MATERIALS: A medium-sized cardboard box with a hole cut in the top that is big enough for the child to put his hand in but small enough that he cannot see inside; some familiar objects, such as a toy car, a small wooden block, a spoon, a small coin purse, a baby shoe, a pencil, and a rock.

NATURALISTIC AND INFORMAL ACTIVITIES: During daily center time, the children should have opportunities to become acquainted with the objects just listed during their play activities. During their play, comment on the objects and supply the appropriate names: "You have used the *rectangular square prism blocks* to build a garage for your car."

ADULT GUIDED ACTIVITIES:
1. Show the children each of the objects. Be sure they know the name of each one. Have them pick up each object and name it.
2. Out of their sight, put the objects in the box.
3. Then do the following:
   Have another set of identical objects. Hold them up one at a time, and say, **"Put your hand in the box. find one like this."**
   Have yet another set of identical objects. Put each one in its own bag, and say, **"Feel what is in here. Find one just like it in the big box."**
   Use just a verbal clue, **"Put your hand in the box. Find the rock (car, block)."**
   Say, **"Put your hand in the box. Tell me the name of what you feel. Bring it out, and we'll see if you guessed it."**

FOLLOW-UP: Once the children understand the idea of the "feeling box," introduce a "mystery box." In this case, place familiar objects in the box, but the children do not know what they are: They must feel them and guess. Children can take turns. Before a child takes the object out, encourage her to describe it (smooth, rough, round, straight, bumpy, it has wheels, and so on). After the child learns about geometric shapes, fill the box with cardboard cutouts, attribute blocks, or three-dimensional models.

Shape: Discrimination of Geometric Shapes

OBJECTIVE: To see that geometric shapes may be the same or different from each other.

MATERIALS: Any or all of the following may be used:

- Magnet board with magnet shapes of various types, sizes, and colors
- Flannelboard with felt shapes of various types, shapes, and colors
- Attribute blocks (blocks of various shapes, sizes, and colors)
- Cards with pictures of various geometric shapes in several sizes (they can be all outlines or solids of the same or different colors)
- Three-dimensional models

NATURALISTIC AND INFORMAL ACTIVITIES: During the daily center time, provide opportunities for the children to explore the materials. Observe whether they use any shape words, sort the shapes, match the shapes, make patterns, or make constructions. Ask them to describe what they have done. Comment using shape words.

ADULT GUIDED ACTIVITIES: The activities are matching, classifying, and labeling.

- *Matching.* Put out several different shapes. Show the child one shape, and say, "**Find all the shapes like this one. Tell me why those belong together.**"
- *Classifying.* Put out several different kinds of shapes, and say, "**Put all the shapes that are the same kind together. Tell me how you know those shapes are all the same kind.**"
- *Labeling.* Put out several kinds of shapes, and say, "**Find all the triangles (squares, circles) or tell me the name of this shape** (point to one at random)."

FOLLOW-UP: Do individual and small group activities. Do the same basic activities with different materials.

Shape: Discrimination and Matching Game

OBJECTIVE: To practice matching and discrimination skills (for the child who has already had experience with the various shapes).

MATERIALS: Cut out some shapes from cardboard. The game can be made harder by increasing the number of shapes used and/or by varying the size of the shapes and the number of colors. Make six bingo-type cards (each one should be different) as well as a spinner card that includes all the shapes used.

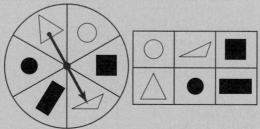

ACTIVITIES:
1. Give each child a bingo card.
2. Have the children take turns spinning the spinner. Anyone whose card has the shape that the spinner points to can cover the shape with a paper square or put a marker on it.

FOLLOW-UP: Once the rules of the game are learned, the children can play it on their own.

Shape: Environmental Geometry

OBJECTIVE: To see that there are geometric shapes all around in the environment.

MATERIALS: The classroom, the school building, the playground, the home, and the neighborhood.

ACTIVITIES:
1. Look for shapes on the floor, the ceiling, doors, windows, materials, clothing, trees, flowers, vehicles, walls, fences, sidewalks, etc.
2. Make a shape table. Cover the top, and divide it into sections. Mark each section with a sample shape. Have the children bring things from home and put them on the place on the table that matches the shape of what they brought.
3. Make "Find the Shape" posters (see Figure 9–7).

asked to draw a floor plan, most children in Western culture start with a rectangle. They can then move on to study the shapes of homes in other cultures. Some Native Americans believed that the circle had great power and thus built their tepees on a circular base. The Kamba people in Africa also built on a circular base. The Yoruba of Nigeria and the Egyptians built rectangular homes. Students can learn how cultural beliefs and lifestyles influence the shapes of houses. Zaslavsky describes how art is a reflection of shape. Art is evident in items such

as decorative pieces, household items, architecture, clothing, and religious artifacts. Art may have symbolic meaning, and art patterns are frequently based on geometric shapes. In Unit 10 we will see how art can reflect spatial concepts.

Evaluation

Through observing during center time and during adult guided experiences, the teacher can see whether the child shows advances in ideas

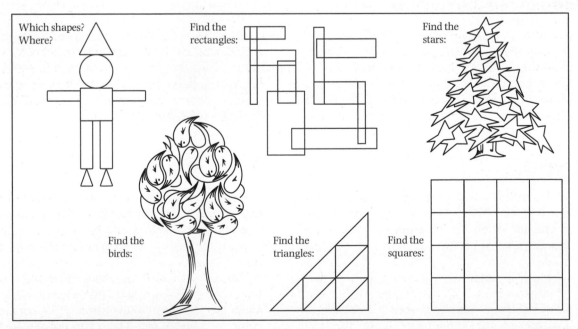

FIGURE 9–7 "Find the shapes."

regarding shape. She observes whether the child uses the word *shape* and other shape words as he goes about his daily activities. When he sorts and groups materials, the teacher notices whether he sometimes uses shape as the basis for organizing. The adult gives the child informal tasks such as "Put the box on the square table," "Fold the napkins so they are rectangle shapes," "Find two boxes that are the same shape," "Look carefully at the shapes of your puzzle pieces," and "Make a design with these different-shaped tiles."

After a period of instruction, the teacher may use interview tasks such as those described in Appendix A.

Summary

Each thing the child meets in the environment has shape. The child explores his world and learns in a naturalistic way about the shape of each object in it. Adults help by giving the child things to view, hold, and feel. Adults also teach the child words that describe shapes and the names of geometric shapes: square, circle, triangle, cylinder, triangular prism, and so on. It is through exploration of shapes and spatial relations (see Unit 10) that the foundation of geometry is laid. Concepts of shape can be applied to developing perceptual motor integration, bilingual lessons, and comparisons of the meaning of shape across cultures.

KEY TERMS

circle	sphere	triangular prism
cylinder	square	
rectangular prism	triangle	

SUGGESTED ACTIVITIES

1. Perform an assessment of a child's concept of shape. Plan and do some activities with the child that will enhance her shape understanding. Report on your evaluation of the results.
2. Make or assemble some materials for a haptic activity. Have the class use the materials and give you feedback. Make any needed changes, and add the activity to your file or notebook.
3. Maria Montessori created some haptic activities. Research her method in the library and by visiting a Montessori school if one is available. Write an evaluation of her materials.

REVIEW

A. A description of 4-year-old Maria's activities on a school day follows next. Identify the shape activities she experiences and decide whether each is naturalistic, informal, or adult guided.

Maria's mother wakes her up at 7:00 a.m. "Time to get up." Maria snuggles her teddy bear, Beady. His soft body feels very comforting. Mom comes in and gets her up and into the bathroom to wash her face and brush her teeth. "What kind of cereal do you want this morning?" Maria responds, "Those round ones, Cheerios." Maria rubs her hands over the slippery surface of the soap before she rubs it on her face.

Maria goes into the kitchen, where she eats her cereal out of a round bowl. Occasionally, she looks out the window through its square panes. After breakfast, Maria gets dressed, and then she and her mother drive to school. Along the way, Maria notices a stop sign, a railroad crossing sign, a school zone sign, buildings with many windows, and other cars and buses.

At the child development center, Maria is greeted by her teacher. She hangs her coat in her cubby and runs over to where several of her friends are building with unit blocks. Maria builds, using combinations of long blocks, short blocks, rectangular blocks, square blocks, and curved blocks. She makes a rectangular enclosure and places some miniature animals in it.

Next, Maria goes to the art center. She cuts out a large and small circle as well as four rectangles. She glues them on a larger sheet of paper. "Look," she says to her teacher, "I made a little person."

The children gather around Miss Collins for a group activity. "Today we will see what kinds of shapes we can make with our bodies." Individually and in small groups, the children form a variety of shapes with their bodies.

For snack, the children have cheese cut into cubes and elliptical crackers. Following snack, Maria goes to a table of puzzles and formboards and selects a geometric shape formboard. After successfully completing the formboard, Maria selects the shape blocks. She sorts and stacks them according to shape. "Look, I made a stack of triangles and a stack of squares."

B. Give an example of shape discrimination, shape labeling, shape matching, and shape sorting.

C. Decide whether each of the following is an example of discrimination, labeling, matching, or sorting:
1. The child is shown an ellipse. "Tell me the name of this kind of shape."
2. The children are told to see how many rectangular prisms they can find in the classroom.
3. The teacher passes around a bag with an unknown object inside. Each child feels the bag and makes a guess about what is inside.
4. The teacher holds up a cylinder block and tells the children to find some things that are the same shape.
5. A child is fitting shapes into a shape matrix board.
6. A small group of children is playing shape lotto.

REFERENCES

Clements, D. H., & Sarama, J. (2000). Young children's ideas about geometric shapes. *Teaching Children Mathematics, 6*(8), 482–488.

Flores, A. (1995). Bilingual lessons in early grades geometry. *Teaching Children Mathematics, 1,* 420–424.

Hannibal, M. A. (1999). Young children's developing understanding of geometric shapes. *Teaching Children Mathematics, 5*(6), 353–357.

National Council of Teachers of Mathematics. (2000). *Principles and standards for school mathematics.* Reston, VA: Author.

National Library of Virtual Manipulatives. (2010). *Geometry (grades pre-K–2).* Retrieved January 31, 2010, from http://nlvm.usu.edu

Zaslavsky, C. (1996). *The multicultural math classroom.* Portsmouth, NH: Heinemann.

FURTHER READING AND RESOURCES

Brown, C. S. (2009). More than just number. *Teaching Children Mathematics, 15*(8), 474–479.

Columba, L., & Waddell, L. (2009/2010). Math by the month: A treasure trove of triangles. *Teaching Children Mathematics, 16*(5), 274 (Grades K-2).

Copley, J. V. (Ed.). (2004). *Showcasing mathematics for the young child* (chap. 3, Geometry). Reston, VA: National Council of Teachers of Mathematics.

Copley, J. V., Jones, C., & Dighe, J. (2007). *Mathematics: The creative curriculum approach.* Washington, DC: Teaching Strategies.

DeBellis, V., Rosenstein, J. G., Hart, E. W., & Kenney, M. J. (2009). *Navigating through discrete mathematics in prekindergarten-grade 5.* Reston, VA: National Council of Teachers of Mathematics.

Del Grande, J. (1993). *Curriculum and evaluation standards for school mathematics: Geometry and spatial sense.* Reston, VA: National Council of Teachers of Mathematics.

Greenes, C. E., & House, P. A. (Eds.). (2001). *Navigating through geometry in prekindergarten–grade 2.* Reston, VA: National Council of Teachers of Mathematics.

Learning Resources. (2007). *Hands-on standards.* Vernon Hills, IL: Author.

Marsh, J., Loesing, J., & Soucie, M. (2004). Math by the month: Gee-whiz geometry. *Teaching Children Mathematics, 11*(4), 208.

National Council of Teachers of Mathematics. (2007). *Curriculum focal points.* Reston, VA: Author.

Taylor-Cox, J. (2009). Teaching with blocks. *Teaching Children Mathematics, 15*(8), 460–463.

Whitin, D. J., & Whitin, P. (2009). Why are things shaped the way they are? *Teaching Children Mathematics, 15*(8), 464–472.

Early Geometry: Spatial Sense

OBJECTIVES

After reading this unit, you should be able to:

- Explain the NCTM expectations regarding spatial sense for prekindergarten through grade 2.
- Define the five spatial sense concepts and tell how each answers specific questions.
- Assess and evaluate a child's spatial concepts.
- Do informal and adult guided spatial activities with young children.

The NCTM (2000) lists several expectations concerning young children's understanding and application of spatial relationships as one of the foundations of early geometry. Young children are expected to (1) describe, name, and interpret relative positions in space and apply ideas about relative position; (2) describe, name, and interpret direction and distance in navigating space and apply ideas about direction and distance; and (3) find and name locations with simple relationships such as "near to" and "in." A sense of spatial relationships along with an understanding of shape (Unit 9) is fundamental to "interpreting, understanding, and appreciating our inherently geometric world" (NCTM, 1989, p. 48). Spatial sense experiences can integrate across content areas (Figure 10–1).

A focal point for prekindergarten and kindergarten is describing spatial relations and space.

Children build structures with blocks and other construction materials and construct collages in two and three dimensions. They learn to verbally label directions and positions in space. They connect geometry, measurement, and number (e.g., "move three steps to the left").

Math, science, and technology are integrated in the area of engineering known as **design technology** (Dunn & Larson, 1990). Young children apply their knowledge of spatial relations to building and construction projects. They are natural engineers who continuously engage in problem-solving activities. Their activities as engineers are primitive but are the basis for what adult engineers do. An engineer can be playful and imaginative, just like a young child. According to Petroski (2003), the professional engineer's fundamental activity is designing. "Design is rooted in imagination and choice—and play" (Petroski, 2003, pp. 4–5).

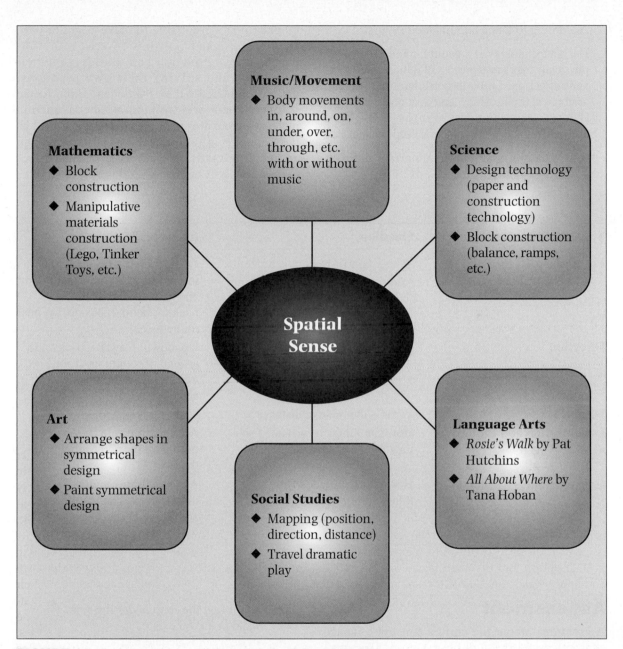

FIGURE 10–1   Integrating spatial sense across the curriculum.

According to Dunn and Larson (1990, p. 5):

Design technology is a natural, intellectually and physically interactive process of design, realization, and reflection. Through consideration of ideas, aesthetics, implications, and available resources, children become imaginative engineers, exploring alternative solutions to contextualized challenges.

Children naturally assemble materials and construct things that fit their needs. They place a blanket over a card table to make a tent or cave and transform an empty box covered with wallpaper scraps into a doll bed. Building on their own ideas and solving their own problems, children can create their own curriculum. At the preoperational level, children need construction materials to explore. At the elementary level as they emerge into concrete operations, design engineering takes on a more formalized structure, which will be discussed later in this text.

Space Concept	Question	Answers
Position	Where (am I, are you, is he)?	On, off; on top of, over, under; in, out; into, out of; top, bottom; above, below; in front of, in back of, behind; beside, by, next to; between
Direction	Which way?	Up, down; forward, backward; around, through; to, from; toward, away from; sideways; across
Distance	What is the relative distance?	Near, far; close to, far from
Organization and Pattern	How can things be arranged so they fit in a space?	Arrange things in the space until they fit or until they please the eye
Construction	How is space made? How do things fit into the space?	Arrange things in the space until they fit; change the size and shape of the space so things will fit

Assessment

A great deal about the child's concept of space can be learned through observation. The adult notes the child's use of space words. Does he respond with an appropriate act when he is told the following?

- Put the book *on* the table.
- Please *take off* your hat.
- You'll find the soap *under* the sink.
- Stand *behind* the gate.
- Sit *between* Kate and Chris.
- Move *away from* the hot stove.
- It's on the table *near* the window.

Does she answer space questions using space words?

- Where is the cat? *On* the bed.
- Where is the cake? *In* the oven.

Young children naturally engage in spatial activities.

rectangular prisms and piles them three high in a row. Next she picks all the red rectangular prisms and piles them in another direction in a row. Next she piles orange rectangular prisms to make a third side to her structure. Finally, she lines up some yellow cylinders to make a fourth side. She places two pigs, a cow, and a horse in the enclosure. Juanita has sorted the blocks by color and shape. She has made a structure with space for her farm animals (a class) and put the animals *in* the enclosure.

With the availability of information on outer space flight in movies and on television, children might demonstrate the concept during their dramatic play activities. For example, they might build a space vehicle with large blocks and fly off to a distant planet or become astronauts on a trip to the moon.

Children begin to integrate position, direction, distance, organization, pattern, and construction through mapping activities. Early mapping activities involve developing more complex spaces such as building houses and laying out roads in the sand

- Which way did John go? He went *up* the ladder.
- Where is your house? *Near* the corner.

The adult should note the child's use of organization and pattern arrangement during his play activities.

- When he does artwork, such as a collage, does he take time to place the materials on the paper in a careful way? Does he seem to have a design in mind?
- Does the child's drawing and painting show balance? Does he seem to get everything into the space that he wants to have it in, or does he run out of space?
- As he plays with objects, does he place them in straight rows, circle shapes, square shapes, and so on?

The teacher should note the child's use of construction materials such as blocks and containers.

- Does the child use small blocks to make structures into which toys (such as cars and animals) can be placed?
- Does she use larger blocks to make buildings into which large toys and children will fit?
- Can she usually find the right size of container to hold things (e.g., a shoe box that makes an appropriately sized bed for her toy bear)?

The teacher should also note the child's use of his own body in space.

- When he needs a cozy place to play, does he choose one that fits his size or does he often get stuck in tight spots?
- Does he manage to move his body without too many bumps and falls?

The individual interview tasks for space will center on relationships and use of space. The following are examples of interview tasks.

SAMPLE ASSESSMENT TASK

3G
Space, Position: Unit 10   **Preoperational Ages 2–3**

METHOD: Interview.

SKILL: Given a spatial relationship word, the child is able to place objects relative to other objects on the basis of that word.

MATERIALS: A small container such as a box, cup, or bowl; an object such as a coin, checker, or chip.

PROCEDURE: **Put the Coin (Checker, Chip) in the Container**. Repeat using other space words: **On, Off of, Out of, In front of, Next to, Under, Over**.

EVALUATION: **Observe** whether the child is able to follow the instructions, and place the object correctly relative to the space word used.

INSTRUCTIONAL RESOURCE: Charlesworth, R. (2011). *Experiences in math for young children* (6th ed.). Belmont, CA: Wadsworth/Cengage Learning.

Block
opmer

SAMPLE ASSESSMENT TASK

4F
Space, Position: Unit 10

METHOD: Interview.

SKILL: Child will be able to use appropriate spatial relation
in space.

MATERIALS: Several small containers and several small objects
glasses and four small toy figures such as a fish, d

PROCEDURE: Ask the child to name each of the objects (so you
differs from yours). Line up the glasses in a row. Pl
one *on*, one *under*, and one *between* the glasses.
fish is." Then, "**Tell me where the dog is. Then, t**
"**Tell me where the mouse is.**" Frequently, childre
it without pointing. Tell me with words."

EVALUATION: Note whether the child responds with position wor
are correct.

INSTRUCTIONAL RESOURCE: Charlesworth, R. (2011). *Experien*
(6th ed.). Belmont, CA: Wadsworth/Cengage Learn

Naturalistic Activities

It is through everyday motor activities that the child
first learns about space. As she moves her body in
space, she learns position, direction, and distance
relationships and also learns about the use of space.
Children in the sensorimotor and preoperational
stages need equipment that lets them place their
own bodies on, off, under, over, in, out, through,
above, below, and so on. They need places to go
up and down, around and through, and sideways
and across. They need things that they can put in,
on, and under other things. They need things that
they can place near and far from other things. They
need containers of many sizes to fill; blocks with
which to build; and paint, collage materials, wood,
clay, cutouts, and such that can be made into patterns and organized in space. Thus, when the child
is matching, classifying, and comparing, she is
learning about space at the same time.

The child
under furnitu
stuck when s
clearance und
to pull hersel
This activity
tor developme
However, ma
or are too hig
bottle case w
it may be tap
colorful Conta
expensive pla
several, and
construction b

Each time
may learn m
stance, Juanit
blocks. The b
shapes. First

---

4. *Where Is Your Friend?*
As in Activity 2, "Find Your Friend," place the children in different places. This time ask *WHERE*
questions. The child must answer in words. For example: ask, "**Where is your friend?**" The child
answers: "Tim is under the table" or "Mary is on top of the playhouse."

FOLLOW-UP: Set up indoor and outdoor obstacle courses for the children to use during playtime.

Space, Relationships, Objects

OBJECTIVE: To be able to relate the position of objects in space to other objects.

MATERIALS: Have several identical containers (cups, glasses, or boxes) and some small objects
such as blocks, pegs, buttons, sticks, and toy animals.

NATURALISTIC AND INFORMAL ACTIVITIES: Observe how children play with objects during center
time. Do they stack their blocks? Do they put dolls in beds? Do they place vehicles in structures?
Comment on their placements: "The red block is *on* two green blocks." "The doll is *in* the bed." Give
instructions: "Sit *next to* Mary." "Put the place mat *under* the dishes." "Put this brush *in* the red paint."
Note whether the children are able to comply.

ADULT GUIDED:
1. *Point To*
   Place objects in various spatial relationships like the one shown in the following diagram. Say:

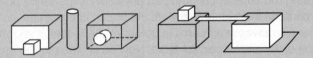

   "**Point to the thing that is in (on, under, between, behind) a box.**"
2. *Put the*
   Set some containers out and place some objects to the side. Tell the child, "**Put the (object
   name) in (on, through, across, under, near) the container.**"
3. *Where Is?*
   Place objects as in activity 1 and/or around the room. Ask, "**Where is (object name)? Tell me
   where the (object name) is.**" Child should reply using a space word.

FOLLOW-UP: Repeat the activity using different objects and containers. Leave the materials out for
the children to use during center time.

Space, Use, Construction—Design Technology/Engineering

OBJECTIVE: To organize materials in space in three dimensions through construction.

MATERIALS: Wood chips, polythene, cardboard, wire, bottle caps, small empty boxes
(e.g., tea, face cream, toothpaste, frozen foods) and other waste materials that can be recycled
for construction projects, glue, tape. cardboard, and/or plywood scraps.

NATURALISTIC AND INFORMAL ACTIVITIES: Provide children with the opportunity to build
structures using construction toys (unit blocks, LEGO, Unifix Cubes, etc.) during center time. Also

provide them with opportunities to make a variety of collages, which provide the children with experience in organizing materials and using glue.

ADULT GUIDED ACTIVITY: Give the child a bottle of glue, a roll of masking tape, and a piece of cardboard or plywood for a base. Let her choose, from the scrap materials, things that can be used to build a structure on the base. Encourage her to take her time, to plan, and to choose carefully which items to use and where to put them.

FOLLOW-UP: Keep plenty of waste materials on hand so that children can make structures when they are in the mood.

Space, Use, Construction—Design Technology/Engineering

OBJECTIVE: To organize materials in three-dimensional space through construction.

MATERIALS: Purchase many kinds of construction materials that help the child to understand space and also improve hand–eye coordination and small muscle skills. Some examples follow:
1. LEGO: jumbo for the younger child, regular for the older child or one with good motor skills.
2. Tinker Toys.
3. Bolt-It.
4. Snap-N-Play blocks.
5. Rig-A-Jig.
6. Octons, Play Squares (and other things with parts that fit together).

NATURALISTIC AND INFORMAL ACTIVITIES: Once the child understands how he can use the toys, leave him alone with the materials and his imagination.

ADULT GUIDED ACTIVITY: Add challenge by having the children think first about what they might like to construct. Older children can draw a sketch of their plan. Next, they can make their project. After they are finished, ask them to reflect on the result. Is it what they had planned? Is it different? In what ways? Do they need to make any changes? When they are satisfied with their construction, they can draw a sketch or (if a camera is available) take a photo to place in their portfolio.

FOLLOW-UP: Encourage the students to engage in further design technology projects.

Space: Mapping

OBJECTIVE: To integrate basic space concepts through simple mapping activities.

MATERIALS: Make a simple treasure map on a large piece of poster board. Draw a floor plan of the classroom, indicating major landmarks (learning centers, doors, windows, etc.) with simple drawings. Draw in some paths going from place to place. Make a brightly colored treasure chest from a shoe box. Make a matching two-dimensional movable treasure chest that can be placed anywhere on the floor plan.

NATURALISTIC AND INFORMAL ACTIVITIES: Children should have opportunities for sand play and unit block play with a variety of vehicles. Note if they construct roads, bridges, tunnels, and so on. Ask, "Where does your road go?" They should have a miniature house with miniature furniture to arrange. Ask, "How do you decide where to place the furniture?" Include maps as a dramatic play prop. Observe whether children find a way to use the maps in their play. How do they use them? Does their activity reflect an understanding of what a map is for?

ADULT GUIDED ACTIVITY: Hide the treasure chest somewhere in the room. Place the small treasure chest on the floor plan. Have the children discuss the best route to get from where they are to the treasure using only the paths on the floor plan. Have them try out their routes to see if they can discover the treasure.

FOLLOW-UP: Let class members hide the treasure and see if they are able to place the treasure chest correctly on the floor plan. Let them use trial and error when hiding the treasure, marking the spot on the plan, and finding the treasure. Make up some other games using the same basic format. Try this activity outdoors. Supply some adult maps for dramatic play and observe how children use them.

MATH TECHNOLOGY
FOR YOUNG CHILDREN

Review one of the following resources using the guidelines suggested in Unit 2:

- *Geometry Bundle* (Tenth Planet). This bundle includes Spatial Relationships, Combining Shapes, Introduction to Patterns, Creating Patterns from Shapes, Mirror Symmetry, and Shapes within Shapes (Hazelton, PA: K–12 Software).
- *My Make Believe Castle*. Each room offers a different challenging activity. The woods are a maze, which provides the child with an opportunity to apply spatial relations skills (Highgate Springs, VT: LCSI).
- *MicroWorlds JR*. Focus is on problem solving, project building, design, and construction (Highgate Springs, VT: LCSI).
- *James Discovers Math*. Includes spatial visualization (Hazelton, PA: K–12 Software).
- *Arthur's Math Games*. Includes geometry (San Francisco: Broderbund at Riverdeep).
- Examine the geometry activities from the National Library of Virtual Manipulatives (http://nlvm.usu.edu).

Ideas for Children with Special Needs

Much of young children's knowledge and understanding of spatial relations comes through their outdoor experiences of running, jumping, and climbing. Children with physical disabilities often miss out on these experiences. There is a movement across the country to construct Boundless Playgrounds (*Boundless Playgrounds*, 2008; *Shane's Inspiration*, 2007). These playgrounds are designed to enable physically challenged children to play alongside their more able-bodied peers. Children with perceptual motor disabilities can work at a chalkboard, whiteboard, or flannel board putting chalk marks or markers above (below, on, etc.) lines or drawings of objects.

Children of all cultures need opportunities for play (de Melendez & Beck, 2007). Music and movement provide opportunities for learning about space and spatial relations. Movement can be inspired by playing instruments from a variety of cultures. Children of all cultures can construct spatial arrangements through their art projects (Zaslavsky, 1996).

Evaluation

Informal evaluation can be done through observation. The teacher should note the following as the children proceed through the day:

- Does the child respond to space words in a way that shows understanding?
- Does she answer space questions and use the correct space words?
- Do her artwork and block building show an increase in organization and use of pattern?
- Does the child handle her body well in space?
- Does her use of geoboards, parquetry blocks, inch cubes, and/or pegboards show an increase in organization and patterning?

After children have completed several space activities, the teacher can assess their progress using the interview tasks described in Appendix A.

Summary

Spatial sense is an important part of geometry. The child needs to understand the spatial relationship between his body and other things. He must also understand the spatial relationship among things around him. Things are related through position, direction, and distance.

Children must also be able to use space in a logical way. They learn to fit things into the space available and to make constructions in space. Playground and art experiences help them build spatial concepts.

KEY TERMS

construction
design technology

direction
distance

organization and pattern
position

SUGGESTED ACTIVITIES

1. Design a piece of equipment (e.g., jungle gym or slide) for large motor skills that offers children a variety of spatial experiences. Explain where and how these experiences might take place.
2. Pretend you have a budget of $500, and select from a catalog the construction toys you would purchase. Provide a rationale for each selection.
3. Add two or more space activities to your file or notebook.

REVIEW

A. Describe how a teacher can assess children's concepts of space by observing their play.
B. The listed items 1–15 are examples of which of the following:
   a. Position
   b. Direction
   c. Distance
   d. Organization
   e. Construction
   f. Mapping
   1. Several children are building with blocks. "Is Carl's building closer to Kate's or to Bob's?"
   2. LEGO construction materials.
   3. "How can we get all these trucks into this garage?"
   4. Mario works with the trucks until he manages to park them all in the garage he has built.
   5. Mary is next to Carlo and behind Jon.
   6. "Are we closer to the cafeteria or to the playground? Let's measure on our school floor plan."
   7. Parquetry blocks.
   8. "Let's play 'London Bridge.' "
   9. "Where am I?" is the central question.
   10. "Which way?" is the focus question.
   11. Geoboards are useful in the development of which spatial concept?
   12. "We don't have enough room for everyone who wants to play house. What can we change?"
   13. "Let's act out *The Three Billy Goats Gruff.*"
   14. The children are building tunnels and roads in the sandbox.
   15. As Angelena swings, she chants: "Up and down, up and down."
C. Explain how the NCTM expectations for spatial sense relate to each of the examples in question B.

REFERENCES

Boundless Playgrounds. Retrieved July 2, 2008, from http://www.boundlessplaygrounds.org (This site has links to 100 boundless playground sites.)

de Melendez, W. R., & Beck, V. (2007). *Teaching young children in multicultural classrooms*. Albany, NY: Thomson Delmar Learning.

Dunn, S., & Larson, R. (1990). *Design technology: Children's engineering*. Bristol, PA: Falmer, Taylor & Francis.

National Council of Teachers of Mathematics. (1989). *Curriculum and evaluation standards for school mathematics*. Reston, VA: Author.

National Council of Teachers of Mathematics. (2000). *Principles and standards for school mathematics*. Reston, VA: Author.

Petroski, H. (2003, January 24). *Early education*. Presentation at the Children's Engineering Convention (Williamsburg, VA). Retrieved November 20, 2004, from http://www.vtea.org

Shane's Inspiration. Retrieved August 1, 2007, from http://www.shanesinspiration.org

Zaslavsky, C. (1996). *The multicultural math classroom*. Portsmouth, NH: Heinemann.

FURTHER READING AND RESOURCES

Andrews, A. G. (2004). Adapting manipulatives to foster the thinking of young children. *Teaching Children Mathematics, 11*(1), 15–17.

Casey, B., & Bobb, B. (2003). The power of block building. *Teaching Children Mathematics, 10*(2), 98–102.

Chalufour, I., Hoisington, C., Moriarty, R., Winokur, J., & Worth, K. (2004). The science and mathematics of building structures. *Science and Children, 41*(4), 30–34.

Children's engineering [Focus issue]. (2002). *Children's Engineering Journal, 1*(1). Retrieved November 20, 2004, from http://www.vtea.org

Children's engineering: Achieving excellence in education [Focus issue]. (2006). *Children's Engineering Journal, 4*(1). Retrieved August 1, 2007, from http://www.vtea.org

Copley, J. V. (Ed.). (2004). *Showcasing mathematics for the young child* (chap. 3, Geometry). Reston, VA: National Council of Teachers of Mathematics.

Geometry and geometric thinking [Focus issue]. (1999). *Teaching Children Mathematics, 5*(6).

Golbeck, S. L. (2005). Research in review: Building foundations for spatial literacy in early childhood. *Young Children, 60*(6), 72–83.

Greenes, C. E., & House, P. A. (Eds.). (2001). *Navigating through geometry in prekindergarten–grade 2*. Reston, VA: National Council of Teachers of Mathematics.

Hewitt, K. (2001). Blocks as a tool for learning: A historical and contemporary perspective. *Young Children, 56*(1), 6–12.

Learning Resources. (2007). *Hands-on standards*. Vernon Hills, IL: Author.

Lindquist, M. M., & Clements, D. H. (2001). Principles and standards. Geometry must be vital. *Teaching Children Mathematics, 7*(7), 409–415.

National Council of Teachers of Mathematics. (2007). *Curriculum focal points*. Reston, VA: Author. Retrieved May 24, 2007, from http://www.nctm.org

Newburger, A., & Vaughn, E. (2006). *Teaching numeracy, language and literacy with blocks*. St. Paul, MN: Redleaf Press.

Pohlman, M. (2010). *Spatial development: A weakness of the American education system begins in early childhood*. Baltimore, MD: Brookes.

Tickle, L. (1990). *Design technology in primary classrooms*. London: Falmer.

Parts and Wholes

OBJECTIVES

After reading this unit, you should be able to:

- Explain and apply the NCTM expectations for part–whole relationships.
- Describe the three types of part–whole relationships.
- Assess and evaluate a child's knowledge of parts and wholes.
- Do informal and adult guided part–whole activities with young children.

Young children have a natural understanding and interest in **parts** and **wholes** that can be used later as a bridge to understanding **fractions**, which are a third-grade focal point (see Unit 23). NCTM (2000) expectations include that young children will develop a sense of whole numbers and represent them in many ways by breaking groups down into smaller parts. They will also understand and represent commonly used fractions such as one-quarter, one-third, and one-half. They should learn that objects and their own bodies are made up of special (unique) parts, that groups of things can be divided into parts, and that whole things can be divided into smaller parts.

Parts of Wholes

- A body has parts (arms, legs, head).
- A car has parts (engine, doors, steering wheel, seats).

- A house has parts (kitchen, bathroom, bedroom, living room).
- A chair has parts (seat, legs, back).

Division of Groups into Parts

- They pass out cookies for snack.
- They deal cards for a game of picture rummy.
- They give each friend one of their toys with which to play.
- They divide their blocks so that each child may build a house.

Division of Whole Things into Parts

- One cookie is broken in half.
- An orange is divided into several segments.
- A carrot or banana is sliced into parts.
- The contents of a bottle of soda pop are put into two or more cups.
- A large piece of paper is cut into smaller pieces.

The young child focuses on the number of things he sees. Two-year-old Pablo breaks up his graham cracker into small pieces. "I have more than you," he says to Mukki, who also has one whole graham cracker. Pablo does not see that although he has more *pieces* of cracker, he does not have more crackers. Ms. Moore shows Chris a whole apple. "How many apples do I have?" "One," says Chris. "Now watch," says Ms. Moore as she cuts the apple into two pieces. "How many apples do I have now?" "Two!" answers Chris. As the child enters concrete operations, he will see that a single apple is always a single apple even though it may be cut into parts.

Gradually the child is able to see that a whole is made up of parts. He also begins to see that parts may be the same (equal) in size and amount or different (unequal) in size and amount. He compares number and size (see Unit 8) and develops the concepts of more, less, and the same. These concepts are prerequisites to the understanding of fractions, which are introduced in the primary grades. An understanding of more, less, and the same underlies learning that objects and groups can be divided into two or more equal parts while still maintaining the same amount. Part–whole concepts can be integrated into other content areas (Figure 11–1).

Assessment

The teacher should observe, as the child works and plays, whether she uses the words *part* and *whole* and whether she uses them correctly. The teacher should note her actions:

SAMPLE ASSESSMENT TASK

3H
Parts and Wholes, Missing Parts: Unit 11   **Preoperational Ages 2–3**

METHOD: Interview.

SKILL: Child is able to tell which part(s) of objects and/or pictures of objects are missing.

MATERIALS: Several objects and/or pictures of objects and/or people with parts missing. Some examples are:

    Objects: A doll with a leg or an arm missing
                 A car with a wheel missing
                 A cup with a handle broken off
                 A chair with a leg gone
                 A face with only one eye
                 A house with no door
    Pictures: Mount pictures of common things on poster board. Parts can be cut off before mounting.

PROCEDURE: Show the child each object or picture. Ask, "**Look carefully. Which part is missing from this?**"

EVALUATION: Observe whether the child is able to tell which parts are missing in both objects and pictures. Does he have the language label for each part? Can he perceive what is missing?

INSTRUCTIONAL RESOURCE: Charlesworth, R. (2011). *Experiences in math for young children* (6th ed.). Belmont, CA: Wadsworth/Cengage Learning.

- Does she try to divide items to be shared equally among her friends?
- Will she think of cutting or breaking something into smaller parts if there is not enough for everyone?

- Does she realize when a part of something is missing (such as the wheel of a toy truck, the arm of a doll, the handle of a cup)?

Interview questions would have the following form.

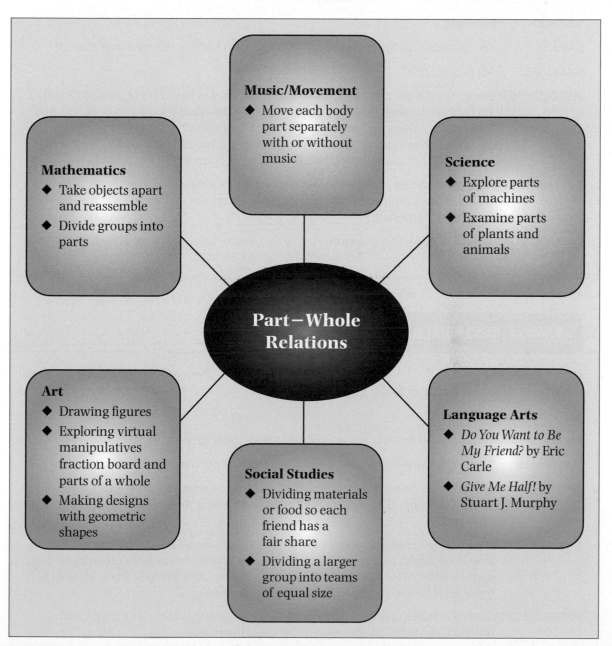

Music/Movement
- Move each body part separately with or without music

Mathematics
- Take objects apart and reassemble
- Divide groups into parts

Science
- Explore parts of machines
- Examine parts of plants and animals

Part–Whole Relations

Art
- Drawing figures
- Exploring virtual manipulatives fraction board and parts of a whole
- Making designs with geometric shapes

Social Studies
- Dividing materials or food so each friend has a fair share
- Dividing a larger group into teams of equal size

Language Arts
- *Do You Want to Be My Friend?* by Eric Carle
- *Give Me Half!* by Stuart J. Murphy

FIGURE 11–1 Integrating part–whole concepts across the curriculum.

SAMPLE ASSESSMENT TASK

5F   **Preoperational Ages 4–5**
Parts and Wholes, Parts of a Whole: Unit 11

METHOD: Interview.

SKILL: The child can recognize that a whole divided into parts is still the same amount.

MATERIALS: Apple and knife.

PROCEDURE: Show the child the apple. Ask, "**How many apples do I have?**" After you are certain the child understands that there is one apple, cut the apple into two equal halves. Ask, "**How many apples do I have now? How do you know?**" If the child says "Two," press the halves together and ask, "**How many apples do I have now?**" Then cut the apple into fourths and eighths, following the same procedure.

EVALUATION: If the child can tell you that there is still one apple when it is cut into parts, she is able to mentally reverse the cutting process, and she may be leaving the preoperational period.

INSTRUCTIONAL RESOURCE: Charlesworth, R. (2011). *Experiences in math for young children* (6th ed.). Belmont, CA: Wadsworth/Cengage Learning.

SAMPLE ASSESSMENT TASK

6D   **Preoperational Ages 5–6**
Parts and Wholes, Parts of Sets: Unit 11

METHOD: Interview.

SKILL: The child can divide a group of objects into smaller groups.

MATERIALS: Three small dolls (or paper cutouts) and a box of pennies or other small objects.

PROCEDURE: Have the three dolls arranged in a row. Say, "**I want to give each doll some pennies. Show me how to do it so each doll will have the same amount.**"

EVALUATION: Note how the child approaches the problem. Does he give each doll one penny at a time in sequence? Does he count out pennies until there are three groups with the same amount? Does he divide the pennies in a random fashion? Does he have a method for finding out if each has the same amount?

INSTRUCTIONAL RESOURCE: Charlesworth, R. (2011). *Experiences in math for young children* (6th ed.). Belmont, CA: Wadsworth/Cengage Learning.

Naturalistic Activities

The newborn infant is not aware that all her body parts are part of her. Her early explorations lead her to find out that her hand is connected via an arm to her shoulder and that those toes she sees at a distance are connected to her legs. As she explores objects, she learns that they also have different parts. As she begins to sort and move objects around, she learns about parts and wholes of groups.

This child is engaged in naturalistic experiences that provide opportunities for activities involving parts and wholes.

The following are some examples of the young child's use of the part–whole idea:

- Two-year-old Pablo has a hotdog on his plate. The hotdog is cut into six pieces. He gives two pieces to his father, gives two to his mother, and keeps two for himself.

- Three-year-old Han is playing with some toy milk bottles. He says to Ms. Brown, "You take two like me."
- Three-year-old Kate is sitting on a stool in the kitchen. She sees three eggs boiling in a pan on the stove. She points as she looks at her mother. "One for you, one for me, and one for Dad."
- Tanya is slicing a carrot. "Look, I have a whole bunch of carrots now."
- Juanita is lying on her cot at the beginning of nap time. She holds up her leg. "Mrs. Raymond, is this part of a woman?"
- Ayi runs up to Mr. Brown. "Look! I have a whole tangerine."

Informal Activities

There are many times during the day when a teacher can help children develop their understanding of parts and wholes. The teacher can use the words *part, whole,* **divide**, and **half**.

- "Today, everyone gets *half* of an apple and *half* of a sandwich."
- "Too bad; *part* of this game is missing."
- "Take this basket of crackers, and *divide* them up so everyone gets the same amount."
- "No, we won't cut the carrots up. Each child gets a *whole* carrot."
- "Give John *half* the blocks so he can build, too."
- "We have only one apple left. Let's *divide* it up."
- "Point to the *part* of the body when I say the name."

Children can be given tasks that require them to learn about parts and wholes. When children are asked to pass something, to cut up vegetables or fruit, or to share materials, they learn about parts and wholes.

one have more? How do you know? If you put all the pennies back in the same container, would you still have the same amount? Let's do it and check the amount." Note whether the children realize that the total amount does not change when the objects in the group are separated. In other words, can they conserve number?

FOLLOW-UP: Increase the number of smaller groups to be made. Use different types of containers and different objects.

Parts and Wholes

OBJECTIVE: To divide whole things into two or more parts.

MATERIALS: Real things or pictures of things that can be divided into parts by cutting, tearing, breaking, or pouring.

NATURALISTIC AND INFORMAL ACTIVITIES: Provide children with plenty of opportunities to explore puzzles, construction toys, easily divisible fruits (such as oranges), etc. Talk about the parts and wholes as in the examples given earlier in this unit.

ADULT GUIDED ACTIVITIES:
1. Have the children cut up fruits and vegetables for snack or lunch. They have a sharp knife so that the job is not frustrating, but be sure they are shown how to cut properly so as not to hurt themselves. Children with poor coordination can tear lettuce, break off orange slices, and cut the easier things such as string beans or bananas.
2. Give the child a piece of paper. Have her cut (or tear) it and then fit the pieces back together. Ask her to count how many parts she made.
3. Give the child a piece of Play-Doh or clay. Have her cut it with a dull knife or tear it into pieces. How many parts did she make?
4. Use a set of plastic measuring cups and a larger container of water. Have the children guess how many of each of the smaller cups full of water will fill the one-cup measure. Let each child try the one-fourth, one-third, and one-half cups, and ask them to count how many of each of these cups will fill the one cup.

FOLLOW-UP: Make or purchase[1] some structured part–whole materials. Examples include the following:
1. Fraction pies: circular shapes available in rubber and magnetic versions.
2. Materials that picture two halves of a whole.
   Halves to Wholes (DLM)
   Match-ups (Childcraft and Playskool)
3. Puzzles that have a sequence of difficulty with the same picture cut into two, three, and more parts.
   Basic Cut Puzzles (DLM)
   Fruit and Animal Puzzles (Teaching Resources)
4. Dowley Doos take-apart transportation toys (Lauri)

---

[1] Addresses are given in Unit 27.

Ideas for Children with Special Needs

Preprimary grade children learn about parts and wholes as an aspect of both their social skills and their mathematics concept development. Children with behavior problems may have difficulty sharing materials but should be provided with many opportunities to do so, for example, passing out materials to a group or giving part of what he is using to another child.

Cultural factors are always important to consider when teaching math. Bonner (2009) provides an example of a culturally responsive math teacher whose African American students were very successful. This teacher's instructional practice was characterized by "warm demanding": "a combination of high expectations, firm and authoritative classroom management, and culturally familiar communication patterns" (p. 3). Major elements in this teacher's instructional approach included applying knowledge of her students' lives, cultures and interests; being caring and demanding, using rituals common to the children's everyday interactions, and constantly reflecting and revising.

MATH TECHNOLOGY
FOR YOUNG CHILDREN

Using guidelines from Unit 2, evaluate one or more of the following resources that are designed to reinforce the concept of parts and wholes:

- *Math Express: Fractions* (preschool–grade 6). A variety of fraction activities (Hazelton, PA: K–12 Software).
- *Richard Scarry's Busytown* (preschool–grade 1). Many construction activities (http://www.childrenssoftwareonline.com).
- *Richard Scarry's Best Activity Center Ever* (ages 3–7). Put Mr. Fumble's billboard back together (http://www.childrenssoftwareonline.com).
- The National Library of Virtual Manipulatives (http://nlvm.usu.edu/) includes activities entitled "fraction bars" and "parts of a whole."

Md-Yunus (2009) points out the importance of culturally appropriate food practice using rice as an example. Rice is frequently used in the sensory table along with beans, pasta, and other foods for math activities. Rice is a basic food in many cultures as are other foods such as dried beans and pasta that are often used in classroom projects. Md-Yunus is concerned that we are teaching children that it is okay to play with and to waste food when they should be taught to respect food.

Evaluation

The adult should observe and note if the child shows increased use of part–whole words and more skills in his daily activities.

- Can he divide groups of things into smaller groups?
- Can he divide wholes into parts?
- Does he realize that objects, people, and animals have parts that are unique to each?
- Can he share things equally with others?

Individual evaluations can be done using the assessment task described earlier in the unit.

Summary

Young children have a natural interest in parts and wholes. This interest and the ideas learned are the foundations of learning about fractions.

The child learns that things, people, and animals have parts. She learns that groups can be divided into parts (groups with smaller numbers of things) and that whole things can be divided into smaller parts or pieces.

Experiences in working with parts and wholes help the young child move from the preoperational level to the concrete view and to understanding that the whole is no more than the sum of all its parts. Such experiences can also teach some essential social skills.

KEY TERMS

divide   half   wholes
fractions   parts

SUGGESTED ACTIVITIES

1. Observe in a Montessori, NAEYC accredited, or university laboratory school classroom. Write a description of all the materials that are designed to teach the concept of part–whole.
2. Assess the part–whole concept as exhibited by one or more young children. Based on the results, plan some part–whole activities. Do the activities with the children, and evaluate the results.
3. Add part–whole activities to your file or notebook.

REVIEW

A. Into which of the following categories do the eight listed items fit? (a) things, people, and animals have parts; (b) sets can be divided into parts; (c) whole things can be divided into smaller parts or pieces.
   1. Chris shares his doughnut.
   2. Pieces of a cat puzzle.
   3. Tina gives Fong some of her crayons.
   4. Larry tears a piece of paper.
   5. Pete takes half of the clay.
   6. Kate puts the yellow blocks in one pile and the orange blocks in another pile.
   7. A teddy bear's leg.
   8. Juanita takes the fork from the place setting of utensils.
B. Describe the types of experiences and activities that support a child's development of the concept of parts and wholes.
C. Explain how a child's knowledge of parts and wholes can be assessed through observation and interview.
D. Decide which of the NCTM expectations for parts and wholes match the examples in question A.

REFERENCES

Bonner, E. P. (2009). Achieving success with African American learners: A framework of culturally responsive mathematics teaching. *Childhood Education, 86*(1), 2–6.

Burton, M. R. (1992). *Tail toes eyes ears nose*. New York: Harper Trophy (children's book that teaches parts of eight animals).

Md-Yunus, S. (2009). Rice, rice, rice in the bin: Addressing culturally appropriate practice in early childhood classrooms. *Childhood Education, 86*(1), 27–31.

National Council of Teachers of Mathematics. (2000). *Principles and standards for school mathematics*. Reston, VA: Author.

FURTHER READING AND RESOURCES

Axworhy, A. (1998). *Guess what I am*. Cambridge, MA: Candlewick Press (children's peephole book; they can guess to whom body parts belong).

Colomb, J., & Kennedy, K. (2005). Your better half. *Teaching Children Mathematics, 12*(4), 180–190.

Copley, J. V. (Ed.). (1999). *Mathematics in the early years*. Washington, DC: National Association for the Education of Young Children.

Copley, J. V. (2000). *The young child and mathematics*. Washington, DC: National Association for the Education of Young Children.

Giles, R. M., Parmer, L., & Byrd, K. (2003). Putting the pieces together: Developing early concepts of fractions. *Dimensions, 31*(1), 3–8.

Kosbob, S., & Moyer, P. S. (2004). Picnicking with fractions. *Teaching Children Mathematics, 10*(7), 375–381.

Lietze, A. R., & Stump, S. (2007). Sharing cookies. *Teaching Children Mathematics, 13*(7), 378–379.

Luciana, B., & Tharlet, E. (2000). *How will we get to the beach?* New York: North-South (children's book that illustrates part–whole of a group).

National Council of Teachers of Mathematics. (2007). *Curriculum focal points*. Reston, VA: Author. Retrieved May 24, 2007, from http://www.nctm.org

Powell, C. A., & Hunting, R. P. (2003). Fractions in the early-years curriculum. *Teaching Children Mathematics, 10*(1), 6–7.

Richardson, K. (1999). *Developing number concepts: Planning guide*. Parsippany, NJ: Seymour.

Riddle, M., & Rodzwell, B. (2000). Fractions: What happens between kindergarten and the army? *Teaching Children Mathematics, 7*(4), 202–206.

Language and Concept Formation

After reading this unit, you should be able to:

- Explain the importance of language to the NCTM process expectations.
- Explain two ways to describe a child's understanding of concept words.
- Describe the philosophy of literacy instruction as it applies to mathematics.
- Use literature, writing, drawing, and speaking to support the development of mathematics language.

The NCTM (2000) standards include expectations in five process areas: **problem solving, reasoning and proof, communication, connections,** and **representation.** In Unit 3 *problem solving* was discussed as the major process focus in mathematics. For the youngest mathematicians, problem solving is the most important means of building mathematical knowledge. Problems usually arise from daily routines, play activities and materials, and stories. As children work with the materials and engage in activities already described, they figure things out using the processes of reasoning, communications, connections, and representation. Logical *reasoning* develops in the early years and is especially important in working with classification and patterns. Reasoning enables students to draw logical conclusions, apply logical classification skills, explain their thinking, justify their problem solutions and

processes, apply patterns and relationships to arrive at solutions, and make sense out of mathematics. *Communication* through oral, written, and pictorial language provides the means for explaining problem-solving and reasoning processes. Children need to provide a description of what they do, why they do it, and what they have accomplished. They need to use the language of mathematics in their explanations. The important *connections* for young mathematicians are the ones between the naturalistic and informal mathematics they learn first and the formal mathematics they learn later in school. Concrete objects can serve as a bridge between informal and formal mathematics. Young children can "*represent* their thoughts about, and understanding of, mathematical ideas through oral and written language, physical gestures, drawings, and invented and conventional symbols" (NCTM, 2000, p. 136).

What the child does—and what the child says—tells the teacher what the child knows about math. The older the child gets, the more important concepts become. The language the child uses and how she uses it provide clues to the teacher regarding the child's conceptual development. However, children may imitate adults' use of words before the concept is highly developed. The child's language system is usually well developed by age 4; by this age, children's sentences are much the same as an adult's and their vocabulary is growing rapidly.

The adult observes what the child does from infancy through age 2 and looks for the child's first understanding and use of words. Between the ages of 2 and 4, the child starts to put more words together into longer sentences. She also learns more words and what they mean.

Questions are used to assess the young child's concept development. Which is the big ball? Which is the circle? The child's understanding of words is checked by having her respond with an appropriate action.

- "Point to the big ball."
- "Find two chips."
- "Show me the picture in which the boy is on the chair."

These tasks do not require the child to say any words. She needs only to point, touch, or pick up something. Once the child demonstrates her understanding of math words by using gestures or other nonverbal answers, she can move on to questions she must answer with one or more words. The adult can ask the child the same questions as before in a way that requires a verbal response.

- (The child is shown two balls, one big and one small.) "Tell me, what is different about these balls?"
- (The child is shown a group of objects.) "Tell me, how many are there in this group?"
- (The child is shown a picture of a boy sitting on a chair.) "Tell me, where is the boy?"

The child learns many concept words as he goes about his daily activities. By the time a child starts kindergarten, he uses many concept words he has learned in a naturalistic way. Examples have been included in

units 5-7 have to be checked. The child uses both comments and questions. Comments might be as follows:

- "Mom, I want two *pieces* of cheese."
- "I have a *bunch* of birdseed."
- "Mr. Brown, this chair is *small*."
- "*Yesterday* we went to the zoo."
- "The string is *long*."
- "This is the *same* as this."
- "The foot fits *in* the shoe."
- "This cracker is a *square* shape."
- "Look, some of the worms are *long* and some are *short*, some are *fat* and some are *thin*."
- "The *first* bean seed I planted is *taller* than the *second* one."
- "Outer space is *far* away."

Questions could be like these examples:

- "How *old* is he?"
- "*When* is Christmas?"
- "*When* will I grow as *big* as you?"
- "*How many* are coming for dinner?"
- "Who has *more*?"
- "What *time* is my TV program?"
- "Is this a school *day*, or is it *Saturday*?"
- "What makes the bubbles when the water gets *hot*?"
- "Why does this roller always go *down* its ramp *faster* than that roller goes *down* its ramp?"
- "Why are the leaves turning *brown* and *red* and *gold* and falling *down on* the ground?"

The answers the child gets to these questions can help increase the number of concept words she knows and can use.

The teacher should use concept words during center time, lunch, and other times when an adult guided concept lesson is not being done. She should also note which words the child uses during free times.

The teacher should encourage the child to use concept words even though he may not use them in an accurate, adult way. Some examples follow:

- "I can count—one, two, three, five, ten."
- "Aunt Helen is coming after my last nap." (indicates future time)

- "I will measure my paper." (holds ruler against the edge of the paper)
- "Last night Grandpa was here." (actually several days ago)
- "I'm six years old." (really 2 years old)
- "I have a million dollars." (has a handful of play money)

Adults should accept the child's use of the words, but they should use the words correctly themselves. Soon the child will develop a higher-level use of words as she is able to grasp higher-level ideas. For a 2- or 3-year-old, any group of more than two or three things may be called a *bunch*. Instead of using *big* and *little*, the child may use family words: "This is the mommy block" and "This is the baby block." Time is one concept that a child takes a long time to grasp (see Unit 15). A young child may use the same word to mean different time periods. The following examples were said by a 3-year-old:

- "*Last night* we went to the beach." (meaning last summer)
- "*Last night* I played with Chris." (meaning yesterday)
- "*Last night* I went to Kenny's house." (meaning three weeks ago)

For this child, *last night* means any time in the past. One by one he will learn that there are words that refer to times past such as last summer, yesterday, and three weeks ago.

Computer activities can also add to the child's vocabulary. The teacher uses concept words when explaining how to use the programs. Children enjoy working at the computer with friends and will use the concept words to communicate with each other as they work cooperatively to solve the problems presented on the screen.

We have already introduced many concept words, and more will appear in the later units. The prekindergarten child continually learns words. The next section presents the concept words that most children can use and understand by the time they complete kindergarten. However, the teacher must be cautious in assessing children's actual understanding of the concept words they use. The use of a concept word does not in itself indicate an understanding of the concept. Children

imitate behavior they hear and see. Real understanding can be determined through an assessment interview.

We'll have a party *tomorrow*.

Concept Words

The words that follow have appeared in Units 5 through 11:

- *One-to-one correspondence*. One, pair, more, each, some, group, bunch, amount.
- *Number and counting*. Zero, one, two, three, four, five, six, seven, eight, nine, ten; how many, count; group; one more than; next; number.
- *Logic and classifying*. Groups; descriptive words for color, shape, size, materials, pattern, texture, function, association, class names, and common features; belong with; goes with; is used with; put with; the same.
- *Comparing*. More, less, big, small, large, little, long, short, fat, skinny, heavy, light, fast, slow, cold, hot, thick, thin, wide, narrow, near, far, later, sooner, earlier, older, younger, newer, higher, lower, loud, soft (sound).
- *Geometry (shape)*. Circle, square, triangle, rectangle, ellipse, rhombus, shape, round, point, square prism (cube), rectangular prism, triangular prism, cylinder, pyramid.
- *Geometry (spatial sense)*. *Where* (on, off, on top of, over, under, in, out, into, out of, top, bottom, above, below, in front of, in back of, behind, beside, by, next to, between); *which way* (up, down, forward, backward, around,

through, to, from, toward, away from, sideways, across); *distance* (near, far, close to, far from); map; floor plan.

- *Parts and wholes.* Part, whole, divide, share, pieces, some, half, one-quarter, one-third.

Words that will be introduced later include the following:

- *Ordering.* First, second, third; big, bigger, biggest; few, fewer, fewest; large, larger, largest; little, littler, littlest; many, more, most; thick, thicker, thickest; thin, thinner, thinnest; last, next, then.

- *Measurement of volume length, weight, and temperature.* Little, big, medium, tiny, large, size, tall, short, long, far, farther, closer, near, high, higher, thin, wide, deep, cup, pint, quart, gallon, ounces, foot, inch, mile, narrow, measure, hot, cold, warm, cool, thermometer, temperature, pounds.

- *Measurement of time and sequence.* Morning, afternoon, evening, night, day, soon, week, tomorrow, yesterday, early, late, a long time ago, once upon a time, minute, second, hour, new, old, already, Easter, Kwanza, Christmas, Passover, Hanukkah, June 10th, Pioneer Days, Cinco de Mayo, birthday, now, year, weekend, clock, calendar, watch, when, time, date, sometimes, then, before, present, soon, while, never, once, sometime, next, always, fast, slow, speed, Monday (and other days of the week), January (and other months of the year), winter, spring, summer, fall.

- *Practical.* Money, cash register, penny, dollar, buy, pay, change, cost, check, free, store, map, recipe, measure, cup, tablespoon, teaspoon, boil, simmer, bake, degrees, time, hours, minutes, freeze, chill, refrigerate, pour, mix, separate, add, combine, ingredients.

- The child can use words before he is presented with them in a formal adult guided activity. The child who speaks can become familiar with words and even say them before he understands the concepts they stand for. As children between ages 5 and 7 shift into concrete operations, they gain a conceptual understanding of more math vocabulary, some of which they have already used and applied in their preoperational way.

- *Primary-level words.* Addition, subtraction, number facts, plus, add, minus, take away, total, sum, equal, difference, amount, altogether, in all, are left, number line, place value, rename, patterns, 1s, 10s, 100s, digit, multiplication, division, equation, times, divide, product, even, odd, fractions, halves, fourths, thirds, wholes, numerator, denominator, hours, minutes, seconds, measure, inches, feet, yards, miles, centimeter, meter, kilometer.

Mathematics and Literacy

Written language learning is also critical during the preschool, kindergarten, and primary years. Children's literature is an important element in the curriculum. Preschoolers need to engage in pre-reading and pre-writing experiences through exploring quality children's literature, story dictation, and story retelling (Morrow & Gambrell, 2004). By first grade, children are expected to be in the beginning stages of becoming readers. The concept of how they should be taught has been a subject of controversy. Wren (2003) summarized the situation as follows: Some educators believe reading should begin with instruction in the rules of printed text (letters, sounds, etc.), whereas others believe reading should develop naturally through experiences with good literature. These two views are referred to as **phonics** versus **whole language**. The **balanced reading** approach, whereby phonics and whole language are used in a balanced fashion, is an attempt to settle the question. However, according to Wren (2003), there is no agreement on what constitutes a balanced reading program. Wren suggests that a truly balanced program should include both phonics and whole language approaches but should be refocused on the needs of children.

The focus needs to shift to the student and the individual learning needs that can be revealed through ongoing, diagnostic assessment. Only when all teachers learn to diagnose student reading skills and respond with focused, deliberate instruction will literacy be available to all children. (p. 8)

Literature experiences can provide a basis for problem solving and concept development.

Literacy instruction has turned away from a strictly whole language philosophy, yet that approach may still be valuable for placing mathematics concepts and skills in meaningful contexts given the emphasis in those disciplines on communication, reasoning, and making connections. Children can listen to good literature that is relevant to mathematics and then experiment with writing. They can explain and discuss, record data, and write about their mathematics explorations. Through these activities, children develop their spoken and written language vocabulary in a meaningful context. Refer to Unit 3 for applications to problem solving.

Literature and Mathematics

A tremendous growth has been seen in the use of children's literature as a springboard to curriculum integration in mathematics instruction. There have long been many books that include mathematics concepts (see Appendix B), but there has recently been an increasing number of major journal articles

that describe literature-centered activities, books that present thematic activities centered on pieces of literature, and books featuring annotated lists of children's books related to mathematics. Examples of such literature have been included in previous units, and more can be found in subsequent units. The Further Reading and Resources section of this unit includes references to articles describing mathematics studies that focus on children's literature.

The book *Whole Language across the Curriculum: Grades 1, 2, 3* (edited by Shirey Raines) focuses on integrated curriculum. It includes a chapter by Charlesworth and Lind (1995) that focuses on mathematics, science, and writing. Included is an example in Claudia Wangsgaard's first-grade classroom in Kaysville, Utah, where the students kept math journals in which they wrote about their solutions to math problems. For example, one day's math activities centered on the book *One Gorilla* by Atsuko Morozumi. The narrative starts with one gorilla who wanders through each page; the book includes scenes in the jungle as well as in other locations. Jungle and nonjungle inhabitants are introduced in groups in numerical order up to ten: two butterflies and one gorilla among the flowers, three budgies and one gorilla in the house, four squirrels and one gorilla in the woods, and so on. The students discussed each illustration, locating the gorilla and counting the other creatures.

The class then divided up into groups of four to work cooperatively on the following problem: *How many creatures were there altogether in this story?* The students used a variety of materials: large sheets of blank paper, tubs of Unifix Cubes, pencils, and crayons. Mrs. Wangsgaard circulated from group to group, providing help as needed. When everyone was finished, the class members reassembled. A reporter from each small group explained the group results, summarizing what was recorded on the group's poster. The groups used several communication procedures, such as drawing the number of Unifix Cubes or making marks to tally the number of creatures. Each group also wrote its procedure. For example:

We did unafick cubes and then we did tally Marcks and there were 56. *Jason, Caitlin, Malorie, and Kady* (p. 171)

This activity provided for cooperative learning and communication of thinking through concrete representations, drawings, and written and oral language. Figure 12–1 illustrates how this activity might be included in a planning web for an extended study of jungle inhabitants using the book *One Gorilla* as the focus.

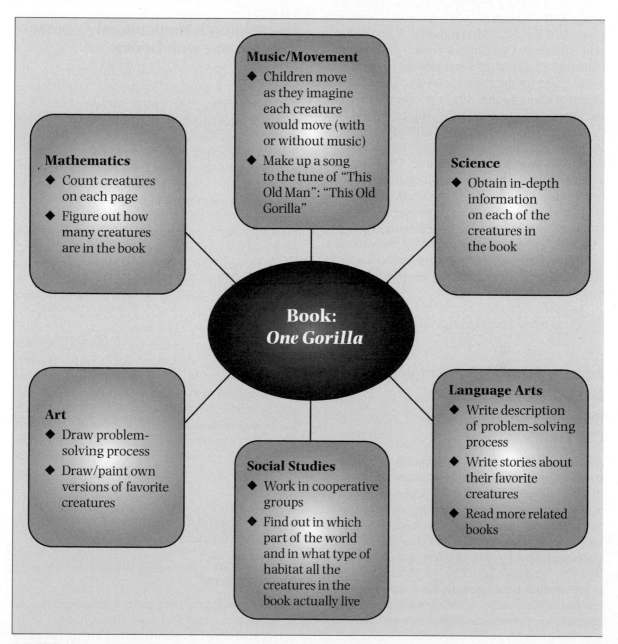

Music/Movement
- Children move as they imagine each creature would move (with or without music)
- Make up a song to the tune of "This Old Man": "This Old Gorilla"

Mathematics
- Count creatures on each page
- Figure out how many creatures are in the book

Science
- Obtain in-depth information on each of the creatures in the book

Book:
One Gorilla

Art
- Draw problem-solving process
- Draw/paint own versions of favorite creatures

Social Studies
- Work in cooperative groups
- Find out in which part of the world and in what type of habitat all the creatures in the book actually live

Language Arts
- Write description of problem-solving process
- Write stories about their favorite creatures
- Read more related books

FIGURE 12–1   An integration across the curriculum with literature as the focus.

Books for Emergent Readers

Zaner-Bloser publishes sets of easy readers that provide beginning readers with the opportunity to apply their math process skills. Each book is related to the NCTM standards. *Harry's Math Books*, authored by Sharon Young, present problems related to real-life experiences in simple repetitive text for the early reader. For example, *The Shape Maker* (Young, 1997) relates making cutout shapes to a kite-making project. *At the Park* (Young, 1998a) moves from identifying circles in the environment to a circle of friends holding hands. *Six Pieces of Cake* (Young, 1998b) relates a whole cake to its parts as pieces are distributed one by one. Other books in the series include concepts such as numeracy and counting skills, skip-counting forward and backward, using fractions, using ordinal numbers, comparing and ordering, sorting and classifying, and performing early operations. The teacher guide suggests extension activities based on each book.

As resources increase on the Web, ideas for literature-related mathematics are increasing.

Ideas for Children with Special Needs

Speech, Language, and Communication

Allen and Cowdery (2005) describe the importance of speech, language, and communication in child development. The purpose of language is communication, and clearly articulated speech makes for the best verbal communication. Other language systems consist of facial expressions, signs, and gestures. For children with hearing disabilities, American Sign Language can be a helpful augmentation for communicating. In an inclusive classroom, the teacher must attend to all children's attempts to communicate. Math can provide many opportunities for communication, as indicated in this unit. Teachers can be alert for children who may need extra help in the areas of speech and language. Allen and Cowdrey point out that, for young ELLs, drill and practice is not as effective as naturally occurring language experience. Books can be an important language mediator.

Maintaining a Multicultural Approach to Language with Books

Whiteford (2009) responds to the question: "Is mathematics a universal language?" Each culture has its own way of teaching mathematics. Children who move to the United States from another country, especially from Asia or Africa, may have learned a different numeral and counting system. Problem solving may not have been emphasized, and procedures may be different. Teachers need to be culturally responsive to their students.

Zaslavsky (1996) points out that literature is a means for participating in lives and cultures, both past and present, of people all over the world. Many picture books are available in translations from English to other languages and vice versa. A simple counting book is *¿Cuantos animales hay?* by Brian Wildsmith (1997). For Spanish speakers, this book supports their first language; for English speakers, there is the joy of learning another language. *Eight Animals on the Town (Ocho Animales)* by Susan M. Elya (2000) presents number names, animal names, and animal foods in English and Spanish. *We All Went on a Safari*, by Laurie Krebs and Julia Cairns (2003), takes the reader on a counting journey through Tanzania. Children of African heritage see the respect given to their culture, and all children learn some Tanzanian vocabulary, customs, and geography. Like the resources listed at the end of this unit, there are many math literacy resources that support a multicultural approach to instruction.

Summary

As children learn, they have a language that is basic to its content and activities. Children learn language through naturalistic, informal, and adult guided activities. Computer activities are excellent for promoting communication among children. Books are a rich source of conceptual language that matches a child's growing understanding. They can also support a multicultural approach to instruction. The whole language philosophy of literacy learning fits well with the emphasis in mathematics on processes of problem solving, representation, communication, reasoning and proof, and making connections. The current focus of reading instruction is a balanced whole language–phonics approach. For young children, books open the door to reading.

KEY TERMS

balanced reading	phonics	representation
communication	problem solving	whole language
connections	reasoning and proof	

SUGGESTED ACTIVITIES

1. Visit a prekindergarten, a kindergarten, and a primary classroom. Observe for at least 30 minutes in each room. Write down every child and adult math word used. Compare the three age groups and teachers for the number and variety of words they use.
2. Observe some young children engaged in concept development computer activities. Record their conversations, and note how many concept words they use.
3. Select one of the concept books mentioned in this unit or from the list in Appendix B. Familiarize yourself with the content. Read the book with one or more young children. Question them to find out how many of the concept words they can use.

REVIEW

A. Explain how language learning relates to mathematics concept learning.
B. Describe how a whole language approach to instruction might increase the concept vocabulary of young children.
C. Describe how the five mathematics process expectations relate to young children's learning.

REFERENCES

Allen, K. E., & Cowdery, G. E. (2005). *The exceptional child: Inclusion in early childhood education* (5th ed.). Albany, NY: Thomson Delmar Learning.

Charlesworth, R., & Lind, K. K. (1995). Whole language and primary grades mathematics and science: Keeping up with national standards. In S. Raines (Ed.), *Whole language across the curriculum: Grades 1, 2, 3* (pp. 146–178). New York: Teachers College Press.

Elya, S. M. (2000). *Eight animals on the town.* New York: Penguin.

Krebs, L., & Cairns, J. (2003). *We all went on a safari: A counting journey through Tanzania.* Cambridge, MA: Barefoot Books.

Morrow, L. M., & Gambrell, L. B. (2004). *Using children's literature in preschool*. Newark, DE: International Reading Association.

National Council of Teachers of Mathematics. (2000). *Principles and standards for school mathematics*. Reston, VA: Author.

Whitefod, T. (2009/2010). Is mathematics a universal language? *Teaching Children Mathematics, 16*(5), 276–283.

Wildsmith, B. (1997). *¿Cuantos animales hay?* New York: Star Bright Books.

Wren, S. (2003). *What does a "balanced approach" to reading instruction mean?* Retrieved November 26, 2004, from http://www.balanced reading.com

Young, S. (1997). *The shape maker*. Columbus, OH: Zaner-Bloser.

Young, S. (1998a). *At the park*. Columbus, OH: Zaner-Bloser.

Young, S. (1998b). *Six pieces of cake*. Columbus, OH: Zaner-Bloser.

Zaslavsky, C. (1996). *The multicultural math classroom*. Portsmouth, NH: Heinemann.

FURTHER READING AND RESOURCES

Bay-Williams, J. M., & Livers, S. (2009). Supporting math vocabulary acquisition. *Teaching Children Mathematics, 16*(4), 238–245.

Dobler, C. P., & Klein, J. M. (2002). Links to literature. First graders, flies, and Frenchman's fascination: Introducing the Cartesian coordinate system. *Teaching Children Mathematics, 8*(9), 540–545.

Ducolon, C. K. (2000). Quality literature as a springboard to problem solving. *Teaching Children Mathematics, 6*(7), 442–446.

Fleege, P. O., & Thompson, D. R. (2000). From habits to legs: Using science-themed counting books to foster connections. *Teaching Children Mathematics, 7*(2), 74–78.

Forbringer, L. L. (2004). The thirteen days of Halloween: Using children's literature to differentiate instruction in the mathematics classroom. *Teaching Children Mathematics, 11*(2), 82–90.

Forrest, K., Schnabel, D., & Williams, M. E. (2005). Math by the book. *Teaching Children Mathematics, 12*(4), 200.

Forrest, K., Schnabel, D., & Williams, M. E. (2006). Mathematics and literature, anyone? *Teaching Children Mathematics, 13*(4), 216.

Gomez-Zwiep, S., & Straits, W. (2006). Analyzing anthropomorphisms. *Science & Children, 44*(3), 26–29.

Hellwig, S. J., Monroe, E. E., & Jacobs, J. S. (2000). Making informed choices: Selecting children's trade books for mathematics instruction. *Teaching Children Mathematics, 7*(3), 138–143.

Henry, K. E. (2004). Links to literature. Math rules in the animal kingdom. *Teaching Children Mathematics, 10*(9), 456–463.

Hesse, P., & Lane, F. (2003). Media literacy starts young: An integrated curriculum approach. *Young Children, 58*(6), 20–26.

Krech, B. (2003). Picture-book math. *Instructor, 112*(7), 42–43.

Kulczewski, P. (2004/2005). Vygotsky and the three bears. *Teaching Children Mathematics, 11*(5), 246–248.

Lowe, J. L., & Matthew, K. I. (2000). Puppets and prose. *Science and Children, 37*(8), 41–45.

Mathematics and literature: Celebrating children's book week, November 15–21, 2004. *Teaching Children Mathematics, 11*(4), 237–240.

McDuffie, A. M. R., & Young, T. A. (2003). Promoting mathematical discourse through children's literature. *Teaching Children Mathematics, 9*(7), 385–389.

Orozco, J., & Kleven, E. (1997). *Diez deditos* [Ten little fingers]. New York: Scholastic Books.

Plummer, D. M., MacShara, J., & Brown, S. K. (2003). The tree of life. *Science and Children, 40*(6), 18–21.

Ponce, G. A., & Garrison, L. (2004/2005). Overcoming the "walls" surrounding word problems. *Teaching Children Mathematics, 11*(5), 256–262.

Robinson, L. (2003). Technology as a scaffold for emergent literacy: Interactive storybooks for toddlers. *Young Children, 58*(6), 42–48.

Rozanski, K. D., Beckmann, C. E., & Thompson, D. R. (2003). Exploring size with *The Grouchy Lady Bug. Teaching Children Mathematics, 10*(2), 84–89.

Rubenstein, R. N., & Thompson, D. R. (2002). Understanding and supporting children's mathematical vocabulary development. *Teaching Children Mathematics, 9*(2), 107–111.

Rudd, L. C., Lambert, M. C., Satterwhite, M., & Amani, Z. (2008). Mathematical language in early childhood settings: What really counts? *Early childhood Education Journal, 36*(1), 75–80.

Sarama, J., & Clements, D. H. (2006). Early math: Connecting math and literacy. *Early Childhood Today, 21*(1), 17.

Sarama, J., & Clements, D. H. (2006). Picture books that build math skills. *Early Childhood Today, 21*(3), 20.

Shih, J. C., & Giorgis, C. (2004). Building the mathematics and literature connection through children's responses. *Teaching Children Mathematics, 10*(6), 328–333.

Thiessen, D. (Ed.). (2004). *Exploring mathematics through literature*. Reston, VA: National Council of Teachers of Mathematics.

Thiessen, D., Matthias, M., & Smith, J. (1998). *The wonderful world of mathematics: A critically annotated list of children's books in mathematics* (2nd ed.). Reston, VA: National Council of Teachers of Mathematics.

Torres-Velasquez, D., & Lobo, G. (2004/2005). Culturally responsive mathematics teaching and English Language Learners. *Teaching Children Mathematics, 11*(5), 249–254.

Welchman-Tischler, R. (1992). *How to use children's literature to teach mathematics*. Reston, VA: National Council of Teachers of Mathematics.

West, S., & Cox, A. (2004). *Literacy play*. Beltsville, MD: Gryphon House.

Whitin, D. J. (2002). The potentials and pitfalls of integrating literature into the mathematics program. *Teaching Children Mathematics, 8*(9), 503–504.

Whitin, D. J., & Whitin, P. (2004). *New visions for linking literature and mathematics*. Urbana, IL: National Council of Teachers of English, and Reston, VA: National Council of Teachers of Mathematics.

Journals such as *Teaching Children Mathematics, Childhood Education, Journal of Early Childhood Education,* and *Young Children* have book review columns in each issue; many of the books reviewed apply to math concepts.

Applying Fundamental Concepts, Attitudes, and Skills

Ordering, Seriation, and Patterning

OBJECTIVES

After reading this unit, you should be able to:

- Define ordering, seriation, and patterning.
- List and describe four basic types of ordering activities.
- Provide for naturalistic ordering, seriation, and patterning experiences.
- Do informal and adult guided ordering, seriation, and patterning activities with young children.
- Assess and evaluate a child's ability to order, seriate, and pattern.
- Relate ordering, seriation, and patterning to the NCTM standard for prekindergarten through grade 2 algebra.

The NCTM (2000, p. 90) standard for prekindergarten through grade 2 algebra includes the expectations that students will order objects by size, number, and other properties; recognize and extend patterns; and analyze how patterns are developed. Young children learn repetitive rhymes and songs and hear stories with predictive language. They develop patterns with objects and eventually with numbers. They recognize change such as in the seasons or in their height as they grow.

NCTM Standard 13 provides that students "recognize, extend, and create a wide variety of patterns" (p. 60). Underlying the concept of patterning are the concepts of comparing, ordering, and seriation. A focal point connection for algebra at the prekindergarten level is that children recognize and duplicate simple pattern sequences of the A–B model. At the

kindergarten level, children identify, duplicate, and extend patterns made with objects or shapes.

Ordering is a higher level of comparing (Unit 8) that is another step toward measurement (Cross, Woods, & Schweingruber, 2009). Ordering involves comparing more than two things or more than two groups. It also involves placing things in a sequence from first to last. In Piaget's terms, ordering is called **seriation**. **Patterning** is related to ordering in that children need a basic understanding of ordering before they can do patterning. It involves making or discovering auditory, visual, and motor regularities. Patterning includes (1) simple patterns such as placing Unifix Cubes in a sequence by color and/or number, (2) number patterns such as days of the week and patterns on the 100s chart, (3) patterns in nature such as spiderwebs and designs on shells, (4) quilt patterns, and (5) graphs. Movement can also be used to develop pattern and sequence through clapping, marching, standing, sitting, jumping, and the like.

Children start to develop ordering and seriation in the sensorimotor stage. Before the age of 2, the child likes to work with nesting toys. *Nesting toys* are items of the same shape but of varying sizes so that each one fits into the larger ones. If they are put into each other in order by size, they will all fit in one stack. Ordering and seriation involve seeing a pattern that follows continuously in equal increments. Other types of patterns involve repeated sequences that follow a preset rule. Daily routine is an example of a pattern that is learned early; that is, infants become cued into night and day and to the daily sequence of diaper changing, eating, playing, and sleeping. As they experiment with rattles,

they might use a regular pattern of movement that involves motor, auditory, and visual sequences repeated over and over. As the sensorimotor period progresses, toddlers line up blocks: placing a large one, then a small one, large, small or perhaps red, green, yellow, red, green, yellow.

An early way of ordering is to place a pattern in one-to-one correspondence with a model, as shown in Figure 13–1. This gives the child the idea of ordering. Next, he learns to place things in ordered rows on the basis of their length, width, height, and size. At first the child can think of only two things at one time. When ordering by length, he places sticks in a sequence as shown in Figure 13–1(C). As he develops and practices, he will be able to use the whole sequence at once and place the sticks as shown in Figure 13–1(D).

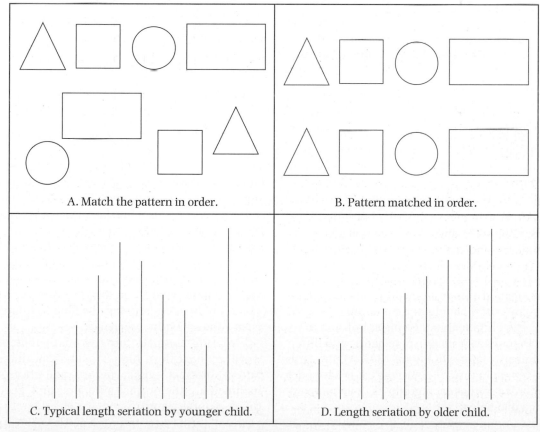

A. Match the pattern in order.   B. Pattern matched in order.

C. Typical length seriation by younger child.   D. Length seriation by older child.

FIGURE 13–1   Ordering by pattern and seriating by size.

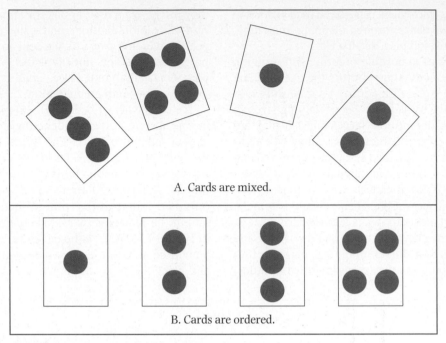

A. Cards are mixed.

B. Cards are ordered.

FIGURE 13–2 Ordering groups.

As the child develops further, he can order things by other characteristics, such as color shades (dark to light), texture (rough to smooth), and sound (loud to soft).

Once the child can place one set of things in order, he can go on to double seriation. For double seriation he must put two groups of things in order. This is a use of matching or one-to-one correspondence (Unit 5).

Groups of things can also be put in order by the number of things in each group. By ordering groups, each having one more thing than the others, the child learns the concept of **one more than**. Figure 13–2 shows some cards with different numbers of dots. In Figure 13–2(A), the cards are mixed; in Figure 13–2(B), the cards have been put in order so that each group has one more dot than the one before.

More complex patterns involve the repetition of a sequence. For example, the teacher might present children with a pile of shapes such as those depicted in Figure 13–1, show the pattern, and then ask them to select the correct shapes to repeat the pattern in a line (rather than matching underneath, one to one). The teacher can develop patterns with Unifix Cubes, cube blocks, beads, alphabet letters, numerals, sticks, coins, and many other items. He can develop auditory patterns with sounds such as hand clapping and drumbeats or motor activities such as the command to jump, jump, and then sit. To solve a pattern problem, children must be able to figure out what comes next in a sequence.

Ordering and patterning words include such words as next, last, biggest, smallest, thinnest, fattest, shortest, tallest, before, and after. Also included are the ordinal numbers: first, second, third, fourth, and so on, to the last thing. Ordinal terms are matched with counting in Figure 13–3. Ordering, seriation, and patterning

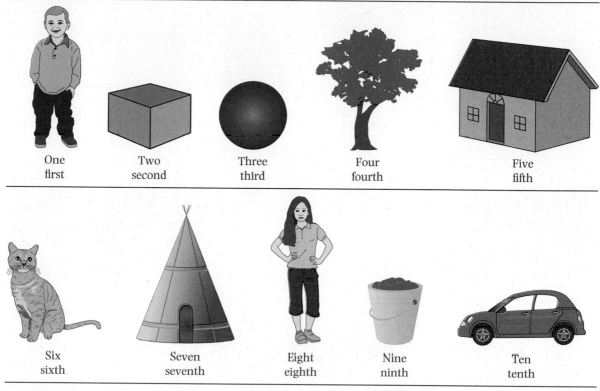

One
first

Two
second

Three
third

Four
fourth

Five
fifth

Six
sixth

Seven
seventh

Eight
eighth

Nine
ninth

Ten
tenth

FIGURE 13–3 Counting numbers and ordinal numbers.

can be integrated into the content areas (see Figure 13–4).

Assessment

While the child plays, the teacher should note activities that might show that the child is learning to order things. Notice how she uses nesting toys. Does she place them in each other so she has only one stack? Does she line them up in rows from largest to smallest? Does she use words such as *first* ("I'm first") and *last* ("He's last") on her own? In her dramatic play, does she go on train or plane rides where chairs are lined up for seats and each child has a place (first, second, last)? Seriation may be reflected in children's drawings. For example, in Figure 13–5, a child has drawn a picture of his family members in order of their height. The

teacher can seriate paint chips from light to dark, for example, from light pink to dark burgundy. He can put sequence stories (such as a child blowing up a balloon) on cards for the child to put in order.

Also during play, the teacher should watch for evidence of patterning behavior. Patterns might appear in artwork such as paintings or collages; in motor activity such as movement and dance; in musical activity such as chants and rhymes; in language activities such as acting out patterned stories (e.g., *The Three Billy Goats Gruff* or *Goldilocks and the Three Bears*); or with manipulative materials such as Unifix Cubes, Teddy Bear Counters, LEGO®, building blocks, attribute blocks, beads for stringing, geoboards, and so on.

Ask the child to order different numbers and kinds of items during individual interview tasks, as in the examples that follow and in Appendix A. Here are examples of three assessment tasks.

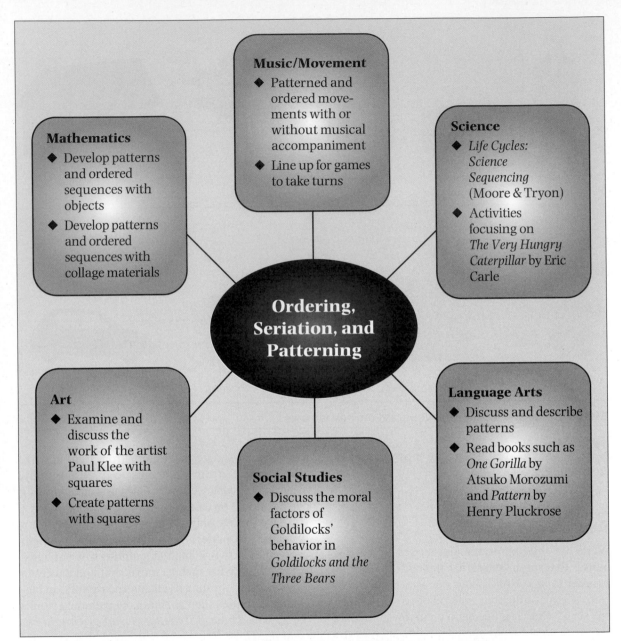

Music/Movement
- Patterned and ordered movements with or without musical accompaniment
- Line up for games to take turns

Mathematics
- Develop patterns and ordered sequences with objects
- Develop patterns and ordered sequences with collage materials

Science
- *Life Cycles: Science Sequencing* (Moore & Tryon)
- Activities focusing on *The Very Hungry Caterpillar* by Eric Carle

Ordering, Seriation, and Patterning

Art
- Examine and discuss the work of the artist Paul Klee with squares
- Create patterns with squares

Social Studies
- Discuss the moral factors of Goldilocks' behavior in *Goldilocks and the Three Bears*

Language Arts
- Discuss and describe patterns
- Read books such as *One Gorilla* by Atsuko Morozumi and *Pattern* by Henry Pluckrose

FIGURE 13–4 Integrating ordering, seriation, and patterning across the curriculum.

FIGURE 13–5 A young child draws his family in order by size.

SAMPLE ASSESSMENT TASK

5G   **Preoperational Ages 4–5**
Ordering, Sequential/Ordinal Number: Unit 13

METHOD: Interview.

SKILL: Child can order up to five objects relative to physical dimensions and identify the ordinal position of each.

MATERIALS: Five objects or cutouts that vary in equal increments of height, width, length, or overall size dimensions.

PROCEDURE: Start with five objects or cutouts. If this proves to be difficult, remove the objects or cutouts; then put out three and ask the same questions. **"Find the (tallest, biggest, fattest or shortest, smallest, thinnest); put them all in a row from tallest to shortest (biggest to smallest, fattest to thinnest)."** If the child accomplishes the task, ask, "Which is first?" "Which is last?" "Which is second?" "Which is third?" "Which is fourth?"

EVALUATION: Note whether the children find the extremes, but mix up the three objects or cutouts that belong in the middle. This is a common approach for preoperational children. Note whether the children approach the problem in an organized way or in a disorganized, unplanned way.

INSTRUCTIONAL RESOURCE: Charlesworth, R. (2011). *Experiences in math for young children* (6th ed.). Belmont, CA: Wadsworth/Cengage Learning.

SAMPLE ASSESSMENT TASK

6H   **Transitional Ages 5–7**
Ordering, Double Seriation: Unit 13

METHOD: Interview.

SKILL: Child will place two sets of ten items in double seriation.

MATERIALS: Two sets of ten objects, cutouts, or pictures of objects that vary in one or more dimensions in equal increments such that one item in each set is the correct size to go with an item in the other set. The sets could be children and baseball bats, children and pets, chairs and tables, bowls and spoons, cars and garages, hats and heads, etc.

PROCEDURE: Suppose you have decided to use hats and heads. First, place the heads in front of the child in random order. Instruct the child to line the heads up in order from smallest to largest. Help them if needed; for example, ask: **"Find the smallest. Good, now which one comes next? and next?"** If the child is able to line up the heads correctly, then place the hats in a random arrangement. Tell the child, **"Find the hat that fits each head, and put it on the head."**

EVALUATION: Note how the children approach the problem—in an organized way or haphazard fashion. Note whether their solution is entirely or only partially correct. If they get a close approximation, repeat the procedure again with seven or five items or to see if they grasp the concept when fewer items are used. A child going into concrete operations should be able to accomplish the task with two groups of ten. Transitional children may be able to perform the task correctly with fewer items in each group.

INSTRUCTIONAL RESOURCE: Charlesworth, R. (2011). *Experiences in math for young children* (6th ed.). Belmont, CA: Wadsworth/Cengage Learning.

SAMPLE ASSESSMENT TASK

6I   **Transitional Period Ages 5–7**
Ordering, Patterning: Unit 13

METHOD: Interview.

SKILL: Child can copy, extend, and describe patterns made with concrete objects.

MATERIALS: Color cubes, Unifix Cubes, Teddy Bear Counters, attribute blocks, small toys, or other objects that can be placed in a sequence to develop a pattern.

PROCEDURE: 1. *Copy patterns*. One at a time, make patterns of various levels of complexity (each letter stands for one type of item such as one color of a color cube, one shape of an attribute block, or one type of toy). For example, A–B–A–B could be red block–green block–red block–green block or big triangle–small triangle–big triangle–small triangle. Show the following series of patterns and tell the child, **"Make a pattern just like this one."** (If the child hesitates, point to the first item and say, **"Start with one like this."**)

    a. A–B–A–B

    b. A–A–B–A–A–B

    c. A–B–C–A–B–C

    d. A–A–B–B–C–C–A–A–B–B–C–C

    2. *Extend patterns*. Make patterns as in item 1, but this time say: **"This pattern isn't finished. Make it longer. Show me what comes next."**

    3. *Describe patterns*. Make patterns as in items 1 and 2. Say, **"Tell me about these patterns. (What comes first? next? next?) If you wanted to continue the pattern, what would come next? next?"**

    4. If the child easily accomplishes the foregoing tasks, try some more difficult patterns such as the following:

    a. A–B–A–C–A–D–A–B–A–C–A–D

    b. A–B–B–C–D–A–B–B–C–D

    c. A–A–B–A–A–C–A–A–D

EVALUATION: Note which types of patterns are easiest for the children. Are they more successful with the easier patterns? With copying? With extending? With describing?

INSTRUCTIONAL RESOURCE: Charlesworth, R. (2011). *Experiences in math for young children* (6th ed.). Belmont, CA: Wadsworth/Cengage Learning.

Naturalistic Activities

Just as children's natural development guides them to sort things, so too it guides them to put things in order and arrange things in patterns. As children sort, they often put the items in rows or arrange them in patterns. For example, Kate picks out blocks that are all of one size, shape, and color and lines them up in a row. She then adds to the row by lining up another group of blocks of the same size, shape, and color. She picks out blue blocks and yellow blocks and lines them up, alternating colors. Pete is observed examining his mother's measuring cups and spoons. He lines them up from largest to smallest. Then he makes a pattern: cup–spoon–cup–spoon–cup–spoon–cup–spoon.

Children construct concepts of ordering, seriation, and patterning as they explore materials during play.

Nesting cups provide for exploration of ordering by size.

As the child's speech ability increases, he uses order words. "I want to be *first*." "This is the *last* one." "Daddy Bear has the *biggest* bowl." "I'll sit in the *middle*." As he starts to draw pictures, he often draws mothers, fathers, and children and places them in a row from smallest to largest.

Informal Activities

Informal teaching can go on quite often during the child's daily play and routine activities. Some examples follow:

- Eighteen-month-old Brad has a set of mixing bowls and measuring cups to play with on the kitchen floor. He puts the biggest bowl on his head. His mother smiles and says, "The *biggest* bowl fits on your head." He tries the smaller bowls, but they do not fit. Mom says, "The *middle-sized* bowl and the *smallest* bowl don't fit, do they?" She sits down with him and picks up a measuring cup. "Look, here is the cup that is the *biggest*. These are *smaller*." She lines them up by size. "Can you find the *smallest* cup?" Brad proceeds to put the cups one in the other until they are in a single stack. His mother smiles, "You have them all in *order*."
- Five-year-old Enrique, four-year-old Chin, and three-year-old Jim come running across the yard to Mr. Brown. "You are all

fast runners." "I was *first*," shouts Enrique. "I was *second*," says Chin. "I was *third*," says Jim. Enrique shouts, "You were *last*, Jim, 'cause you are the *littlest*." Jim looks mad. Mr. Brown says, "Jim was both *third* and *last*. It is true Jim is the *littlest* and the *youngest*. Enrique is the *oldest*. Is he the *biggest*?" "No!" says Jim, "He's *middle size*."

- Mary is sharing some small candies some of her friends and her teacher. "Mr. Brown, you and I get five because we are the *biggest*. Diana gets four because she's the *next* size. Pete gets three. Leroy gets two, and Brad gets one. Michael doesn't get any 'cause he is a baby." "I see," says Mr. Brown, "you are dividing them so the *smallest* people get the least and the *biggest* get the most."

- Mrs. Red Fox tells her first graders that she would like them to line up boy–boy–girl–girl.

- Second grader Liu Pei decides to draw a picture each day of her bean sprout that is the same height as it is that day. Soon she has a long row of bean sprout pictures, each a little taller than the one before. Mr. Wang comments on how nice it is to have a record of the bean sprout's growth from the day it sprouted.

- Miss Collins tells the children, "You have to take turns on the swing. Tanya is *first* today."

These examples show how the adult can make comments that help the child see her own use of order words and activities. Many times in the course of the day, opportunities come up where children must take turns. These times can be used to the fullest for teaching order and ordinal number. The teacher can place many kinds of materials for children that help them practice ordering. Some of these materials are self-correcting, such as the Montessori cylinders (see Figure 27–2): Each cylinder fits in only one place.

Children's literature provides structured pattern and sequence experiences.

Adult Guided Activities

Adult guided experiences with ordering and patterning can be done with many kinds of materials. The teacher can purchase or make these materials. Things of different sizes are easy to find at home or school. Measuring cups and spoons, mixing bowls, pots and pans, shoes, gloves, and other items of clothing are easily available in several different sizes. Paper and cardboard can be cut into different sizes and shapes. Paper towel rolls can be made into cylinders of graduated sizes. The artistic teacher can draw pictures of the same item in graduated sizes. Already drawn materials such as Richardson's (1999) Unifix Cube train patterns, counting boards, or working space papers can be used for patterning. The following are basic activities that can be done with many different kinds of objects, cutouts, and pictures.

Jorge, a kindergartner, enjoys exploring patterns with Virtual Manipulatives online (http://nlvm.usu.edu): *color pattern* challenges Jorge to arrange colors to complete a pattern and *pattern blocks* provides him opportunities to build patterns with virtual pattern blocks.

MATH TECHNOLOGY FOR YOUNG CHILDREN

Using one of the evaluation systems suggested in Unit 2, evaluate one or more of the following resources in terms of each item's value for learning about ordering and/or patterning.

- *Math Blaster* (ages 4–6; Hazelton, PA: K–12 Software). Includes pattern completion activities.
- *Introduction to Patterns* (http://store.sunburst.com). Includes exploration of linear and geometric patterns and creation of patterns.
- *MicroWorlds JR* (Highgate Springs, VT: LCSI). Includes pattern exploration.
- *Millie's Math House* (San Francisco: Riverdeep-Edmark). Compare and match sizes and see and hear patterns.
- National Library of Virtual Manipulatives (http://nlvm.usu.edu). Color patterns, pattern blocks.

Activities

Ordering and Patterning: The Basic Concept

OBJECTIVE: To help the child understand the idea of order and sequence.

MATERIALS: Large colored beads with a string for the teacher and each child.

NATURALISTIC AND INFORMAL ACTIVITIES: Have the container of beads available during center time. As the children explore the beads, note if they develop patterns based on color. Comment such as, "First you lined up the blue beads and then the red beads"; "You lined up two yellow, two red, and two blue beads."

ADULT GUIDED ACTIVITIES: The beads are put in a box or bowl, which each child can reach. Say, **"Watch me. I'm going to make a string of beads."** Start with three beads. Add more as each child learns to do each amount. Lay the string of three beads down where each child can see it: **"Now you make one like mine. Which kind of bead should you take first?"** When the first bead is on: **"Which one is next"?** When two are on: **"Which one is next?"**
Use patterns of varying degrees of complexity.

1. A–B–A–B
2. A–B–C–A–B–C
3. A–A–B–A–A–C–A–A–D
4. Make up your own patterns.

FOLLOW-UP:

1. Make a string of beads. Pull it through a paper towel roll so that none of the beads can be seen. Say, **"I'm going to hide the beads in the tunnel. Now I'm going to pull them out. Which one will come out first? Next? Next?"** and so on. Then pull the beads through, and have the children check as each bead comes out.
2. Dye some macaroni with food coloring. Set up a pattern for a necklace. The children can string the macaroni to make their own necklaces in the same pattern.

Ordering/Seriation: Different Sizes, Same Shape

OBJECTIVE: To make comparisons of three or more items of the same shape and different sizes.

MATERIALS: Four to ten squares cut with sides 1 inch, 1¼ inch, 1½ inch, and so on.

NATURALISTIC AND INFORMAL ACTIVITIES: Have a container of the squares and other shapes in a sequence of sizes available during center time. Note how the children use the shapes. Do they sequence them by size? Comment such as: **"You put the biggest square first; You put all the same sizes in their own piles."**

ADULT GUIDED ACTIVITY: Lay out the shapes. **"Here are some squares. Stack them up so the biggest is on the bottom."** Mix the squares up again. **"Now, put them in a row starting with the smallest."**

FOLLOW-UP: Do the same thing with other shapes and materials.

Ordering/Seriation: Length

OBJECTIVE: To make comparisons of three or more things of the same width but of different lengths.

MATERIALS: Sticks, strips of paper, yarn, string, Cuisenaire Rods, drinking straws, or anything similar cut in different lengths such that each item has the same difference in length from the next one.

NATURALISTIC AND INFORMAL ACTIVITIES: Have containers of each type of material available during center time. Place some of the items in the art center to be used for collages. Note how the children explore the materials. Do they line them up in sequence? Comment such as: "You put the largest (smallest) first"; "Tell me about what you made."

ADULT GUIDED ACTIVITY: Place the sticks in a mixed order. **"Line these up from shortest to longest (longest to shortest)."** Help if needed. **"Which one comes next? Which one of these is longest? Is this the next one?"**

FOLLOW-UP: Do this activity with many different kinds of materials.

Ordering/Seriation: Double Seriation

OBJECTIVE: To match, one-to-one, two or more ordered sets of the same number of items.

MATERIALS: *Three Bears* flannelboard figures or cutouts made by hand: mother bear, father bear, baby bear, Goldilocks, three bowls, three spoons, three chairs, and three beds.

NATURALISTIC AND INFORMAL ACTIVITIES: Have the flannelboard and story pieces available during center time. Note how the children use the material. Do they tell the story? Do they line up the pieces in sequence? Comment if they hesitate: "What comes next in the story?" Note if they sequence and/or match the materials by size: "You matched up each bear with its chair, bowl, bed."

ADULT GUIDED ACTIVITY: Tell the story. Use all the order words: biggest, middle-sized, smallest, next. Follow up with questions: **"Which is the biggest bear? Find the biggest bear's bowl (chair, bed, spoon)."** Use the same sequence with each character.

FOLLOW-UP: Let the children act out the story with the felt pieces or cutouts. Note if they use the order words; change their voices; and match each bear to the correct bowl, spoon, chair, and bed.

Ordering: Groups

OBJECTIVE: To order groups of one to five objects.

MATERIALS: Glue buttons or draw dots on five cards.

NATURALISTIC AND INFORMAL ACTIVITIES: Have the cards available during center time. Note if the children sequence them from one to five items. Ask them: "How many buttons (dots) there are on each card"; "Which cards have more than one?"

ADULT GUIDED ACTIVITY: Lay out the cards. Put the card with one button in front of the child. **"How many buttons are on this card?"** Child answers. Say, **"Yes, there is one button. Find the card with one more button."** If child picks out the card with two, say, **"You found one more. Now find the card with one more button."** Keep on until all five are in line. Mix the cards up. Give the stack to the child. **"Line them all up by yourself. Start with the smallest group."**

FOLLOW-UP: Repeat with other materials. Increase the number of groups as each child learns to recognize and count larger groups. Use loose buttons (chips, sticks, or coins), and have the child count out her own groups. Put each set in a small container or on a small piece of paper.

Order: Ordinal Numbers

OBJECTIVE: To learn the ordinal numbers *first, second, third*, and *fourth*. (The child should be able to count easily to four before doing this activity.)

MATERIALS: Four balls or beanbags, four common objects, four chairs.

NATURALISTIC AND INFORMAL ACTIVITIES: Have the materials available during center time or gym time as appropriate. Note how the children use them. Note if they figure out that they must take turns. Comment such as, "You are doing a good job taking turns. Mary is first, José is second, Larry is third, and Jai Li is fourth."

ADULT GUIDED ACTIVITIES:

1. Use games that require children to take turns. Just keep in mind that young children cannot wait very long. Limit the group to four children, and keep the game moving fast. For example, give each of the four children one beanbag or one ball. Say: "**How many bags are there? Let's count. One, two, three, four. Can I catch them all at the same time? No, I can't. You will have to take turns: you are first, you are second, you are third, and you are fourth.**" Have each child say his number, "**I am (first, second, third, and fourth). Okay, first, throw yours.**" (Throw it back.) Second, throw yours. (Throw it back.) After each has had his turn, have all of them do it again. This time have them tell you their ordinal number name.

2. Line up four objects. Say, "**This one is first, this one is second, this one is third, this one is fourth.**" Ask the children: "**Point to the (fourth, first, third, second).**"

3. Line up four chairs. "**We are going to play bus (plane, train).**" Name a child, _____ "**You get in the third seat.**" Fill the seats. Go on a pretend trip. "**Now we will get off. Second seat get off. First seat get off. Fourth seat get off. Third seat get off.**"

FOLLOW-UP: Make up some games that use the same basic ideas. As each child knows first through fourth, add fifth, then sixth, and so on.

Patterning: Auditory

OBJECTIVE: To copy and extend auditory patterns.

MATERIALS: None needed.

NATURALISTIC AND INFORMAL ACTIVITIES: Note if the children engage in spontaneous chants and rhymes. Encourage them by joining in their rhythmic activities.

ADULT GUIDED ACTIVITIES: Start a hand-clapping pattern. Ask the children to join you. Say, "**Listen to me clap.**" Clap, clap, (pause), clap (repeat several times). Say, "**You clap along with me.**" Keep on clapping for 60–90 seconds, so everyone has a chance to join in. Say, "**Listen. When I stop, you finish the pattern.**" Do three repetitions, and then stop. Say, "**You do the next one.**" Try some other patterns such as "Clap, clap, slap the elbow" or "Clap, stamp the foot, slap the leg."

FOLLOW-UP: Help the children develop their own patterns. Have them use rhythm instruments (e.g., drums, jingle bells, or sound cans) to develop patterns.

Patterning: Objects

OBJECTIVE: To copy and extend object patterns.

MATERIALS: Several small plastic toys such as vehicles, animals, or peg people; manipulatives such as Unifix Cubes, inch cubes, or attribute blocks; or any other small objects such as coins, bottle caps, eating utensils, or cups.

NATURALISTIC AND INFORMAL ACTIVITIES: Provide opportunities to explore many kinds of materials such as those listed above. After the children have had some structured pattern activities, note if they develop patterns during their independent activity periods. Do they call your attention to their pattern constructions? Can they describe their constructions when you ask them to?

ADULT GUIDED ACTIVITIES: Have the children explore ways to make patterns with the objects. Have them see how many different kinds of patterns they can make.

FOLLOW-UP: Find additional ideas for pattern activities in this unit's Further Reading and Resources listing.

Patterning: Exploring Patterns in Space

OBJECTIVE: To organize materials in space in a pattern.

MATERIALS: Many kinds of materials are available that will give the child experiences with making patterns in space.
1. *Geoboards* are square boards with attached pegs. Rubber bands of different colors can be stretched between the pegs to form patterns and shapes.
2. *Parquetry* and *pattern blocks* are blocks of various shapes and colors that can be organized into patterns.
3. *Pegboards* are boards with holes evenly spaced. Individual pegs can be placed in the holes to form patterns.
4. *Color inch cubes* are cubes with 1-inch sides. They are available in sets with red, yellow, blue, green, orange, and purple cubes.

NATURALISTIC AND INFORMAL ACTIVITIES: Provide children time for exploring materials during center time. Note the patterns the children construct. Do they call your attention to their pattern constructions? Can they describe their constructions when you ask them to?

ADULT GUIDED ACTIVITIES:
1. Have the children experiment freely with the materials and create their own patterns.
2. Purchase or make patterns for the children to copy.

FOLLOW-UP: After showing the children how to use the materials, leave them out during center time.

Patterning: Organizing Patterns in Space

OBJECTIVE: To organize materials in space in a pattern.

MATERIALS: Construction paper, scissors, and glue.

NATURALISTIC AND INFORMAL ACTIVITIES: Children should already have been involved with many activities (naturalistic as well as informal and adult guided) and have had many opportunities to work in small groups before they are assigned the following activity.

ADULT GUIDED ACTIVITY: Provide a poster-size piece of construction paper and an assortment of precut construction paper shapes (e.g., squares, triangles, circles). Suggest that the children, working in small groups, create as many different patterns as they can and glue them on the big piece of paper.

FOLLOW-UP: Offer the activity several times. Use different colors for the shapes, use different sizes, and change the choice of shapes.

Ideas for Children with Special Needs

An understanding of patterns and ordering provides the children a foundation for understanding algebraic relationships. A multisensory approach to instruction can be used to meet the needs of all children. The art of many cultures includes special patterns (Zaslavsky, 1996). Children can make stamped repeated patterns with sponges and other materials. They can also use stencils for creating patterns. Pattern blocks can be explored. Children can be introduced to the patterns common to a variety of cultures. They might bring materials that include patterns from home.

Children with perceptual motor challenges may benefit from extra time using large colored beads. Beads are usually available in six colors and three shapes. For the first step the children can select five or six beads of any color or shape to practice stringing. Once the children feel comfortable with stringing, they can begin to string patterns. They can start with the simplest patterns such as all cubes, all spheres, or all cylinders in one color and gradually move to A–B and more complex patterns in small steps. Sequence terms can be applied to instructions—for example, "First blue, second yellow."

For auditory learners, more opportunities for auditory patterns can support their understanding of pattern and ordering. Rhymes with repeated patterns work well with these children. Kinesthetic learners do well with patterned movement activities such as two steps, two jumps, and so on. Children can also use movement to work with sequence; for example, they can line up "first, second, third," and so forth, to do patterned movement or take turns doing patterns.

Evaluation

Note whether children's use of ordering and patterning words—and their involvement in ordering and patterning activities—has increased during play and routine activities. Without disrupting the children's activities, ask questions or make comments and give suggestions:

- Who is the biggest? (The smallest?)
- (As the children put their shoes on after their nap) Who has the longest shoes? (The shortest shoes?)
- Who came in the door first today?
- Run fast. See who can get to the other side of the gym first.
- (The children are playing train) Well, who is in the last seat? She must be the caboose. Who is in the first seat? She must be the engineer.
- Everyone can't get a drink at the same time. Line up with the shortest person first.
- Great, you found a new pattern to make with the Unifix Cubes!
- Sam made some patterns with the ink pad and stamps.

Richardson (1999, pp. 78–79) suggests that the adult should note whether children can do the following

- Copy patterns.
- Extend patterns.
- Create patterns.
- Analyze a given pattern.

The assessment tasks in this unit and in Appendix A can be used for individual evaluation interviews.

Summary

The process of comparing more than two things is called ordering or seriation. There are four basic types of ordering activities. The first is to put things in sequence by size. The second is to make a one-to-one match between two sets of related things. The third is to place sets of different numbers of things in order from the least to the most. The last is ordinal numbers (first, second, third, etc.). Some children may need extra ordering and sequencing experiences.

Patterning is related to ordering and includes auditory, visual, and physical motor sequences that are repeated. Patterns may be copied, extended, or verbally described. Children can learn about patterns common to a variety of cultures.

KEY TERMS

one more than
ordering

patterning

seriation

SUGGESTED ACTIVITIES

1. Observe children at school. Note those activities that show that the children are learning order and patterning. Share your observations with the class.
2. Add ordering and patterning activities to your Activity File.
3. Assemble the materials needed to do the ordering and patterning assessment tasks described in this unit. Try out the tasks with several young children. What did the children do? Share the results with the class.

REVIEW

A. List at least seven of the major characteristics of ordering/seriation.
B. Describe the major characteristics of patterning.
C. Decide whether the listed descriptions are examples of the following ordering and patterning behaviors: (a) size sequence, (b) one-to-one comparison, (c) ordering groups, (d) using ordinal words or numbers, (e) basic concept of ordering, (f) using double seriation, (g) patterning.
   1. Child arranges tokens in groups: one in the first group, two in the second, three in the third, and so on.
   2. Pablo says, "I'm last."
   3. Maria lines up sticks of various lengths from shortest to longest.
   4. Kate is trying to place all the nesting cups inside each other in order by size.
   5. Child chants, "Ho, ho, ho. Ha, ha, ha. Ho, ho, ho. Ha, ha, ha."
   6. Jim strings blue beads in this manner: large-small-large-small-large-small.
   7. Fong places a white chip on each red chip.
   8. Nancy places the smallest flower in the smallest flowerpot, the middle-sized flower in the middle-sized flowerpot, and the largest flower in the largest flowerpot.
   9. Mr. Mendez says, "Today we will line up with the shortest child first."
   10. Child parks cars: yellow car, blue car, yellow car, blue car.
   11. Tanja tells Josie, "I'm first this time."
   12. In the Montessori class, children construct the pink tower with the largest cube at the bottom, the next smaller cube second, and so on, until they use all the cubes.
D. Summarize the NCTM expectations for algebra that are described in this unit.

REFERENCES

Cross, C. T., Woods, T. A., & Schweingruber, H. (2009). *Mathematics learning in early childhood*. Washington, DC: National Academies Press.

National Council of Teachers of Mathematics. (2000). *Principles and standards for school mathematics*. Reston, VA: Author.

Richardson, K. (1999). *Developing number concepts: Counting, comparing, and pattern (Book 1)*. Parsippany, NJ: Seymour.

Zaslavsky, C. (1996). *The multicultural math classroom*. Portsmouth, NH: Heinemann.

FURTHER READING AND RESOURCES

AIMS Educational Products. AIMS Education Foundation, P.O. Box 8120, Fresno, CA 93747-8120.

Cadzow-Wardell, L. (2009/2010). White trillium. *Teaching Children Mathematics, 16*(5), 264–267.

Copley, J. V., Jones, C., & Dighe, J. (2007). *Mathematics: The creative curriculum approach*. Washington, DC: Teaching Strategies.

Dubon, L. P., & Shafer, K. G. (2010). Storyboards for meaningful patterns. *Teaching Children Mathematics, 16*(6), 325–329.

Greenes, C. E., Cavanagh, M., Dacey, L., Findell, C. R., & Small, M. (2001). *Navigating through algebra in prekindergarten–kindergarten*. Reston, VA: National Council of Teachers of Mathematics.

Greenes, C. E., Dacey, L., Cavanagh, M., Findell, C. R., Sheffield, L. J., & Small, M. (2003). *Navigating through problem solving and reasoning in prekindergarten–kindergarten*. Reston, VA: National Council of Teachers of Mathematics.

Learning Resources. (2007). *Hands-on standards*. Vernon Hills, IL: Author.

National Council of Teachers of Mathematics. (2007). *Curriculum focal points*. Reston, VA: Author.

Richardson, K. (1984). *Developing number concepts using Unifix Cubes*. Menlo Park, CA: Addison-Wesley.

Richardson, K. (1999). *Developing number concepts: Planning guide*. Parsippany, NJ: Seymour.

Ziemba, E. J., & Hoffman, J. (2005/2006). Sorting and patterning in kindergarten: From activities to assessment. *Teaching Children Mathematics, 12*(5), 236–241.

Measurement: Volume, Weight, Length, and Temperature

After reading this unit, you should be able to:

- Explain how measurement skills develop in five stages.
- Assess and evaluate the measurement skills of a young child.
- Do informal and adult guided measurement with young children.
- Provide children with naturalistic measurement experiences.
- Explain the NCTM standard for measurement as it applies to preschool/kindergarten children.

The NCTM (2000, p. 102) expectations for children in the beginning stages of **measurement** include recognizing the attributes of **length**, **volume**, **weight**, and time as well as comparing and ordering objects according to these attributes. This unit addresses these attributes plus the attributes of **temperature**. Time is addressed in Unit 15. By the time they reach kindergarten, young children are expected to understand measurement with nonstandard units such as multiple copies of objects of the same size (e.g., paper clips). Measurement connects geometry and number and builds on children's experiences with comparisons

(Unit 8). Length is the major focus for younger children, but experiences with volume, weight, and temperature are also important. Estimation is an important measurement tool in the early stages. The curriculum focal point (NCTM, 2007) for measurement in prekindergarten is identifying measurable attributes and comparing objects using these attributes; in kindergarten, the focal point for measurement is ordering objects by measurable attributes such as length and weight. Two objects might be compared with a third.

Measurement is one of the most useful math skills. It involves assigning a number to things, so they can be compared on the same attributes. Numbers can be assigned to attributes such as volume, weight, length, and temperature, for example, the child drinks *one cup* of milk. Numbers can also be given to time measurement. However, time is not an attribute of things and so is presented separately (Unit 15). **Standard units** such as pints, quarts, liters, yards, meters, pounds, grams, and degrees tell us exactly how much (*volume*); how heavy (*weight*); how long, wide, or deep (*length*); and how hot or cold (*temperature*). A number is put with a standard unit to let us make a comparison: Two quarts contain more than one quart, two pounds weigh less than three pounds, one meter is shorter than four meters, and 30° is colder than 80°.

Stages of Development

The concept of measurement develops through five stages, as outlined in Figure 14–1. The first stage is a **play stage**. The child imitates older children and adults. She plays at measuring with rulers, measuring cups, measuring spoons, and scales as she sees others do. She pours sand, water, rice, beans, and peas from one container to another as she explores the properties of volume. She lifts and moves things as she learns about weight. She notes that those who are bigger than she can do many more activities and thus has her first concept of length (height). She finds that her short arms cannot always reach what she wants them to reach (length). She finds that she has a preference for cold or hot food and cold or hot bathwater and begins to learn about temperature. This first stage begins at birth and continues through the sensorimotor period into the preoperational period.

The second stage in the development of the concept of measurement is the one of making **comparisons** (Unit 8). This is well under way by the preoperational stage. The child is always comparing: bigger–smaller, heavier–lighter, longer–shorter, and hotter–colder.

The third stage, which comes at the end of the preoperational period and at the beginning of concrete operations, is one in which the child learns to use what are called **arbitrary units**; that is, anything the child has can be used as a unit of measure. She will try to find out how many coffee cups of sand will fill a quart milk carton. The volume of the coffee cup is the arbitrary unit. She will find out how many toothpicks long her foot is. The length of the toothpick is the arbitrary unit. As she goes through the stage of using arbitrary units, she learns concepts that she will need to understand standard units.

When the child enters the period of concrete operations, she begins to see the need for using standard units. She can see that to communicate with someone in a way the other person will understand, she must use the same units the other person uses. For example, the child says that her paper is nine thumbs wide. Another person cannot find another piece of the same width unless the child and her thumb are there to measure it. But if she says her paper is eight and one-half inches wide, another person will know exactly the width of the paper. In this case, the thumb is an arbitrary unit, and the inch is a *standard unit*. The same is true for other units as well. When cooking, standard measuring cups and spoons must be used for the recipe to turn out correctly. If any coffee cup or teacup and just any spoon are used when

Piagetian Stage	Age	Measurement Stage
Sensorimotor and Preoperational	0–7	1. Plays and imitates
		2. Makes comparisons
Transitional: Preoperational to Concrete Operations	5–7	3. Uses arbitrary units
Concrete Operations	6+	4. Sees need for standard units
		5. Uses standard units

FIGURE 14–1 Stages in the development of the concept of measurement.

following a recipe, the measurement will be arbitrary and inexact, and the chances of a successful outcome will be poor. The same can also be said of building a house. If nonstandard measuring tools are used, the house will not come out as it appears in the plans, and one carpenter will not be communicating clearly with another.

The last stage in the development of the concept of measurement begins in the concrete operations period. In this last stage, the child begins to use and understand the standard units of measurement such as inches, meters, pints, liters, grams, degrees, and so on.

Obviously, prekindergartners and most kindergartners are still exploring the concept of measurement. Prekindergartners are usually in stages 1 (play and imitation) and 2 (making comparisons). The kindergartners begin in stage 2 and move into stage 3 (arbitrary units). During the primary grades, students begin to see the need for standard units (stage 4) and move into using standard units (stage 5). Measurement can be integrated into the other content areas (see Figure 14–2).

How the Young Child Thinks about Measurement

A review of Piaget will help explain why young children do not understand standard units in the sensorimotor and preoperational stages. Recall from Unit 1 that the young child is fooled by appearances. He believes what he sees before him. He does not keep old pictures in mind as he will do later. He is not yet able to conserve (or save) the first way something looks when its appearance is changed. When the ball of clay is made into a snake, he thinks the volume (the amount of clay) has changed because it looks smaller to him. When the water is poured into a differently shaped container, he thinks there is more or less—depending on the height of the glass. Because he can focus on only one attribute at a time, the most obvious dimension determines his response.

Two more examples are shown in Figure 14–3. In the first task, the child is fooled when a crooked road is compared with a straight road. The straight road looks longer (conservation of length). In the

second task, size is dominant over material, and the child guesses that the Ping-Pong ball weighs more than the hard rubber ball. He thinks that because the table tennis ball is larger than the hard rubber ball, it must be heavier.

The young child becomes familiar with the words of measurement and learns which attributes can be measured. He learns mainly through observing older children and adults as they measure. He does not need to be taught the standard units of measurement in a formal way. The young child needs to gain a feeling that things differ on the basis of "more" and "less" of some attributes. He gains this feeling mostly through his own observations and firsthand experimental experiences.

Assessment

To assess measurement skills in the young child, the teacher observes the child. The teacher notes whether the child uses the term measure in the adult way. He notes whether she uses adult measuring tools in her play as she sees adults use them. He looks for the following kinds of incidents:

- Mary is playing in the sandbox. She pours sand from an old bent measuring cup into a bucket and stirs it with a sand shovel. "I'm measuring the flour for my cake. I need three cups of flour and two cups of sugar."
- Juanita is seated on a small chair. Kate kneels in front of her. Juanita has her right shoe off. Kate puts Juanita's foot on a ruler. "I am measuring your foot for your new shoes."
- The children have a play grocery store. Jorge puts some plastic fruit on the toy scale. "Ten pounds here."
- Azam is the doctor, and Bob is his patient. Azam takes an imaginary thermometer from Bob's mouth. "You have a hot fever."

Individual interviews for the preoperational child may be found in Unit 8. For the child who is near concrete operations (past age 5), the conservation tasks in Unit 1 and Appendix A may be used to determine if children are conservers and thus probably ready to use standard units of measurement.

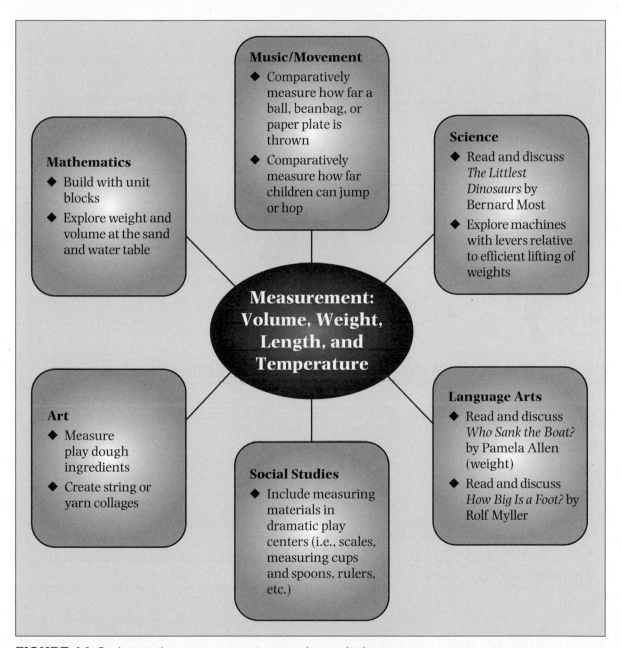

FIGURE 14–2 Integrating measurement across the curriculum.

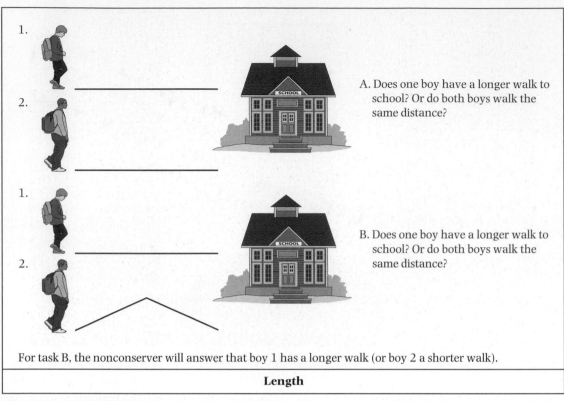

A. Does one boy have a longer walk to school? Or do both boys walk the same distance?

B. Does one boy have a longer walk to school? Or do both boys walk the same distance?

For task B, the nonconserver will answer that boy 1 has a longer walk (or boy 2 a shorter walk).

Length

PING-PONG BALL   HARD RUBBER BALL

Here are two balls. Do you think they weigh the same, or is one heavier?

The preperational child will be fooled by size and will say the bigger ball weighs more.

Weight

FIGURE 14–3 Conservation of length and weight.

Naturalistic Activities

Young children's concepts of measurement develop, for the most part, from their natural everyday experiences exploring the environment, discovering its properties, and so constructing their own knowledge. The examples in the assessment section of this unit demonstrate how children's play activities reflect their concepts of measurement. Mary has seen and may have helped someone make a cake. Kate has been to the shoe store and knows the clerk must measure the feet before he brings out a pair of shoes to try on the customer. Jorge has seen the grocer weigh fruit. Azam knows that a thermometer tells how "hot" a fever is. The observant young child picks up these

Children explore the fundamentals of measurement as they play at the sand and water table.

ideas on his own without being told specifically that they are important.

The child uses his play activities to practice what he has seen adults do. He also uses play materials to learn ideas through experimentation and trial and error. Water, sand, dirt, and mud can teach the child about volume. As he pours these substances from one container to another, he learns about *how much*, or amount. The child can use containers of many sizes and shapes: buckets, cups, plastic bottles, dishes, bowls, and coffee cans. Shovels, spoons, strainers, and funnels can also be used with these materials. When playing with water, the child can also learn about weight if he has some small objects, such as sponges, rocks, corks, small pieces of wood, and marbles, that may float or sink. Any time a child tries to put something in a box, envelope, glass, or any other container, he learns something about volume.

The child can begin to learn the idea of linear measure (length, width, and height) and area in his play. The unit blocks that are usually found in the early childhood classroom help the child learn the idea of units. He will soon learn that each block is a unit of another block. Two, four, or eight of the small blocks are the same length when placed end to end as one of the longest blocks. As he builds enclosures (houses, garages, farmyards, and so on), he is forced to pick his blocks so that each side is the same length as the one across from it.

The child learns about weight and balance on the teeter-totter. He soon learns that it takes two to go up and down. He also learns that it works best when the two are near the same weight and are the same distance from the middle.

The child makes many contacts with temperature. He learns that his soup is hot, warm, and then, as it sits out, cold. He likes cold milk and hot cocoa. He learns that the air may be hot or cold. If the air is hot, he may wear shorts or just a bathing suit. If the air is cold, he will need a coat, hat, and mittens.

Adult scaffolding helps children construct measurement concepts.

Kindergartners can carry out nonstandard measurement activities.

Informal Activities

The young child learns about measurement through the kinds of experiences just described. These activities provide children with many opportunities for informal teaching. One job for the adult as the child plays is to help her by pointing out properties of materials that the child may not be able to find on her own. For instance, if a child says she must have all the long blocks to make her house large enough, the teacher can show her how several small blocks can do the job. She can show the child how to measure how much string will fit around a box before she cuts off a piece to use.

The teacher can also take these opportunities to use measurement words such as the names of units of measurement and the words listed in Unit 12. She can also pose problems for the child. Some examples are:

- How can we find out if we have enough apple juice for everyone?
- How can we find out how many paper cups of milk can be poured from a gallon container?
- How can we find out if someone has a high fever?
- How can we find out without going outside if we need to wear a sweater or coat?
- How can we find out who is the tallest boy in the class? The child who weighs the most?

- How many of these place mats will fit around the table?
- Who lives the longest distance from school?

It is the teacher's responsibility to provide environmental opportunities for exploring and discovering measurement concepts.

Adult Guided Activities

The young child learns most of his basic measurement ideas through his play and home activities that come through the natural routines of the day. He gains a feeling for the need for measurement and learns the language of measurement. Adult guided activities must be chosen with care. The activities should make use of the child's senses. They should be related to what is familiar to the child and expand what he already knows. They should pose problems that will show him the need for measurement. They should give the child a chance to use measurement words to explain his solution to the problem. The following activities are examples of these kinds of experiences and the naturalistic and informal experiences that serve as their foundation.

Activities

Measurement: Volume

OBJECTIVES:
- To learn the characteristics of volume.
- To see that volume can be measured.
- To learn measurement words used to tell about volume (more, less, too big, too little, the same).

MATERIALS:
- Sandbox (indoors and/or out), water table (or sink or plastic dishpans).
- Many containers of different sizes: bottles, cups, bowls, milk cartons, cans (with smooth edges), boxes (for dry materials).
- Spoons, scoops, funnels, strainers, beaters.
- Water, sand, marbles, seeds, or anything else that can be poured.

NATURALISTIC AND INFORMAL ACTIVITIES: Allow plenty of time for the children to experiment with the materials listed above during center time. Observe if children are into the pretend play measurement stage, are making comparisons, or mention any standard units. Ask questions or make comments, such as: "How many of the blue cups of sand will fill up the purple bowl?"; "Which bottle will hold more water?"; and "You filled that milk carton up to the top."

ADULT GUIDED ACTIVITIES:
1. Have several containers of different kinds and sizes. Fill one with water (or sand or pebbles). Pick out another container. Ask the children: **"If I pour this water from this bottle into this other bottle, will the second bottle hold all the water?"** After each child has made her prediction, pour the water into the second container. Ask a child to tell what she saw happen. Continue with several containers. Have the children line them up from the one that holds the most to the one that holds the least.

2. Pick out one standard container (coffee cup, paper cup, measuring cup, or tin can). Have one or more larger containers. Say, **"If I want to fill the big bowl with sand and use this paper cup, how many times will I have to fill the paper cup and pour sand into the bowl?"** Write down the children's predictions. Let each child have a turn to fill the cup and pour sand into the bowl. Record by making slash marks how many cups of sand are poured. Have the children count the number of marks when the bowl is full. Compare this amount with what the children thought the amount would be.

FOLLOW-UP: Do the same types of activities using different sizes of containers and common objects. For example, have a doll and three different-sized boxes. Have the children decide which box the doll will fit into.

Measurement: Weight

OBJECTIVES:
- To learn firsthand the characteristics of weight.
- To learn that weight and size are different attributes (big things may have less weight than small things).
- To learn that light and heavy are relative terms.

MATERIALS:
- Things in the classroom or brought from home, for example, manipulatives, paper clips, buttons, crayons, pencils, small toys.
- A teeter-totter, a board and a block, a simple pan balance.
- Sand, sawdust, small shells, pebbles, seeds.
- A ball collection with balls of different sizes and materials: ball bearings, table tennis, golf, solid rubber, foam rubber, Styrofoam, balsa wood, cotton, balloons.

NATURALISTIC AND INFORMAL ACTIVITIES: During center time, provide opportunities for the children to experiment with a simple pan balance using a variety of materials. Note if they use any weight vocabulary (such as heavy or light). Ask them to explain their actions. Outdoors or in the gym, provide a teeter-totter. Note how they find ways to balance. Ask them what happens when children of different weights or different numbers of children sit on each end.

ADULT GUIDED ACTIVITIES:
1. Have the child name things in the room that he can lift and things he cannot lift. Which things can he not lift because of size? Which because of weight? Compare things such as a stapler (small and heavy) and a large paper bag (large and light). Have the children line up things from heaviest to lightest.
2. Have the children experiment with the teeter-totter. How many children does it take to balance the teacher? Make a balance with a block and a board. Have the child experiment with different things to see which will make the board balance.
3. Use a fixed-position pan balance for firsthand experiences with all types of things.
    a. Have the child try balancing small objects such as paper clips, hair clips, bobby pins, coins, toothpicks, cotton balls, and so on, in the pans.
    b. Take the collection of balls and pick out a pair. Have the child predict which is heavier (lighter). Let him put one in each pan to check his prediction.

c. Put one substance such as sand in one pan. Have the child fill the other pan with seeds until the pans balance. Ask, **"Is the amount (volume) of sand and seeds the same?"**

d. Have equal amounts of two different substances such as sand and sawdust in the balance pans. Ask, **"Do the pans balance?"**

FOLLOW-UP: Make some play dough with the children. Have them measure out one part flour and one part salt. Mix in some powder tempera. Add water until the mixture is pliable but not too sticky. Have the students measure cooking and baking ingredients. See Unit 17 for cooking ideas. Read *Who Sank the Boat?* by Pamela Allen (1982).

Measurement: Length and Height

OBJECTIVES:
- To learn firsthand the concepts of length and height.
- To help the child learn the use of arbitrary units.

MATERIALS:
- The children's bodies.
- Things in the room that can be measured, for example, tables, chairs, doors, windows, shelves, books.
- Balls of string and yarn, scissors, construction paper, markers, beans, chips, pennies, other small counters, pencils, toothpicks, ice-cream-bar sticks, unit blocks.

NATURALISTIC AND INFORMAL ACTIVITIES: During center time, note if the children engage in any comparison or play length measurement activities. Unit blocks are especially good for naturalistic and informal measurement explorations. For example, observe whether children, when using unit blocks, appear to use trial and error to make their blocks fit as they wish. Comment, "You matched the blocks so your house has all the sides the same length."

ADULT GUIDED ACTIVITIES:
1. Present the child with problems where she must pick out something of a certain length. For example, a dog must be tied to a post. Have a picture of the dog and the post. Have several lengths of string and have the child find out which string is the right length. Ask, **"Which rope will reach from the ring to the dog's collar?"**
2. Say, **"Look around the room"**, and ask, **"Which things are close? Which things are far away?"**
3. Have several children line up and have a child point out which is the tallest and the shortest. Have the children line up from tallest to shortest. Ask the child to draw pictures of friends and family in a row from shortest to tallest.
4. Draw lines on construction paper. Ask, **"How many paperclips (chips, toothpicks, or other small things) will fit on each line? Which line has more paperclips? Which line is longest?"** Gradually use paper with more than two lines.
5. Put a piece of construction paper on the wall from the floor up to about 5 feet. Have each child stand next to the paper. Mark their heights and label the marks with their names. Check each child's height each month. Note how much each child grows over the year.
6. Create an arbitrary unit such as a pencil, a toothpick, a stick, a long block, or a piece of yarn or string. Have the child measure things in the room to see how many units long, wide, or tall the things are.

FOLLOW-UP: Keep the height chart out, so the children can look at it and talk about their heights. Read *The Littlest Dinosaurs* by Bernard Most (1989) and *How Big Is a Foot?* by Rolf Myller (1972).

Measurement: Temperature

OBJECTIVES:
- To give the child firsthand experiences that will help him learn that temperature is the relative measure of heat.
- To learn that the thermometer is used to measure temperature.
- To experience hot, warm, and cold as related to things, weather, and the seasons of the year.

MATERIALS: Ice cubes, hot plate, teakettle or pan, pictures of the four seasons, poster board, markers, scissors, glue, construction paper, old magazines with pictures, real thermometers (body, indoors, and outdoors).

NATURALISTIC AND INFORMAL ACTIVITIES: Note children's talk regarding temperature. Make comments, such as: "Be careful, the soup is very hot" and "It's cold today, you must button up your coat." Ask questions such as, **"Do we need to wear mittens or gloves today?"**

ADULT GUIDED ACTIVITIES:
1. Have the children decide whether selected things in the environment are hot, cold, or warm—for example, ice and boiling water, the hot and cold water taps, the radiators, the glass in the windows, their skin, and so on.
2. Show pictures of summer, fall, winter, and spring. Discuss the usual temperatures in each season. What is the usual weather? What kinds of clothes are worn? Make a cardboard thermometer. At the bottom put a child in heavy winter clothes, above put a child in a light coat or jacket, then a child in a sweater, then one in short sleeves, then one in a bathing suit.
3. Each day discuss the outside temperature relative to what was worn to school.
4. Give the children scissors and old magazines. Have them find and cut out pictures of hot things and cold things. Have them glue the hot things on one piece of poster board and the cold things on another.
5. Show the children three thermometers: one for body temperature, one for room temperature, and one for outdoor use. Discuss when and where each is used.

FOLLOW-UP: Discuss and record outside temperature each day in some way (as in Activity 3 or on a graph as discussed in Unit 16).

Ideas for Children with Special Needs

Measurement lends itself very well to the first cooperative learning activities. Two children can form a buddy group and work together with the younger children comparing attributes (such as grouping objects into long and short) and with the kindergartners measuring with nonstandard units. The adult can put children of different cultures and of different abilities into buddy pairs. He can assign each child a responsibility: for example, one could handle the measuring tool and the other could record the measurements.

MATH TECHNOLOGY FOR
YOUNG CHILDREN

All young children can benefit from technology experiences. Use one of the evaluation schemes suggested in Unit 2 to evaluate any of these resources:

- *Key Skills Math Shapes, Numbers, and Measurement* (http://www.campus tech.com). Measures of time and temperature.
- *Ani's Rocket Ride* (Evanston, IL: APTE). Includes exploration of a balancing scale.
- *Light Weights/Heavy Weights* (NASA explores, http://media.nasaexplores.com). Activities for comparing relative weights of common objects.
- *James Discovers Math* (http://www. smartkidssoftware.com). Includes measurement.
- Turtle Pond and Pan Balance Shapes Activities and As People Get Older, They Get Taller, Block Pounds ad Lady Bug Lengths Lessons at http://Illuminations. nctm.org

Evaluation

The adult should note the children's responses to the activities given to them. She should observe them as they try out the materials and should note their comments. She must also observe whether they are able to solve everyday problems that come up using informal measurements such as comparisons. Use the individual interviews in Unit 8 and Appendix A.

Summary

The concept of measurement develops through five stages. Preoperational children are in the early stages: play, imitation, and comparing. They learn about measurement mainly through naturalistic and informal experiences that encourage them to explore and discover. Transitional children move into the stage of experimenting with arbitrary units. During the concrete operations period, children learn to use standard units of measurement. Measurement activities lend themselves to cooperative learning groups with two members.

KEY TERMS

arbitrary units	measurement	temperature
comparisons	play stage	volume
length	standard units	weight

SUGGESTED ACTIVITIES

1. Observe young children during group play. Note and record any measurement activities you observe. Identify the stage of measurement understanding that is represented by each activity.

2. Plan two or three measurement activities. Assemble the necessary materials, and use the activities with a group of young children.

3. Add several measurement activities to your File/Notebook.

REVIEW

A. List, in order, the five stages of measurement.
B. Describe each of the five stages of measurement.
C. Identify the level of measurement described in each of the following incidents:
   1. Johnny says, "My block building is bigger than yours."
   2. Linda checks the thermometer. "It's 32 degrees today—very cold!"
   3. Cindy, Juanita, and Li pour dry beans in and out of an assortment of containers.
4. "I weigh 60 pounds. How much do you weigh?"
5. "Dad, it would take two of my shoes to make one as long as yours."
D. Explain how a young child's measurement skills can be assessed.
E. Describe the NCTM (2000, 2007) expectations for measurement for preschool/kindergarten children.

REFERENCES

Allen, P. (1982). *Who sank the boat?* New York: Sandcastle Books.

Most, B. (1989). *The littlest dinosaurs*. San Diego, CA: Harcourt Brace.

Myller, R. (1972). *How big is a foot?* New York: Atheneum.

National Council of Teachers of Mathematics. (2000). *Principles and standards for school mathematics*. Reston, VA: Author.

National Council of Teachers of Mathematics. (2007). *Curriculum focal points*. Reston, VA: Author.

FURTHER READING AND RESOURCES

Copley, J. V. (Ed.). (2004). *Showcasing mathematics for the young child* (chap. 5, Measurement). Reston, VA: National Council of Teachers of Mathematics.

Copley, J. V., Glass, K., Nix, L., Faseler, A., DeJesus, M., & Tanksley, S. (2004). Early childhood corner: Measuring experiences for young children. *Teaching Children Mathematics, 10*(6), 314–319.

Cox, D., & Lo, J. (2009). Math by the month: Comparing sizes. *Teaching Children Mathematics, 16*(4), 204–205.

Dacey, L., Cavanagh, M., Findell, C. R., Greenes, C. E., Sheffield, L. J., & Small, M. (2003). *Navigating through measurement in prekindergarten–grade 2*. Reston, VA: National Council of Teachers of Mathematics.

Dougherty, B. J., & Venenciano, L. C. H. (2007). Measure up for understanding. *Teaching Children Mathematics, 13*(9), 452–456.

Lubinski, C. A., & Thiessen, D. (1996). Exploring measurement through literature. *Teaching Children Mathematics, 2*, 260–263.

Mailley, E., & Moyer, P. S. (2004). Investigations: The mathematical candy store: Weight matters. *Teaching Children Mathematics, 10*(8), 388–391.

McGregor, J. (1996). Math by the month: How do you measure up?: K–2. *Teaching Children Mathematics, 3*, 84.

Taylor-Cox, J. (2009). Teaching with blocks. *Teaching children mathematics, 15*(8), 460–463.

Teaching and learning measurement [Focus Issue]. (2006). *Teaching Children Mathematics, 13*(3).

West, S., & Cox, A. (2001). *Sand and water play*. Beltsville, MD: Gryphon House.

Young, S., & O'Leary, R. (2002). Creating numerical scales for measuring tools. *Teaching Children Mathematics, 8*(7), 400–405.

Measurement: Time

After reading this unit, you should be able to:

- Describe what is meant by time sequence.
- Describe what is meant by time duration.
- Explain the three kinds of time.
- Do informal and adult guided time measurement activities with young children.
- Explain the NCTM expectations for preschool and kindergarten students' understanding of time.

The NCTM standards (2000) for measurement include expectations for the understanding of time. Preschool and kindergarten children are learning the attributes of time such as **sequence** and **duration**. *Sequence* of time concerns the order of events and is related to the ideas about ordering, presented in Unit 13. While the child learns to sequence things in patterns, he also learns to sequence events. He learns that small, middle-sized, and large beads go in order for a pattern sequence. He gets up, washes his face, brushes his teeth, dresses, and eats breakfast for a time sequence. *Duration* of time has to do with how long an event takes (seconds, minutes, hours, days, a short time, a long time).

Kinds of Time

There are three kinds of time a child has to learn. Unlike weight, volume, length, and temperature,

time is a hard measure to learn because the child cannot see and feel it.

There are fewer clues to help the child. The young child relates time to three things: **personal experience**, **social activity**, and **culture**.

In her *personal experience*, the child has her own past, present, and future. The past is often referred to as "When I was a baby." "Last night" may mean any time before right now. The future may be "After my night nap" or "When I am big." The young child has difficulty with the idea that there was a time when mother and dad were little and she was not yet born.

Time in terms of *social activity* is a little easier to learn and makes more sense to the young child. The young child tends to be a slave to order and routine. A change of schedule can be very upsetting. This is because time for her is a sequence of predictable events. She can count on her morning activities being the same each day when she wakes up. Once she gets to school, she learns that there is order there, too: first she takes off her coat and hangs it up, next she is greeted by her teacher, then she goes to the big playroom to play, and so on, through the day.

A third kind of time is **cultural time**, which is fixed by clocks and calendars. Everyone learns this kind of time. It is a kind of time that the child probably does not really understand until she is in the concrete operations period. She can, however, learn the language (seconds, minutes, days, months, and so on) and the names of the timekeepers (clock, watch, calendar). She can also learn to recognize a timekeeper when she sees one.

Language of Time

Learning time depends on language no less than learning any part of math. Time and sequence words are listed in Unit 12 and are listed again here for easy reference.

- **General words**: time, age
- **Specific words**: morning, afternoon, evening, night, day, noon
- **Relational words**: soon, tomorrow, yesterday, early, late, a long time ago, once upon a time, new, old, now, when, sometimes, then, before, present, while, never, once, next, always, fast, slow, speed, first, second, third, and so on
- **Duration words**: clock and watch (minutes, seconds, hours); calendar (date, names of days of the week, names of the month, names of seasons, year)
- **Special days**: birthday, Passover, Juneteenth, Cinco de Mayo, Kwanzaa, Ramadan, Easter, Christmas, Thanksgiving, vacation, holiday, school day, weekend

Time concept experiences can be integrated into the other content areas (see Figure 15–1).

Assessment

The teacher should observe the child's use of time language. She should note if he makes an attempt to place himself and events in time. Does he remember the sequence of activities at school and at home? Is he able to wait for one thing to finish before going on to the next? Is he able to order things (Unit 13) in a sequence?

The following are examples of the kinds of interview tasks that are included in Appendix A.

Naturalistic Activities

From birth onward, children are capable of learning time and sequence. In an organized, nurturing environment, infants learn quickly that when they wake up from sleep, they are held and comforted, their diapers are changed, and then they are fed. Their first sense of time duration comes from how long it takes for each of these events. Infants soon have a sense of how long they will be held and comforted, how long it takes for a diaper change, and how long it takes to eat. Time for the infant is a sense of sequence and duration of events.

The toddler shows his understanding of time words through his actions. When he is told "It's lunchtime," he runs to his high chair. When he is told it is time for a nap, he may run the other way. He will notice cues that mean it is time to do something new: toys are being picked up, the table is set, or Dad appears at the door. He begins to look for these events that tell him that one piece of time ends and a new piece of time is about to start.

As the child develops spoken language, he will use time words. He will make an effort to place events and himself in time. It is important for adults to listen and respond to what he has to say. The following are some examples.

- Carlos (18 months old) tugs at Mr. Flores's pants leg; "Cookie, cookie." "Not yet Carlos. We'll have lunch first. Cookies are after lunch."
- Kai (age 20 months) finishes her lunch and gets up. "No nap today. Play with dollies." Ms. Moore picks her up; "Nap first. You can play with the dolls later."
- "Time to put the toys away, Kate." Kate (age 30 months) answers, "Not now. I'll do it a big later on."
- Chris (3 years old) sits with Mrs. Raymond. Chris says, "Last night we stayed

SAMPLE ASSESSMENT TASK

5H   **Preoperational Ages 4–5**
Time—Labeling and Sequence: Unit 15

METHOD: Interview.

SKILL: Shown pictures of daily events, the child can use time words to describe the action in each picture and place the pictures in a logical time sequence.

MATERIALS: Pictures of daily activities such as meals, nap, bath, playtime, bedtime.

PROCEDURE: Show the child each picture. Say, "**Tell me about this picture. What's happening?**" After the child has described each picture, place all the pictures in front of him, and tell the child, "**Pick out (show me) the picture of what happens first each day.**" After the child selects a picture, ask him, "**What happens next?**" Continue until all the pictures are lined up.

EVALUATION: When describing the pictures, note whether the child uses time words such as breakfast time, lunchtime, playtime, morning, night, and so on. Note whether he uses a logical sequence in placing the pictures in order.

INSTRUCTIONAL RESOURCE: Charlesworth, R. (2011). *Experiences in math for young children* (6th ed.). Belmont, CA: Wadsworth/Cengage Learning.

SAMPLE ASSESSMENT TASK

4I   **Preoperational Ages 3–6**
Time—Identify Clock or Watch: Unit 15

METHOD: Interview.

SKILL: The child can identify a clock and/or watch and describe its function.

MATERIALS: One or more of the following timepieces: conventional clock and watch, digital clock and watch. Preferably at least one conventional and one digital should be included. If real timepieces are not available, use pictures.

PROCEDURE: Show the child the timepieces or pictures of timepieces. Ask, "**What is this? What does it tell us? What is it for? What are the parts, and what are they for?**"

EVALUATION: Note whether the child can label watch(es) and clock(s) and how much she is able to describe about the functions of the parts (long and short hands, second hands, alarms set, time changer, numerals). Note also if the child tries to tell time. Compare her knowledge of conventional and digital timepieces.

INSTRUCTIONAL RESOURCE: Charlesworth, R. (2010). *Experiences in math for young children* (6th ed.). Belmont, CA: Wadsworth/Cengage Learning.

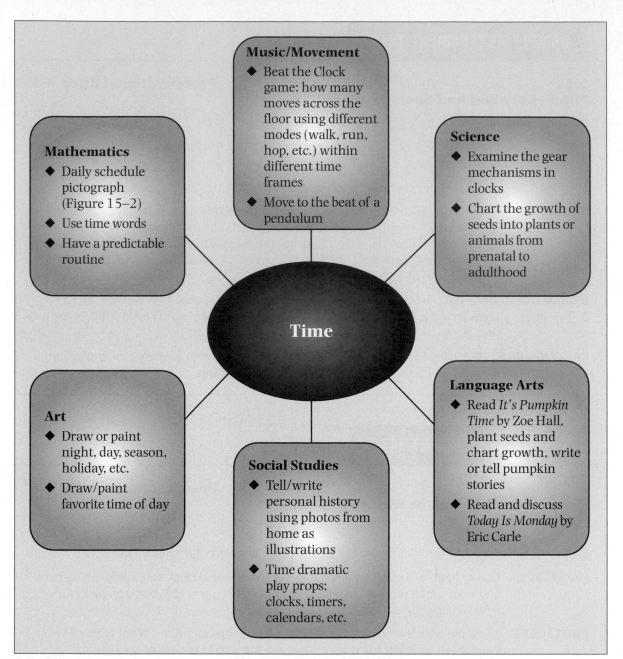

FIGURE 15–1 Integrating time experiences across the curriculum.

at the beach house." "Oh yes," answers Mrs. Raymond, "You were at the beach last summer, weren't you?" (For Chris, anything in the past happened "last night.")

- Mr. Flores is showing the group a book with pictures of the zoo. Richard (4 years old) com-

ments, "I want to go there yesterday." Mr. Flores says, "We'll be going to the zoo on Friday."

- Rosa (6 years old) says, "One time, when I was real small, like three or something, _____." Her teacher listens as Rosa relates her experience.

A consistent routine is the basis of the young child's understanding of time.

It is important for the young child to have a predictable and regular routine because it is through this routine that the child gains his sense of time duration and time sequence. It is also important for him to hear time words and to be listened to when he tries to use his time ideas. It is especially important that his own time words be accepted. For instance Kate's "a big later on" and Chris's "last night" should be accepted. Kate shows an understanding of the future and Chris of the past even though they are not as precise as an adult would be.

Informal Activities

The adult needs to capitalize on the child's efforts to gain a sense of time and time sequence. Reread the situations described in the previous section. In each, the adults do some informal instruction. Mr. Flores reminds Brad of the coming sequence. So do Ms. Moore and the adult with Kate. Mrs. Raymond accepts what Chris says but also uses the correct time words "last summer." It is important that adults listen to and expand on what children say.

The adult serves as a model for time-related behavior. The teacher checks the clock and the calendar for times and dates. She uses the time words listed in the Language of Time section. She makes statements and asks questions.

- "*Good morning*, Tom."
- "*Goodnight*, Mary. See you *tomorrow*."
- "What did you do over the *weekend*?"
- "Who will be our guest for lunch *tomorrow*?"
- "*Next week* on *Tuesday* we will go to the park for a picnic."
- "Let me check the *time*. No wonder you are hungry. It's almost *noon*."
- "You are the *first* one here *today*."

Children will observe and imitate what the teacher says and does even before they understand the ideas completely.

An excellent tool for informal classroom time instruction is a daily picture/word schedule placed in a prominent place. Figure 15–2 is an example of such a schedule. Children frequently ask, "When do we _____?" "What happens after this?" and so on. Teachers can take them to the pictorial schedule and help them find the answer for themselves. "What are we doing now?" "Find (activity) on the schedule." "What comes next?" Eventually, children will just have to be reminded to "Look at the schedule," and they will answer their own questions.

Adult Guided Activities

Adult guided time and sequence activities include sequence patterns with beads, blocks, and other objects; sequence stories; work centering around the calendar; and work centering around clocks. Experiences with pattern sequence and story sequence can begin at an early age. The infant enjoys looking at picture books, and the toddler can listen to short stories and begin to use beads and clocks to make her own sequences. The more adult guided

pattern, story, calendar, clock, and other time activities described next are for children older than 4½ years.

Ideas for Children with Special Needs

Working with diverse families, time is an important factor to keep in mind, because different cultures vary in their view of time. It is important to respect these views and try to work with families that view time in different ways. Westerners, particularly Americans and Europeans, view scheduling and organization of time as critical in managing any organization, including schools and classrooms. Clocks, watches, and calendars run Western culture. Time is viewed as a commodity not to be wasted, and being late is considered rude. Yet other cultures have different views. For example, Latin Americans, Middle Easterners, and Native Americans view time as being more indefinite. The Chinese are also less concerned with time and schedules. When these two kinds of views meet, conflict and confusion can result. If we are socialized to depend on clock time, then promptness is valued. If we are geared to natural events such as the rising and setting of the sun or the time it takes to finish the job, then promptness is not so important. As it applies to schooling, some families may not (at least initially) value being "on time." The importance of not missing essential instructional events can be explained, but children and parents should not be punished; instead, they should be helped to see the importance of Western beliefs and uses of time to being successful in Western culture.

Evaluation

The teacher should note whether the child's use of time words increases. He should also note whether her sense of time and sequence develops to a more

DAILY SCHEDULE

8:00–8:30 A.M.
Breakfast

8:30–9:00 A.M.
Playtime
Outdoors or in Gym

9:00–9:15 A.M.
Group Meeting

9:15–10:30 A.M.
Center Activities

10:30–10:45 A.M.
Snack

10:45–11:15 A.M.
Playtime
Outdoors or in Gym

FIGURE 15–2a: A picture/word daily schedule supports the development of the concept of time sequence. (continued on next page).

11:15–11:45 A.M
Story and Language
Development Group Activities

11:45–12:00 A.M
Wash Hands, Go to
Lunch

12:00–12:30 P.M
Lunch

12:30–1:00 P.M
Playtime
Outdoors or in Gym

1:00–2:00 P.M
Rest

2:00–3:00 P.M
Art, Music, Writing,
Reading

3:00–3:30 P.M
Clean-up
Prepare to Leave or
Go to Extended Day

FIGURE 15–2b *continued*

Activities

Time: Sequence Patterns, What Is *Next*?

OBJECTIVE: To be able to understand and use the sequence idea of *next*.

MATERIALS: Any real things that can be easily sequenced by category, color, shape, size, etc. For example:
- Wooden beads and strings.
- Plastic eating utensils.
- Poker chips or buttons or coins.
- Shapes cut from cardboard.
- Small toy animals or people.

NATURALISTIC AND INFORMAL ACTIVITIES: If they have had opportunities to explore the materials, the children should be familiar with the names of all the items and be able to identify their colors. For example, a child selects all the horses from a container of animals: "You have all the horses: brown ones (teacher points), black (teacher points), and white (teacher points)."

ADULT GUIDED ACTIVITIES: Use plastic eating utensils for this activity. Use knives (K), forks (F), and spoons (S) in three colors (C1, C2, and C3). Set up a pattern to present to the child. Present many kinds of patterns, including any of the following.
- *Color*: C1–C2–C1–C2 …
      C2–C3–C3–C2–C3–C3 …
- *Identity*: K–F–S–K–F–S …
      K–S–S–K–S–S …

Say to the child: "**This pattern is knife–fork–spoon**" (or whatever pattern is set up). Ask, "**What comes next?**" Once the child has the idea of pattern, set up the pattern and say, "**This is a pattern. Look it over. What comes next?**"

FOLLOW-UP: Do the same activity with some of the other materials suggested. Also try it with the magnet board, flannelboard, and chalkboard.

Time: Sequence Stories

OBJECTIVE: To learn sequences of events through stories.

MATERIALS: Picture storybooks[1] that have clear and repetitive sequences of events, such as:
- *The Gingerbread Man*
- *The Three Little Pigs*
- *The Three Billy Goats Gruff*
- *Henny Penny*
- *Caps for Sale*
- *Brown Bear, Brown Bear*
- *Polar Bear, Polar Bear*

---

[1] References are given in Appendix B.

NATURALISTIC AND INFORMAL ACTIVITIES: Place the books in the library center where children can make selections during center time, rest time, or book time. Note which children appear to be familiar with the stories as they turn the pages pretending to read to themselves, a friend, or a doll or stuffed animal.

ADULT GUIDED ACTIVITIES: Read the stories several times until the children are familiar with them. Begin by asking, "**What happens next?**" before going on to the next event. Have the children say some of the repeated phrases such as "Little pigs, little pigs, let me come in," "Not by the hair on my chinny-chin-chin," "Then I'll huff and I'll puff and I'll blow your house in." Have the children try to repeat the list of those who chase the gingerbread man. Have them recall the whole story sequence.

FOLLOW-UP: Obtain some sequence story cards, such as Life Cycles Puzzles and Stories from Insect Lore or Lakeshore's Logical Sequence Tiles and Classroom Sequencing Card Library. Encourage children to reenact and retell the stories and events that are read to them. Encourage them to pretend to read familiar storybooks. This kind of activity helps with comprehending the stories and the sequences of events in them.

Time: Sequence Activity, Growing Seeds

OBJECTIVE: To experience the sequence of the planting of a seed and the growth of a plant.

MATERIALS: Radish or lima bean seeds, Styrofoam cups, a sharp pencil, a 6-inch paper plate, some rich soil, a tablespoon.

NATURALISTIC AND INFORMAL ACTIVITIES: During center time, provide dirt and small shovels, rakes, pots, and so on, in the sand and water table. Talk with the children about what else they might need to grow something. Note if they talk about planting seeds.

ADULT GUIDED ACTIVITIES:
1. Give the child a Styrofoam cup. Have her make a drainage hole in the bottom with the sharp pencil.
2. Set the cup on the paper plate.
3. Have the child put dirt in the cup up to about an inch from the top.
4. Have the child poke three holes in the dirt with her pointer finger.
5. Have her put one seed in each hole and cover the seeds with dirt.
6. Have the child add one tablespoon of water.
7. Place the pots in a sunny place, and watch the seeds' sequence of growth.
8. Have the children water the plants each day. Ask them to record how many days go by before the first plant pops through the soil.

FOLLOW-UP: Plant other types of seeds. Make a chart or obtain a chart that shows the sequence of growth of a seed. Discuss which steps take place before the plant breaks through the ground. In the fall, use the book *It's Pumpkin Time* by Zoe Hall (1999) to introduce a seed project and explain how we get the pumpkins we carve for Halloween.

Time: The First Calendar

OBJECTIVE: To learn what a calendar is and how it can be used to keep track of time.

MATERIALS: Cut a one-week calendar from poster board with sections for each of the seven days, identified by name. In each section, cut tabs with a razor blade to hold signs made to be slipped under the tabs to indicate special times and events or the daily weather. These signs may have pictures of birthday cakes, items seen on field trips, umbrellas to show rainy days, the sun to show fair days, and so on.

NATURALISTIC AND INFORMAL ACTIVITIES: In the writing center or in the dramatic play center, place a number of different types of calendars. Note if the children know what they are and if they use them in their pretend play activities. Ask them to explain how they are using the calendars. Where else have they seen them? Who uses them?

ADULT GUIDED ACTIVITIES: Each day discuss the calendar. Use the following key questions:
- **Who knows today's name?**
- **Who remembers yesterday's name?**
- **Who knows tomorrow's name?**
- **What special day comes this week (birthday, holiday, field trip)?**
- **What did we do yesterday?**
- **Do we go to school on saturday and sunday?**
- **How many days until_____?**
- **How many days of the week do we go to school?**
- **What day of the week is the first day of school?**
- **What day of the week is the last day of school?**

CAUTION: You do not have to ask every question every day, nor spend more than 2–3 minutes. The calendar is still an abstract item for young children (see Beneky, Ostrosky, & Katz, 2008; Schwartz, 1994).

FOLLOW-UP: Read *Today Is Monday* by Eric Carle (1993). Discuss which foods the students like to eat on each day of the week. They could draw/dictate/write their own weekly menus.

Time: The Use of the Clock

OBJECTIVE: To find out how the clock is used to tell us when it is time to change activity.

MATERIALS: School wall clock and a handmade or a purchased large clock face such as that made by the Judy Company.

NATURALISTIC AND INFORMAL ACTIVITIES: Place a large wooden toy clock in the dramatic play center. Note if the children use it as a dramatic play prop. Do they use time words? Do they make a connection to the clock on the classroom wall or to the daily schedule picture?

ADULT GUIDED ACTIVITY: Point out the wall clock to the children. Show them the toy clock face. Let them move the hands around. Explain how the clock face is made just like the real clock face. Show them how you can set the hands on the clock face so that they are the same as the ones on the real clock. Each day set the clock face for important times (e.g., cleanup, lunch, time to get up from the nap). Explain that when the real clock and the clock face have their hands in the same place, it will be time to (do whatever the next activity is).

FOLLOW-UP: Do this every day. Soon each child will begin to catch on and check the clocks. Instead of asking "When do we get up from our nap?" they will be able to check for themselves.

Time: Beat the Clock Game

OBJECTIVE: To learn how time limits the amount of activity that can be done.

MATERIALS: Minute Minder or similar timer.

NATURALISTIC AND INFORMAL ACTIVITIES: Note how children react to time limit warnings (e.g., five minutes until cleanup). Use a signal (bell, buzzer, dim the lights, etc.) as a cue. Note if the children react with an understanding of time limits (five minutes until we go outside).

ADULT GUIDED ACTIVITIES: Have the child see how much of some activity he can do in a set number of minutes—for example, in three, four, or five minutes.
1. How many pennies can be put in a penny bank one at a time?
2. How many times can he bounce a ball?
3. How many paper clips can he pick up one at a time with a magnet?
4. How many times can he move across the room: walking, crawling, running, going backward, sideways, etc. Set the timer between three and five minutes. When the bell rings, have the child stop. Then count to find out how much the child accomplished.

FOLLOW-UP: Try many different kinds of activities and different lengths of time. Have several children do the tasks at the same time. Who does the most in the time given?

Time: Discussion Topics for Language

OBJECTIVE: To develop use of time words through discussion.

MATERIALS: Pictures collected or purchased. Pictures could show the following:
- Day and night.
- Activities that take a long time and a short time.
- Picture sequences that illustrate times of day, yesterday, today, and tomorrow.
- Pictures that illustrate seasons of the year.
- Pictures that show early and late.

NATURALISTIC AND INFORMAL ACTIVITIES: During center time, place the time pictures on a table. Observe as the children examine the pictures. Note if they use any time words. Ask them to describe the pictures.

ADULT GUIDED ACTIVITIES: Discuss the pictures using the key time words.

FOLLOW-UP: Put pictures on the bulletin board that the children can look at and talk about during their center time.

MATH TECHNOLOGY FOR
YOUNG CHILDREN

Use one of the evaluation schemes suggested in Unit 2 to evaluate one of the following resources:

- *Trudy's Time and Place House* (San Francisco: Riverdeep-Edmark). Includes clocks and calendars.
- *Shapes, Numbers, and Measurement* (http://www.campustech.com). Includes time and temperature activities.
- *James Discovers Math* (http://www.smartkids.com). Includes telling time.
- *Telling Time by the Hour Sheet* (Arlington, MA: Dositey Corporation).
- *Destination Math* (http://www.riverdeep.net). Includes length, weight, clock, and calendar time.
- *Match-Time CD-ROM* (http://www.k12software.com). Time concepts.
- *Time—Analog and Digital Clocks, and Time-Match Clocks at National Library of Virtual Manipulatives* (http://nlvm.usu.edu).

mature level: Does she remember the order of events? Can she wait until one thing is finished before she starts another? Does she talk about future and past events? How does she use the calendar? The clock? The sequence stories? The teacher may use the individual interview tasks in this unit and Appendix A.

Summary

The young child begins to learn that time has duration and that time is related to sequences of events. The child first relates time to his personal experience and to his daily sequence of activities. It is not until the child enters the concrete operations period that he can use units of time in the ways that adults use them.

For the most part, the young child learns his concept of time through naturalistic and informal experiences. When he is about the age of 4½ or 5, he can do adult guided activities as well. It is important to understand that some families from non-Western cultures may not view time as Westerners do.

KEY TERMS

cultural time
duration
duration (time) words
general (time) words

personal experience
relational (time) words
sequence
social activity

special days
specific (time) words

SUGGESTED ACTIVITIES

1. Observe some young children engaged in group play. Record any examples of time measurement that take place. What stage of measurement did each incident represent?
2. Plan and gather materials for at least one time sequence and one time measurement activity.

Do the activities with a small group of young children. Report the results in class.
3. Add some time measurement activities to your File/Notebook.

REVIEW

A. Describe and compare time sequence and time duration.
B. Decide if the children's comments that follow reflect (a) time sequence, (b) time duration, or (c) neither sequence nor duration:
 1. A child playing with a ball says, "The ball went up high."
 2. Mario asks his dad, "Please read me a bear story at bedtime."
 3. Janie says, "I stayed with Grandma for three nights."
 4. Lindsey says, "I love to play with Daddy for hours and hours."
 5. Li says, "It's lunchtime, everybody."
 6. Donny says, "This box weighs a million tons."
 7. Tina sighs, "It took me a long time to draw the pictures in my dog book."

C. Explain the three kinds of time. Include an example of each type.
D. Decide which of the words in the following list are (a) general time words, (b) specific time words, (c) relational words, (d) duration words, or (e) special day words:
 1. Yesterday
 2. Three hours
 3. This afternoon
 4. Easter
 5. Twice
 6. Four years old
 7. Birthday
 8. Two minutes
 9. Today
E. Explain the NCTM (2000) expectations for preschool/kindergarten time understanding.

REFERENCES

Beneke, S. J., Ostrosky, M. M., & Katz, L. G. (2008). Calendar time for young children: Good intentions gone awry. *Young Children, 63*(3), 12–16.
Carle, E. (1993). *Today is Monday*. New York: Scholastic Books.
Hall, Z. (1999). *It's pumpkin time*. New York: Scholastic Books.

National Council of Teachers of Mathematics. (2000). *Principles and standards for school mathematics*. Reston, VA: Author.
Schwartz, S. (1994). Calendar reading: A tradition that begs remodeling. *Teaching Children Mathematics, 1*(2), 104–109.

FURTHER READING AND RESOURCES

Barnes, M. K. (2006). "How many days 'til my birthday?" Helping kindergarten students understand calendar connections and concepts. *Teaching Children Mathematics, 12*(6), 290–295.
Church, E. B. (1997, January). "Is it time yet?" *Early Childhood Today*, 33–34.
Copley, J. V. (Ed.). (2004). *Showcasing mathematics for the young child* (chap. 5, Measurement). Reston, VA: National Council of Teachers of Mathematics.
Dacey, L., Cavanagh, M., Findell, C. R., Greenes, C. E., Sheffield, L. J., & Small, M. (2003). *Navigating through measurement in*

prekindergarten–grade 2. Reston, VA: National Council of Teachers of Mathematics.
Friederitzer, F. J., & Berman, B. (1999). The language of time. *Teaching Children Mathematics, 6*(4), 254–259.
Harms, J. M., & Lettow, L. J. (2007). Nurturing children's concepts of time and chronology through literature. *Childhood Education, 83*(4), 211–218.
Pliske, C. (2000). Natural cycles: Coming full circle. *Science and Children, 37*(6), 35–39, 60.
Shreero, B., Sullivan, C., & Urbano, A. (2002). Math by the month: Calendar math. *Teaching Children Mathematics, 9*(2), 96.

Interpreting Data Using Graphs

OBJECTIVES

After reading this unit, you should be able to:

- Explain the use of graphs.
- Describe the three stages that young children go through in making graphs.
- List materials to use for making graphs.
- Describe the NCTM expectations for preschool and kindergarten level graphing activities and understanding.

The NCTM (2000, p. 108) expectations for data analysis for prekindergarten and kindergarten focus on the ability of children to sort and classify objects according to their attributes, organize data about the objects, and describe the data and what they show. "The main purpose of collecting data is to answer questions when the answers are not immediately obvious" (NCTM, 2000, p. 109). Children's questions should be the major source of data. The beginnings of data collection are included in the fundamental concepts learned and applied in classifying in a logical fashion (see Unit 7).

Data collection activities can begin even before kindergarten, as students collect sets of data from their real-life experiences and depict the results of their data collection in simple graphs. Consider the following example from Ms. Moore's classroom.

Ms. Moore hears George and Sam talking in loud voices. She goes near them and hears the following conversation:

GEORGE: "More kids like green than blue."
SAM: "No! No! More like blue!"
GEORGE: "You are all wrong."
SAM: "I am not. You are wrong."

Ms. Moore goes over to the boys and asks, "What's the trouble, boys?" George replies, "We have to get paint to paint the house Mr. Brown helped us build. I say it should be green. Sam says it should be blue."

Sam insists, "More kids like blue than green."

Ms. Moore asks, "How can we find out? How do we decide on questions like who will be our next president?" George and Sam looked puzzled. Then George says, "I remember when Mom and Dad voted. We could have the class vote." Sam agreed that this would be a good idea. Ms. Moore then asked them how they might have all the students vote. George and Sam were afraid that if they asked for a show of hands their classmates might just copy whoever voted first. Ms. Moore then suggested that they put out a green box and a blue box and a bowl of green and blue cube blocks. George's eyes lit up. "I see then each person could vote by putting either a blue block in the blue box or a green block in the green box." Sam agreed.

After setting up the boxes and blocks, Sam and George go around the room. They explain the problem to each child. Each child comes over to the table, chooses one block of the color he likes better, and places the block in the matching box. When the voting is completed, George and Sam empty the boxes and stack the blocks as shown in Figure 16–1.

Ms. Moore asks the boys what the vote shows. Sam says, "The green stack is higher. More children like the idea of painting the house green." "Good," answers Ms. Moore, "Would you like me to write that down for you?" Sam and George chorus, "Yes!"

"I have an idea," says George, "Let's make a picture of this for the bulletin board so everyone will know. Will you help us, Ms. Moore?"

Ms. Moore shows them how to cut out squares of green and blue papers to match each of the blocks used. The boys write "green" and "blue" on a piece of white paper and then paste the green squares next

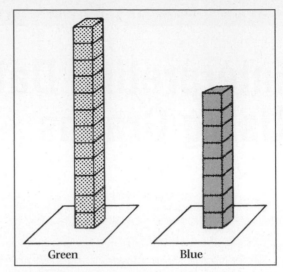

FIGURE 16–1 A three-dimensional graph that compares children's preferences for green or blue.

to the word "green" and the blue squares next to the word "blue." Ms. Moore shows them how to write the title: "Choose the Color for the Playhouse." Then they glue the description of the results at the bottom. The results can be seen in Figure 16–2.

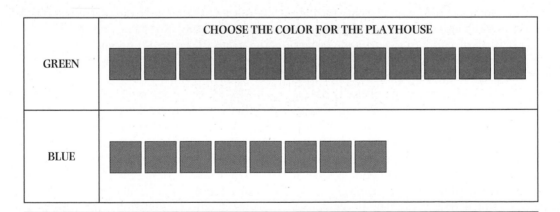

FIGURE 16–2 The color preference graph is copied using squares of green and blue paper, and the children dictate their interpretation.

In the preceding example, the teacher helped the children solve their problem by helping them make two kinds of graphs. **Graphs** are used to show visually two or more comparisons in a clear way. When a child makes a graph, he uses basic skills such as classification, counting, comparing quantities, one-to-one matching, and communicating through describing data. By making a concrete structure or a picture that shows some type of information, they visualize a variety of different quantities. Graphing provides an opportunity to apply several fundamental concepts and skills, as illustrated in Figure 16–3.

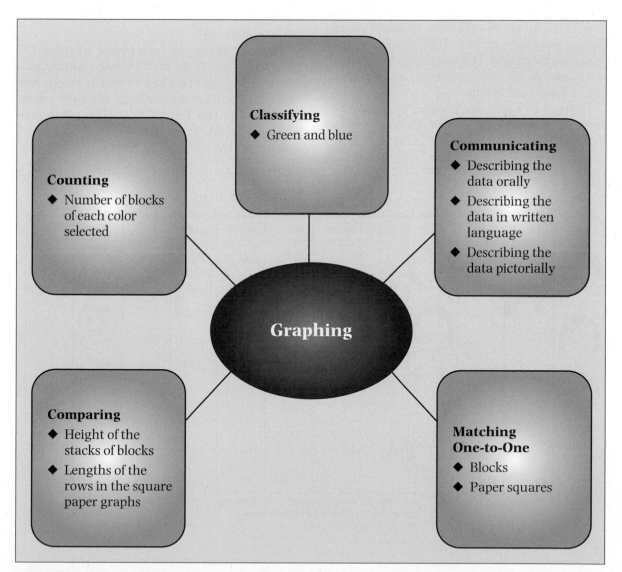

FIGURE 16–3   Graphing can be used to describe data in any of the content areas and provides an opportunity to apply fundamental concepts and skills.

Stages of Development for Making and Understanding Graphs

The types of graphs young children can construct progress through five stages of development. The first three stages are described in this unit; the fourth is included in Unit 20, and the fifth in Unit 25. In **stage one, object graphs**, the child uses real objects to make her graph. Sam and George used cube blocks. At this stage only two things are compared. The main basis for comparison is one-to-one correspondence and visualization of length and height.

In **stage two, picture graphs**, more than two items are compared. In addition, a more permanent record is made—such as when Sam and George glued squares of colored paper on a chart for the bulletin board. An example of this type of graph is shown in Figure 16–4. The teacher has lined off 12 columns on poster board (or large construction paper). Each column stands for one month of the year. The teacher gives each child a paper circle. Crayons, water markers, glue, and yarn scraps are available, so each child can draw her own head and place it on the month for her birthday. When each child has put her "head" on the graph, the children can compare the months to see which month has the most birthdays.

In **stage three, square paper graphs**, the children progress through the use of more pictures to block charts. They no longer need to use real objects but can start right off with cutout squares of paper. Figure 16–5 shows this type of graph. In this stage, the children work more independently.

Jan.	Feb.	March	April	May	June	July	August	Sept.	Oct.	Nov.	Dec.

April has the most birthdays. There are four.
March and October have no birthdays.
Three months have three.
One month has two.
Five months have one.

FIGURE 16–4 "When is your birthday?"

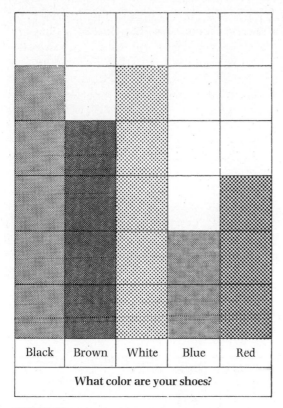

Black	Brown	White	Blue	Red

What color are your shoes?

FIGURE 16–5   A block graph made with paper squares.

Discussion of a Graph

As the children talk about their graphs and dictate descriptions for them, they use the following concept words:

less than	the same as
more than	none
fewer than	all
longer, longest	some
shorter, shortest	a lot of
the most	higher
the least	taller

Materials for Making Graphs

Many kinds of materials can be used for the first-stage graphs. An example has been shown in which cube blocks were used. Other materials can also be used.

At first it is best to use materials that can be kept in position without being knocked down or pushed apart by young children. Stands can be made from dowel rods. A washer or curtain ring is then placed on the dowel to represent each thing or person (Figure 16–6(A)). Strings and beads can be used. The strings can be hung from hooks or a rod; the lengths are then compared (Figure 16–6(B)). Unifix Cubes (Figure 16–6(C)) or pop beads (Figure 16–6(D)) can also be used.

Once the children have worked with the more stable materials, they can use the cube blocks and any other things that can be lined up. Poker chips, bottle caps, coins, spools, corks, and beans are good for this type of graph work (Figure 16–7).

At the second stage, graphs can be made with these same materials, but with more comparisons made. Then the children can go on to more permanent recording by gluing down cutout pictures or markers of some kind (Figure 16–8).

At the third stage, the children can use paper squares. This prepares the way for the use of squared paper (see Unit 20).

Many interesting graphing materials are available on the Internet and in the form of software. See the technology box that follows.

Topics for Graphs

Children can research any type of student question and put the information into graphical form. For example, a group of kindergartners collected information about their school bus (Colburn & Tate, 1998), and another group of young children studied a tree that grows on their campus (El Harim, 1998).

Once children start making graphs, they often think of problems to solve on their own. The following are some comparisons that might be of interest:

- Number of brothers and sisters.
- Hair color, eye color, clothing colors.
- Kinds of pets children have.

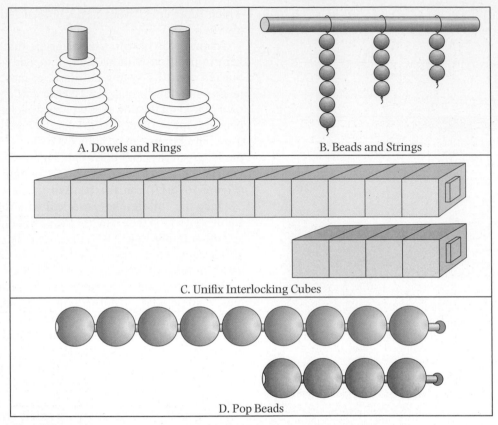

A. Dowels and Rings

B. Beads and Strings

C. Unifix Interlocking Cubes

D. Pop Beads

FIGURE 16–6 Four examples of three-dimensional graph materials.

MATH TECHNOLOGY FOR
YOUNG CHILDREN

Use one of the evaluation schemes suggested in Unit 2 to evaluate one of the following graphing resources (all from Sunburst: 1-800-321-7511; fax, 1-888-800-3028).

- *Numbers Recovered*. Includes creating and interpreting graphs.
- *Graphers*. Manipulation and creation of a variety of graphs.
- *Tabletop Jr.* Grouping, sorting, and classifying data; graphing and interpreting data; measurement.
- *The Graph Club*. For creative projects and displays of data.

Also explore online:

- At NCTM Illuminations see *Bar Grapher* and *Circle Grapher*. Also look through Data Analysis and Probability Web Links (NCTM.org).
- At the National Library of Virtual Manipulatives Data Analysis and Probability site, see *Bar Chart* and *Pie Chart* (nlvm.usu.edu).

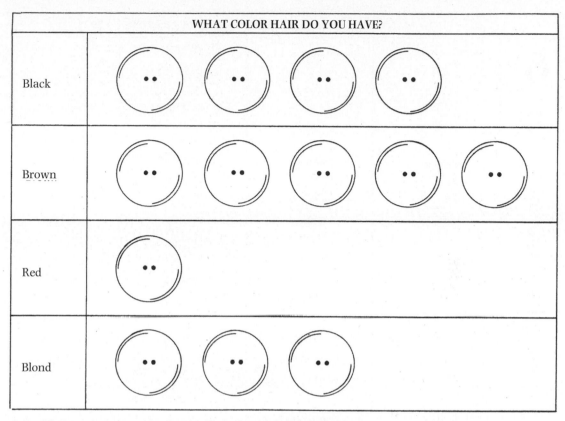

FIGURE 16–7 Graph made with buttons glued to cardboard.

- Heights of children in the class.
- Number of children in class each day.
- Sizes of shoes.
- Favorite TV programs (or characters).
- Favorite foods.
- Favorite colors.
- Favorite storybooks.
- Type of weather each day for a month.
- Number of cups of water or sand that will fill different containers.
- Time, in seconds, to run across the playground.
- Number of baby hamsters class members predict that their female hamster will bear.
- Number of days class members predict that it will take for their bean seeds to sprout.
- Data obtained regarding sinking and floating objects (Unit 10).

- Comparison of the number of seeds found in an apple, an orange, a lemon, and a grapefruit.
- Students' predictions regarding which items will be attracted by magnets.
- Frequency with which different types of insects are found on the playground.
- Distance that rollers will roll when ramps of different degrees of steepness are used.
- Comparison of the number of different items that are placed in a balance pan to weigh the same as a standard weight.
- Frequency count of each color in a bag of M&M's, Skittles, or Trix.
- Frequency with which the various combinations of yellow and orange show up when the counters (orange on one side and yellow on the other) are shaken and then tossed out on the table.

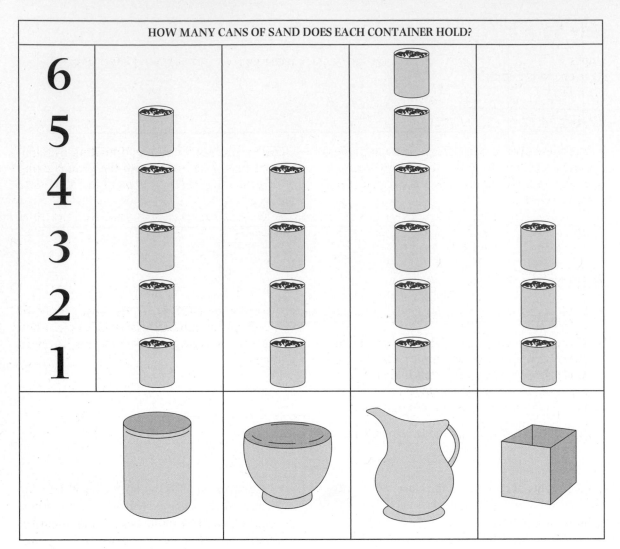

FIGURE 16–8   Graph made with paper cutouts.

Summary

Making graphs provides children an opportunity for using some basic math skills in a creative way. Children can put into picture form the results of classifying, comparing, counting, and measuring activities. Graphs also serve as a means of integrating mathematics with other content areas, such as science and social studies, by providing a vehicle for depicting and analyzing data.

The first graphs are three-dimensional and are made with real objects. The next are made with pictures, and the next with paper squares. Children can discuss the results of their graph projects and dictate a description of the graph's meaning to be put on the bulletin board alongside the graph.

KEY TERMS

graphs

stage one, object graphs

stage three, square paper graphs

stage two, picture graphs

SUGGESTED ACTIVITIES

1. Interview several prekindergarten and kindergarten teachers. Find out if and how they use graphs in their classrooms. Report your findings in class.
2. With a small group of 4–6-year-olds, discuss some topics that might be of interest for collecting information and making a graph. Then make the graph with the group. Bring the graph to class, and explain the process to the class.
3. Add ideas for graphs to your Activity File/Notebook.

REVIEW

A. Explain the importance and values of graph making.
B. There are three levels of making and understanding graphs that are appropriate for prekindergarten and kindergarten students. Name and describe each of these stages.
C. Sketch out three graphs that are representative of (respectively) each of the three beginning stages of graph making.

D. Describe the NCTM (2000) expectations for preschool and kindergarten students constructing and analyzing information displayed in graphs.

REFERENCES

Colburn, K., & Tate, P. (1998). The big, yellow laboratory. *Science and Children, 36*(1), 22–25.

El Harim, J. L. (1998). A tremendous learning experience. *Science and Children, 35*(8), 26–29.

National Council of Teachers of Mathematics. (2000). *Principles and standards for school mathematics*. Reston, VA: Author.

FURTHER READING AND RESOURCES

Copley, J. V. (Ed.). (2004). *Showcasing mathematics for the young child* (chap. 6, Data Analysis). Reston, VA: National Council of Teachers of Mathematics.

Cengiz. N., & Grant, T. J. (2009). Children generate their own representations. *Teaching Children Mathematics, 15*(7), 438–444.

Cook, C. D. (2008). I scream. you scream: Data analysis with kindergartners, *Teaching Children Mathematics*, *14*(9), 538–542.

Curcio, F. R., & Folkson, S. (1996). Exploring data: Kindergarten children do it their way. *Teaching Children Mathematics, 2*, 382–385.

Greenes, C. E., Dacey, L., Cavanagh, M., Findell, C. R., Sheffield, L. J., & Small, M. (2003). *Navigating through problem solving and reasoning in prekindergarten–kindergarten*. Reston, VA: National Council of Teachers of Mathematics.

Lacefield, W. O., III. (2009). The power of representation: Graphs and glyphs in data analysis lessons for young children. *Teaching Children Mathematics, 15*(6), 324–326.

Lamphere, P. (1994). Classroom data. *Teaching Children Mathematics, 1*, 28–31.

Litton, N. (1995). Graphing from A to Z. *Teaching Children Mathematics, 2*, 220–223.

Sheffield, L. J., Cavanagh, M., Dacey, L., Findell, C. R., Greenes, C. E., & Small, M. (2002). *Navigating through data analysis and probability in prekindergarten–grade 2*. Reston, VA: National Council of Teachers of Mathematics.

Whitin, D. J., & Whitin, P. (2003). Talk counts: Discussing graphs with young children. *Teaching Children Mathematics, 10*(3), 142–149.

Integrating the Curriculum through Dramatic Play and Thematic Units and Projects

After reading this unit, you should be able to:

- Describe how children apply and extend concepts through dramatic play.
- Describe how children apply and extend concepts through thematic units and projects.
- Encourage dramatic role-playing that promotes concept acquisition.
- Recognize how dramatic role-playing and thematic units and projects promote interdisciplinary instruction and learning.
- Use dramatic play and thematic units and projects as settings for science investigations, mathematical problem solving, social learning, and language learning.
- Connect the math standards to integrated curriculum.

The NCTM (2000) standards for mathematics focus on content areas skills, understandings, and processes that can be applied across the curriculum. Children can apply and experience problem solving, reasoning, communication, connections, and hands-on learning through *dramatic play, thematic and project approaches*, and an **integrated curriculum**. **Play** is the major medium through which children learn (Unit 1). They experiment with grown-up roles, explore materials, and develop rules for their actions (Eisenhauer & Feikes, 2009). Curriculum that meets the national standards can be implemented using **thematic units and projects** that integrate mathematics, science, social studies, language arts, music, and movement. The teacher (Isbell, 1995) and/or the child (Helm & Katz, 2001; Katz & Chard, 1989) may select themes. Integrated curriculum can also support state standards (Akerson, 2001; Clark, 2000; Decker, 1999).

Integrated curriculum can easily include mathematics. Remember that mathematics is composed of fundamental concepts that are used for thinking in all the content areas (Whitin & Whitin, 2001, 2008).

These concepts are used to investigate the world. According to the authors, the adults can provide authentic, real-world learning experiences to children using two strategies: (1) having children make direct observations and (2) posing questions or "wonders" based on these observations (Whitin & Whitin, 2001, p. 1, 2008).

For example, a first-grade class went outside in February to look for insects. They wondered why they did not find any. This question led to the study of the life cycles of insects, which applied the children's knowledge of time. A month later they found insects in abundance. The students took measurements (length) to find out how far grasshoppers can jump. Their observations caused them to wonder why spiders make webs in corners (spatial relations). Eventually, the class made a map of the best places to find bugs. This type of activity exemplifies a student-selected project that applies mathematics to answer questions developed from observation (Whitin & Whitin, 2001, 2008).

The purpose of this unit is to demonstrate how dramatic play and thematic units can enrich children's acquisition of concepts and knowledge, not only in mathematics but also in the other content areas. Furthermore, these areas offer rich settings for social learning, science investigations, and mathematical problem solving. This unit emphasizes the natural play of young children as the basis for developing thematic units that highlight the potentials for an interdisciplinary curriculum for young children. Peggy Ashbrook (2009) describes how children can engage in a science investigation exploring safe odors. They can integrate math by making a chart of the smells they investigated and placing a tally mark by their favorite. They can count up the tally marks for each food and graph the result. Geist and Geist (2008) integrate music and math while Whitin and Piwko (2008) integrate poetry and math.

Concepts and skills are valuable to children only if they can be used in everyday life. Young children spend most of their waking hours involved in play. Play can be used as a vehicle for applying concepts. Young children like to feel big and do "big person" things. They like to pretend they are grown up and want to do as many grown-up things as they can. Role-playing can be used as a means for children to apply what they know as they take on a multitude of grown-up roles.

Dramatic role-playing is an essential part of thematic units. For example, using food as the theme for a unit could afford opportunities for children not only to apply concepts and carry out science investigations and mathematics problem solving but also to try out adult roles and do adult activities. Children can grow food and shop for groceries; plan and prepare meals, snacks, and parties; serve food; and enjoy sharing and eating the results of their efforts. Teachers can offer children opportunities that provide experiences for social education as they learn more about adult tasks, have experiences in the community, and learn about their own and other cultures. Teachers can use these experiences to assess and evaluate children through observation.

Butterworth and Lo Cicero (2001) described a project that grew from the interests of 4- and 5-year-old Latino children in a transitional kindergarten class. The teachers used the Reggio Emilia approach (Edwards, Gandini, & Forman, 1998) in developing the project. That is, they began with the children's culture. In this case they had the children tell stories about their trips to the supermarket and transformed these stories into math problems. The market provided a setting that led the children naturally to talk about quantity and money. After presenting their stories, the children reenacted them through dramatic play. They pretended to buy fruit and take it home to eat. Setting the table naturally posed problems in rational counting and one-to-one correspondence. The project continued on into more complex problems and other types of child-selected dramatic play.

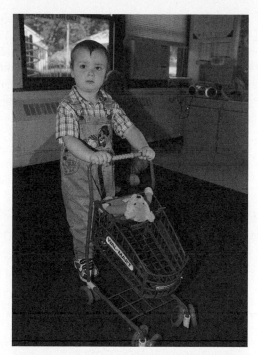

With his grocery cart and his "babies," this boy is ready to shop.

As their dramatic play experience increases, children can add more realistic props and personalities to a setting. This girl has learned that she needs a cash register to "ring out" a customer who is buying these tacos.

Dramatic Role-Playing

When children are engaged in dramatic role-playing, they practice what it is like to be an adult. They begin with a simple imitation of what they have observed. Their first roles reflect what they have seen at home. They bathe, feed, and rock babies. They cook meals, set the table, and eat. One of their first outside experiences is to go shopping, which is soon reflected in dramatic play. They begin shopping by carrying things in bags, purses, and other large containers. At first, they carry around anything that they can stuff in their containers. Gradually, they move into using more realistic props such as play money and empty food containers. Next, they might build a store with big blocks and planks. Eventually, they learn to play cooperatively with other children. One child might be the mother, another the father, another the child, and another the store clerk. As the children move toward this stage, teachers can provide more props and background experiences that will expand the raw material children have for developing their role-playing. Problem-solving skills are refined as children figure out who will take which role, provide a location for the store and home, and develop the rules for the activity.

Children can learn about adult roles through field trips to businesses such as restaurants, banks, the post office, and stores both in the local neighborhood and in the extended community. Museums, construction sites, hospitals, fire stations, and other places offer experiences that can enrich children's knowledge of adult roles. Books, tapes, films, and classroom visitors can also provide valuable experiences for children. Following such experiences, teachers can provide props to support children's dramatic role-playing. They can also set up each type of business or service center in the classroom with appropriate props.

Some examples of dramatic play centers and props follow:

- Set up a toy store by having the children bring old toys from home, which they could pretend to buy and sell.
- Set up a grocery store using items that might otherwise be discarded, such as empty food containers, which the children could bring from home. The children could make food

from play dough, clay, or papier-mâché. Plastic food replicas can be purchased.

- Organize a clothing store into departments for children, ladies, and men; children can bring discarded clothing and shoes from home.
- Stock a jewelry store with old and pretend jewelry (such as macaroni necklaces and cardboard watches).
- Stock services centers such as the post office, fire station, police station, automobile repair shop, hospital, beauty shop, and the like, with appropriate props.
- Build transportation vehicles such as space vehicles, automobiles, trucks, and buses with large blocks, lined-up chairs, or commercially made or teacher-made steering wheels and other controls.
- Set up a zoo, veterinarian's office, circus, farm, or pet shop. Have children bring stuffed animals from home to live in the zoo, visit the vet, act in the circus, live on the farm, or be sold in the pet shop. Classify the animals as to which belong in each setting. Children can predict which animals eat the most, are dangerous to humans, are the smartest, and so on. Provide play money to pay for goods and services.
- Organize health and medical service centers. Provide props for medical play. Tie these plays in with discussions of good nutrition and other health practices. The children can "pay the bill" for the services, and the medical staff can tell the patients their temperatures and count their heart beats.
- Create space science vehicles. Provide props for space travel (e.g., a big refrigerator carton that can be made into a spaceship, paper bag space helmets, and so on). Provide materials for making mission control and designing other planetary settings. Students can count down to lift off, decide how many passengers and crew can make the trip, and estimate the miles to their destination and the time for the trip.
- Create water environments. Provide toy boats, people, rocks for islands, and the like. Discuss floating and sinking. Outdoors, use water for firefighter play and watering the garden. Have a container (bucket or large dishpan) that can

be a fishing hole, and use waterproof fish with a safety pin or other metal object attached so they can be caught with a magnet fish bait. Investigate why the magnet/metal combination makes a good combination for pretend fishing. Count how many fish each child catches.

- Set up simple machines. Vehicles, a packing box elevator, a milk carton elevator on a pulley, a plank on rollers, and so on, make interesting dramatic play props, and their construction and functioning provide challenging problems for investigation.

Concepts are applied in a multitude of play activities such as those just described. The following are some examples:

- One-to-one correspondence can be practiced by exchanging play money for goods or services.
- Sets and classifying are involved in organizing each dramatic play center in an orderly manner (e.g., placing all the items in the drugstore in the proper place).
- Counting can be applied to figuring out how many items have been purchased and how much money must be exchanged.
- Comparing and measuring can be used to decide if clothing fits, to determine the weight of fruits and vegetables purchased, to check a sick person's temperature, and to decide on which size box of cereal or carton of milk to purchase.
- Spatial relations and volume concepts are applied as items purchased are placed in bags, boxes, and/or baskets and as children discover how many passengers will fit in the space shuttle or can ride on the bus.
- Number symbols can be found throughout dramatic play props—for example, on price tags, play money, telephones, cash registers, scales, measuring cups and spoons, thermometers, rulers, and calculators.

Pocket calculators are excellent props for dramatic play. Children can pretend to add up their expenses, costs, and earnings. As they explore calculators, they will learn how to use them for basic mathematical operations. Methods for introducing calculators are described in Units 18 through 20. (See resources in Figure 17–1.)

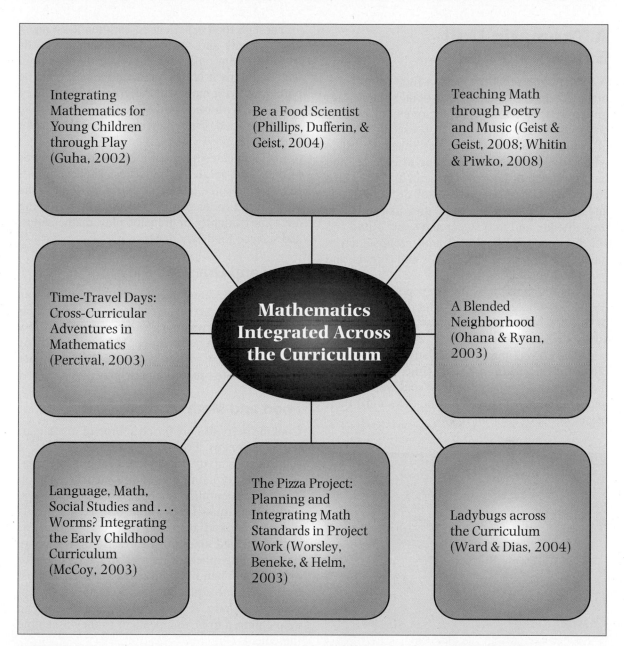

FIGURE 17–1   Examples of resources for integrating mathematics across the curriculum.

A Thematic Unit Example: Food

A thematic unit that focuses on food can involve many science, mathematics, social studies, language arts, art, music, and movement experiences. As scientists, children observe the growth of food, the physical changes that take place when food is prepared, and the effects of food on the growth of humans and animals. They also compare the tastes and smells of different foods and categorize them into those they like and those they dislike; and into sweet and sour; liquid and solid; "junk" and healthful; and groups such as meat and dairy products, breads and cereals, and fruits and vegetables.

As mathematicians, children pour, measure, count, cut wholes into parts, and divide full pans or full bowls into equal servings. They count the strokes when mixing a cake, make sure the oven is on the correct temperature setting, and set the clock for the required baking time. At the store, they exchange money for food and weigh fruits and vegetables. They count the days until their beans sprout or the fruit ripens.

These boys are dramatizing based on their cooking experiences.

Through food experiences, children learn much about society and culture. They can make foods from different cultures. They learn where food is grown, how it is marketed, and how it must be purchased with money at the grocery store. They cooperate with one another and take turns when preparing food. Then they share what they make with others.

Children can sing about food and draw pictures of their food-related experiences. They can move like an eggbeater, a stalk of wheat blowing in the wind, or a farmer planting seeds. The following are some examples of dramatic play, mathematics, and science food experiences.

Food and Dramatic Play

In the home living center at school, children can purchase, cook, serve, and eat food as part of their role-playing. It was suggested in Unit 14 that a simple measuring activity could be to make flour and salt dough. Children can make the dough into pretend food to use as dramatic play props.

Food and Math

Cooking activities are a rich source of mathematics experiences. Following a recipe provides a sequencing activity. Each ingredient must be measured exactly using a standard measuring tool. The correct number of cups, tablespoons, eggs, and so on, must be counted out. Baked foods must be cooked at the correct temperature for the prescribed amount of time. Some foods are heated, while others are placed in the refrigerator or freezer. When the food is ready to eat, it must be divided into equal portions so that each person gets a fair share. A simple pictograph recipe can help children to be independent as they assemble ingredients (Figure 17–2).

Children who live in the country or who have a garden have additional opportunities to apply math concepts to real-life experiences. They can count the number of days from planting the seed until the food is ready to be picked. They can measure the growth of the plants at regular intervals. They can also measure the number of cucumbers

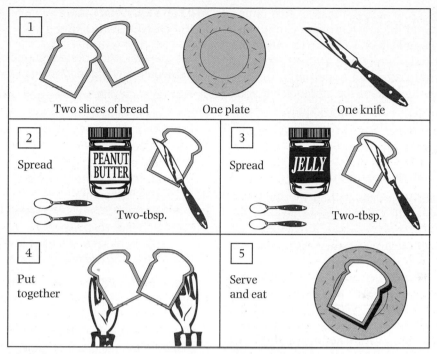

FIGURE 17–2   A pictograph for making a peanut butter and jelly sandwich.

harvested and the weight of the potatoes. If the child lives where livestock can be kept, he can count the daily number of eggs gathered, weigh the young calf each week, and count the amount of money collected for products sold.

Setting the table at the home living center or for a real meal provides an opportunity for children to apply math skills. They can calculate the number of people to be seated and served and match it with the amount of tableware and the number of chairs, napkins, and place mats needed. Putting utensils and dishes away is an experience in sorting things into sets. Pictographs can be used to provide clues about where each type of item should be placed.

Food and Science

Each of the activities described under the previous section also involves science. The adult can ask the children to predict what will happen when the wet ingredients (oil and milk) are mixed with the dry ingredients (flour, baking powder, and salt) when making the play dough biscuits. Children can then make the mixture; observe and describe its texture, color, and density; and compare their results with their predictions. Next, they can predict what will happen when the dough is baked in the oven. When it is taken out, they can observe and describe the differences that take place during the baking process. The adult can also ask the children what would happen if the oven is too hot or if the biscuits are left in too long.

If the children have the opportunity to see eggs produced, it can lead to a discussion of where the eggs come from and what would happen if the eggs were fertilized. They could observe the growth from seed to edible food as vegetables are planted, cultivated, watered, and picked. Applesauce exemplifies several physical changes: from whole to parts, from solid chunks to soft lumps and to smooth and thick as cutting, heating, and grinding each has an effect. Children can also note the change in taste before and after the sugar is added. Stone soup offers an opportunity for discussing the significance of the stone. What does the stone add to the soup? Does a stone have nutrients? What really makes the soup taste good and makes it nutritious?

Food and Social Studies

Each of the activities described involves social studies as well. City children might take a trip to the farm. For example, a trip to an orchard to get apples for applesauce is an enriching and enjoyable experience. They might also take a trip to the grocery store to purchase the ingredients needed in their recipes. Then they can take turns measuring, cutting, adding ingredients, or whatever else is required as the cooking process proceeds. Stone soup is an excellent group activity because everyone in the class can add an ingredient. Invite people from different cultures to bring foods to class and/or help the children make their special foods. Children can note similarities and differences across cultures.

Ideas for Children with Special Needs

The multicultural curriculum can include learning about the favorite foods of different cultures. Children can make a variety of ethnic dishes. They can construct graphs of their favorite foods and write their favorite recipes. Young children can come up with delightful recipes for a class cookbook. Projects can center on the study of ethnic groups, geographical area, and customs of different cultures. Parents can contribute to these projects. Costumes, dolls, musical instruments, and other diverse cultural artifacts can be included in the dramatic play center.

MATH TECHNOLOGY
FOR YOUNG CHILDREN

Use the evaluation system suggested in Unit 2 to evaluate any of the following resources:

- *Rainbow Fish* (ages 3–7; http://childrenssoftwareonline.com).
- *Ani's Rocket Ride* (http://www.apte.com).
- *Coco's Math Project 2* (http://mathequity.terc.edu).
- *Math Missions* (Scholastic, http://www.kidsclick.com).
- *Richard Scarry's Busytown* (Simon & Schuster, http://www.childrenssoftwareonline.com).
- *Shopping Math* (http://www.dositey.com).

Devise a plan for using one of these resources to stimulate a thematic unit or project that includes dramatic play. Find out whether there are any online resources that could be used to support a thematic unit or project.

Summary

Dramatic play and thematic units and projects provide math, science, and social studies experiences that afford children an opportunity to apply concepts and skills. They can predict, observe, and investigate as they explore these areas. As children play home, store, and service roles, they match, count, classify, compare, measure, and use spatial relations concepts and number symbols. They also practice the exchange of money for goods and services. Through dramatic play they try out grown-up roles and activities.

Through thematic units and projects, mathematics can be integrated with other content areas. The thematic experiences provide real-life connections for abstract concepts. For teachers, these activities offer valuable opportunities for naturalistic and informal instruction as well as time to observe children and assess their ability to use concepts in everyday situations.

KEY TERMS

dramatic	integrated	play
role-playing	curriculum	thematic units and projects

SUGGESTED ACTIVITIES

1. Observe young children at play in school. Note if any concept experiences take place during dramatic role-playing or while doing thematic activities. Share what you observe with your class.
2. Review several cookbooks (the ones suggested in this unit and/or others), and examine recipes recommended for young children. Explain to the class which recipe books you think are most appropriate for use with young children.
3. Add a section to your Activity File for dramatic play and thematic projects. Include five food experiences that enrich children's concepts and promote the application of concepts.

REVIEW

A. Briefly answer each of the following questions:
   1. Why should dramatic role-playing be included as a math, science, and social studies concept experience for young children?
   2. Why should food activities be included as math, science, and social studies concept experiences for young children?
   3. How can teachers encourage dramatic role-playing that includes concept experiences?
   4. Describe four food activities that can be used in the early childhood math, science, and social studies program.
   5. Explain how thematic units promote an integrated curriculum.

B. Describe the props that might be included in three different dramatic play centers.

C. Describe the relationship between the integrated curriculum and the math standards.

REFERENCES

Akerson, V. L. (2001). Teaching science when your principal says, "Teach Language Arts." *Science & Children, 38*(7), 42–47.

Ashbrook, P. (2009). Safe smelling. *Science & Children, 47*(2), 19–20.

Butterworth, S., & Lo Cicero, A. M. (2001). Storytelling: Building a mathematics curriculum from the culture of the child. *Teaching Children Mathematics, 7*(7), 396–399.

Clark, A. M. (2000). Meeting state standards through the project approach. *Eric/EECE Newsletter, 12*(1), 1–2.

Decker, K. A. (1999). Meeting state standards through integretion. *Science & Children, 36*(6), 28–32, 69.

Edwards, C., Gandini, L., & Forman, G. (Eds.). (1998). *The hundred languages of children: The Reggio Emilia approach—Advanced reflections.* Greenwich, CT: Ablex.

Eisenhauer, M. J., & Feikes, D. (2009). Dolls, blocks, and puzzles: Playing with mathematical understandings. *Young Children, 64*(3), 18–24.

Geist, K., & Geist, E. A. (2008). Do re mi, 1-2-3: That's how easy math can be. *Young Children, 63*(2), 20–25.

Helm, J. H., & Katz, L. G. (2001). *Young investigators: The project approach in the early years.* New York: Teachers College Press.

Isbell, R. (1995). *The complete learning center book.* Beltsville, MD: Gryphon House.

Katz, L. G., & Chard, S. C. (1989). *Engaging children's minds: The project approach.* Norwood, NY: Ablex.

National Council of Teachers of Mathematics. (2000). *Principles and standards for school mathematics.* Reston, VA: Author.

Whitin, D. J., & Piwko, M. (2008). Mathematics and poetry: The right connection. *Young Children, 63*(2), 34–39.

Whitin, D., & Whitin, P. (2001). Where is the mathematics in interdisciplinary studies? *Dialogues* [On-line serial]. Retrieved July 17, 2008, from http://www.nctm.org/resources/content.aspx?id=1684

Whitin, D., & Whitin, P. (2008). *Where is the mathematics in interdisciplinary studies?* Retrieved July 18, 2008, from http://www.nctm.org

FURTHER READING AND RESOURCES

Guha, S. (2002). Integrating mathematics for young children through play. *Young Children, 57*(3), 90–92.

McCoy, M. K. (2003). Language, math, social studies, and … worms? Integrating the early childhood curriculum. *Dimensions of Early Childhood, 31*(2), 3–8.

Percival, I. (2003). Time-travel days: Cross-curricular adventures in mathematics. *Teaching Children Mathematics, 9*(7), 374–380.

Ward, C. D., & Dias, M. J. (2004). Ladybugs across the curriculum. *Science and Children, 41*(7), 40–44.

Worsley, M., Beneke, S., & Helm, J. H. (2003). The pizza project: Planning and integrating math standards in project work. In D. Koralek (Ed.), *Spotlight on young children and math* (pp. 35–42). Washington, DC: National Association for the Education of Young Children.

Theme, Project, and Integration

Clements, D. H., & Sarama, J. (2006). Math all around the room! *Early Childhood Today, 21*(2), 25–30.

Cook, H., & Matthews, C. E. (1998). Lessons from a "living fossil." *Science and Children, 36*(3), 16–19.

Draznin, Z. (1995). *Writing math: A project-based approach.* Glenview, IL: Goodyear Books.

Edelson, R. J., & Johnson, G. (2003/2004). Music makes math meaningful. *Childhood Education, 80*(2), 65–70.

Fogelman, Y. (2007). The early years: Water works. *Science and Children, 44*(9), 16–18.

Forrest, K., Schnabel, D., & Williams, M. (2006). Water wonders, K–2. *Teaching Children Mathematics, 12*(5), 248.

Johnson, G. L., & Edelson, R. J. (2003). Integrating music and mathematics in the elementary classroom. *Teaching Children Mathematics, 9*(8), 474–479.

Krogh, S., & Morehouse, P. J. (2007). *The early childhood curriculum: Inquiry learning through integration.* New York: McGraw-Hill.

Shreero, B., Sullivan, C., & Urbano, A. (2002). Math in art. *Teaching Children Mathematics, 9*(4), 218–220.

Smith, R. R. (2002). Cooperation and consumerism: Lessons learned at a kindergarten mini-mall. *Teaching Children Mathematics, 9*(3), 179–183.

Warner, L., & Morse, P. (2001). Studying pond life with primary-age children: The project approach in action. *Childhood Education, 77*(3), 139–143.

Yagi, S., & Olson, M. (2007). Supermarket math: K–2. *Teaching Children Mathematics, 13*(7), 376.

Cooking and Food

Albyn, C. L., & Webb, L. S. (1993). *The multicultural cookbook for students.* Phoenix, AZ: Oryx.

Better Homes and Gardens New Junior Cookbook (7th ed.). (2004). Des Moines, IA: Meredith.

Christenberry, M. A., & Stevens, B. (1984). *Can Piaget cook?* Atlanta, GA: Humanics.

Cloke, G., Ewing, N., & Stevens, D. (2001). Food for thought. *Teaching Children Mathematics, 8*(3), 148–150.

Colker, L. J. (2005). *The cooking book.* Washington, DC: National Association for the Education of Young Children.

Cook, D. (2006). *Family fun cooking with kids.* Burbank/Glendale, CA: Disney.

Cooking with Kids. A parent helper. Retrieved July 17, 2008, from http://www.pbs.org/parents/parenthelpers/cooking.html

Dahl, K. (1998). Why cooking in the curriculum? *Young Children, 53*(1), 81–83.

Faggella, K., & Dixler, D. (1985). *Concept cookery.* Bridgeport, CT: First Teacher Press.

Howell, N. M. (1999). Cooking up a learning community with corn, beans and rice. *Young Children, 54*(5), 36–38.

Metheny, D., & Hollowell, J. (1994). Food for thought. *Teaching Children Mathematics, 1,* 164.

Owen, S., & Fields, A. (1994). Eggs, eggs, eggs. *Teaching Children Mathematics, 1,* 92–93.

Partridge, E., Austin, S., Wadlington, E., & Bitner, J. (1996). Cooking up mathematics in the kindergarten. *Teaching Children Mathematics, 2,* 492–495.

Ray, R. (2004). Cooking rocks: *Rachael Ray 30 minute meals for kids.* New York: Lake Isle Press.

Richardson, M. V., Hoag, C. L., Miller, M. B., & Monroe, E. E. (2001). Children's literature and mathematics: Connections through cooking. *Focus on Elementary, 14*(2), 1–6.

Rothstein, G. L. (1994). *From soup to nuts: Multicultural cooking activities and recipes.* New York: Scholastic Books.

Taylor, S. I., & Dodd, A. T. (1999). We can cook! Snack preparation with toddlers and twos. *Early Childhood Education Journal, 27*(1), 29–33.

Symbols and Higher-Level Activities

Symbols

1 2 3 4 5 6 7 8 9 10

OBJECTIVES

After reading this unit, you should be able to:

- List the six number symbol skills.
- Describe the four basic types of self-correcting number symbol materials.
- Set up an environment that supports naturalistic and informal number symbol experiences for children.
- Do adult guided number symbol activities with children.

Number symbols are called **numerals**. Each numeral represents an amount and acts as a shorthand for recording *how many*. The young child sees numerals all around him (Figure 18–1). He has some idea of what they are before he can understand and use them. He sees that there are numerals on his house, the phone, the clock, and the car license plate. He may have one or more counting books. He may watch a children's TV program in which numeral recognition is taught. Sometime between the ages of 2 and 5, a child learns to name the numerals from 0 to 10. However, the child is usually 4 or older when he begins to understand that each numeral stands for a group of things of a certain amount that is always the same. He may be able to tell the name of the symbol "3" and count three objects, but he may not realize that the "3" can stand for the three objects or the **cardinal meaning** of three (see Figure 18–2).

It can be confusing to the child to spend time on drills with numerals before he has had many concrete experiences with basic math concepts. Most experiences with numerals should be naturalistic and informal.

The Number Symbol Skills

Young children acquire six number symbol skills during the preoperational period.

- They learn to recognize and say the name of each numeral.
- They learn to place the numerals in order: 0–1–2–3–4–5–6–7–8–9–10.
- They learn to associate numerals with groups: "1" goes with one thing.
- They learn that each numeral in order stands for one more than the numeral that comes

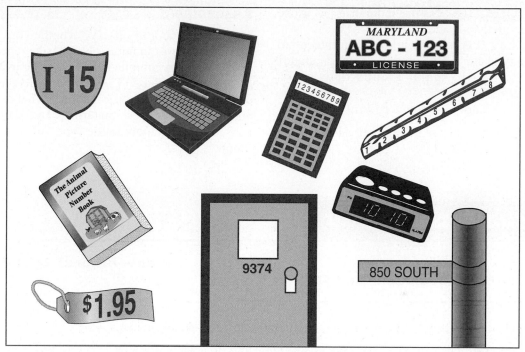

FIGURE 18–1 Numerals are everywhere in the environment.

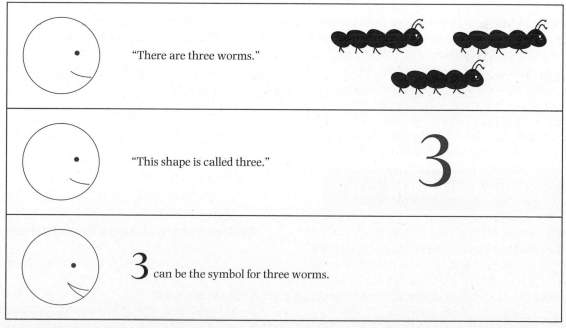

FIGURE 18–2 The child counts the objects, learns the symbol, and realizes that the symbol can represent the group.

before it (i.e., 2 is one more than 1, 3 is one more than 2, and so on).

- They learn to match each numeral to any group of the size the numeral stands for and to make groups that match numerals.
- They learn to reproduce (write) numerals.

The first four skills are included in this unit, and the last two in Unit 19.

Assessment

The teacher should observe whether the child shows an interest in numerals. Does he repeat the names he hears on television? Does he use self-correcting materials? (These are described in this unit's Informal Activities section.) What does he do when he uses these materials? Individual interviews would include the types of tasks that follow.

SAMPLE ASSESSMENT TASK

4J
Symbols, Recognition: Unit 18

Preoperational Ages 3–6

METHOD: Interview.

SKILL: Child is able to recognize numerals 0 to 10 presented in sequence.

MATERIALS: 5″ × 8″ cards with one numeral from 0 to 10 written on each.

PROCEDURE: Starting with 0, show the child each card in numerical order from 0 to 10.
Ask, "**What is this? Tell me the name of this.**"

EVALUATION: Note if the child uses numeral names (correct or not), indicating she knows the kinds of words associated with the symbols. Note which numerals she can label correctly.

INSTRUCTIONAL RESOURCE: Charlesworth, R. (2011). *Experiences in math for young children* (6th ed.). Belmont, CA: Wadsworth/Cengage Learning.

SAMPLE ASSESSMENT TASK

6J
Symbols, One More Than: Unit 18

Preoperational Ages 5 and Older

METHOD: Interview.

SKILL: Child is able to identify numerals that are "one more than."

MATERIALS: 5″ × 8″ cards with one numeral from 0 to 10 written on each.

PROCEDURE: Place the numeral cards in front of the child in order from 0 to 10. Ask, **"Tell me which numeral means one more than two. Which numeral means one more than seven? Which numeral means one more than four?" (If the child answers these questions,** then try "less than.")

EVALUATION: Note whether the child is able to answer correctly.

INSTRUCTIONAL RESOURCE: Charlesworth, R. (2011). *Experiences in math for young children* (6th ed.). Belmont, CA: Wadsworth/Cengage Learning.

SAMPLE ASSESSMENT TASK

5L   **Preoperational Ages 4–6**
Symbols, Sequencing: Unit 18

METHOD: Interview.

SKILL: Child is able to sequence numerals from 0 to 10.

MATERIALS: 5″ × 8″ cards with one numeral from 0 to 10 written on each.

PROCEDURE: Place all the cards in front of the child in random order. Say, **"Put them in order.** Ask, **Which comes first? Next? Next?"**

EVALUATION: Note whether the child seems to understand that numerals belong in a fixed sequence. Note how many are placed in the correct order and which, if any, are labeled.

INSTRUCTIONAL RESOURCE: Charlesworth, R. (2011). *Experiences in math for young children* (6th ed.). Belmont, CA: Wadsworth/Cengage Learning.

Naturalistic Activities

As the young child observes his environment, he sees numerals around him. He sees them on clocks, phones, houses, books, food containers, TV programs, money, calendars, thermometers, rulers, measuring cups, license plates, and on many other objects in many places. He hears people say number names, as in the following examples:

- My phone number is 622-7732.
- My house number is 1423.
- My age is 6.
- I have a five-dollar bill.
- The temperature is 78 degrees.
- Get a five-pound bag of rabbit food.
- We had three inches of rain today.
- This pitcher holds eight cups of juice.

Usually children start using the names of the number symbols before they actually match them with the symbols.

- Tanya and Juanita are ready to take off in their spaceship. Juanita does the countdown, "Ten, nine, eight, three, one, blast off!"
- Tim asks Ms. Moore to write the number 7 on a sign for his race car.

- Ako notices that the thermometer has numbers written on it.
- Becca is playing house. She takes the toy phone and begins dialing, "One-six-two. Hello dear, will you please stop at the store and buy a loaf of bread?"
- "How old are you, Pete?" "I'm six," answers 2-year-old Pete.
- "One, two, three, I have three dolls."
- Tanya is playing house. She looks up at the clock. "Eight o'clock and time for bed," she tells her doll. (The clock actually says 9:30 a.m.)

Children begin to learn number symbols as they look and listen and then, in their play, imitate what they have seen and heard.

Informal Activities

During the preoperational period, most school activities with numerals should be informal. Experimentation and practice in perception with sight and touch are most important. Children's activities with self-correcting manipulative materials provide these experiences. **Self-correcting materials** are those the child can use by trial and error to solve a problem without adult's assistance. The material is made in such a way that it can be used successfully with very little help. **Manipulative materials** are things that have parts and pieces that the child can pick up and move to solve the problem the materials present. The teacher observes the child as she works. He notes whether the child works in an organized way and whether she sticks with the material until she has finished the task.

There are four basic types of self-correcting manipulative math materials that can be used for informal activities. The teacher can buy or make these materials. The four basic groups of materials include those that teach discrimination and matching, those that teach sequence (or order), those that give practice in association of symbols with groups, and those that combine association of symbols and groups with sequence. Examples of each type are illustrated in Figures 18–3 through 18–5.

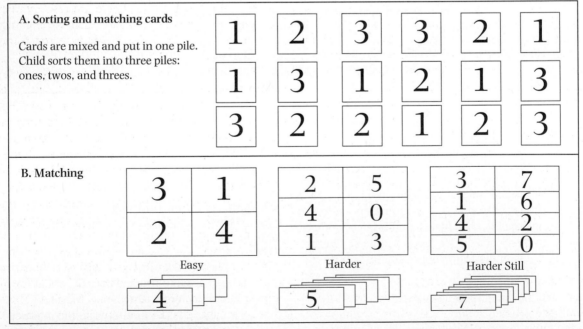

FIGURE 18–3 Sorting and matching.

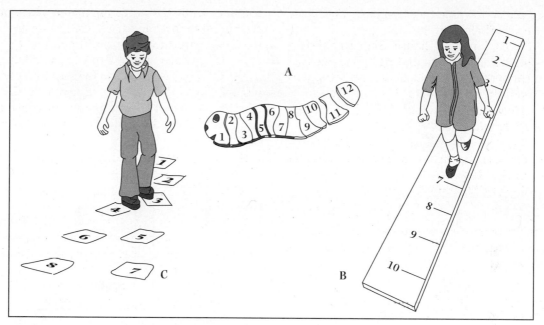

FIGURE 18–4 Materials that help the child learn numeral sequence.

The child can learn to discriminate one numeral from the other by sorting packs of numeral cards. She can also learn which numerals are the same as she matches. Another type of material that serves this purpose is a lotto-type game. The child has a large card divided equally into four or more parts. She must match individual numeral cards to each numeral on the big card. These materials are shown in Figure 18–3(A and B). She can also experiment with felt, plastic, magnetic, wooden, rubber, and cardboard numerals.

There are many materials that teach sequence or order. The teacher may set up these materials so that parts can only be put together in such a way that, when the child is done, she sees that the numerals are in order in front of her. An example is the Number Worm from Childcraft (Figure 18–4A) and Number Sequencing Puzzles from Lakeshore. The teacher can also teach sequence using a number line or number stepping-stones. The Childcraft giant Walk-On Number Line and the Didax floor Number Line let the child walk from one numeral to the next in order (Figure 18–4B). The teacher

can set out numerals on the floor (e.g., Stepping Stones from Childcraft) that the child must step on in order (Figure 18–4C). There are also number sequence wooden inset puzzles (such as Constructive Playthings' Giant Number Puzzle and Number Art Puzzle).

The hand calculator lends itself to informal exploration of numerals. First, show the students how to turn the calculator on and off. Tell them to watch the display window and then turn on the calculator. A "0" will appear first. Explain to them that when they first turn on their calculators a "0" will always appear. Then ask them to turn on their calculators and tell you what they see in the window. Have them practice turning their calculators on and off until you are sure they all understand this operation. Next, tell them to press "1." Ask them what they see in the window. Note if they tell you they see the same number. Next, have them press "2." A "2" will appear in the window next to the "1." Show them that they just need to press the C key to erase. Then let them explore and discover on their own.

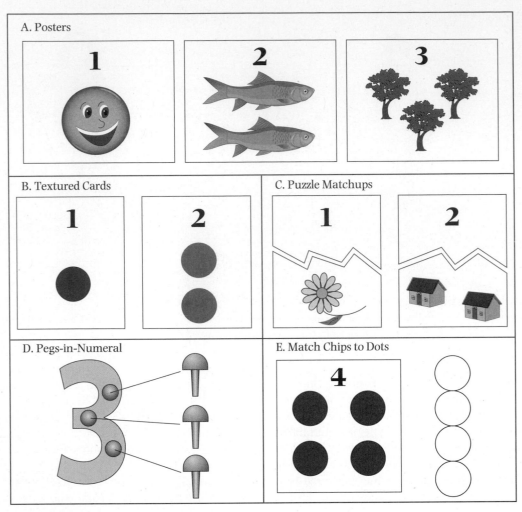

FIGURE 18–5 Numeral and group association.

Help them by answering their questions and posing questions to them such as, "What will happen if _____?"

The teacher can purchase many materials that help the child associate each numeral with the group that goes with it. He can place large posters on the bulletin board (can be found at http://abcteach.com/directory/basics/math/math_posters/) that give a visual association (Figure 18–5A). Children can see and touch numerals on textured cards, such as Didax Tactile Number Cards. The teacher can make numeral cards using sandpaper for the sets of dots and for the numerals (Figure 18–5B). Other materials require the child to use visual and motor coordination. She may have to match puzzle-like pieces (such as Number-Picture-Word Puzzles from Constructive Playthings; Figure 18–5C). She may put pegs in holes (such as Peg Number Boards from Lakeshore, Figure 18–5D). Unifix inset pattern boards require the same type of activity. The teacher can make cards that have numerals and dots the size of buttons or other counters. The child could place a counter on each dot (Figure 18–5E).

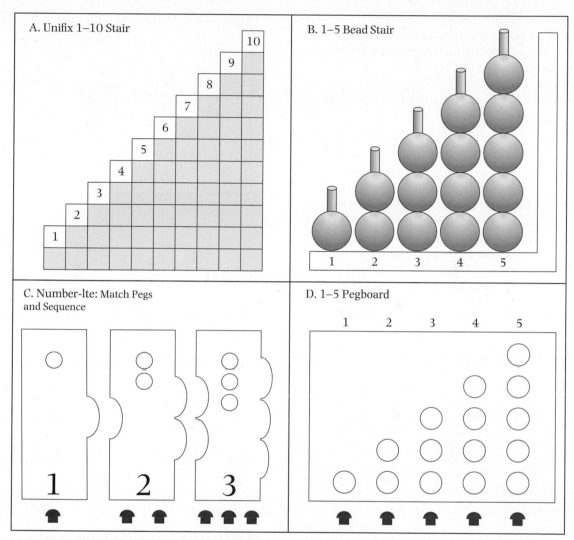

A. Unifix 1–10 Stair

B. 1–5 Bead Stair

C. Number-lte: Match Pegs and Sequence

D. 1–5 Pegboard

FIGURE 18–6 Sequence and association.

Materials that give the child experience with sequence and association at the same time are also available. Examples of these materials are shown in Figure 18–6. The basis of these materials is that the numerals are in a fixed order and the child adds some sort of counter that can be placed only in the right amount. Unifix® stairs are like the in-set patterns but are stuck together (Figure 18–6A).

Other materials illustrated are counters on rods (Figure 18–6B), sequence pegs in holes (Figure 18–6C), or 1–5 pegboard (Figure 18–6D).

The teacher's role with these materials is to show the child how they can be used and then step back and watch. After the child has learned to use the materials independently, the teacher can make comments and ask questions.

- How many pegs are on this one?
- Can you tell me the name of each numeral?
- You put in the four pegs that go with that numeral 4.
- How many beads are there here? (point to stack of one) How many here? (stack of two, and so on)
- Good, you separated all the numerals into piles. Here are all 1s, and here are all 2s.

The teacher can also introduce numerals informally as part of daily counting activities. For example, the class can keep track of the first 100 days of school (see Unit 6). Children can make a 100-number line around the room. They add the appropriate numeral each day to a number line strip after they have agreed on how many straws they have accumulated. The strip should be wide enough so that large-sized numerals (that the students can easily see) can be glued or written on it.

The children can draw special symbols representing special days, such as birthdays, Halloween, Thanksgiving, and so on, below the appropriate numeral on the line. The number line then serves as a timeline recording the class history. A weekly or monthly calendar may also be placed on the bulletin board next to the 100-days display. Calendars were introduced in Unit 15.

| 1 | 2 | 3 | 4 | 5 | 6 | 7 | 8 | 9 | 10 |

Through this informal use of materials, most children will learn to recognize and say the name of each numeral, to place the numerals in order, to see that each numeral stands for one more than the one before it, and to associate numerals with amounts. However, some children will need the adult guided activities described next.

Numeral	Amount in Group
0	
1	X
2	XX
3	XXX
4	XXXX
5	XXXXX
6	XXXXXX
7	XXXXXXX
8	XXXXXXXX
9	XXXXXXXXX
10	XXXXXXXXXX

Adult Guided Activities

By the time young children finish kindergarten, they should be able to do the following activities:

- Recognize the numerals from 0 to 10 or more.
- Place the numerals from 0 to 10 or more in order.
- Know that each numeral represents a group one larger than the numeral before (and one less than the one that comes next).
- Know that each numeral represents a group of things.

They may not always match the right numeral to the correct amount, but they will know that there is such a relationship. The 5-year-old child who cannot do one or more of the tasks listed needs some adult guided scaffolding.

Activities

Numerals: Recognition

OBJECTIVE: To learn the names of the number symbols.

MATERIALS: Write the numerals from 0 to 10 on cards.

NATURALISTIC AND INFORMAL ACTIVITIES: Place the cards in the math center for the children to explore. Note if children label and/or sequence the numerals or in any way demonstrate a knowledge of the symbols and what they mean. Ask questions such as, "What are those?" "Do they have names?"

ADULT GUIDED ACTIVITY: This is an activity that a child who can name all the numbers can do with a child who needs help. Show the numerals one at a time in order. Say, "**This numeral is called _____. Let's say it together**: _____." Repeat this for each numeral. After 10, say, "**I'll hold the cards up one at a time. You name the numeral.**" Go through once. Five minutes at a time should be enough.

FOLLOW-UP: Give the child a set of cards to review on his own.

Numerals: Sequence and One More Than

OBJECTIVE: To learn the sequence of numerals from 0 to 10.

MATERIALS: Flannelboard or magnet board, felt or magnet numerals, felt or magnet shapes (such as felt primary cutouts or magnetic geometric shapes).

NATURALISTIC AND INFORMAL ACTIVITIES: Place the numerals and shapes in the math center for the children to explore. Note if the children make groups and place numerals next to the groups. Ask questions such as, "How many does this numeral mean?" "Why does this numeral go next to this group?" "Tell me about your groups."

ADULT GUIDED ACTIVITY: Put the "0" up first at the upper left-hand corner of the board. Ask, "**What is this numeral called?**" If the child cannot tell you, say: **This is called zero**. Put the 1 numeral up next to the right. Ask, "**What is this numeral called**?" If the child cannot tell you, say: **This is 1. Say it with me. One**. Continue to go across until the child does not know two numerals in a row. Then, go back to the beginning of the row. Say, "**Tell me the name of this numeral. Yes, zero.**" Ask, "**What is the name of the next one? Yes, it is 1, so I will put one rabbit here.**" Put one rabbit under the 1. Ask, "**The next numeral is one more than 1. What is it called?**" After the child says "two" on his own or with your help, let him pick out two shapes to put on the board under the "2." Keep going across until you have done the same with each numeral he knows, plus two that he does not know.

FOLLOW-UP: Have the child set up the sequence. If he has trouble, ask: "**What comes next? What is one more than _____?**" Leave the board and the numerals and shapes out during playtime. Encourage the children who know how to do this activity to work with a child who does not.

Numerals: Recognition, Sequence, Association with Groups, One More Than

OBJECTIVE: To help the child to integrate the concepts of "association with groups" and "one more than" while learning the numeral names and sequence.

MATERIALS: Cards with numerals 0 to 10 and cards with numerals and groups 0 to 10.

NATURALISTIC AND INFORMAL ACTIVITIES: Place the cards in the math center for the children to explore. Note if the children make matches and/or sequences. Ask, "Can you tell me about what you are doing with the cards?"

ADULT GUIDED ACTIVITIES:

1. Say, **"I'm going to put down some cards. Each one has a numeral on it. They go up to 10. Say the names with me if you know them."**
2. Say, **"Here is another set of cards with numerals."** Give the cards with numerals and groups to the child. Say, **"Match these up with the other cards. Let's say the names as you match."**

FOLLOW-UP: Let the child do this activity on his own. Encourage him to use the self-correcting materials also.

Most of the resources described in Unit 6 include numeral recognition. See also the following technology box for additional recommendations. Number symbols can be incorporated in other content areas (Figure 18–7).

MATH TECHNOLOGY FOR
YOUNG CHILDREN

Use an evaluation system as suggested in Unit 2 to review and evaluate one of the following resources (see Unit 6 resources as well).

- *James Discovers Math* (http://www. smartkidssoftware.com). Includes number recognition.
- *Winnie the Pooh Ready for Math* (http:// www.amazon.com). Includes number recognition.
- *Arthur's Kindergarten* (http://www. smartkidssoftware.com). Activities in many areas including number.
- *1, 2, 3 Count With Me* (http://store. sesameworkshop.org/product/show). Video starring Ernie.
- *Learn About Numbers and Counting* (Elgin, IL: Sunburst). Includes counting and other concepts and skills.

Ideas for Children with Special Needs

Cristina Gillanders (2007) examined the factors that enabled an English-speaking prekindergarten teacher to successfully teach Latino ELLs. First and foremost were the teacher's efforts to develop a positive relationship with the students. The teacher took the time to learn some Spanish. Her use of Spanish, however meager, in the classroom gave the Latino children social status. The Latino children were then accepted by the English-speaking students as play partners. The teacher's experience as a second language learner gave her empathy for the Latino students' struggles with learning English. Providing one-to-one attention and a consistent routine helped the Latino children feel comfortable. The teacher spoke some Spanish in the classroom and included Spanish materials in her program. Some of the English-speaking children became enthralled with the bilingual songs and videotapes included in the program. She also enlisted the help of the Latino children in translations. Spanish became valued in the classroom and supported cross-language cooperative play. How does this example relate to mathematics? In any classroom the quality of the social/emotional climate is important. In math, presenting some concepts using Spanish or other

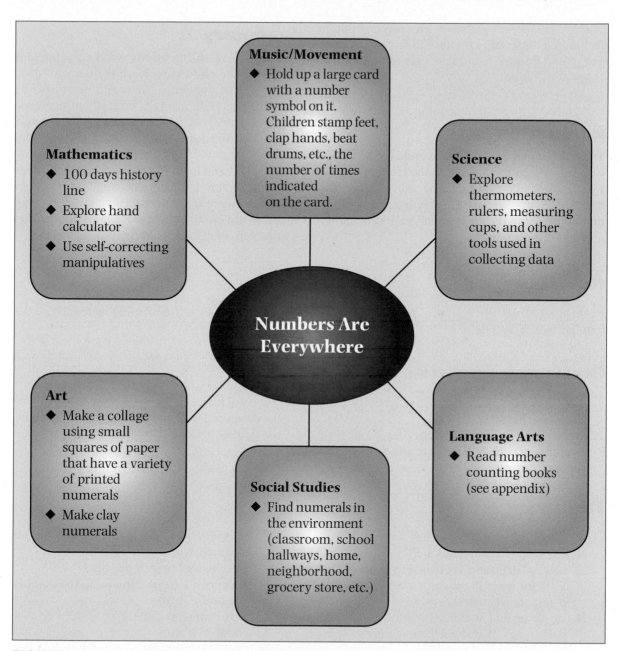

FIGURE 18–7 Integrating number symbol experiences across the curriculum.

primary language vocabulary can make children feel more comfortable because their primary language and culture become a valued part of the classroom culture.

Evaluation

The teacher may question each child as she works with the self-correcting materials. He should note which numerals she can name and whether she names them in sequence. He may interview her individually using the assessment questions in this unit and in Appendix A.

Summary

Numerals are the symbols used to represent amounts. The child must learn the name of each numeral. The sequence, or order, must also be learned. The child needs to understand that each numeral represents a group that is one larger than the one before (and one less than the one that comes next).

Most children learn the properties and purposes of numerals through naturalistic and informal experiences. There are many excellent self-correcting materials that can be bought or made for informal activities. Any adult guided activities should be brief.

KEY TERMS

cardinal meaning
manipulative materials

numerals

self-correcting materials

SUGGESTED ACTIVITIES

1. Add numeral activities to your Activity File/Notebook.
2. Make a number symbol game. Try it out with 4- and 5-year-olds. Report to the class on the children's responses.

3. Go to a school supply or toy store, and evaluate the developmental appropriateness of the number symbol materials you find.

REVIEW

A. Answer each of the following:
   1. Explain what numerals are.
   2. List and define the six number symbol skills.
   3. Explain what is meant by self-correcting manipulative materials.
   4. Describe and sketch examples of the four basic types of self-correcting number symbol manipulative materials.
   5. Describe the teacher's role in the use of self-correcting number symbol materials.
B. What type of number symbol knowledge might children gain from each of the following numeral materials?

1. Magnet board, 0–5 numerals, and various magnetic animals
2. Matchmates (match plaques)
3. A set of 11 cards containing the number symbols 0 to 10
4. Lotto numeral game
5. Number Worm
6. Pegs-in-Numerals
7. Unifix 1–10 Stair
8. Walk on Line
9. Number-Ite
10. 1-2-3 Puzzle
11. Hand calculator
12. Personal computer

REFERENCE

Gillanders, C. (2007). An English-speaking pre-kindergarten teacher of young Latino children: Implications of the teacher–child relationship on second language learning. *Early Childhood Education Journal, 35*(1), 47–54.

FURTHER READING AND RESOURCES

American Association for the Advancement of Science (AAAS). (2007). *Atlas of science literacy: Project 2061* (Vol. 2). Washington, DC: Author.

Box it or bag it mathematics (K–2). Portland, OR: Math Learning Center.

Bridges in mathematics (K–2). Portland, OR: Math Learning Center.

Brizuela, B. M. (2004). *Mathematical development in young children: Exploring notations*. New York: Teachers College Press.

Copley, J. V. (Ed.). (1999). *Mathematics in the early years*. Washington, DC: National Association for the Education of Young Children.

Copley, J. V. (2000). *The young child and mathematics*. Washington, DC: National Association for the Education of Young Children.

Epstein, A. S. (2007). *The intentional teacher*. Washington, DC: National Association for the Education of Young Children.

Fosnot, G. T., & Cameron, A. (2007). *Games for early number sense*. Portsmouth, NH: Heinemann.

Gallenstein, N. L. (2003). *Creative construction of mathematics and science concepts in early childhood*. Olney, MD: Association for Childhood Education International.

Haylock, D., & Cockburn, A. (2003). *Understanding mathematics in the lower primary years: A guide for teachers of children 3–8* (2nd ed.). Thousand Oaks, CA: Chapman.

Mix, K. S., Huttenlocher, J., & Levine, S. C. (2002). *Quantitative development in infancy and early childhood*. New York: Oxford University Press.

National Council of Teachers of Mathematics. (2000). *Principles and standards for school mathematics*. Reston, VA: Author.

Richardson, K. (1999). *Developing number concepts: Counting, comparing, and pattern* (Book 1). Parsippany, NJ: Seymour.

Wakefield, A. P. (1998). *Early childhood number games*. Boston: Allyn & Bacon.

Groups and Symbols

After reading this unit, you should be able to:

- Describe the three higher-level tasks that children do with groups and symbols.
- Set up an environment that provides for naturalistic and informal groups and symbols activities.
- Plan and do adult guided groups and symbols activities with young children.
- Assess and evaluate a child's ability to use math groups and symbols.

The activities in this unit build on many of the ideas and skills presented in earlier units: matching, numbers and counting, sets and classifying, comparing, ordering, and symbols. A curriculum focal point (NCTM, 2007) for kindergarten is the use of written numerals to represent quantities and solve simple quantitative problems.

The experiences in this unit will be most meaningful to the child who can already do the following activities:

- Match things one-to-one and match groups of things one-to-one.
- Recognize groups of one to four without counting and count groups up to at least ten things accurately.
- Divide large groups into smaller groups and compare groups of different amounts.

- Place groups containing different amounts in order from least to most.
- Name each of the numerals from 0 to 10.
- Recognize each of the numerals from 0 to 10.
- Be able to place each of the numerals in order from 0 to 10.
- Understand that each numeral stands for a certain number of things.
- Understand that each numeral stands for a group of things one more than the numeral before it and one less than the numeral after it.

When the child has reached the objectives in the preceding list, she can then learn to do the following activities:

- Match a symbol to a group; that is, if she is given a set of four items, she can pick out or write the numeral 4 as the one that goes with that group.

- Match a group to a symbol; that is, if he is given the numeral 4, he can make or pick out a group of four things to go with it.
- Reproduce symbols; that is, she can learn to write the numerals.

The movement from working with groups alone to working with groups and symbols and finally to symbols alone must be done carefully and sequentially. Mary Baratta-Lorton (1979) describes three levels of increasing abstraction and increasing use of symbols: the concept level, connecting level, and symbolic level. These three levels can be pictured as follows:

Concept level	ΔΔΔΔ	Number sense—child has concept of amounts.
Connecting level	ΔΔΔΔ 4	Child connects group amount with numeral.
Symbolic level	4	Child understands numeral is the symbol for an amount.

Units 6, 7, and 8 worked at the concept level. The connecting level, which was introduced informally, is the major focus of this unit. The symbolic level will be introduced in Unit 20.

Assessment

If the children can do the tasks in the assessments in Units 5 through 11, 13, and 18, then they have the basic skills and knowledge necessary to connect groups and symbols. In fact, they may be observed doing some symbol and grouping activities on their own if materials are made available for them to explore in the math center. The following are some individual interview tasks.

SAMPLE ASSESSMENT TASK

6M   **Preoperational/Concrete Ages 5–7**
Groups and Symbols, Match Symbols to Groups: Unit 19

METHOD: Interview.

SKILL: Child will be able to match symbols to groups using numerals from 0 to 10 and groups of amounts 0 to 10.

MATERIALS: 5″ × 8″ cards with numerals 0 to 10, ten objects (e.g., chips, cube blocks, buttons).

PROCEDURE: Lay out the cards in front of the child in numerical order. One at a time, show the child groups of each amount in this order: 2, 5, 3, 1, 4. Say, "**Pick out the numeral that tells how many things are in this group.**" If the child does these tasks correctly, go on to 7, 9, 6, 10, 8, 0 using the same procedure.

EVALUATION: Note which groups and symbols the child can match. The responses will indicate where instruction can begin.

INSTRUCTIONAL RESOURCE: Charlesworth, R. (2011). *Experiences in math for young children* (6th ed.). Belmont, CA: Wadsworth/Cengage Learning.

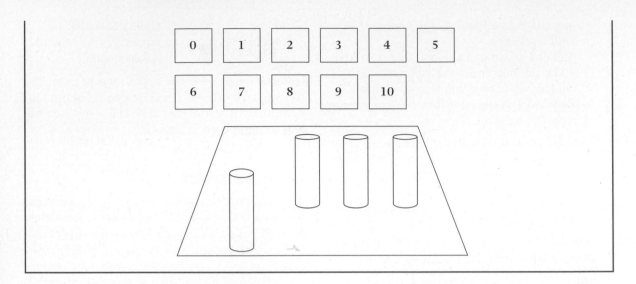

SAMPLE ASSESSMENT TASK

6L   **Preoperational/Concrete Ages 5–7**
Groups and Symbols, Match Groups to Symbols: Unit 19

METHOD: Interview.

SKILL: Child will be able to match groups to symbols using groups of amounts 0 to 10 and numerals from 0 to 10.

MATERIALS: 5″ × 8″ cards with numerals 0 to 10, 60 objects (e.g., chips, cube blocks, coins, buttons).

PROCEDURE: Lay out the numeral cards in front of the child in a random arrangement. Place the container of objects within easy reach. Say, "**Make a group for each numeral.**" Let the child decide how to organize the materials.

EVALUATION: Note for which numerals the child is able to make groups. Note how the child goes about the task. For example, does he sequence the numerals from 0 to 10? Does he place the objects in an organized pattern by each numeral? Can he recognize some amounts without counting? When he counts does he do it carefully? His responses will indicate where instruction should begin.

INSTRUCTIONAL RESOURCE: Charlesworth, R. (2011). *Experiences in math for young children* (6th ed.). Belmont, CA: Wadsworth/Cengage Learning.

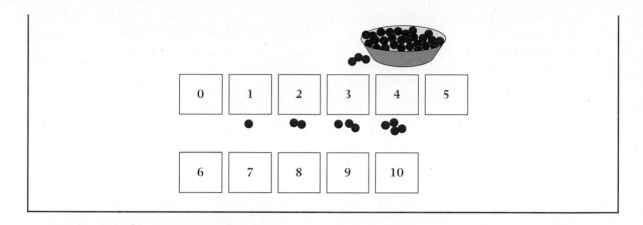

6K   **Preoperational/Concrete Ages 5–7**
Groups and Symbols, Write/Reproduce Numerals: Unit 19

METHOD: Interview.

SKILL: Child can reproduce (write) numerals from 0 to 10.

MATERIALS: Pencil, pen, black marker, black crayon, white paper, numeral cards from 0 to 10.

PROCEDURE: Say, "**Here is a piece of paper. Pick out one of these (point to writing tools) you would like to use. Now, write as many numbers as you can.**" If the child is unable to write from memory, show him the numeral cards. Say, "**Copy any of these that you can.**"

EVALUATION: Note how many numerals the child can write and if they are in sequence. If the child is not able to write the numerals with ease, then at this time writing is probably not an appropriate mode of response to problems; instead, have him do activities in which he can place movable numerals or markers on the correct answers.

INSTRUCTIONAL RESOURCE: Charlesworth, R. (2011). *Experiences in math for young children* (6th ed.). Belmont, CA: Wadsworth/Cengage Learning.

Naturalistic Activities

As the children learn that groups and symbols go together, it will be reflected in their daily play activities.

- Mary and Dean have set up a grocery store. Dean has made price tags, and Mary has made play money from construction paper. They have written numerals on each price tag and piece of money. Sam comes up and picks out a box of breakfast cereal and a carton of milk. Dean takes the tags, "That will be four dollars." Sam counts out four play dollar bills. Dean takes a piece of paper from a notepad and writes a "receipt." "Here, Sam."

- Brent has drawn a picture of a birthday cake. There are six candles on the cake and a big numeral 6. "This is for my next birthday. I will be six."
- The flannelboard and a group of primary cutouts have been left out in a quiet corner. George sits deep in thought as he places the numerals in order and counts out a group of cutouts to go with each numeral.

Each child uses what she has already learned in ways that she has seen adults use these skills and concepts.

Informal Activities

The child can work with groups and numerals best through informal experiences. Each child needs a different amount of practice. By making available many materials that the child can work with on his own, the teacher can help each child have the amount of practice he needs. Each child can choose to use the group of materials that he finds the most interesting.

The basic activities for matching symbols to groups and groups to symbols require the following kinds of materials.

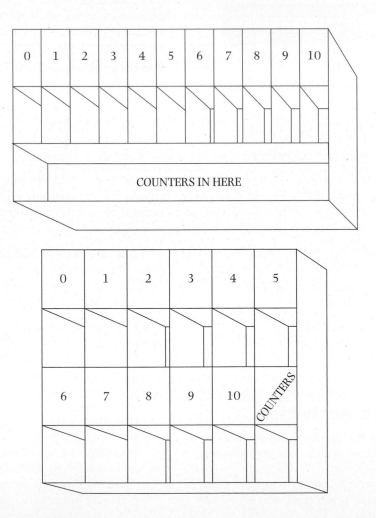

1. Materials in which the numerals are fixed and counters are available for making the groups. These are called *counting trays* and may be made or purchased. They may be set up with the numerals all in one row or in two or more rows.
2. Materials in which there are movable containers on which the numerals are written and counters of some kind. There might be pennies and banks, cups and buttons, cans and sticks, or similar items.
3. Individual numeral cards with a space for the child to make a group to match.
4. Groups of real things or pictures of things that must be matched to numerals written on cards.

The teacher can show each child each new set of materials. He can then have a turn to work with them. If the teacher finds that a child is having a hard time, she can give him some help and make sure that he takes part in some adult guided activities.

Informal experiences in which the child writes numerals come up when the child asks how to write his age, phone number, or address. Some children who are interested in writing may copy numerals they see in the environment—on the clock and calendar or on the numeral cards used in matching and group-making activities. The teacher should encourage these children and help them if needed. The teacher can make or buy a group of sandpaper numerals. The child can trace these with his finger to get the feel of the shape and the movement needed to make the numeral. Formal writing lessons should not take place until the child's fine muscle coordination is well developed. For some children this might not be until they are 7 or 8 years of age.

Games provide an enjoyable way for children to apply their knowledge of the relationships between groups and number symbols.

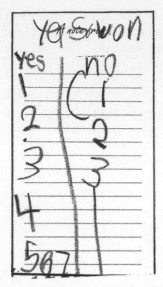

Summer has drawn seven dresses. She
and Grandma vote "yes" or "no" on each
dress to indicate whether or not it is "good."
Used with mother's permission

Adult Guided Activities

Adult guided activities with symbols and groups
for the young child are done in the form of games.
One type of game has the child match groups and
numerals using a theme such as "Letters to the Post
Office" or "Fish in the Fishbowl." A second is the basic
board game. A third type of game is the lotto or bingo
type. In each case, the teacher explains and demonstrates the game. Once the children know the rules,
two or more can play on their own. One example of
each game is described. With a little imagination, the
teacher can think of variations. The last three activities are for the child who can write numerals. Fosnot
and Cameron (2007) provide a variety of games that
support number sense and groups and symbols.

Counting books are another resource for connecting groups and symbols. In most counting
books, the numerals are included with each group
to be counted. The teacher must take caution in
selecting counting books. Ballenger, Benham, and
Hosticka (1984) suggest the following criteria for
selecting counting books.

1. The numerals should always refer to *how
   many* and not to the numerals' ordinal position or sequence.
2. The numeral names should also always
   refer to *how many*.
3. The narrative on the page should clearly
   identify the group of objects the numeral
   is associated with.
4. The illustrations of objects to be counted
   and connected to the numeral on each
   page should be clear and distinct.
5. When ordinals are being used, the starting position (e.g., first) should be clearly
   identified.
6. When identifying ordinal positions, the
   correct terms should be used (e.g., first,
   second, third, and so on).
7. When numerals are used to indicate ordinal position, they should be written as 1st,
   2nd, 3rd, and so on.
8. The numerals should be uniform in size
   (not small numerals for small groups and
   larger numerals for larger groups).

Counting books provide motivation for connecting groups and numerals.

9. The book should emphasize the concept of one-to-one correspondence.
10. When amounts above 10 and their associated numerals are illustrated, the amounts should be depicted as a group of 10 plus the additional items.

Jacqueline McDonald (2007) provides several criteria for selecting counting books to provide a variety of experiences for the children:

- Note if there are quantities above 10 in the book.
- Note if there are opportunities to conserve number.
- Note if a variety of different items are included for counting.
- Note if there are skip counting opportunities (i.e., count by 2's, 5's, 10's, and so on)
- Note if number and quantity are explored in a diversity of cultures and languages.
- Note if there is a grouping model of "10 plus" with numbers larger than ten.
- Note if the illustrations encourage counting on.
- Note if math language (see Unit 12) can be applied.
- Note if zero is used appropriately.

Activities

Groups and Symbols: Fish in the Fishbowl

OBJECTIVE: To match groups and symbols for the numerals 0 to 10.

MATERIALS: Sketch 11 fishbowls about 7″ × 10″ on separate pieces of cardboard or poster board. On each bowl write one of the numerals from 0 to 10. Cut out 11 fish, one for each bowl. On each fish, put dots—from 0 on the first to 10 on the last.

NATURALISTIC AND INFORMAL ACTIVITIES: Place the fish and fishbowls in the math center for the children to explore. Note if they make any matches as they play with them. Do they notice the dots and numerals and attempt to make matches? If they make matches, ask them to tell you about them.

ADULT GUIDED ACTIVITY: Play with two or more children. Line up the fishbowls (a chalk tray is a good place). One at a time, have each child choose a fish, sight unseen. Have her match her fish to its own bowl.

FOLLOW-UP:
1. Make fish with other kinds of sets such as stripes or stars.
2. Line up the fish, and have the children match the fishbowls to the right fish.

Groups and Symbols: Basic Board Games

OBJECTIVE: To match groups and symbols.

MATERIALS: The teacher can purchase or make the basic materials, which would include:

- A piece of poster board (18″ × 36″) for the game board
- Clear Contac or laminating material
- Marking pens
- Spinner cards, plain 3″ × 5″ file cards, or a die
- Place markers (chips, buttons, or other counters)

Figure 19–1 shows materials for three basic games. Set up the game boards with a theme for interest such as the race car game. Themes might be "Going to School," "The Road to Happy Land," or whatever the teacher or children can imagine.

NATURALISTIC AND INFORMAL ACTIVITIES: Put the games out, one at a time, during center time. Note if any of the children are familiar with these types of games. Take note of what they do. Do they know about turn taking? Do they know how to use the spinners and count the jumps? Do they make up rules?

ADULT GUIDED ACTIVITY: The basic activity is the same for each game. Each child picks a marker and puts it on START. Then each in turn spins the spinner (or chooses a card or rolls the die) and moves to the square that matches.

FOLLOW-UP:
1. Have the children learn to play the games on their own.
2. Make new games with new themes. Make games with more moves and using more numerals and larger groups to match.
3. Let the children make up their own rules.

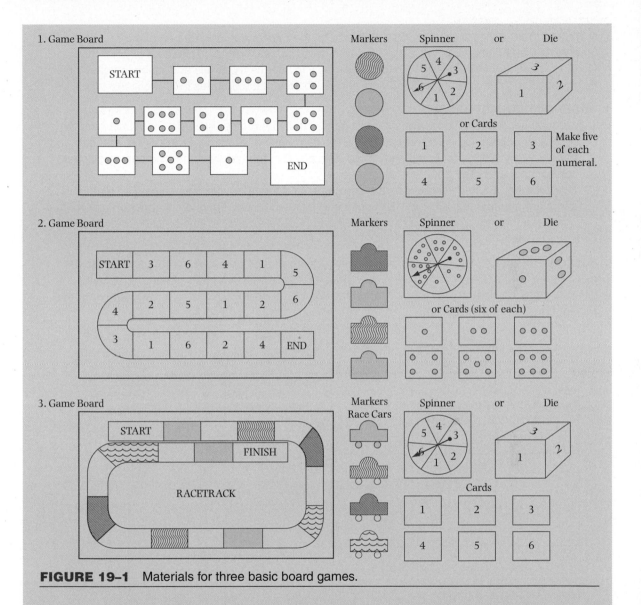

FIGURE 19–1 Materials for three basic board games.

Groups and Symbols: Lotto and Bingo Games

OBJECTIVE: To match groups and symbols.

MATERIALS: For both games, there should be six basic game cards, each with six or more squares (the more squares, the longer and harder the game). For lotto, there is one card to match each square. For bingo, there must also be markers to put on the squares. For bingo, squares on the basic game cards are repeated; for lotto, they are not.

NATURALISTIC AND INFORMAL ACTIVITIES: Put the games out, one at a time, during center time. Note if any of the children are familiar with these types of games. Take note of what they do. Do they know about turn taking? Do they know how to use the materials and make matches? Do they recognize the numerals on the bingo cards? Do they make up rules?

ADULT GUIDED ACTIVITIES:

1. *Lotto game.* Each child receives a basic game card. The matching cards are shuffled and held up one at a time. The child must call out if the card has her mark on it (dot, circle, triangle) and then match the numeral to the right group. The game can be played until one person fills her card or until everyone does.

2. *Bingo game.* Each child receives a basic game card together with nine chips. The matching set cards are shuffled and are then held up one at a time. The child puts a chip on the numeral that goes with the group on the card. When someone gets a row full in any direction, the game starts again.

FOLLOW-UP: Make more games using different picture groups and adding more squares to the basic game cards. Bingo cards must always have the same (odd) number of squares in both directions (i.e., grids that are three-by-three, five-by-five, or seven-by-seven). Select games from Fosnot and Cameron (2007).

1. Lotto Game

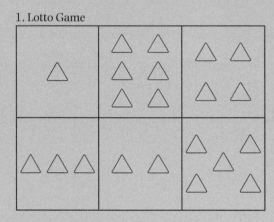

Make six cards for six players.

Matching cards:
Make a set for each big card.

2. Bingo Game

1	2	3
8	0	4
7	6	5

2	5	3
7	0	9
4	6	1

6	1	5
9	0	4
7	10	8

10	2	6
3	0	4
8	1	7

10	6	1
9	0	7
8	3	2

7	3	9
2	0	8
1	6	5

4	5	9
8	0	1
10	3	2

10	3	8
1	0	2
6	4	5

Markers: ● ● ● (54 chips)

Matching cards:
11 cards with sets 0 to 10:

  and so on.

Groups and Symbols: My Own Number Book

OBJECTIVE: To match groups and symbols.

MATERIALS: Booklets made with construction paper covers and several pages made from newsprint or other plain paper, hole puncher and yarn or brads to hold book together, crayons, glue, scissors, and more paper or stickers.

NATURALISTIC AND INFORMAL ACTIVITIES: Provide the children with opportunities to make their own books in the writing center. Have them read number books, and have them explore the books independently.

ADULT GUIDED ACTIVITY: The child writes (or asks the teacher to write) a numeral on each page of the book. The child then puts a group on each page. Groups can be made using
1. Stickers
2. Cutouts made by the child
3. Drawings done by the child

FOLLOW-UP: Have the children show their books to one another, and then take the books home. Also read to the children some of the number books listed in Appendix B.

Groups and Symbols: Writing Numerals to Match Groups

OBJECTIVE: To write the numeral that goes with a group.

MATERIALS: Objects and pictures of objects, chalk and chalkboard, crayons, pencils, and paper.

NATURALISTIC AND INFORMAL ACTIVITIES: Have the children explore many numerals and groups and numeral materials. Numeral models should be available in the writing center for the children to observe and copy.

ADULT GUIDED ACTIVITY: Show the child some objects or pictures of objects. Say, "**Write the numeral that tells how many _____ there are.**" The child then writes the numeral on the chalkboard or on a piece of paper.

FOLLOW-UP: Get some clear acetate. Make some set pictures that can be placed in acetate folders for the child to use on her own. Make acetate folders by taking a piece of cardboard and taping a piece of acetate of the same size on with some plastic tape. The child can write on the acetate with a nonpermanent marker and then erase her mark with a tissue or a soft cloth.

Computers and calculators can also be used for helping children acquire the groups and symbols connection. Most of the technology resources listed in Units 6 and 18 as supportive of counting and symbol recognition also connect groups and symbols. These resources should also be evaluated with the same criteria suggested for books. With their calculators, students could play games such as closing their eyes, pressing a key, identifying the numeral, and then selecting or constructing a group that goes with the numeral. Many self-correcting computer/calculator-type toys are also available that children enjoy using.

Groups and symbol activities may be included in other content areas. See Figure 19–2 for examples.

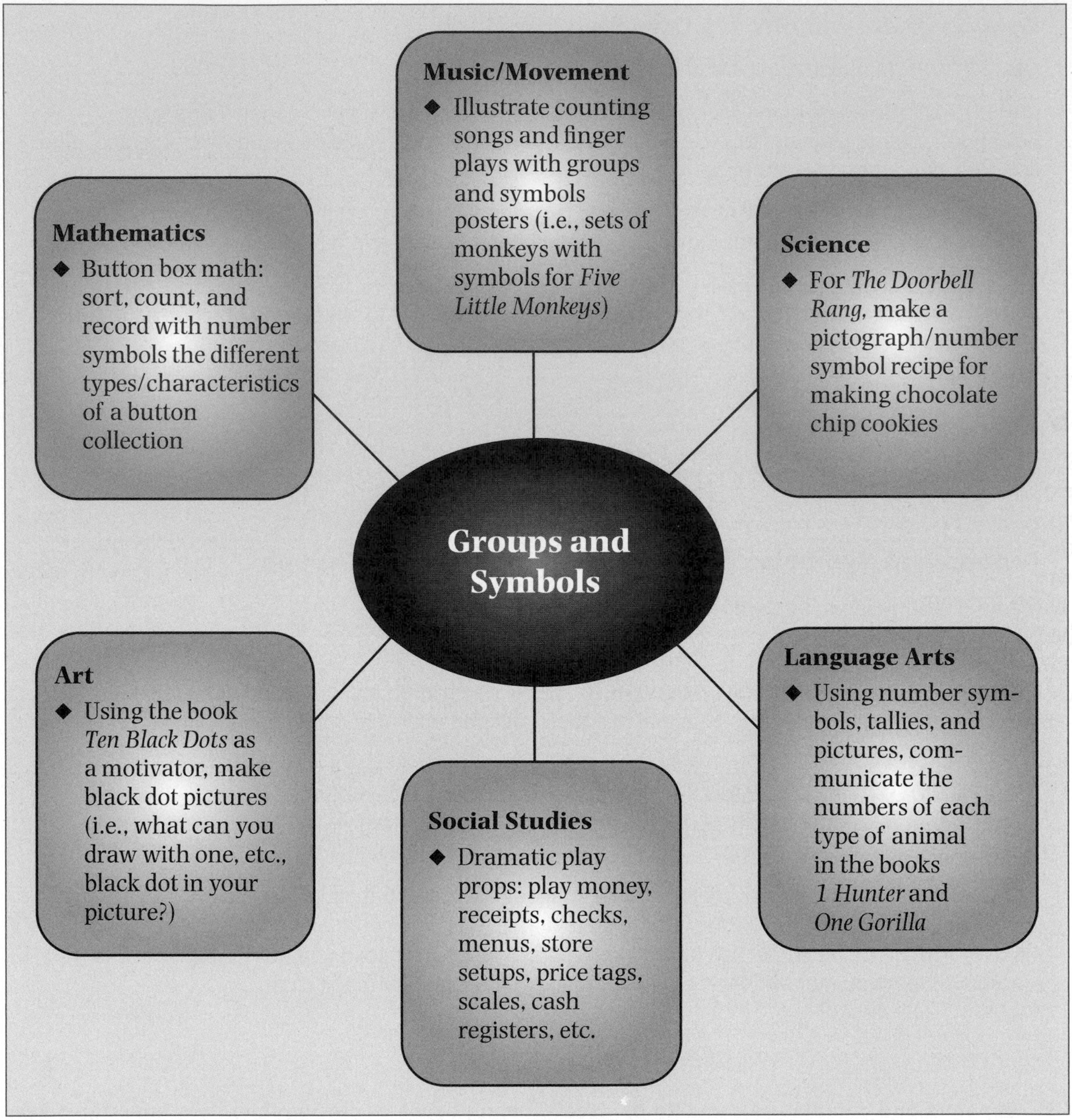

Music/Movement

◆ Illustrate counting songs and finger plays with groups and symbols posters (i.e., sets of monkeys with symbols for *Five Little Monkeys*)

Mathematics

◆ Button box math: sort, count, and record with number symbols the different types/characteristics of a button collection

Science

◆ For *The Doorbell Rang,* make a pictograph/number symbol recipe for making chocolate chip cookies

Groups and Symbols

Art

◆ Using the book *Ten Black Dots* as a motivator, make black dot pictures (i.e., what can you draw with one, etc., black dot in your picture?)

Social Studies

◆ Dramatic play props: play money, receipts, checks, menus, store setups, price tags, scales, cash registers, etc.

Language Arts

◆ Using number symbols, tallies, and pictures, communicate the numbers of each type of animal in the books *1 Hunter* and *One Gorilla*

FIGURE 19–2 Integrating groups and symbols experiences across the curriculum.

MATH TECHNOLOGY FOR
YOUNG CHILDREN

Review one or more technology resources listed as links in NCTM Illuminations or PBSKids that connect groups and symbols. Use one of the procedures suggested in Unit 2 and the criteria suggested in this unit for children's counting books to evaluate the resource.

Technology provides a means for making symbol/group connections.

Ideas for Children with Special Needs

Purchase or make many materials that provide experiences for children that support making the connection between the symbols and the groups they represent. Verbal counting comes before the written symbol is introduced. Some children will take longer to learn the written number sequence before connecting them with groups. The following are examples of materials and activities that can be used to support number recognition and sequence:

1. Make or buy cards with numbers (be sure that there are several cards for each number). Have the children divide cards and then turn them over one at a time, identifying matches.

2. In kindergarten, learning one's street address and phone number provides a meaningful context for number identification. Provide each child with two sentence strips: one with address and one with phone number.

3. Numbers above nine may be difficult for children with poor concepts of spatial awareness. Use color cueing to indicate concepts of left and right. Teens can be especially difficult: whereas the "2" provides a clue in the twenties, the numeral "1" does not say "teen."

4. Number sequencing can be done individually, in small groups, or by the whole class. During a class meeting, give several children large-size number cards and ask them to line up in sequence. Individual or pairs of children can work at a table with numbers on $3'' \times 5''$ cards. Use felt boards as well. Calendars can be used for matching.

5. Use two calendars of the same month. Keep one intact and mounted and cut up the other for matching. Children can name each numeral as matched.

Once children can identify and name numerals in sequence, they can begin to associate the written number symbols with number concepts. A variety of activities have been described in this unit, and some additional ideas follow:

1. Make a hopscotch pattern on the ground. Write a number in each square. The child can jump or hop from square to square in order, stopping to clap the number in each square.

2. Child can trace around his hand and then number each finger.

3. Provide the child with random written number symbols and some counting objects. Have him count out the amount that goes with each symbol.

4. Provide the child with a sheet of paper with numbers written along the left side. Next to each number the child can:
   a. Draw the correct number of objects.
   b. Place the correct number of stickers.
   c. Place the correct number of objects.

Evaluation

With young children, most evaluation can be done by observing their use of the materials for informal activities. The adult can also notice how the children do when they play games with rules.

For children about to enter first grade, an individual interview using the assessment interviews in this unit and in Appendix A.

Summary

When the child works with groups and symbols, he puts together the skills and ideas he learned earlier. He must match, count, classify, compare, order, and associate written numerals with groups.

He learns to match groups to symbols and symbols to groups. He also learns to write each number symbol. The child uses mostly materials that can be used informally on his own. He can also learn from board games, number books, computer games, and calculator activities.

SUGGESTED ACTIVITIES

1. Add groups and symbols assessment tasks to your Assessment File/Notebook and activities to your Activity File/Notebook.
2. Make groups and symbols instructional materials. Use them with prekindergarten, kindergarten, and first-grade students. Share the results with the class.
3. Go to a bookstore, the children's literature library, and/or your local public library. Identify three or more counting books and evaluate them using the criteria suggested by Ballenger and colleagues (1984) and McDonald (2007).

REVIEW

A. List and describe the skills a child should have before doing the activities suggested in this unit or in higher-level units.
B. Decide which of the following incidents are examples of (a) matching a symbol to a group, (b) reproducing symbols, or (c) matching a group to a symbol.
   1. Mario is writing down his phone number.
   2. Kate selects three Unifix Cubes to go with the numeral 3.
   3. Fong selects the magnetic numeral 6 to go with the six squares on the magnet board.
C. Describe three kinds of materials that are designed to be used for matching symbols to groups and groups to symbols.
D. If 4-year-old John tells you that he wants to know how to write his phone number, what should you do?
E. Describe two adult guided groups and symbols activities.
F. List some materials that young children could use for reproducing symbols.
G. Describe two informal groups and symbols activities young children might be engaged in.
H. What criteria should be used when selecting books and software to use in helping children acquire the groups and symbols connection?

REFERENCES

Ballenger, M., Benham, N. B., & Hosticka, A. (1984). Children's counting books. *Childhood Education, 61*(1), 30–35.

Baratta-Lorton, M. (1979). *Workjobs II.* Menlo Park, CA: Addison-Wesley.

Fosnot, C. T., & Cameron, A. (2007). *Games for early number sense.* Portsmouth, NH: Heinemann.

McDonald, J. (2007). Selecting counting books. *Young Children, 62*(3), 38–40.

National Council of Teachers of Mathematics. (2007). *Curriculum focal points.* Reston, VA: Author.

FURTHER READING AND RESOURCES

Box it or bag it mathematics (K–2). Portland, OR: The Math Learning Center.

Bridges in mathematics (K–2). Portland, OR: Math Learning Center.

Brizuela, B. M. (2004). *Mathematical development in young children: Exploring notations.* New York: Teachers College Press.

Copley, J. V. (Ed.). (2004). *Showcasing mathematics for the young child* (chap. 2, Number and Operations). Reston, VA: National Council for Teachers of Mathematics.

Copley, J. V., Jones, C., & Dighe, J. (2007). *Mathematics: The creative curriculum approach.* Washington, DC: Teaching Strategies.

Cutler, K. M., Gilkerson, D., Parrott, S., & Bowne, M. T. (2003). Developing games based on children's literature. *Young Children, 58*(1), 22–27.

Gallenstein, N. L. (2003). *Creative construction of mathematics and science concepts in early childhood.* Olney, MD: Association for Childhood Education International.

Haylock, D., & Cockburn, A. (2003). *Understanding mathematics in the lower primary years: A guide for teachers of children 3–8* (2nd ed.). Thousand Oaks, CA: Chapman.

Mix, K. S., Huttenlocher, J., & Levine, S. C. (2002). *Quantitative development in infancy and early childhood.* New York: Oxford University Press.

National Council of Teachers of Mathematics. (2000). *Principles and standards for school mathematics.* Reston, VA: Author.

Richardson, K. (1984). *Developing number concepts using Unifix Cubes.* Menlo Park, CA: Addison-Wesley.

Richardson, K. (1999). *Developing number concepts: Counting, comparing, and pattern* (Book 1). Parsippany, NJ: Seymour.

Richardson, K. (1999). *Developing number concepts: Planning guide.* Parsippany, NJ: Seymour.

Wakefield, A. P. (1998). *Early childhood number games.* Boston: Allyn & Bacon.

Zaslavsky, C. (1996). *The multicultural math classroom.* Portsmouth, NH: Heinemann.

See also the games and materials resources suggested in Units 18 and 27, and the books suggested in Appendix B.

UNIT 20

Higher-Level Activities and Concepts

OBJECTIVES

After reading this unit, you should be able to:

- List the ten areas in which higher-level concept activities are described in this unit.
- Describe the three higher levels of classification.
- Plan higher-level activities for children who are near the stage of concrete operations.

The experiences in this unit include further applications of skills that children learned through the activities described in the previous units. These experiences support more complex application of the processes of problem solving, reasoning, communication, connections, and representation (NCTM, 2000; see also Unit 12). They are appropriate for preschool/kindergarten students who are developing at a fast rate and can do the higher-level assessment tasks with ease or for the older students who still need concrete experiences. The ten areas presented are **algebra, classification, shape, spatial relations, concrete whole number operations, graphs, symbolic level** activities, **quantities above ten, estimation,** and **design technology**.

Assessment

Assessment determines where the children are in their ZPD (see Unit 1), that is, where they can

work independently and where they can complete tasks with support from scaffolding by an adult or a more advanced peer.

The teacher looks at the child's level in each area. Then he makes a decision as to when to introduce these activities. When the teacher introduces any one activity to one child, it could capture the interest of another child who might be at a lower developmental level. Therefore, it is not necessary to wait for all the children to be at the highest level to begin. Children at lower levels can participate in these activities as observers and contributors. The higher-level child can serve as a model for the lower-level child. The lower-level child might be able to do part of the task following the leadership of the higher-level child. For example, if a floor plan of the classroom is being made, the more advanced child might design it while everyone draws a picture of a piece of furniture to put on the floor plan. The more advanced child might get help from the less advanced child when she makes a graph.

The less advanced child can count and measure; the more advanced child records the results. Children can work in pairs to solve concrete addition, subtraction, multiplication, and division problems. They can move into higher levels of symbol use and work with numerals and quantities greater than ten. They can also work together exploring calculators and computer software.

By the end of kindergarten, children should have an understanding of number (Marshall, 2006). That is, number sense should be well established. Children should understand the idea of "twoness," "threeness," and so forth. They need to understand that the concept of number is independent of size, shape, and color. They need to find groups everywhere that are two, three, four, five, and so on. They must understand that arrangement in space (conservation of number) is independent of amount. They need to examine and construct groups using different objects. The book *What Comes in 2's, 3's, and 4's?* by Suzanne Aker (1990) demonstrates the concept of number in pictures. With number understood, students are ready to move on to more abstract ideas that are based on an understanding of number. *One Hundred Hungry Ants* by Pinczes (1993) demonstrates how 100 is still 100 when broken down into smaller groups, and *Miss Bindergarten Celebrates the 100th Day* by Slate (1998) shows how 100 is still 100 no matter how it is composed.

Algebraic Thinking

Many people view algebra as a blockade to their progress in understanding mathematics and as a mindless abstract manipulation of symbols. The NCTM has promoted a new vision of algebra as "a way of thinking, a method of seeing and expressing relationships" (Moses, 1997). It sees algebra as a way of thinking that goes beyond numerical reasoning and as one that can begin in the elementary grades.

For preprimary-level children, algebraic thinking is reflected in their discovery of patterns as they sort and group objects, combine groups and count totals, build with blocks, and use objects as symbolic representations. As young children explore these materials, they construct generalizations that reflect an increasing understanding of patterns and relationships (Curcio & Schwartz, 1997).

Children figure out how to balance their block buildings. They discover that ten groups of ten is 100. Exploring with a pan balance, they find that if they put certain objects on each side, the pans will balance. They find that groups will break down into smaller sets and still be the same number. These discoveries are the outcome of the beginnings of algebraic thinking. As children move into higher-level activities, it is important to continue to provide them with opportunities to explore and discover.

Classification

The higher levels of classification are called **multiple classification, class inclusion**, and **hierarchical classification**. Multiple classification requires the child to classify things in more than one way and to solve matrix problems. Figures 20–1 and 20–2 illustrate the two types of multiple classification. In Figure 20–1, the child is shown three shapes, each in three sizes and in three colors. He is asked to put the ones together that belong together. He is then asked to find another way to organize the shapes.

The preoperational child will not be able to do this. He centers on his first sort. Some games are suggested that will help the child move to concrete operations.

Figure 20–2 illustrates matrix problems. Figure 20–2A shows a simple two-by-two matrix. In this case, both size and number must be considered to complete the matrix. The problem can be made more difficult by making the matrix larger (there are always the same number of squares in each row, both across and up and down). Figure 20–2B shows a four-by-four matrix. The easiest problem is to fill in part of a matrix. The hardest problem is to fill in a whole blank matrix, as illustrated in Figure 20–2C.

The preoperational child cannot see that one class may be included within another (*class inclusion*).

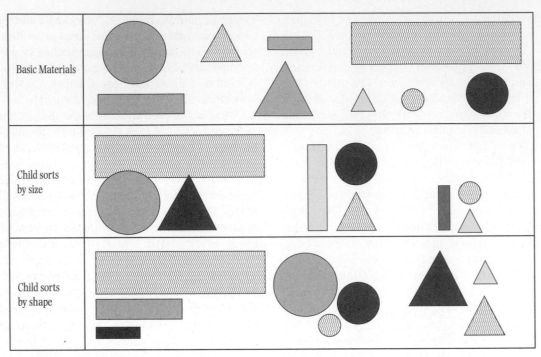

FIGURE 20–1 Multiple classification involves sorting one way and then sorting again using different criteria.

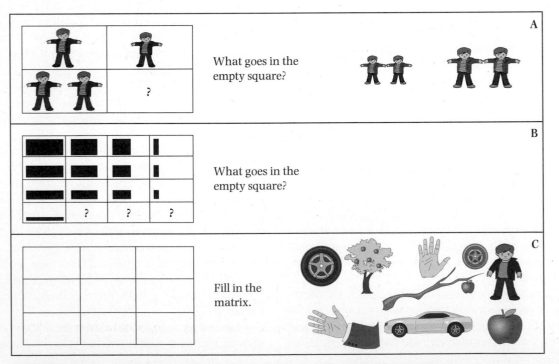

FIGURE 20–2 The matrix problem is another type of multiple classification.

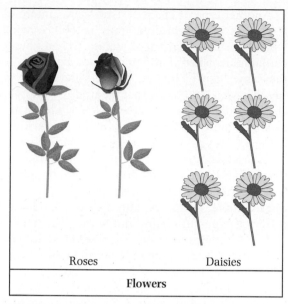

Roses   Daisies

Flowers

FIGURE 20–3 Class inclusion is the idea that one class can be included in another.

For example, the child is shown ten flowers: two roses and eight daisies. The child can divide the flowers into two groups: roses and daisies. He knows that they are all flowers. When the teacher asks him if there are more flowers or more daisies, he will answer, "More daisies." He is fooled by what he sees and centers on the greater number of daisies. He is not able to hold in his mind that daisies are also flowers. This problem is shown in Figure 20–3.

Hierarchical classification involves classes within classes. For example, black kittens ⊂ kittens ⊂ house cats ⊂ cats ⊂ mammals (here "⊂" denotes "subgroup" or "are contained within"). As can be seen in Figure 20–4, this forms a *hierarchy* or a series of ever-larger classes. Basic-level concepts are usually learned first. This level includes categories such as dogs, monkeys, cats, cows, and elephants (see Figure 20–4). Superordinate-level concepts such as mammals, furniture, vehicles,

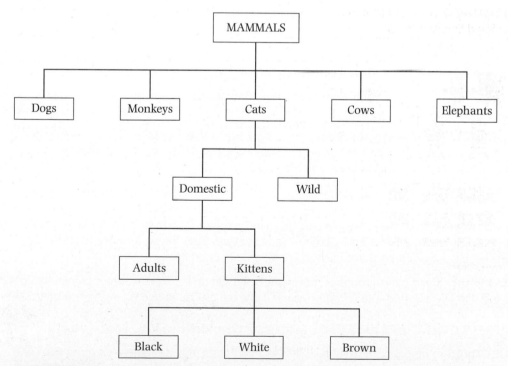

FIGURE 20–4 In a hierarchical classification, all things in each lower class are included in the next higher class.

and so on, are learned next. Finally, children learn subordinate categories such as domestic cats and wildcats or types of chairs such as dining room, living room, rocking, kitchen, folding, and so on.

Another interesting aspect of young children's concept learning is their view of which characteristics the members of a class have in common. Although preoperational-level children tend to be perceptually bound when they attempt to solve many types of conceptual problems, they are able to classify based on category membership when they are shown things that are perceptually similar. For example, 4-year-olds were shown pictures of a blackbird; a bat, which looked much like the blackbird; and a flamingo. They were told that the flamingo gave its baby mashed-up food and the bat gave its baby milk. When they were asked what the blackbird fed its baby, they responded that it gave its baby mashed-up food. In this case, the children looked beyond the most obvious physical attributes.

Another type of characteristic that is interesting to ask young children about is their view of what is inside members of a class. When young children are asked if all members of a class have the same "stuff" inside, preschoolers tend to say that yes, they have; that is, all dogs, people, chairs, and dolls are the same inside. Children are aware of more than just observable similarities. By second grade, they can discriminate between natural and synthetic items; that is, they realize that living things such as dogs, people, or apples are, for the most part, the same inside as other dogs, people, or apples, although the insides of different types of chairs, dolls, or other manufactured items are not necessarily the same. For younger children, category membership overwhelms other factors.

The following activities will help the transitional child (usually ages 5–7) to enter concrete operations.

Activities

Higher-Level Classification: Multiple Classification, Reclassify

OBJECTIVE: To help the transitional child learn that groups of objects or pictures can sometimes be sorted in more than one way.

MATERIALS: Any group of objects or pictures of objects that can be classified in more than one way, for example, pictures or cardboard cutouts of dogs of different colors (brown and white), sizes (large and small), and hair lengths (long and short).

ADULT GUIDED ACTIVITY: Place the dogs in front of the child. Ask, "**Which dogs belong together**?" or "**Are they the same**?" Note whether she groups the dogs by size, color, or hair length. Ask, "**Now, what is another way to put them in groups? Can they be put like (name another way)**?" Put them in one pile again if the child is puzzled. Say, "**Okay, now try to sort the _____ from the _____.**" Repeat this using different criteria each time.

FOLLOW-UP: Make other groups of materials. Set them up in boxes where the child can get them out and use them during free playtime. Make some felt pieces to use on the flannelboard.

Higher-Level Classification: Multiple Classification, Matrices

OBJECTIVE: To help the transitional child see that things may be related on more than one criterion.

MATERIALS: Purchase or make a matrix game. Start with a two-by-two matrix and gradually increase the size (three-by-three, four-by-four, etc.). Use any of the criteria from Unit 10 such as color, size, shape, material, pattern, texture, function, association, class name, common feature, or number. Make a game board from poster board or wood. Draw or paint permanent lines. Use a flannelboard, and make the lines for the matrix with lengths of yarn. Figure 20–5 shows an example of a three-by-three board. Start with three-dimensional materials, then cutouts, and then cards.

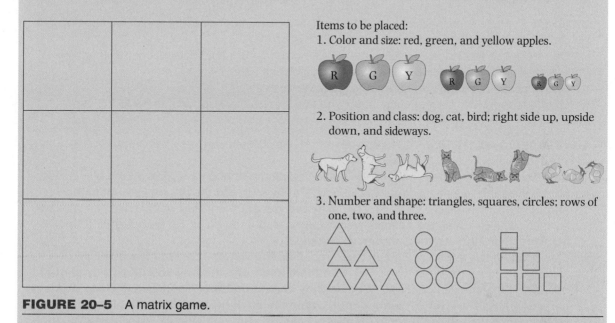

Items to be placed:
1. Color and size: red, green, and yellow apples.

2. Position and class: dog, cat, bird; right side up, upside down, and sideways.

3. Number and shape: triangles, squares, circles; rows of one, two, and three.

FIGURE 20–5   A matrix game.

ADULT GUIDED ACTIVITIES: Start with the matrix filled except for one space, and ask the child to choose from two items the one that goes in the empty space. Ask, "**Which one of these goes here**?" After the child places the item, say, "**Why does it belong there?**" Once the child understands the task, leave more spaces empty until it is left for the child to fill in the whole matrix.

FOLLOW-UP: Add more games that use different categories and larger matrices.

Higher-Level Classification: Class Inclusion

OBJECTIVE: To help the transitional child see that a smaller set may be included within a larger set.

MATERIALS: Seven animals. Include two kinds (such as horses and cows, pigs and chickens, dogs and cats). There should be four of one animal and three of the other. They can be cutouts or toy animals.

ADULT GUIDED ACTIVITY: Place the animals within an enclosure (a yarn circle or a fence made of blocks). Ask, "**Who is inside the fence**?" Children will answer "horses," "cows," "animals." Ask, "**Show me which ones are horses (cows, animals). Are there more horses or more animals? How do you know? Let's check**" (use one-to-one correspondence).

FOLLOW-UP: Play the same game. Use other categories such as plants, types of material, size, and so on. Increase the size of the sets.

Higher-Level Classification: Hierarchical

OBJECTIVE: To help the transitional child see that each thing may be part of a larger category (or set of things).

MATERIALS: Make some sets of sorting cards. Glue pictures from catalogs and/or workbooks onto file cards or poster board. For example:
- One black cat, several house cats, cats of other colors, one tiger, one lion, one panther, one bobcat, one dog, one horse, one cow, one squirrel, one bear
- One duck, three swans, five other birds, five other animals
- One teaspoon, two soupspoons, a serving spoon, two baby spoons, three forks, two knives

ADULT GUIDED ACTIVITIES: Place the cards where the children can see all of them. Give the following instructions:
1. Say, "**Find all the animals. Find all the cats. Find all the house cats. Find all the black cats.**" Mix up the cards, and lay them out again. Say, "**Put them in groups the way you think they should be.**" When the child is done, ask, "**Why did you put them that way?**" Mix them up, and lay them out. Ask, "**If all the animals were hungry, would the black cat be hungry? If the black cat is hungry, are all the animals hungry?**"
2. Say, "**Find all the animals. Find all the birds. Find the waterbirds. Find the duck.**" Mix up the cards, and lay them out again. Say, "**Put them in groups the way you think they should be.**" When the child is done, ask, "**Why do they belong that way?**" Mix them up, and lay them out again. Ask, "**If all the birds were cold, would the duck be cold? If the duck were cold, would all the waterbirds be cold? If all the animals were cold, would the waterbirds be cold?**"
3. Say, "**Find all the things that we eat with. Find all the knives. Find all the forks. Find all the spoons.**" Mix them up, and lay them out again. Say, "**Put them in groups the way you think they belong.**" When the child is done, ask, "**Why do they belong that way?**" Mix them up, and lay them out again. Ask, "**If all the spoons are dirty, would the teaspoon be dirty? If all the things we eat with were dirty, would the big spoon be dirty? If the teaspoon is dirty, are all the other things we eat with dirty too?**"

FOLLOW-UP: Make up other hierarchies. Leave the card sets out for the children to sort during play. Ask them some of the same kinds of questions informally.

Higher-Level Classification: Multiple Classification

OBJECTIVE: To help the transitional child learn to group things in a variety of ways using logical reasoning.

MATERIALS: *What to Wear?* an emergent reader book by Sharon Young. The book depicts a boy who has two shirts, two pairs of shorts, and two caps, with each item a different color. The problem presented to the reader is figuring out how many different outfits the boy can put together.

ADULT GUIDED ACTIVITIES: The *Teacher Guide for Harry's Math Books, Set B* (Young, 1998a) suggests a number of activities that can be done to support the concepts in *What to Wear?* Here are some examples:

1. Have the children discuss the ways they can sort clothes, such as school clothes/play clothes/dress-up clothes or clean clothes/dirty clothes.
2. Use cutouts to see that, although only two of each type of clothing are in the book, the children can construct more than two outfits.
3. Make connections with other areas such as meal combinations with two main dishes, two vegetables, two potatoes, two desserts, and two drinks.
4. Have the students draw the eight different outfits they can derive from the book.

FOLLOW-UP: Provide real clothing in the dramatic play center. Note how many combinations of outfits the students can put together.

Shape

Once the child can match, sort, and name shapes, she can also reproduce shapes. This can be done informally. Some materials that can be used are discussed next.

Purchase or make **Geoboards**, a square board with headed screws or pegs sticking up at equal intervals. Give the child a supply of rubber bands, and have the child experiment in making shapes by stretching the rubber bands around the pegs.

Put out a container of pipe cleaners, Wikki Stix, or straws. Ask the children to make as many different shapes as they can. Have them glue these shapes onto construction paper. Strips of paper, toothpicks, string, and yarn can also be used to make shapes.

Pattern blocks are an important material for children to use in exploring shape (Wilson, 2001). For beginners, provide puzzle frames that indicate the shapes to be used to fill the frame. For more advanced students, provide frames where the pattern block shapes are partially indicated. Provide children who can select pieces to fill in the puzzle without trial and error with puzzle frames with no hints as to which pattern block shapes will fill the frame. Offer children who master these advanced frames the challenge of filling the frames in more than one way.

Spatial Relations

After playing the treasure hunt game described in Unit 11, children can learn more about space by reproducing the space around them as a floor plan or map. Start with the classroom for the first map. Then move to the whole building, the neighborhood, and the town or city. Be sure the children have maps among their dramatic play props.

Activities

Higher-Level Activities: Spatial Relations, Floor Plans

OBJECTIVE: To relate position in space to symbols of position in space.

MATERIALS: Large piece of poster board or heavy paper, markers, pens, construction paper, glue, crayons, scissors, some simple sample floor plans.

ADULT GUIDED ACTIVITY:

1. Show the children some floor plans. Ask, "**What are they? What are they for? If we make a floor plan of our room, what would we put on it?**" Make a list.

2. Show the children a large piece of poster board or heavy paper. Say, "**We can make a plan of our room on here. Each of you can make something that is in the room, just like on our list. Then you can glue it in the right place. I've marked in the doors and windows for you.**" As each child draws and cuts out an item (a table, shelf, sink, chair), have her show you where it belongs on the plan and glue it on.

FOLLOW-UP: After the plan is done, leave it on the wall so the children can look at it and talk about it. They can also add more things to the plan. Use the same procedure later to make a plan of the building. Teacher and children should walk around the whole place. They should talk about which rooms are next to each other and which rooms are across from each other. Use sticks or straws to lay out the plan.

Higher-Level Activities: Spatial Relations, Maps

OBJECTIVE: To relate position in space to symbols of position in space.

MATERIALS: Map of the city, large piece of poster board or heavy paper, marking pens, construction paper, glue, crayons, scissors.

ADULT GUIDED ACTIVITY: Show the children the map of the city (or county in a rural area). Explain that this is a picture of where the streets would be if the children were looking down from a plane or a helicopter. Label each child's home on the map, and mark where the school is. Talk about who lives closest and who lives farthest away. Print each child's address on a card and have her review it each day. Help her mark out the streets and roads. Have the children cut out and glue down strips of black paper for the streets (and/or roads). Each child can draw a picture of her home and glue it on the map. Keep the map up on the wall for children to look at and talk about. As field trips are taken during the year, add each place to the map.

FOLLOW-UP: Encourage the children to look at and talk about the map. Help them add new points of interest. Help children who would like to make their own maps. Bring in maps of the state, the country, and the world. Try to purchase U.S. and world map puzzles.

Design Technology

Unit 10 described design technology as a natural component of children's play. Kindergartner, Josh, is constructing with Marble Works. He tells his friends, "This is my invention," as he admires his work and tests its functioning with marbles. A small group is engaged in creating art projects with recycled materials (Eichinger, 2009). The more advanced 5- and 6-year-olds may be challenged by more complex design technology problems.

In these more advanced design technology projects, children go through several steps:

- A problem is identified.
- Ideas are generated for ways of investigating and solving the problem.
- A plan of action is devised.
- A product is designed.
- The product is made and tested.
- Students reflect on the results of their process and product.

Problems may be worked on by individuals or small groups.

The youngest children should start with simple projects that focus on one item, such as designing an airplane, building a house, or constructing a miniature piece of playground equipment. Supplied with small boxes and other recycled materials, tape, and glue, children's imaginations take off. The Virginia Children's Engineering (n.d.) Council website provides detailed instructions for design technology projects. For kindergarten, plans are provided for four designs: Building a Letter, Shapes All Around Us, Magnet Motion, and Old-Fashioned Paper Dolls (download the teacher resource guide via http://CTEresource.org).

Children Designing and Engineering provides (n.d.) some samples of more complex long-term projects. For example, the students decide to construct a safari park. They investigate the types of animals to be included and their size, habitats, and diets. The students then plan how to construct an appropriate habitat and proceed with construction. Next they identify the needs of the workers and visitors. Then they design and build an official safari vehicle. Finally, they plan an Opening Day event. At each step the students reflect on the results and offer constructive criticism.

Budding engineers can join the Kids Design Network (KDN). This website (http://www.dupagechildrensmuseum.org) is sponsored by the Dupage Children's Museum. Children are presented with design problems that encourage investigation, invention, problem solving, design, and the actual building of a product. Members can communicate with an engineer through text chat and an interactive whiteboard. There is no cost to belong.

Graphs

The fourth level of graphs introduces the use of squared paper. The child may graph the same kind of things as discussed in Unit 16. He will now use squared paper with squares that can be colored in or filled with glued-in paper squares. These squares should be introduced only after the child

has had many experiences of the kinds described in Unit 16. The squares should be large. A completed graph might look like the one shown in Figure 20–6.

FIGURE 20–6 The child who has had many experiences with simpler graphs can make square paper graphs.

Concrete Whole Number Operations

Once children have a basic understanding of one-to-one correspondence, number and counting, and comparing, they can sharpen their problem-solving skills with concrete whole number operations. They can solve simple addition, subtraction, division, and multiplication problems using concrete materials. You can devise some simple problems to use as models as described in Unit 3. Some examples are in the box that follows. Provide the children with ten counters (pennies, chips, Unifix Cubes, and so on) or the real items or replicas of the real items described in the problems. The children will gradually catch on and begin devising their own problems, such as those described by Skinner (1990).

As children grow and develop and have more experiences with whole number operations, they learn more strategies for solving problems. They gradually stop using the less efficient strategies and retain the more efficient ones. For example, 4- and 5-year-olds usually begin addition with the *counting all* strategy. That is, for a problem such as "John has three cars and Kate gives him two more; how many does John have now?" the 4- or 5-year-old will count all the cars (one–two–three–four–five). Fives will gradually change to *counting on*; that is, considering that John has three cars, they then count on two more (four–five). Even older children who are using recall (3 + 2 = 5) will check with counting all and counting on. When observing children working with division, note whether they make use of their concept of one-to-one correspondence (e.g., when giving three people equal numbers of cookies, does the child pass out the cookies, one at a time, consecutively to each of the three recipients?). Teacher guided activities involve the students drawing problem solutions as in the examples that follow.

Carrot and Raisin Problem: You can have carrots and raisins. You have seven things. What is on your plate? [(Schulman, L., & Eston, R. (1998, October). A problem worth revisiting. *Teaching children mathematics*.)] Work of Ember used with parental permission.

Name Rhett

When the Doorbell Rang

Cookie Problem: Mother baked twelve cookies. Divide them fairly among four children. [(Based on the story *The doorbell rang* by Pat Hutchins, 1986, New York: Scholastic.)] Work of Rhett used with parental permission.

One More Child by Sharon Young (1998b) takes the emergent reader through the process of adding on one from one to four. This affords an opportunity to see the logic that when you add one more, the total is the next number in order. The students can use objects or a calculator to continue adding ones. Suggest they add several ones and discover how many they obtain. The book *Six Pieces of Cake* (Young, 1998c) takes the emergent reader through the subtraction process in which, one by one, pieces of cake are taken off a plate.

The Symbolic Level

Children who can connect groups and symbols (Unit 19), identify numerals 0 to 9, and do concrete addition and subtraction problems can move to the next step, which is connecting groups and symbols in addition and subtraction.

As children continue to create their own problems and work on teacher-created problems, encourage them to communicate their findings. Suggest that they draw, write, and use numerals to show their results. They can use cards with numerals written on them and gradually write the numerals themselves. Children can work in pairs on problems and trade problems with other students.

Addition

- If Mary has three pennies and her mother gives her one more penny, how many pennies will Mary have?
- George wants two cookies for himself and two for Richard. How many cookies should he ask for?

Subtraction

- Mary has six pennies. She gives three pennies to her sister. How many does she have now?
- George has six cookies. He gives Richard three. How many does he have left?

Multiplication

- Mary gives two pennies to her sister, two to her brother, and two to her friend Kate. How many pennies did she give away?
- Tanya had three friends visiting. Mother said to give each one three cookies. How many cookies should Tanya get from the cookie jar?

Division

- Lai has three dolls. Two friends come to play. How many dolls should she give each friend so each of them will have the same number?
- Lai's mother gives her a plate with nine cookies. How many cookies should Lai and each of her two friends take so each of them has the same number?

Problems can be devised with stories that fit thematic topics.

As the children work with these concrete symbol/set addition and subtraction problems, they will begin to store the basic facts in their memories and retrieve them without counting. They can then do problems without objects. Just have the objects on hand in case they are needed to check the answers.

Excellent resources for games and materials are *Games for Early Number Sense* (Fosnot & Cameron, 2007), *Minilessons for Early Addition and Subtraction* (Fosnot & Uittenbogaarg, 2007), *Constructing Number Sense, Addition, and Subtraction* (Fosnot & Dolk, 2001), *The Young Child and Mathematics* (Copley, 2000), *Developing Number Concepts: Addition and Subtraction, Book 2* (Richardson, 1999), *Developing Number Concepts Using Unifix Cubes* (Richardson, 1984), *Navigating through Problem Solving and Reasoning in Prekindergarten–Kindergarten* (Greenes et al., 2003), *Showcasing Mathematics for the Young Child* (Copley, 2004), *Hands-on Standards* (2007), and *A Head-Start on Science* (Ritz, 2007). The book *What's Your Problem?* (Skinner, 1990) provides a means for encouraging children to develop their own problems. Unit 21 provides a more detailed description of the procedure for introducing the symbols needed for whole number operations.

Calculators are also useful as tools for experimentation. Children will learn to make connections between problem solving and the signs on the calculator (i.e., $+$, $-$, and $=$).

Quantities Above Ten

Once children can count ten objects correctly, can identify the numerals 1 to 10, have a good grasp of one-to-one correspondence, and can accurately count by rote past ten, they are ready to move on to counting quantities above ten. They can acquire an understanding of quantities above ten by exploring the relationship of groups of ten with additional amounts. For example, they can count out ten Unifix Cubes and stick them together. Then they can pick one more Unifix Cube. Ask if they know which number comes after 10. If they cannot provide an answer, tell them that 11 comes after 10. Have them take another cube. Ask if they know what comes after 11. If they do not know the answer, tell them 12. Go as far as they can count by rote accurately. When they get to 20, have them put their cubes together, lay them next to the first 10, and compare the number of cubes in the two rows. See if they can tell you that there are two 10s. Give them numeral cards for 11 to 19. See if they can discover that the right-hand numeral matches up with how many more than 10 that numeral stands for.

Once the children understand through 19, they can move on to 20, 30, 40, and so on. By exploring the number of 10s and 1s represented by each numeral, they will discover the common pattern from 20 to 99; that is, the 2 in 20 means two 10s, and no 1s, the 2 in 21 means two 10s and the 1 means one 1, and so on, and that the same pattern holds true through 99. See Fosnot and Cameron (2007) and Fosnot and Uittenbogaarg (2007) for games.

Estimation

Estimation for young children involves making a sensible and reasonable response to the problem of how many are in a quantity or how much of a measurement something is. It is the "process of thinking about a 'how many' or 'how much' problem and possible solutions" (Lang, 2001, p. 463). Children might estimate how many objects (e.g., candies, teddy bears, screws) are in a jar or how many shoes tall the bookcase is. To come up with a reasonable response, children must already have developed number, spatial, and measurement sense. Without these prerequisite concepts they will make wild guesses rather than reasonable estimates.

Lang (2001) suggests several ways to assist children so they can make reasonable estimates. A *referent* can be used such as, "If I know how tall John is, I can estimate how tall the bookcase is if he stands next to it." *Chunking* involves taking a known measurement and using it as a guide for estimating a larger measurement. For example, if the children know how long ten Unifix Cubes are, they can use this information to estimate the length of the table in cubes. Unitizing is another type of chunking where, if one part is known, then the whole can be estimated. For example, if a cup of pennies fills a jar half full, then two cups will fill the whole jar. If the number of pennies in the cup is known, then the number to fill the jar can be estimated. It is important that children understand the language of comparison (Units 8 and 12) to give and receive communications regarding their estimates.

Ideas for Children with Special Needs

Unit 21 describes a progression suggested by Kathy Richardson for moving from concrete arithmetic to algorithms. For some children, a useful step for beginning arithmetic is to play a thinking game. Using numbers 2 to 9, the children are asked a series of questions. The children are asked "What number comes *after* 6?" Next, "What number comes *before* 6?" and finally "What is 6 and one more?" Patterns are also useful in helping children move into arithmetic. For example, when making a bead pattern, the child must think, "How many more beads will I need to complete my pattern?"

MATH TECHNOLOGY FOR YOUNG CHILDREN

Explore the National Laboratory for Virtual Manipulatives and the NCTM Illuminations sites for virtual manipulatives that support higher-level concept development.

Summary

This unit builds on the concepts and skills presented in the previous units. Areas are reviewed and children moved to higher levels that will shift them into concrete operations and primary grade arithmetic.

KEY TERMS

algebra	design technology	multiple classification
class inclusion	estimation	quantities above ten
classification	geoboards	shape
concrete whole number	graphs	spatial relations
operations	hierarchical classification	symbolic level

SUGGESTED ACTIVITIES

1. Observe in a kindergarten classroom. Note any behaviors that suggest that any of the children are ready for higher-level concept activities. Share your observations with the class.
2. Interview one or more kindergarten teachers. Ask them to describe the concept activities available for students who are entering the concrete operations period.
3. Include higher-level concept activities in your Activity File/Notebook.

REVIEW

A. Describe areas in this unit that provide higher-level concept activities.
B. Characterize the three higher levels of classification.
C. Which of the following examples can be identified as (a) multiple classification, (b) class inclusion, or (c) hierarchical classification?
  1. Basset hound, dog, animal.
  2. Matrix that varies horizontally by size and vertically by color.
  3. Two cars and three airplanes; are there more airplanes or more vehicles?
  4. Texture, weight, and material.
  5. Markers, pens, pencils, and things you can write with.
  6. Three apples and one banana; are there more apples or more fruit?
D. Read the following descriptions carefully. Identify the higher-level activity the child seems to be engaged in, and suggest how the teacher should respond.
  1. Kate says, "Donny lives on the other side of the street from me."
  2. Liu takes the Unifix Cubes and places them in groups of three.
  3. Cindy takes some cube blocks and toy cars and places them on the balance scale.
  4. Bret points to the orange in the picture book and says, "Look at that round orange."
  5. Liu says that chocolate ice cream is the best. Kate says vanilla is best. Kate insists that most children like vanilla ice cream better than chocolate.
  6. "John, give me two more blocks so that I will have six, too."
  7. Mrs. Jones notices that Sam is laboriously drawing four oranges and five apples. Then he writes a numeral 4 by the oranges and the number 5 by the apples. Finally he writes in invented spelling, "thrs 9 froots."
  8. Mrs. Carter notices that 5-year-old George can rote count to 99 accurately.
  9. Tanya explains that all people have blood, bones, and fat inside, but all dolls are filled with cotton.
  10. We counted out 20 jelly beans in this scoop. How can we use that information to estimate how many jelly beans this jar will hold when it is full?
  11. Look back through all the ideas for children with special needs. Set up a plan for children with disabilities and ELLs and for ensuring that your classroom meets the needs of culturally diverse students.

REFERENCES

Aker, S. (1990). *What comes in 2's, 3's, and 4's.* New York: Aladdin.

Children Designing and Engineering. (n.d.). *What is CD&E?* Retrieved November 20, 2004, from http://www.childrendesigning.org

Copley, J. V. (2000). *The young child and mathematics.* Washington, DC: National Association for the Education of Young Children.

Copley, J. V. (2004). *Showcasing mathematics for the young child.* Reston, VA: National Council of Teachers of Mathematics.

Curcio, F. R., & Schwartz, S. L. (1997). What does algebraic thinking look like with preprimary children? *Teaching Children Mathematics, 3*(6), 296–300.

Eichinger, J. (2009). *Activities linking science and math K-4.* Arlington, VA: National Science Teachers Association (Activity 7).

Fosnot, C. T., & Cameron, A. (2007). *Games for early number sense.* Portsmouth, NH: Heinemann.

Fosnot, C. T., & Dolk, M. (2001). *Young mathematicians at work: Constructing number sense, addition, and subtraction.* Portsmouth, NH: Heinemann.

Fosnot, C. T., & Uittenbogaard, W. (2007). *Mini-lessons for early addition and subtraction.* Portsmouth, NH: Heinemann.

Greenes, C. E., Dacey, L., Cavanagh, M., Findell, C. R., Sheffeld, L. J., & Small, M. (2003). *Navigating through problem solving and reasoning in prekindergarten–kindergarten.* Reston, VA: National Council of Teachers of Mathematics.

Lang, F. K. (2001). What is a "good guess" anyway? Estimation in early childhood. *Teaching Children Mathematics, 7*(8), 462–466.

Learning Resources. (2007). *Hands-on standards.* Vernon Hills, IL: Author.

Marshall, J. (2006). Math wars 2: It's the teaching, stupid! *Phi Delta Kappan, 87*(5), 356–363.

Moses, B. (1997). Algebra for a new century. *Teaching Children Mathematics, 3*(6), 264–265.

National Council of Teachers of Mathematics. (2000). *Principles and standards for school mathematics.* Reston, VA: Author.

Pinczes, E. J. (1993). *One hundred hungry ants.* New York: Scholastic Books.

Richardson, K. (1984). *Developing number concepts: Using Unifix Cubes.* Menlo Park, CA: Addison-Wesley.

Richardson, K. (1999). *Developing number concepts: Addition and subtraction* (Book 2). Parsippany, NJ: Seymour.

Ritz, W. C. (Ed.). (2007). *A head start on science.* Arlington, VA: NSTA Press.

Skinner, P. (1990). *What's your problem?* Portsmouth, NH: Heinemann.

Slate, J. (1998). *Miss Bindergarten celebrates the 100th day.* New York: Puffin Books.

Virginia Children's Engineering Council. (n.d.). *Inspiring the next generation.* Retrieved November 20, 2004, from http://www.vtea.org

Wilson, D. C. (2001). Patterns of thinking in pattern block play. *Building Blocks News, 3*, 2.

Young, S. (1998a). *Teacher guide for Harry's math books*, Set B. Columbus, OH: Zaner-Bloser.

Young, S. (1998b). *One more child.* Columbus, OH: Zaner-Bloser.

Young, S. (1998c). *Six pieces of cake.* Columbus, OH: Zaner-Bloser.

Young, S. (1998d). *What to wear?* Columbus, OH: Zaner-Bloser.

FURTHER READING AND RESOURCES

Box it or bag it mathematics (K–2). Portland, OR: Math Learning Center.

Bridges in mathematics (K–2). Portland, OR: Math Learning Center.

Buschman, L. (2002). Becoming a problem solver. *Teaching Children Mathematics, 9*(2), 98–103.

Children's Engineering Journal, http://www.vtea.org

Clements, D. H., & Sarama, J. (2000). Predicting pattern blocks on and off the computer. *Teaching Children Mathematics, 6*(7), 458–461.

Clements, D. H., Swaminathan, S., Hannibal, M. A. Z., & Sarama, J. (1999). Young children's concepts of shape. *Journal for Research in Mathematics Education, 30*(2), 192–212.

Copley, J. V. (Ed.). (1999). *Mathematics in the early years*. Washington, DC: National Association for the Education of Young Children.

Dunn, S., & Larson, R. (1990). *Design technology: Children's Engineering*. Bristol, PA: Falmer, Taylor & Francis.

Falkner, K. P., Levi, L., & Carpenter, T. R. (1999). Children's understanding of equality: A foundation for algebra. *Teaching Children Mathematics, 6*(4), 232–236.

Gallenstein, N. L. (2004). Creative discovery through classification. *Teaching Children Mathematics, 11*(2), 103–108.

Greenes, C. E., Cavanagh, M., Dacey, L., Findell, C. R., & Small, M. (2001). *Navigating through algebra in prekindergarten–kindergarten*. Reston, VA: National Council of Teachers of Mathematics.

Holly, K. A. (1997). Math by the month: Patterns and functions. *Teaching Children Mathematics, 3*(6), 312.

Johanning, D., Weber, W. D., Heidt, C., Pearce, M., & Horner, K. (2009/2010). The *Polar Express* to early algebraic thinking. *Teaching Children Mathematics, 16*(5), 300–307.

Outhred, L., & Sarelich, S. (2005). Problem solving by kindergartners. *Teaching Children Mathematics, 12*(3), 146–154.

Petroski, H. (2003, January 24). *Early education*. Presentation at the Children's Engineering Convention (Williamsburg, VA). Retrieved November 20, 2004, from http://www.vtea.org

Sheffield, L. J., Cavanagh, M., Dacey, L., Findell, C. R., Greenes, C. E., & Small, M. (2002). *Navigating through data analysis and probability in prekindergarten–grade 2*. Reston, VA: National Council of Teachers of Mathematics.

Shulman, L., & Eston, R. (1998). A problem worth revisiting. *Teaching Children Mathematics, 5*(2), 72–77.

Taylor-Cox, J. (2001). How many marbles in the jar? Estimation in the early grades. *Teaching Children Mathematics, 8*(4), 208–214.

Mathematics Concepts and Operations for the Primary Grades

Operations with Whole Numbers

OBJECTIVES

After reading this unit, you should be able to:

- Define the whole number operations of addition, subtraction, multiplication, and division.
- Introduce the whole number operations to primary grade children.
- Administer whole number operations assessment tasks.
- Introduce whole number operations notation and number sentence format following a three-step process.
- Develop instructional activities and materials for whole number operations at the primary level.

This unit looks at arithmetic, which includes the areas that were conventionally the core of the elementary grades mathematics program, that is, the **whole number operations** of addition, subtraction, multiplication, and division (Charlesworth & Senger, 2001). Today, however, the term *mathematics* refers to all the related concepts and skills included in this text—algebra, geometry, number sense, data analysis, and so on. Elementary and early childhood mathematics is a much more inclusive content area than it used to be.

The NCTM (2000) standard on number and operations includes expectations for the understanding of operations and how they relate to each other and for fluent computation and making reasonable estimates (discussed in Unit 20). During the primary grades, students should understand a variety of means for adding and subtracting, the relationship

between these two operations, the effects of adding and subtracting whole numbers, and situations in which they can use multiplication and division. Children should develop skill at whole number computation for addition and subtraction, be able to use the basic addition and subtraction number combinations, and use many different computation tools such as "objects, mental computation, estimation, paper and pencil, and calculators" (p. 78).

The curriculum focal points (Mirra, 2009; NCTM, 2007) for the primary level are organized by grades 1, 2, and 3. The focal points for grade 1 in number and operations are:

- Developing understandings of addition and subtraction strategies and facts.
- Connecting with concepts of 10s and 1s and solving two-digit problems.

The focal points for grade 2 in number and operations are:

- Developing quick recall of addition and related subtraction facts.
- Developing fluency with multidigit addition and subtraction.
- Connecting with a beginning understanding of multiplication.
- Connecting with applying the understanding of number to solve a variety of problems.

The focal points for grade 3 in number and operations are:

- Developing understandings of multiplication and division.
- Understanding and using basic multiplication and division facts.
- Connecting with algebra by developing an understanding of the patterns in multiplication and division.
- Connecting with data analysis using the whole number operations in collecting data and graphing.

Today, the most complex calculations are done with calculators and computers. However, the teachers encourage children to use estimation and mental computation. To understand each operation, children must learn how to solve problems using conventional and/or invented **algorithms**, which are step-by-step procedures for solving problems (Warshauer & Warshauer, 2001, p. 23). Once children establish this understanding, they can accomplish more by working on how to set up problems and then using technology to do the calculations. This unit describes methods for introducing children to whole number operations and whole number notation at a basic level. Once children understand the concepts, they can move on to more complex operations using calculators and computers to perform calculations.

Children naturally engage in the whole number operations of addition, subtraction, multiplication, and division prior to reaching the primary grades.

Units 18 through 20 describe the beginnings of the whole number operations as children grow out of naturalistic and informal experiences. Prior to entering first grade, young children also usually have an understanding of number symbols as they represent quantities. During the primary period (grades 1–3), children gradually learn the meaning of **action symbols** such as + (add), − (subtract), × (multiply), ÷ (divide), = (equals), < (less than), and > (greater than).

Teachers are expected to use state- and locally developed lists of objectives and selected textbooks to provide a structure for planning instruction. Unfortunately, primary teachers tend to rely too heavily on textbooks, workbooks, and photocopied support materials. Conventionally, students are expected to be able to do paper-and-pencil arithmetic even though it might be developmentally inappropriate. Opportunities for using exploration as a route to constructing concepts and operations are too seldom observed in the primary classroom. Students usually sit at individual desks with social interaction kept at a minimum (if allowed at all).

Constance Kamii is a major critic of the conventional approach to mathematics instruction in the primary grades. She presents her point of view in her books *Young Children Reinvent Arithmetic* (2000), *Young Children Continue to Reinvent Arithmetic, Second Grade* (2003), and *Young Children Reinvent Arithmetic, Third Grade* (1994). As a Piagetian, Kamii believes that—just as our ancestors did—children reinvent arithmetic through their own actions and needs rather than learning through what someone else tells them. Children need to reinvent arithmetic through naturalistic and informal exploration with naturally occurring problems and through group games. Adults should encourage them to invent their own procedures and use their own thinking. Kamii explains that paper-and-pencil worksheet approaches remove the child from his logical thinking, which is the heart of arithmetic. Kamii's emphasis on group games and social interaction as the basis for understanding arithmetic has its roots in Piaget's view that social interaction is essential as a stimulus for constructing knowledge. The following are examples of children solving problems through peer interaction:

- Three nonconservers are going to drink juice. The server pours juice into glass A. Now he must pour equal amounts into glasses B and C, which are different in size and shape from each other and from glass A. The children discuss how to do this in a fair manner and arrive at a solution: Use glass A as a measuring cup to fill the other two glasses.
- Derrick has written $7 + 4 = 10$, and Brent has written $7 + 4 = 12$. Their teacher has them explain to each other why they think that their respective answers are correct. Soon they discover that they are both wrong.

A danger in primary math instruction is that students will be pushed too fast before they have developed the cognitive capacity to understand the logical reasoning that underlies the operations. Keep in mind that children must be in the concrete operations period before they can successfully meet primary-level expectations. Beginning in kindergarten, standardized testing is performed each year, and teachers are pressured to teach the concepts and skills that are included in the tests. This pressure leads teachers to instruct arithmetic as a rote memory activity that has no logical meaning to the children. Children should be allowed to move at their own pace through primary math just as they did prior to entering first grade. They should also be allowed to invent their own procedures for solving problems. Herbert Ginsburg (1977) claims that young children naturally invent their own methods and should be able to use and experiment with them. For example, young children usually learn on their own to use counting methods for addition. When adding $2 + 2$, the child might say, "One, two, three, four" using fingers or objects. If left on their own, they will eventually stop counting because they've internalized $2 + 2 = 4$.

Carpenter, Carey, and Kouba (1990) point out that children enter first grade with informal concepts of the whole number operations. They also state the importance of observing the processes children use in solving problems. The authors believe that symbols should be introduced only to represent concepts that children already know. Instruction should begin with observations of naturalistic and informal activities.

Fuson, Grandau, and Sugiyama (2001) support the importance of informal teaching. "Such informal teaching can be done while children play, eat, get dressed, go up and down stairs, jump, and otherwise move through the day" (p. 522). During these activities, adults and more advanced peers can model mathematical concepts and skills, which children can then combine with understandings obtained during adult guided mathematics activities. Games can also support the transition into formal mathematics (see Fosnot & Dolk, 2001; Fosnot & Uittenbogaard, 2009).

This text describes a sequence of concept instruction with the caution to the teacher to bear in mind that children move at their own pace. As in previous units, it describes naturalistic, informal, and adult guided activities. Adult guided activities emphasize the use of concrete materials, with paper and pencil introduced through children's natural interests when they are ready.

Basic Combinations (Facts) and Algorithms

Isaacs and Carroll (1999) pose several questions about the value and purpose of learning the **basic facts** (or combinations) in the early grades. Will making first graders learn the addition facts interfere with their mathematical thinking? What kinds of instructional practices can build their understanding and quick recall? Can children learn the facts through problem-solving activities, or is drill and practice needed? Isaacs and Carroll go on to provide answers to these questions. Knowing the facts is certainly essential to furthering mathematical understanding, but drill and practice and timed tests lead only to stress and anxiety. We should instead build on the knowledge children bring to school and support them in developing strategies for learning the basic facts. Children enter the primary grades with counting skills and an understanding that quantities can be broken down into parts. They can learn facts through solving problems using their understanding of counting and parts and wholes. Building concrete models supports understanding and remembering. Having students share strategies will move them toward more efficient ones. Useful practice that is brief and nonstressful—such as games, computers, or even flash cards—can support the learning of basic facts.

Baroody (2006) contrasts the conventional drill and practice approach to instruction with the number sense approach to learning the facts with understanding. Children usually learn the facts in three phases (Baroody, 2006, p. 22) as follows:

- *Phase 1*. Uses object counting (blocks, fingers, tally marks) or verbal counting—for 5 + 2 the child says 5 and then counts on, using two fingers, to get 7 (typical first grader).
- *Phase 2*. Uses reasoning strategies to arrive at the answer to an unknown combination—for 5 + 4 the child thinks 4 + 4 = 8 and so one more would be 9 (typical second grader).
- *Phase 3*. Mastery is achieved as answers come quickly and accurately—for 5 + 4 = 9 the child responds without counting and reasoning (typical third grader).

The number sense view promotes learning the facts through discovering patterns and relationships that interconnect the basic combinations. Phases 1 and 2 serve this purpose by supporting the exploration and discovery that lead to seeing the patterns in each group of number facts. Adults should support children's use of informal strategies and focus on families of facts and their relationships. Children will gradually become more efficient. According to Baroody (2006), practice should be meaningful and should allow for flexible strategies.

Assessment should be process-oriented in the primary grades; that is, children can use a number of strategies for solving problems. By the end of third grade and the beginning of fourth grade,

children should be able to recall the addition and subtraction facts quickly and automatically.

Algorithms may be thought of as procedures, efficient methods, or rules for computation (Curcio & Schwartz, 1998). Several questions arise when it comes to instructional practice. Should algorithms be taught before, along with, or after children have had the opportunity to invent some of their own strategies? Curcio and Schwartz suggest that we begin with the children's own strategies and, through questioning, guide their reasoning toward more efficient and possibly conventional methods.

Computational Fluency

An important goal for the primary grades is developing **computational fluency** with whole numbers (NCTM, 2000). Russell (2000) provides guidelines for developing computational fluency. Fluency involves three ideas: efficiency, accuracy, and flexibility. Efficiency means the student can proceed directly without being distracted from his goal. Accuracy depends on being careful and double-checking results. Flexibility means being able to try out more than one strategy for solving problems. Fluency goes beyond memorizing one procedure or algorithm. As they learn more basic facts, they can apply this knowledge to recording their methods of problem solving. Children in grades K–2 should be encouraged to invent computational methods as they invent strategies to solve problems (Reys & Reys, 1998). Children in the early grades should be encouraged to invent their own problem-solving procedures (Heuser, 2005).

Action and Relational Symbols

At the primary level, children are usually introduced to the action and relational symbols. **Action symbols** show that some quantities have been or will be acted upon, or changed, in some way (+, −, ÷, ×); **relational symbols** show that quantities are in some way related (=, <, >). These symbols appear in **number sentences** that symbolize an operation, such as:

- $2 + 3 = 5$ (two things put together in a group with three things is the same amount as five things).
- $5 > 2$ (five is more than, or greater than, two).

Kamii and DeClark (Kamii, 1994, 2003; Kamii & DeClark, 2000) have found that young children often learn to deal with these symbols without a genuine understanding of how they relate to real quantities. Children should work with operations mentally through concrete experiences before connecting these operations to symbols and using complete conventional written number sentences such as $1 + 5 = 6, 5 - 3 = 2, 6 > 2$, and so on.

Kamii suggests that full number sentences (e.g., $4 + 2 = 6$) should not be introduced to children until second grade (Kamii, 2003; Kamii & DeClark, 2000). Children should be encouraged to devise their own notation systems and apply them as a bridge to formal notation. Children need experiences in joining and separating quantities and verbalizing about their actions prior to really understanding what symbols represent. Just filling in blanks in a workbook or marking answers in a standardized test booklet does not indicate that children understand the deeper meaning of number sentences.

Children often need concrete help such as manipulatives or fingers when first doing written problems.

In summary, formal number sentences should be introduced gradually. First, children should have extensive exploratory experiences that provide them with opportunities to invent their own solutions to everyday problems. They should be encouraged to find their own systems of recording solutions using their own notation. Teachers should develop the language of number sentences through word problems that come from real-life experiences. They should introduce formal number sentences when children have developed to the level where they can understand that number sentences are a shorthand representation for words. Teachers should introduce numeral notation first, then operational signs, and finally relational signs. Richardson's books (1984, 1999) are excellent resources for methods and materials that can be used for accomplishing these tasks. Discussions that follow describe some of these ideas for introducing formal symbolic notation.

Instructional Strategies

Fraivillig (2001) outlines instructional strategies for advancing children's mathematical thinking. Effective teaching includes three aspects: eliciting, supporting, and extending children's solution methods. This framework is called advancing children's thinking (ACT). *Eliciting* (p. 456) involves supporting a variety of solutions for any problem by listening to children, encouraging elaboration, being accepting of errors, promoting collaborative problem solving, and being sure everyone has an opportunity to report. *Supporting* (p. 457) involves pointing out problems that are similar, providing background knowledge, supporting students as they review their strategies, putting symbolic representations of solutions on the board, and encouraging children to ask for help. *Extending* (p. 457) requires maintaining high standards and expectations for all children, encouraging the drawing of generalizations, listing all solutions on the board to promote reflection, encouraging children to try alternative solutions and more efficient solutions, and promoting enthusiasm for challenge. Overall, the learning must take place in a safe environment in which all students feel comfortable and respected.

Assessment

Observations and interviews can be used to assess children's progress in constructing operations with whole numbers. Assessment should be done through concrete activities with real-life or pretend situations. Assessment should be incorporated into instruction. Paper-and-pencil tests are not appropriate for primary students until they can read and comprehend story problems on their own. Assessment examples will be provided as each whole number operation is discussed.

To find out if children are ready to move on to whole number operations, use the assessment interviews in Appendix A, Concrete Operations: Level 8. These tasks include conservation of number, knowledge of symbols and sets, multiple classification, and class inclusion.

Addition

Constructing the concept of addition requires the children to understand that adding is putting together groups of objects to find out how many there are. It also involves learning the application of terms such as **total**, **sum**, and **equals** as well as the operation signs (+ and =) that represent these terms, and connecting these amounts to symbols. Before children make these connections, they must understand quantity and what happens when quantities are combined.

Assessment

Assessing children's understanding of addition is more than finding out if they know the so-called number facts. It is important to observe the process each child goes through in dealing with quantities. Observing the process and questioning children regarding what they have done will reveal what they do and do not understand. Their mistakes are informative and can be used to help them develop a more accurate knowledge of arithmetic.

Observations can be made during naturalistic and informal activities. Dean figures out that if he has two dimes and his grandmother gives him four more, he will have six dimes. Liu Pei decides that if there are three children at one table, two at another, and four at a third, then she will need nine pieces of paper to pass out. Ann realizes that, instead of counting everyone to find out if there are enough pencils, she can record the number at each table, find the total, and compare it with the number of pencils in the box.

Observations can also be made during adult guided activities. Sara's teacher tells her to take groups of six cube blocks and place them in as many combinations of group sizes as she can. Does Sara realize that, however she arranges six objects (in groups of three and three; one and five; two, two, and two; two and four; or six and zero), there are still six altogether? The children are playing a card game called "Double War." Each player has two stacks of cards, which are turned over two cards at a time. The player with the higher sum gets the other player's two cards. The teacher can observe the children's strategies and whether they help one another. He can also suggest that they write and/or draw descriptions of their strategies.

As with the assessment of other math concepts, addition can also be measured using an interview approach. The following is a sample task.

SAMPLE ASSESSMENT TASK

9A
Addition, Combining Sets
up to 10: Unit 21

Concrete Operations Ages 6–8

METHOD: Interview.

SKILL: Child is able to combine sets to form new sets up to ten.

MATERIALS: Twenty counters (cube blocks, Unifix Cubes, chips): ten of one color and ten of another.

PROCEDURE: Have the child select two groups of counters from each color so that the total is ten or less. Say, **"Put three yellow cubes over here and five blue cubes over here."** Child completes task. Say, **"Now tell me, if you put all the cubes in one bunch, how many cubes do you have altogether? How do you know?"** Do this with combinations that add up to 1 through 10.

EVALUATION: Note if the child is able to make the requested groups with or without counting. Note the strategy the child uses to decide on the sum.
1.   Does he begin with one and count all the blocks?
2.   Does he count on? That is, in the example given, does he put his two small groups together and then say, "Three blocks, four, five, six, seven, eight. I have eight now"?
3.   Does he just say, "Eight, because I know that three plus five is eight"?

INSTRUCTIONAL RESOURCE: Charlesworth, R. (2011). *Experiences in math for young children* (6th ed.). Belmont, CA: Wadsworth/Cengage Learning.

Instruction

Instruction begins with naturalistic and informal experiences that familiarize children with quantities and how they relate to one another. Students can be guided toward constructing their own concepts if they are provided with games and word or story problems to solve and are encouraged to make up their own problems.

In *Young Children Reinvent Arithmetic* (2000), Constance Kamii and Georgia DeClark describe a number of types of games that can support the development of addition concepts. The following are examples of activities.

Activities

Addition: Double War

OBJECTIVE: Constructing combinations of addends (i.e., 1 + 1, 1 + 2, etc.) up to four.

MATERIALS: Two decks of cards with different patterns on the back.

PLAYING THE GAME: Start using the cards with addends up to four (aces, twos, threes, and fours). Have two children play together. To play the game, ask the children to begin with half the cards in each of the two decks, which are stacked facedown next to each other in front of them. Without looking at the cards, ask them to simultaneously turn over the top two cards from each deck. Have each find the total of her two cards. Have the child with the highest total keep all four cards.

FOLLOW-UP: Add the cards with the next higher addends as the children become adept with the first four. If the game takes too long, remove some of the smaller addends as the larger ones are included. Have the students write and/or draw descriptions of their strategies.

Addition: Board Games

OBJECTIVE: Constructing combinations of addends up to six.

MATERIALS: A pair of dice, a marker for each player (four), and a board game. Purchase or make board games. Design games themes that fit units in science and social studies. Some basic board-game patterns and the materials needed for construction are described in Unit 19. Design board games at the primary level with more spaces than those in Unit 19 because older students may move farther on each turn and will have longer attention spans.

PLAYING THE GAME: Have each player, in turn, roll the dice, find the sum of the roll, and move the marker that many spaces.

FOLLOW-UP: Bring in new games as the students become skilled at playing the old ones. As the students become adept at playing board games, purchase or make some with pitfalls. In other words, on some spaces the player might have to move backward or lose a turn (i.e., when a player lands on a red space, he rolls the dice again, and the player moves backward the sum of the dice; or, when a player lands on a certain space, he loses a turn).

Unit 3 describes the importance of problem solving. Placing operations in the context of real-life situations makes them come alive for the students, so they can see the practical applications of mathematics. Richardson (1984, 1999) suggests that the children act out stories using real objects from around the room as props. For example, Derrick brings six books from the library center and Theresa brings four. "How many did they bring altogether?" Derrick and Theresa actually demonstrate by going to the library center and obtaining the number of books in the problem. Trang Fung joins Dean and Sara. "How many children were there to start with?" "How many are there now?" Again, the children act out the situation. Richardson (1999) provides resources for acting out story problems with Unifix Cubes and other objects.

Carpenter and colleagues (1990) identify four types of addition problems.

Join, result unknown. Kim has two cars. Mario gives her five more cars. How many cars does Kim have altogether?

Separate, start unknown. Kim has some cars, and she gives two to Mario. Now she has five cars. How many cars did Kim have to start with?

Part–part–whole, whole unknown. Kim has two yellow cars and five blue cars. How many cars does she have?

Compare, compare quantity unknown. Mario has two cars. Kim has five more cars than Mario. How many cars does Kim have?

The authors caution that textbooks often contain only join and separate problems even though all four types should be introduced. A further caution is that these types are not formulas to be memorized but just problem variations that children need to explore.

As children become more advanced, the numbers can be larger and more addends can be included. More complex, **nonroutine problems** should also be used (see Unit 3).

Once the children have had some experiences with teacher-made problems, they can create their own problems.

Activities

Addition: Story Problems

OBJECTIVE: To construct the concept of addition by solving story problems.

MATERIALS: Twenty small toys that fit a current unit. For example:
- Miniature dinosaurs during a dinosaur unit
- Miniature dogs, cats, horses, etc., during a pet unit
- Miniature farm animals during a farm unit
- Miniature vehicles during a safety unit

DEVELOPING THE PROBLEMS: Let the students act out the problems as you tell the stories.
- **Find three plant-eating dinosaurs. Find four meat-eating dinosaurs. How many dinosaurs do you have?**
- **Mary has some puppies. She sells three puppies. Now she has two puppies left. How many did she have to start with?**
- **Officer Smith gave tickets to the drivers of two cars for speeding. Officer Vargas gave the drivers of three cars tickets for going too slow on the interstate. How many tickets did the officers give?**
- **Farmer Smith has five horses. Farmer Valdez has three more horses than farmer Smith. How many horses does farmer Valdez have?**
- **Four puppies went out to play. Two puppies jumped in a mud puddle. How many muddy feet were there? How many dry feet?**

FOLLOW-UP: Create problems to fit units and other activities and events.

Addition: Creating Problems Using Dice or a Fishbowl

OBJECTIVE: The children will create their own addition problems.

MATERIALS: A pair of dice or a container (fishbowl) full of numerals written on small pieces of cardboard cut into fish shapes, objects such as cube blocks, chips, or Unifix Cubes.

PLAYING THE GAME: Either by rolling the dice or picking two fish, have each child obtain two addends. Let him count out the amount for each addend and then tell how many objects or fish he has.

FOLLOW-UP: Once students are having an easy time making up problems using the dice or the written numerals as cues, suggest that they write or dictate their favorite problem, draw it, and write or dictate the solution. For example, Brent's dog is expecting pups. He writes, "I have one dog. I hope she has five pups." Then he draws his dog and the five pups. He writes, "Then I will have six dogs."

Using number symbols is referred to as **notation**. Gradually, you can connect number symbols to problems as you find that the children understand the process of addition and understand class inclusion. Although most first graders can fill in the blanks correctly on worksheets, this does not indicate that they really

understand what notation means. To find out if a child really understands notation, present a problem such as the following.

Show the child several (four, five, or six) counters. Then show how you add some (two, three, or four) more. Then say, "Write on your paper what

I did." Even at the end of first grade, you will find very few children who will write the correct notation (i.e., 5 + 3 = 8). It is very common for first graders to write the first and last numeral (5 8) or to write all three (5 3 8) and omit the action symbols. They may also be unable to tell you what they did and why. It is important that the use of notation be an integral part of concrete problem-solving activities.

Richardson (1984, 1999) suggests that formal instruction in connecting symbols to the process of addition begins with modeling of the writing of equations. After acting out a problem such as the one described previously, write the problem on the whiteboard and explain that this is another way to record the information. For example, "Another way to write three cows plus six cows makes nine cows is: 3 + 6 = 9 (three plus six equals nine)." Help the children learn what the plus sign means by playing games and doing activities that require the use of the plus sign with the equals sign. For example, try the following activity.

Activities

Addition: Using Notation at the Connecting Level

OBJECTIVE: Children will connect symbols to problems using numerals and the plus operation symbol.

MATERIALS: Objects to count and one die.

PLAYING THE GAME: Have children take turns rolling the die to find out how many to add. For example, a three is rolled. Have each child count out three counters. Write 3 on the board. A five is rolled. The students count out groups of five to put with their groups of three. Write 3 + 5.

FOLLOW-UP: After working with you in small groups, students can work independently with problems written on cards: 2 + 3, 4 + 6, and so on. As you go by, observe what they do, and ask them to read the problems to you.

Children sometimes look upon the equals sign as indicating that the answer is coming next rather than understanding that it indicates there is the same amount on each side of the equation. This concept can be clarified using a balance scale to explore equality.

When the children are comfortable with connecting the symbols to the problems and using the plus symbol, they can begin to write the notation themselves. Start with problems in which you write the notation, and have the children copy what you do before they go on to independent work. For example, have everyone pick five groups of five counters each. Then tell them to separate each

group of five counters as many ways as they can, and you write the results.

1 + 4 = 5	1	2	1	2	5
2 + 3 = 5	+4	+3	1	2	+0
1 + 1 + 3 = 5	5	5	+3	+1	5
2 + 2 + 1 = 5			5	5	
5 + 0 = 5					

After you write each equation, have the children write it on a piece of paper and put it next to the counters they have counted out. Follow up by having the students work independently, finding out how many ways they can break the amounts up to six and write the equations. When they are doing well up to six, have them move on to seven and above.

Subtraction

To conceptualize subtraction is to develop an understanding that subtracting involves taking objects away to find out how many are left or comparing groups of objects to find out the difference between them. It also involves learning the application of terms such as minus, difference, and equal as well as the action signs ($-$ and $=$) that represent these terms. Subtraction also involves thinking about **more than** ($>$) and **less than** ($<$) and the symbols that stand for these relationships. It also includes connecting to symbols as a shorthand notation for concrete operations. As with addition, before children make the connections to and between symbols, they must understand quantity and what happens when something is taken away from a group or when two groups are compared.

Assessment

Assessing children's understanding of addition is more than finding out if they know the so-called number facts. It is important to observe the process each child goes through in dealing with quantities. Observing the process and questioning children regarding what they have done will reveal what they do and do not understand. Their mistakes are informative and can be used to help them develop a more accurate knowledge of arithmetic.

As with addition, assessing children's understanding of subtraction should involve more than mere number facts. Observing and questioning children about their processes for dealing with quantities will indicate the level of their knowledge.

Observations can be made during naturalistic and informal activities. Chan figures out that if there are ten more minutes until school is out and Ms. Hebert says that they will start to get ready to leave in five minutes, then they will have five minutes to get ready. Jason has ten bean seeds. He decides that he can give Ann four because the six he will have left will be enough for his seed-sprouting experiment. Six children are allowed to work in the science center at one time. Brent notices that there are only four children at the science center now. He suggests to Derrick that they hurry over while there is room for two more. Vanessa observes that there is room for eight children in the library center, whereas six at a time may work in the math center. Thus there is room for two more in the library center than in the math center.

Observations can also be made during adult guided activities. Dean is trying to figure out how many different amounts he can take away from five. Mrs. Red Fox notes that Dean is well organized and systematic as he constructs one group of five after another and takes a different amount away until he has the combinations five minus zero, one, two, three, four, and five. Derrick and Liu Pei are playing "Double War." They have to subtract the amount that is smaller from the amount that is larger. Mr. Wang can note whether the children can figure out the correct differences and whether they help one another.

Subtraction can be assessed using an interview approach. The following is a sample task.

SAMPLE ASSESSMENT TASK

9B   **Concrete Operations Ages 6–8**
Subtraction, Sets of Ten and Less: Unit 21

METHOD: Interview.

SKILL: Child is able to subtract groups to make new groups using groups of ten and smaller.

MATERIALS: Twenty counters (cube blocks, Unifix Cubes, chips): ten of one color and ten of another and a small box or other small container.

PROCEDURE: Pick out a group of ten or fewer counters. Say, "**I have seven cubes. I'm going to hide some in the box.**" (Hide three in the box.) "**Now how many do I have left? How many did I hide?**" If the child cannot answer, give him seven of the other color cubes and ask him to take three away and tell you how many are left. Do this with amounts of ten and less. For the less mature or younger child, start with five and less.

EVALUATION: Note if the child is able to solve the problem and the process used. Note whether the child has to count or whether he just knows without counting.

INSTRUCTIONAL RESOURCE: Charlesworth, R. (2011). *Experiences in math for young children* (6th ed.). Belmont, CA: Wadsworth/Cengage Learning.

Instruction

Just as with addition, instruction should involve informal experiences that familiarize children with how quantities are related to each other. Again, providing students with games or story problems can help them to construct their own concepts and problems. Once the students evidence an understanding of addition, introduce subtraction. Children can work with both addition and subtraction problems so that they can learn the clues for deciding which operation to use.

The game "Double War" can be modified and played as a subtraction game by having the player with the largest difference between her pair of cards keep all four cards. As with addition, begin with numbers up to four and then gradually include higher numbers as the children become adept at the game. Purchase or devise board games that use subtraction as the operation that indicates which way to move. Make a board game in which all the moves are backward. The theme might be running away from a wild animal or going home from a friend's house. Or dice could be thrown, and each move would be the difference between the two.

Of course, word or story problems are an essential ingredient in the instruction of subtraction, just as they are for addition. Set or act out problems in real-life contexts. For example, suppose

Derrick and Theresa have brought ten books from the library center. Continue the activity by asking children to take different numbers of books back to the library center and to find out how many are left after each trip. Place children in groups of different sizes. If there are five children in this group and three in this group, ask them, "Which group has more? How many more? How will we find out?"

A number of different basic patterns can be used for subtraction story problems. Carpenter and colleagues (1990) identify seven types of subtraction problems, as follows.

1. *Join, change unknown*. Kim has three cars. How many more cars will she need to have eight altogether?
2. *Join, start unknown*. Kim has some cars, and Mario gives her three more cars. Now she has eight cars. How many cars did Kim have to start with?
3. *Separate, result unknown*. Kim had eight cars and she gave Mario three cars. How many cars does Kim have left?
4. *Separate, change unknown*. Kim had eight cars and gave some to Mario. Now she has five cars. How many did she give to Mario?
5. *Part–part–whole, part unknown*. Kim has eight cars. Five are yellow and the rest are green. How many are green?

6. *Compare, difference unknown.* Kim has eight cars and Mario has three cars. How many more cars does Kim have than Mario?
7. *Compare, referent unknown.* Kim has eight cars. She has five more cars than Mario. How many cars does Mario have?

As with addition, once the children have experiences with teacher-devised story problems, they can dictate or write their own. The dice/fishbowl game can be modified for subtraction. Children can also dictate or write original problems, draw them, and write or dictate the solutions.

Introduce subtraction notation gradually. Connect number symbols to problems as you find that the children have understood the process of subtraction. To find out if a child really understands notation, use the same type of procedure as for

addition. In other words, show the child several counters (five, six, or seven). Have her tell you how many you have. Hide one or more of the counters, and ask the child to show you on paper what you did. Do not be surprised if very few late first graders and only some second graders will be able to write the correct equation.

Formal introduction of subtraction can begin with modeling. Act out a problem and then explain that there is another way to record the information. Write the number sentence for the problem on the chalkboard. For example, "Another way to write five rabbits take away three rabbits is $5 - 3 = 2$ (five minus three equals two)." Help the children learn what the minus sign means by playing games and doing activities that require its use with the equals sign. For example, try the following activity.

Activities

Subtraction: Using Notation at the Connecting Level

OBJECTIVE: The children will connect symbols to problems using numerals and the minus action symbol.

MATERIALS: Objects to count and two dice.

PLAYING THE GAME: Have the children take turns rolling the dice to find out which numbers to subtract. Have them first identify the larger number and count out that amount of counters. Write [larger number −]. Then have the children remove the smaller number of counters. Continue writing [larger number − smaller number]. Then have the children identify how many are left in the original pile. Complete the equation [larger number − smaller number = difference]. For example, the children roll six and two. They make a group of six counters, and you write $6 -$. Then they remove two counters, and you continue writing: $6 - 2$. Then they identify the difference (four). You finish the equation: $6 - 2 = 4$.

FOLLOW-UP: After working with you in small groups, students can work independently with problems written on cards: $5 - 1$, $3 - 2$, etc. Have them make up problems using dice or pulling numbers out of a fishbowl. As you observe what the children are doing, stop and ask them to read the problems to you.

As with addition, when the students are comfortable with connecting the symbols to the problems and using the minus symbol, they can begin to write the notation themselves. Start with problems where you write the notation, and have the children copy you before they go on to independent work. For example, have everyone pick six counters. Have them see what kinds of problems appear as different amounts are taken away. After each problem, take a new group of six so the problems can be compared. You write the results of each takeaway on the chalkboard (e.g., $6 - 1 = 5$); have the children copy it on a piece of paper and put it next to the counters they have counted out. Follow up by having the students work independently. Find out how many subtraction problems they can discover starting with groups of different amounts up through six. When they are doing well up to six, have them move on to seven and above.

The notations for greater (more) than ($>$) and less than ($<$) are conventionally introduced in first grade along with subtraction, but children usually do not really understand them until grade 3. For the most part, students in early primary grades work with *more* and *less* using concrete materials such as those described in Unit 8. As they begin to understand the concepts, the children can apply them in playing games. For example, lotto and bingo boards (see Unit 19) can be used. For bingo, the players can roll a die and cover a square on their card containing a number or set that is more than or less than the number rolled. For lotto, they would pick a numeral or set card and again cover a card on the board that was either more than or less than the numeral or set on the card. As students become familiar with the action symbols, cards could be used that indicate that they pick an amount or numeral that is $>$ (more or greater than) or $<$ (less than) one of those on the card. They could then move on to using cards that indicate an amount such as [__ $>$ 2] or [__ $<$ 5] and thus be required to use addition or subtraction to arrive at a selection.

Children need to understand that addition and subtraction are related (Fosnot & Dolk, 2001). They may both apply to the same problem. For example, in a problem where people get on and off a bus, people must be added to the passengers and people may be subtracted from the passengers to get the total at the end of the ride. Some problems may look like addition when they really involve subtraction. For example, Juan needs $5.00 to buy a toy. He has $3.00. How much more does he need? Addition and subtraction should be taught at the same time, so children can develop an intuitive understanding of their relationship.

Multiplication

Conceptualizing multiplication requires that the students understand what equal quantities are. Then they can proceed to learn that multiplication is a shorthand way of adding equal quantities. That is, 4×3 is the same as $3 + 3 + 3 + 3$. Multiplication also involves learning the application of terms such as **factors** (the two numbers that are operated on) and **product** (the result of the operation). Students also learn the action terms **times** and *equals* and connect them to the action signs ($\times$ and $=$). Multiplication with concrete objects was introduced prior to the primary level and continues at this level for most primary students. Notation and the more formal aspects may be introduced toward the end of the primary level, but students are not usually proficient at the most fundamental level until fourth grade.

Assessment

Assessing children's understanding of multiplication, as with the other whole number operations, is more than finding out if children know the number facts. It is important to observe the process each child goes through in dealing with quantities and to ask questions that will reveal the thoughts behind their actions.

Observations can be made during naturalistic and informal activities. Use the terms *rows, stacks*, and *groups* to refer to equal groups that will be added. There is no rush to use the term *times*. Many children learn to recite the times tables by heart without any understanding of what *times* really means. Children must first understand that, when they multiply, they are not counting individual objects but rather groups of objects. Watch for incidents when children work with equal groups. For example, Dean comments that every child at his table has three carrot sticks. Theresa makes sure that each of the six children working in the science center receives four bean seeds to plant. Chan tells Ms. Hebert that he has purchased three miniature dinosaurs for each of the five friends invited to his birthday party. She asks him if he can figure out how many he bought altogether.

Multiplication can also be assessed using an interview approach. The following is a sample task.

SAMPLE ASSESSMENT TASK

9F   **Concrete Operations Ages 7–8**
Multiplication, Readiness: Unit 21

METHOD: Interview.

SKILL: Child is able to demonstrate readiness for multiplication by constructing equal groups of different sizes from groups of the same size.

MATERIALS: Twenty counters (cube blocks, Unifix Cubes, chips).

PROCEDURE: Make two groups of six counters each. Ask the child, "**Make three groups of two chips (blocks, cubes) each with this bunch of six chips (blocks, cubes).**" When the child finishes (right or wrong), point to the other group of counters. "**Now make two groups of three with these chips (blocks, cubes).**"

EVALUATION: Note if the child is able to make the two different subgroups. Children who are not ready for multiplication will become confused and not see the difference between the two tasks.

INSTRUCTIONAL RESOURCE: Charlesworth, R. (2011). *Experiences in math for young children* (6th ed.). Belmont, CA: Wadsworth/Cengage Learning.

Instruction

Just as with addition and subtraction, instruction in multiplication begins with naturalistic and informal experiences that familiarize children with quantities and how they relate to each other. Students can be guided toward constructing their own concepts if they are provided with games and story problems to solve and are encouraged to make up their own problems. Richardson (1984, 1999) suggests that the children should first be asked to look for equal groups in the environment. How many tables have four chairs? How many girls have two barrettes in their hair? How many children have three cookies for dessert? How many parts of the body can they identify that come in groups of two? What parts do cars have that come in groups of four?

Of course, word or story problems are an essential ingredient in the instruction of multiplication, just as they are for subtraction and addition. Set or act out problems in real-life contexts. Dean gives four children two crayons each. How many crayons did he pass out? Chan makes three stacks of books. He puts three books in each stack. How many books does he have? Ann gives each of the five people at her table four pieces of paper. How many pieces of paper did she pass out?

Build models of multiplication problems with the students. Stack counters, put in rows, and place in groups as illustrated in Figure 21–1. For example, working with inch cubes:

- Make three stacks of four cubes each.
- Make four rows of five cubes each.
- Make six groups of two cubes each.

Introduce notation gradually. Connect number symbols to problems as you find that the children have understood the process of multiplication. Formal introduction of multiplication can begin with modeling. Act out a problem, and then explain that there is another way to record the information. Write the number sentence for the problem on the chalkboard. For example: "Another way to write 'Dean gave four children two crayons each' is [4 groups of 2 = 8]. Another way to write 'Chan has three stacks of three books' is [3 stacks of 3 = 9]." Do several problems in this manner. Then introduce the multiplication sign. First model. Explain that there is an even shorter way to write problems. Erase "stacks of" or "groups of" and write $\times$ in its place. Then write problems on the board and have the children work them out with their counters. Next, have them work out problems and copy you as you write the whole equation, that is [4 $\times$ 2 = 8]. Finally, have them make models and write the equations on their own.

The following is an example of an independent activity that can be done with multiplication using notation.

To find out if a child really understands notation, use the same type of procedure as you use for addition and subtraction. For example, show

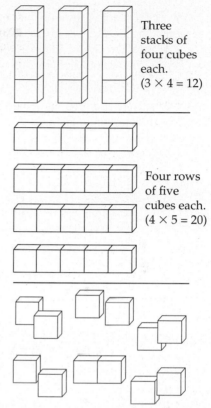

Three stacks of four cubes each. (3 $\times$ 4 = 12)

Four rows of five cubes each. (4 $\times$ 5 = 20)

Six groups of two cubes each. (6 $\times$ 2 = 12)

FIGURE 21–1 Equal stacks, rows, and groups are the basis of multiplication.

the child three or more equivalent groups and explain that you are going to put the groups together into one group. Ask him to write what you did. If you showed three groups of four, he should write [3 $\times$ 4 =12].

Activities

Multiplication: Using Notation at the Connecting Level

OBJECTIVE: The children will connect symbols to problems using numerals and the times action symbol.

MATERIALS: Counters, a die, several small containers, a sheet for recording the problems.

ACTIVITY: Have children work on their own writing equations. First let them decide how many containers to use. Have them roll the die or just pick a number. Have them line up the cups and then, starting with zero and one at a time, fill the cups and write the resulting equation. For example, if they pick four cups, they would first put zero blocks in each cup and write the equation, then one block in each, then two, three, and so on. Their work would look like that shown in Figure 21–2.

FOLLOW-UP: Develop some more independent activities using the resources suggested on the Online Companion for this unit.

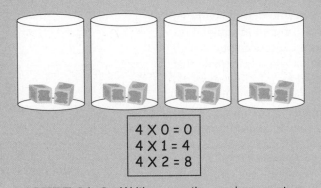

$$4 \times 0 = 0$$
$$4 \times 1 = 4$$
$$4 \times 2 = 8$$

FIGURE 21–2 Writing equations using counters and containers.

Division

Division is an activity that children engage in frequently during their natural everyday activities (see Unit 25). They are encouraged to share equally, and they are often asked to pass out items so that everyone has the same amount. Formal instruction in division is usually introduced toward the end of the primary period during the third grade, but children are not expected to be proficient in doing division problems until the fifth grade. Division is used to solve two types of problems.

1. *Grouping* is the process used to find out how many subgroups of a particular size a larger group contains. For example, George has 15 blocks. He wants to make towers that are five blocks high. How many can he make?
2. *Sharing* is the process of dividing a larger group into a particular number of groups to find out how many items will be included in

that number of subgroups. Six children will work in the science center exploring the reaction of different types of items when they are touched by magnets. There are 32 items. How many will each child get? Are there any left over?

The children do not have to distinguish between these types of problems, which serve mainly as a guide for making up problems for them to explore. Eventually they will learn the terminology of division: **dividend ÷ divisor = quotient** and, if some are left over, **remainder**.

Assessment

Assessing children's understanding of division focuses on the processes they use to group and to share. The following task can be used to assess the child's understanding of grouping and sharing.

SAMPLE ASSESSMENT TASK

9I
Division, Basic Concept: Unit 21

Concrete Operations Ages 7–8

METHOD: Interview.

SKILL: Child can demonstrate an understanding that division consists of grouping or sharing objects.

MATERIALS: Thirty counters (cube blocks, Unifix Cubes, chips) and five small containers (such as clear plastic glasses).

PROCEDURE: Put out eight chips and four containers. Say, "**Divide up the chips so that each cup has the same amount.**" When the chips are divided, ask, "**How many cubes do you have in each cup?**" The child should respond "Two in each cup" rather than "I have two, two, and two." Try the same procedure with more cups and larger amounts to divide. Then try it with uneven amounts. Note if the child becomes confused or can recognize that there are more cups than are needed. Also do some sharing problems; for example, put out 16 chips. Ask, "**I want to give three friends the same amount of chips. How many will each one receive? Are there any left over?**"

EVALUATION: Note how the children handle the problem. Do they proceed in an organized fashion? Can they deal with the remainders?

INSTRUCTIONAL RESOURCE: Charlesworth, R. (2011) *Experiences in math for young children* (6th ed.). Belmont, CA: Wadsworth/Cengage Learning.

Instruction

Division also begins with naturalistic and informal experiences. The teacher can give children many tasks that give them division experiences. Passing out items, putting items into groups to be shared, and finding out if there is enough for everyone are opportunities for children to develop the division concept. The teacher can use games and story problems as guides in supporting the child's construction of the concept of division as she ventures into more formal activities.

As with the other whole number operations, begin formal instruction by doing concrete problems. As Richardson (1984) suggests, tell the children stories and have them act them out. Start with real objects from the classroom. Here are two examples.

- Ann has 16 pieces of paper. Each child in her group needs four pieces. How many children can receive four pieces of paper?
- Jason, Chan, and Vanessa want to feed the guinea pig. The guinea pig gets six pellets of food. How many pellets can each child give it?

Next, have the children act out similar stories, using counters to represent real objects. Have the children make many models by constructing rows and stacks and dividing them into groups.

Activities

Division: Making Models

OBJECTIVE: The children will construct models of division.

MATERIALS: Counters (cube blocks, Unifix Cubes, chips) and several 16-ounce clear plastic cups.

ACTIVITY: Using different amounts initially and having the children divide them up into groups of different sizes and into different numbers of groups, have the students do many problems using the following patterns:

1. **Make a row (train) with (number of) blocks (cubes, chips). How many stacks of (number) can you make? Divide your row (train) of (number) into (number of) rows. How many cubes (blocks, chips) are in each row?**
2. **Get (number) cups. Divide (number) cubes into each cup so that there is the same amount of cubes in each cup.**
   Continue with different numbers of cups and counters.

FOLLOW-UP: Develop some more independent activities using the resources suggested on the Online Companion for this unit.

Introduce division notation with modeling. Act out problems just as you did with the other whole number operations.

- "John has twelve crackers." Write [12] on the board. "He has three friends. He wants to give himself and each friend the same number of crackers." Write [12 ÷ 4]. "Each child got three crackers." Write [12 ÷ 4 = 3].
- "The children are going to explore how pendulums work. There are four pendulums and eight children. How many children will have to share each pendulum? Eight children (write 8) divided by four pendulums (write [8 ÷ 4]) equals two children must share each pendulum" (write [8 ÷ 4 = 2]).

After you have modeled several problems, let the children go to the next step by acting out the problems and copying what you write. Next, give them problems they can act out with counters and write the equations themselves. When the children have completed the equations, write them on the board and they can check theirs. Check each child's model and equation. Note whether there are any difficulties, and help children figure out how to act out and write the equation correctly. Move on to giving the children written problems (i.e., 10 ÷ 2), and ask them to act the problems out using counters. Finally, have them make up their own problems, act them out, draw them, and write them.

To find out if a child really understands notation, use the same procedure as suggested for the other whole number operations. Namely, act out division and then ask the children to write what you did. For example, count out 15 counters and divide them into five groups of three. See whether the children can write [15 ÷ 5 = 3] and tell you that 15 divided into five groups makes three in each group.

Integration with Other Content Areas

Whole number operations can be applied in the other major content areas, as depicted in Figure 21–3. With an art project, for example, students can create squared paper designs, count the number of each color used in their design, and add the total number of squares included. For science, they can do environmental math such as graphing the contents of the trash can in the classroom and determining which type of trash is found in the largest amount. Social studies offers many opportunities, such as adding up the cost of a meal in a restaurant, dividing food into equal portions, or finding out how many of an item will be needed if each person in the group gets a fixed amount. Books, as previously described in Unit 12, offer many opportunities for solving whole number problems.

PROBLEM SOLUTIONS

Four monsters are at a party. There are eight little cakes with cherries on top. How many cakes will each monster get?

Three dinasaurs each had two mittens. How many mittens altogether?

6 mittens because theres three dinosaurs and each one gets two so count be twos 2, 4, 6

Creepy crawly had 10 legs to walk with. He lost several legs and had only six left. How many legs did Creepy lose?

4 because 6 + 4 = 10 and 10 take away four = 6 so its four 4

A third grader easily solves these kindergarten problems and can explain her solutions.
Problems from L. Outhred & S. Sardelich (2005). Problem solving by kindergartners. *Teaching Children Mathematics, 12*(3), 146–152.
Work of Summer Potter used with parent's permission.

Technology

Computers and hand calculators are useful tools for supporting the exploration of whole number operations and the properties of whole numbers. There are a multitude of software and Internet resources available for working with basic whole number operations. Most of these programs are designed to help children remember the basic addition, subtraction, multiplication, and division facts. Many have interesting graphics that catch the children's attention and make drill and practice fun. With the capability of letting the children know right away whether the response is correct, the programs give the children immediate feedback and allow them to move along at their own pace.

During preprimary activities, children have explored some of the basic calculator capabilities.

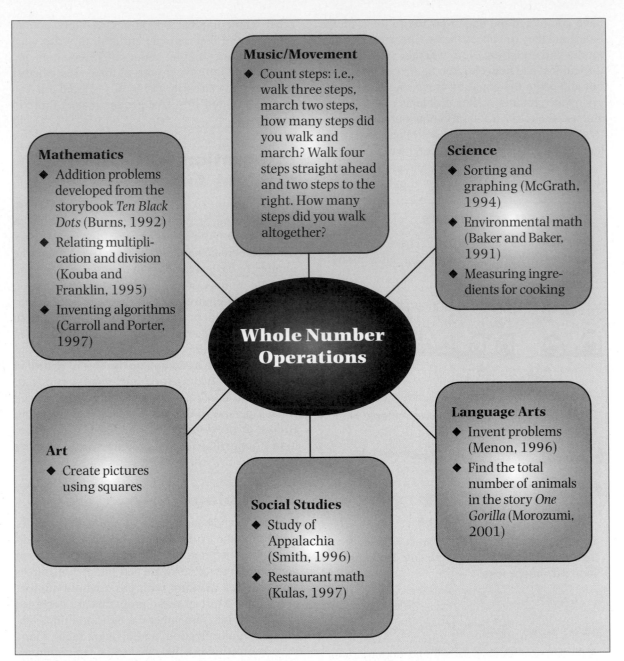

FIGURE 21–3 Integrating whole number operations across the curriculum.

COUNT WITH YOUR CALCULATOR

Push ©⓪⊕②⊜

What do you see?_____

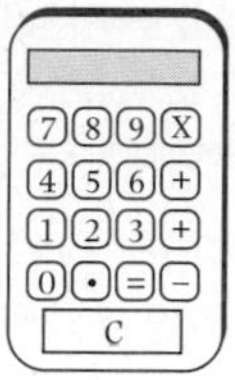

Push ⊜ again

What do you see?_____

What will the calculator show if you

Push ⊜ again?_____

Do it. Were you correct?_____

Push ⊜⊜⊜ .

Guess what the calculator will show each time._____

What happened?_____

Complete the following. Then use your calculator to see if you are correct.

Push ©⓪⊕③⊜

The calculator will show_____

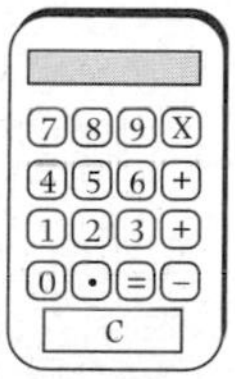

Push

⊜ _____

⊜ _____

⊜ _____

Push ©⓪⊕④⊜

The calculator will show_____

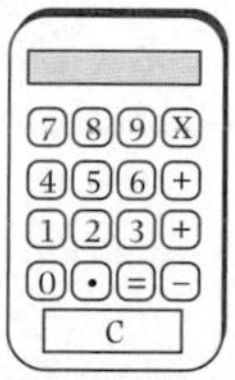

Push

⊜ _____

⊜ _____

⊜ _____

FIGURE 21–4   The calculator can be used to count by equal multiples.

During primary activities, the calculator can be used for further exploration, for checking and comparing with manual calculations, and for problem solutions. A basic activity with the calculator is the exploration of multiples. Young children are fascinated with rhymes such as "Two, four, six, eight, who do we appreciate?" This type of counting is called **skip counting**. Skip counting in this example defines the multiples of two—that is, all the numbers that result when a series is multiplied by two ($2 \times 2 = 4$, $2 \times 3 = 6$, $2 \times 4 = 8$, etc.). Children can explore these properties with the calculator through calculator counting (Figure 21–4).

Ideas for Children with Special Needs

In the primary grades, children are expected to become proficient readers. This is a special challenge for ELLs, and the challenge is compounded when they are given written or oral math problems to solve. Garrison, Ponce, and Amarel (2007) explored how mathematics teachers can find ways to help ELLs understand both the language and the mathematical concepts. Garrison and colleagues studied the results of a problem-based approach featuring adaptations for ELLs compared with

MATH TECHNOLOGY
FOR YOUNG CHILDREN

Review some whole number operations resources using the format described in Unit 2. You might try one of the following resources if available.

- *Flash Action Software—Addition and Subtraction* (ages 6 and up; Grand Haven, MI: School Zone Publishing).
- *Math Missions: The Race to Spectacle City Arcade* (ages 5–8; New York: Scholastic, http://www.kidsclick.com).
- *Stickybear Math Town Bilingual* (ages 5–10; Hazelton, PA: K–12 Software). Addition, subtraction, multiplication, and division.
- *Key Skills for Math: Addition and Subtraction* (grades 1–3; http://store.sunburst.com).
- *Destination Math* (K–1; http://www.riverdeep.net).
- *Mighty Math Zoo Zillions* (K–2; http://www.riverdeep.net).
- *Mighty Math Carnival Countdown* (K–2; http://www.riverdeep.net).
- *Math Express: Addition, Division, Multiplication, Subtraction* (pre-K–6; http://www.k12software.com).
- *Math Resources from PBS. Mathline lessons.* (pbs.org).
- *PBS Parents Guide to Early Math Grades PreK-2.* (pbs.org).

more traditional instruction—with no ELL adaptations—in two first-grade classrooms that included ELLs. "Our study found that students in the problem-based class were better and more persistent problem solvers than their peers in the traditional mathematics class" (Garrison et al., 2007, p. 13).

The teacher started the year with simple problems using familiar vocabulary. These first problems were in the present tense, and any new words were discussed. Children first worked independently and then were put into pairs. A successful child was paired with a struggling child. Finally, children shared their strategies with the whole class. Gradually the problems became more complex. By combining the teaching of English with mathematics, the class gained in both areas.

Tabor and Canonica (2008) were challenged to teach division to their special education students. These students had many misconceptions and computational difficulties. They focused on division as sharing and as the inverse of multiplication. Students shared objects and then wrote equations that illustrated their sharing. Then they moved on to writing sharing stories. They drew models of their problems and described their solutions. These and other tasks provided the students with the freedom to select numbers they felt comfortable with at their level.

Evaluation

Evaluation, just as with assessment, should be done first with concrete tasks and should involve observing both the process and the product. The tasks in Appendix A and in this unit can be used for evaluation as well as for initial assessment. Standardized achievement tests should not be administered until the students have the concepts internalized with concrete activities. For guidelines for testing young children, see the National Association for the Education of Young Children (NAEYC, 1991) position statement on standardized testing of children aged 3–8.

Summary

Children begin to develop the whole number operations of addition, subtraction, multiplication, and division through naturalistic and informal experiences during the preprimary years. As children's cognitive development takes them into the concrete operational level, they are ready to move into learning about action symbols and written notation. Problem solving with whole numbers involves the learning of basic facts and algorithms as well as developing computational fluency. Conventionally, children start with addition and subtraction in the beginning of the primary period (grade 1). They move on to more complex addition and subtraction and to multiplication in the second grade. They start with division in the third grade. Children begin each operation with informal activities and acting out problems using concrete objects and then move gradually into using formal notation and written problems. Story or word problems that put the operations into real-life contexts are the core around which the whole number operations are constructed in the young child's mind. ELLs can improve mathematical skill and increase their language skill through a problem-solving approach to mathematics.

KEY TERMS

action symbols	less than (<)	remainder
algorithms	more than (>)	skip counting
basic facts	nonroutine problems	sum
computational fluency	notation	times
dividend	number sentences	total
divisor	product	whole number operations
equals	quotient	
factors	relational symbols	

SUGGESTED ACTIVITIES

1. Develop at least two of the independent activities suggested by Kathy Richardson and/or the group games described by Constance Kamii or Catherine Fosnot in their respective books. Add the instructions to your Activity File. If possible, try out the activities with one or more primary grade children. Report to the class regarding what you developed, whom you tried it with, what happened, and how well you believe it worked.

2. Do a comparison of concrete versus paper-and-pencil modes of math assessment. Select three whole number operations assessment tasks from this unit or Appendix A. Devise a paper-and-pencil test that includes the same kinds of problems. Use the interview tasks with two primary students. Return a week later and use the conventional paper-and-pencil test with the same two students. Take careful notes on the process the students use to solve the problems. Write a report describing the two types of assessment tasks; the results, including the students' performance; and your comparison and evaluation of the two methods of assessment.

3. Observe in two or more primary classrooms during times when math activities are occurring. Your report to the class should include a description of what you observed, how the instruction compared with the methods described in this unit, and suggestions for any changes you would make if you were teaching in those classrooms.

REVIEW

A. Explain why it is essential that children have the opportunity to construct their own whole number algorithms.

B. Match the action symbols in Column I with the words they stand for in Column II.

Column I	Column II
1. +	a. multiply, times
2. −	b. equals
3. ×	c. more than or greater than
4. ÷	d. add, plus
5. =	e. less than
6. <	f. divide
7. >	g. subtract, minus

C. Select the following statements that are correct:
1. Constance Kamii believes that children learn arithmetic by being told about it.

2. Kamii believes that group games are excellent vehicles for supporting the construction of math concepts.
3. Paper-and-pencil worksheets are excellent for helping children develop the logic of arithmetic.
4. Kamii believes that children should always work alone at their desks when learning math.

D. Explain why standardized testing is a threat to the development of logical thinking.
E. When introducing whole number sentences (equations), a three-stage sequence should be followed. List the steps.
F. Explain briefly the instructional processes for addition, subtraction, multiplication, and division.

REFERENCES

Baroody, A. J. (2006). Why children have difficulties mastering the basic number combinations and how to help them. *Teaching Children Mathematics, 13*(1), 22–31.

Carpenter, T., Carey, D., & Kouba, V. (1990). A problem-solving approach to the operations. In J. N. Payne (Ed.), *Mathematics for the young child* (pp. 111–131). Reston, VA: National Council of Teachers of Mathematics.

Charlesworth, R., & Senger, E. (2001). Arithmetic. In L. S. Grinstein & S. I. Lipsey (Eds.), *Encyclopedia of mathematics* (pp. 37–43). New York: RoutledgeFalmer.

Curcio, F. R., & Schwartz, S. L. (1998). There are no algorithms for teaching algorithms. *Teaching Children Mathematics, 5*(1), 26–30.

Fosnot, C. T., & Dolk, M. (2001). *Young mathematicians at work: Constructing number sense, addition, and subtraction*. Portsmouth, NH: Heinemann.

Fosnot, C. T., & Uittenbogaard, W. (2009). *Minilessons for early addition and subtraction*. Portsmouth, NH: Heinemann.

Fraivillig, J. (2001). Strategies for advancing children's mathematical thinking. *Teaching Children Mathematics, 7*(8), 454–459.

Fuson, K. C., Grandau, L., & Sugiyama, P. A. (2001). Achievable numerical understandings for all young children. *Teaching Children Mathematics, 7*(9), 522–526.

Garrison, L., Ponce, G. A., & Amaral, O. M. (2007). Ninety percent of the game is half mental. *Teaching Children Mathematics, 14*(1), 12–17.

Ginsburg, H. (1977). *Children's arithmetic*. New York: Van Nostrand.

Heuser, D. (2005). Teaching without telling: Computational fluency and understanding through invention. *Teaching Children Mathematics, 11*(8), 404–412.

Isaacs, A. C., & Carroll, W. M. (1999). Strategies for basic-facts instruction. *Teaching Children Mathematics, 5*(9), 508–515.

Kamii, C. K. (1994). *Young children reinvent arithmetic, third grade*. New York: Teachers College Press.

Kamii, C. K. (2003). *Young children continue to reinvent arithmetic, second grade* (2nd ed.). New York: Teachers College Press.

Kamii, C. K., & DeClark, G. (2000). *Young children reinvent arithmetic*. New York: Teachers College Press.

Mirra, A. (2009). *Focus in prekindergarten— Grade 2: Teaching with curriculum focal points*. Reston, VA: National Council of Teachers of Mathematics.

National Association for the Education of Young Children (NAEYC) and National Association of Early Childhood Specialists in State Departments of Education (NAECSSDE). (1991). Guidelines for appropriate curriculum content and assessment in programs serving children ages 3 through 8: A position statement. *Young Children, 46*(3), 21–38.

National Council of Teachers of Mathematics. (2000). *Principles and standards for school mathematics*. Reston, VA: Author.

National Council of Teachers of Mathematics. (2007). *Curriculum focal points*. Reston, VA: Author.

Reys, B. J., & Reys, R. E. (1998). Computation in the elementary curriculum: Shifting the emphasis. *Teaching Children Mathematics, 5*(4), 236–241.

Richardson, K. (1984). *Developing number concepts using Unifix Cubes.* Menlo Park, CA: Addison-Wesley.

Richardson, K. (1999). *Developing number concepts: Book 2. Addition and subtraction.* Parsippany, NJ: Seymour.

Russell, S. J. (2000). Developing computational fluency with whole numbers. *Teaching Children Mathematics, 7*(3), 154–158.

Tabor, S. B., & Canonica, M. (2008). Sharing "cat games" and cookies: Special education students investigate division. *Teaching Children Mathematics, 15*(1), 55–61.

Warshauer, H. K., & Warshauer, M. L. (2001). Algorithms. In L. S. Grinstein & S. I. Lipsey (Eds.), *Encyclopedia of mathematics* (pp. 23–24). New York: RoutledgeFalmer.

FURTHER READING AND RESOURCES

Barlow, A. T., & Gates, J. M. (2006/2007). The answer is 20 cookies. What is the question? *Teaching Children Mathematics, 13*(5), 252–255.

Behrend, J. L. (2003). Learning-disabled students make sense of mathematics. *Teaching Children Mathematics, 9*(5), 269–273.

Boerst, T. A., & Schielack, J. F. (2003). Toward understanding of "computational fluency." *Teaching Children Mathematics, 9*(6), 292–293.

Bresser, R. (2003). Helping English-language learners develop computational fluency. *Teaching Children Mathematics, 9*(6), 294–299.

Buchholz, L. (2004). Learning strategies for addition and subtraction facts: The road to fluency and the license to think. *Teaching Children Mathematics, 10*(7), 362–367.

Burns, M., & Silbey, R. (2001, April). Math journals boost real learning. *Instructor,* 18–20.

Carroll, W. M., & Porter, D. (1997). Invented strategies can develop meaningful mathematical procedures. *Teaching Children Mathematics, 3*(7), 370, 374.

DeBellis, V. A., Rosenstein, J. G., Hart, E. W., & Kenney, M. J. (2009). *Navigating through discrete mathematics in prekindergarten—Grade 5.* Reston, VA: National Council of Teachers of Mathematics.

DeGroot, C., & Whalen, T. (2006). Investigations. Longing for division. *Teaching Children Mathematics, 12*(8), 410–418.

Eichinger, J. (2009). *Activities linking science with math K-4.* Arlington, VA: NSTA Press.

Findell, C. R., Cavanagh, M., Dacey, L., Greenes, C. E., Sheffield, L. J., & Small, M. (2004). *Navigating through problem solving and reasoning in grade 1.* Reston, VA: National Council of Teachers of Mathematics.

Ittigson, R. (2002). Helping students become mathematically powerful. *Teaching Children Mathematics, 9*(2), 91–95.

Kamii, C., & Anderson, C. (2003). Multiplication games: How we made and used them. *Teaching Children Mathematics, 10*(3), 135–141.

Kamii, C., & Lewis, B. A. (2003). Single-digit subtraction with fluency. *Teaching Children Mathematics, 10*(4), 230–236.

Kamii, C., Lewis, B. A., & Booker, B. M. (1998). Instead of teaching missing addends. *Teaching Children Mathematics, 4*(8), 458–461.

Kamii, C. K., Lewis, B. A., & Livingston, S. J. (1993). Primary arithmetic: Children inventing their own procedures. *Arithmetic Teacher, 41*(4), 200–203.

Mann, R., & Miller, N. (2003). Responses to the marble mayhem problem: A solution evolution. *Teaching Children Mathematics, 9*(9), 516–520.

Morozumi, A. (2001). *One gorilla.* New York: Farrar, Strauss, & Giroux.

Murphy, M. S. (2009). Mathematics and social justice in grade 1: How children understand inequality and represent it. *Young Children, 64*(3), 12–17.

O'Connell, S. (2000). *Introduction to problem solving: Strategies for the elementary math classroom.* Portsmouth, NH: Heinemann.

Polly, D., & Ruble, L. (2009). Learning to share equally. *Teaching Children Mathematics, 15*(9), 558–563.

Postlewait, K. B., Adams, M. R., & Shih, J. C. (2003). Promoting meaningful mastery of addition and subtraction. *Teaching Children Mathematics, 9*(6), 354–357.

Reys, B. J., & Arbaugh, F. (2001). Clearing up the confusion over calculator use in grades K–5. *Teaching Children Mathematics, 8*(2), 90–94.

Small, M., Sheffield, L. J., Cavanagh, M., Dacey, L., Findell, C. R., & Greenes, C. E. (2004). *Navigating through problem solving and reasoning in grade 2.* Reston, VA: National Council of Teachers of Mathematics.

Varol, F., & Farran, D. C. (2006). Early mathematical growth: How to support children's mathematical development. *Early Childhood Education Journal, 33*(6), 381–388.

Wells, P. J., & Coffey, D. C. (2005). Are they wrong? Or did they just answer a different question? *Teaching Children Mathematics, 12*(4), 202–207.

Whitenack, J. W., Knipping, N., Novinger, S., & Underwood, G. (2001). Second graders circumvent addition and subtraction difficulties. *Teaching Children Mathematics, 8*(4), 228–233.

Whitin, D. J. (2006). Problem posing in the elementary classroom. *Teaching Children Mathematics, 13*(1), 14–18.

Wilcox, V. B. (2008). Questioning zero and negative numbers. *Teaching Children Mathematics, 15*(4), 202–206.

Wu, Z., An, S., King, J., Ramirez, M., & Evans, S. (2009). Second grade "Professors." *Teaching Children Mathematics, 16*(1), 34–40.

Zaslavsky, C. (1998). *Math games and activities from around the world.* Chicago: Chicago Review Press.

See also the monthly issues of *Teaching Children Mathematics* for activities, materials, and reviews of software and websites.

Children often need concrete help such as manipulatives or fingers when they first do written problems.

Patterns

After reading this unit, you should be able to:

- Describe patterning as it applies to primary age mathematics.
- Explain why the cognitive developmental level of primary children makes looking for patterns an especially interesting and appropriate activity.
- Assess primary grade children's understanding of patterning.
- Plan and teach patterning activities for primary grade children.

As described in Unit 13, the NCTM (2000, p. 90) standard for prekindergarten through grade 2 algebra includes the expectations that students will order objects by size, number, and other properties; recognize and extend patterns; and analyze how patterns are developed. Young children learn repetitive rhymes and songs and hear stories with predictive language. They develop patterns with objects and eventually with numbers. They recognize change such as in the seasons or in their height as they grow. During the primary grades, children make a transition into more complex patterning activities such as comparing patterns, learning number patterns, extending complex patterns, and gaining an understanding of **equality** (that two quantities are the same amount).

The curriculum focal points (NCTM, 2007) continue to make connections with pre-algebra during the primary grades. During first grade, problem solving connects number and operations and algebra. Children also learn about number patterns such as odd and even and those discovered in the 1-to-100 chart. At the second-grade level, children use number patterns to extend their understanding of number and operations. During third grade, a part of pre-algebra readiness is the understanding of multiplication and the relationship between multiplication and division.

Ordering, or putting things into a sequence, is basic to patterning. **Patterning** is the process of discovering auditory, visual, and motor regularities. There are many regularities in the number system that children must understand. During the primary years, children work with more complex problems with concrete materials, connect concrete patterns to symbols, and learn to recognize some of the patterns and higher-level sequences in the number system.

This unit focuses on extending the concept of patterning to more complex patterns and connecting symbols and patterns. It also describes activities for looking at patterns in the environment.

Assessment

Refer to Unit 13 for a description of naturalistic and informal patterning behaviors that can be observed during children's activities. By the primary grades, children should be able to copy and extend patterns with ease. During the primary grades, they develop the ability to extend patterns further, make more complex patterns, become more adept at describing patterns with words, build their own patterns, and see patterns in numbers. See Unit 13 for a sample assessment task procedure for pattern copying, extending patterns, and describing patterns and more difficult extensions. The following are examples of higher-level assessment tasks.

SAMPLE ASSESSMENT TASK

9K   **Concrete Operations Ages 6–8**
Patterns, Extension in Three Dimensions: Unit 22

METHOD: Interview.

SKILL: The child can extend complex patterns in three dimensions by predicting what will come next.

MATERIALS: Inch or centimeter cubes, Unifix Cubes, or other counters that can be stacked.

PROCEDURE: Present the child with various patterns made of stacked counters. Ask the child to describe the pattern and continue it as far as he can. Stack the blocks as shown in the following figure one pattern at a time:

a.

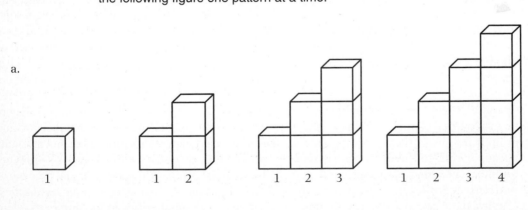

b.

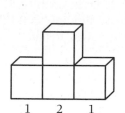 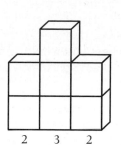 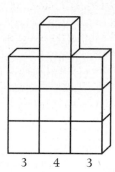

| 1 | 2 | 1 | | 2 | 3 | 2 | | 3 | 4 | 3 |

c.

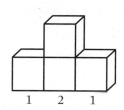 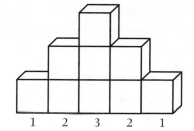

| 1 | 2 | 1 | | 1 | 2 | 3 | 2 | 1 |

Creating patterns begins with concrete materials such as Unifix Cubes.

For each pattern ask, **"Tell me about this pattern. What comes next? How do you know? Continue the pattern for me."**

EVALUATION: Note whether the child can continue each pattern and state his rationale. Note where the child might need further help and practice.

INSTRUCTIONAL RESOURCE: Charlesworth, R. (2011). *Experiences in math for young children* (6th ed.). Belmont, CA: Wadsworth/Cengage Learning.

SAMPLE ASSESSMENT TASK

9M
Patterns, Multiple Numbers: Unit 22   **Concrete Operations Ages 7–9**

METHOD: Interview.

SKILL: The child can use a 1-to-100 chart to discover and predict number multiple patterns.

MATERIALS: Inch or centimeter cubes, Unifix Cubes, or other counters, and a 1-to-100 chart (Figure 22–1).

PROCEDURE: Start a pattern using multiples of two blocks. Tell the child, "**Circle or mark the amount in my group on the chart**." If the child has a problem, show her the numeral 2, and circle it for her if necessary. Next to the group of two blocks, construct a group of four blocks. Use the same procedure. Continue up to 10. Then say, "**Show me which numbers you would circle if I kept continuing with this pattern**." When children can predict accurately with multiples of two, try threes, fours, fives, and so on.

EVALUATION: Note whether the children can connect the numbers in the pattern to the numerals on the chart and whether they can predict what comes next. If they cannot accomplish these tasks, note where their errors are: Do they need more help with basic pattern construction? With counting? With connecting sets to symbols? With finding numbers on the chart?

INSTRUCTIONAL RESOURCE: Charlesworth, R. (2011). *Experiences in math for young children* (6th ed.). Belmont, CA: Wadsworth/Cengage Learning.

Activities

Children who have reached concrete operations are in a stage of cognitive development where they are naturally seeking out the rules and regularities in the world. Patterning activities fit the natural inclinations and interests of children in this stage. While they are engaged in calendar and "100 days" activities, children are challenged to note number patterns and count by multiples (i.e., two, four, six, eight, …). They also enjoy arranging paper shapes into quilt patterns. The following examples are activities adapted from Richardson (1984, 1999) and Baratta-Lorton (1976). Patterning examples are also included in Greenes, Cavanagh, Dacey, Findell, and Small (2001) and DeBellis, Rosenstein, Hart, and Kenney (2009).

1	2	3	4	5	6	7	8	9	10
11	12	13	14	15	16	17	18	19	20
21	22	23	24	25	26	27	28	29	30
31	32	33	34	35	36	37	38	39	40
41	42	43	44	45	46	47	48	49	50
51	52	53	54	55	56	57	58	59	60
61	62	63	64	65	66	67	68	69	70
71	72	73	74	75	76	77	78	79	80
81	82	83	84	85	86	87	88	89	90
91	92	93	94	95	96	97	98	99	100

FIGURE 22–1 1-to-100 chart.

Creating patterns begin with concrete materials such as Unifix Cubes.

Activities

Patterning: Increasing Patterns

OBJECTIVE: To copy and extend patterns using objects.

MATERIALS: Counters such as chips, cube blocks, or Unifix Cubes; paper; and pencil.

ACTIVITY: Examples of patterns that can be developed are given in the following figure. In each case, model the first three elements in the pattern; then ask the children to predict what comes next and to extend the pattern as far as they can. Have the children write down the pattern in numerals under each element and compare the patterns with both the objects and the numeral representations.

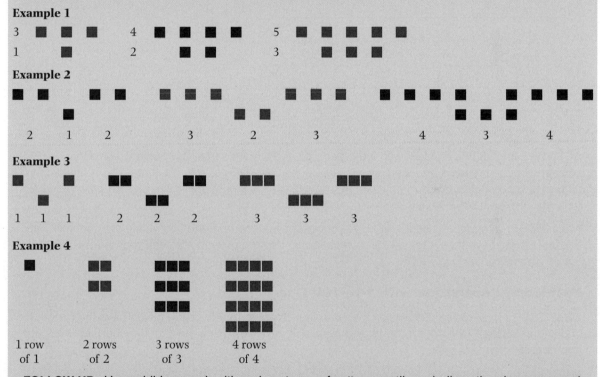

Example 1

Example 2

Example 3

Example 4

1 row of 1   2 rows of 2   3 rows of 3   4 rows of 4

FOLLOW-UP: Have children work with various types of patterns until you believe they have grasped the concept. Then present the higher-level pattern activities that follow.

Patterning: Task Cards

OBJECTIVE: To copy and extend patterns using task cards.

MATERIALS: Counters such as chips, inch or centimeter cubes, or Unifix Cubes; task cards, for example, those with the first three steps in a pattern.

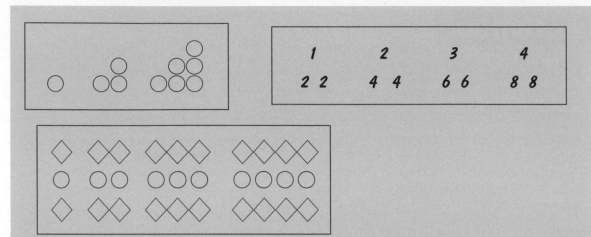

Task cards with the first step in a pattern.

ACTIVITY: Provide the children with the task cards and a good supply of counters. Have the children copy the models and then proceed to extend the patterns. With the three-step models, the pattern is set. With the one-step models, ask the children to create their own rules for extending the patterns. Always have them explain their pattern to you.

FOLLOW-UP: When the children have the concept of working from the abstract to the concrete with the task cards, have them create their own patterns, first with objects and then drawing them using the objects as models.

Patterning: Activities with 1-to-100 Chart

OBJECTIVE: To perceive patterns on the chart in pictorial form. For children who have the concept of place value (see Unit 24) for the 1s and 10s place, activities using the 1-to-100 chart activities are appropriate.

MATERIALS: Copies of the 1-to-100 chart (see Figure 22–1) and counters.

ACTIVITY: On the chart, ask the children to color in or mark the amounts in their patterns, such as the one shown in the figure.

Ask the children then to mark off on the chart the amount in each part of the pattern: 5, 10, 15, 20, and so on.

FOLLOW-UP: Have the children transfer to the charts from patterns you provide and then move on to patterns they devise themselves.

Patterning: Exploring Natural Materials

OBJECTIVE: To be able to observe and describe patterns in natural materials.

MATERIALS: Fruits and vegetables such as cabbage, onion, orange, lemon, grapefruit, and apple; magnifying glass; pencil and paper.

ACTIVITY: Let the children explore and examine the whole fruits and vegetables. Encourage them to describe what they see and feel. Suggest that they examine the fruits and vegetables with the magnifying glass and draw them if they wish. After a few days, ask them to predict what each item looks like inside. Then cut each one in half. Talk about what they discover. Compare what they see with what they predicted. Suggest that they draw the inside patterns.

FOLLOW-UP: Have each child use his picture to make a "What's inside?" book. Have him write or dictate what he knows about each item.

Patterning: Multiples Graphs

OBJECTIVE: To collect data regarding natural patterns and depict the data on graphs.

MATERIALS:
1. Number line templates. These templates are made from heavy tagboard. The numbers are written across. A hole is cut or punched below each one so that the numbers can be copied.

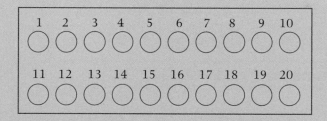

2. Large sheets of manila paper, rulers, crayons, markers, and picture magazines.

ACTIVITY: With the children, discuss the following questions:
• How many eyes do five people have among them?
• How many legs do three chairs have among them?

With their rulers, have the children draw horizontal lines about 3–4 inches apart on a large piece of manila paper. Have them copy their number line at the bottom of the paper using a template. Have them draw or cut out and paste pictures on their paper as shown in Figure 22–2. Then have them record the number of eyes (legs) down the right side of the paper and circle the corresponding numerals on the number line. Ask them to examine the number line and describe the pattern they have made.

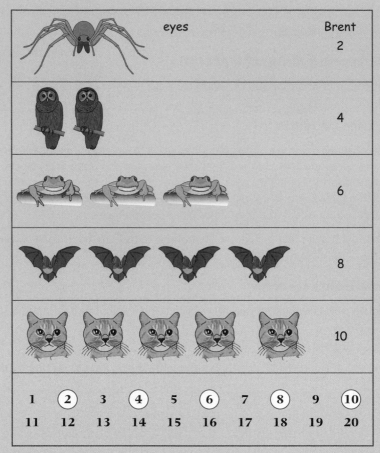

FIGURE 22–2   Multiples graph.

FOLLOW-UP: Have the children think of other items they could graph in multiples to create patterns.

Patterning: Division

OBJECTIVE: To make division patterns.

MATERIALS: Large pieces of paper (11″ × 18″), smaller pieces of paper (4¼″ × 5½″), scissors, crayons or markers, and glue.

ACTIVITY: With the whole group, start with a large piece of paper. Have a child cut the paper in half and give one half to another child. Then have each child cut the paper in half and give one part away. Keep a record of the number of cuts and the number of children until everyone has a piece of paper. Next, give each child a large piece of paper and a small piece of paper. Have them glue the smaller piece at the top of the larger sheet (Figure 22–3). Have them take another small piece, cut it in half, and glue the two parts on the large paper below the first whole piece (Figure 22–3). Have them take another small piece, cut it in half, and then cut each half in half. Glue these four parts on the large sheet. Let them continue as long as they wish. Have them record the number of pieces in each row on the right-hand side of the chart.

FOLLOW-UP: Have the more advanced children cut three parts each time and see what kind of pattern they make.

Other patterning activities can be developed using manipulatives such as pattern blocks. Pattern blocks are available in a variety of sizes, thicknesses, and colors. Many supplementary materials are also available such as tracing templates, stickers, rubber stamps, and puzzles (see the Creative Publications catalog in Unit 27). You can also make your own materials. Pattern blocks can be used to make quilt designs. Patterning activities can also be developed from children's literature (see Appendix B for book list). As with other concepts, patterning activities can be integrated across the curriculum (Figure 22–4).

As already described in Unit 21, calculator activities are interesting ways to look at number patterns. After some practice with patterns as suggested in Unit 21, have the children discover and extend patterns with their calculators; for example, make up some more patterns for the children to explore with calculators.

Clements and Sarama (2000) describe the "predict and cover" activity, which can be done both on and off the computer. First the children explore pattern blocks, developing their own designs. Then they are provided with specific shapes and asked to predict and select which pattern blocks will cover the shapes provided. Patterning activities can be found online at Virtual Manipulatives (http://nlvm.usu.edu) and at Illuminations (http://illuminations.nctm.org). Several advantages of doing the activity on the computer are as follows: It gives children more flexibility, work can be saved and retrieved, children can design their own patterns, and tasks are broken down in ways that clarify mathematical mental actions.

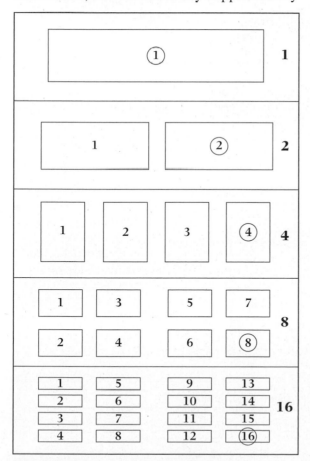

FIGURE 22–3   Patterning: division.

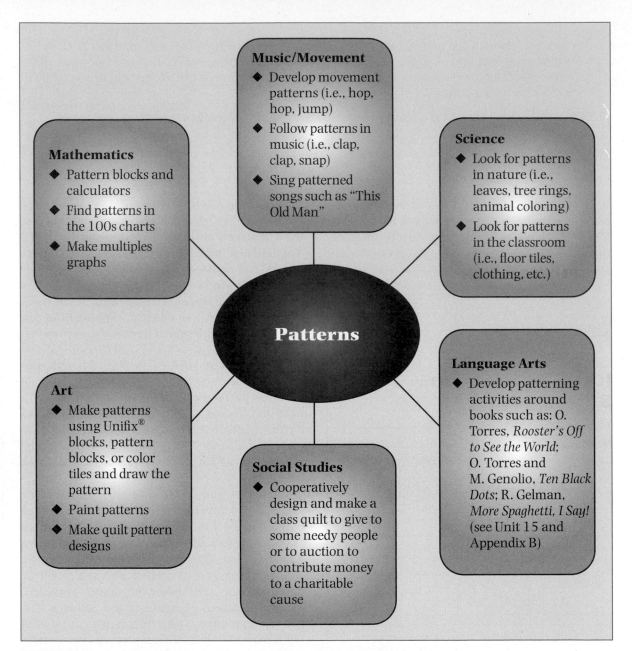

FIGURE 22–4 Integrating patterning experiences across the curriculum.

Calculators can provide opportunities to explore number patterns.

As with other math concepts, pattern software is also available. See the activities at the end of this unit and Unit 13 for suggestions.

Ideas for Children with Special Needs

This unit and each of those following in this section describe the practical developmental implications of a different disability. This unit focuses on the blind child (Lewis, 2003). When considering any disability it is important to avoid stereotypes. Every child is an individual. Children with visual disabilities must depend on their other senses for information. Rhymes and routines are essential for the visually impaired young child. The adult should talk during routines, describing what is happening. Give-and-take games can be very educational. Objects can be incorporated into routines and rhymes, because touch is an important element in a blind child learning about the environment. The adult should label and explain toys. Spatial relationships (such as putting a cup on the table or climbing on a chair) should be practiced. In the classroom, the blind child needs time to explore. A peer can be helpful as a mentor. Consistent routines are very important. During the primary grades, reading is a major focus and children who are blind learn Braille. The concrete materials used in mathematics instruction are extremely useful for the child who is blind. He may need extra time to become familiar with materials and learn to organize them. Texture can be very helpful. For example, patterns using rough and smooth or pattern blocks of different shapes are appropriate adaptations.

FIND THE RULE AND FINISH THE PATTERN
Use your calculator.

<u>7</u>, <u>9</u>, <u>11</u>

PRACTICE PATTERN: 1, 3, 5, _____, _____, _____   RULE: +2

1. Rule: +2
   Pattern: 2, 4, 6, _____, _____, _____
2. Rule: +3
   Pattern: 3, 6, 9, _____, _____, _____
3. Rule: _____
   Pattern: 2, 5, 8, _____, _____, _____
4. Rule: _____
   Pattern: 12, 16, 20, _____, _____, _____
5. Rule: _____
   7, 9, _____, 13, _____, _____, _____
6. Rule: _____
   5, _____, 15, _____, _____, 30, 35, _____, _____

Evaluation

Note how the children deal with the suggested pattern activities. Do they count each part out loud? Do they seem to be doing the patterning logically through application of their number sense concept (i.e., through subitizing)? When asked, can they explain the pattern? Use the assessment tasks in Appendix A for individual evaluation interviews.

Summary

Primary level children extend the work they did with patterning at earlier levels. Now they begin to identify and work with patterns in the number system as they connect numerals to patterns and develop number patterns using counting and calculators. Number patterns are the basis for multiplication and division.

Key Terms

equality   ordering   patterning

Suggested Activities

1. Administer the sample assessment tasks to a first grader, a second grader, and a third grader. Write a report describing what you did, how the children responded, and how they compared with one another. Include suggestions for further activities for each child.
2. Assemble the materials for one or more of the suggested instructional activities. Try out the activities with a small group of primary children. Report to the class on what you did and how the children responded. Evaluate the children's responses and the appropriateness of the activities. Describe any changes you would make when you use these activities another time.
3. Using the evaluation system from Unit 2, evaluate one or more of the previously mentioned online resources and one of the following in terms of its value for learning about patterning.
   • *Introduction to Patterns* (pre-K–1; http://store.sunburst.com)
   • *Creating Patterns from Shapes* (grades 1–2; http://store.sunburst.com)

Review

A. Describe patterning as it applies to primary age mathematics. Give at least one example.
B. Explain why the cognitive developmental level of primary children makes looking for patterns an especially appropriate and interesting activity.
C. Match the types of activities to the following examples:
   1. Copy and extend patterns using objects.
   2. Copy and extend patterns using task cards.
   3. Observe and describe patterns in natural materials.
   4. Collect data from naturally occurring objects, and depict the data on a graph.
   5. Make a division pattern.

Examples:

   a. Chan carefully draws the pattern that appears in half of an orange.
   b. Sara examines three groups of blocks and proceeds to create the group she believes should come next.
   c. Theresa draws lines across a large sheet of paper, copies her number line with a

template, and then looks through a magazine for animals with four legs.

d. Vanessa has a large sheet of paper and several smaller sheets. First she glues one small sheet at the top of the large sheet and writes the numeral 1 to the right.

e. Brent examines some patterns drawn on a card. Then he takes some Unifix Cubes, makes the same designs, and adds two more.

D. Describe how a 1-to-100 chart might be used to assist in illustrating multiple number patterns.

REFERENCES

Baratta-Lorton, M. (1976). *Mathematics their way*. Menlo Park, CA: Addison-Wesley.

Clements, D. H., & Sarama, J. (2000). Predicting pattern blocks on and off the computer. *Teaching Children Mathematics, 6*(7), 458–462.

DeBellis, V. A., Rosenstein, J. G., Hart, E. W., & Kenney, M. J. (2009). *Navigating with discrete mathematics in kindergarten—grade 5*. Reston, VA: National Council of Teachers of Mathematics.

Greenes, C., Cavanagh, M., Dacey, L., Findell, C., & Small, M. (2001). *Navigating through algebra in prekindergarten–grade 2*. Reston, VA: National Council of Teachers of Mathematics.

Lewis, V. (2003). *Development and disability* (2nd ed.). Malden, MA: Blackwell.

National Council of Teachers of Mathematics. (2000). *Principles and standards for school mathematics*. Reston, VA: Author.

National Council of Teachers of Mathematics. (2007). *Curriculum focal points*. Reston, VA: Author.

Richardson, K. (1984). *Developing number concepts using Unifix Cubes*. Menlo Park, CA: Addison-Wesley.

Richardson, K. (1999). *Developing number concepts: Book 1. Counting, comparing and pattern*. Parsippany, NJ: Seymour.

FURTHER READING AND RESOURCES

Billings, E. M., Tiedt, T. L., & Slater, L. H. (2007/2008). Algebraic thinking and pictorial growth patterns. *Teaching Children Mathematics, 14*(5), 302–308.

Box it or bag it mathematics. (K–2). Portland, OR: Math Learning Center.

Brahier, D. J. (2003). Patterns at your fingertips. *Teaching Children Mathematics, 9*(9), 521–528.

Bridges in mathematics. (K–2). Portland, OR: Math Learning Center.

Britton, B. (2006). Patterns galore! *Teaching Children Mathematics, 12*(6), 296–302.

Burris, A. C. (2005). *Understanding the math you teach*. Upper Saddle River, NJ: Pearson-Merrill/Prentice-Hall.

Cadzow-Wardell, L. (2009/2010). White trillium. *Teaching Children Mathematics, 16*(5), 264–266.

Chen, J., & McNamee, G. D. (2007). *Bridging: Teaching and learning in early childhood classrooms, pre-K–3*. Thousand Oaks, CA: Corwin.

Copley, J. V. (Ed.). (2004). *Showcasing mathematics for the young child*. Reston, VA: National Council of Teachers of Mathematics.

Cross, C. T., Woods, T. A., & Schweingruber, H. (2009). *Mathematics learning in early childhood*. Washington, D.C.: The National Academies Press.

Dubon, L. P., & Shafer, K. G. (2010). Storyboards for meaningful patterns. *Teaching Children Mathematics, 16*(6), 325–329.

Findell, C. R., Cavanagh, M., Dacey, L., Greenes, C. E., Sheffield, L. J., & Small, M. (2004). *Navigating through problem solving and reasoning in grade 1*. Reston, VA: National Council of Teachers of Mathematics.

Greenes, C. E., Cavanagh, M., Dacey, L., Findell, C. R., Sheffield, L. J., & Small, M. (2003). *Navigating through problem solving and reasoning in prekindergarten–kindergarten.* Reston, VA: National Council of Teachers of Mathematics.

Greenes, C. E., Cavanagh, M., Dacey, L., Findell, C. R., & Small, M. (2001). *Navigating through algebra in prekindergarten–grade 2.* Reston, VA: National Council of Teachers of Mathematics.

Lee, J. (2007). Context in mathematical learning. Problems and possibilities. *Teaching Children Mathematics, 14*(1), 40–44.

MacDonald, S. (2001). *Block play: The complete guide to learning and playing with blocks.* Beltsville, MD: Gryphon House.

Mirra, A. (2009). *Teaching with curriculum focal points: pre-K-2.* Reston, VA: National Council of Teachers of Mathematics.

Reynolds, A., Cassel, D., & Lillard, E. (2006). A mathematical exploration of grandpa's quilt. *Teaching Children Mathematics, 12*(7), 340–345.

Small, M., Sheffield, L. J., Cavanagh, M., Dacey, L., Findell, C. R., & Greenes, C. E. (2004). *Navigating through problem solving and reasoning in grade 2.* Reston, VA: National Council of Teachers of Mathematics.

Fractions

OBJECTIVES

After reading this unit, you should be able to:

- Explain how the concept of fractions is based on an understanding of part–whole relationships.
- Explain why primary children should not be rushed into using fraction notation.
- Assess primary children's understanding of the concept of fractions.
- Plan and teach fraction lessons appropriate for primary children.

Unit 11 explained that young children have a natural understanding and interest in **parts** and **wholes** that can be used later as a bridge to understanding **fractions**. The NCTM (2000, p. 78) expectations include that young children will develop a sense of whole numbers and represent them in many ways by breaking groups down into smaller parts. By the end of second grade, the children should understand and be able to represent commonly used fractions such as ¼, ⅓, and ½.

Fractions become a focal point (NCTM, 2007) in number and operations during third grade. During third grade, children develop an understanding of fractions and fraction equivalence. They understand how fractional parts relate to the whole. They study a variety of models and solve fraction problems.

As described in Unit 11, the fundamental concept of *parts* and *wholes* is the basis for the understanding of fractions. Through naturalistic,

informal, and adult guided experiences, preprimary children become familiar with three aspects of the part–whole concept: Things have special parts, a whole object can be divided into parts, and groups of things can be divided into smaller groups. They also become familiar with the application of the terms *more, less*, and *same*. During the primary level, young children expand on the concrete activities they engaged in during the preprimary level. It is important not to introduce notation and symbols too soon. Even 9-year-olds have difficulty with fractions at the symbolic level. This would indicate that, for most children, fraction symbols cannot safely be introduced until the end of the primary period (the latter part of grade 3) and may not be fully understood until well into the intermediate level (grade 4 or higher). Fraction problems cannot be solved by counting as can whole number problems. This factor makes them much more abstract and thus more difficult.

At the presymbolic level, children's work with fractions should be limited to **halves, thirds**, and **fourths**. These are the fractions we deal with most frequently in life, and once children understand them, they should be able to transfer this knowledge to fractions in general. Children can learn fraction terminology relative to concrete experiences without being concerned with the corresponding symbols. Terms such as *one-half, one-third,* and *one-fourth* can be associated with parts of concrete objects and subgroups of large groups of concrete objects. During the primary period, children continue to work with fractions as part–whole relationships. They can work with volume, regions, length, and groups. Experiences with foods (such as cutting up a carrot) and cooking (measuring ingredients) involve volume. Regions are concrete and easy to work with. They involve working with shapes such as circles, rectangles, squares, and triangles. Length can also be divided into parts. Long, narrow pieces of paper, string, thread, and ribbon are useful for this type of activity. When working with groups, a whole group of objects serves as the unit to be divided into smaller subgroups.

Payne, Towsley, and Huinker (1990, pp. 175–200) sum up the sequence in the development of conceptual knowledge of fractions. As you have already seen, 3–5-year-old children work with the concept of parts and wholes; 5–8-year-olds work on equal parts and on oral (*not* written) names. In other words, children learn to use terms such as *halves, thirds, fourths,* and the like. They also use terms such as *part,* **pieces,** *whole,* and **almost whole.**

Assessment

Unit 11 described both observational and interview tasks for assessing part–whole concepts. When children understand that a whole can be divided into parts, that when a quantity is divided its whole is conserved, and that the size of each part gets smaller as the number of equal divisions increases, they are ready to understand fractions. If children evidence some of the behaviors described in Unit 11 as indicating that they understand the part–whole concept and are able to respond successfully to the Unit 11 assessment tasks, then try the following kinds of higher-level assessment tasks.

SAMPLE ASSESSMENT TASK

9N   **Concrete Operations Ages 6–8**
Fractions, Equivalent Parts: Unit 23

METHOD: Interview.

SKILL: The child can divide a rectangle into smaller equal parts.

MATERIALS: A supply of paper rectangles of equal size (8½″ × 2¾″) in four different colors and a pair of scissors.

PROCEDURE: Show the child a paper rectangle. Say, "**This is a rectangle**." Place two more rectangles (color #2) below the first one. Ask, "**Here are two more rectangles. Are all three the same size?**" Be sure the child agrees. Let him compare them to be sure. Say, "**Now I'm going to fold one of the rectangles** (color #2) **so both parts are the same.**" Fold the rectangle. Say, "**Now you fold this other one**

(also color #2) **just like I did**." Offer assistance if necessary. The three rectangles should look like this:

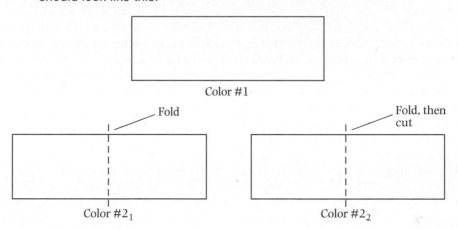

Color #1

Fold

Fold, then cut

Color #2₁

Color #2₂

Ask, "**Are the parts of** (color #2) **rectangle the same size as the parts of this one?** (also color #2) **show me how you know. I'm going to cut this one** (second color #2) **on the fold. How many parts do I have now? If I put them back together, will they be the same size as this whole rectangle? As your** (color #1) **rectangle? What is a special name for this amount of the whole rectangle?**" Point to the half. If the response is one-half, go through the procedure again with one-third and one-fourth, using colors #3 and #4, respectively.

EVALUATION: Note whether the child has to check on the equivalency of the three rectangles. Can he keep in mind that the parts still equal the whole, even when cut into two or more parts? Does he know the terms *one-half, one-third*, and/or *one-fourth*?

INSTRUCTIONAL RESOURCE: Charlesworth, R. (2011). *Experiences in math for young children* (6th ed.). Belmont, CA: Wadsworth/Cengage Learning.

SAMPLE ASSESSMENT TASK

90   **Concrete Operations Ages 6–8**
Fractions, One-Half of a Group: Unit 23

METHOD: Interview.

SKILL: The child can divide a set of objects into smaller groups when she is given directions using the term *one-half*.

MATERIALS: Ten counters (cube blocks, chips, Unifix Cubes, or other concrete objects).

PROCEDURE: Place the counters in front of the child. Say, "**I have some** (name of counters). **Divide these so that we each have one-half of the group.**" If the child completes this task easily, go on to nine counters and ask her to divide the group into thirds. Then go on to eight counters and ask her to divide the group into fourths.

EVALUATION: Note the method the child uses. Does she use counting, or does she pass the counters out: "One for you and one for me"? Does she really seem to understand the terms *one-half, one-fourth*, and *one-third*?

INSTRUCTIONAL RESOURCE: Charlesworth, R. (2011). *Experiences in math for young children* (6th ed.). Belmont, CA: Wadsworth/Cengage Learning.

Activities

Unit 11 emphasized naturalistic and informal activities as the foundation for adult guided experiences. These activities should be encouraged and continued. Primary children continue to need time to explore materials and construct their concept of parts and wholes through their own actions on the environment. There are many materials that children can explore independently in developing the foundations for understanding fractions. Children can organize any of the usual kinds of counting objects as a group, which they can then divide (or partition) into smaller groups. Some materials for dividing single objects or shapes into parts are illustrated in Figure 23–1. The examples include

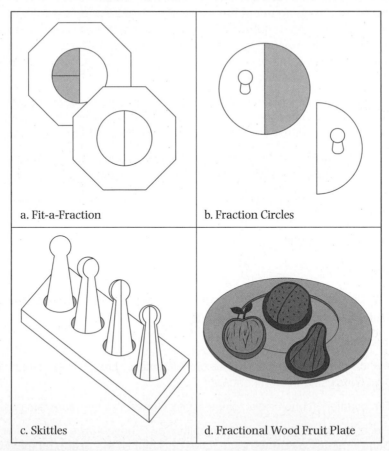

a. Fit-a-Fraction

b. Fraction Circles

c. Skittles

d. Fractional Wood Fruit Plate

FIGURE 23–1 Examples of materials that can be used to explore how whole things can be divided into equal parts.

Fit-a-Fraction (Lakeshore), Fraction Circles and Skittles (Nienhuis-Montessori), and Fractional Wood Fruit Plate (ETA). Figure 23–2 illustrates materials that promote the construction and comparison of parts and wholes. These materials include Unit Blocks (Community Playthings), Cuisinaire Rods (Cuisinaire of America), puzzles (Lakeshore), and LEGO (Lakeshore).

Following are adult guided activities that can be used to develop fraction concepts.

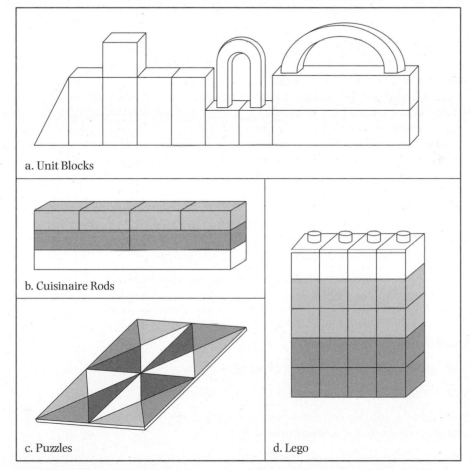

a. Unit Blocks

b. Cuisinaire Rods

c. Puzzles

d. Lego

FIGURE 23–2 Materials that promote the construction and comparison of parts and wholes.

Activities

Fractions: Construction Paper Models

OBJECTIVE: To conceptualize fractional parts of wholes using construction paper and/or poster board models.

MATERIALS: Make your own models out of construction paper and/or poster board. Use a different color for each fractional part—for example, a blue whole circle, a red circle the same size cut into halves, a yellow circle cut into thirds, and a green circle cut into fourths.

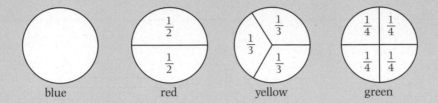

Use the same colors to make a set of fraction rectangles and a set of fraction squares.

ACTIVITY: Let the children explore the sets of fraction models. After they have worked with them several times, ask them some questions.

- **What have you learned about these shapes?**
- **How many red pieces make a circle the same size as the blue circle? How many yellow pieces? How many green pieces?**
- **Use the same procedure with the rectangles and the squares.**

FOLLOW-UP: Label the parts as halves, thirds, and fourths of the wholes. Provide the students with matching construction paper shapes, and have them make their own models by folding. Start with rectangles and squares.

Fractions: Comparing Sizes

OBJECTIVE: To compare sizes of halves, thirds, and fourths.

MATERIALS: Same as in previous activity.

ACTIVITY: Put out the models one set at a time. Ask the children, "**Which is larger—a half, a third, or a fourth? How many fourths make one-half?**"

FOLLOW-UP: Provide models of other fractions for children who have a good understanding of halves, fourths, and thirds.

Fractions: Parts of Groups

OBJECTIVE: To divide groups of objects into subgroups of halves, thirds, and fourths.

MATERIALS: Draw, color, and cut out a mother rabbit, four child rabbits, and twelve carrots (see Figure 23–3 for patterns).

ACTIVITY: Place the mother rabbit, two child rabbits, and four carrots in front of the children. Say, "**Mother rabbit has four carrots and wants to give each of her children half of the carrots. Help her by dividing the carrots between the two children so each has half.**" Give the children time to complete the task. Say, "**Now suppose she has four carrots and four children** (bring out two more

FIGURE 23–3 Patterns for the "parts of groups" activity.

children). **Show me how they can share the carrots so each has one-fourth of the carrots."** As long as the children are interested, continue the activity using different numbers of child rabbits and different amounts of carrots. Emphasize that the carrots must be shared so that it is fair to everyone.

FOLLOW-UP: Make other groups of materials (such as children and apples and dogs and bones). Move on to other fractions when the children can do these problems easily.

Fractions: Liquid Volume

OBJECTIVE: To compare fractional parts of liquid volume.

MATERIALS: Several sets of color-coded standard measuring cups, if available, and a pitcher of water. If color-coded cups are not available, mark each size with a different color (e.g., 1 cup with blue, ½ cup with red, ⅓ cup with yellow, ¼ cup with green).

ACTIVITY: Give each child a set of measuring cups. Let them examine the set and tell you what they notice. After discussion and examination, have everyone pick up their 1-cup size and their ½-cup size. Ask, **"How many of these small cups of water will fill the large cup?"** Let the children predict. Ask, **"Fill your small cup with water. Pour the water in your large cup. Is the large cup full? Pour in another small cup of water. Is the large cup full now? How many of the smaller cups were needed to fill the larger cup?"** Follow the same procedure with the ⅓- and ¼-size cups.

FOLLOW-UP: Reverse the procedure. Starting with the full 1-cup measure, have the children count how many ½, ⅓, and ¼ cupfuls it takes to empty the full cup. Do the same activity using rice, birdseed, or sand instead of water.

Fractions: Length

OBJECTIVE: To compare fractional parts of lengths.

MATERIALS: Cuisinaire Rods.

ACTIVITY: Provide the children with a basket full of Cuisinaire Rods. After they have had an opportunity to explore the rods, suggest that they select a long rod and find out which lengths of rods can be placed next to it to show halves, thirds, and fourths.

FOLLOW-UP: Follow the same procedure with whole straws and straws cut into halves, fourths, and thirds. Try the activity with other materials such as string, ribbons, and paper strips.

Fractions: Using Literature

OBJECTIVE: To analyze the fractional components of relevant children's literature as an application of the concept of fractions.

MATERIALS: Children's trade books that contain fractional concepts, writing and drawing implements, paper, chalk, and chalkboard.

ACTIVITY: Read books such as *When the Doorbell Rang* (Hutchins, 1986). Provide problem situations such as making a chart that shows how, as more children come, each gets fewer cookies. Have the children draw pictorial representations of what is happening. For further suggestions and a list of additional books, see Conaway and Midkiff (2004), Colker (2005), and Whitin and Whitin (2004), as well as others listed in Unit 12.

FOLLOW-UP: Use additional books. Children will become more independent and see more and more ways of looking at fractions.

Fractions: Story Problems

OBJECTIVE: To have the children create and solve fraction story problems.

MATERIALS: One or more model problems; paper, pencils, crayons, markers, and scissors; chart paper for model problems.

ACTIVITY: Have the students brainstorm real-life situations in which things must be divided into equal parts. Encourage them to write or dictate their own problems, draw a picture of the problem, and write out the solution. If they cannot come up with their own problems, provide one or two models they can work through with you. Here are some models (have each problem written on chart paper):

1. **Two children found six pennies. One child took three pennies.** Ask, **"What fractional part of the pennies was left for the other child?"** Draw two stick figure children. Draw six pennies on another piece of paper. Glue three pennies by one child and three by the other. Ask, **"What part of the pennies does each child have? Yes, one-half."** Write: "Each child has one-half of the pennies" (Figure 23–4).
2. **Brent invites three friends over for pizza. If each child gets a fair share, how will the pizza look when it is cut up?** Give each child a paper pizza. Ask them to fold the pizzas into the right size and number of parts. Cut up one of the pizzas, and glue the parts on the chart. Write: "Each child gets one-fourth."

FOLLOW-UP: Encourage the children to create and illustrate their own fraction problems.

"Each child has one half of the pennies."

FIGURE 23–4 The teacher can write and illustrate a model story problem that involves the partitioning of a group.

Fractions: Geoboard Shapes

OBJECTIVE: To divide geoboard shapes into equal parts.

MATERIALS: Geoboards, geoboard shape patterns, and rubber bands.

ACTIVITY: Have the children use rubber bands to make rectangles and squares on their geoboards and then divide those shapes into equal parts using additional rubber bands.

FOLLOW-UP: Question the children regarding how they know that their shapes are divided into equal parts. Note whether they use the number of geoboard pegs as a clue to making their parts equal. *To Half or Half Not* is a collection of geoboard activities, which can be found at Mathline http://www.pbs.org/mathline. Another online resource for geoboard material is at http://socrates. acadiau.ca. Search for geoboard fraction activities.

For the more advanced students, introduce notation. Show them how one-half can be written as ½, which means one part out of two. Then ask how they think they might write one-third as one part out of three, two-thirds as two parts out of three, and so on. Have them write the numerical fractions that match the parts of some of the materials suggested earlier in the unit.

Children can make the connection between fractions and decimals through further concrete activities. Avoid placing any emphasis on decimal points. Work with 10ths and 100ths using models and diagrams in the same manner as you did with the larger fractions. Show through models how 1/10 and 1/100 can also be written as .1 and .01. Students with a strong conceptual foundation can move into operations with fractions and decimals by the fourth grade.

Fraction concepts can be integrated across the curriculum, as depicted in Figure 23–5.

MATH TEHNOLOGY FOR YOUNG CHILDREN

Using the guidelines from Unit 2, evaluate resources designed to reinforce the concept of fractions.

- *Math Express: Fractions* (preschool–grade 6; Eugene, OR: Visions Technology). Fraction skills cover identifying, converting, and comparing fractions; adding, subtracting, multiplying, and dividing fractions; mixed numbers; telling time; adding/subtracting time; and counting money.
- *Richard Scarry's Busytown—Best Math Program Ever* (preschool–grade 1; Hazelton, PA: K–12 Software). Includes fraction activities.
- *Tenth Planet: Fractions Collections Bundle* (grades 2–7; http://store.sunburst.com). Interactive demonstrations and practice activities build skills and understanding of fractions and part-number concepts.
- *Tenth Planet: Representing Fractions* (grades 2–4; http://store.sunburst.com). Students work with one interpretation of a fraction—namely, as a relationship between a whole and its parts. Work with fractions in symbolic and visual representations.
- *Virtual Manipulatives*, *Number and Operations* (pre-K–2; http://nlvm.usu.edu). Fraction bars, naming fractions, parts and whole, visualizing fractions, pie chart.
- *Funbrain* has fraction activities at four levels of difficulty (http://www.funbrain.com/fract).

Ideas for Children with Special Needs

With deaf children, communication is a major consideration (Lewis, 2003). Being able to communicate with sign language provides many advantages for the deaf child. Deaf children who sign have been found to be academically and socially advanced. If the deaf child is in a regular classroom, then he will need an interpreter. Bilingual deaf children—those who are proficient in sign and oral language—have an advantage. Deaf children should be introduced to written language at an early age. Allen and Cowdery (2005) make a number of recommendations for teachers of young deaf children, which include the following:

- While speaking, look children directly in the face. Get down to their level.
- Speak slowly and clearly.
- Use some gestures but not so many that the child is distracted from lipreading.
- In a group, seat the child across from the teacher.
- Get the child's attention by tapping softly on shoulder or hand.
- Use concrete examples when giving instructions.
- Read story books with clear, brightly colored illustrations.
- Keep routines sequenced and on a regular schedule.

Using concrete materials for math is essential for communicating concepts to the deaf child.

Evaluation

Continue to note whether the children apply what they have learned about fractions during their everyday activities. Be sure to provide situations in which the children have to share individual items or groups of items equally with others. Note whether they can use their concept of fractions in these situations. Also note if the children apply their concept of fractions during measuring experiences that are a part of food preparation and science investigations. Administer the assessment tasks described in Appendix A.

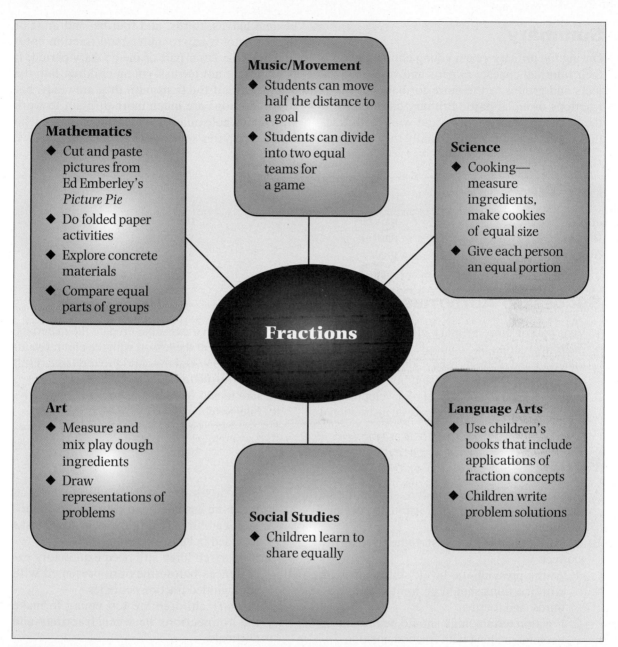

FIGURE 23–5 Integrating fraction experiences across the curriculum.

Summary

During the primary years, young children expand their informal concept of parts and wholes of objects and groups to the more formal concept of fractions or equal parts. Primary children learn the vocabulary of fractions and work with fractions at the concrete level. Usually they do not go beyond halves, thirds, and fourths, and most of them are not ready to understand fraction notation until the latter part of the primary period. It is important not to rush young children into the abstract use of fractions until they are ready, because fractions are much more difficult to work with than whole numbers. Teaching children who are deaf requires some special considerations.

KEY TERMS

almost whole	halves	thirds
fourths	part(s)	whole(s)
fractions	pieces	

SUGGESTED ACTIVITIES

1. Visit one or more primary classrooms during math instruction on fractions. Take note of the materials and methods used. Compare what you observe with what is suggested in the text.
2. Assess a primary child's level of development in the concept of fractions. Prepare an instructional plan based on the results. Prepare the materials, and implement the lesson with the child. Evaluate the results. Did the child progress as a result of your instruction?
3. Be sure to add fraction activities to your Activity File/Notebook.

REVIEW

A. Explain why primary children should not be rushed into working with fraction and decimal notation.
B. Identify the following statements that are correct:
   1. At the presymbolic level, children's work with fractions should be limited to halves, thirds, and fourths.
   2. Fraction terminology should be introduced to children along with fraction notation.
   3. At the presymbolic level, primary children can work with volume, regions, lengths, and groups.
   4. Food experiences are excellent opportunities for children to work with volume.
   5. Begin assessment with the tasks in this unit. It can be assumed that primary-level children can already do the lower-level tasks included in Unit 14.
   6. Primary children still need exploratory experiences before they are presented with adult guided fraction activities.
   7. Primary children are too young to make the connections between fractions and decimals.
C. Label items 1–4 as examples of one of the following: (a) objects can be partitioned into groups, (b) a whole object can be divided into equal parts, or (c) a liquid can be divided into equal parts.

1. Liu Pei carefully folds rectangular pieces of paper in half and then in half again and cuts accurately on each line.
2. Ann has six crackers. She wants to be sure that she and both of her friends receive an equal amount. She decides that they should each have two crackers.
3. Jason has a 1-cup measure of milk. Ms. Hebert tells him that they will need one-half cup of milk for their recipe. Jason selects a smaller cup that says ½ on the handle and fills it with milk from the larger cup.
4. Trang Fung is experimenting with the Fit-a-Fraction set.

REFERENCES

Allen, K. E., & Cowdery, G. E. (2005). *The exceptional child: Inclusion in early childhood education* (5th ed.). Albany, NY: Thomson Delmar Learning.

Colker, L. J. (2005). *The cooking book*. Washington, D.C.: National Association for the Education of Young Children.

Conaway, B., & Midkiff, R. B. (2004). Connecting literature, language and fractions. In D. Theissen (Ed.), *Exploring mathematics through literature* (pp. 69–78). Reston, VA: National Council of Teachers of Mathematics.

Hutchins, P. (1986). *When the doorbell rang*. New York: Greenwillow.

Lewis, V. (2003). *Development and disability* (2nd ed.). Malden, MA: Blackwell.

National Council of Teachers of Mathematics. (2000). *Principles and standards for school mathematics*. Reston, VA: Author.

National Council of Teachers of Mathematics. (2007). *Curriculum focal points*. Reston. VA: Author.

Payne, J. N., Towsley, A., & Huinker, D. (1990). Fractions and decimals. In J. N. Payne (Ed.), *Mathematics for the young child* (pp. 175–200). Reston, VA: National Council of Teachers of Mathematics.

Whitin, D. J., & Whitin, P. (2004). *New visions for linking literature and mathematics*. Reston, VA: National Council of Teachers of Mathematics.

FURTHER READING AND RESOURCES

Anderson, C. L., Anderson, K. M., & Wenzel, E. J. (2000). Oil and water don't mix but they do teach fractions. *Teaching Children Mathematics, 7*(3), 174–178.

Burris, A. C. (2005). *Understanding the math you teach*. Upper Saddle River, NJ: Pearson-Merrill/Prentice-Hall.

Chen, J., & McNamee, G. D. (2007). *Bridging: Assessment for teaching and learning in early childhood classrooms, pre-K–3*. Thousand Oaks, CA: Corwin.

Emberley, E. (1984). *Picture pie: A circle drawing book*. Boston: Little, Brown.

Flores, A., Samson, J., & Yanik, H. B. (2006). Quotient and measurement interpretations of rational numbers. *Teaching Children Mathematics, 13*(1), 34–39.

Giles, R. M., Parmer, L., & Byrd, K. (2003). Putting the pieces together: Developing early concepts of fractions. *Dimensions of Early Childhood, 31*(1), 3–8.

Goral, M. B., & Wiest, L. R. (2007). An arts-based approach to teaching fractions. *Teaching Children Mathematics, 14*(2), 74–80.

Irvin, B. B. (2008). *Geometry and fractions with geoboards*. Obtain from ETA Cuisenaire.

Kosbob, S., & Moyer, P. S. (2004). Picnicking with fractions. *Teaching Children Mathematics, 10*(7), 375–378.

Leitze, A. R., & Stump, S. (2007). Sharing cookies. *Teaching Children Mathematics, 13*(7), 378–379.

Moone, G., & de Groot, C. (2007). Fraction action. *Teaching Children Mathematics, 13*(5), 266–271.

Moyer, P. S., & Mailley, E. (2004). *Inchworm and a half:* Developing fraction and measurement concepts using mathematical representations. *Teaching Children Mathematics, 10*(5), 244–252.

Neumer, C. (2007). Mixed numbers made easy: Building and converting mixed numbers and improper fractions. *Teaching Children Mathematics, 13*(9), 488–492.

Norton, A. H., & McCloskey, A. V. (2008). Modelling students' mathematics using Steffe's fraction schemes. *Teaching Children Mathematics, 15*(1), 48–54.

Ortiz, E. (2000). A game involving fraction squares. *Teaching Children Mathematics, 7*(4), 218–222.

Powell, C. A., & Hunting, R. P. (2003). Fractions in the early years curriculum: More needed, not less. *Teaching Children Mathematics, 10*(1), 6–7.

Siebert, D., & Gaskin, N. (2006). Creating, naming and justifying fractions. *Teaching Children Mathematics, 12*(8), 394–400.

Stump, S., & Tayeh, C. (2006). Problem solvers: Making brownies and solutions to the better box problem. *Teaching Children Mathematics, 13*(3), 162.

Numbers above 10 and Place Value

OBJECTIVES

After reading this unit, you should be able to:

- Define place value, renaming, and regrouping.
- Identify developmentally appropriate instruction for place-value and two-digit whole number operations.
- Assess children's understanding of numbers above ten and place value.
- Provide developmentally appropriate instruction for place-value and addition and subtraction with two-digit numbers.

As described in Unit 21, the NCTM (2000, p. 78) standard on number and operations includes expectations for the understanding of operations and how they relate to one another and for fluent computation and making reasonable estimates (discussed in Unit 20). During the primary grades, students should reach an understanding of a variety of means for adding and subtracting, the relationship between these two operations, the effects of adding and subtracting whole numbers, and the situations in which multiplication and division are used. Children should develop skill at whole number computation for addition and subtraction, be able to use the basic addition and subtraction number combinations, and use many different computation tools such as "objects, mental computation, estimation, paper and pencil, and calculators" (p. 78). This unit proceeds on to working with numbers above ten and addition and subtraction of double-digit whole numbers.

The focal points (NCTM, 2007) for number and operations for first grade include developing an understanding of whole numbers from 10 to 100 in relation to groups of ten and one. During grade 2, students develop an understanding of the base-ten numeration system and place-value concepts. They are able to depict equivalent representations of numbers, such as showing 25 to be two tens and one five. In grade 3, students extend their understanding of place value to numbers up to 10,000.

During the latter part of the preoperational period (see Unit 20), children who are adept at manipulating quantities up to ten can move on to working with quantities above ten. Through manipulating groups of ten and quantities between zero and ten, children move through the teens and up to 20. Some will pick up the pattern of the 20s, 30s, and so on, up through the 90s. As children enter concrete operations, they perfect their informal knowledge of numbers above ten and move on to whole number operations with such numbers. To fully understand what they are doing when they use whole number operations involving numbers above ten, they must be able to conceptualize **place value**: the understanding that the same numeral represents different amounts depending on which position it is in. For example, consider the numbers 3, 30, and 300. In the first instance, *3* stands for three 1s and is in the 1s' place. In 30, *3* stands for three 10s and is in the 10s' place. In 300, *3* stands for three 100s and is in the 100s' place. In the latter two numbers, 0 indicates that there is no quantity in the place it holds. In the number 32, *3* is in the 10s' place and *2* is in the 1s' place. An understanding of place value underlies the understanding of certain **trading rules** that govern place value and enable whole number operations to be accomplished. Examples of trading rules include:

- Ten 1s can be traded for one 10.
- One 10 can be traded for ten 1s.
- Ten 10s can be traded for 100.
- One hundred 1s can be traded for 100.

The place-value concept enables us to represent any value using only 10 numerals (0–9).

Place value is one of the most difficult concepts for young children to grasp. Being able to rote and rational count above ten is only a beginning step on the way to an understanding of place value. Children need many counting experiences (as described in Unit 6) and many experiences with concrete models in order to develop the place-value concept. All too often, children are rushed into the place-value operations involved in **regrouping** (formerly called borrowing and carrying) as a rote memory activity without the necessary underlying conceptualization. By understanding place value, children will realize that when they take one from the 10s' column, they are actually taking one group of 10 and that when they add numbers in the 1s' column and arrive at a sum

above nine, the amount they move to the 10s' column represents one or more groups of ten. Understanding place value will also help them to see that the placement of numerals is critical in determining value. For example, *sixty-eight* can be written as 68 (six 10s and eight 1s) and as 60 + 8 but *not* as 86. The sequence for writing numbers follows fixed rules just like a word sentence. In other words, "Ball boy the throws" does not follow the conventions of correctly written English. In the same fashion, *one hundred twenty-one* is not written as 10021. This unit focuses on how to guide children to an understanding of this concept.

Place-value problems are a challenge for primary grade students.

Assessment

For young children, understanding place value is a difficult task. They will normally flounder for a while, seeming to understand the concept in some situations and not in others. Teachers should be patient and accepting and offer the children time and appropriate experiences. The following examples of assessment tasks can be used to discover where the children are on the road to understanding two-digit numbers and the concept of place value.

SAMPLE ASSESSMENT TASK

9P
Place Value, Groups of Ten: Unit 24
Concrete Operations Ages 7–8

METHOD: Interview.

SKILL: Child is able to count groups of 11 or more objects and tell how many 10s are in the groups.

MATERIALS: A container of 100 counters (e.g., chips, cubes, or sticks).

PROCEDURE: Place the container of counters in front of the child. Say, "**here are a bunch of counters. Count out as many of them as you can.**" If the child counts out 11 or more ask, "**how many 10s do you think you have? How many 1s?**"

EVALUATION: If the child answers correctly, then she probably has the concept of place value for 10s. An incorrect answer indicates that, although she may be able to rational count groups of objects greater than ten, she does not yet understand the meaning of each of the numerals in her response.

INSTRUCTIONAL RESOURCE: Charlesworth, R. (2011). *Experiences in math for young children* (6th ed.). Belmont, CA: Wadsworth/Cengage Learning.

SAMPLE ASSESSMENT TASK

9Q
Place Value, Grouping to Identify an Amount: Unit 24
Concrete Operations Ages 7–8

METHOD: Interview.

SKILL: The child is able to form two or more subgroups of ten objects, each with some remaining from the original group, and then tell how many he has without counting each individual object.

MATERIALS: A container of 100 counters (e.g., chips, cubes, or sticks).

PROCEDURE: Place a pile of counters (start with about 35) in front of the child. Say, "**make as many groups of ten as you can.**" Ask, "**how many** (counters) **do you have altogether?**"

EVALUATION: Note if the child can come up with the answer by counting the number of groups of ten and adding on the number of 1s or if instead he must count each object to be sure of the total. If the child can determine the answer without counting by 1s, this indicates that he is developing the concept of place value.

INSTRUCTIONAL RESOURCE: Charlesworth, R. (2011). *Experiences in math for young children* (6th ed.). Belmont, CA: Wadsworth/Cengage Learning.

On average, first graders can learn to read, write, and understand two-digit numbers; second graders three-digit numbers; and third graders four-digit numbers. However, a broad range of normal variation will exist within any particular group. The best rule of thumb in assessment is to be sure that children understand one-digit numbers before going on to two-digit, two before three, and so on.

Activities

The following activities are adapted from the selection of resources listed at the end of this unit. Young children need many experiences with place value and in manipulating objects whose number exceeds ten before proceeding to whole number operations with two-digit numbers. Start with counting activities such as those suggested in Unit 6. Then move on to the kinds of activities described in the following pages. The first two activities focus on constructing an understanding of the properties of amounts greater than ten.

Once the children reach a good understanding of counting and subdividing groups greater than ten, they are ready for activities that gradually move them into the complexities of place value.

Activities

Numerals Greater Than 10: Conservation of Large Numbers

OBJECTIVE: To understand, when given a group of more than ten objects, that the number of objects remains the same no matter how they are arranged.

MATERIALS: Each child will need a container with 50 or more counters (i.e., cubes, chips, or sticks) and a place-value board (cf. Richardson, 1984, p. 212). A place-value board is a piece of paper divided into two sections so that groups can be placed on one side and loose counters on the other side. To make a place-value board, take a 9″ × 12″ piece of paper or tagboard and then glue or staple a 6″ × 9″ piece of colored paper on one half. Draw a picture in the upper right-hand corner of the white side so that the child will know how to place the board in the correct position.

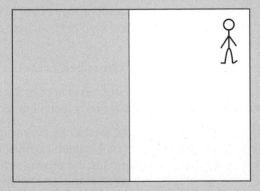

Unifix Cubes are excellent for this activity because they can be snapped together. However, cubes or chips that can be stacked or sticks that can be held together with a rubber band may also be used.

ACTIVITY: Tell the children to put some amount of counters greater than ten on the white side of their place-value board. Suggest the children work in pairs so they can check each other's counting. When they agree that they have the same amount, say, "**make a group of ten** (counters) **and put it on the** (color) **side of your board. How many loose** (counters) **do you have left?**" "**How many** (counters) **do you have altogether?**" Note how many children realize that they still have the same number of counters. Ask, "**do you have enough** (counters) **to make another ten?**" Note if they respond correctly. If they do make another ten, ask again how many loose cubes they have and if the total is still the same. To connect their arrangements to number symbols, write the arrangements on the board: "three 10s and four 1s" and "two 10s and fourteen 1s."

FOLLOW-UP: Do the same activity using containers to put the counters in. Label each container "10." If you use small counters such as tiny chips, bottle caps, or beans, this would be a more efficient way to keep the groups separated. See Richardson (1984, 1999a, 1999b) for additional variations on this activity.

Numerals Greater Than 10: Measuring

OBJECTIVE: To work with large numbers through nonstandard measurement activities (see Unit 18 for background information).

MATERIALS: Small objects that can be used as nonstandard units, paper and pencil to record measurements, and measurement cards (as suggested by Richardson, 1984). Each measurement card depicts something in the classroom that can be measured.

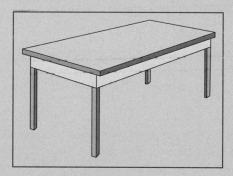 

ACTIVITY: Have the children measure the items with the objects, group the objects into 10s, and then figure out how many they have used. Ask them to record the results on their paper.

> The chair is 24 paper clips tall.
> The table is 36 paper clips wide.

FOLLOW-UP: Have the children measure the same items using different nonstandard units and compare the number of units. See Richardson (1984, 1999a, 1999b) for further activities.

Activities

Place Value: Constructing Models of Two-Digit Numbers

OBJECTIVE: To develop models of two-digit numbers using the place-value board.

MATERIALS: Place-value board (described in previous activity) and a supply of cards with individual numerals, 0–9, written on each card. Provide the child(ren) with at least two sets of numerals and a supply of counters that can be readily stacked, snapped, or bundled into groups of ten. One child working alone will need 100 counters. If children are working in small groups and sharing the counters, add 50 counters per child.

ACTIVITY: Have the children put the place-value boards in front of them. Provide them with an ample supply of numerals in a small container, and place the container of counters where it is convenient for everyone to reach. Say, **"close your eyes and pick two numerals. Put one on your board on the** (color) **side and one on your board on the white side. Make a model of the numeral you have selected."**

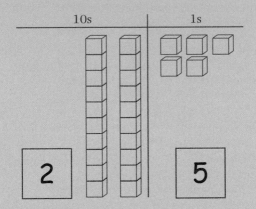

FOLLOW-UP: Have the students repeat this activity with different number combinations. Have them work alone, in pairs, and/or in small groups. Have them do the same activity using base-ten blocks after they have been introduced. (Base-ten blocks will be described later in this chapter.) The same activity can be adapted to work with 100s and 1,000s when the children are ready. The activity could also be done using spinners, one for each place value.

Place Value: Estimation with Common Items

OBJECTIVE: To estimate amounts and apply knowledge of place value to finding out how close the estimate is.

MATERIALS: A container of common items such as a bag of peanuts, dry beans, or cotton balls; a box of paper clips, rubber bands, or cotton swabs; a jar of bottle tops, clothespins, pennies, or other common items; some small cups, bowls, or plastic glasses; flip-chart numerals or paper and pencil to write results. (Flip-chart numerals can be made by writing numerals 0–9 on cards, punching two holes at the top of each card, and putting the cards on rings.)

ACTIVITY: *Estimating* is the math term for guessing or predicting the answer to a math problem. Show the children the container of objects. Let them hold it, examine it, but not open it. Say, "**look closely at this** (item)." Ask, "**how many (items) do you think are in this** (container)?" You record or have the children record each child's guess. Open the container. Say, "**count out groups of ten (item) and put them in the** (cups, glasses, and so on). **Find out how many groups of ten there are altogether. Each time you count out ten, turn over a number on your flip chart**," or if the children can write, say, "**write the number that tells how many 10s you have.**"

FOLLOW-UP: Once the children catch on, put out the estimate of the week. Have the children record their guesses on a chart. Then on Friday, have them open the container and find out the actual amount. Make a graph showing the distribution of estimates.

	10s	20s	30s	40s	50s	50s
4					59	
3			39		56	64
2		27	39	45	55	63
1		25	32	40	51	60

For more large number activities and examples, see Chapter 4 in Fosnot and Dolk (2001).

Base-ten blocks provide a different kind of model for working with the place-value concept. It is important that children work with various types of materials in model construction so that they do not think there is only one way to view place value with concrete materials. So far we have described making models with discrete items. Base-ten blocks depict each place with a solid model. Units (or 1s) are individual cubes, rods (or 10s) are the equivalent of ten unit cubes stuck together in a row, flats (or 100s) are the equivalent of ten rods stuck together, and cubes (or 1,000s) are the equivalent of ten flats stacked and glued together (see Figure 24–1).

Trading is another procedure for working with place value. Primary children need many

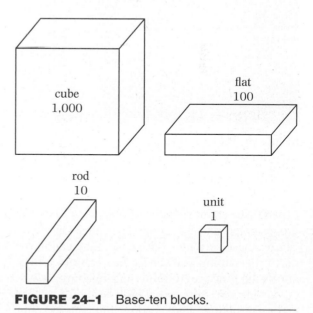

FIGURE 24–1   Base-ten blocks.

Activities

Place Value: Base-Ten Blocks

OBJECTIVE: To work with place value using base-ten blocks.

MATERIALS: A classroom set of base-ten blocks.

ACTIVITY: Use the base-ten blocks for the activities previously described by adding on another step. Each time the child makes a group of ten, she can record it by selecting a rod. She can then count the rods at the end to find out how many groups of ten she has found.

FOLLOW-UP: Many auxiliary materials can be purchased that provide activities with base-ten blocks besides those that come with the Teacher's Guide. Base-ten blocks and teachers' guides can be purchased from suppliers such as Dale Seymour, Creative Publications, ETA, Cuisinaire, and DIDAX Educational Resources (see addresses in Unit 27).

In the computer laboratory, students can experiment with virtual mathematics place-value activities.

experiences counting piles of objects, trading for groups of ten, and describing the results. Once they can do these activities with ease, they can move on to regrouping and renaming. Too often they are pushed into regrouping and renaming without an adequate conceptual base built on counting and constructing many groups of ten and relating them (and any 1s remaining) to written numerals. Regrouping happens when one or more items are added or taken away so that an amount moves to the next 10, next 100, next 1,000, and so on. That is, a group might break down into two 10s and six 1s, or 26. Five more units are added so there are now 11 units. Ten units are then moved to the 10s' place, leaving one unit in the 1s' place. There are now three 10s and one unit, or 31. **Renaming** of the group has also occurred. It has now been *renamed* 31.

Reverse trading takes place if units are removed. For example: suppose seven units are to be taken away from the three 10s and one unit; a 10 would be moved over to the units, making eleven units, and seven units could then be removed, leaving two 10s and four 1s, or 24. Primary-grade children need to do many trading activities with concrete materials before moving on to paper-and-pencil computations. These trades can be practiced with concrete items, such as cubes and chips, the beads on an abacus, or base-ten blocks. Chip trading materials can be purchased from Dale Seymour.

Activities

Place Value: Trading Activities

OBJECTIVE: To construct the concepts of regrouping and renaming through trading activities.

MATERIALS: A supply of paper squares consisting of 100 reds (units) and 30 blues (10s); a place-value board with a 1s' and 10s' place.

ACTIVITY: Have the children put their place-value boards in front of them. Place a supply of red and blue paper squares where they can be easily reached. Say, "**the blue squares are 10s and the red squares are 1s.**" Hold up a large 27. Say, "**show me how you can make a model of this number on your board.**" Have the children try several examples. When you are sure they understand that the reds are 1s and the blues are 10s, go on to regrouping. Go back to 27. Say, "**make 27 on your boards again. Now, suppose someone gives you five more 1s. Take five more. What happens to your 1s?**" Encourage them to describe what happens. Remind them that there cannot be more than nine in the 1s' place. Eventually someone will realize that 32 should be modeled with three 10s and two 1s. Have the children discuss what they might do to get a model that has three 10s and two 1s by trading. Say, "**suppose you trade 10 reds for 1 blue. Where should the blue be placed?**" Once everyone has the blue in the 10s' place, ask, "**suppose someone needs four 1s. How could you give them four?**" Encourage them to discuss this problem with one another, and ask your questions until someone discovers that another trade will have to be made. Have everyone trade in a blue for ten reds, take four away, and see that they now have two blues and eight reds (28).

FOLLOW-UP: Create some story problems, and have the children solve them using trading. Then move on to adding and taking away two-digit quantities. Also provide students with pairs of two-digit numbers and have them invent problems using the numbers.

When the children practice trading to regroup and rename on their place-value boards, they are actually adding and subtracting informally. Richardson (1984) explains how to carry this activity over to addition and subtraction of two-digit numbers. Richardson believes that it is confusing to begin two-digit addition and subtraction with numbers that do *not* have to be regrouped, such as

$$
\begin{array}{cccc}
22 & 53 & 46 & 18 \\
+35 & +14 & -34 & -13 \\
\hline
57 & 67 & 12 & 5
\end{array}
$$

This type of addition and subtraction may lead children to believe that adding or subtracting with two digits is exactly the same operation as with one digit. The result may be responses such as the following:

$$
\begin{array}{cccc}
25 & 48 & 72 & 37 \\
+16 & +34 & -35 & -28 \\
\hline
311 & 712 & 43 & 11
\end{array}
$$

Note in these examples that the children have added or subtracted each column as though it were an individual one-digit problem. Introduce two-digit addition as follows.

PUT 26 CUBES
ON YOUR BOARD.

NOW GET 18
CUBES, AND
PUT THEM
NEXT TO YOUR
BOARD.

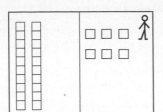
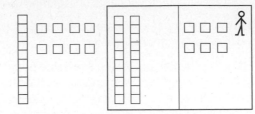

NOW PUT THEM TOGETHER.
HOW MANY 10s? HOW
MANY 1s?
YES, WE HAVE THREE 10s
AND FOURTEEN 1s.
DO WE HAVE ENOUGH TO
MAKE ANOTHER 10?

(Give them time to move
10 cubes.) NOW WE HAVE
FOUR 10s AND SIX 1s
HOW MANY IS THAT? YES,
THAT IS 44.

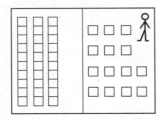
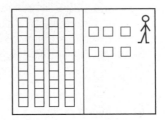

Repeat this process several times with different pairs of two-digit numbers: Sometimes the sum contains more than nine units and sometimes it does not. When the children understand the process without symbols, connect the symbols by writing them on the board as you go through the process.

Introduce subtraction of two-digit numbers in parallel fashion. For example, have the children put out 42 cubes and then tell them they need to take away 25. They will discover that they have to break up a 10 to accomplish this task. After doing many examples without written numbers, go through some problems in which you connect the quantities to numbers at each step, thus gradually introducing the notation. Then have them do mixed sets of problems. Finally, move on to story problems.

Problems and activities that apply place-value concepts can be integrated across the curriculum (Figure 24–2).

Kamii's Approach

The activities suggested in this unit follow a fairly structured sequence while promoting construction of concepts through exploration. Kamii and colleagues (Kamii, Lewis, & Livingston, 1993) have been working with primary children using open-ended activities that provide for more child trial and error and self-sequencing. Interviewing primary students who had been through conventional workbook/textbook instruction, they discovered that students were able to do regrouping and renaming as a rote process without really knowing the meaning

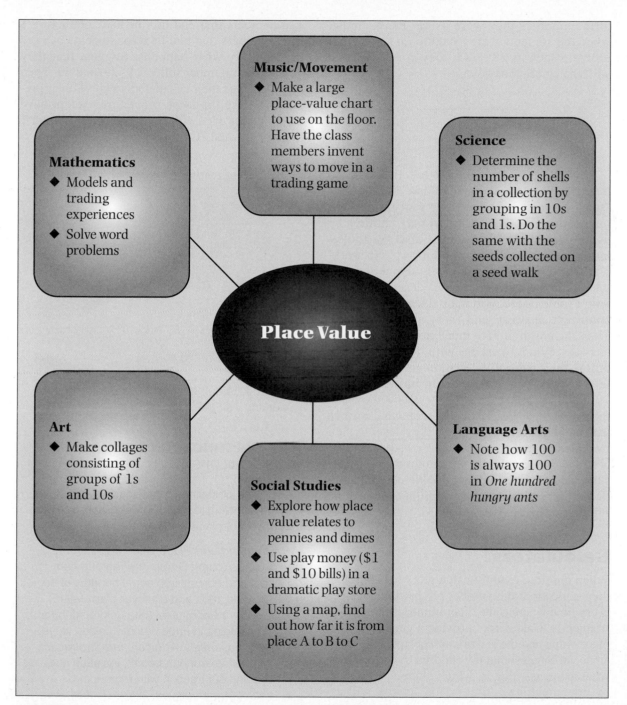

FIGURE 24–2   Integrating experiences with place value and quantities above ten across the curriculum.

of the numbers they were using. For example, when the students were asked to do a two-digit problem such as 28 + 45, they could come up with the correct answer:

$$\begin{array}{r} 1 \\ 28 \\ +45 \\ \hline 73 \end{array}$$

However, when asked what the 1 in 13 means, they said it meant "one" rather than "ten." Kamii has had greater success in communicating this concept to primary children by using games and letting them discover the relationship of the digits on their own. No workbooks or worksheets are used, and neither are the kinds of concrete activities described in this unit. Problems are written on the board, children contribute answers, and every answer is listed. Then the children give their rationales for their answers. When working with double-digit addition, their natural inclination is to start on the left. They add the 10s; write the answer; add the 1s; and, if necessary, move any 10s over, erasing the original answer in the 10s' column. Through trial and error and discussion, they develop their own method and construct their own place-value concept. Place value is not taught as a separate skill needed prior to doing double-column addition. This method sounds intriguing and is more fully described in Kamii (2003).

Calculators

When children explore calculators for counting, they notice that the number on the right changes every time whereas the other numbers change less frequently. Calculators provide a graphic look at place value and the relation of each place to those adjacent. Suggest that the children try ten and note what happens—that is, which place changes, and by how much each time? This activity will assist children in seeing what the 10s' place means. Concepts constructed using manipulatives can be reinforced with calculator activities. By adding

1 to numbers that end in nine and subtracting 1 from numbers that end in zero, students can see immediately what happens. Suggest that they guess which number follows 9, 29, and 59. Then have them use their calculators to check their predictions. Use the same procedure, except have them predict what will happen if they subtract 1 from 20, 40, and 70.

A hand calculator can be a useful tool for working with place value.

MATH TECHNOLOGY FOR YOUNG CHILDREN

Using the guidelines from Unit 2, evaluate any of the following resources designed to reinforce concepts of place value.

- *Grouping and Place Value* (http://store. sunburst.com). Group and regroup numbers and objects into equal bundles of 1s, 10s, and 100s and discover place value.
- *Numbers Recovered* (http://store.sunburst. com). Helps in understanding place value.
- *Math Essentials: Addition and Subtraction* (http://store.sunburst.com). Includes addition and subtraction with regrouping.
- *Virtual Manipulatives*, *Numbers and Operations* (pre-K–2; http://nlvm.usu.edu). Base-ten blocks, chips abacus, color chips.

Ideas for Children with Special Needs

Children with motor disabilities such as spina bifida (SB), cerebral palsy (CP), or developmental coordination disorder (DCD) are challenged by any type of motor skills task (Lewis, 2003). They may not be able to interact with objects in any conventional way depending on the degree of their disability. However, they can develop cognitive understanding with the right kind of support. Ways have to be found for them to act on their environment. Technology can be designed that allows children with motor disabilities to use whatever movement they have available to assist them in learning and communicating. These children require close attention from adults, who should provide prompting and cueing as they work. In class, teachers need to emphasize the children's strengths.

Children with perceptual problems may have difficulties perceiving the commonalities among numbers above nine. They may need to have the teens lined up vertically so the common element of 1 (in the 10s' place) can be seen. Color coding can be helpful. These children commonly make reversals (e.g., confusing 13 and 31). With numbers of two or more symbols, it is important for children to understand spatial terms such as left, right, middle, first, last, and beginning. Some children may need extra help with auditory memory. The teacher may say "fifty-two," but the child may perceive only the "two."

Children may find it interesting to learn how we arrived at base ten for our number system and the systems other cultures use for recording and calculating. Zaslavsky (1996) explains how finger counting is common practice in many cultures. In others, both fingers and toes are used, and so the base is 20. Once large amounts become involved, each culture has had to invent a method of recording and calculating. Tally marks on bone or wood have been used for thousands of years. The bar codes used so commonly today are based on groups of tally marks of two

heights. Knots on string is another method used to record amounts. The abacus, first developed in China, allows for calculating large numbers using rows of beads.

Evaluation

An evaluation technique suggested by Kamii (2003) shows if children really understand place value in two-digit numbers.

> Show the child a three-by-five-inch card with 16 written on it. Ask, "What does this say?" After the child says 16, count out 16 chips. With the top of a pen circle the 6 of the 16. "What does this *part* (the 6) mean? Show me with the chips what this *part* (the 6) means." Circle the 1 of the 16. "What does this *part* (the 1) mean? Show me with the chips what this *part* (the 1) means." (p. 161)

Kamii reports that, after conventional instruction with workbooks and possibly some manipulatives, all first and second graders can answer correctly regarding the 6. However, of the primary children Kamii interviewed, none of the late first graders, 33% of late third graders, and only 50% of late fourth graders said that the 1 means 10. Children who learned about place value through constructing it themselves using Kamii's method did considerably better. At the end of the second grade, 66% said that the 1 means 10 and 74% said that the 5 in 54 means 50.

Whichever instructional method you use, be sure to observe carefully the process each child uses. Question children frequently about what they are doing to be sure that they really understand the concepts and are not just answering in a rote manner.

Summary

Learning about place value and working with two-digit whole number operations that require regrouping and renaming are two of the most difficult challenges the primary-level child faces. Conventionally, they are taught using a workbook approach with few (if any) manipulatives to support the instruction. Also, they are conventionally introduced too early and become rote memory activities for those who have the facility to remember the steps necessary to come up with correct answers. Less capable students flounder in a lack of understanding.

Most mathematics educators believe that children learn the concepts and skills needed to understand place value—as well the processes of regrouping and renaming—through practice in solving problems that use concrete materials. Kamii (2003) takes a different approach, using no concrete materials but guiding children through trial and error and discussion. Children with perceptual and/or motor disabilities will have a need for special assistance.

KEY TERMS

place value
regrouping

renaming

trading rules

SUGGESTED ACTIVITIES

1. Visit one or more primary classrooms and observe the math instruction. Describe the methods observed. Is place value and/or two-digit addition and subtraction being taught? How? Is the method developmentally appropriate? Are the children ready for these concepts? Do they seem to understand?
2. Using Kamii's technique, interview one first grader, one second grader, and one third grader. Describe the results. Compare the performance of the children you interviewed with those Kamii interviewed. What did you learn from this experience?
3. Review the first-, second-, and third-grade levels of two or more elementary math textbook

series. At what level are place value, two-digit addition and subtraction, regrouping, and renaming introduced? What methods of instruction are used? Compare the textbook methods with those described in this unit. What are the similarities and differences? Explain why you would or would not like to use these textbooks.
4. Prepare materials for one of the activities suggested in this unit. Try out the activity with a child or small group of children that you believe to be at the right stage for it. Write a report explaining what you did, who you did it with, what happened, and your evaluation of the activity and the children's responses.
5. Keep your Activity File/Notebook up-to-date.

REVIEW

A. Define the following terms.
   1. Place value
   2. Regrouping
   3. Renaming
B. Identify which of the following are descriptions of place value being taught as described in this unit.

1. A kindergarten teacher is drilling her class on 1s', 10s', and 100s' places using a worksheet approach.
2. A second-grade teacher gives one of her students 35 Unifix Cubes and asks him to make as many groups of ten as he can.

3. A primary teacher is beginning instruction on two-digit addition with simple problems such as 12 + 41, so the students will not have to regroup and rename right away.

4. Some primary children are exploring with calculators. Their teacher has suggested they take a list of the numbers 19, 29, 39, and 49 and predict what will happen if 1 is added to each. Then they are to try these operations with their calculators, write down what happens, and share the results with the other children and the teacher.

C. Explain your answers to question B.

D. List three kinds of materials that can be used for making place-value models.

E. In what ways does Kamii's approach to teaching place value differ from the conventional one?

F. Check yourself on place value.

1. Identify the number of 100s, 10s, and 1s in each numeral.

	100s	10s	1s
37			
4			
276			

2. In the numeral 3,482, the 4 means ___, the 8 means ___, and the 2 means ___.

3.
```
   1
  67   The 1 above the 6 means:
 +17   _____
  84
```

REFERENCES

Fosnot, C. T., & Dolk, M. (2001). *Young mathematicians at work*. Portsmouth, NH: Heinemann.

Kamii, C. (2003). *Young children continue to reinvent arithmetic, 2nd grade* (2nd ed.). New York: Teachers College Press.

Kamii, C., Lewis, B, A., & Livingston, S. J. (1993). Primary arithmetic: Children inventing their own procedures. *Arithmetic Teacher, 41*(4), 200–203.

Lewis, V. (2003). *Development and disability* (2nd ed.). Malden, MA: Blackwell.

National Council of Teachers of Mathematics. (2000). *Principles and standards for school mathematics*. Reston, VA: Author.

National Council of Teachers of Mathematics. (2007). *Curriculum focal points*. Reston, VA: Author.

Richardson, K. (1984). *Developing number concepts using Unifix Cubes*. Menlo Park, CA: Addison-Wesley.

Richardson, K. (1999a). *Developing number concepts: Book 2. Addition and subtraction*. Parsippany, NJ: Seymour.

Richardson, K. (1999b). *Developing number concepts: Book 3. Place value, multiplication, and division*. Parsippany, NJ: Seymour.

Zaslavsky, C. (1996). *The multicultural math classroom*. Portsmouth, NH: Heinemann.

FURTHER READING AND RESOURCES

Barker, L. (2009). Ten is the magic number! *Teaching Children Mathematics, 15*(6), 336–345.

Burris, A. C. (2005). *Understanding the math you teach: Content and methods for prekindergarten through grade 4*. Upper Saddle River, NJ: Merrill-Pearson/Prentice-Hall.

Huinker, D. (2002). Calculators as learning tools for young children's explorations of number. *Teaching Children Mathematics, 8*(6), 316–321.

Irving, K. J. (2003). The MegaPenny project. *Teaching Children Mathematics, 10*(3), 158–161.

Kari, A. R., & Anderson, C. B. (2003). Opportunities to develop place value through student dialogue. *Teaching Children Mathematics, 10*(2), 78–82.

Perry, J. A., & Atkins, S. L. (2002). It's not just notation: Valuing children's representations. *Teaching Children Mathematics, 9*(4), 196–201.

Princzes, E. J. (1993). *One hundred hungry ants*. New York: Scholastic Books.

Reys, B. J., & Arbaugh, F. (2001). Clearing up the confusion over calculator use in grades K–5. *Teaching Children Mathematics, 8*(2), 90–94.

Ross, S. R. (2002). Place value: Problem solving and written assessment. *Teaching Children Mathematics, 8*(7), 419–423.

Sztajn, P. (2002). Celebrating 100 with number sense. *Teaching Children Mathematics, 9*(1), 212–217.

Uy, F. L. (2003). The Chinese numeration system and place value. *Teaching Children Mathematics, 9*(5), 243–247.

Wickett, M. (2009). Tuheen's thinking about place value. *Teaching Children Mathematics, 16*(4), 256.

Geometry, Data Collection, and Algebraic Thinking

After reading this unit, you should be able to:

- List the basic concepts of geometry that young children learn informally at the primary level.
- Assess children's readiness for primary-level geometry and data collection experiences.
- Plan and carry out developmentally appropriate primary-level geometry, data collection, algebraic thinking, estimation, and probability instruction.
- To construct and interpret graphs and tables.

Standards (NCTM, 2000) for geometry (Units 9 and 10), data analysis (Units 7 and 16), and algebra (Units 7, 8, 13, and 20) were introduced, and these topics were discussed previously. The initial level of algebraic thinking lies in understanding patterns and relationships. These expectations continue into the primary grades, when children are expected to further their capabilities to recognize, name, build, draw, compare, and sort two- and three-dimensional shapes. Further, they should gain some understanding of **symmetry**, be able to create mental images of geometric shapes, recognize shapes from different perspectives, relate ideas in geometry to number and measurement, and locate geometric shapes in the environment.

Primary-level children are expected to move further in understanding data analysis by being able to describe and explain the meaning of data and make predictions from data. The expectations for understanding probability are only at an informal level.

The focal points (NCTM, 2007) for primary grades include an emphasis on integration of several of the topics in this unit. For first grade, a focal point in geometry is composing and decomposing shapes. Connections include using geometric shapes for informal measurement and on bar graphs in addition to connecting patterns (such as odd and even numbers) as a basis for algebra. A curriculum focal point for second-grade number and operations is learning methods of estimation. Children make connections to geometry as they collect data related to space. They obtain more knowledge of number patterns that lead to later algebraic understanding. A third-grade focal point in geometry is describing and analyzing two-dimensional shapes so that children develop an understanding of congruence and symmetry. Multiplication and division and their relationship connect with algebra readiness. Whole number operations are applied during data analysis: constructing and analyzing frequency tables, bar graphs, picture graphs, and line plots to solve problems.

Weather is the current science topic in Mr. Gonzales's third-grade class in northern Utah. This morning the children are huddled over copies of the past week's weather forecasts they clipped out of Ogden's local morning paper. They are reading the forecast section to find out what kind of information is included and to discuss how they might organize some of the data presented. They note that the day's forecast is included along with the normal highs and lows for that date. There is a regional forecast for Utah and a forecast map and description of the weather for the entire United States. Selected national and global temperatures along with precipitation and outlook are included in a table. The nation's highs and lows are also reported. The children compile a list of this information and discuss what they can learn and what information might be interesting for them to record.

Chan's great-great-grandparents came to Utah from Beijing, People's Republic of China. Chan has noticed that Ogden and Beijing are at about the same latitude. He decides to record the high temperatures in Beijing for eight days and compare them with those in Ogden for the same time period. First Chan made a chart and then a graph to depict the information from the chart. Then he wrote a description of the information obtained from the graphs. To complete this activity, he applied his mathematical knowledge (measurement, counting, graph making) to an activity that integrates science (the topic of weather), social studies (geography), and reading

Cities	Dates/Temperatures							
	22	23	24	25	26	27	28	29
Beijing	28	28	37	37	41	41	45	37
Ogden	36	27	26	26	33	33	42	44

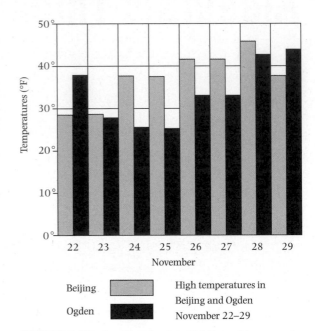

High temperatures in Beijing and Ogden, November 22–29

FIGURE 25–1 Chan's data table and bar graph.

and language arts (reading and comprehending the article and writing about the information obtained). Figure 25–1 depicts what Chan might have produced.

Groundwork for this type of activity was laid in Units 9, 10, 16, and 20. Primary children must have this groundwork before moving on to the activities described in this unit. Children need a basic understanding of shape and space, which they apply to the early graphing and mapping experiences during the preoperational period, before they can move on to higher-level graphing and geometry concepts. Children should know the basic characteristics of shapes and be able to identify geometric shapes such as circles, triangles, squares, rectangles, and prisms when they enter the primary level. They should also have the spatial concepts of position, direction, and distance relationships and be able to use space for making patterns and constructions. During the primary years, they should continue with these basic experiences, and adults should guide them to more complex levels.

Children study geometry in a general, informal way during the elementary grades. Spatial concepts are reinforced, and the senses are sharpened. During the primary years, the children continue to develop geometric concepts mainly at an intuitive level. However, geometric figures are used to teach other concepts, so children should be familiar with them. For example, multiplication is frequently illustrated in a rectangular grid.

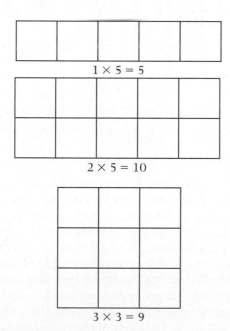

$1 \times 5 = 5$

$2 \times 5 = 10$

$3 \times 3 = 9$

Fractions are commonly illustrated using geometric shapes (see Unit 23) as shown in the following figure.

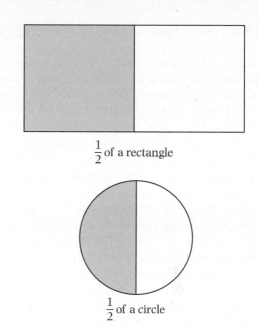

$\frac{1}{2}$ of a rectangle

$\frac{1}{2}$ of a circle

Number lines (which will be described later in this unit) are conventionally used to help children visualize *greater than*, *less than*, betweenness, and the rules of addition and subtraction. For example, the number line shown in the following figure is used to illustrate that $2 + 3 = 3 + 2$.

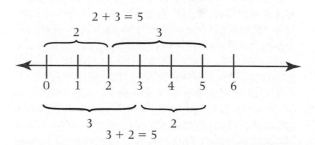

$2 + 3 = 5$

$3 + 2 = 5$

Collecting and organizing data continue to be important applications of mathematics. Graphing is closely related to geometry in that it makes use of geometric concepts such as line and shape. Note that the graphs depicted in this book are based on squares and rectangles. More advanced graphs are based on circles, and others involve the use of line segments to connect points. Tables are the necessary first step in organizing complex data prior to illustrating it on a graph. Charts are closely related to graphs.

In the twenty-first century, we look at algebra as "a way of thinking, a method of seeing and expressing relationships" (Moses, 1997). Algebra provides a way to organize and generalize the patterns we observe in everyday activities. Through learning how to develop relationships, we can understand the regularities not just in mathematics but also in science, history, economics, language, and other areas.

Moses (1997) suggests that algebraic thinking can begin in the early primary grades using geometric concepts such as perimeter and investigations involving square tiles, string, pipe cleaners, and grid paper. Students can identify geometric and number patterns as they explore these relationships. Schifter, Russell, and Bastable (2009) looked at children's early algebraic thinking— "learning representations, connections, and generalizations in the elementary school grades." Discussing and providing reasons for their problem solutions increased children's mathematical understanding and achievement.

The February 1997 issue of *Teaching Children Mathematics* was devoted to this topic. Algebra was defined in the NCTM (2000) standards and in the navigation publications for prekindergarten through grade-2 algebra (Greenes, Cavanagh, Dacey, Findell, & Small, 2001).

Technology can also be used to support the development of algebraic thinking. Technology involves applications of a broad base of skills. As previously pointed out, design technology is an integration of technology, engineering, mathematics, and science. The Science, Technology, Engineering, and Mathematics (**STEM**) movement is growing in strength. See the March 2010 issue of *Science & Children* that focuses on STEM. Another integration is the application of a variety of skills and concepts in the development of robotics projects (Clark, 2002; Murray & Bartelmay, 2005).

In sum, knowledge of geometry, constructing tables and graphs, and algebraic thinking are closely related basic tools for organizing data. The remainder of the unit describes geometry, graphing, using charts and tables, and algebraic thinking at the primary level. Also described are LEGO and its relationship with **LOGO** programming, estimation, and probability.

Assessment

Children's readiness for the following primary-level activities should be assessed using the assessment tasks that accompany Units 9 and 10. It is also measured by observing children's capacities to accomplish the graphing activities in Unit 16 and the higher-level graphing and spatial relations (mapping) activities in Unit 20. It is not safe to assume that children have had all the prerequisite experiences before they arrive in your primary classroom. You might have to start with these earlier levels before moving on to the activities suggested in this unit.

Activities

This section begins with geometry and mapping; it then describes LOGO computer applications to mapping and to robotics and design technology. The unit then goes on to the topics of charts and tables, algebraic thinking, estimation, and probability.

Geometry

Primary children are not ready for the technicalities of geometry, but they can be introduced informally to some of the basic concepts. They can learn about **points** as small dots on paper or on the chalkboard. During a story or a mapping activity, the children get introduced to **curves** as smooth but not straight paths that connect two points. **Lines** appear as number lines, in measurement activities, and as the sides of geometric figures. Children perceive *angles* (space made by the meeting of two straight lines) in geometric figures. *Congruency* or sameness of size and shape is what children deal with when they match and compare the sizes and shapes

of various figures, such as when they sort attribute blocks or make collages from paper shapes.
Symmetry (correspondence of parts of a figure
on opposite sides of a point, line, or plane) is
what children are working with when they do the
paper folding suggested in the unit on fractions.
The terms *point(s), line(s),* and *curve(s)* may be
used with young children without going into the
technicalities. The terms *congruency, symmetry,*
and *angle* will be introduced to them beyond the
primary level and are not essential to working
with the concepts informally. The readings and
resources listed at the end of the unit contain a
multitude of ideas for activities that will lay
the basis for the formal study of geometry. The
following are some examples.

Activities

Geometry: Geoboard Activities

OBJECTIVE: To provide experience exploring the qualities of plane figures.

MATERIALS: Geoboards and rubber bands. Geoboards may be purchased or made. A geoboard is
a square board with round head screws or smooth, slender cylinders (pegs) made of plastic placed
at equal intervals so that it appears to be made up of many squares of equal size. Commercial
geoboards have five rows of five pegs each.

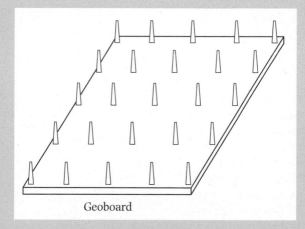

Geoboard

ACTIVITIES:
1. Put out the geoboards and an ample supply of rubber bands of different sizes and colors
   (special rubber bands may be purchased with the geoboards). Allow plenty of time for the
   children to explore the materials informally. Suggest that they see how many different kinds of
   shapes they can make.
2. Give each child a geoboard and one rubber band. Say, "**make as many different shapes as
   you can with one rubber band.**" Encourage children to count the sides of their shapes and to
   count the number of pegs in each side. Suggest that they make a drawing of each shape.
3. Give each child a rubber band and an attribute block. Say, "**make a shape just like the block's
   shape.**" Start with squares and rectangles, and then triangles and hexagons.

4. On graph paper made to match the geoboard, draw patterns that the children can copy with their rubber bands. An example follows:

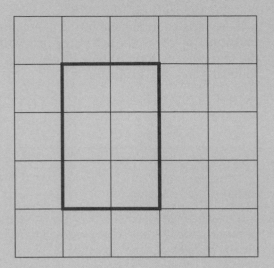 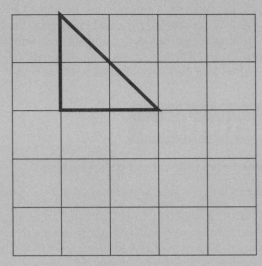

5. Have the children draw patterns on graph paper that matches the size of the geoboards. Demonstrate on the chalkboard first to be sure they realize that they need to make their lines from corner to corner. Have them try out their capabilities on some laminated blank graphs first. Then have them copy their own patterns on the geoboards. Encourage them to exchange patterns with other children.

FOLLOW-UP: Provide more complicated patterns for the children to copy. Encourage those who are capable of doing so to draw and copy more complicated patterns, possibly even some that overlap. Have them draw overlapping patterns with different-colored pencils or crayons and then construct the patterns with rubber bands of matching colors.

Geometry: Activities with Solids

OBJECTIVE: To explore the characteristics of solid geometric figures.

MATERIALS: A set of geometric solids (available from ETA, Kaplan, Nienhuis Montessori, DIDAX Educational Resources, Creative Publications, Dale Seymour, Cuisinaire, etc.).

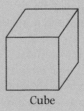

Cube

Cylinder

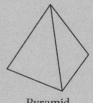

Cone

Pyramid

Sphere

ACTIVITIES: Let the children explore the solids and note the similarities and differences. Once they are familiar with them, try the following activities.

Put out three of the objects. Describe one and see if the children can guess which one it is.

- **It is flat all over, and each side is the same.** (Cube)
- **It is flat on the bottom. Its sides look like triangles.** (Pyramid)
- **It is flat on the bottom, the top is a point, and the sides are smooth.** (Cone)
- **Both ends are flat and round, and the sides are smooth.** (Cylinder)
- **It is smooth and round all over.** (Sphere)

FOLLOW-UP: Have the children take turns being the person who describes the geometric solid. Put up a ramp. Have the students predict which solids will slide and which will roll. Then try them out. See if the children realize that some may roll or slide depending how they are placed.

Geometry: Symmetry

OBJECTIVE: To provide experiences for exploring symmetry.

MATERIALS: Construction paper symmetrical shapes. (See Figure 25–2, on page 370, for some patterns.) The following are some suggested shapes; use your imagination to develop others.

ACTIVITY: Give the children one shape pattern at a time. Have them experiment with folding the shapes until the halves match.

FOLLOW-UP:
1. Have the children use the shapes they have folded to make a three-dimensional collage. Say, **"put glue on just one half of your folded paper."**

2. Give the children paper squares and rectangles. Show them how they can fold them in the middle and then cut the sides so they come out with a figure that is the same on both halves. These figures can also be used to make three-dimensional collages.

FIGURE 25–2   Patterns for exploring symmetry.

Geometry: Number Lines

OBJECTIVE: To apply the concept of a line as a visual picture of addition and subtraction and of *more than* and *less than*.

MATERIALS: A laminated number line for each child, a large laminated number line that can be used for demonstration (or a permanent number line on the whiteboard), markers (i.e., chips) to mark places on the number lines.

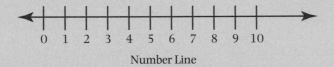

Number Line

ACTIVITIES:
1. *Greater and less than*. Say**, "put a marker on the 4. Find a number that is greater than 4. Put a marker on it."** Discuss which numbers were selected. How did they know which numbers were greater than four? Go through the same procedure with the other numbers. Then go through the procedure looking for numbers less than a given number.
2. *Addition*. Ask, **"how can we show two plus four on the number line?"** Encourage the children to try to figure it out. If they cannot, then demonstrate. Say, **"first I'll put a marker on 2.**

Now I'll count over four spaces. Now I'm at 6. How much is two plus four?" Have the children try several problems with sums of ten or less.

3. *Subtraction*. Ask, "**how can we show five minus two on the number line**?" Encourage the children to try to figure it out. If they cannot, then demonstrate. Say, "**first I'll put a marker on the 5. Now which way should I go to find five minus two?**" Have them try several problems using numbers ten or less.

FOLLOW-UP: Have the children illustrate equivalent sums and differences on the number line (e.g., $3 + 4 = 1 + 6$, $8 - 4 = 7 - 3$). Have them also make up number line problems for themselves. Suggest that they use the number line to find the answer whenever they need help with a one-digit problem.

Geometry: Comparing Road and Straight-Line Distances

OBJECTIVE: To see the relationship between a direct route and the actual route between points on a map. (This activity is for the more advanced primary students who have learned how to use standard measurement tools.)

MATERIALS: Maps of your state for everyone in the class, 1-foot rulers, and marking pens.

ACTIVITIES: Have the students explore the maps. See if they can find the legend and if they can tell you what the various symbols mean. Be particularly sure that they know which kinds of lines are roads, how you find out the mileage from one place on the map to another, and how many miles an inch represents on the map. Spend some time finding out how far it is from your town or city to some of the nearby towns and cities. Have the class agree on two places in the state they would like to visit. Using their rulers and marking pens, have them draw a line from your city to the nearest place selected, from that place to the other location selected, and from there back home. They should then have a triangle. Have everyone figure out the mileage by road and then by direct flight by measuring the lines. Add up the three sides of the triangle. Add up the three road routes. Find the difference between the road trip and the direct route. Discuss why the roads are not as direct as the lines.

FOLLOW-UP: Encourage interested students to compare road and direct distances to other points in the state.

Robotics: LEGO and LOGO

LOGO computer language can provide experience with geometry and technology at a number of levels. With just a few simple commands and minimal instruction, children can explore, play, and create an infinite number of geometric shapes and designs. With a little more adult guided approach, they can learn how to plan out patterns ahead of time and use more complex instructional commands. The cursor, referred to as the **turtle** in LOGO, can be moved about in many directions and at different angles to make straight or curved lines. Children develop problem-solving skills when they work on figuring out how they will make the turtle go just where they want it to in order to come up with a particular design or figure.

Children's building with LEGO building bricks and their exploration of LOGO are combined in connection with math, science, or technology via **LEGO/LOGO**, LEGO Mindstorms, and LEGO

Dacta robotics, which provide children with the opportunity to explore physics, technology, and mathematics. The children have a choice of many tasks that range from assembling a simple traffic light to complex projects such as bridges, playground rides, construction equipment, and vehicles. In the original version, the computer was programmed to control operation of the LEGO machines. More recently, National Instruments, LEGO Dacta, and Tufts University have developed a ROBOLAB system that enables students to write computer programs and transfer them into programmable LEGO bricks. Even kindergartners can create their own robot designs. LEGO Mindstorms includes several robotics products with sets for building *Star Wars* robots and many others. With the invention of the programmable bricks, the robots no longer need to be bound to the computer.

Design Technology

Design technology was introduced in Units 17 and 20 (see also Dunn & Larson, 1990; Petroski, 2003). Primary-grade students can follow more adult guided directions and work on projects individually or in small cooperative groups. The Virginia Children's Engineering Council, the Virginia *Children's Engineering Journal*, and Children Designing and Engineering provide information and activities that provide problems for design technology. Children Designing and Engineering (n.d.) and the Virginia Children's Engineering Council (n.d.) provide some samples of more complex long-term projects. Unit 20 described an example of a safari park project obtained from Children Designing and Engineering. The same site includes several additional projects. The Virginia Children's Engineering Council website also provides projects for students in kindergarten through third grade. As already mentioned, the STEM movement is increasing interest in projects relating Science, Technology, Engineering, and Mathematics. STEM projects might include designing gravity racers (Wilcox, Roberts, & Wilcox, 2010),

designing an insect keeper (Moore, Chessin, & Theobald, 2010), building houses (Bautista & Peters, 2010), and building with sand (Ashbrook, 2010). Lottero-Perdue, Lovelidge, and Bowling (2010) describe the engineering design process.

Collecting and Analyzing Data and Constructing Graphs

Students can collect data, categorize the results, and depict the results in a graphical representation for analysis. Graphing includes constructing graphs, reading information on graphs, and interpreting what the information on a graph means. The data used for making graphs need to be something of interest to the students. Unit 16 presents a list of possible graphing subjects that young children might enjoy working on. Other subjects will grow out of their current interests and activities.

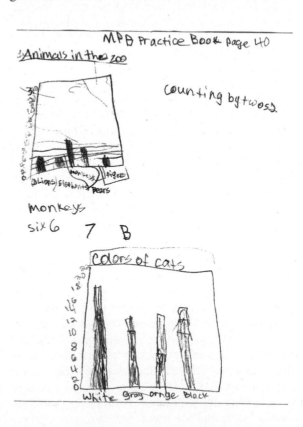

The four most popular types of graphs are picture graphs, bar graphs or histograms, **line graphs**, and circle or pie graphs. The graphs described in previous units fall into the first two categories and are the easiest for young children to construct and interpret. Although pie graphs are beyond the primary level, some primary level children can begin to work with line graphs.

These children record their observations for further analysis.

Line graphs demand concrete operational thinking because children must focus on more than one aspect of the data at the same time. Line graphs are made on a squared paper grid and apply the basic skills that children would learn by first doing the squared paper activities with the geoboard. They are especially good for showing variations such as rainfall, temperature, and hours of daylight. In Figure 25–3, Chan's temperature data are translated from the bar graph to the line graph. Note that the left side and the bottom are called the **axes** and that each must be labeled. In this case, the left side is the temperature axis and the bottom is the axis representing days of the week. To find the correct point for each temperature on each day, the child has to find the point where the two meet, mark the point, and connect it to the previous point and the next point with a line. If two or more types of information are included on the same

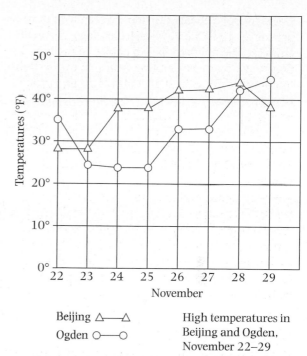

FIGURE 25–3   Chan's data depicted in a line graph.

graph, then usually geometric symbols are used to indicate which line goes with which set of data. Jeanne Vissa (1987) suggests some creative ways to introduce the use of coordinate (or line) graphing to young children.

Charts and Tables

Charts and **tables** are constructed to organize data before they are graphed. A simple chart consists of tally marks such as those depicted in the chart on floating and sinking objects in Unit 7 (see Figure 7–4). This information could be translated into a single-variable graph showing frequency of floating or sinking for each object or into a double-variable graph (i.e., a double-bar or double-line graph) showing both tendencies. The simple tables shown in Figure 25–1 were used to organize the temperature data prior to constructing the graphs.

Activities

Graphing: Introducing Coordinates

OBJECTIVE: To introduce finding coordinates on a graph.

MATERIALS: A large supply of stickers of various kinds. On the bulletin board, construct a large 5 × 5 square coordinate graph. Make the grids using black tape. Place stickers at the intersections of various coordinates (Figure 25–4).

FIGURE 25–4 Coordinate graphing can be introduced using a grid with stickers placed at points to be identified.

ACTIVITIES: Say, **"This is the city. Driving into the city the corner is here at 0, 0. I want to go to** (name one of the stickers). **Tell me how many blocks over and how many blocks up I will have to go."** Suppose that the sticker is on 2, 3. Say, **"yes, I have to go over two blocks and up three. This point is called 2, 3."** Draw the children's attention to how the numbers on the bottom and the sides correspond to the point. Go back to 0, 0 and have the children direct you to other points on the graph. Let the children take turns telling you the coordinates of a sticker they would like to have. When they are able to give the correct coordinates, have them get a matching sticker to keep.

FOLLOW-UP: During center time, encourage children to explore the coordinate map on their own or with a friend. Suggest they trace trips to different corners with their fingers. Let the children who understand the concept of coordinates use coordinate paper to complete symmetrical shapes (Figure 25–5) and name the coordinates.

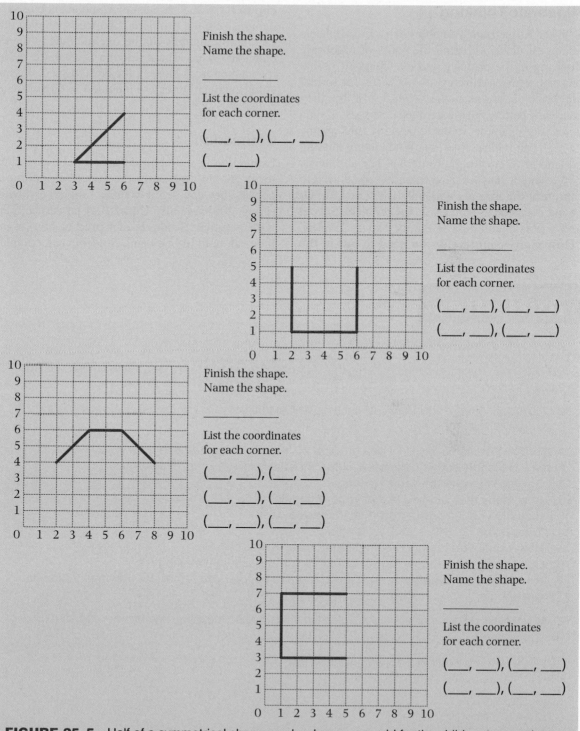

FIGURE 25–5   Half of a symmetrical shape can be drawn on a grid for the children to complete.

Algebraic Thinking

Schifter, Russell, and Bastable (2010) and Michaele Chappell (1997) outline the roots of algebraic thinking in the primary grades. Chappell points out that primary children are not ready for formal algebraic equations such as $x + 5 = 8$, but they can learn patterns using geometric shapes as variables. For example, in the "guess my rule" game, $\square + \square$ can indicate two $\square$s. When doing missing addend problems (e.g., Tonio has 12¢ and needs 25¢ to buy a candy bar), a triangle can be used to represent the missing addend: $12 + \triangle = 25$. Or counters can be used to set up the problem. Set out and write 12 counters + empty cup = 25. Ask, **"How many counters do we need to put in the cup to have 25?"** A balance could also be used to demonstrate the problem. Chappell believes that the gate to algebra can be opened during the elementary years. The following is a sample activity adapted from those in the NCTM special issue. Additional activities are included in Greenes and colleagues (2001).

Estimation

Estimation is an important activity at the primary level. As children enter the concrete operations period, they can begin to make rational estimates (Lang, 2001; see also Unit 20). A jar can be filled with pennies. Students can predict how many they can hold in one hand. Students can compare

Activities

Algebraic Thinking: Building Rectangles[1]

OBJECTIVE: To introduce the patterns that determine the area of a rectangle using nonstandard units.

MATERIALS: Square tiles from sets such as TexTiles (Creative Publications) or Algebra Tiles (Cuisinaire).

ACTIVITY: Provide each child with a group of 20 tiles. Say, **"use some of your square tiles to make a rectangle with a base of two tiles."** Ask the following kinds of questions.
1. **Did you all make the same rectangle?**
2. **How many tiles did you use in your rectangle?**
3. **How did you figure out how many tiles you used?**
4. **What is the height of your rectangle?**
5. **How would you build a rectangle that uses 18 tiles?**
6. **Can you figure out how high it would be without actually making it?**
7. **If you know how high you want a rectangle to be, can you figure out how many tiles you will need?**

EVALUATION: Note the different strategies the students use (counting one by one, counting by twos, or others).

FOLLOW-UP: Try some of the other activities described in the articles suggested at the end of the unit.

---

[1] Adapted from Yackel (1997).

estimates. Each student can then take a handful, count them, and compare the amounts with their estimates (Olson & Easley, 1996). Finally, using their handfuls as a base, they can estimate how many pennies the jar holds. Show the students a jar filled with interlocking cubes. Have them guess how many there are. Then remove ten cubes and connect them into a train. Now the students have more information. Ask them to make a new estimate. Continue making trains of ten until the jar is empty (Burns, 1997).

Probability

According to NCTM (2000), the concept of probability is extremely informal at the primary level. It is suggested that children be challenged to answer questions about what is *most likely* and what is *least likely*. For example, in Minnesota in January, is it more likely to snow or rain? Children can tally throws of the dice or the results of tossing a small group of two-sided discs (yellow on one side and red on the other). They will note that some numbers or colors come up more often than others, though they are not yet ready to learn how to calculate probabilities.

Integration across the Content Areas

The concepts described in this unit can be applied across the content areas. Many of the articles suggested at the end of the unit provide examples of activities that integrate mathematics with other content areas.

Ideas for Children with Special Needs

Children with Down syndrome (DS) also need special attention and accommodations (Lewis, 2003). They tend to be relatively slow in language

MATH TECHNOLOGY FOR
YOUNG CHILDREN

Using the guidelines from Unit 2, evaluate one or more of the following software programs (all are available at http://store.sunburst.com) or other resources listed.

- *Easy Sheet* (grades 3–12). An easy-to-use spreadsheet program.
- *Introduction to Patterns*. Students discover many types of patterns.
- *Combining Shapes*. Students manipulate shapes.
- *Creating Patterns from Shapes*. Students explore radiating and tiling patterns.
- *Mirror Symmetry*. Advances students' understanding of geometric properties and spatial relationships.
- *Graphers*. Students manipulate a variety of data analysis and graphing activities.
- *The Graph Club* 2.0. Students can collect data and construct their own graphs.
- *Lemonade for Sale* (grades 2 and 3).
- *Shape Up!* (pre-K–6). Supports creativity in two- and three-dimensional shape worlds. Students can put shapes together, change their size, change orientation in space, change colors, and so on. This program can write labels, stories, or descriptions and print out pages.
- *Toy Store* (grades 2–5). Students create bar graphs and interpret and collect data.
- *Zap! Around Town* (K–3). For developing mapping and direction skills.

See also the tools available from Illuminations (http://illuminations.nctm.org) and Virtual Manipulatives (http://nlvm.usu.edu).

development as a result of poor short-term memory, especially for auditory material, and poor long-term memory for verbal and spatial material. Such children need lots of repetition of new skills along with review of previously learned skills. Lessons need to be simple and should include a minimum number of materials and instructions. The range of DS abilities is broad, so careful assessment is necessary for appropriate planning. Breaking tasks into small steps is a technique used effectively with DS children (Gargiulo & Kilgo, 2007).

Evaluation

Note whether children can follow directions and maintain their involvement in the activities. Observing the process in these activities is critical. When children are not able to do an activity, it is important to note where the process breaks down. Does the child have the basic idea but just needs a little more practice and guidance? Does the activity seem to be beyond the child's capabilities at this time? These activities require advanced cognitive and perceptual motor development, so children should not be pushed beyond their developmental level. If children work in pairs or small groups of varied ability, the more advanced can assist the less advanced.

Summary

Primary experiences with geometry, spatial sense, graphs, tables, charts, algebraic thinking, estimation, and probability build on preprimary experiences with shape, spatial sense, simpler graphs and charts, and patterns. Primary level geometry is an informal, intuitively acquired concept. Children gain familiarity with concepts such as line, angle, point, curve, symmetry, and congruence. Geoboard activities are basic at this level.

Geometric and number concepts can be applied to graphing. Advanced children can develop more complex bar graphs and move on to line graphs. Charts and tables are used to organize data, which can then be visually depicted in a graph. LEGO/LOGO, LEGO Mindstorms, LEGO Dacta robotics, and design technology provide opportunities for more complex experiences combining mathematics, science, and technology. All these activities promote algebraic thinking.

KEY TERMS

axes	lines	STEM
charts	line graphs	symmetry
curves	LOGO	tables
LEGO/LOGO	points	turtle

SUGGESTED ACTIVITIES

1. Assess some primary children's readiness for the types of geometry and graphing activities discussed in this unit. Describe the results and your evaluation of their degree of readiness. Plan some activities that would be appropriate for the children you assessed. If possible, use these activities with the children. Evaluate the results. Did the children respond as you expected? Was your assessment accurate? What modifications, if any, would you make the next time? Why?

2. Provide the students in this course with some data. Have them develop some charts or tables using the data. Then have them make some line graphs. Do they have any problems in developing graphs?

3. Add geometry, data collection, technology, and algebraic thinking activities to your Activity File.

REVIEW

A. List the concepts and experiences that are prerequisite to the geometry and graphing concepts and activities described in this unit.

B. Make three diagrams that illustrate how fractions are visually depicted using geometric shapes.

C. Use a number line to show that $4 + 5 = 3 + 6$.

D. Match the terms in Column I with the definitions in Column II.

Column I	*Column II*
1. Point	a. Correspondence of parts of a figure on opposite sides of a point, line, or plane
2. Curve	b. The space made by the meeting of two straight lines
3. Line	c. An idea that is represented on paper by a dot
4. Angle	d. Sameness of size and shape
5. Congruency	e. Represented on paper using a straightedge ruler and pencil
6. Symmetry.	f. A smooth but not straight line

E. Make a sketch of a geoboard, and explain its purpose.

F. Find the following points on an integer-valued (x, y) graph: $(0, 0), (3, 2), (3, 4), (0, 3), (4, 1), (1, 2)$.

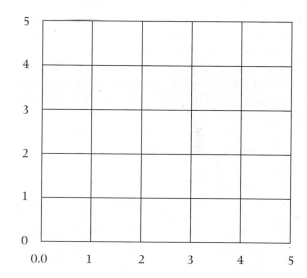

G. Make a line graph using the following data.
High Temperatures, May 15–20

City	Saturday	Sunday	Monday	Tuesday	Wednesday	Thursday
New York	73	72	74	64	61	60
Cairo	102	111	107	95	93	102

What conclusions can you make from examining the graph?

H. Explain how algebraic thinking can be included in the curriculum for elementary grades.

I. At what level does probability fit into the pre-K–3 curriculum?

J. Explain the value of design technology for primary students.

REFERENCES

Ashbrook, P. (2010). Building with sand. *Science & Children, 47*(7), 17–18.

Bautista, N. U., & Peters, K. N. (2010). First-grade engineers. *Science & Children, 47*(7), 38–42.

Burns, M. (1997, April). Number sense. *Instructor,* 49–54.

Chappell, M. E. (1997). Preparing students to enter the gate. *Teaching Children Mathematics, 3,* 266–267.

Children Designing and Engineering. (n.d.). What is CD&E? Retrieved November 20, 2004, from http://www.childrendesigning.org

Clark, L. J. (2002). Real world robotics. *Science & Children, 40*(2), 38–42.

Dunn, S., & Larson, R. (1990). *Design technology: Children's engineering.* Bristol, PA: Falmer, Taylor & Francis.

Gargiulo, R., & Kilgo, J. (2007). *Young children with special needs* (2nd ed.). Albany, NY: Thomson Delmar Learning.

Greenes, C., Cavanagh, M., Dacey, L., Findell, C., & Small, M. (2001). *Navigating through algebra in prekindergarten–grade 2.* Reston, VA: National Council of Teachers of Mathematics.

Lewis, V. (2003). *Development and disability* (2nd ed.). Malden, MA: Blackwell.

Lang, F. K. (2001). What is a "good guess" anyway? Estimation in early childhood. *Teaching Children Mathematics, 7*(8), 462–466.

Lottero-Perdue, P. S., Lovelidge, S., & Bowling, E. (2010). Engineeing for all. *Science & Children, 47*(7), 24–27.

Moore, V. J., Chessin, D. A., & Theobald, B. (2010). Insect keepers. *Science & Children, 47*(7), 28–32.

Moses, B. (1997). Algebra for a new century. *Teaching Children Mathematics, 3*, 264–265.

Murray, J., & Bartelmay, K. (2005). Inventors in the making. *Science & Children, 42*(4), 40–44.

National Council of Teachers of Mathematics. (2000). *Principles and standards for school mathematics.* Reston, VA: Author.

National Council of Teachers of Mathematics. (2007). *Curriculum focal points.* Reston, VA: Author.

Olson, M., & Easley, B. (1996). Plentiful penny projects to ponder. *Teaching Children Mathematics, 3*, 184–185.

Petroski, H. (2003, January 24). *Early education.* Presentation at the Children's Engineering Convention (Williamsburg, VA). Retrieved November 20, 2004, from http://www.vtea.org

Schifter, D., Russell, S. J., & Bastable, V. (2009). Early algebra to reach the range of learners. *Teaching Childen Mathematics, 16*(4), 230–237.

Virginia Children's Engineering Council. (n.d.). Inspiring the next generation. Retrieved November 20, 2004, from http://www.vtea.org

Vissa, J. (1987). Coordinate graphing: Shaping up a sticky situation. *Arithmetic Teacher, 35*(3), 6–10.

Wilcox, D. R., Roberts, S., & Wilcox, D. (2010). Gravity racers. *Science & Children, 47*(7), 19–23.

Yackel, E. (1997). A foundation for algebraic reasoning in the early grades. *Teaching Children Mathematics, 3*, 276–280.

FURTHER READING AND RESOURCES

General Resources

Burris, A. C. (2005). *Understanding the math you teach.* Upper Saddle River, NJ: Pearson-Merrill/Prentice-Hall.

Findell, C. R., Cavanagh, M., Dacey, L., Greenes, C. E., Sheffield, L. J., & Small, M. (2004). *Navigating through problem solving and reasoning in grade 1.* Reston, VA: National Council of Teachers of Mathematics.

Findell, C. R., Small, M., Cavanagh, M., Dacey, L., Greenes, C. E., & Sheffield, L. J. (2001). *Navigating through geometry in prekindergarten–grade 2.* Reston, VA: National Council of Teachers of Mathematics.

Greenes, C., Cavanagh, M., Dacey, L., Findell, C., & Small, M. (2001). *Navigating through algebra in prekindergarten–grade 2.* Reston, VA: National Council of Teachers of Mathematics.

Greenes, C. E., & House, P. A. (Eds.). (2003). *Navigating through problem solving and reasoning in prekindergarten–kindergarten.* Reston, VA: National Council of Teachers of Mathematics.

Sheffield, L. J., Cavanagh, M., Dacey, L., Findell, C. R., Greenes, C. E., & Small, M. (2002). *Navigating through data analysis and probability in prekindergarten–grade 2*. Reston, VA: National Council of Teachers of Mathematics.

Small, M., Sheffield, L. J., Cavanagh, M., Dacey, L., Findell, C. R., & Greenes, C. E. (2004). *Navigating through problem solving and reasoning in grade 2*. Reston, VA: National Council of Teachers of Mathematics.

Geometry/Spatial Sense

Ambrose, R. C., & Falkner, K. (2002). Developing spatial understanding through building polyhedrons. *Teaching Children Mathematics, 8*(8), 442–447.

Brewer, E. J. (1999). Geometry and art. *Teaching Children Mathematics, 6*(4), 220–224, 236.

Dobler, C. P., & Klein, J. M. (2002). First graders, flies, and a Frenchman's fascination: Introducing the Cartesian coordinate system. *Teaching Children Mathematics, 8*(9), 540–545.

Geometry and geometric thinking [Focus issue]. (1999). *Teaching Children Mathematics, 5*(6).

Hale, C. (2003, April). Art workshop: Kids design striking geometric artwork in the style of M. C. Escher. *Instructor*, 31–33.

Linquist, M. M., & Clements, D. H. (2001). Geometry must be vital. *Teaching Children Mathematics, 7*(7), 409–415.

Lord, T. R., & Clausen-May, T. (2002). Giving spatial perception our full attention. *Science & Children, 39*(5), 22–25.

Marsh, J., Loesing, J., & Soucie, M. (2004). Gee-whiz geometry. *Teaching Children Mathematics, 11*(4), 208–209.

Whitin, D. J., & Whitin, P. (2009). Why are things shaped the way they are? *Teaching Children Mathematics, 15*(8), 464–472.

Collecting and Organizing Data

Ashbrook, P. (2006). The early years: Communication about collections. *Science & Children, 44*(3), 18–20.

Braude, S. (2007). The tree of animal life. *Science & Children, 45*(1), 42–51.

Cengiz, N., Grant, T. J. (2009). Children generate their own representations. *Teaching Children Mathematics, 15*(7), 438–444.

Crane, P. (2004). On observing the weather. *Science & Children, 41*(8), 32–36.

DeBellis, V. A., Rosenstein, J. G., Hart, E. W., & Kenney, M. J. (2009). *Navigating through discrete mathematics in prekindergarten—grade 5*. Reston, VA: National Council of Teachers of Mathematics (Chapter 6).

Eichinger, J. (2009). *Activities linking science with math*. Arlington, VA: NSTA (Vertex graphs).

Frykholm, J. A. (2001). Eenie, meenie, minie, moe ... Building on intuitive notions of chance. *Teaching Children Mathematics, 8*(2), 112–118.

Hutchison, L., Ironsmith, M., Snow, C. W., & Poteat, G. M. (2000). Third-grade students investigate and represent data. *Early Childhood Education Journal, 27*(4), 213–218.

Manchester, P. (2002). The lunchroom project: A long-term investigative study. *Teaching Children Mathematics, 9*(1), 43–47.

Mokros, J., & Wright, T. (2009). Zoos, aquariums, and expanding students' data literacy. *Teaching Children Mathematics, 15*(9), 524–530.

Whitin, D. J., & Whitin, P. (2003). Talk counts: Discussing graphs with young children. *Teaching Children Mathematics, 10*(3), 142–149.

Estimation and Probability

Beck, S. A., & Huse, V. E. (2007). A virtual spin on the teaching of probability. *Teaching Children Mathematics, 13*(9), 486.

Guess, graphs, and numbers. (1997, January). *Teaching K–8*, 35.

Technology

Canada, D. L. (2009). Fraction photo frenzy. A new exploration. *Teaching Children Mathematics, 15*(9), 552–557.

Clements, D. H., & Meredith, J. S. (1993). One point of view: A talk with LOGO turtle. *Arithmetic Teacher, 41*(4), 189–191.

Clements, D. H., & Sarama, J. (1997). Computers support algebraic thinking. *Teaching Children Mathematics, 3*, 320–325.

Clements, D. H., & Sarama, J. (2000). Predicting pattern blocks on and off the computer. *Teaching Children Mathematics, 6*(7), 458–461.

Clements, D. H., & Sarama, J. (2000). Young children's ideas about geometric shapes. *Teaching Children Mathematics, 6*(8), 482–488.

Eichinger, J. (2009). *Activities linking science with math.* Arlington, VA: NSTA (Chapter 7).

Learning and teaching mathematics with technology [Focus issue]. (2002). *Teaching Children Mathematics, 8*(6).

Parker, D. L. (2003). Take care of mother earth: Technology and the environment. *Teaching Children Mathematics, 9*(7), 414–419.

Woleck, K. R. (2003). Tricky triangles: A tale of one, two, three researchers. *Teaching Children Mathematics, 10*(1), 40–44.

Algebraic Thinking

Bay-Williams, J. M. (2001). What is algebra in elementary school? *Teaching Children Mathematics, 8*(4), 196–200.

Blanton, M. L., & Kaput, J. J. (2003). Developing elementary teachers' "Algebra eyes and ears." *Teaching Children Mathematics, 10*(2), 70–77.

Burns, M. (2002, October). Algebra in the elementary grades? Absolutely! *Instructor*, 24–28.

Femiano, R. B. (2003). Algebraic problem solving in the primary grades. *Teaching Children Mathematics, 9*(8), 444–449.

Hynes, M. E., Dixon, J. K., & Adams, T. L. (2002). Rubber-band rockets. *Teaching Children Mathematics, 8*(7), 390–395.

Koester, B. A. (2003). Prisms and pyramids: Constructing three-dimensional models to build understanding. *Teaching Children Mathematics, 9*(8), 436–442.

Lubinski, C. A., & Otto, A. D. (1997). Literature and algebraic reasoning. *Teaching Children Mathematics, 3*, 290–295.

Moyer, P. S. (2001). Patterns and symmetry: Reflections of culture. *Teaching Children Mathematics, 8*(3), 140–144.

Reeves, C. A. (2006). Putting fun into functions. *Teaching Children Mathematics, 12*(5), 250–259.

Rivera, F. D. (2006). Changing the face of arithmetic: Teaching children algebra. *Teaching Children Mathematics, 12*(6), 306–311.

Soares, J., Blanton, M. L., & Kaput, J. J. (2005/2006). Thinking algebraically across the curriculum. *Teaching Children Mathematics, 12*(5), 228–235.

Steckoth, J. J. (2009/2010). From calculating to calculus. *Teaching Children Mathematics, 16*(5), 292–299.

Measurement with Standard Units

OBJECTIVES

After reading this unit, you should be able to:

- List the reasons that measurement is an essential part of the primary mathematics program.
- Know when to introduce standard units of measurement for length, time, volume, area, temperature, and money.
- Name the two types of standard units of measurement that are used in the United States.
- Plan and carry out developmentally appropriate primary level measurement instruction.

Measurement is an extremely important aspect of mathematics. It is a practical activity that is used in everyday life during experiences such as cooking, shopping, building, and constructing. In the primary curriculum, it is essential to gathering data in science and can also be applied in other areas. Measurement is a major vehicle for integrating mathematics with other content areas. It is also a vehicle for reinforcing other math skills and concepts: The number line is based on length, a popular multiplication model is much like area, and measurement is an area that lends itself naturally to problem-solving activities. Counting, whole number operations, and fractions are used to arrive at measurements and report the results. This unit will build on the basic concepts of measurement described in Units 14, 15, and 17. This unit focuses on the instruction and activities for introducing the concept of standard units and applying that concept to length, volume, area, weight, temperature, time, and money measurement.

The National Council of Teachers of Mathematics (2000) lists several expectations for primary-grade children's accomplishments in measurement. Primary-grade children are expected to select an appropriate unit and tool for the attribute being measured, be able to measure objects that require a repeated use of the same tool (e.g., three cups of flour with a cup measure, three-foot table with a foot ruler), use a variety of tools for measuring, and be able to make comparisons and estimates of standard unit measurements.

During the primary grades, measurement is an important connection from number and operations to algebra and geometry. During grade 1, measurement is a means for obtaining data to be analyzed to solve problems. During grade 2, linear measurement is a focal point that connects with geometry. During grade 3, children use their knowledge of fractions as they connect to making finer measurements. Measurement of area is a focal point in grade 4 and measurement of volume in grade 5.

Unit 14 described five stages in the development of the measurement concept (see Figure 14–1). During the sensorimotor and preoperational periods, children's measurement activities center on play and imitation and making comparisons (e.g., long–short, heavy–light, full–empty, hot–cold, early–late, rich–poor). During the transition period from ages 5–7, children enjoy working with arbitrary units. During concrete operations (which an individual usually enters at age 6 or older), children can begin to see the need for standard units (stage 4) and to develop skills in using them (stage 5). Standard units are not introduced for each concept at the same time. In general, the following guidelines can be observed.

- *Length (linear measure).* The units of inch/ foot and centimeter/meter are introduced in the beginning of primary and are used for measurement during grade 2.
- *Area.* Area is introduced informally with nonstandard units in grade 1 and ties in with multiplication in grade 3.
- *Time.* Time measurement devices and vocabulary are introduced prior to primary, but it is generally the end of primary before conventional time is clearly understood and a nondigital (analog) clock can be read with accuracy.
- *Volume (capacity).* Volume is learned informally during pouring activities, and accuracy is stressed during preprimary cooking. The concept of units of volume is usually introduced in grade 2.
- *Weight.* The standard measurement for weight is usually introduced in grade 3.
- *Temperature.* Temperature units are identified in grade 2, by which time children may begin to read thermometers, but it is usually beyond primary before children can measure temperature with accuracy and understanding.

- *Money.* Coins and bills are identified prior to primary and symbols are associated in early primary, but value does not begin to be understood until the end of primary.

The goal in the primary grades is to introduce the meaning of measurement, needed terminology, important units, and most common measurement tools.

Both **English units** (customary in the United States) and **metric units** are introduced during the primary years. Although the metric system is much easier to use because it is based on 10s and is used as the principal system in most countries, it has not been adopted as the official measure in the United States. In the 1970s there was a movement toward U.S. adoption of the system, but it died out and the U.S. Metric Commission was abolished in 1984. However, children must learn the metric system because it is so widely used around the world as well as in industry and science.

Assessment

Concrete operational thinking is essential for children to understand the need for and the use of standard units. Conservation tasks for length (see Figure 14–3), weight (see Figure 14–3), and volume were illustrated earlier in the text. Unit 14 suggested observational assessment guidelines for finding out what children at the early stages of understanding measurement know about volume, weight, length, and temperature. Interview tasks for time can be found in Unit 15. Be sure that children can apply nonstandard measure before moving on to standard measure.

Instruction

The concept of measurement develops through measurement experiences. Lecture and demonstration are not adequate for supporting the development of this concept. Also, it is important to take a sequenced approach to the introduction of standard units. Adhere to the following steps:

1. Do comparisons that do not require numbers (see Unit 8).
2. Use nonstandard arbitrary units (see Unit 14).

    a. Find the number of units by counting.

    b. Report the number of units.

3. Compare the thing measured to the units used (e.g., a table's width is measured with paper clips or drinking straws).

4. Introduce standard units appropriate for the same type of measurement.

    a. Find the number of units using standardized measuring instruments (i.e., ruler, scale, cup, liter, thermometer).

    b. Report the number of units.

Introduction of new standard measurement techniques and instruments should always be preceded by comparisons and nonstandard measurement with arbitrary units. Naturalistic and informal measurement experiences should be encouraged at all levels.

The Concept of Unit

Children's ability to measure rests on their understanding of the concept of **unit**. Many children have difficulty in perceiving that units can be other than one. In other words, one-half foot could be a unit, three centimeters could be a unit, two standard measuring cups could be a unit, one mark on a thermometer equals two degrees, and so on.

    The concept of unit can be developed using nonstandard units of measurement first. Children learn that measurement can be made with an arbitrary unit but that the arbitrary units must be equal to one another when making a specific measurement. For example, when paper clips are used for measurement, each one must be the same length. Paper clip is not the unit; rather, a paper clip of some specific length is the unit. Using arbitrary but equal units to measure objects, children construct the concept of unit. The concept is reinforced using different arbitrary units (one kind at a time) and then by comparing the results in terms of the number of units. For example, the children measure Lai's height using Unifix Cubes, identical drinking straws, and the class math textbook. Soon they realize that measurement with smaller units requires more units than that with larger units. When the students move on to standard units, they can compare the number of units needed to measure using teaspoons versus a standard cup measure, inches versus a yardstick, and so on.

    Children should be aware that they must be accurate when using units, either arbitrary or standard. For example, there cannot be gaps or spaces between units when measuring length, which is why it is a good idea to start with Unifix Cubes, Lots-A-Links, or some other units that can be stuck together and easily lined up. Once children are able to measure using as many units as needed to measure the whole length, capacity, and so on, they can advance to using one or more units that must be moved to make a complete measurement. For example, they could make a 10-Unifix-Cube length measure, place it on the item to be measured, mark where it ends, move the measure to that point, keep going until finished, and then add the 10s and any remaining cubes to arrive at the length in cubes. For capacity, they can fill individual measuring cups and then count the number of empties after filling a larger container, or use one cup and keep a record of how many cupfuls filled the larger container. As children discover these shortcuts to measurement, they will be able to transfer this knowledge over to standard unit measure and understand the rationale behind foot rulers, meter- and yardsticks, and quart and liter measures.

Measuring Instruments

With the introduction of standard units comes the introduction of measuring instruments. Rulers, scaled instruments (scales, graduated cylinders, thermometers), and clocks are the tools of standard measurement. Children have problems with these instruments unless they understand what they are measuring and what it means to measure. It is wise to begin with simple versions of the instruments, which are marked only with the unit being used. For example, if the unit is the centimeter, use a ruler that is marked only with centimeters (no millimeters). If the unit is an inch, use a ruler marked only with inches (no ½, ¼, or smaller parts of each inch marked). Be sure the children understand how units are marked.

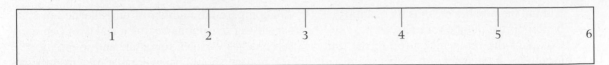

FIGURE 26–1   Six-inch ruler.

For example, on a ruler, the numbers come after the unit, not before. Most 9-year-olds will say that the ruler illustrated in Figure 26–1 is 5 inches (rather than 6 inches) long. You must be sure that children understand that each number tells how many units have been used. Children need many experiences measuring objects shorter than their ruler before they move on to longer objects with which they will have to measure, mark, and move the ruler. They will also need to be able to apply their addition skills. For example, if a child is using a 12-inch ruler and measures something that is 12 inches plus 8 inches, can she add 12 + 8? Measuring to the nearest quarter, eighth, or sixteenth of an inch requires that the child understand fractions.

Scaled instruments present a problem because not every individual unit is marked. For example, thermometers are marked every two degrees. A good way to help children understand this concept is to have them make their own instruments. They can make graphs using different scales or make their own graduated cylinders. They can do the latter by taking a large glass and putting a piece of masking tape down the side, as shown in Figure 26–2.

Take a smaller container, fill it with spoonfuls, count how many it holds, and empty it into the glass. Mark the level of the water and the number of spoonfuls. Fill the small container, empty into the glass, and mark again. In the example, the small container holds five teaspoons of water. This measure can be used to find out how much other containers will hold.

Analog clocks are one of the most difficult instruments for children to understand. Although there are only three measures (hours, minutes, and seconds), the circular movement of the hands makes reading the face difficult. McMillen and

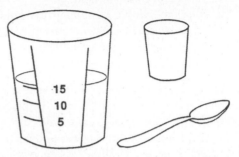

FIGURE 26–2   Items used to illustrate the concept of scaled instruments.

Hernandez (2008) describe a method designed to help second-grade students understand the meanings of the short and long hands on the analog clock. Two one-handed clocks were used. The activities were designed to help the students understand the relationship of minutes and seconds to each other, to groups of five, and to 12 hours. For example, to get a feeling for one minute, students predicted how many times they could bounce a ball, how far they could run, and how many Unifix Cubes they could connect in one minute. Children vary greatly as to when they are finally able to read a clock face accurately. There is no set age for being able to tell time. Skills needed to tell time must be learned over many years and through practice with clock faces with movable hands. Digital clocks are easier to read but do not provide the child with a visual picture of the relationship between time units.

Money also offers difficulties because the sizes of the coins do not coincide with their value (i.e., the dime is smaller than the penny and the nickel). Bills provide no size cues but do have numerical designations that relate one bill to the other. Relating the coins to the bills is a difficult task for young children.

Summer's
1$ chores
windows
clean litter box 1$
make Bed 50¢
get ready for bed 1$
bring laundry down to wash 1$
help put Groceries 1$
put dishes away 1$
put things away 1$

at Grandmas house
summer's
chores

Summer lists chores to be done at
Grandma's house for $1.00 per chore.

Summer (age nine) is very interested in making money. She makes a list of chores she can do at Grandma's house and receive some cash.

Measurement Activities

This section includes activities that will help children construct the concepts of measuring length, volume (capacity), area, weight (mass), temperature, time, and money using standard units. Refer to previous units in this text for the comparison and arbitrary (nonstandard) measurement experiences that must occur prior to introducing standard units of measurement. Also, remember to work on the concepts of the units used for each type of measurement as well as actual measurement.

An understanding of volume measurement begins with explorations in the sandbox.

Activities

Standard Measurement: Linear

OBJECTIVES: To be able to use standard units of measurement to compare lengths of objects; to discover that the smaller the units, the more will be needed to measure a distance; and to use a ruler for measuring objects.

MATERIALS: Rulers (inch/foot, yardstick, centimeter, meterstick); tape measures; paper, pencils, crayons, markers, and poster board; and the book *How Big Is a Foot?* by Myller (1972).

ACTIVITIES: Introduce these activities to children following many exploratory experiences that involve comparing objects visually and with arbitrary units. Have children measure the same objects using both arbitrary and standard units to emphasize the need for standard units. The first activity is designed to develop an understanding of this need.

1. Say, "**You have measured many things around the room, including yourselves, and made comparisons. What you compare against is called your *unit of measurement*. What are**

some units of measurement you have used?" (Children should name items used such as paper clips, Unifix Cubes, books, etc.) **"When you tell how long or how tall something is, you have to tell which unit of measure you used. Why? What problem could occur if you are telling this information to someone who cannot see your unit of measure?"** Encourage discussion. For example, they might suggest that if they are measuring with Unifix Cubes you send the person a cube, or if they are measuring with a piece of string you send the person a piece of string of the same length. Next, read *How Big Is a Foot?* and discuss the problem the king encountered. For ideas on how to use this book, see Lubinski and Thiessen (1996).

Now the students should begin to understand why standard units of measurement are necessary. Clarify this point by summing up: **"If everyone in the world knows exactly what the units of measurement are, it is much easier to explain how long, wide, and tall something is. That is why we have standard units of measurement. We use inches, feet, and yards."** (Pass around foot rulers and yardsticks for children to examine and compare.) **"In most places in the world, in science laboratories, and in factories, centimeters, decimeters, and meters are used."** Pass around metersticks. Point out that the base-ten blocks they have been using are marked off in centimeters (1s units) and in decimeters (10s units), and that ten 10s placed end to end is a meter. Have them test this with the metersticks and the base-ten blocks. Say, **"These units are the same everywhere and do not change. Get into pairs and measure each other's body parts using your rulers and tape measures. Before you start, make a list of the parts you plan to measure. Have the students call out the names of the parts they plan to measure."** When they finish, have them compare their results.

2. Have the children use their foot rulers and two other units (such as a shoe and a pencil) to measure the same objects. Have them record the results in a table.

Object	Length			
	Feet	*Inches*	*Shoes*	*Pencils*
Table				
Windowsill				
Bookshelf				

Discuss the results and what they mean.

3. Have the children make their own inch and centimeter rulers. Provide them with strips of cardboard 6 inches long, and have them mark the results off in units as shown in the figure.

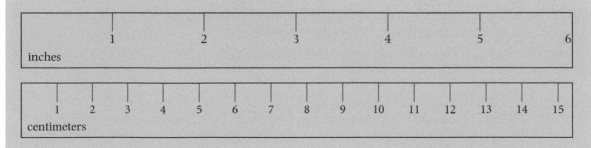

Ask the children to make comparative measures around the classroom. Then send the rulers home along with a note to the parents.

Dear Parents,

We are working with different ways of measuring length. Your child is bringing home an inch ruler and a centimeter ruler and is supposed to measure six things at home with each ruler and record the results. Please help your child if necessary. Have your child share the results with you and explain the differences in the number of inches versus the number of centimeters of length found for each object. Thanks for your help with this project.

Sincerely,

Jon Wang, Second Grade Teacher

Object	Length	
	Inch ruler	Centimeter ruler
1.		
2.		
3.		
4.		
5.		
6.		

FOLLOW-UP: Do many more linear measurement activities using standard units, as suggested in the resources at the end of the unit.

Standard Measurement: Volume

OBJECTIVES: To be able to use standard units of measurement to compare volumes of materials; to learn that the smaller the units, the more will be needed to measure the volume; to learn how to use standard measures of volume such as teaspoons, tablespoons, cups, pints, quarts, and liters.

MATERIALS: Containers of many different sizes (boxes, baskets, buckets, jars, cups, bowls, pans, bottles, plastic bags, and so on) and standard measures of volume (set of customary and set of metric measuring cups, liter and quart measures, customary and metric measuring spoons).

ACTIVITIES: Introduce these activities to children following many exploratory experiences of comparing volumes visually and with arbitrary units. Have children measure the same container's capacities with both arbitrary and standard units to emphasize the need for standard units. The first activity is designed to develop an understanding of this need.

1. Discuss volume following the same format as was used for linear measurement. Say, "**You have explored the volume or space inside of many containers by filling and emptying containers of different sizes and shapes. What kinds of units have you used?**" Encourage them to name some of the smaller units that they used to fill larger containers. See if they can

generalize from the length discussion that problems in communication arise when standard units are not used. Pass around the standard measurement materials. Encourage the children to talk about the characteristics of these materials. Do they recognize that they have used these types of things many times to measure ingredients for cooking? Do they notice the numbers and scales marked on the materials?

2. Using the standard units, have the children find out the capacities of the containers previously used for exploration. Have them use materials such as water, rice, beans, and/or sand for these explorations. They should record their findings in a table such as the following one:

Container	Number of units to fill
Using small juice glass	*Using standard cup measure*
1.	
2.	
3.	
4.	
5.	
6.	

FOLLOW-UP: Continue to do exploratory measurement of capacity. Also, continue with cooking activities, giving the children more responsibility for selecting the needed measurement materials.

Standard Measurement: Area

OBJECTIVE: To explore area in a concrete manner and its relationship to linear measurement.

MATERIALS: Inch and centimeter cubes, two-dimensional patterns (with and without squares), paper grids, and paper squares (or purchase Learning Measurement Inch by Inch from Lakeshore).

ACTIVITIES: Children can explore area with squared paper and cubes long before formal instruction. Remember that area-type activities are frequently used as the visual representations of multiplication.

1. On poster board, make some shapes such as those shown in the following figure that are in inch or centimeter units. Have the children find out how many inch or centimeter cubes will cover the whole shape.

SHAPES WITH SQUARES MARKED

SHAPES WITHOUT SQUARES MARKED

2. Make a supply of paper grids (inch or centimeter squares, about 5 × 4 squares) and construction paper squares. Have the children make up their own areas by pasting individual squares on the grid. Have them record on the grid how many squares are in their area (or use Learning Measurement Inch by Inch.)

FOLLOW-UP: If you have introduced rulers to the children, ask them to measure the lines on the grids and patterns with their rulers. Discuss how they might figure out how many square inches or centimeters are on a plane surface using their rulers.

Standard Measurement: Weight

OBJECTIVE: To be able to use standard units of measurement to compare the weights of various materials and to use balance and platform scales.

MATERIALS: Balance scales with English and metric weights, a set of platform scales, a metric, and/or customary kitchen scale; paper and pencil for recording observations; and many objects and materials that can be weighed.

ACTIVITIES: The children should have already explored weight using comparisons.
1. Say, "**When you look at two objects, you can guess if they are heavy or light, but you don't really know until you lift them because size can fool you. You could easily lift a large balloon, but a rock of the same size would be too heavy to lift**" (have a balloon and a rock available for them to lift, if possible). "**A marshmallow would be easier to lift than a lump of lead of the same size. The lead and the rock have more stuff in them than the balloon and the marshmallow. The more stuff there is in something, the harder a force in the earth called gravity pulls on it. When something is weighed, we are measuring how hard gravity is pulling on it. You have compared many kinds of things by putting one kind of thing on one side of a balance scale and another on the other side. Now you will work with customary and metric weights in your pan balance on one side and things you want to weigh on the other side.**" Discuss the sets of pan balance weights, and have them available for the children to examine. Explain that all of them are made of the same material so that size is relative to weight. Have the children weigh various objects and materials (water, rice, beans, and so on). Compare the weights of a cup of water versus a cup of rice or a cup of beans. Which weighs more? How much more? Remind the children that they will have to add the amounts for each weight to get a total. Suggest that they work in pairs, so they can check each other's results.
2. Show the children how to read the dial on the kitchen scale. Provide a variety of things to weigh.
3. If a platform scale for people is available, have everyone in the class weighed, record the results, and have the children make a graph that depicts the results.
4. Have the children go through newspaper grocery-store advertisements and cut out pictures of items that have to be weighed at the store to find their cost.
5. Have the children weigh two objects at the same time. Remove one and weigh the remaining object. Subtract the weight of the single object from the weight of the two. Now weigh the other object. Is the weight the same as when you subtracted the first weight from the total for both objects?

FOLLOW-UP: Continue putting out interesting things to weigh. Make something with a metric recipe that specifies amounts by weight rather than volume.

Standard Measurement: Temperature

OBJECTIVE: To be able to use standard units of measurement to compare temperatures and to learn how to use a thermometer to measure temperature.

MATERIALS: Large demonstration thermometer, small thermometers for student use, outdoor thermometer.

ACTIVITIES: These activities assume that children have talked about and have had experiences with hot, warm, and cold things and hot, comfortable, and cold weather.
1. Let the children examine the demonstration thermometer. Have them decide why there are two scales (Fahrenheit and Celsius) and how each is read. Discuss their experiences with thermometers (e.g., when they are ill or go to the doctor for a checkup, for measuring the outdoor and indoor air temperature, for controlling the thermostat on their furnaces and air conditioners).
2. Provide some hot water and ice cubes. Ask the children to measure the temperature of the water and record the result. Have them add an ice cube, let it melt, have them measure again, and record the result. Keep adding ice cubes and recording the results. Have the children make a line graph to illustrate how the ice affects the temperature. Is any other factor affecting the water temperature? (Answer: the air temperature.) Compare the results with the temperature of tap water.
3. If possible, post an outdoor thermometer outside the classroom window and have the children record the temperature each day in the morning, at noon, and at the end of the day. After a week, have them make some graphs depicting what they found out. Ask interested students to write daily weather reports for posting on the bulletin board.

FOLLOW-UP: Have interested children record the daily weather forecasts from the radio, TV, or newspaper. Compare the forecast temperatures with those recorded at school.

Standard Measurement: Time

OBJECTIVE: To be able to use standard units of time measurement and to read time accurately from an analog clock.

MATERIALS: Large clock model with movable hands (e.g., the well-known Judy Clock), miniature model clocks that can be used individually during small group activities, a 60-minute timer that can be used to help develop a sense of time duration, a class monthly calendar (teacher made or purchased).

ACTIVITIES:
1. Children should have some sense of time sequence and duration by the time they reach the primary level. A timer is still useful to time events such as "Five minutes to finish up" or "Let's see if anyone can finish before the 10-minute timer rings." The major task for the primary child is understanding the clock and what it tells us and eventually learning how to work with time in terms of the amount of time from one clock reading to another. Children can work together with the Judy Clock or with their smaller models, moving the hands and identifying the time. Much of clock knowledge comes from everyday activities through naturalistic and informal

experiences. You can support these experiences by having a large wall clock in your classroom and having visual models of important times during the day that the children can match to the real clock. For example, the daily schedule might be put on the wall chart with both a conventional clock face and the digital time indicated for each major time block, as shown in the following figure.

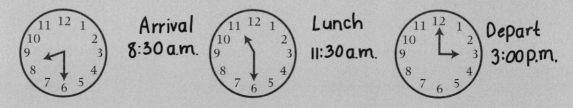

Arrival 8:30 a.m.   Lunch 11:30 a.m.   Depart 3:00 p.m.

2. Clock skills may be broken down as follows:
    a. Identify the hour and the minute hands and the direction in which they move.
    b. Be able to say the time on the clock at the hour, and be able to place the hands of the clock for the hour. Know that the short hand is on the hour, and the long hand is on 12.
    c. Identify that it is after a particular hour.
    d. Count by 5s.
    e. Tell the time to the nearest multiple of 5.
    f. Count on from multiples of 5 (10, 11, 12, . . .).
    g. Write time in digital notation (3:15).
    h. Tell time to the nearest minute, and write it in digital notation.
    i. Match the digital clock's time to a conventional clock's time.
    j. Identify time before a particular hour and count by 5s to tell how many minutes it is before that hour.
3. Each child can make a clock to take home. Use a poster board circle or paper plate. Provide each child with a paper fastener and a long and short hand. Have them mark the short hand with an *H* and the long hand with an *M*. Send a note home to the parents suggesting some clock activities they can do with their child.
4. Provide the children with blank calendars each month that they can fill in with important dates (holidays, birthdays, etc.).

FOLLOW-UP: Continue to read children stories that include time concepts and time sequence. For more advanced students who understand how to read clocks and keep track of time, have them keep a diary for a week recording how much time they spend on activities at home (eating, sleeping, doing homework, reading, watching TV, playing outdoors, attending soccer practice, going to dancing lessons, etc.). Ask them to add up the times at the end of the week and rank the activities, in terms of time spent on them, from most to least. They might even go on to figure out how much time per month and year they spend on each activity if they are consistent from week to week. See McMillen and Hernandez (2008) for lessons on understanding the analog clock.

A monthly calendar supports a child's developing understanding of time.

Standard Measurement: Money

OBJECTIVE: To be able to tell the value of money of different denominations, associate the symbol ¢ with coins and $ with dollars, find the value of a particular set of coins, and be able to write the value of particular sets of coins and bills.

MATERIALS: Paper money and coin sets, pictures of coins, Money Bingo game (Trend Enterprises).

ACTIVITIES: Money is always a fascinating subject for young children. Money activities can be used not only to learn about money but also to provide application for whole numbers and later for decimal skills.

1. Dramatic play continues to be an important vehicle of learning for primary children. First graders enjoy dramatic play centers such as those described in Unit 22. Second and third graders begin to be more organized and can design their own dramatic play activities using available props. They enjoy writing plays and acting them out. Play money should always be available in the prop box.
2. Make some price tags (first with amounts less than $1, later with more). Have the children pick tags out of a box one at a time and count out the correct amount of play money.
3. Have the children go through catalogs and select items they would like. Have them list the items and the prices and add up their purchases. Younger children can write just the dollar part of the prices.

FOLLOW-UP: Play Money Bingo. The bingo cards have groups of coins in each section. Cards with different amounts of cents are picked, and the children have to add up their coins to find out if they have a match.

Ideas for Children with Special Needs

The last disability considered in this section of the book are the autism spectrum disorders (ASDs). Awareness of the prevalence of these disorders has increased greatly in recent years ("As awareness," 2007). This group of developmental disabilities includes autistic disorder, pervasive developmental disorder, and Asperger's syndrome. The symptoms of these disorders vary, but afflicted children typically have social and communication disorders and may display challenging behaviors. The focus for teaching ASD children is getting them socially involved. Intellectually they range from gifted to severely challenged.

According to Lewis (2003), communication with these children must be clear and simple. Tasks need to be broken down into small steps. The most common instructional methods are applied behavioral analysis, applied verbal analysis, and floor time (Gargiulo & Kilgo, 2007). All these methods require constant attention to the child.

In this text we have looked at the wide variety of disabilities children may display. Some typical children may have difficulties with mathematics that can be identified in the early grades. Mathematics Recovery (MR) (Wright, Martland, Stafford, & Stanger, 2002) is a program for helping first graders (6- or 7-year-olds) who are struggling with mathematics. The one-on-one instruction is individualized and problem based. Wright and colleagues present a detailed plan for working with difficult students.

Evaluation

Evaluation of children's progress with measurement should be done using concrete tasks; here are some examples. Give the children a list of three items in the classroom to measure. Arrange a set of measuring cups, material to measure, and a container to measure into; then ask each child to turn in his answer. Set up a scale with three items of known weight, have each child weigh each item individually, and record the amount. Put out three model thermometers with different temperatures and have each child, in turn, tell you the readings and whether they indicate hot, comfortable, or cold. Show the child the time on a model clock and ask him to tell you the time and explain how he knows. Have each child identify coins and then put them together to make various amounts, making the amounts appropriate to the child's level at the time.

MATH TECHNOLOGY
FOR YOUNG CHILDREN

Using the guidelines from Unit 2, evaluate one or more of the following resources.

- *Numbers Undercover* (K–3; http://store. sunburst.com). Time, measurement, and money mysteries.
- *Math Blaster* (ages 5–7; http://store. sunburst.com). Includes time, money, and measurement.
- *Lemonade for Sale* (http://store.sunburst. com). Work with bar graphs and money.
- *The Penny Pot* (http://store.sunburst.com). Basic money concepts.
- *Key Skills for Math* (http://store.sunburst. com). Shapes, numbers, and measurement.
- *Learn about Physical Science: Matter, Measurement, Mixture* (http://store.sunburst.com).
- *Magic School Bus: Whales and Dolphins* (Redmond, WA: Microsoft). Measure and weigh whales and dolphins.
- *Trudy's Time and Place House* (http://www. riverdeep.net). Explores geography and time.
- *LeapFrog Cash Register* (Emeryville, CA: LeapFrog Enterprises). Coin identification, money values, quantities, numbers, and counting.
- *Measures* (http://www.dositey.com). Time measuring activities.
- *Shopping Math* (http://www.dositey.com). Buying toys.
- *MatchTime* (preschool–6; http://www. K12software.com).
- *Light Weights/Heavy Weights* (K–4; www. nasaexplores.com). Weight prediction.
- *See also NLVM, Measurement: Geoboard, Money, and Time* (http://nlvm.usu.edu).

Summary

Measurement skills are essential for successful everyday living. People need to know how to measure length, volume, area, weight, temperature, time, and money. These concepts develop gradually through many concrete experiences from gross comparisons (e.g., long–short, heavy–light, hot–cold, early–late) to measurement with arbitrary units and finally to measurement with standard English (customary) and/or metric units. Measurement activities are valuable opportunities for applying whole number skills and fraction knowledge (and later decimals) as well as for obtaining data that can be graphed for visual interpretation. Measurement concepts are acquired through practice with real measuring tools and real things to measure. Lecture and demonstration alone are not adequate methods of instruction.

KEY TERMS

English units	metric units	unit

SUGGESTED ACTIVITIES

1. On your Activity File cards for this unit, make note of the prerequisite activities in Units 14, 15, and 17.
2. Prepare materials for the suggested evaluation tasks. Evaluate one first-grade, one second-grade, and one third-grade student on their understanding of standard units of measurement. Write a report describing your evaluation: Record the children's responses and compare the three children's levels of understanding. Plan instructional activities based on the results of your interviews with the primary children. If possible, use the activities with the children.
3. Develop a plan for a measurement center that can serve a first-, second-, or third-grade classroom. Include one station for each type of measurement discussed (or five stations for one type of measurement). If possible, procure the materials and set up the center in a classroom for a week. Keep a record of what the children do in the center. At the end of the week, evaluate the center. Was it appropriate? Were the materials in the center set up in such a way that the children could work independently? Did children return again? Did they try the activities at each station? Would you do it the same way next time? Why? What changes would you make?

REVIEW

A. List two reasons that measurement is an essential part of the primary mathematics curriculum.
B. There are five stages children pass through on their way to understanding and using standard units of measurement. Put the steps in the correct developmental order.
   1. Understands the need for standard units
   2. Works with arbitrary units
   3. Applies standard units of measurement

4. Makes gross comparisons (e.g., heavy–light, hot–cold)
5. Plays and imitates

C. Children are not ready to understand all the different units of standard measure at the same time. Match the measurement concepts on the left with the usual time of readiness on the right.

Measurement concept	Time when ready for standard units
1. Length	a. In grade 2.
2. Time	b. Introduced in grade 2 but well beyond primary when accuracy is achieved.
3. Volume	c. Introduced gradually starting in preprimary, but not done accurately until the end of primary or later (instrument is difficult to understand).
4. Area	d. Value is not really understood until the end of primary.
5. Weight	e. Units introduced in grade 1, measurement in grade 2.
6. Temperature	f. Introduced in grade 3.

7. Money   g. Mainly informal during primary but important for visual representation of multiplication.

D. Name the two types of units used in the United States. Which is the conventional (customary) standard?

E. Why should U.S. students learn the metric system even if it is not the standard in the United States?

F. Which cognitive developmental stage must children have reached before they are able to understand and apply standard units of measurement?

G. List the most important factors in understanding the concept of *unit*.

H. Provide two or more examples of the difficulties associated with using measuring instruments. Explain how these difficulties can be eased.

I. Select a type of measurement. Describe how you would introduce measurement of that type by following the sequence of instruction described in this unit.

J. Describe three types of disabilities discussed in Units 21 through 26 of this book.

REFERENCES

As awareness and concern grow, autism moves into public spotlight. (2007). *ACD Developments, 21*(2), 1, 9, 10–12.

Gargiulo, R., & Kilgo, J. (2007). *Young children with special needs* (2nd ed.). Albany, NY: Thomson Delmar Learning.

Lewis, V. (2003). *Development and disability* (2nd ed.). Malden, MA: Blackwell.

Lubinski, C. A., & Thiessen, D. (1996). Exploring measurement through literature. *Teaching Children Mathematics, 2*, 260–263.

McMillen, S., & Hernandez, B. O. (2008). Taking time to understand telling time. *Teaching Children Mathematics*, 15(4), 248–255.

Myller, R. (1972). *How big is a foot?* New York: Atheneum.

National Council of Teachers of Mathematics. (2000). *Principles and standards for school mathematics*. Reston, VA: Author.

Wright, R. J., Martland, J., Stafford, A. K., & Stanger, G. (2002). *Teaching number*. Thousand Oaks, CA: Chapman.

The Math Environment

children, friends, businesspeople, and others to add to your junk box. Once people know you collect odds and ends, they will remember you when they are ready to throw something away. Examples include:

- Aluminum foil, pie plates, and frozen food containers are useful for numerous activities.
- Film cans make smell and sound containers.
- Hardware supplies are always welcome for the tool center; plastic tubing, garden hoses, and funnels are ideal for water play and making musical instruments.
- Candles, thumbtacks, paper clips, and other "sink or float" items come in handy.
- Oatmeal containers make drums; shoe boxes are great for dioramas and general organization and storage.
- Toys, clocks, and kitchen tools can be added to the machine center and used for dramatic play.
- Pipe cleaners are always useful for art; buttons and other small objects are needed for classifying and comparing.
- Straws, balloons, paper cups, pieces of fabric, and wallpaper are objects for the touch box.
- Some stores invite teachers to collect their old carpet and wallpaper sample books.
- Always keep an eye out for feathers, unusual rocks, shells, seed-growing containers, plastic eggs—the list is endless.
- Items that can be counted, sorted, graphed, and so on, such as plastic lids from bottles, jars, and other containers; thread spools, pinecones, seashells, buttons, and seeds are all useful.
- Egg cartons and frozen food containers can be used for sorting.
- String, ribbon, sticks, and so on, can be used for comparing lengths and for informal measuring.
- Small boxes can be used for construction projects.

See Unit 29 for additional suggestions.

Some teachers send home a list of "junk" items at the beginning of the year. Parents are asked to bring or send available items to school. Such a list will be easy to complete when you become familiar with "good junk" and have an idea of some of the items that you will use during the year. In addition, parents are usually responsive to special requests such as ingredients for cooking activities.

Purchased Equipment

There are a multitude of commercially available materials for mathematics. Some materials are versatile and can be used in developing more than one concept. Basic materials include unit blocks with miniature animals, people, and vehicles; construction materials (Figure 27–2); Unifix Cubes; LEGO; Multilinks; pegboards and pegs; picture lotto games; beads and strings; attribute blocks; geoboards; balance scales; a thermometer; a flannelboard and a magnet board with felt and magnet pieces for concept activities; Montessori Cylinder Blocks (Figure 27–3); a manipulative clock; base-ten blocks; and fraction pies. Hand calculators and computers should also be available. Search through the major catalogs (Figure 27–1), and decide what you can afford. Also consider assembling and making materials (see the resource lists at the end of each unit).

Organizing and Storing Materials

As you collect and develop materials for teaching math, storage might become a problem. Most commercial kits have neat, ready-made labeled boxes, but the "junk box" system will need some organizing.

One way to manage a variety of materials is to place them in shoe boxes or other similar containers. The boxes contain the materials needed to teach one or more specific concepts. If the containers are clearly marked, they can be very convenient. The trick is to keep everything you need in the appropriate container—for example, homemade equipment materials, task cards, materials to duplicate, and bulletin board ideas. To be effective, the container should display a materials list on the outside. In this way, you have a self-contained kit for teaching math.

An example of a carefully organized shelf

Blockbusters	Crystal Climbers	Wonderforms	Block Head
Lego	Rig-A-Jig	Geo-D-Stix	Snap-N-Play Blocks
Free Form Posts	Color Cone	Connector	Channel Blocks
Sprocketeers	Tectonic	Wood'n Molds	Wee Waffle Blocks
Tinkertoys	Structo-Brics	Poki Blocks	Struts
Toy Makers	Giant Structo-Cubes	Multi-fit	Duplo
Cloth Cubes	Floresco	Disco Shapes	Gear Circus
Snap Wall	Ring-A-Majigs	Snap Blocks	Create It
Lock & Stack Blocks	Crystal Octons	Bristle Blocks	LASY Construction Kits
Giant Interlockers	Ji-gan-tiks	Bristle Bears	Giant Double Towers
Unifix Cubes	Mobilo	Brio Builder	Gears! Gears!
Unit Blocks	Locktagons	Flexo	Frontier Logs 'N Blocks
Flexibricks	Connect-A-Cube	Klondikers	Marble Run
Play Shapes	Tuff Tuff Blocks	Beam and Boards	Construction Rug
Stackobats	Polydron	Hex-A-Links	Sturdiblocks
Magnetic Blocks	Play Squares	Pipe Construction	Giant Edu-Blocks
Form-A-Tions	3D Geoshapes	Bendits	Soft Big-Blocks
Poly-M	Learning Links	K'Nex	Galaxy Builder
Omnifix	Tower-ifics	Habitat	Building Clowns
Multilinks	Edu-Builder	Busy Blocks	Building Shapes
Jumbo Cuisinaire Rods	Groovy Parts	Space Wheels	Bolt Builder
Mega Blocks	Octagons	Magnastiks	Light Table and Accessories
Lincoln Logs	Girders	Keeptacks	Beads
Baufix	Play-Panels	Balancing H Blocks	Cuisinaire Rods

FIGURE 27-2   Construction materials for math.

What is the purpose or objective?

Who will be using this learning center?

What are the concepts children should learn?

What are the skills children should learn?

What activities will take place?

What materials need to be available?

What are the learning objectives?

How will children's progress be evaluated?

FIGURE 27–4 Questions to ask when planning a learning center.

replacement? Are there materials for all concepts in the program and for naturalistic, informal, and adult guided experiences? Are both indoor and outdoor materials and equipment in good condition? With this information, make decisions as to what is on hand and what needs to be purchased. In preprimary, when children have shorter attention spans, it is recommended that a variety of small sets of materials (enough for two or three children to share at one time) be purchased. In the primary grades, start with a classroom set of Unifix materials. These materials are among the most versatile because they can be used for teaching almost every primary mathematics concept. Many accessories are available and there are numerous resources, already mentioned in this text, from which to select activities. Gradually add base-ten blocks, fraction materials, and other manipulatives.

Another source is materials that teachers and/ or volunteer parents can make. Parents may donate waste materials: Ask parents to save egg cartons, buttons, boxes and other containers, bottle caps, yarn, ribbon, and other materials that can be used in the math program (see the list in Unit 29). Parents might also donate inexpensive items such as toothpicks, golf tees, playing cards, funnels, measuring cups, and so on. Lumber companies might donate scrap lumber. Restaurant supply companies will often sell teachers trays, various-sized containers, and the like, at low prices. Try to convince your principal to let you spend your share of supply money on concrete manipulative materials and supplies for making two-dimensional manipulatives rather than spending on workbooks and copy paper. Resources for ideas for teacher-made materials are listed at the end of each unit, and some frequently used catalogs are shown in Figure 27–1. Figure 27–4 contains a list of questions to guide the planning of a learning center.

Technology

Computer software suggestions have been inserted throughout the text. Ideally, each classroom should have two or three computers where children can take turns exploring a variety of software and online resources. There should be time for searching the Web for information and using e-mail to communicate with others regarding problems to solve and information to share. Many early childhood mathematics journals have software reviews in every issue as well as frequent reports from teachers describing how their students use technology. Further suggestions are included in Unit 28.

While computers have long been an important vehicle for mathematics instruction (Cross, Woods, & Schweingruber 2009), other technology adaptations for young children are growing. In a special focus issue of Young Children (E-learning for educators, 2004), the challenges for educators are described.

> Interactive media have come of age. The range of interactive entertainment products, intended to be used by children in and out of school settings, is growing: CD-ROMs, computers, the Internet, video games, interactive toys …, and a variety of wireless software for cell phones and other wireless devices. (Wartella, Caplovitz, & Lee, 2004, p. 1)

At age 9, Summer does searches on the computer and talks, texts, and takes and sends photos with her cell phone. Those adults who did not grow up using technology have a lot to learn.

Children from pre–K to grade 12 use many types of technology in classrooms. From PBS Kids, children can explore engineering math with the *Curious George Discovery Guide* (pbskids.org). Interactive whiteboards provide young children with many exciting learning experiences (Lisenbee, 2009). High school students are solving algebra problems on their smartphones (Davis, 2010) while educators are developing lessons for elementary students adapted to cell phones (Manzo, 2010). Jerry Everhart (2009) describes how video file sharing website YouTube can be incorporated into science lessons. Digital cameras are popular classroom tools beginning in preschool. Second graders collected information in the zoo using digital cameras (Davison, 2009). Technology is spreading rapidly into homes and schools.

Materials for Children with Special Needs

Gargiulo and Kilgo (2005) provide suggestions for materials that will support the learning of children with disabilities. Self-correcting materials as suggested in previous units can be especially effective for children with disabilities. Many Montessori materials are self-correcting. Computer software may provide immediate feedback. Teacher-made materials can have flaps or windows that reveal the correct answer. Children with physical or multiple disabilities can be provided with battery or electronic materials that operate off switches. Some can be operated by a puff of air or a head movement.

Materials should also provide for cultural diversity. They should reflect the students' cultures, languages, communities, and disabilities. According to de Melendez and Beck (2007), multicultural planning is child-centered, developmentally based, and culturally responsive. Considerations include the children's individual and cultural characteristics, language, social and emotional development, cognitive development, and physical and motor capabilities. Stereotypes should be avoided. Media, pictures, manipulatives, and books should not promote bias toward any group but should promote respect for diversity. For example, languages besides English should be represented in literature, songs, and rhymes and used in the classroom. Ethnic artifacts should be used. Accommodations should be made for children with special needs.

Summary

Stimulating math lessons do not happen by accident. The materials selected to teach math—and the format in which they are presented—are essential for successful learning. Whether materials are purchased or scrounged, they must be flexible and appropriate to the developmental age of the child and the type of math learning that is required. Learning centers are designed and used to meet specific teaching objectives and must be evaluated in terms of their effectiveness. Technology is taking an increasingly important role as a tool in instruction.

Lists of resource books for teachers and further reading lists are included in this unit. Lists of children's books are located in Appendix B.

SUGGESTED ACTIVITIES

1. Construct a math learning center. Use the center with a group of children, and share the effectiveness of the materials with the class.
2. Participate in a small group in class, and compare math materials lists. Make cooperative decisions as to what math materials should be purchased if a new prekindergarten, kindergarten, and/or primary classroom is to be furnished. Each group should consider cost as well as purpose.
3. Go to the library. Find and read at least ten children's picture books that contain math concepts (see Appendix B for suggestions). Write a description of each one. Tell how each book could be used with children.

4. Assemble two different homemade math resources that young children can use. Select the materials from books, journals, and/or the Internet. Share the materials with the class. Be prepared to show the students how they can make the resources.

5. Add a math materials list to each of the units in your Activity File/Notebook.

REVIEW

A. Why are learning centers essential for math learning?

B. What are the two main types of math materials?

C. List some useful items for a math junk box.

D. Describe each of the following materials:
   1. Concrete manipulative math materials
   2. Abstract representational math materials

E. Respond to each of the following situations:
   1. Mrs. Anderson has four lotto games with some of the cards missing, two geoboards with five rubber bands, and a few unit blocks in her preschool classroom. Mr. Brown has three complete lotto games, a set of Unifix Cubes, a set of unit blocks, a big tub of a variety of jar lids, and three shape puzzles. Give your opinion of the quality of math materials in each classroom. Why do you believe as you do?

   2. Miss Collins says she does not believe it is appropriate to teach math to young children. When you observe in her kindergarten, you see children playing at a water table with various containers. Others are weighing toy cars on a balance scale. Is Miss Collins teaching math? If so, explain how.

   3. Mr. Dominic teaches first grade. He is going to set up a math center and has been given $500 to purchase basic materials. He asks for your help. What would you suggest?

   4. Mrs. Edwards teaches second grade. She has just read this book. She is trying hard to provide a developmentally appropriate math environment but cannot decide how to begin. What suggestions would you give her?

REFERENCES

Cross, C. T., Woods, T. A., & Schweingruber, H. (Eds.). (2009). *Mathematics learning in early childhood*. Washington, DC: National Academies Press.

Davis, M. R. (2010). Solving algebra on smartphones. *Education Week, 29*(6), 20–23. Retrieved 3/19/10 from www.edweek.org.

Davison, S. (2009). A picture is worth a thousand words. *Science & Children, 46*(5), 36–39.

de Melendez, W. R., & Beck, V. (2007). *Teaching young children in multicultural classrooms* (2nd ed.). Albany, NY: Thomson Delmar Learning.

E-learning for educators [Special Section]. (2004). *Young Children, 59*(3), 10–44.

Everhart, J. (2009). YouTube in the science classroom. *Science & Children, 46*(9), 32–35.

Gargiulo, R., & Kilgo, J. (2005). *Young children with special needs* (2nd ed.). Albany, NY: Thomson Delmar Learning.

Lisenbee, P. (2009). Whiteboards and websites; Digital tools for the early childhood curriculum. *Young Children, 64*(6), 92–95.

Manzo, K. K. (2010). Educators struggle to design mobile-learning content. *Education Week, 29*(26) 28–29. Retrieved online 3/18/10 from www.edweek.org.

McNeil, N. M., & Uttal, D. H. (2009). Rethinking the use of concrete materials in learning:

Perspectives from development and education. *Child Development Perspectives, 3*(3), 137–139.

Wartella, E., Caplovitz, A. G., & Lee, J. H. (2004). From *Baby Einstein* to *Leapfrog*, from *Doom* to the *Sims*, from instant messaging to Internet chatrooms: Public interest in the role of interactive media in children's lives. *SRCD Social Policy Report, 18*(4).

FURTHER READING AND RESOURCES

Burris, A. C. (2005). *Understanding the math you teach.* Upper Saddle River, NJ: Pearson-Merrill/Prentice-Hall.

Carin, A. A., & Sund, R. B. (1992). *Teaching science through discovery.* New York: Macmillan.

Chen, J. (2007). *Bridging: Assessment for teaching and learning in early childhood classrooms, Pre-K–3.* Thousand Oaks, CA: Corwin.

Copley, J. V., Jones, C., & Dighe, J. (2007). *Mathematics. The creative curriculum approach.* Washington, DC: Teaching Strategies.

Dacey, L., & Eston, R. (2002). *Show and tell: Representing and communicating mathematical ideas in K–2 classrooms.* Sausalito, CA: Math Solutions.

Gallenstein, N. L. (2003). *Creative construction of mathematics and science concepts in early childhood.* Olney, MD: Association for Childhood Education International.

Glanfield, F., Bush, W. S., & Stenmark, J. K. (Eds.). (2003). *Mathematics assessment: A practical handbook for grades K–2.* Reston, VA: National Council of Teachers of Mathematics.

Haylock, D., & Cockburn, A. (2003). *Understanding mathematics in the lower primary years* (2nd ed.). Thousand Oaks, CA: Chapman.

Isbell, R., & Exelby, B. (2001). *Early learning environments that work.* Beltsville, MD: Gryphon House.

Jacobs, V. R., Bennett, T. R., & Bullock, C. (2000). Selecting books in Spanish to teach mathematics. *Teaching Children Mathematics, 6*(9), 582–587.

Jasmine, G. (2000). *Early childhood activities with internet connections.* Westminster, CA: Teacher Created Materials.

Mix, K. S., Huttenlocher, J., & Levine, S. C. (2002). *Quantitative development in infancy and early childhood.* New York: Oxford University Press.

National Council of Teachers of Mathematics. (2000). *Principles and standards for school mathematics.* Reston, VA: Author.

National Council of Teachers of Mathematics. (2001–2004). *Navigations Series, pre-K–2.* Reston, VA: Author.

National Research Council. (1999). *Selecting instructional materials: A guide for K–12.* Washington, DC: National Academies Press.

Richardson, K. (1999). *Developing number concepts: Planning guide.* Parsippany, NJ: Seymour.

Richardson, K. (1984). *Developing number concepts using Unifix Cubes.* Menlo Park, CA: Addison-Wesley.

Thiessen, D. (Ed.). (2004). *Exploring mathematics through literature.* Reston, VA: National Council of Teachers of Mathematics.

Wakefield, A. P. (1998). *Early childhood number games.* Boston: Allyn & Bacon.

West, S., & Cox, A. (2001). *Sand and water play.* Beltsville, MD: Gryphon House.

Whitin, D. J., & Whitin, P. (2004). *New visions for linking literature and mathematics.* Urbana, IL: National Council of Teachers of English, and Reston, VA: National Council of Teachers of Mathematics.

Wright, R. J., Martland, J., Stafford, A. K., & Stanger, G. (2002). *Teaching number: Advancing children's skills and strategies.* Thousand Oaks, CA: Chapman.

Note: Resource reviews appear in each issue of *Teaching Children Mathematics* as well as in other early childhood periodicals.

Math in Action

OBJECTIVES

After reading this unit, you should be able to:

- Understand the value of children working together cooperatively.
- Plan and use blocks for math experiences.
- Describe the benefits of using blocks with primary age children.
- Plan and use woodworking for math experiences.
- Plan and use math games and activities with young children.
- Plan and use outdoor activities with young children.
- Understand how technology can contribute to active mathematics learning.
- Explain the value of culturally relevant mathematics activities.

As reviewed in Units 1 and 3, action in mathematics involves hands-on problem solving and inquiry. The National Council of Teachers of Mathematics (NCTM, 2000) describes five process standards: problem solving, reasoning and proof, communication, connections, and representation. This unit provides an overview of the kinds of activities that should be observed in action in early childhood classrooms.

Math goes on all the time in the developmentally appropriate classroom for young children. The block builder, like any engineer, builds her building so it will stand up and serve a planned function. The young carpenter measures wood and swings his hammer to get the most power when he hits the nail. Children do finger plays and action songs and explore the outdoors while they apply math concepts. As children move into concrete operations, math in action include more complex group games and activities and the introduction of team sports and pre-planned building and science projects.

Children continue to be active learners in the primary grades. This is a fact from research based on Piagetian theory. Unfortunately, the active opportunities blocks and outdoor explorations provide are not always considered in curriculum plans for primary age children; this is a mistake. Remember, primary age children are still concrete operation thinkers who learn to understand the world around them through actively engaging in explorations.

Block play and outdoor explorations provide children with many opportunities to investigate, test, and change objects. It is from these interactions that children build their own model of the world. (Refer to concept development in Units 1 through 4 to refresh your memory.)

This unit focuses on the interrelationship of blocks, woodworking, songs, action games, problem solving, outdoor activities, technology, and culturally relevant activities that meet the affective, cognitive, and psychomotor learning needs of the young child. The emphasis is on active learning both indoors and outdoors.

A math lesson that meets the NCTM standards should include the following factors (Burrill, 1997): manipulatives, cooperative groups, a teacher who is a facilitator, the use of technology, opportunities to write, and strong connections to the children's world. Activities that meet these criteria can provide a program that will avoid the *Math Curse* (Scieszka & Smith, 1995). As described in Unit 2, math in action includes hands-on projects for both individual and group work. Both individuals and groups of two or more can organize their work using the K-W-L-D model (Shaw, Chambless, Chessin, Price, & Beardain, 1997). "K" involves recording what is *known* from studying the problem to be solved. "W" stands for *what* I (we) want to find out; that is, identify the question. The "L" step involves recording what the student or group of students has *learned*. In the final "D" step, the answer is stated and *defended* and the process of problem solving is described—what I (we) did. An important aspect of a problem-solving approach to math is allowing plenty of time for students to think through and discuss their solution processes. Even in the midst of lively discussion, a long pause in the conversation may be needed for students to reflect on the problems so that they can create their own unique solutions.

Blocks

Blocks are probably the play material most used by young children. Unfortunately, blocks are seldom seen in classrooms beyond the kindergarten level, even though they have the potential to function as valuable concept-building materials for primary children. Research reported by Wolfgang, Stannard, and Jones (2001) indicates that young children's block play performance during preschool is a predictor of mathematics achievement in middle school and high school.

Children apply basic concepts as they explore the relationships among the various sizes and shapes in a set of unit blocks (Figure 28–1). They note that two of one size may equal one of another—some are longer and some shorter, some are square, some are rectangular, others are triangular, and still others are curved. They are working with fractions and parts and wholes. MacDonald (2001) lists 29 mathematics concepts and skills that children can construct

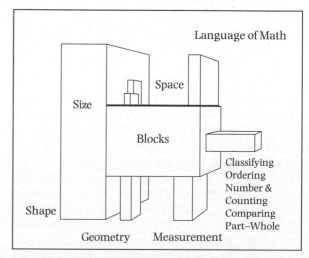

FIGURE 28–1 Children can construct many concepts as they work with blocks.

and apply when building with unit blocks. Furthermore, block play enhances concepts and skills in science, art, literacy, physical development, social studies, and socioemotional development (MacDonald, 2001).

The block area needs plenty of space. Neatly organize the blocks and the small vehicles, people dolls, and animals that enhance the accompanying dramatic play activities on low shelves where the children can easily reach them. Mark shelves with outlines of each block shape so that the children can return the blocks to the proper place (and practice some one-to-one correspondence). Start the year with a small, easy-to-handle set. As time goes by, introduce more blocks and more shapes. Facilitate exploration by asking questions and making comments. For example, Mrs. Red Fox notes that Trang Fung has used all square blocks in her structure, whereas Sara has developed her structure with larger units. Mrs. Red Fox says, "It looks like each of you have your favorite-sized blocks."

Blocks can be purchased in sets of various sizes. There are a variety of shapes and sizes in each set. The basic unit is a brick-shaped rectangle that is 1″ × 2¾″ × 5½″. The variety of shapes and sizes is listed in Figure 28–2. Unit blocks should be made of good, strong, hard wood with beveled edges so that they will not wear down or splinter. They should be smoothly sanded. The sizes must be precise so that building can be done effectively. Unit block sets are very expensive, but with good care they last for many years. Keep them dry and free of dust. Occasionally they should be oiled or waxed.

At the beginning stage, the child may just handle the blocks and carry them from place to place. At the second stage, the children make rows and lines of blocks. At the third stage, children build bridges. At the fourth stage, children make simple enclosures. At the fifth stage, the children make patterns that may be balanced and symmetric. At the sixth stage, the children name the structures and use them for dramatic play. At the last stage, the children make structures that represent familiar buildings, such as their own home or even their whole city.

Children enjoy using other types of building materials besides unit blocks. Many preschools

	Name	Nursery	Kgn. & Primary
	Square	40	80
	Unit	96	192
	Double Unit	48	96
	Quadruple Unit	16	32
	Pillar	24	48
	Half Pillar	24	48
	Small Triangle	24	48
	Large Triangle	24	48
	Small Column	16	32
	Large Column	8	16
	Ramp	16	32
	Ellipse		8
	Curve	8	16
	¼ Circle		8
	Large Switch & Gothic Door		4
	Small Switch		4
	Large Buttress		4
	½ Arch & Small Buttress		4
	Arch & ½ Circle		4
	Roofboard		24
	Number of Shapes	12	23
	Number of Pieces	344	760

FIGURE 28–2 Childcraft block sets.

have large, hollow, wood blocks. At a lower cost, there are cardboard blocks. Cardboard boxes can enhance the imaginative activity of young children. Large boxes can be the focus of walking *around*, climbing *in*, and climbing *over*. Boxes can be moved about and combined in many different ways, providing experiences with weight, size, shape, and volume. Sheets and blankets can add to the variety of structures. Blocks and boxes provide a rich opportunity for math in action.

Blocks Encourage Thinking

Blocks force children to distinguish, classify, and sort. This can be seen as a group of second graders learns the different properties of blocks by re-creating a field trip to the zoo. As they plan and build the zoo, they deal with the fact that each block has different qualities. They consider size, shape, weight, thickness, width, and length. As construction progresses, the blocks become fulcrums and levers. Guiding questions such as "Can you make a ramp for unloading the rhinoceros?" and "Where will you put the access road for delivering food to the animals?" will help children focus on an aspect of construction. Some children create zoo animals, workers, and visitors to dramatize a day at the zoo.

Allow time for children to verbalize why they are arranging the zoo in a particular way. This will encourage children to share their problem-solving strategy and will help them clarify their thinking. By observing the children at play, you will also gain insight into their thought processes.

Blocks and Marbles

Balance and action can be seen as children assemble plastic ramps and chutes with commercial toys such as Marbleworks. Children gain a familiarity with concepts such as gravity, acceleration, and momentum and can observe the relationship between time and speed when they design and create a maze of movement by fitting pieces together. To further introduce children to the principle of cause and effect, ask: **What action starts the marble moving?** Then have children predict the way in which the marble will move. Creating different

pathways and exploring how the marble moves on them can be exciting.

Complex block and marble sets seem to fascinate primary age children. With these sets, children arrange wooden sections to allow marbles to travel through holes and grooved blocks of different lengths. Children enjoy controlling the movement of the marble down the construction and creating changes that determine the direction and speed of the marble. Children can make their own marble runs from decorative molding that is available in paneling supply stores. The track can be nailed onto boards, taped down, or held for observing the movement of marbles (some will move at breakneck speeds). Have your students add a tunnel, try different types of balls, and find ways to use friction to slow down the marbles.

Another Type of Construction

Constructions introduce children to the conditions and limitations of space. They learn to bridge space with appropriate-sized blocks and objects and to enclose space in different ways. The following ideas involve creating your own construction set with straws.

Use large straws for straw construction, and connect them with string, pipe cleaners, or paper clips. String is the most difficult to use but makes the most permanent construction. Simply stick the string in one end of the straw and then suck on the other end. The string will come through.

You will have to form a triangle with three straws. A triangle is the only shape made with straws that is rigid enough for building. If you are using string as a connector, tie the ends together to form a triangle, or thread three straws on one string to form the triangle.

Pipe cleaners as connectors are another method for building with straws. Push a pipe cleaner halfway into the end of one straw, and then slip another straw over the other end of the pipe cleaner. Double up the pipe cleaners for a tighter fit. Children can twist and turn this construction in many ways.

Many teachers recommend paper clips as ideal connectors in straw building. Open a paper clip, bend out the two ends, and slip each end into a straw. Paper clips are rigid and allow for complex building. You might have to add as many as three paper clips to give the structure strength. Paper clips may also be chained for a flexible joint between two straws. Challenge children to think and construct. Ask: **How tall a structure can you make? Why did your structure collapse? Can you make a bridge?**

When the straw frame stands by itself, test it. Ask, **Can you think of a way to test the strength of your structure?** Place a paper clip through a paper cup and hang it somewhere on the straw structure. Ask, **How many paper cups can your structure support? How many paper clips will make the frame work?**

Block City

Blocks in the classroom provide many opportunities for children to integrate their basic reading and writing, science, math skills and concepts, and social studies into the construction process. Opportunities for integration abound as children explore the busy life of a block city.

Mr. Wang's second-grade children created a city of blocks. Buildings had to be accurate in the city, and each child builder represented herself in the daily acting out of city life. The block building sessions were preceded by class discussion as the children planned the daily block activities. Accessories (labeled boxes of food, clothing, computers, typewriters, and the like) were constructed from a variety of materials. Children played the roles of shopkeepers, bankers, and other workers. They made decisions such as where the people in the block city would get their money.

When the children had to put out an imaginary fire, they immediately saw a problem. How would they get water to the blaze? This discovery led to an investigation of how water gets into hydrants, utility covers, and water pipes. The children responded to the emergency by adding plastic tubing to the city as well as wire for electricity and telephones.

Not only was the city becoming more realistic, it was becoming less magical. Children no longer thought that water magically appeared when the water faucet was turned on. They knew that a system of pipes carried the water. In fact, the workings of a city in general became less magical. Many common misconceptions were dispelled, and an understanding of how a city functions began to develop.

Second graders built New York City (Benedis-Grab, 2010). They learned about building materials. They applied concepts of size, shape, measurement, and time.

Children construct the town of Hudgensville.

The Edible Village

Mrs. Moore's first-grade students integrated the study of their neighborhood with block building. After determining the different sections of the neighborhood and buildings they needed to create, each child was assigned a building. The class created their neighborhood with blocks made of graham crackers. They used flattened caramels for roadways and lollipops for streetlights. Coconut spread over white icing gave the illusion of snow.

The students mixed yellow and green food coloring into icing to create differently colored buildings. Recipes for icing provided opportunities to use measurements and follow directions in sequence. Writing about the creation of the village and what might be happening within graham cracker walls became a springboard for discussion.

Children made decisions about what should and should not be included in the village. They determined the authenticity of buildings and building size. This activity is especially appropriate for primary age children. Children in this age group are able to incorporate more detail and can be exposed to another's viewpoint. For example, the teacher asked, "How will the people know that school is open?" Children began asking one another, "Do we need a hospital? What about a gas station?"

If your city or town is located near a river or lake, be sure to include it in construction. Paper straw bridges could be added, and the geography of your area could be explored. You will find that as the children develop questions, they are motivated to find the answers because they need to know something for construction of the city. Thus, the block experience also becomes a first research experience for them.

Woodworking

Most young children enjoy working with wood. Woodworking provides hands-on experience with measurement, balance, power, and spatial and size relationships. Children use informal measurement as they check to see if they have a piece of wood that is the one they need and if they have a nail that is the correct length. As children move into the primary level, they can apply standard measurement: "I will need 12 pieces of 12-by-8-inch plywood for my birdhouse." The more advanced primary children can follow simple instructions and use patterns to make projects.

For effective woodworking, the classroom should have a sturdy workbench, good-quality real tools, and assorted pieces of soft wood. The workbench should be large enough for at least two children to work at the same time. Woodworking must always be closely supervised. Workbenches

designed for children can be purchased from the major school supply companies, or a large old tree stump can be used.

The basic components of a high-quality tool set for 4- and 5-year-olds are illustrated in Figure 28–3. Older children can use a greater variety of tools. The tools should be easily accessible when in use but kept in a locked closet or on a high shelf when not in use. Beginners do best with short nails with large heads.

Soft wood such as pine is easy for children to work with. When introducing sawing, the wood should be put in a vise so it will hold steady, and so the child's hands will not be in the line of the saw.

Experienced woodworkers enjoy creating projects using odds and ends with their wood. Wheels can be made from bottle caps and windows from plastic lids. Scraps of cloth or ribbon

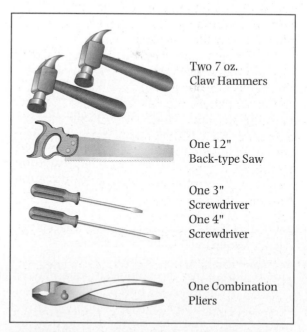

Two 7 oz. Claw Hammers

One 12" Back-type Saw

One 3" Screwdriver
One 4" Screwdriver

One Combination Pliers

FIGURE 28–3 Basic woodworking tools for 4- and 5-year-olds: Start with these tools and add more as children become more proficient.

can be glued on to the wood. Children can apply their math vocabulary as they explain their finished projects.

Math Games

As described in Unit 19, board games provide children with opportunities for counting and one-to-one correspondence. They also provide opportunities for developing social skills such as cooperation and following rules.

Young children enjoy playing games. Some 4-year-olds and most 5-year-olds enjoy playing board games. For the preschooler, games should be simple with a minimum of rules. As children get older they enjoy creating their own board games. The rules are often flexible and change frequently. They may make play money applying their knowledge of money and cards that tell how many jumps they can make.

Board games provide an excellent way to teach math. Candyland, Numberland Counting Game, Chutes and Ladders, Fraction Brothers Circus, Memory, Picture Dominoes, Picture Nines (a domino game), Candyland Bingo, Triominos, Connect Four, Count-a-Color, Farm Lotto, and other bingo and lotto boxed games can be purchased. Board game patterns can be obtained from early childhood publications and **Internet** sites. For more advanced children, basic concepts can be practiced using board games such as Multiplication/Division Quizmo, Addition/Subtraction Mathfacts Game, Multiplication/Division Mathfacts Game, UNO, UNO Dominoes, Yahtzee, and IMMAWhiz Math Games. Two games that help children learn money concepts are Pay the Cashier and Count Your Change.

Lakeshore has wooden board games that provide materials for the youngest game players. Number Bingo can be purchased from Constructive Playthings. Early Childhood Direct carries Color and Shape Bingo, Bingo Bears, a set of readiness math games, and some more advanced games (Number Start, Number Detective, Playcount).

Other basic board games were described in Unit 19. Card games primary children enjoy include those suggested by Kamii (see Unit 21) and those that are perennial favorites such as Go Fish, Concentration, Crazy Eights, Old Maid, Flinch, Solitaire, and Fantan. Look through catalogs, and examine games at exhibitors' displays when you attend professional meetings. A vast selection is available. Marilyn Burns (2009) provides instructions for four math games for primary-grade students.

Young children enjoy bowling games and games that involve aiming. Dropping clothespins into a container or throwing beanbags through a hole or into a container are appropriate for young children. Once they learn the game, they can keep track of their successes using Unifix Cubes or making tally marks to keep score.

Outdoors or in the gym, children can have races. They can estimate how far they can throw a ball, a beanbag, or a paper plate. Primary children can measure with a yardstick and compare their estimates with their actual throwing distances.

Primary children enjoy jumping rope. They enjoy jumping to jingles such as "Mabel, Mabel." During the primary years, children are in the stage of industry versus inferiority. The struggle between these forces leads them into a natural interest in competitive activities, such as the games listed earlier, and into team sports and races. Adults must find ways for each of the children to achieve so that they do not experience inferiority feelings. Primary children enjoy races that give them practice in time and distance relationships. Hurdle jumping can begin with high and low jumps and then move into standard measures of height. Balls, beanbags, or Frisbees can be thrown and the distances compared and measured. Team sports require scorekeeping and an understanding of *more, less*, and *ordinal relations* (i.e., who is up first, second, and so on).

Primary children also enjoy math puzzlers and brainteasers that give them practice in problem solving. Some of these types of problems were introduced in Unit 3. The following are additional examples.

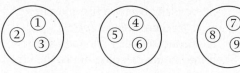

Move one so each set has a sum of 15.

Magic Triangles

Write the numbers 1 through 6 in the circles of the triangle shown in the following figure in such a way as to have a total of 9 (or 10 or 11 or 12) on each side.

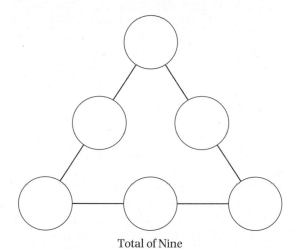

Total of Nine

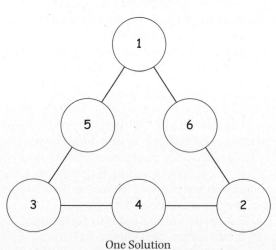

One Solution

The Lady and the Tiger

How many different squares can you count?

How many different triangles can you count?

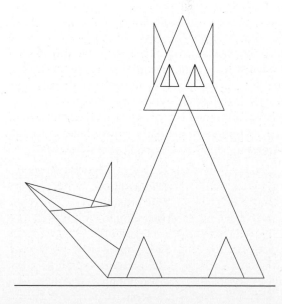

Your Number

Ask someone to think of a number, but keep it secret. Now tell him to double the number, add eight to the result, divide by two, and subtract the original number. Then have him write down the answer but tell him not to show it to you until you predict the answer. The answer will always be 4.

Young children enjoy games. Board, target, and action games offer them opportunities to apply math concepts. Through observation of children playing games, adults can obtain information regarding a child's development of math skills and concepts. Each issue of *Teaching Children Mathematics* includes a thematic section called "Math by the Month" that poses problems for elementary students beginning with kindergarten through grade 2. For example, in January 2009/January 2010 (Columba & Waddell, 2009/2010), the theme was "A treasure trove of triangles." Four problems were presented: one focused on finding triangles in a quilt, another was a geoboard activity, a third focused on drawing as many triangles as possible on centimeter grid paper in 30 seconds, and the fourth involved sorting pattern blocks.

Finger Plays and Action Songs

Many finger plays and action songs include the application of math concepts. Children may have to hear the song or finger play several times before they join in. If the teacher keeps repeating it, the students will gradually learn and participate. Favorite finger plays are "Five Little Monkeys Jumping on the Bed" and "Five Little Ducks Swimming in a Pond." A longtime favorite song is "Johnny Works with One Hammer." Children particularly enjoy counting rhymes (Arenson, 1998). Two examples are as follows.

> One potato,
> Two potato,
> Three potato,
> Four;
> Five potato,
> Six potato,
> Seven potato,
> More.

> Here is the beehive (fist closed),
> Where are the bees?
> Hidden away where nobody sees,
> Soon they come creeping out of the hive,
> (open fingers one at a time)
> One! Two! Three! Four! Five!

See the resources listed at the end of the unit. Finger plays and action songs help children learn math concepts through body actions.

Math in the Environment

The outdoors provides many opportunities for children's mathematics applications. Children can count the number of windows they can see from the playground. They can do informal measurements of playground equipment and distances across the playground. They can measure shadows at different times of the day. Trailblazers (2010) provide opportunities for children to create math trails in their environment. Children and/or teachers devise a series of directions that include math concepts such as the following:

1. Walk to the front door. Count how many steps you took.
2. Go out the door and walk to the church. Stop at the church. Count the number of windows in the front of the church.
3. Walk by the park. How many swings do you see?
4. Look at the fence around the park. Which shapes do you see?

Baker and Baker (1991) suggest many outdoor activities in their book *Counting on a Small Planet*. For example, in the activity "All That Rubbish," children examine the rubbish left in their lunch boxes after they have eaten. They chart the results over time and develop conclusions regarding their rubbish. Other investigations include noise pollution, water use and abuse, wind, and other outdoor topics.

A first-grade unit on the rain forest provided many mathematics applications (Thornton, Dee, Damkoehler, Gehrenbeck, & Jones, 1995). The study of the rain forest provided opportunities to advance the students' number sense as they created a sense of the space the rain forest occupied, built a classroom rain forest, and used related problem-solving experiences. The students kept journals, made graphs, and did some estimating.

Solving Mathematics Problems

A critical activity in mathematics is problem solving, as detailed in Unit 3. Many examples of children's problem-solving approaches can be found in the *Teaching Children Mathematics* journal articles. The *Navigation* series on problem solving and reasoning provides examples of problems to be solved (see Findell et al., 2004; Greenes et al., 2003; Small et al., 2004). Prekindergartners and kindergartners can be provided with problems involving number relationships, patterning, nonstandard measurement, and simple data analysis (Greenes et al., 2003). First graders can work with algebraic relationships, geometric relationships, data graphing, and measurement (Findell et al., 2004). Second graders can move on to more complex problems in number, algebra, geometry, measurement, and reasoning about data relationships (Small et al., 2004). Beginning problem solvers use drawings and/or manipulatives to reach solutions whereas more advanced students gradually invent numerical processes.

Interview a Spider

Children enjoy becoming reporters and interviewing various wildlife. After discussing what a reporter does and the techniques of interviewing, teams of children can decide on an animal they want to interview.

Planning for Outdoor Learning

Taking children outdoors can be a challenge if you are not prepared. To ensure the greatest value from this experience, teachers of all age groups should consider the following:

1. Think about your purpose for including outdoor experiences. How will children benefit? What type of preparation do the children need before they go outdoors?

Children enjoy seeing how fast they can jump rope and how many times they can jump rope without a mistake.

2. What are the logistics? Will you walk, drive, or ride in cars or in a bus? What type of clothing is needed? Should you take snacks and lunch? Are there people to contact? What are the water and toilet facilities? How much help do you need?
3. Which math concepts will be developed? What do you hope to accomplish?
4. Have you planned what you will be teaching before the experience, during the activity, and after the experience?
5. How much talking do you really need to do?
6. How will you evaluate the experience?
7. What types of follow-up learning will be provided? What subjects can you integrate into the experience?

Attention Grabbers Devices for grabbing the attention of a group can be physical, such as pulling out a surprise object from your bag when you want to discuss a topic.

More subtle attention grabbers include:

1. Look intently at an object to focus group attention on the same object.
2. Have children remind you of tasks, carry various items, assist with the activity, and lead in other tasks. This participation helps keep their attention.
3. Lowering your voice when you want to make a point works well in the classroom and outdoors.
4. Change your position. Sit down with the children when they begin to wander, and regroup them.
5. Give the children specific items to look for or match, notes to take, or specific jobs. Children tend to lose interest if they do not have a task. Use small notebooks.

Additional Control Strategies Although you might be proficient at controlling children indoors, the outdoors can be quite a different matter. Here are a few tips:

1. Before the outdoor experience, set up a firm set of rules (as you do indoors). As you know, it is far easier to relax rules than the other way around.
2. When children become too active, try an attention grabber or initiate an activity designed to give children a chance to run. For example, "Run to the big pine tree and back to me." Relays with rocks as batons will also expend excess energy.
3. Have a prearranged attention signal for activities that require wandering. A whistle, bell, or hand signals work well.
4. When one child is talking and others desperately want your attention, place your hand on their hand to let them know that you recognize them.
5. Let different children enjoy leading the adventure. Occasionally, remove yourself

from the line, take a different place in line, and go in a different direction. In this way, you lead the group in a new direction with different children directly behind you.

6. Play *follow the leader* with you as the leader as you guide the line where you want it to go. If there is snow on the ground, have the children walk like wolves: Wolves walk along a trail in single file, putting their feet in the footprints of the wolf ahead of them.
7. Be flexible. If something is not working, just change the activity. Later you can analyze why something was not working the way you had planned.

Exciting outdoor activities do not happen by chance. Begin by planning carefully what you want the children to learn. Then teach the lesson, and evaluate the children's learning and your preparation. You will be off to a good start as an outdoor science educator.

Technology

Relevant technology has been suggested throughout this text. Exciting adventures await students as they use the Internet. The **World Wide Web** (WWW) provides opportunities for teachers to share ideas while students can expand their knowledge. For example, a science teacher in Virginia whose students were interested in comparing Atlantic coast shells with shells found in other parts of the world assisted them in connecting with schools in other countries through the Internet (Holden, 1996). The students made contact through e-mail and exchanged beach materials. Another teacher focused on mathematical thinking by having her students investigate pet ownership around the world through the Internet (Lynes, 1997). The students applied several standards areas: problem solving, communication, reasoning, and connections. The Global Schoolhouse provides access to collaborative projects and communication tools (classroom conferencing, mailing lists, and discussion boards). Teachers had students use digital cameras and whiteboards to demonstrate solutions to fraction problems (Canada, 2009). Primary-grade students integrated concrete and virtual manipulatives (Rosen & Hoffman, 2009).

Instructional Technology in Action

Instruction technology offers many opportunities for children to learn more about the world around them than would be possible in the confines of the classroom or schoolyard. There are numerous pieces of software available for young children that encourage their critical thinking and problem solving. For example, young children can plan towns, roads, parks, and more using *Stickybear Town Builder* (for grades K–3) or *SimTown* (ages 8–12). The popular children's magazine *Highlights* offers interactive computer software, which includes a science corner, hidden pictures, and rebus stories. In using *Thinkin' Things* software, children build higher-level thinking skills as they determine secret rules, make logical comparisons, and determine patterns. *Sammy's Science House* offers pre-K to grade-2 children a gadget builder as well as opportunities to sort and classify plants and animals, to sequence events in a filmlike fashion, and to explore different weather conditions.

The Internet and the WWW offer opportunities for students to interact with other students from across the world, to see images otherwise inaccessible, and to play educational games. Most Web **browsers** (e.g., Internet Explorer, Mozilla Firefox, Netscape, Safari) and Web **search engines** (e.g., Google, Yahoo!, Webcrawler, Lycos) offer some sort of "Just for Kids" option on their home page. You can also find great websites using a browser to initiate a search. For example, you could enter the phrase "kids and math" in the search field and see what links are listed. Once you locate any site that you want your children to use, be sure to **bookmark** that site; this bookmark (or similar feature; browsers vary) allows you to recall the site later without having to do a search or type an Internet address or **URL**.

There are many resources available to find out more about using the WWW in your classroom. Wentworth Worldwide Media offers a number of useful products. First, a guide titled *Educator's Internet Companion* has information on how to find websites with lesson plans and how to share ideas with others via the Web; it also provides many WWW addresses, so you can start "surfing the Web" right away. Second, a special newsletter titled *Classroom Connect* offers nine monthly issues jam-packed with ideas, WWW addresses, and lesson-plan ideas.

If your school does not have access to the Web, there are options for you to explore that use WWW sites. For example, *WebWhacker* software allows the user to **download** entire sites for later use on a computer that is not connected to the Internet. However, not all sites will download, and the download process can be rather lengthy.

MATH TECHNOLOGY FOR YOUNG CHILDREN

Evaluate a technology resource for young children that emphasizes one of the concepts or skills discussed in this unit. Choose from the following list and/or from the recommended resources in other units.

- *Sammy's Science House* (pre-K–2; San Francisco: Edmark). Order through Broderbund or Riverdeep.
- *SimTown* (ages 8–12; Maxis).
- *Stickybear Town Builder* (K–3; Norfolk, CT: Optimum Resource). Order from K–12 Software.
- *Thinkin' Things 1* and *Thinkin' Things 2* (ages 4–13; San Francisco: Edmark). Order through Broderbund or Riverdeep.

Other software selections you might explore:

- *WebWhacker* (adults; Houston, TX: Forefront Direct). Utility for downloading websites.
- The *Educator's Internet Companion*, *Classroom Connect*, and the *Educators' Internet CD Club* are available from Wentworth Worldwide Media (address in Appendix B).

Nonetheless, for those that can download, it is wonderful to be able to **surf** websites without even having an Internet connection! Additionally, *Classroom Connect* offers software (the *Educator's Internet CD Club*) that includes entire websites and lesson plans without the need for Internet access.

Culturally Relevant Mathematics

Remember that the first NCTM (2000) principle is that of equity. "Excellence in mathematics education requires equity—high expectations and strong support of all students" (p. 12). Respect for and accommodation to differences is essential to instruction in mathematics. As a follow-up to support and elaborate on the equity principle, a special issue of *Teaching Children Mathematics* (Barta, 2001) consists of articles that look at various aspects of mathematics and culture.

In Unit 2, ethnomathematics—the natural mathematics that children learn in their culture—was described. Information regarding ethnomathematics can be obtained from the International Study Group on Ethnomathematics website (Eglash, 2001). It is essential to discover and build on the mathematics that children bring to school. It is also necessary to use culturally relevant materials and activities. For example, many of the books suggested throughout this text reflect cultural diversity (see especially Unit 12 and Appendix B). Some books are written in English but focus on other cultures. For example, in the book *Round Is a Mooncake* (Thong, 2000), a young girl seeks out shapes in a Chinese American setting. In *Feast for Ten* (Fallwell, 1993), an African American family is followed while shopping for, cooking, serving, and eating a meal. Other books are written in other languages as translations of English-language classics or as stories written originally in other languages. Books in Spanish are increasing in number and are reviewed frequently in *Young Children*. Advice on selecting mathematics-related books in Spanish is the subject of an article by Jacobs, Bennett, and Bullock (2000).

Culturally relevant mathematics can be integrated with science and social studies. Internet activities such as those just described can provide opportunities to learn about other geographic areas and their cultures while obtaining science knowledge and applying mathematics knowledge. Upper-grade or younger advanced students can study and compare the mathematical systems of other cultures such as Native American, Roman, and Egyptian. They can compare calendars of various cultures, such as Chinese, Jewish, and Muslim (Zaslavsky, 2001). White (2001) describes how first graders explored geometry by comparing fabrics from different cultures.

Summary

Math in action means children exploring the environment, which is done through woodworking, block constructing, game playing, problem solving, and exploring the outdoor areas in their environment. Math in action means children saying, singing, and acting out math language and concepts.

When children make block-building decisions, they are thinking like engineers. They focus on a problem and use the thinking skills of math to arrive at a solution. Block building and other indoor and outdoor explorations give children an opportunity to learn by manipulating and acting on their environment as they build their own model of the world.

The outdoor environment can be used to extend and enhance indoor lessons or as a specific place for engaging children in challenging learning. Suggestions have been given about how to work directly with outdoor learning as well as strategies for focusing children's attention on outdoor learning and encouraging higher-level math thinking. Once children learn how to study outdoors, they will enjoy the fascinating world around them. Technology provides increasing opportunities for children to learn about the world and apply mathematical skills and concepts through software applications and through the broad domain opened up by the Internet. Equity is an essential principle of mathematics instruction. Focusing on children's cultural mathematics and comparisons with the mathematics of other cultures shows respect for diversity.

KEY TERMS

bookmark
browser
download

Internet
search engines
surf

URL
World Wide Web

SUGGESTED ACTIVITIES

1. Observe some preschool, kindergarten, and/or primary students playing with blocks. See if you can categorize the developmental stages of their block building. Report on your observations in class.
2. Visit a local hardware store or a local discount store hardware department. Record the types of tools available and their prices. Compare your findings with the prices of similar toys in educational catalogs.
3. Find five math finger plays, songs, and/or rhymes. Teach them to the other members of the class.
4. Locate a classroom that has access to the Internet. Find out if the students are using the Internet in any math-related activities.

REVIEW

A. Explain the benefits of block play for young children.
B. List several types of block accessory toys.
C. Describe how to set up a woodworking area.
D. At which stage of block building is each of the following examples?
   1. Putting blocks in rows
   2. Carrying blocks around
   3. Building structures for dramatic play
   4. Building simple enclosures
E. List some popular early childhood board games.
F. Explain how finger plays and action songs can support math concept development.
G. Explain the value of the World Wide Web to math instruction.
H. What are the benefits of including outdoor activities with primary age children?
I. Describe at least two factors that support cultural equity.

REFERENCES

Arenson, R. (Illus.). (1998). *One, two, skip a few! First number rhymes.* New York: Barefoot Books.

Baker, A., & Baker, J. (1991). *Counting on a small planet: Activities for environmental mathematics.* Portsmouth, NH: Heinemann.

Barta, J. (Ed.). (2001). Mathematics and culture [Special issue]. *Teaching Children Mathematics, 7*(6).

Benedis-Grab, G. (2010). The built environment. *Science & Children, 47*(6), 22–26.

Burns, M. (2009, March-April). 4 win-win math games. *Instructor, 118*(5).

Burrill, G. (1997, April). Show me the math! *NCTM News Bulletin, 3.*

Canada, D. (2009). Fraction photo frenzy. *Teaching Children Mathematics, 15*(9), 552–557.

Columba, L., & Waddell, L. (2009/2010). A treasure trove of triangles. *Teaching Children Mathematics, 16*(5), 272.

Eglash, R. (2001). News from the net: The international study group on ethnomathematics. *Teaching Children Mathematics, 7*(6), 336.

Fallwell, C. (1993). *Feast for 10.* New York: Clarion.

Findell, C. R., Cavanagh, M., Dacey, L., Greenes, C. E., Sheffield, L. J., & Small, M. (2004). *Navigating through problem solving and reasoning in grade 1.* Reston, VA: National Council of Teachers of Mathematics.

Greenes, C. E., Dacey, L., Cavanagh, M., Findell, C. R., Sheffield, L. J., & Small, M. (2003). *Navigating through problem solving and reasoning in prekindergarten–kindergarten.* Reston, VA: National Council of Teachers of Mathematics.

Holden, J. C. (1996). The science exchange program. *Science and Children, 34*(3), 20–21.

Jacobs, V. R., Bennett, T. R., & Bullock, C. (2000). Selecting books in Spanish to teach mathematics. *Teaching Children Mathematics, 6*(9), 582–587.

Lynes, K. (1997). Tech time: Mining mathematics through the Internet! *Teaching Children Mathematics, 3*(7), 394–396.

MacDonald, S. (2001). *Block play: The complete guide to learning and playing with blocks.* Beltsville, MD: Gryphon House.

National Council of Teachers of Mathematics. (2000). *Principles and standards for school mathematics.* Reston, VA: Author.

Rosen, D., & Hoffman, J. (2009). Integrating concrete and virtual manipulatives. *Young Children, 64*(3), 26–33.

Scieszka, J., & Smith, L. (1995). *Math curse.* New York: Viking.

Shaw, G. M., Chambless, M. S., Chessin, D. R., Price, V., & Beardain, G. (1997). Cooperative problem solving: Using K-W-D-L as an organizational technique. *Teaching Children Mathematics, 3,* 482–486.

Small, M., Sheffield, L. J., Cavanagh, M., Dacey, L., Findell, C. R., & Greenes, C. E. (2004). *Navigating through problem solving and reasoning in grade 2.* Reston, VA: National Council of Teachers of Mathematics.

Thong, R. (2000). *Round is a mooncake.* San Francisco: Chronicle Books.

Thornton, C. A., Dee, D., Damkoehler, D. D., Gehrenbeck, H., & Jones, G. A. (1995). The children's rain forest. *Teaching Children Mathematics, 2*(3), 144–148.

Trailblazers. (2010, March). *Teaching Children Mathematics.* Retrieved from www.nctm.org.

White, D. Y. (2001). Kenta, kilts, and kimonos: Exploring cultures and mathematics through fabrics. *Teaching Children Mathematics, 7*(6), 354–359.

Wolfgang, C. H., Stannard, L. L., & Jones, I. (2001). Block play performance among preschoolers as a predictor of later school achievement in mathematics. *Journal of Research in Childhood Education, 15*(2), 173–180.

Zaslavsky, C. (2001). Developing number sense: What can other cultures tell us? *Teaching Children Mathematics, 7*(6), 312–319.

FURTHER READING AND RESOURCES

Planning the Environment and the Curriculum

Copley, J. V. (Ed.). (1999). *Mathematics in the early years.* Washington, DC: National Association for the Education of Young Children.

Copley, J. V. (2000). *The young child and mathematics.* Washington, DC: National Association for the Education of Young Children.

Richardson, K. (1999). *Developing number concepts: Planning guide.* Parsippany, NJ: Seymour.

Learning Together

Artzt, A. F., & Newman, C. M. (1990). *How to use cooperative learning in the mathematics class.* Reston, VA: National Council of Teachers of Mathematics.

Barone, M. M., & Taylor, L. (1996). Peer tutoring with mathematics manipulatives: A practical guide. *Teaching Children Mathematics, 3*(1), 8–15.

Green, D. A. (2002). Last one standing: Creative, cooperative problem solving. *Teaching Children Mathematics, 9*(3), 134–139.

Schussheim, J. Y. (2004). Large-scale family math nights: A primer for collaboration. *Teaching Children Mathematics, 10*(5), 254–257.

Blocks, Construction, and Woodworking

Benenson, G., & Neujahr, J. L. (2002). *Mechanisms and other systems.* Portsmouth, NH: Heinemann.

Benenson, G., & Neujahr, J. L. (2002). *Packaging and other structures.* Portsmouth, NH: Heinemann.

Benenson, G., & Neujahr, J. L. (2002). *Signs, symbols, and codes.* Portsmouth, NH: Heinemann.

Casey, B., & Bobb, B. (2003). The power of block building. *Teaching Children Mathematics, 10*(2), 98–102.

Dunn, S., & Larson, R. (1990). *Design technology.* London: Falmer Press.

Hirsch, E. (Ed.). (1984). *The block book.* Washington, DC: National Association for the Education of Young Children.

Johnson, P. (1992). *Pop-up engineering.* London: Falmer Press.

Skeen, P., Garner, A. P., & Cartwright, S. (1984). *Woodworking for young children.* Washington, DC: National Association for the Education of Young Children.

Wellhousen, K., & Kieff, J. (2001). *A constructivist approach to block play in early childhood.* Clifton Park, NY: Thomson Delmar Learning.

Zubrowski, B. (1981). *Messing around with drinking straw construction.* Boston: Little, Brown.

Games

Church, E. B. (2004). Glorious outdoor games. *Early Childhood Today, 18*(8), 6–12.

Cutler, K. M., Gilkerson, D., Parrott, S., & Bowne, M. T. (2003). Developing games based on children's literature. *Young Children, 58*(1), 22–27.

Feldman, J. R. (1994). *Complete handbook of indoor and outdoor games for young children.* Englewood Cliffs, NJ: Prentice-Hall.

Kamii, C. (1994). *Young children continue to reinvent arithmetic, 3rd grade.* New York: Teachers College Press.

Kamii, C. (1999). *Young children reinvent arithmetic* (2nd ed.). New York: Teachers College Press.

Kamii, C. (2003). *Young children continue to reinvent arithmetic, 2nd grade* (2nd ed.). New York: Teachers College Press.

Kamii, C., & DeVries, R. (1980). *Group games in early education.* Washington, DC: National Association for the Education of Young Children.

Shamrock math game. (2003, March). *Instructor,* 26.

Worstell, E. V. (1961). *Jump the rope jingles.* New York: Collier Books.

Finger Plays, Songs, and Rhymes

Aruego, J., & Dewey, A. (Illus.). (1989). *Five little ducks.* New York: Crown.

Christelow, E. (1991). *Five little monkeys sitting in a tree.* New York: Clarion.

Croll, C. (2001). *Fingerplays and songs for the very young.* New York: Random House.

Cromwell, L., & Hibner, D. (1976). *Finger frolics.* Livonia, MI: Partner Press.

Finkel, S., & Seberg, K. (1996). *Circle time math.* Carthage, IL: Teaching and Learning.

Haines, B. J. E., & Gerber, L. L. (2000). *Leading young children to music* (6th ed.). Columbus, OH: Pearson-Merrill/Prentice-Hall.

Kitson, J. (2000). *Fabulous holiday and seasonal fingerplays.* Clifton Park, NY: Thomson Delmar Learning.

Pica, R. (1999). *Moving & learning across the curriculum.* Clifton Park, NY: Thomson Delmar Learning.

Schiller, P., & Moore, T. (1993). *Where is thumbkin?* Beltsville, MD: Gryphon House.

Umansky, K., & Fisher, C. (1999). *Nonsense counting rhymes.* Oxford: Oxford University Press. Weimer, T. E. (1993). *Space songs for children.* Greenville, SC: Pearce-Evetts.

Problem Solving

Buschman, L. (2002). Becoming a problem solver. *Teaching Children Mathematics, 9*(2), 98–103.

Buschman, L. (2003). Children who enjoy problem solving. *Teaching Children Mathematics, 9*(9), 539–544.

Buschman, L. (2004). Teaching problem solving in mathematics. *Teaching Children Mathematics, 10*(6), 302–309.

Hoosain, E., & Chance, R. H. (2004). Problem-solving strategies of first graders. *Teaching Children Mathematics, 10*(9), 474–479.

Technology

Britton, E., DeLong-Cotty, B., & Levenson, T. (2005). *Bringing technology education into K–8 classrooms: A guide to curricular resources about the designed world.* Thousand Oaks, CA: Corwin Press.

Clements, D. H. (1999). Young children and technology. In *Dialogue on early childhood science, mathematics and technology education* (pp. 92–105). Washington, DC: American Association for the Advancement of Science.

Computer technology tool kit. (1997). White Plains, NY: Addison-Wesley Longman Supplementary Division.

The educator's guide to the Internet. (1997). White Plains, NY: Addison-Wesley Longman Supplementary Division.

Haugland, S. W., & Wright, J. L. (1997). *Young children and technology: A world of discovery.* Boston: Allyn & Bacon.

Haury, D. L., & Milbourne, L. A. (1999). Internet resources. In S. J. Rakow (Ed.), *ERIC Review: K–8 Science and Math Education, 6*(2), 66–67.

Integrating computers into your classroom: Elementary education, math, and science. (1997). White Plains, NY: Addison-Wesley Longman Supplementary Division.

Steffe, L. P. (Ed.). (1994). Mathematical learning in computer microworlds [Special issue]. *Journal of Research in Childhood Education, 8*(2).

Unifix software basic version (ver. 1). (1996). Rowley, MA: Didax.

Usiskin, Z. (Ed.). (1999, May/June). Groping and hoping for a consensus on calculator use. *Mathematics Education Dialogues.*

Action Books, Articles, and Videos

Brown, S. (1997). First graders write to discover mathematics' relevancy. *Young Children, 52*(4), 51–53.

Church, E. B. (2004). Tasty no-bake cooking. *Early Childhood Today, 18*(8), 30–36.

Heuser, D. (2000). Mathematics workshops: Mathematics class becomes learner centered. *Teaching Children Mathematics, 6*(5), 288–295.

Hildebrand, C., Ludeman, C. J., & Mullin, J. (1999). Integrating mathematics with problem solving using the mathematician's chair. *Teaching Children Mathematics, 5*(7), 434–441.

Kroll, L., & Halaby, M. (1997). Writing to learn mathematics in the primary school. *Young Children, 52*(4), 54–60.

Leitze, A. R. (1997). Connecting process problem solving to children's literature. *Teaching Children Mathematics, 3*(7), 398–405.

Merz, A. H., & Thomason, C. (2002). Sizing up the river. *Teaching Children Mathematics, 9*(3), 149–155.

Murray, A. (2001). Ideas on manipulative math for young children. *Young Children, 56*(4), 28–29.

Overholt, J. L., Dickson, S., & White-Holtz, J. (1999). *Big math activities for young children.* Clifton Park, NY: Thomson Delmar Learning.

Raleigh, J., Rigdon, D., & Goodman, S. (2001). Summer fun. *Teaching Children Mathematics, 7*(9), 528–529.

Reading Rainbow (literature videos). Phone: 800-228-4630.

Smith, N. L., Babione, C., & Vick, B. J. (1999). Dumpling soup: Exploring kitchens, cultures, and mathematics. *Teaching Children Mathematics, 6*(3), 148–152.

Swindal, D. N. (2000). Learning geometry and a new language. *Teaching Children Mathematics, 7*(4), 246–250.

Warfield, J. (2001). Teaching kindergarten children to solve word problems. *Early Childhood Education Journal, 28*(3), 161–168.

West, S., & Cox, A. (2004). *Literacy play.* Beltsville, MD: Gryphon House.

Wickett, M. S. (1997). Links to literature. Serving up number sense and problem solving: *Dinner at the panda palace. Teaching Children Mathematics, 3*(9), 476–480.

Studying the Environment

LeBeau, S. (1997). Mathematics and the environment. *Teaching Children Mathematics, 3*(8), 440–441.

Mann, R. (2003). Responses to the "A Walk in the Park Problem." *Teaching Children Mathematics, 10*(1), 54–59.

Sisson, E. A. (1981). *Nature with children of all ages.* New York: Prentice-Hall.

UNIT 29

Math in the Home

After reading this unit, you should be able to:

- Explain the importance of the home as an educational setting.
- Be knowledgeable about strategies for family involvement in math.
- Provide families with strategies and activities for teaching children at home.
- Describe a variety of activities that relate math to a child's everyday life.

The home is the first educational setting. Learning happens on a daily basis in the home: Children learn as they cook, set the table, sort laundry, pour sand and water, and build with blocks. Teachers of young children are in a unique position to help families make good use of these home learning opportunities. This unit provides guidelines for parents and other family members as teachers. It focuses on specific suggestions for emphasizing math as a vehicle for family learning.

Parents and other family members need to understand that children are eager to learn and can learn if provided with experiences that are developmentally appropriate. As teachers of young children, you can assist parents in recognizing that they do not need to go overboard purchasing expensive materials when there are a multitude of learning opportunities that center on everyday activities using resources naturally present in the environment.

Approaches to Family Involvement in Math

Encourage family members to find math in their homes. A large part of a child's time is spent in school, but the majority of time is still spent outside the classroom. Every day at home is filled with opportunities for children to explore and ask questions that encourage their thinking. It should be stressed that family entertainment does not have to be passive, such as watching TV. Activities that incorporate daily routines such as cooking, playing games, doing simple projects, and finding materials to bring to school, are opportunities for discovery, math, and family fun.

Getting the Family Involved

Changes in our economy and lifestyles have resulted in a multitude of family configurations that were rare or nonexistent in the past. A large percentage of mothers of young children work either to boost the family income or because they are the principal breadwinner, so they are not as available as their counterparts were in the past. Fathers work longer hours, sometimes holding down two jobs, and are also less able than in the past to participate in school-based activities. Family involvement in education has changed from the view that parents could be active participants only by coming to school and assisting with classroom activities and attending parent meetings and conferences. These are still important activities, but involvement has been expanded to include all family members and caregivers and to focus on opening lines of communication. Families are now provided with home learning tasks that can be performed as part of everyday living. Further, the use of home visits as a means for developing a good relationship with families is moving up from prekindergarten into the elementary school. The home visitor can model math activities in the home, suggest home materials that can be used for math, and explain how parents can boost their children's math achievement. Research indicates that family involvement influences math achievement (Cross, Woods, & Schweingruber, 2009). Children's pre-kindergarten experiences relate to school achievement. Teachers need to build on this knowledge. The following are suggestions for getting families involved and engaging them in their roles as teachers.

A first step could be the publication of a newsletter that could be sent home each month telling about the past month's events and including information about upcoming activities (see Figure 29–1 for a sample). Future activities could be described and/or sent in the form of a monthly calendar. Children can contribute to the newsletter. They can draw pictures and dictate and/or write news stories describing their experiences at school. Two or three children can contribute to each newsletter. Suggested home activities may be included in the newsletter and/or sent home as a separate booklet. See the NAEYC publication *Family-Friendly Communication for Early Childhood Programs* (Diffily & Morrison, 1996).

Kindergarten News

Published by Mr. Jones's Class ***Carver School***
October 1, 2005

School Gets Off to a Good Start

The day after Labor Day, the children started kindergarten. Eight children came each day to get acquainted with the room and find out what we do in kindergarten. Several children have contributed descriptions of what they liked best about coming to kindergarten.

José: I like being bigger than the 4-year-old classes.
Mimi: I like painting and playing house.
Ronny: My favorite was drawing and writing with markers on big paper and playing with trucks and blocks.
Nina: I liked finding my new friend Marcus.

Buddy the Bunny Joins Us

Last week, we had a late arrival in our class. Mr. Ortiz, who manages a pet store at the mall, brought us a black-and-white rabbit with a cage and a supply of food. The class discussed a number of names. The majority voted for the name Buddy ("'cause he will be our best friend"). Buddy is very friendly and enjoys fresh vegetables. If your child asks to bring a carrot or a little piece of lettuce, please send it, if possible. The children are taking turns bringing treats for Buddy.

The Month Ahead

We are looking forward to fall. We are reading the outdoor temperature every morning and recording the data on a graph. We watch each day for the leaves to change. Our observations are written and drawn in our daily class journal. We are planning a walk around the block to collect samples of the leaves that fall from the trees. We will report next month on what we see and what we find.

FIGURE 29–1 Sample classroom newsletter.

Getting parents or other family members to school for a meeting can be difficult. However, it is important that they become acquainted with the activities, the environment, their child's teacher, and families of other students. Meetings should provide important information and involve active experiences that will give families an understanding of appropriate educational experiences that can be followed up in the home.

The students should be actively involved in the planning so that their excitement and enthusiasm for the event will spill over to their parents. A program that has shown a great deal of success is Family Math (Lachance, 2007; Coates & Stenmark, 1997; Stenmark, Thompson, & Cossey, 1986). Parents come to school and do math activities with their children. They are then provided with instructions for follow-up activities they can do at home. Another procedure is to hold a Math Fun Day (Carey, 1990). For a Fun Day, several activities are set up in a large area, such as a gym or cafeteria. Families can be invited to take part as volunteer helpers and as active participants with their children. By having the Fun Day extend over several hours, busy people can more likely find a time when they can join in. See other resources listed at the end of this unit.

Families can also be asked to send waste materials to school as needed. The items listed in Figure 29–3 as aids to learning math at home are

---

Take Home Activity

Hello Family!

We have been working with groups of the amounts 0 to 10. *Ten Black Dots* is one of the books we are using to relate literature and math.

What can you do with ten black dots? This is a question we have worked on. In the book, rhymes suggest answers such as:

1. One dot can make a sun or a moon when day is done.
2. Two dots can make the eyes of a fox or the eyes of keys that open locks.

We have been working with black dots in class. Now it's time to do a job at home.

Home Job

1. Talk to your child about how dots can be used to make a picture. Make a list of ideas. Ten black dots are included below.

2. Have your child draw a picture including one or more black dots. Have the child write or dictate for you one or two sentences about the picture. A page is attached for writing and drawing.

FIGURE 29–2 Ten Black Dots take-home activity. Based on *Ten Black Dots* (Crews, 1986); created by Rosalind Charlesworth.

Note: A page can be attached for writing and drawing at home.

also useful at school. Each child can bring a pack of small brown paper lunch bags to school at the beginning of the year; then, if an item is needed, the children can draw and/or write the name of the item on the bag, take it home, and ask their parents to put the item in the bag to take to school. Do not be concerned if the younger children write symbols that are not conventional pictures or words—they will know what it is and can read the symbol to adults.

Family members who have the time may volunteer to assist in the classroom. Those who are not free during the day or who prefer not to be involved in the classroom are often delighted to make games and other materials at home. There should always be an open invitation for family members to visit school.

Parents or other major caregivers need to meet with their child's teacher in one-to-one conferences to exchange information about children's activities and progress. At these times, teacher and parent or other family member (and even the child) can review the student's portfolio of work and discuss goals for the future. At the same time, family members can describe what they have been doing at home with the child and relate any home events that may be affecting the child's behavior.

Homework becomes an important type of activity in the primary grades. Children can work their way into the more formal homework activities by bringing things requested from home as a part of their prekindergarten and kindergarten experiences. These activities help them develop responsibility and accustom parents to supporting classroom instruction. Homework should always be an extension of what has been taught at school. It may involve bringing some material to school; doing a simple project; or obtaining some information from a newspaper, magazine, or reference book. Be sure that all the information needed to guide the child to complete the assignment is included in the instructions. Assignments for young children should be something that can be easily completed in 10–15 minutes. Even kindergarten teachers are being pressured to provide homework assignments. These assignments should be

interactive, requiring a parent or sibling to assist. Figure 29–2 is an example of an activity that works very well with kindergartners. Articles by Burton and Baum (2009), Kliman (1999), and Kline (1999) provide ideas for home math support and activities. The February 1998 issue of *Teaching Children Mathematics* focuses on parent and community involvement (Edge, 1998).

An increasingly popular method for promoting developmentally appropriate home learning activities involves putting together small kits of materials that children can check out and take home for two or three days (Czerniak, 1994; Merenda, 1995; Seo & Bruk, 2003). Each kit includes materials and instruction for a home activity and some means for parents and children to return a report on the outcome. Many of the activities suggested later in this unit could be made into take-home kits.

Resources are available on the Internet that teachers can download to share with families or that families with Internet connections can download themselves. Government sites such as the U.S. Department of Education (DOE) have many excellent resources that can be downloaded free of charge in both English and Spanish. The Lawrence Hall of Science at the University of California, Berkeley, is the site for Equals and Family Math (lawrencehallofscience.org/equals and/kidsite). Activities can be downloaded and activity books purchased.

Guidelines for Families as Teachers at Home

Many families have questions about how they can provide learning experiences at home. They need to be reassured that naturalistic and informal experiences are at the heart of home learning. All during early childhood, play is the major vehicle for learning, both at school and at home. Exploration and discovery through play allow children to construct concepts. Adults should be encouraged to be positive models for their children. If adults are enthusiastic learners, their children are more likely to be enthusiastic learners, too.

From the Kitchen

egg cartons
cereal boxes and other empty food boxes
margarine tubs
milk cartons
milk jugs
plastic lids
pumpkin seeds
nuts
nutshells
straws
dry peas, beans, rice
coffee can and lids
other food and juice cans
baby food jars
potato chip cans
frozen food cartons
yogurt, cottage cheese,
    sour cream, or dip containers
milk bottle lids
individual small cereal boxes
soft drink bottle caps
plastic holder (soft drink six-pack carrier)
paper plates
coffee grounds
plastic bottles or jugs (soap, bleach, etc.)
plastic or metal tops or lids
Styrofoam meat plates (trays)
plastic bag twists
cardboard rolls (paper towels, foil, etc.)
kitchen scales
plastic forks, spoons
cleaned and dried bones

From All Around the House

sponges
magazines with pictures
catalogs (general, seed, etc.)
old crayons
shoe boxes and other small boxes (bar soap,
    toothpaste, aspirin, tape, etc.)
other cardboard boxes
    (not corrugated)
corrugated cardboard
cardboard tablet backs
scraps of wallpaper, carpeting
Contact paper
toothbrushes (for spattering paint)
lumber scraps
gift wrap (used or scraps)
gift wrap ribbon and bows
old greeting cards (pictures)
newspapers
jewelry
wire
clothesline
clocks
watches
small appliances
rubber or plastic hose
plastic tubing
plastic tubs
nails and screws
wood scraps
tools

From Outside

pebbles	bird feathers
rocks and stones	acorns
twigs, sticks, bark	animal teeth
leaves and weeds	insects
pinecones and nuts	mosses
seeds	abandoned nests
corn kernels and husks	nonpoisonous plants
soybeans	
flowers	
clay, mud, dirt, sand	
seashells	

From Sewing Scraps

buttons
snaps
fabric
felt
thread
yarn
lace
ribbon
trim
rickrack
spools

FIGURE 29–3 Math materials found at home.

Families can provide a close relationship where exploration is encouraged and where one-to-one conversation can enrich the young child's math language development. Adults and older children must be cautioned to be patient and allow young children the opportunity to explore, reflect, and construct concepts. They need to understand that children learn through repetition. Children do the same activities over and over before they assimilate what the experience has to offer and feel confident in their understandings. Families also need to realize that children learn through concrete experiences. They need to learn how to use simple household items and waste materials (Figure 29–3) as the focus for learning.

Provide examples of naturalistic, informal, and adult guided home learning experiences. *Naturalistic experiences* are those in which a concept is applied in an everyday activity, such as sorting laundry, counting out tableware, or watching the clock to get to an appointment on time. *Informal experiences* take place when the alert adult finds a way to involve the child in an activity such as asking the child to set the table, measure out cooking ingredients, learn his telephone number, and count the money in his piggy bank. The adult can also sing a song or chant a rhyme on the spur of the moment and provide materials the child can use on his own (such as blocks, sets of dishes, construction materials, and the like). *Adult guided activities* are not usually appropriate before age 3. Adults need to take care that, when they introduce activities, they do not pressure the child if he seems uninterested or not ready. Suggest that adults pull back and try again in two or three weeks. Emphasize that the youngest children need time to explore materials before adults present preplanned questions or problems to them. Hansen (2005) describes daily learning opportunities with art, food, bath, blocks, chores, games, books, and other home activities. Primary grade children can be helped with their homework as adults provide hints and ask open-ended questions that support the children's thinking processes and enable them to arrive at their own problem solutions.

Math in the Home, Yard, Neighborhood, and Park

Many math activities can be done in the home, backyard, neighborhood, park, or even on a vacation trip. Any of the following activities could be included in a home newsletter and/or activity booklet or monthly calendar. Activities begin with daily home routines and then move into other areas.

Daily Routines

Families should be encouraged to emphasize the skills of math as they go about their daily routines. Here are some examples.

1. As laundry is sorted and socks are matched, talk about the differences and similarities in the articles. Then fold the clothes, and put them in the correct places. Ask, "**Where do the pants go? Where shall we put the T-shirts?**" Even small children will begin the process of classification as they note the differences in characteristics.

2. Children can examine their bodies counting and measuring the parts. They have five toes on each foot; they have two eyes, two arms, etc. They can measure the parts with string or yarn and compare the lengths.

3. When kitchen utensils are returned to drawers after washing or food is put away after a shopping trip, discuss why they go where they do. Say, "**Where shall we put the spoons? Should the crackers go in the cupboard or the refrigerator?**" Some parents might want to lay items such as spoons, spatulas, or cups on the table and see how many ways children can devise to group items: for example, things you eat with, things you cook with, things you drink with, and so on.

4. Begin a button collection for classifying, counting, and crafts. Have children sort buttons by size, color, and number of holes. Trace around the buttons to make designs. Paste the buttons on cardboard, and paint them. Graph the button attributes.

5. Collect scraps of wood, and make things with the wood. Give children a hammer and some nails and say, "**Let's make something with this wood**." When the wood sculpture is completed, have the child name it and propose a function.

Cooking with Children

Cooking provides many opportunities for parents to provide children with practical applications of math. When someone is cooking, the child can measure the ingredients, observe them as they change form during cooking (or mixing), and taste the final product.

Children should be given as much responsibility for the food preparation as possible. This might include shopping for the food; washing; possibly cutting (carefully supervised, of course); reading and following the recipe; baking, cooking, or freezing; setting the food on the table; and cleaning up. The more the parent does, the less the child learns.

Try making an easy pizza. You will need muffins, tomato sauce, oregano, mozzarella cheese slices, and meat or mushrooms. Spread half of the muffin with a tablespoon of tomato sauce. Add a pinch of oregano. Put meat or mushroom on the sauce and then add a layer of cheese. Place the little pizza on a cookie sheet and bake for 10 minutes at 425°.

Children enjoy getting creative with food. Create Bugs on a Log by spreading peanut butter on pieces of celery. Top off the "log" with raisin "bugs."

Make Summer Slush. Freeze a favorite fruit juice in ice cube trays. After the cubes are hard, place them in the blender, and blend. Add extra juice if needed for a slushy consistency.

Save the seeds from a jack-o'-lantern or a Thanksgiving pumpkin pie. Clean them thoroughly and then dip them in a solution of salt water (1 tablespoon salt in 1½ cups of water). Drain off the water, and spread the seeds on an ungreased cookie sheet. Bake at 350°. Stir every five minutes to be sure that they dry out and toast lightly on all sides. When lightly toasted, remove from oven, cool, crack, and eat.

Curious George's favorite is to spread a banana with peanut butter and roll it in ground nuts or wheat germ. Quarter an apple and spread peanut butter on the cut sides. Roll the apple slices in one or more of the following: wheat germ, raisins, coconut, ground nuts, or sesame seeds.

Math Activities Here and There

The following are a selection of home math activities. For more ideas, see the resources listed at the end of the unit.

Find the Numerals Using a newspaper page of grocery advertisements, find and mark numbers that are alike; for example, "Find all the fours." The child with well-developed motor skills can cut out the numerals and glue those that are alike on separate sheets of paper to make a number book.

A Monthly Caterpillar Cut out and number one circle for each day of the month. Make a caterpillar head from one additional circle. Tape the head to the refrigerator or cabinet door. Each day, add the appropriately numbered circle. Point to and count the numbers.

Traveling Numerals When driving or walking along highways and streets, have the child watch for numerals to identify.

Snack Shapes Cut sandwiches into circles, squares, rectangles, and/or triangles. Buy crackers in a variety of shapes.

Fraction Food When the parent or the child is cutting foods (especially bananas or carrots), suggest that the foods be cut in two pieces (halves), three pieces (thirds), and so on. Introduce fraction vocabulary.

How Many? Play counting games, such as "How many doorknobs in this room?" "How many legs on the kitchen chairs?" "How many numbers on the microwave?" and so on.

Measure Things   Encourage the child to describe the size of things using comparison words: *big(-ger, -gest), small(-er, -est), tall (-er, -est), short (-er, -est), wide (-r, -st), narrow (-er, -est),* and the like. Keep a record of the child's height and weight with a wall measurement poster, so the numbers can be checked at any time. Compare the children's measurements with their siblings, friends, and adults. Have the younger child do informal measurements of things in the house and outdoors using paper clips, toothpicks, body parts (such as hands or feet), string, and so on. Have the older (primary level) child use a clearly labeled ruler.

Learn about Money   Play simple games. For example, play "store" using objects such as empty food containers or the child's toys. Mark each item with a price tag in an amount that is understandable at the child's developmental level: in pennies for younger children and in larger amounts for older children. Work with pennies at first, and have the child count out the number of pennies needed to buy an item. When the child is successful with pennies, introduce the nickel as equal to five pennies. Price some items above 5¢, and have the child work with pennies and nickels. Go on to dimes, quarters, and dollars when the child is ready. The older children enjoy *Monopoly*.

Growing Things   Children enjoy caring for and observing their own plants as they grow. Bean seeds usually grow fast and do well under any circumstances. Place three bean seeds in a plastic bag with air holes or in a plastic cup along with a wet paper towel. This will allow the roots and stems to be observed. Keep a record of the plants' growth. Point out the roots, stems, and leaves. Keep the paper towel wet.

Bathtub Fun   Keep a supply of safe plastic containers and plastic boats in the bathroom. Let the child explore these materials during bath time.

Shape Hunt   Search for shapes in the environment, both indoors and out.

Picture Sort   Collect pictures of animals, vehicles, people, etc. Have children sort by size, shape, color, or other attributes.

Eye Spy   Encourage both observational and questioning skills. Take turns describing objects in the room and have the other person(s) guess what it is by asking up to 20 questions.

Math in Nature

The outdoors affords many opportunities for family activities that center on nature. Whether in urban, suburban, or small-town settings, the outdoors affords rich opportunities for observation and interaction.

A Family Bird Walk

A bird walk will heighten the observational skills of everyone involved. Families can categorize birds by characteristics such as:

- Hop when they move on the ground.
- Peck at the ground.
- Hold their heads to one side and appear to be listening to something in the ground.
- Flap their wings a lot when they fly.
- Glide and hardly move their wings.
- Climb on the side of trees.
- Fly alone.
- Fly with many other birds.
- Make a lot of noise.
- Eat alone.
- Blend in well with the grass, trees, or sky.
- Swim in the pond.

Select a favorite bird, and find out as much as you can about it. This can be a family project. Use birdcall audio tapes or videotapes to identify the birds that you have seen and heard on the bird walk. Children will enjoy creating bird stories, art projects, and puzzles as well as reading more about the birds they have observed. For helpful information on identifying birds and creating a backyard habitat, see Burke (1983), Cook (1978), Cosgrove (1976), and Kress (1985).

Trees and Seeds

In the backyard, the neighborhood, or the park, children can find leaves, seeds, and cones. A tree walk can prove very interesting. Carry a paper or plastic bag for collecting treasures. First talk about what you might collect, and then begin your hunt. Children can use some of their collection to make a collage; they can glue items onto cardboard. They can sort the items and count and graph the groups. Visit a tree and discuss the parts: trunk, bark, branches, leaves or needles, pods or cones, and roots. Observe the tree in different seasons of the year. Draw pictures of the tree, and describe it in each season.

Sort Rocks or Shells

Collect rocks and/or shells and encourage the child to sort them by color, shape, size, texture, etc. Compare them by weight. If you do not live near the beach, you can purchase collections of shells online.

Exploring Math with Technology

The resources listed in most units are available for parental purchase and online downloading or interaction. Hand calculators may be explored at home using the same types of activities suggested in Unit 22. Also, children's TV channel websites such as *PBS Kids, Noggin,* and *Disney* have many online activities using the characters that are familiar to children from their daily television viewing. At the *Sesame Street* site, children can practice counting with the Count's Number of the Day activities or Journey to Ernie for problem solving with matching and pattern recognition. At the *Mr. Rogers' Neighborhood* site, there are simple recipes for cooking and projects such as making a bird feeder or a rocket ship. On the "Lawrence Hall of Science Kidsite," there are activities such as *Measure Yourself* and *How Old is a Penny?* The Family Math Site activities can be downloaded such as *Mixtures* for young children and *The Balloon Ride for* older children.

Summary

Mathematics can provide many opportunities for informal family sharing. Family members can encourage children to explore, ask questions, and think about the world around them. A single guiding question from an adult can turn a daily routine into a learning experience. As children cook, observe, sort, investigate, construct, and explore software and the Internet, they are using the skills needed to learn mathematics. Rocks, trees, shells, and other outdoor inhabitants make ideal subjects for observation and exploration. Technology provides many opportunities for math experiences.

SUGGESTED ACTIVITIES

1. Add 15 home math activities to your Activity File/Notebook: five each for prekindergarten, kindergarten, and primary.
2. Plan a workshop for families on math in the home. Present the workshop to the class.
3. Interview at least three parents. Ask them what types of math activities they do with their children. Find out what problems, concerns, or needs they might have in doing math with their children.

REVIEW

A. Why is the home a good place to emphasize math?

B. List and describe three opportunities for learning math in the home.

C. How does cooking relate to integration of science and math?

D. Describe two family nature activities involving math.

REFERENCES

Burke, K. (1983). *How to attract birds.* San Francisco: Ortho Books. (A well-illustrated book with an informative text about providing food, water, and nest sites for both eastern and western birds.)

Burton, M., & Baum, A.C. (2009). Engage families in meaningful mathematics. *Teaching Children Mathematics, 16*(1), 12–15.

Carey, J. H. (1990). Science fun: Have a field day in the gym. *Science and Children, 28*(2), 16–19.

Coates, G. D., & Stenmark, J. K. (1997). *Family math for young children.* Berkely, CA: Lawrence Hall of Science.

Cook, B. C. (1978). *Invite a bird to dinner.* New York: Lathrop. (A children's book about feeding birds with good ideas for making feeders out of everyday materials.)

Cosgrove, I. (1976). *My recipes are for the birds.* New York: Doubleday. (A book full of recipes, featuring treats such as Cardinal Casserole, Finch Fries, and Dove Delight.)

Crews, D. (1986). *Ten black dots.* New York: Mulberry.

Cross, C. T., Woods. T. A., & Schweingruber, H. (Eds.). (2009). *Mathematics learning in early childhood.* Washington, DC: National Academies Press.

Czerniak, C. M. (1994). Backpack science. *Science and Children, 32*(1), 46–47.

Diffily, D., & Morrison, K. (Eds.). (1996). *Family-friendly communication for early childhood programs.* Washington, DC: National Association for the Education of Young Children.

Edge, D. (Ed.). (1998). Beyond the classroom: Linking mathematics learning with parents, communities, and business and industry [Special issue]. *Teaching Children Mathematics, 4*(6).

Hansen, L. E. (2005). ABCs of early math experiences. *Teaching Children Mathematics, 12*(4), 208–212.

Kliman, M. (1999). Parents and children doing mathematics at home. *Teaching Children Mathematics, 6*(3), 140–146.

Kline, K. (1999). Helping at home. *Teaching Children Mathematics, 5*(8), 456–460.

Kress, S. W. (1985). *The Audubon Society guide to attracting birds.* New York: Scribner's.

Lachance, A. (2007). Family math nights: Collaborative celebrations of mathematical learning. *Teaching Children Mathematics, 13*(8), 404–408.

Merenda, R. C. (1995). A book, a bed, a bag: Interactive homework for "10." *Teaching Children Mathematics, 1*(5), 262–266.

Seo, K., & Bruk, S. J. (2003). Promoting young children's mathematical learning through a new twist on homework. *Teaching Children Mathematics, 10*(1), 26–31.

Stenmark, D. D., Thompson, V., & Cossey, R. (1986). *Family math.* Berkeley, CA: University of California Press.

FURTHER READING AND RESOURCES

Teacher Resources

Boling, K. B., & Larson, C. N. (2002). Horizons: A mother–daughter mathematics club. *Teaching Children Mathematics, 8*(5), 284–289.

Clements, D. H., & Sarama, J. (2005). Math play: How young children approach math. *Early Childhood Education Today, 19*(4), 50–57.

Hall, J. B., & Acri, R. P. (1995). A fourth-grade family math night. *Teaching Children Mathematics, 2*(1), 8–10.

Kyle, D. W., McIntyre, E., & Moore, G. H. (2001). Connecting mathematics instruction with the families of young children. *Teaching Children Mathematics, 8*(2), 80–86.

Lazerick, B., & Seidel, J. D. (1996). Tech times news from the net. Helping your child learn math. *Teaching Children Mathematics, 3*(3), 141.

Schussheim, J. Y. (2004). Large-scale family math nights: A primer for collaboration. *Teaching Children Mathematics, 10*(5), 254–257.

Strutchens, M. E. (2002). Multicultural literature as a context for problem solving: Children and parents learning together. *Teaching Children Mathematics, 8*(8), 448–454.

Washington, V., Johnson, V., & McCracken, J. B. (1995). *Grassroots success! Preparing families and schools for each other.* Washington, DC: National Association for the Education of Young Children.

Weiss, H. B. (1999). Partnerships among families, early childhood educators, and communities to promote early learning in science, mathematics and technology. In *Dialogue on early childhood science, mathematics, and technology education.* Washington, DC: American Association for the Advancement of Science.

Witzel, B. S. (Winter 2008–2009). A response: Highlighting key elements of the national mathematics advisory panel's blueprint, *Childhood Education, 85*(2), 118–119.

Family Resources

Allison, L., & Weston, M. (1993). *Eenie meenie miney MATH.* Boston: Little, Brown.

Barber, J., Parizeau, N., & Bergman, L. (2002). *Spark your child's success in math and science: Practical advice for parents.* Berkeley, CA: Lawrence Hall of Science.

Bennett, S., & Bennett, R. (1993). *The official playroom activity book.* New York: Random House.

Colker, L. J. (2005). *The cooking book.* Washington, DC: National Association for the Education of Young Children.

Kenschaft, P. C. (1997). *Math power: How to help your child love math, even if you don't.* Reading, MA: Addison-Wesley Longman.

PBS Parents. Many activities and guidelines. Retrieved August 4, 2008, from http://www.pbs.org

Polonsky, L. (1995). *Math for the very young: A handbook of activities for parents and teachers.* New York: Wiley.

Wanamaker, N., Hearn, K., & Richard, S. (1979). *More than graham crackers.* Washington, DC: National Association for the Education of Young Children.

Wellnitz, W. R. (1992). *Science in your backyard.* Blue Ridge Summit, PA: TAB Books.

Math

Axelrod, A. (1997). *Pigs will be pigs: Fun with math and money.* Simon & Schuster, Alladin Picture Books.

Brunetto, C. F. (1997). *MathART projects and activities.* (grades 3–5). New York: Scholastic.

Churchman, S. (2006). *Bringing math home: A parent's guide to elementary school math: Games, activities, projects.* Chicago: Zephyr Press.

Egan, L. H. (no date). *25 Super cool math board games.* (grades 3–6). Jefferson City, MO: Scholastic Professional Books.

Franco, B. (no date). *Counting caterpillars and other math poems*. New York: Sholastic.

Schiller, P., & Peterson, L. (1997). *Count on math: Activities for small hands and lively minds*. Beltsville, MD: Gryphon House, Inc.

Schiro, M., & Walker, A. (1995). *Mega-fun math games: 70 quick-and-easy games to build math skills*. (grades 2–5). New York: Scholastic.

Stenmark, J. K., Coates, G., & Rose, C. (1997). *Family math for young children: Comparing*. (Equals series). Berkeley, CA: University of California Press.

Taylor-Cox, J. (2005). *Family math night: Math standards in action*. Larchmont, NY: Eye on Education.

Wickelgren, W. A., & Wickelgren, I. (2001). *Math coach: A parent's guide to helping children succeed in math*. New York: Berkeley Books, Penguin Putnam.

Williams, A., & Cunningham, D. *Preschool math*. Beltsville, MD: Gryphon House.

Cooking

Better Homes and Gardens. *(2004). New junior cookbook*. DesMoines, IA: BGH.com, Meredith Corporation.

Cook, D. (2006). *Family fun. Cooking with kids*. New York: Disney PublishAmerica.

Davis, T. (2004). *Look and cook: A cookbook for children*. New York: Abrams.

Ibbs, K. (2004). *DK children's cookbook*. New York: DK Publishing.

Johnson, K. D. (2009). *How kids can have fun in the kitchen: A child's first cookbook*. Frederick, MD: Enterprises, Inc.

Nissenberg, H., & Nissenberg, S. K. (1998). *I made it myself!: Mud cups, pizza puffs, and over 100 other fun and healthy recipes for kids to make*. Minneapolis, MN: Chronimed Publishing.

Ray, R. (2004). *Cooking rocks! Rachael Ray 30-minute meals for kids*. Available from Amazon.com

Wilkes, A. (1997). *Children's quick and easy cookbook*. New York: DK Publishing.

Research

Cannon, J., & Ginsburg, H. P. (2008). "Doing the math": Maternal beliefs about early mathematics vs. language learning. *Early Education and Development, 19*(2), 238–260.

Lee, J. S., & Ginsburg, H. P. (2007). Preschool teachers' beliefs about appropriate early literacy and mathematics education for low- and middle-socioeconomic status children. *Early Education and Development, 18*(1), 111–143.

Skwarchuk, S. (2009). How do parents support preschoolers' numeracy learning experiences at home? *Early Childhood Education Journal, 37*(3), 189–198.

Webb, P., & Austin, P. (2009). The family maths programme: parents' perceptions of what influences their engagement, enjoyment, and confidence within a complex learning community. *Education as Change, 13*(1), 27–44.

Appendices

Appendix A

Developmental Assessment Tasks*

* Tasks that have been used as samples in the text.

Sensorimotor: Level 1

1A

**Sensorimotor
Age 2 months**

General Development

METHOD: Interview.

SKILLS: Perceptual/motor.

MATERIALS: Familiar object/toy such as a rattle.

PROCEDURES/EVALUATIONS:
1. Talk to the infant. Notice if he seems to attend and respond (by looking at you, making sounds, and/or changing facial expression).
2. Hold a familiar object within the infant's reach. Note if he reaches out for it.
3. Move the object through the air across the infant's line of vision. He should follow it with his eyes.
4. Hand the small toy to the infant. He should hold it for two to three seconds.

1B

**Sensorimotor
Age 4 months**

General Development

METHOD: Observation.

SKILLS: Perceptual/motor.

MATERIALS: Assortment of appropriate infant toys.

PROCEDURES/EVALUATIONS:
1. Note each time you offer the infant a toy. Does she usually grab hold of it?
2. Place the infant where it is possible for her to observe the surroundings (such as in an infant seat) in a situation where there is a lot of activity. Note if her eyes follow the activity and if she seems to be interested and curious.

1C

**Sensorimotor
Age 6 months**

General Development

METHOD: Interview and observation.

SKILLS: Perceptual/motor.

MATERIALS: Several nontoxic objects/toys including infant's favorite toy.

PROCEDURES/EVALUATIONS:
1. One by one, hand the infant a series of nontoxic objects. Note how many of his senses he uses for exploring the objects. He should be using eyes, mouth, and hands.

2. Place yourself out of the infant's line of vision. Call out to him. Note if he turns his head toward your voice.
3. When the infant drops an object, note whether he picks it up again.
4. When the infant is eating, notice if he can hold his bottle in both hands by himself.
5. Show the infant his favorite toy. Slowly move the toy to a hiding place. Note if the infant follows with his eyes as the toy is hidden.

1D   **Sensorimotor**
                                                                         Age 12 months

General Development

METHOD: Interview and observation.

SKILLS: Perceptual/motor and receptive language.

MATERIALS: Two bells or rattles; two blocks or other small objects; two clear plastic cups; pillow or empty box; a cookie, if desired.

PROCEDURES/EVALUATIONS:

1. Note if the infant will imitate you when you perform the following activities (for each task, provide the infant with a duplicate set of materials).
   a. Shake a bell (or a rattle).
   b. Play peek-a-boo by placing your open palms in front of your eyes.
   c. Put a block (or other small object) into a cup; take it out of the cup, and place it next to the cup.
2. Partially hide a familiar toy or a cookie under a pillow or a box as the child watches. Note whether the infant searches for it.
3. Note whether the infant is creeping, crawling, pulling up to her feet, trying to walk, or is actually walking.
4. Note whether the infant responds to the following verbal commands:
   a. NO, NO.
   b. GIVE ME THE (name of object).

Sensorimotor: Level 2

2A   **Sensorimotor**
                                                                         Ages 12–18 months

General Development

METHOD: Interview and observation.

SKILLS: Perceptual/motor and receptive language.

MATERIALS: Several safe containers and a supply of safe, nontoxic objects.

PROCEDURES/EVALUATIONS:
1. Give the child several containers and the supply of small objects. Note if he fills the containers with objects and dumps them out repeatedly.
2. Tell the child, *"point to your nose, head, eyes, foot, stomach."*
3. Hide a familiar object completely. Note whether the child searches for it.

2B   **Sensorimotor**
                                                                          Ages 18–24 months

General Development

METHOD:	Interview and observation.
SKILLS:	Perceptual/motor and receptive and expressive language.
MATERIALS:	Child's own toys (or other assortment provided by you, such as a ball, toy dog, toy car, blocks, baby bottle, doll, and the like).

PROCEDURES/EVALUATIONS:
1. During playtime observations, note if the child is beginning to organize objects in rows and put similar objects together in groups.
2. Ask the child to point to familiar objects. *"Point to the ball (chair, doll, car)."*
3. Note whether the child begins to name the parts of her body (usually two parts at 18 months).

Preoperational: Level 3

3A*   **Preoperational**
                                                                                  Ages 2–3

One-to-One Correspondence: see Unit 8 for task

3B   **Preoperational**
                                                                                  Ages 2–3

Number Sense and Counting: Unit 9

METHOD:	Interview.
SKILL:	Child understands the concept of "twoness" and can rational count at least two objects.
MATERIALS:	Ten counters (cube blocks, Unifix Cubes, or other objects).

PROCEDURES:
1. Ask, *"how old are you?"*
2. Give the child two objects. *"How many (name of objects) are there?"* If the child succeeds, try three objects. Go on as far as the child can go.

EVALUATION:
1. May hold up appropriate number of fingers or answer "two" or "three."
2. Should be able to rational count two objects (or possibly recognize two without counting).

3C   **Preoperational**
                                                                            Ages 2–3

Logic and Classifying, Informal Sorting: Unit 10

METHOD:	Observation and informal interviewing.
SKILL:	While playing, the child groups toys by various criteria such as color, shape, size, class name, and so on.
MATERIALS:	Assortment of normal toys for 2- to 3-year-olds.
PROCEDURE:	As the child plays, note whether toys are grouped by classification criteria (see Unit 10). Ask, *"Show me the red blocks. Which car is the biggest? Find some square blocks."*
EVALUATION:	The child should naturally group by similarities, should be able to group objects by at least one or two colors, and should be able to find objects from the same class.

3D   **Preoperational**
                                                                            Ages 2–3

Comparing, Informal Measurement: Unit 11

METHOD:	Interview.
SKILL:	Child can respond to comparison terms applied to familiar objects.
MATERIALS:	Pairs of objects that vary on comparative criteria, such as

large–small	cold–hot
heavy–light	fat–skinny
long–short	higher–lower

PROCEDURE:	Show the child the pairs of objects one pair at a time. Ask, *"Point to the big (ball). Point to the small or little (ball)."* Continue with other pairs of objects and object concept words.
EVALUATION:	Note how many of the objects the child can Identify correctly.

3E

Preoperational
Ages 2–3

Comparing, Number: Unit 11

METHOD:	Interview.
SKILL:	Shown a set of one and six or more, the child can identify which set has more.
MATERIALS:	Twenty counters (e.g., pennies, Unifix Cubes, cube blocks).
PROCEDURE:	Place two groups of objects in front of the child: one group with a set of one object and one group with a set of six or more. Ask, ***"Which has more (object name)? Point to the one with more."***
EVALUATION:	Note if the child identifies the group that contains more.

3F

Preoperational
Ages 2–3

Shape, Matching: Unit 12

METHOD:	Interview.
SKILL:	Child can match an object or cutout shape to another of the same size and shape.
MATERIALS:	Attribute blocks or shape cutouts; one red circle, square, and triangle; one green circle, square, and triangle. All should be the same relative size.
PROCEDURE:	Place the three green shapes in front of the child. One at a time, show the child each of the red shapes and tell the child, ***"Find a green shape that is the same as this red one."***
EVALUATION:	The child should be able to make all three matches.

3G*

Preoperational
Ages 2–3

Space, Position: see Unit 13 for task

3H*

Preoperational
Ages 2–3

Parts and Wholes, Missing Parts: see Unit 14 for task

3I   **Preoperational**
                                                                            Ages 2–3

Ordering, Size: Unit 17

METHOD: Interview.

SKILL: Child can order three objects that vary in one size dimension.

MATERIALS: Three objects of the same shape that vary in one size dimension, such as diameter.

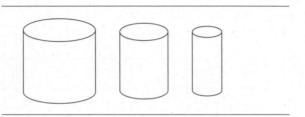

Paper towel rolls can be cut into proportional lengths (heights) for this task. More objects can be available in reserve to be used for more difficult seriation tasks.

PROCEDURE: *"Watch what I do."* Line up the objects in order from fattest to thinnest (longest to shortest, tallest to shortest). *"Now I'll mix them up. (Do so.) Put them in a row like I did."* If the child does the task with three objects, try it with five.

EVALUATION: Note whether the objects are placed in a correct sequence.

3J   **Preoperational**
                                                                            Ages 2–3

Measuring, Volume: Unit 18

METHOD: Observation.

SKILL: Child evidences an understanding that different containers hold different amounts.

MATERIALS: A large container filled with small objects such as small blocks, paper clips, table tennis balls, or teddy-bear counters or with a substance such as water, rice, or legumes; several different size small containers for pouring.

PROCEDURE: Let the children experiment with filling and pouring. Note any behavior that indicates they recognize that different containers hold different amounts.

EVALUATION: Children should experiment, filling containers and pouring back into the large container, pouring into larger small containers, and into smaller containers. Note behaviors such as whether they line up smaller containers and fill each from a larger container or fill a larger container using a smaller one.

Preoperational: Level 4

4A

**Preoperational
Ages 2–3**

One-to-One Correspondence, Same Things/Related Things: Unit 8

METHOD: Interview.

SKILLS:
1. Child can match, in one-to-one correspondence, pairs of objects that are alike.
2. Child can match, in one-to-one correspondence, pairs of objects that are related but not alike.

MATERIALS:
1. Four different pairs of matching objects (such as two toy cars, two small plastic animals, two coins, two blocks).
2. Two groups of four related objects such as four cups and four saucers, four cowboys and four horses, four flowers and four flowerpots, four hats and four heads.

PROCEDURES:
1. Matching like pairs. Place the objects in front of the child in a random array. *"Find the things that belong together."* If there is no response, pick up one. *"Find one like this."* When the match is made, *"Find some other things that belong together."* If there is no spontaneous response, continue to select objects, and ask the child to find the one like each.
2. Matching related pairs. Place two related groups of four in front of the child in a random array. *"Find a cup for each saucer (or a cowboy for each horse)."*

EVALUATIONS:
1. Note if the child matches spontaneously and if he makes an organized pattern (such as placing the pairs side by side or in a row).
2. Note if the child is organized and uses a pattern for placing the objects (such as placing the objects in two matching rows).

4B

**Preoperational
Ages 3–4**

Number Sense and Counting, Rote and Rational: Unit 9

METHOD: Interview.

SKILL: Child can rote and rational count.

MATERIALS: Twenty counters (e.g., cube blocks, pennies, Unifix Cubes).

PROCEDURE: First have the child rote count. *"Count for me. Start with one and count."* If the child hesitates, *"one, two, _____. What comes next?"* Next ask, "how old are you?" Finally, place four counters in front of the child. *"Count the (objects).*

How many (_____) are there?" If the child cannot count four items, try two or three. If she counts four easily, put out more counters, and ask her to count as many as she can.

EVALUATION: Note if she can rote count more than five and rational count at least five items. When she rational counts more than four, she should keep track of each item by touching each methodically or moving those counted to the side.

4C
**Preoperational
Ages 3–4**

Logic and Classifying, Object Sorting: Unit 10

METHOD: Interview.

SKILL: Child can sort objects into groups using logical criteria.

MATERIALS: Twelve objects: two red, two blue, two green, two yellow, two orange, two purple. There should be at least five kinds of objects; for example:

Color	Object 1	Object 2
red	block	car
blue	ball	cup
green	comb	car
yellow	block	bead
orange	comb	cup
purple	bead	ribbon

In addition, you will need six to ten small containers (bowls or boxes).

PROCEDURE: Place the 12 objects in random array in front of the child. Provide him with the containers. *"Put the toys that belong together in a bowl (box). Use as many bowls (boxes) as you need."*

EVALUATION: Note whether the child uses any specific criteria as he makes his groups.

4D*
**Preoperational
Ages 3–4**

Comparing, Number: see Unit 11 for task

4E*	Preoperational Ages 3–4
Shape, Identification: see Unit 12 for task	

4F*	Preoperational Ages 3–4
Space, Position: see Unit 13 for task	

4G*	Preoperational Ages 3–6
Rote Counting: see Unit 9 for task	

4H*	Preoperational Ages 3–6
Rational Counting: see Unit 9 for task	

4I*	Preoperational Ages 3–6
Time, Identify Clock or Watch: see Unit 19 for task	

4J*	Preoperational Ages 3–6
Symbols, Recognition: see Unit 23 for task	

Preoperational: Level 5

5A	Preoperational Ages 4–5
One-to-One Correspondence, Same Things/Related Things: Unit 8 Do tasks in 4A (1 and 2) using more pairs of objects.	

5B   **Preoperational**
                                                             Ages 4–5

Number Sense and Counting, Rote and Rational: Unit 9
See 4B, 4G, and 4H.

5C   **Preoperational**
                                                             Ages 4–5

Comparing, Number: Unit 11

METHOD: Interview.

SKILL: The child can compare the amounts in groups up to five and label the ones that are
                  more, less, and fewer.

MATERIALS: Ten counters (e.g., chips, inch cubes, Unifix Cubes).

PROCEDURE: Present the following groups for comparison in sequence:

                  1 versus 5

                  4 versus 1

                  2 versus 5

                  3 versus 2

                  5 versus 4

                  Each time a pair of groups is presented, ask, ***"Does one group have more?"*** If the
                  answer is yes, ***"Point to the group that has more. Ask, "How do you know that
                  group has more?"*** If the child responds correctly to *more,* present the pairs again
                  using LESS and FEWER.

EVALUATION: Note for which comparisons the child responds correctly. Can she give a logical
                  reason for her choices (such as "Four is more than one" or "I counted them")?
                  Does she place them in one-to-one correspondence?

5D*   **Preoperational**
                                                             Ages 4–5

Comparing, Informal Measurement: see Unit 11 for task

5E*   **Preoperational**
                                                             Ages 4–5

Shape, Geometric Shape Recognition: see Unit 12 for task

5F*   **Preoperational**
                                                                   Ages 4–5

Parts and Wholes, Parts of a Whole: see Unit 14 for task

5G*   **Preoperational**
                                                                   Ages 4–5

Ordering, Sequential/Ordinal Number: see Unit 17 for task

5H*   **Preoperational**
                                                                   Ages 4–5

Time, Labeling, and Sequence: see Unit 19 for task

5I   **Preoperational**
                                                                   Ages 4–5

Practical Activities, Money: Unit 22

METHOD: Observation and interview.

SKILL: Child understands that money is exchanged for goods and services and can identify nickel, dime, penny, and dollar bill.

MATERIALS:
1. Play money and store props for dramatic play.
2. Nickel, dime, penny, and dollar bill.

PROCEDURE:
1. Set up play money and props for dramatic play as described in Unit 22. Observe the child, and note if he demonstrates some concept of exchanging money for goods and services and of giving and receiving change.
2. Show the child a nickel, dime, penny, and dollar bill. ***"Tell me the name of each of these."***

EVALUATION: Note the child's knowledge of money during dramatic play and note which, if any, of the pieces of money he recognizes.

The following tasks can be presented first between ages 4 and 5 and then repeated as the child's concepts and skills grow and expand.

5J*

**Preoperational
Ages 4–6**

Logic and Classifying, Free Sort: see Unit 10 for task

5K*

**Preoperational
Ages 4–6**

Logic and Classifying, Clue Sort: see Unit 10 for task

5L*

**Preoperational
Ages 4–6**

Symbols, Sequencing: see Unit 23 for task

5M

**Preoperational
Ages 4–5**

Naturalistic and Informal Activities

METHOD: Observation.

SKILL: Child can demonstrate a knowledge of math concepts and skills during naturalistic and informal activities.

MATERIALS: Math center (three-dimensional and two-dimensional materials), sand/water/legume pouring table, dramatic play props, unit blocks and accessories, cooking center, math concept books.

PROCEDURE: Develop a recording system and keep a record of behaviors such as the following.

- Chooses to work in the math center.
- Selects math concept books to look at.
- Chooses to work in the cooking center.
- Selects working with sand, water, or legumes.
- Can give each person one napkin, one glass of juice, and so on.
- Spontaneously counts objects or people.
- While playing, spontaneously separates objects or pictures into logical groups.
- Spontaneously uses comparison words (e.g., This one is *bigger*).
- Chooses to build with blocks.
- Knows the parts of people and objects.

- Demonstrates a knowledge of *first, biggest, heaviest,* and other order concepts.
- Does informal measurement such as identifying hot and cold, a bigger container and a smaller container, and so on.
- Evidences a concept of time (What do we do next? Is it time for lunch?).
- Points out number symbols in the environment.
- Uses the language of math (whether he or she understands the concepts or not).

EVALUATION: Child should show an increase in frequency of these behaviors as the year progresses.

Preoperational: Level 6

6A*

One-to-One Correspondence: see Unit 8 for task

Preoperational
Ages 5–6

6B

Number Sense and Counting, Rote and Rational: Unit 9

Preoperational
Ages 5–6

METHOD: Interview.

SKILL: Child can rote and rational count.

MATERIALS: Fifty counters (e.g., chips, cube blocks, Unifix Cubes).

PROCEDURES:
1. Rote counting. ***"Count for me as far as you can."*** If the child hesitates, say ***"one, two, _____. What's next?"***
2. Rational counting. Present the child with 20 objects. ***"How many _____ are there? Count them for me."***

EVALUATION:
1. *Rote.* By age 5, the child should be able to count to 10 or more; by age 6, to 20 or more. Note if any number names are missed or repeated.
2. *Rational.* Note the degree of accuracy and organization. Does she place the objects to ensure that no object is counted more than once or that no object is missed? Note how far she goes without making a mistake. Does she repeat any number names? Skip any? By age 6, she should be able to go beyond 10 objects with accuracy.

6C

**Preoperational
Ages 5–6**

Shape, Recognition and Reproduction: Unit 12

METHOD:	Interview.
SKILL #1:	Identify shapes, Task 4E.
SKILL #2:	Child can identify shapes in the environment.
MATERIALS:	Natural environment.
PROCEDURE:	*"Look around the room. Find as many shapes as you can. Which things are square shapes? Circles? Rectangles? Triangles?"*
EVALUATION:	Note how observant the child is. Does she note the obvious shapes, such as windows, doors, and tables? Does she look beyond the obvious? How many shapes and which shapes is she able to find?
SKILL #3:	Child will reproduce shapes by copying.
MATERIALS:	Shape cards (as in Task 4E); plain white paper; a choice of pencils, crayons, and markers.

PROCEDURE:
1. COPY THE CIRCLE.
2. COPY THE SQUARE.
3. COPY THE TRIANGLE.

EVALUATION: Note how closely each reproduction resembles its model. Is the circle complete and round? Does the square have four sides and square corners? Does the triangle have three straight sides and pointed corners?

6D*

**Preoperational
Ages 5–6**

Parts and Wholes, Parts of Sets: see Unit 14 for task

6E

**Preoperational
Ages 5–6**

Ordering, Size and Amount: Unit 17

METHOD:	Interview.
SKILLS:	Child can order ten objects that vary in one criteria and five sets with amounts from one to five.

MATERIALS:

1. *Size.* Ten objects or cutouts that vary in size, length, height, or width. An example for length is shown below.

2. *Amount.* Five sets of objects consisting of one, two, three, four, and five objects each.

PROCEDURES:

1. *Size.* Place the ten objects or cutouts in front of the child in a random arrangement. ***"Find the (biggest, longest, tallest, or widest). Put them all in a row from _____ to _____."***
2. Amount. Place the five sets in front of the child in a random arrangement. ***"Put these in order from the smallest bunch (group) to the largest bunch (group)."***

EVALUATIONS:

1. *Size.* Preoperational children will usually get the two extremes but may mix up the in-between sizes. Putting ten objects in the correct order would be an indication that the child is entering concrete operations.
2. *Amount.* Most 5-year-olds can order the five sets. If they order them easily, try some larger amounts.

6F   **Preoperational**
                                                                               Ages 5–6

Measurement; Length, Weight, and Time: Units 18 and 19

METHOD: Interview.

SKILLS: Child can explain the function of a ruler, discriminate larger from heavier, identify clocks and explain their function.

MATERIALS:

1. *Length.* A foot ruler.
2. *Weight.* A plastic golf ball and a marble or other pair of objects where the larger is the lighter.
3. *Time.* A clock (with a conventional face).

PROCEDURES:

1. Show the child the rules. ***"What is this? What do we do with it? Show me how it is used."***
2. Give the child the two objects, one in each hand. Ask, ***"Which is bigger? Which is heavier? Why is the small _____ heavier?"***
3. Show the child the clock. ***"What is this? Why do we have it? Tell me how it works."***

EVALUATION: Note how many details the child can give about each of the measuring instruments. Is she accurate? Can she tell which of the objects is heavier? Can she provide a reason for the lighter being larger and the smaller heavier?

6G

Preoperational
Ages 5–6

Practical Activities, Money: Unit 22

METHOD: Interview.

SKILL: Child can recognize money and tell which pieces of money will buy more.

MATERIALS:
1. Pictures of coins, bills, and other similar items.
2. Selection of pennies, nickels, dimes, and quarters.

PROCEDURES:
1. Show the child the pictures. **"Find the pictures of money."** After he has found the pictures of money, ask, **"what is the name of this?"** as you point to each picture of money.
2. Put the coins in front of the child. Ask, **"which will buy the most? If you have these five pennies** (put five pennies in one pile) **and I want two cents for a piece of candy, how many pennies will you have to give me for the candy?"**

EVALUATION: Note which picture of money the child can identify. Note if he knows which coins are worth the most. Many young children equate worth and size and thus think a nickel will buy more than a dime.

Check back to 5J, 5K, and 5L; then go on to the next tasks. The following tasks can be presented first between ages 5 and 6 and then repeated as the child's concepts and skills grow and expand.

6H*

Preoperational/Concrete
Ages 5–7

Ordering, Double Seriation: see Unit 17 for task

6I*

Preoperational/Concrete
Ages 5–7

Ordering, Patterning: see Unit 17 for task

6J*

Preoperational
Ages 5 and older

Symbols, One More Than: see Unit 23 for task

6K*   **Preoperational/Concrete**
                                                                          Ages 5–7

Sets and Symbols, Write/Reproduce Numerals: see Unit 24 for task

---

6L*   **Preoperational/Concrete**
                                                                          Ages 5–7

Sets and Symbols, Match Sets to Symbols: see Unit 24 for task

---

6M*   **Preoperational/Concrete**
                                                                          Ages 5–7

Sets and Symbols, Match Symbols to Sets: see Unit 24 for task

---

6N   **Preoperational/Concrete**
                                                                          Ages 5–6

Naturalistic and Informal Activities: Units 1–25

METHOD:	Observation.
SKILL:	Child demonstrates a knowledge of math concepts and skills during naturalistic and informal activities.
MATERIALS:	See Task 5M.
PROCEDURE:	See Task 5M. Add the following behaviors to your list.

- Demonstrates an understanding of *more than, the same amount*, and *less than* by responding appropriately to questions such as, "Do we have the same number of children as we have chairs?"
- Can match a set to a symbol and a symbol to a set (e.g., if the daily attendance total says 22, he can get 22 napkins for snack).
- Can do applied concrete whole-number operations (e.g., if four children plan to draw and two more children join them, he knows that there are now six children; or if he has three friends and eight cars to play with, he figures out that each friend can use two cars).

EVALUATION: Child should show an increase in frequency of these behaviors as the year progresses.

Math Language: Level 7

By the time the child is between 5½ and 6½ years of age, she should be using most of the words listed in Unit 15. The following tasks can be used to find out which words the child uses in an open-ended situation. Show each picture individually. Say, "I have some pictures to show you. Here is the first one. Tell me about it." For each picture, tape-record or write down the child's responses. Later list all the math words. Compare this with the list of math words she uses in class.

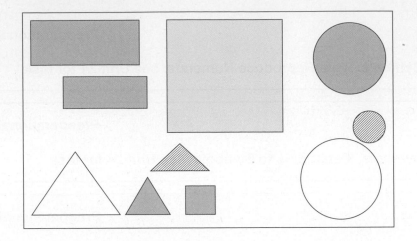

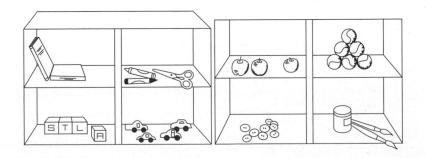

Concrete Operations: Level 8

The following tasks are all indicators of the child's cognitive developmental level. The child who can accomplish all these tasks should be ready for the primary-level instruction described in Section 5.

8A   **Concrete Operations**
                                                                          Ages 6–7

Conservation of Number: Unit 1

METHOD: Interview.
SKILL: Child can solve the number conservation problem.
MATERIALS: Twenty chips, blocks, or coins, all the same size, shape, and color.

PROCEDURE: Set up a row of nine objects. Then proceed through the following four tasks.

1. **"Make a row just like this one** (point to yours)."

   Child   □ □ □ □ □ □ □ □ □

   Adult   □ □ □ □ □ □ □ □ □

   "Does one row have more blocks (chips, coins), or do they both have the same amount? How do you know?" If child agrees to equality, go on to the next tasks.

2. **"Now watch what I do."** (Push yours together.)

   Child   □   □   □   □   □   □   □   □   □

   Adult   □ □ □ □ □ □ □ □ □

   "Does one row have more blocks, or do they both have the same amount? Why?" (If the child says one row has more, **"Make them have the same amount again."**) (If the child says they have the same amount, tell him, **"Line them up like they were before I moved them."**) Go on to task 3 and task 4 following the same steps.

3. Task 3

   Child   □ □ □ □ □ □ □ □

   Adult   □ □ □ □   □ □ □ □ □

4. Task 4

   Child   □ □ □ □ □ □ □ □

   Adult   □ □ □ □ □ □ □ □ □

EVALUATION: If the child is unable to do task 1 (one-to-one correspondence), do not proceed any further. He needs to work further on this concept and needs time for development. If he succeeds with task 1, go on to 2, 3, and 4. Note which of the following categories fit his responses.

Nonconserver 1. Indicates longer rows have more but cannot give a logical reason (e.g., the child may say, "I don't know," "My mother says so," or gives no answer).

Nonconserver 2. Indicates longer rows have more and gives logical reasons, such as "It's longer," "The long row has more," and the like.

Transitional. Says both rows still have the same amount but has to check by counting or placing in one-to-one correspondence.

Conserver. Completely sure that both rows still have the same amount. May say, "You just moved them."

8B

**Concrete Operations
Ages 6–7**

Symbols and Sets, Matching and Writing: Units 23, 24

METHOD: Interview.

SKILL: Child can match sets to symbols and write symbols.

MATERIALS: Cards with numerals 0 to 20, a supply of counters, paper, and writing implements.

PROCEDURES:

1. Present the child with sets of counters. Start with amounts under ten. If the child can do these, go on to the teens. "**Match the numbers to the sets.**"
2. Put the numeral cards and counters away. Give the child a piece of paper and a choice of writing instruments. "**Write as many numbers as you can. Start with zero.**"

EVALUATION: Note how high the child can go in matching sets and symbols and in writing numerals.

8C   **Concrete Operations**
                                                              Ages 6–7

Multiple Classification: Unit 25

METHOD: Interview.

SKILL: Child can group shapes by more than one criterion.

MATERIALS: Make 36 cardboard shapes:

1. Four squares (one each red, yellow, blue, and green).
2. Four triangles (one each red, yellow, blue, and green).
3. Four circles (one each red, yellow, blue, and green).
4. Make three sets of each in three sizes.

PROCEDURE: Place all the shapes in a random array in front of the child. "**Divide (sort, pile) these shapes into groups, any way you want to.**" After the child has sorted on one attribute (shape, color, or size) say, "**now divide (sort, pile) them another way.**" The preoperational child will normally refuse to conceptualize another way of grouping.

EVALUATION: The preoperational child will center on the first sort and will not try another criterion. The concrete operations child will sort by color, shape, and size.

8D   **Concrete Operations**
                                                              Ages 6–7

Class Inclusion: Unit 25

METHOD: Interview.

SKILL: Child can perceive that there are classes within classes.

MATERIALS: Make a set of materials using objects, cutouts, or pictures of objects such as the following.

1. Twelve wooden beads of the same size and shape that differ only in color (e.g., four red and eight blue).
2. Twelve pictures of flowers: eight tulips and four daisies.
3. Twelve pictures of animals: eight dogs and four cats.

PROCEDURE: Place the objects (pictures) in front of the child in random order. "**Put the** (object name) **together that are the same.**" Then after they have grouped into two sub-categories ask, "**Are there more (wooden beads, flowers,** or **animals) or more (blue beads, tulips,** or **dogs)?**" Have them compare the overall class or category with the larger subclass.

EVALUATION: The preoperational child will have difficulty conceptualizing parts and wholes of sets at the same time.

Concrete Operations: Level 9

9A*   **Concrete Operations**
Ages 6–8

Addition, Combining Sets up to 10: see Unit 27 for task

9B*   **Concrete Operations**
Ages 6–8

Subtraction, Sets of 10 and Less: see Unit 27 for task

9C   **Concrete Operations**
Ages 6–8

Addition and Subtraction, Understanding Notation: Unit 27

METHOD: Interview or small group.

SKILL: Child understands the connection between notation and concrete problems.

MATERIALS: Counters (e.g., chips, Unifix Cubes, cube blocks), pencil, and paper.

PROCEDURE: Each child should have a supply of counters, pencils, and paper. "**Take three red** (name of counter). **Now put two green** (name of counter) **with the three red. Write a number sentence that tells what you did.**" When finished, "**put the red and green** (counters) **back. Take out six yellow** (counters). **Separate three of the yellow** (counters) **from the six. Write a number sentence that tells what you did.**" Continue with more addition and subtraction problems. Written story problems could be given to children who know how to read.

EVALUATION: Note if the children are able to use the correct notation, that is, $3 + 2 = 5$ and $6 - 3 = 3$.

9D

Concrete Operations
Ages 6–8

Addition and Subtraction, Create Problems: Unit 27

METHOD:	Interview or small group.
SKILL:	Given a number sentence, the child can create a problem.
MATERIALS:	Counters (e.g., chips, Unifix Cubes, cube blocks), pencil, and paper.
PROCEDURE:	Give the children the number sentences below. Tell them to make up a story to go with each sentence using their counters to represent the characters in the story. Nonreaders/nonwriters can dictate their stories; reader/writers can write the stories themselves. Number sentences:

1. $3 + 5 = 8$ **2.** $6 - 4 = 2$

EVALUATION:	Note if the dictated or written problem relates correctly to the number sentence.

9E

Concrete Operations
Ages 6–8

Addition and Subtraction, Translating Symbols into Concrete Actions: Unit 27

METHOD:	Interview or small group.
SKILL:	The child can translate written problems into concrete actions.
MATERIALS:	Counters (e.g., chips, Unifix Cubes, cube blocks), pencil, paper, and several addition and subtraction problems.

PROBLEMS:

1. $9 - 4$	**6.** $6 - 3$
2. $4 + 5$	**7.** $4 - 1$
3. $3 + 2$	**8.** $2 + 6$
4. $8 - 6$	**9.** $5 + 3$
5. $1 + 7$	**10.** $7 - 2$

PROCEDURE:	Give each child a supply of counters, a pencil, and paper with one or more written problems like those above. It is best to give the problems one at a time the first time. Then give more as the children become more proficient. Point to the first problem, if there is more than one. "**Look at this problem. Show me the problem with** (counters). **Now write the answer. Read the problem and the answer to me.**" If they do this one correctly, have them continue on their own. Ask them to show you if there are any problems they can do without the cubes.
EVALUATION:	Note whether the children do the problems correctly and especially whether they are accurate in translating the signs. For example, for problem 1, a child might take nine counters and then take four more, ignoring the "minus" sign. Some children might be able to tell you that (say) $2 + 6 = 8$ but not be able to show you with the counters. This behavior indicates the children have learned to use the symbols in a rote fashion but do not understand the concepts that the symbols stand for.

9F*   **Concrete Operations**
                                                      Ages 7–8

Multiplication, Readiness: see Unit 27 for task

9G   **Concrete Operations**
                                                      Ages 7–8

Multiplication, The Process: Unit 27

METHOD: Interview.
SKILL: Child understands the process of multiplication.
MATERIALS: Counters (e.g., chips, Unifix Cubes, cube blocks), pencil, and paper.
1. Show the child patterns of counters such as

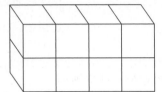 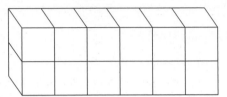

For each pattern, "**Write an equation** (or **number sentence**) **that tells about this pattern**."
2. "**With your** (counters), **show me two times two**." (Try 3 × 4, 5 × 2, and so on).

EVALUATION:
1. Note if the child writes (a) 2 × 4 = 8 or 4 × 2 = 8 (b) 2 × 6 = 12 or 6 × 2 = 12. It is not uncommon for a child to write 3 × 4 = 12 for the second equation. This response would indicate she has memorized 3 times 4 equals 12 without a basic understanding of the multiplication concept.
2. For 2 × 2, the child should make two groups of two; for 3 × 4, three groups of four; for 5 × 2, five groups of two. Some children will reverse the numbers, such as two groups of five for the last problem. Other children may just make two groups, such as a group of five and a group of two for 5 × 2.

9H   **Concrete Operations**
                                                      Ages 7–8

Multiplication, Using Symbols: Unit 27

METHOD: Interview.
SKILL: Child can solve written multiplication problems.
MATERIALS: Counters (e.g., chips, Unifix Cubes, cube blocks), pencil, and paper.

PROCEDURE: One at a time, give the child written multiplication problems. Tell her, "**Work out the problem with counters and write down the answer**."

EVALUATION: Note whether the child makes the appropriate number of sets of the right amount. Note whether the child does the correct operation. Sometimes children will forget and add instead of multiply. That is, a child might write $3 \times 2 = 5$.

9I*

Concrete Operations
Ages 7–8

Division, Basic Concept: see Unit 27 for task

9J

Concrete Operations
Ages 7–8

Division, Symbols: Unit 27

METHOD: Interview.

SKILL: Child understands the use of symbols in division problems.

MATERIALS: Counters (e.g., chips, Unifix Cubes, cube blocks), pencil, and paper.

PROCEDURE: Give the child a division story problem. For example: "Chan has eight bean seeds. He wants to plant two in each small pot. How many pots will he need?" "**Read the problem, and solve it. Write the number sentence for the problem on your paper**."

EVALUATION: Note if the child can write the correct number sentence. If she can't do the problem from memory, does she figure out that she can use her counters or draw a picture to assist in finding the answer?

9K*

Concrete Operations
Ages 6–8

Patterns, Extension in Three Dimensions: see Unit 28 for task

---

9L

Concrete Operations
Ages 7–8

Patterns, Creation: Unit 28

METHOD: Interview.

SKILL: Child can create patterns using discrete objects.

MATERIALS: Concrete objects such as chips, Unifix Cubes, or cube blocks.

PROCEDURE: "**Using your** (counters), **make your own pattern as you have done with pattern starters I have given you**." When the child is finished, "**Tell me about your pattern.**"

EVALUATION: Note if the child has actually developed a repeated pattern and if she is able to describe the pattern in words.

9M* Concrete Operations
Ages 7–9

Patterns, Number Multiples: see Unit 28 for task

9N* Concrete Operations
Ages 6–8

Fractions, Equivalent Parts: see Unit 29 for task

9O* Concrete Operations
Ages 6–8

Fractions, One-Half of a Group: see Unit 29 for task

9P* Concrete Operations
Ages 7–8

Place Value, Groups of 10: see Unit 30 for task

9Q* Concrete Operations
Ages 7–8

Place Value, Grouping to Identify an Amount: see Unit 30 for task

---

9R Concrete Operations
Ages 7–8

Place Value, Symbols to Concrete Representations: Unit 30

METHOD: Interview or small group.

SKILL: Child can translate from written numerals to concrete representations.

MATERIALS: Base-ten blocks or similar material (e.g., Unifix Cubes, sticks, or straws and rubber bands for bundling); eight or ten cards, each with a double-digit number written on it (e.g., 38, 72, 45, 83, 27, 96, 51, 50).

PROCEDURE: **"Using your base-ten blocks, make groups for each numeral."** After each group has been constructed, **"Tell me how you know that you have (number)."**

EVALUATION: Note if the child constructs the correct amount of 10s and units and can explain accurately how the construction is represented by the numeral.

9S   **Concrete Operations**
Geometry, Graphs, Charts, and Tables: Unit 31
See the prerequisite concepts and skills in Units 12, 13, 20, and 25 and Assessment Tasks 3F, 3G, 4E, 5E, and 6C.

9T   **Concrete Operations**
Measurement with Standard Units: Unit 32
See prerequisite concepts in Units 18 and 19 and Assessment Tasks 3J, 4I, 5H, 5I, level 7, 8A, and 8B.

9U   **Concrete Operations**
                                                                            Ages 6, 7, 8
Solving Problems: Unit 27

METHOD: Provide the students with problems such as can be found in the resource lists at the end of Unit 3.

SKILL: Developing problem solutions.

MATERIALS: Pencils and paper, counters (if needed), and problems.

PROCEDURE: Provide the students with oral and written problem versions such as the following. *Four little piggies run out to play. Two piggies jump in a mud puddle and get muddy feet. The other two piggies just stick their snouts in the mud.* **"How many muddy feet and muddy snouts are there all together?"**

EVALUATION: Note the procedures used by the students. Do they draw the pigs and count out the feet and snouts? Do they use counters for the pig parts? Do they use tally marks? Do they write out the numerals and add?

9V	**Concrete Operations**

Writing Problems: Unit 15

METHOD: Observation, interview; review of children's written products.

SKILL: Children can write and/or draw their own problems and solutions to problems presented to them in their math journals. They can also record their general feelings about mathematics and their descriptions of what they have learned.

MATERIALS: Notebook and writing tools (pencils, pens, crayons, felt-tip pens).

PROCEDURE: Students should have regular daily opportunities to record their mathematics experiences in their math journals. The journals might contain solutions to problems they have identified and problems derived from class work such as from literature selections. They can also be encouraged to record how they are feeling about mathematics and explain what they are learning.

EVALUATION: Have the students read their entries to you and review what they have produced. Look for evidence of their mathematical thinking and their approach to problem solving. Also look for their feelings about math and their view of what they know. Note growth in written expression and organization of illustrated problem solutions. Discuss with the children entries they choose to select for inclusion in their portfolio.

REFERENCES AND RESOURCES

General Resources

Baroody, A. J. (1988). *Children's mathematical thinking.* New York: Teachers College Press. (Includes many examples of children's common mistakes and misconceptions)

Bredekamp, S., & Rosegrant, T. (Eds.). (1995). *Reaching potentials: Transforming early childhood curriculum and assessment* (Vol. 2). Washington, DC: National Association for the Education of Young Children. (Defines appropriate assessment strategies for young children)

Copley, J. V. (1999). Assessing mathematical understanding of the young child. In *Mathematics in the early years* (pp. 182–188). Reston, VA: National Council of Teachers of Mathematics, and Washington, DC: National Association for the Education of Young Children. (Provides an overview of early childhood mathematics assessment)

Evan-Moor. (2006). *Math assessment tasks. Quick check activities.* Monterey, CA: Author. (Paper-and-pencil and pictorial assessments)

Glanfield, F., Bush, W. S., & Stenmark, J. K. (Eds.). (2003). *Mathematics assessment: A practical handbook.* Reston, VA: National Council of Teachers of Mathematics.

Huniker, D. (Ed.). (2006). *Prekindergarten–grade 2 mathematics assessment sampler.* Reston, VA: National Council of Teachers of Mathematics. (Assessment tasks and guidelines for evaluation of student responses)

Mindes, G. (2007). *Assessing young children* (3rd ed.). Clifton Park, NY: Cengage Delmar Learning. (Overview of early childhood assessment)

National Council of Teachers of Mathematics. (2000). *Principles and standards for school mathematics.* Reston, VA: Author.

Richardson, K. (1984). *Developing number concepts using Unifix Cubes.* Menlo Park, CA:

Addison-Wesley. (Each chapter ends with a section on analyzing and assessing children's needs)

Webb, N. L. (1993). (Ed.). *Assessment in the mathematics classroom: 1993 yearbook*. Reston, VA: National Council of Teachers of Mathematics. (Contains a series of chapters relevant to assessment in general and relative to grade level and specific skill areas)

Kathy Richardson Materials

Kathy Richardson's materials always take an assessment approach.

Richardson, K. (1990). *A look at children's thinking: Videos for K–2 mathematics*. Norman, OK: Educational Enrichment.

Richardson, K. (1999). *Developing number concepts: Addition and subtraction*. White Plains, NY: Seymour.

Richardson, K. (1999). *Developing number concepts: Counting, comparing and pattern*. White Plains, NY: Seymour.

Richardson, K. (1999). *Developing number concepts: Place value, multiplication and division*. White Plains, NY: Seymour.

Richardson, K. (1999). *Developing number concepts: Planning guide*. White Plains, NY: Seymour.

Children's Books and Software with Math Concepts

Bibliography for Adult Reference

Note: See Unit 15.

Burns, M. (1992). *Mathematics and literature (K–3).* White Plains, NY: Cuisinaire Co.

Chalufour, I., & Worth, K. (2004). *Building structures with young children.* Washington, DC: National Association for the Education of Young Children.

Ducolon, C. K. (2000). Quality literature as a springboard to problem solving. *Teaching Children Mathematics, 6*(7), 442–446.

Fleege, P. O., & Thompson, D. R. (2000). From habits to legs: Using science-themed counting books to foster connections. *Teaching Children Mathematics, 7*(2), 74–78.

Hellwig, S. J., Monroe, E. E., & Jacobs, J. S. (2000). Making informed choices: Selecting children's trade books for mathematics instruction. *Teaching Children Mathematics, 7*(3), 138–143.

Jacobs, V. R., Bennet, T. R., & Bullock, C. (2000). Selecting books in Spanish to teach mathematics. *Teaching Children Mathematics, 6*(9), 582–587.

Sheffield, S. (1995). *Math and literature (K–3): Book 2.* Sausalito, CA: Math Solutions.

Thiessen, D., Matthias, M., & Smith, J. (1998). *The wonderful world of mathematics: A critically annotated list of children's books in mathematics* (2nd ed.). Reston, VA: National Council of Teachers of Mathematics.

Thiessen, D. (Ed.). (2004). *Exploring mathematics through literature.* Reston, VA: National Council for Teachers of Mathematics.

Welchman-Tischler, R. (1993). *How to use children's literature to teach mathematics.* Reston, VA: National Council of Teachers of Mathematics.

West, S., & Cox, A. (2004). *Literacy play.* Beltsville, MD: Gryphon House.

Whitin, D. J., & Wilde, S. (1992). *Read any good math lately? Children's books for mathematical learning.* K–6. Portsmouth, NH: Heinemann.

Whitin, D. J., & Wilde, S. (1995). *It's the story that counts: More children's books for mathematical learning, K–6.* Portsmouth, NH: Heinemann.

Whitin, D. J., & Whitin, P. (2004). *New visions for linking literature and mathematics.* Urbana, IL: National Council of Teachers of English and Reston, VA: National Council of Teachers of Mathematics.

See Zaner-Bloser's *Reading and Math* series.

Also see end-of-unit references and monthly reviews in *Teaching Children Mathematics.*

Fundamental Concepts

One-to-One Correspondence

Jocelyn, M. (1999). *Hannah and the seven dresses.* East Rutherford, NJ: Penguin Putnam; **5, 15.**

Marzollo, J. (1994). *Ten cats have hats.* Jefferson City, MO: Scholastic Professional; **5, 6.**

Slobodkina, E. (1968). *Se venden gorras.* New York: Harper; **5, 26.**

Slobodkina, E. (1976). *Caps for sale.* New York: Scholastic. Ages 3–6; **5, 12.**

The three bears. (1973). New York: Golden Press. Ages 2–5; **5, 6, 13.**

The Three Billy Goats Gruff. (1968). New York: Grosset & Dunlap. Ages 2–5; **5, 6.**

Wade, L. (1998). *The Cheerios® play book.* New York: Simon & Schuster; **5.**

Number Sense and Counting

Many of the books listed in this section include ordinal numbers. Most also include number symbols.

Aker, S. (1990). *What comes in 2's, 3's, and 4's?* New York: Simon & Schuster. Ages 4–6; **6.**

Anno, M. (1982). *Anno's counting house.* New York: Philomel. Ages 4–7; **6.**

Anno, M. (1986). *Anno's counting book.* New York: Harper-Collins. Ages 4–6; **6.**

Aurego, J., & Dewey, A. (1989). *Five little ducks.* New York: Crown; **6.**

Baker, K. (1994). Count to ten with big fat hen. San Diego: Harcourt Brace Voyager; **6.**

Ballart, E. (1992). *Let's count.* Charlottsville, VA: Thomasson-Grant; **6, 24.**

Bang, M. (1983). *Ten, nine, eight.* New York: Greenwillow. Ages 3–5; **6.**

Blumenthal, N. (1989). *Count-a-saurus*. New York: Four Winds Press. Ages 3–6; **6.**

Boynton, S. (1978). *Hippos go berserk*. Chicago: Recycled Paper Press. Ages 3–6; **6, 8, 20, 21.**

Brusca, M. C., & Wilson, T. (1995). *Tres amigos: Un cuento para cantar* [Three friends: A counting book]. New York: Holt, Rinehart, & Winston; **6.**

Carle, E. (1969). *The very hungry caterpillar*. Mountain View, CA: Collins and World. Ages 3–56, 13, 15.

Carle, E. (2005). *10 little rubber ducks*. New York: HarperCollins. **6.**

Carle, E. (1968). 1, 2, 3 to the zoo. New York: Scholastic. **6.**

Carter, D. A. (1988). *How many bugs in a box?* New York: Simon & Schuster. Ages 3–6; **6.**

Cave, K. (2003). *One child, one seed: A South African counting book*. New York: Henry Holt; **6.**

Christelow, E. (1989). *Five little monkeys jumping on the bed*. New York: Clarion; **6.**

Christelow, E. (1991). *Five little monkeys sitting in a tree*. New York: Clarion; **96.**

Crews, D. (1985). *Ten black dots, revised*. New York: Greenwillow. Ages 4–6; **6.**

Cutler, D. S. (1991). *One hundred monkeys*. New York: Simon & Schuster. Ages 3–6; **6.**

Dunbar, J. (1990). *Ten little mice*. San Diego, CA: HBJ. Ages 3–6; **9.**

Elkin, B. (1968, 1971). *Six foolish fishermen*. New York: Scholastic. Ages 3–6; **6.**

Elkin, B., & Kratky, L. J. (Trans.). (1986). *Seis pescadores disparatados* [Six foolish fishermen]. Chicago: Children's Press; **6.**

Elya, S.M. (2002). *Eight animals on the town*. New York: Penguin Group. **6** (Integrates Spanish vocabulary)

Falwell, C. (1993). *Feast for 10*. New York: Clarion; **6.**

Feelings, M. (1976). *Moja means one: Swahili counting book* New York: Dial. Ages 3–6; **9.**

Felton, C., & Felton, A. (2003). *Where's Harley?* New York: Kane Press; **6.**

Flemming, D. (1992). *Count*. New York: Holt; **6.**

Friskey, M. (1946). *Chicken little count to ten*. New York: Harcourt, Brace. Ages 3–8; **6, 18, 19.**

Frith, M. (1973). *I'll teach my dog 100 words*. New York: Random House. Ages 3–6; **6.**

Gag, W. (1928, 1956, 1977). *Millions of cats*. New York: Coward-McCann. Ages 3–5; **6, 8, 12.**

Getty Museum. (n.d.). *1 to 10 and back again: A Getty Museum counting book*. Los Angeles: Author; **6, 18, 19.**

Gibson, R. (1998). *I can count*. London: Usborne Playtime; **6, 18, 19.**

Grindley, S. (1996). *Four black puppies*. Cambridge, MA: Candlewick; **6.**

Grossman, V. (1991). *Ten little rabbits*. San Francisco: Chronicle Books. Ages 3–6; **6.**

Hamm, D. J. (1991). *How many feet in the bed?* New York: Simon & Schuster. Ages 3–6; **6.**

Heller, N. (1994). *Ten old pails*. New York: Greenwillow; **9.** Hewavisenti, L. (1991). *Fun with math: Counting*. Chicago: Franklin Watts; **6.**

Hoban, T. (1999). *Let's count*. New York: Greenwillow/William Morrow; **6.**

Howe, C. (1983). *Counting penguins*. New York: Harper. Ages 3–5; **6.**

Hudson, C. W. (1987). *Afro-bets 1, 2, 3 book*. Orange, NJ: Just Us Productions; **6, 18, 19.**

Hulme, J. N. (1991). *Sea squares*. Waltham, MA: Little, Brown. Ages 4–6; **6.**

Jenkins, E. (2001). *Five creatures*. New York: Farrar, Straus, & Giroux; **6.**

Jonas, A. (1995). *Splash!* New York: Greenwillow; **6.**

Keats, E. J. (1972). *Over in the meadow*. New York: Scholastic. Ages 3–5; **6.**

Kitamura, S. (1986). *When sheep cannot sleep? The counting book*. New York: Farrar, Straus, & Giroux. Ages 2–5; **6.**

Krebs, L. (2003). *We all went on safari. A counting journey through Tanzania*. Cambridge, MA: Barefoot Books; **6.** (Includes information on Masai, Tansanian wild life, and Swahili vocabulary).

Leedy, L. (1985). *A number of dragons*. New York: Holiday House. Ages 1–3; **6.**

Lowell, S. (1992). *The three little javelinas*. New York: Scholastic; **6.**

Lester, H. (2001). *Score one for the sloths*. New York: Scholastic. **6.**

MacDonald, S. (2000). *Look whooo's counting.* New York: Scholastic; **6.**

Mayer, M., & McDermott, G. (1987). *The Brambleberrys animal book of counting.* Honesdale, PA: Boyds Mill Press. Ages 3–6; **6.**

Lewin, B. (1981). *Cat count.* New York: Scho9lastic 6.

McGrath, B. B. (1994). *The m&m's counting book.* Watertown, MA: Charlesbridge; **6, 16, 21.**

Michelson, R. (2000). *Ten times better.* Tarrytown, NY: Marshall Cavendish; **6.**

Micklethwait, L. (1993). *I spy two eyes: Numbers in art.* Fairfield, NJ: Greenwillow Books; **6.**

Moerbeek, K., & Dijs, C. (1988). *Six brave explorers.* Los Angeles: Price Stern Sloan. Ages 4–6; **6.**

Moss, L. (1995). *Zin! Zin! Zin! A violin.* New York: Scholastic; **6, 12.**

Parish, S. (1998). *1, 2, 3 of Australian wildlife.* Archerfield BC, Queensland, Australia: Steve Parish Publishing. **6, 24, 25.**

Pomerantz, C. (1984). *One duck, another duck.* New York: Greenwillow. Ages 3–7; **6.**

Prodan, J. R. (2000). *Count with me.* Pittsburgh, PA: Darrance Publishing; **6.**

Roth, C. (1999). *Ten clean pigs, ten dirty pigs.* New York: North-South Books; **6.**

Ryan, P. M., & Pallotta, J. (1996). *The crayon counting book.* Watertown, MA: Charlesbridge; **6.**

Samton, S. W. (1991). *Moon to sun.* Honesdale, PA: Boyds Mill Press; **6.**

Samton, S. W. (1991). *On the river.* Honesdale, PA: Boyds Mill Press. Ages 4–6; **6.**

Samton, S. W. (1991). *The world from my window.* Honesdale, PA: Boyds Mill Press; **6.**

Sayre, A. P., & Sayre, J. (2003). *One is a snail, ten is a crab.* Cambridge, MA: Candlewick Press; **6.**

Scarry, R. (1975). *Best counting book ever.* New York: Random House. Ages 2–8; **6, 15.**

Sendak, M. (1975). *Seven little monsters.* New York: Scholastic; **6.**

Seuss, Dr. (1938). *The 500 hats of Bartholomew Cubbins.* Eau Claire, WI: Hale and Co. Ages 3–7; **6.**

Seuss, Dr. (1960). *One fish, two fish, red fish, blue fish.* New York: Random House. Ages 3–7; **6, 8, 12, 14.**

Sheppard, J. (1990). *The right number of elephants.* New York: Harper-Collins. Ages 4–6; **6.**

Slobodkina, E. (1940, 1947, 1968). *Caps for sale.* New York: Young Scott; **6, 26.**

Slobodkina, E. (1940, 1947, 1968, translation 1995). *Se venden gorras.* New York: Harper Arco Iris; **6, 26.**

Steiner, C. (1960). *Ten in a family.* New York: Alfred A. Knopf. Ages 3–5; **6.**

Stoddart, G., & Baker, M. (1982). *One, two number zoo.* London: Hodder & Stoughton. Ages 5–7;6.

Storms, R. (1986). *1, 2, 3: A teaching train book.* Miami, FL: Ottenheimer; **6.**

Tafuri, N. (1986). *Who's counting?* New York: Greenwillow. Ages 2–5; **6.**

Thorne-Thomsen, K., & Rocheleau, P. (1999). *A Shaker's dozen counting book.* San Francisco: Chronicle Books; **6, 26.**

Thornhill, J. (1989). *The wildlife 1-2-3: A nature counting book.* New York: Simon & Schuster. Ages 3–6; **6.**

Tucker, K. (2003). *The seven Chinese sisters.* New York: Scholastic. **6, 13.**

Ungerer, T. (1962). *The three robbers.* New York: Antheum. Ages 3–5; **6.**

Von Noorden, D. (1994). *The lifesize animal counting book.* New York: Dorling Kindersley; **6.**

Walton, R. (1993). *How many How many How many.* Cambridge, MA: Candlewick Press; **6.**

Wildsmith, B. (1965). *Brian Wildsmith's 1, 2, 3's.* New York: Franklin Watts. Ages 3–5; **6.**

Wildsmith, B. (1996). *?Cuantos animals hay?* New York: Star Bright Books. **6.**

Wilson, K., & Rankin, J. (2003). *A frog in the bog.* New York: Scholastic. **6.**

Zaslavsky, C. (1999). *Count on your fingers African style.* New York: Writers and Readers Publishing; **6.**

Classification

Cabrera, J. (1997). *Cat's colors.* New York: Puffin; **7.**

Fiammenghi, G. (1999). *A collection for Kate.* New York: Kane; **6, 7, 8.**

Gordon, M. (1986). *Colors.* Morristown, NJ: Silver-Burdett. Ages 2–6; **7.**

Hill, E. (1982). *What does what?* Los Angeles: Price/Stern/Sloan. Ages 2–4; **7.**

Hoban, T. (1978). *Is it red? Is it yellow? Is it blue?* New York: Greenwillow. Ages 2–5; **7.**

Hughes, S. (1986). *Colors.* New York: Lothrop. Ages 2–4; **7.**

Johnson, J. (1985). *Firefighters A–Z.* New York: Walker. Ages 5–8; **7. 17.**

Wildsmith B. (1967). *Brian Wildsmith's wild animals.* New York: Franklin Watts. Ages 3–8; **7.**

Wildsmith, B. (1968). *Brian Wildsmith's fishes.* New York: Franklin Watts. Ages 3–8; **7.**

Winthrop, E. (1986). *Shoes.* New York: Harper & Row. Ages 3–7; **7, 17.**

Comparing

Bourgeois, P., & Clark, B. (1987). *Big Sarah's little boots.* New York: Scholastic. Ages 3–5; **8.**

Brenner, B. (1966). *Mr. Tall and Mr. Small.* Menlo Park, CA: Addison-Wesley. Ages 4–7; **8.**

Broger, A., & Kalow, G. (1977). *Good morning whale.* New York: Macmillan. Ages 3–6; **8.**

Carle, E. (1977). *The grouchy ladybug.* New York: Crowell. Ages 3–5; **8.**

Eastman, P. D. (1973). *Big dog, little dog.* New York: Random House. Ages 3–4; **8.**

Gordon, M. (1986). *Opposites.* Morristown, NJ: Silver-Burdett. Ages 3–5; **8.**

Graham, A., & Wood, W. (1991). *Angus thought he was big.* Hicksville, NY: Macmillan Whole-Language Big Book Program. Ages 3–5; **8.**

Grender, I. (1975). *Playing with shapes and sizes.* New York: Knopf/Pinwheel Books. Ages 3–6; **8, 9.**

Hoban, T. (1972). *Push pull, empty full.* New York: Macmillan. Ages 3–5; **8.**

Horn, A. (1974). *You can be taller.* Boston: Little, Brown. Ages 3–5; **8.**

Hughes, S. (1985). *Bathwater's hot.* New York: Lothrop. Ages 1–2; **8.**

Hughes, S. (1985). *Noises.* New York: Lothrop. Ages 1–2; **8.**

Lewis, J. (1963). *The tortoise and the hare.* Chicago: Whitman. Ages 4–8; **8, 14.**

Lionni, L. (1968). *The biggest house in the world.* New York: Pantheon. Ages 2–6; **8.**

McMillan, B. (1986). *Becca backward, Becca forward.* New York: Lothrop. Ages 3–6; **8.**

Miller, N. (1990). *Emmett's snowball.* New York: Henry Holt. K–3 and above; **8.**

Most, B. (1989). *The littlest dinosaurs.* New York: Harcourt Brace; **8.**

Novak, M. (2005). *Too many bunnies.* New Milford, CT: Roaring Book Press; **8.**

Presland, J. (1975). *Same and different.* Purton Wilts, England: Child's Play (International), Ltd. Ages 4–7; **8.**

Scarry, R. (1976). *Short and tall.* New York: Golden Press. Ages 2–7; **8.**

Scarry, R. (1986). *Big and little: A book of opposites.* Racine, WI: Western. Ages 3–7; **8.**

Shapiro, L. (1978). *Pop-up opposites.* Los Angeles: Price/Stern/Sloan. Ages 3–5; **8.**

Early Geometry: Shape

Anno, M. (1991). *Anno's math games III.* New York: Philomel. K–6; **9, 20. 25.**

Budney, B. (1954). *A kiss is round.* New York: Lothrop, Lee, & Shepard. Ages 2–6; **9.**

Carle, E. (1974). *My very first book of shapes.* New York: Crowell. Ages 3–6; **9.**

Dodds, D. A. (1994). *The shape of things.* Cambridge, MA: Candlewick Press; **9.**

Ehlert, L. (1990). *Color farm.* New York: Harper-Collins; **9, 17, 20.**

Emberley, E. (1961). *A wing on a flea: A book about shapes.* Boston: Little, Brown. Ages 5–8; **9.**

Emberley, E. (1970). *Ed Emberley's drawing book of animals.* Boston: Little, Brown. Ages 6–8; **9.**

Emberley, E. (1972). *Ed Emberley's drawing book: Make a world.* Boston: Little, Brown. Ages 6–8; **9.**

Emberley, E. (1995). *El ala de la polilla: Un libro de figuras* [The wing on a flea: A book about shapes]. New York: Scholastic; **9.**

Hefter, R. (1976). *The strawberry book of shapes.* New York: Weekly Reader Books. Ages 3–7; **9.**

Hewavisenti, L. (1991). *Shapes and solids.* Chicago: FranklinWatts; **9, 25.**

Hoban, T. (1974). *Circles, triangles, and squares.* New York: Macmillan. Ages 5–8; **9.**

Hoban, T. (1983). *Round and round and round.* New York: Greenwillow. Ages 3–6; **9.**

Hoban, T. (1986). *Shapes, shapes, shapes.* New York: Greenwillow. Ages 3–7; **9.**

Hoban, T. (1997). *Look book.* New York: Morrow Junior Books; **9.**

Hoban, T. (2000). *Cubes, cones, cylinders, and spheres.* New York: HarperCollins; **9.**

MacKinnon, D. (1992). *What shape?* New York: Dial; **9.**

MacKinnon, D., & Sieveking, A. (2000). *Eye Spy Shapes: A peephole book.* Watertown, MA: Charlesbridge; **9.**

Rau, D. M. (2002). *A star in my orange: Looking for nature's shapes.* Brookfield, CT: Millbrook Press; **9.**

Shapes: Circle/Square/Triangle (3 books). (1992). New York: Books for Young Readers. Ages 3–6; **9.**

Sullivan, J. (1963). *Round is a pancake.* New York: Holt, Rinehart, & Winston. Ages 3–5; **9.**

Supraner, R. (1975). *Draw me a square, draw me a triangle, & draw me a circle.* New York: Simon & Schuster/Nutmeg. Ages 3–6; **9.**

Teulade, P. (1999). *El más bonito de todos regalos del mundo* [The most beautiful gift in the world]. Barcelona, Spain: Editorial Corimbo; **9.**

Thong, R. (2000). *Round is a mooncake: A book of shapes.* San Francisco: Chronicle Books; **9.**

Early Geometry: Space

Barton, B. (1981). *Building a house.* New York: Greenwillow. Ages 4–7; **10, 11, 15.**

Berenstain, S., & Berenstain, J. (1968). *Inside, outside, upside down.* New York: Random House. Ages 3–7; **10.**

Brown, M. (1949). *Two little trains.* New York: Scott, Foresman. Ages 2–4; **10, 12.**

Carle, E. (1972). *The secret birthday message.* New York: Crowell. Ages 3–7; **10.**

Dunrea, O. (1985). *Fergus and the bridey.* New York: Holiday. Ages 4–7; **10.**

Hill, E. (1980). *Where's Spot?* New York: Putnam's Sons. Ages 2–4; **10.**

Lionni, L. (1983). *Where?* New York: Pantheon. Ages 2–3; **10.**

Maestro, B., & Maestro, G. (1976). *Where is my friend?* New York: Crown. Ages 2–4; **10.**

Martin, B., Jr. (1971). *Going up, going down.* New York: Holt, Rinehart, & Winston. Ages 6–8; **10, 6.**

Russo, M. (1986). *The line up book.* New York: Greenwillow. Ages 3–5; **10.**

Teulade, P. (1999). *El más bonito de todos regalos del mundo* [The most beautiful gift in the world]. Barcelona, Spain: Editorial Corimbo; **10.**

Weimer, T. E. (1993). *Space songs for children.* Greenville, SC: Pearce-Evetts. Ages 5–7; **10.**

Parts and Wholes

Axworthy, A. (Illustrator). (1998). *Guess what I am.* Cambridge, MA: Candlewick; **14.**

Burton, M. R. (1988). *Tail Toes Eyes Ears Nose.* New York: Harper Trophy; **11.**

Carle, E. (1987). *Do you want to be my friend?* New York: Harper Trophy; **11.**

Dubov, C. S. (1986). *Alexsandra, where are your toes?* New York: St. Martin's Press. Ages 1½–3; **11.**

Dubov, C. S. (1986). *Alexsandra, where is your nose?* New York: St. Martin's Press. Ages 1 ½–3; **11.**

Hutchins, P., & Marcuse, A. (Trans.) (1994). *Llaman a la puerta* [The doorbell rang]. New York: Mulberry; **11, 21.**

Le Tord, B. (1985). *Good wood bear.* New York: Bradbury. Ages 4–7; **11.**

Luciana, B., & Tharlet, E. (2000). *How will we get to the beach?* New York: North-South Books; **11.**

Mathews, L. (1979). *Gator pie.* New York: Scholastic. Ages 4–7; **11, 20.**

Language

Arenson, R. (Illustrator). (1989). *One, two, skip a few: First number rhymes.*

Brooklyn, NY: Barefoot Poetry Collections; **12.**

Bemelmans, L. (1969). *Madeline*. New York: Viking. Ages 4–7; **12, 5, 6, 15.**

Duvoisin, R. (1974). *Petunia takes a trip*. New York: Knopf/Pinwheel. Ages 4–7; **18, 12, 14.**

Figueredo, D. H. (2000). *Big snowball fight*. New York: Lee & Low Books; **12.**

Hoff, S. (1959). Julius. New York: Harper & Row. Ages 4–7; **12.**

Mathematics in the kitchen, Mathematics at the farm, Mathematics in buildings, Mathematics on the playground, Mathematics in the circus ring. (1978). Milwaukee: MacDonald–Raintree. Ages 3–7; **12.**

McKellar, S. (1993). Counting rhymes. New York: Dorling Kindersley; **12, 21.**

Orozco, J. (1997). *Diez Deditos* (Ten little fingers. Rhymes and action songs from Latin America.) New York: Scholastic. **12**

Shelby, A. (1990). *We keep a store*. New York: Orchard Books. All ages; **12, 17.**

Umansky, K., & Fisher, C. (1999). *Nonsense counting rhymes*. Oxford: Oxford University Press; **12.**

Application of Fundamental Concepts

Ordering, Seriation, and Patterning

Aker, S. (1990). *What comes in 2's, 3's, & 4's?* New York: Aladdin; **13, 18, 19.**

Asbjörsen, P. C., & Moe, J. E. (1957). *The three billy goats gruff*. New York: Harcourt, Brace, Jovanovich. Ages 2–5; **6, 8, 12, 13.**

Brett, J. (1987). *Goldilocks and the three bears*. New York: Dodd, Mead. Ages 3–5; **13.**

Clements, A. (1992). *Mother Earth's counting book*. New York: Simon & Schuster. Ages 5 and up; **13, 20, 22.**

Hoban, T. (1992). *Look up, look down*. New York: Greenwillow. Ages 5–8; **13.**

Ipcar, C. (1972). *The biggest fish in the sea*. New York: Viking. Ages 3–6; **13.**

Macauly, D. (1987). *Why the chicken crossed the road*. Boston: Houghton-Mifflin. Ages 4–8; **13.**

Maestro, B., & Maestro, G. (1977). *Harriet goes to the circus*. New York: Crown. Ages 5–8; **13.**

Mahy, M. (1987). *17 kings and 42 elephants*. New York: Dial. Ages 2–6; **6, 13.**

Martin, B., Jr. (1963). *One, two, three, four*. New York: Holt, Rinehart, & Winston. Ages 5–7; **6, 13.**

Martin, B., Jr. (1970). *Monday, Monday, I like Monday*. New York: Holt, Rinehart, & Winston. Ages 5–8; **13, 15.**

Measurement: Volume, Weight, and Length

Allen, P. (1983). *Who sank the boat?* New York: Coward. Ages 3–5; **14.**

Anderson, L. C. (1983). *The wonderful shrinking shirt*. Niles, IL: Whitman. Ages 3–5; **14.**

Bennett, V. (1975). *My measure it book*. New York: Grosset & Dunlap. Ages 3–5; **14.**

Demi. (1997). *One grain of rice*. New York: Scholastic; **14.**

Faulkner, K. (2000). *So big! My first measuring book*. New York: Simon & Schuster; **14.**

Henkes, K. (1995). *The biggest boy*. New York: Greenwillow; **14.**

Lionni, L. (1960). *Inch by inch*. New York: Astor-Honor. Ages 3–5; **14.**

McMillan, B. (1987). *Step by step*. New York: Lothrop. Ages 3–6; **14, 15.**

Myller, R. (1972). *How big is a foot?* New York: Atheneum. Ages 6–8; **14.**

Parkinson, K. (1986). *The enormous turnip*. Niles, IL: Whitman. Ages 4–7; **14.**

Russo, M. (1986). *The lineup book*. New York: Greenwillow. Ages 2–4; **14.**

Schlein, M. (1954). *Heavy is a hippopotamus*. New York: Scott. Ages 3–6; **14.**

Shapp, M., & Shapp, C. (1975). *Let's find out about what's light and what's heavy*. New York: Franklin Watts. Ages 6–8; **14.**

Ward, L. (1952). *The biggest bear*. Boston: Houghton-Mifflin. Ages 3–5; **14, 15.**

Zion, G. (1959). *The plant sitter*. New York: Harper & Row. Ages 3–6; **14, 15.**

Measurement: Time

Bancroft, H., & Van Gelde, R. G. (1963). *Animals in winter.* New York: Scholastic. Ages 3–6; **15, 26.**

Barrett, J. (1976). *Benjamin's 365 birthdays.* New York: Atheneum. Ages 3–6; **15, 26.**

Berenstain, S., & Berenstain, J. (1973). *The bear's almanac.* New York: Random House. Ages 3–6; **15, 26.**

Bonne, R. (1961). *I know an old lady.* New York: Scholastic. Ages 3–5; **15, 26.**

Brown, M. (1984). *Arthur's Christmas.* Boston: Little, Brown. Ages 6–8; **15, 26.**

Brown, M. W. (1947). *Goodnight moon.* New York: Harper & Row. Ages 3–6; **15.**

Carle, E. (1977). *The very hungry caterpillar.* New York: Collins & World. Ages 3–5; **15.**

Carle, E. (1993). *Today is Monday.* New York: Scholastic; **15.**

Carle, E., & Marcuse, A. E. (trans.). (1994). *La oruga muy hambrienta* [The hungry caterpillar]. New York: Philomel; **15.**

Carle, E., & Mlawer, T. (Trans.). (1996). *La mariquita malhumorada* [The grouchy ladybug]. New York: HarperCollins; **15.**

Castle, C. (1985). *The hare and the tortoise.* New York: Dial. Ages 5–8; **15, 26.**

Chalmers, M. (1988). *Easter parade.* New York: Harper. Ages 3–6; **15, 26.**

DePaola, T. (1986). *Merry Christmas, Strega Nona.* San Diego, CA: Harcourt, Brace. Ages 3–6; **15, 26.**

Duvoisin, R. (1956). *The house of four seasons.* New York: Lothrop, Lee, & Shepard. Ages 3–6; **15, 26.**

Flournoy, V. (1985). *Patchwork quilt.* New York: Dial. Ages 4–8; **15, 26.**

Hall, B. (1973). *What ever happens to baby animals?* New York: Golden Press. Ages 2–5; **13, 15.**

Hauge, C., & Hauge, M. (1974). *Gingerbread man.* New York: Golden Press. Ages 2–5; **13, 15.**

Hayes, S. (1986). *Happy Christmas Gemma.* New York: Lothrop. Ages 2–5; **15.**

Hooper, M. (1985). *Seven eggs.* New York: Harper & Row. Ages 3–5; **5, 13, 15.**

Kelleritti, H. (1985). *Henry's Fourth of July.* New York: Greenwillow. Ages 3–6; **15.**

Kraus, R. (1972). *Milton the early riser.* New York: Prentice Hall. Ages 2–5; **15.**

Krementz, J. (1986). *Zachary goes to the zoo.* New York: Random House. Ages 2–8; **15, 26.**

Leslie, S. (1977). *Seasons.* New York: Platt & Munk. Ages 2–5; **15.**

McCully, E. A. (1985). *First snow.* New York: Warner. Ages 3–5; **15.**

Miles, B. (1973). *A day of autumn.* New York: Random House. Ages 3–5; **15.**

Older, J. (2000). *Telling time.* Watertown, MA: Charlesbridge; **15, 26.**

Ormerodi, J. (1981). *Sunshine.* New York: Lothrop, Lee, & Shepard. Ages 2–6; **15.**

Pearson, S. (1988). *My favorite time of year.* New York: Harper & Row. Ages 3–7; **15.**

Porter Productions. (1975). *My tell time book.* New York: Grosset & Dunlap. Ages 5–7; **15, 26.**

Prelutsky, J. (1984). *It's snowing! It's snowing!* New York: Greenwillow. Ages 4–7; **15.**

Provensen, A., & Provensen, M. (1976). *A book of seasons.* New York: Random House. Ages 3–5; **15, 26.**

Richards, K. (2000). *It's about time, Max!* New York: Kane Press; **15.**

Robison, A. (1973). *Pamela Jane's week.* Racine, WI: Whitman Books, Western Publishing. Ages 2–5; **15.**

Rockwell, A. (1985). *First comes spring.* New York: Crowell. Ages 2–6; **15, 26.**

Rutland, J. (1976). *Time.* New York: Grosset & Dunlap. Ages 2–7; **15, 26.**

Scarry, R. (1976). *All day long.* New York: Golden Press. Ages 3–6; **15, 26.**

Schlein, M. (1955). *It's about time.* New York: Young Scott. Ages 3–7; **15, 26.**

Schwerin, D. (1984). *The tomorrow book.* New York: Pantheon. Ages 3–6; **15.**

Todd, K. (1982). *Snow.* Reading, MA: Addison-Wesley. Ages 3–8; **15, 26.**

Tudor, T. (1957). *Around the year.* New York: Henry Z. Walck. Ages 3–5; **15.**

Tudor, T. (1977). *A time to keep: The Tasha Tudor book of holidays.* New York: Rand McNally. Ages 3–6; **15.**

Vincent, G. (1984). *Merry Christmas, Ernest & Celestine.* New York: Greenwillow. Ages 4–8; **15, 26.**

Wolff, A. (1984). *A year of birds.* New York: Dodd, Mead. Ages 3–6; **15.**

Zolotow, C. (1984). *I know an old lady.* New York: Greenwillow. Ages 4–8; **15, 26.**

Graphing

Dussling, J. (2003). *Math matters, Fair is fair!* New York: Kane Press; **16, 25.**

Nagda, A. W., & Bickel, C. (2000). *Tiger math: Learning to graph from a baby tiger.* New York: Henry Holt; **16, 25.**

Practical Activities/Integration

Cohn, J. M., & Elliott, D. L. (1992). *Recycling for math.* Berkeley, CA: Educational Materials Associates. For teachers of kindergarten and up; **17.**

Lesser, C. (1999). *Spots: Counting creatures from sky to sea.* San Diego, CA: Harcourt Brace; **17.**

Shelby, A. (1990). *We keep a store.* New York: Orchard Books. All ages; **12, 22.**

Wallace, N. E. (2000). *Paperwhite.* Boston, MA: Houghton- Mifflin; **17.**

Money

Asch, F. (1976). *Good lemonade.* Ontario, Canada: Nelson, Foster, & Scott. Ages 6–8; **26.**

Brenner, B. (1963). *The five pennies.* New York: Random House. Ages 6–7; **17, 26.**

Brisson, P. (1993). *Benny's pennys.* New York: BantamDoubleday; **17, 20, 26.**

Credle, E. (1969). *Little pest Pico.* Ontario, Canada: Nelson, Foster, & Scott. Ages 6–8; **26.**

deRubertis, B. (1999). *Deena's lucky penny.* New York: Kane Press; **17, 26.**

Gill, S., & Tobola, D. (2000). *The big buck adventure.* Watertown, MA: Charlesbridge; **17, 26.**

Hoban, L. (1981). *Arthur's funny money.* New York: Harper & Row. Ages 4–7; **17, 26.**

Kirn, A. (1969). *Two pesos for Catalina.* New York: Scholastic. Ages 6–8; **17, 26.**

Martin, B., Jr. (1963). *Ten pennies for candy.* New York: Holt, Rinehart, and Winston. Ages 5–7; **17, 26.**

Rockwell, A. (1984). *Our garage sale.* New York: Greenwillow. Ages 3–5; **17.**

Slobodkina, E. (1940, 1947, 1968). *Caps for sale.* New York: Young Scott; **6, 17, 26.**

Slobodkina, E. (1940, 1947, 1968, translation 1995). *Se venden gorras.* New York: Harper Arco Iris; **6, 17, 26.**

Thornburgh, R. (1999). *Count on Pablo.* New York: Kane; **17, 20, 26.**

Food (also see Unit 22)

Brown, M. (1947). *Stone soup.* New York: Charles Scribner's. Ages 3–5; **17, 26.**

Carle, E. (1970). *Pancakes, pancakes.* New York: Knopf. Ages 3–5; **17.**

De Rubertis, B. (2006). La limonada de Lulu. New York: Kane Press. **17, 26.**

Ehlert, L. (1987). *Growing vegetable soup.* San Diego, CA: Harcourt, Brace, Jovanovich. Ages 3–6; **17, 26.**

Fleming, D. (1992). *Lunch.* New York: Henry Holt. **17.**

Hoban, R. (1964). *Bread and jam for Frances.* New York: Scholastic. Ages 3–7; **17.**

McCloskey, R. (1948). *Blueberries for Sal.* New York: Viking. Ages 3–6; **17.**

Norquist, S. (1985). *Pancake pie.* New York: Morrow. Ages 4–8; **17, 26.**

Sendak, M. (1962). *Chicken soup with rice.* New York: Harper & Row. Ages 3–5; **17.**

Sendak, M. (1970). *In the night kitchen.* New York: Harper & Row. Ages 4–6; **17, 26.**

Seymour, P. (1981). *Food.* Los Angeles: Intervisual Communications. Ages 2–5; **17.**

Thayer, J. (1961). *The blueberry pie elf.* Edinburgh, Scotland: Oliver & Boyd. Ages 4–7; **17, 26.**

Cookbooks (also see Unit 22)

Can be adapted to all ages.

See Colker listed in Unit 22.

Ault, R. (1974). *Kids are natural cooks.* Boston: Houghton-Mifflin; **22, 32, 38.**

Better Homes and Gardens new junior cookbook. (1979). Des Moines, IA: Meredith; **17, 26.**

Kementz, J. (1985). *The fun of cooking.* New York: Knopf; **17, 26.**

Pratt, D. (1998). *Hey kids, you're cookin' now: A global awareness cooking adventure.* [On-line]Available: http://www.Amazon.com, 17, 26.

Rothstein, G. L. (1994). *From soup to nuts: Multicultural cooking activities and recipes.* New York: Scholastic; **17, 26.**

Sesame Street cookbook. (1978). New York: Platt & Munk; **17, 26.**

Shepard, E. H. (1993). *Winnie-the-Pooh's teatime cookbook.* [On-line] Available: http://www. Amazon.com 17, 26.

Walker, B., & Williams, G. (1995). *Little house cookbook.* [On- line] Available: http://www. Amazon.com 17, 26.

Walt Disney's Mickey Mouse cookbook. (1975). New York: Golden Press; **17, 26.**

Warner, P. (1999). *Healthy snacks for kids (Nitty Gritty Cookbooks).* [On-line] Available: http:// www.Amazon.com 17, 26.

Williamson, S., & Williamson, Z. (1992). *Kids cook! Fabulous food for the whole family.* Charlotte, VT: Williamson Publishing Co; **17, 26.**

Symbols and Higher-Level Activities

Groups and Symbols

Aker, S. (1990). *What comes in 2's, 3's, & 4's?* New York: Aladdin; **18, 19, 20.**

Alain (Bruslein, A). (1964). *One, two, three going to sea.* New York: Scholastic. Ages 5–7; **18, 19, 20, 21.**

Anno, M. (1977). *Anno's counting book.* New York: Crowell. Ages 5–7; **18, 19, 20.**

Balet, J. B. (1959). *The five Rollatinis.* Philadelphia: Lippincott. Ages 4–7; **18, 19, 20.**

Chang, A. (2000). *Grandfather counts.* New York: Lee & Low Books; **18, 19, 20.**

Cuyler, M. (2000). *100th day worries.* New York: Simon & Schuster; **18, 19, 20.**

Duvoisin, R. (1955). *1000 Christmas beards.* New York: Knopf. Ages 3–7; **18, 19, 20.**

Duvoisin, R. (1955). *Two lonely ducks.* New York: Knopf. Ages 4–7; **18, 19, 20.**

Federico, H. (1963). *The golden happy book of numbers.* New York: Golden Press. Ages 3–7; **18, 19, 20.**

Franco, B. (1999). *The tortoise who bragged: A Chinese tale with trigrams.* Sunnyvale, CA: Stokes Publishing; **20.**

Francoise (Seignobosc, F.) (1951). *Jean-Marie counts her sheep.* New York: Charles Scribner's Sons. Ages 3–6; **18, 19, 20.**

Friskey, M. (1940). *Seven diving ducks.* New York: McKay. Ages 4–6; **18, 19, 20.**

Garne, S. T. (1992). *One white sail.* New York: Green Tiger Press. Ages 5–8; **18, 19, 20.**

Getty Museum. (n.d.). *1 to 10 and back again: A Getty Museum counting book.* Los Angeles: Author; **6, 18, 19, 20.**

Gibson, R. (1998). *I can count.* London: Usborne Playtime; **6, 18, 19, 20.**

Gollub, M. (2000). *Ten Oni drummers.* New York: Lee & Low; **18, 19, 20.**

Guettier, B. (1999). *The father who had ten children.* East Rutherford, NJ: Dial/Penguin; **18, 19, 20.**

Hoban, T. (1987). *Letters & 99 cents.* New York: Greenwillow. Ages 4–8; **18, 19, 20, 26.**

Hudson, C. W. (1987). *Afro-bets 1, 2, 3 book.* Orange, NJ: Just Us Productions; **6, 18, 19.**

Hulme, J. N. (1993). *Sea squares.* New York: Hyperion; **6, 18, 19, 20.**

Johnson, S. T. (1998). *City by numbers.* New York: Viking/Penguin; **23.**

Keats, E. J. (1971). *Over in the meadow.* New York: Scholastic. Ages 3–5; **18, 19.**

Kherdian, D., & Hogrogian, N. (1990). *The cat's midsummer jamboree.* New York: Philomel. Ages 5–8; **18, 19, 20.**

LeSeig, T. (1974). *Whacky Wednesday.* New York: Random House. Ages 5–8; **20.**

McNutt, D. (1979). *There was an old lady who lived in a 1.* Palo Alto, CA: Creative Publications. Ages 4–6; **6, 18, 19.**

Merriam, E. (1993). *12 ways to get to 11.* New York: Aladdin; **19, 20, 21.**

Miller, V. (2002). *Ten red apples: A Bartholomew Bear counting book.* Cambridge, MA: Candlewick Press; **18, 19, 20.**

Numbers: Match-up flip book. (1984). St. Paul, MN: Trend. Ages 4–8; **23, 24.**

Suen, A. (2000). *100 day.* New York: Lee & Low Books; **18, 19, 20.**

Thaler, M. (1991). *Seven little hippos.* Old Tappan, NJ: Simon & Schuster. Ages 5–8; **18, 19, 20.**

Zaslavsky, C. (1999). *Count on your fingers African style.* New York: Writers and Readers Publishing; **20.**

Mathematics Concepts and Activities for the Primary Grades

As already noted, many of the books listed are appropriate for preprimary and primary children. Many books that are read- along books for the younger children become books for individual reading for older children. A few additional titles are included here.

Aber, & Allen, J. Carrie. *Esta a la altura. (measuring).* Kane Press. **26.**

Anderson, L. (1971). *Two hundred rabbits.* New York: Penguin Books. Ages 7–9; **21.**

Barry, D. (1994). *The Rajah's rice: A mathematical folktale from India.* New York: Freeman; **26.**

Base, G. (2006). *Uno's Garden.* (K-8). Time Warner Book group. **21.**

Belov, R. (1971). *Money, money, money.* New York: Scholastic. Ages 6–8; **26.**

Boynton, S. (1987). *Hippos go berserk.* Chicago: Recycled Paper Press: **24.**

Branco, B., & Salerno, S. (2003). *Mathematickles.* Riverside, NJ: Simon & Schuster; **3.**

Bruce, S., & Billin-Frye. !Todos ganan! (division). New York: Kane Press. **21.**

Bruchac, J., & London, J. (1992). *Thirteen moons on turtle's back: A Native American year of moons.* New York: Philomel; **26.**

Calmenson, S., & Cole, J. (1998). *Get well gators!* New York: Morrow Junior Books; **21.**

Cave, K., & Riddel, C. (1992). *Out for the count: A counting adventure.* New York: Simon & Schuster. Ages 6–8; **21, 24.**

Cobb, A. (2000). *The long wait.* New York: Kane Press; **24.**

Dahl, M. (2006). *Know your number series.* (6 books). Mankato, MN: Picture Window Books. **20, 24.**

Dahl, R. (1990). *Esio trot.* New York: Viking. Ages 7–8; **26.**

Darwin, S., Grout, B., & McCoy, D. (Eds.). (1992). *How do octopi eat pizza pie?* Alexandria, VA: Time-Life for Children. Ages 6–9; **21, 25, 26.**

Darwin, S., Grout, B., & McCoy, D. (Eds.). (1992). *Look both ways.* Alexandria, VA: Time-Life for Children. Ages 6–9; 21, 25, 26.

Dennis, J. R. (1971). *Fractions are parts of things.* New York: Crowell. Ages 7–8; **23.**

Driscoll, L. (2003). *The blast off kid.* New York: Kane Press; **21.**

Eboch, C. (2007). *Science measurements: How heavy? How long? How hot?* Mankato, MN: Picture Window Books. **26.**

Friedman, A. (1994). *A cloak for the dreamer.* Jefferson City, MO: Scholastic Professional; **25.**

Friskey, M. (1963). *Mystery of the farmer's three fives.* Chicago: Children's Press. Ages 6–8; **21.**

Gibson, R. (1998). *I can count.* London: Usborne Playtime; **24.**

Gill, S., & Tobolo, D. (2000). *The big buck adventure.* Watertown, MA: Charlesbridge; **3.**

Gordon, J. R. (1991). *Six sleepy sheep.* Honesdale, PA: Boyds Mill Press. Ages 6–8, 21, 22.

Harper, D. (1998). *Telling time with big mama cat.* San Diego: Harcourt Brace; **26.**

Hawkins, C. (1984). *Take away monsters.* New York: Putnam's Sons. Ages 3–5; **20, 21.**

Heide, F. P. (1994). *The bigness contest.* Boston: Little, Brown; **26.**

Hewavisenti, L. (1991). *Measuring.* Chicago: Franklin Watts; **26.**

Hindley, J. (1994). *The wheeling and whirling-around book.* Cambridge, MA: Candlewick Press; **25.**

Hoban, T. (1998). *More, fewer, less.* New York: Greenwillow; **24.**

Hulme, J. N. (1995). *Counting by kangaroos: A multiplication concept book.* New York: Scientific American Books; **21, 22.**

Jocelyn, M. (2000). *Hannah's collections.* East Rutherford, NJ: Putnam; **22, 25.**

Johnson, J. (1995). *How big is a whale?* Skokie, IL: Rand McNally; **26.**

Johnson, J. (1995). *How fast is a cheetah?* Skokie, IL: Rand McNally; **26.**

Kopp, J. (2000). *Math on the menu: Real-life problem solving for grades 3–5.* Berkeley, CA: Lawrence Hall of Science; **3.**

Krudwig, V. L. (1998). *Cucumber soup* [Sopa de pepino]. Golden, CO: Fulcrum Publishing; **14, 26.**

Leedy, L. (1994). *Fraction action.* New York: Holiday House; **23.**

Lewis, J. P. (2002). *Arithme-tickle.* Orlando, FL: Harcourt; **3.**

Llewellyn, C. (1992). *My first book of time.* New York: Dorling Kindersley; **26.**

Maestro, B. (1993). *The story of money.* New York: Clarion Books. Ages 6–9; **26.**

Maestro, B. (1999). *The story of clocks and calendars: Marking a millennium.* New York: Lothrop, Lee, & Shepard Books; **26.**

Martin, B., Jr. (1963). *Five is five.* New York: Holt, Rinehart, & Winston. Ages 6–8; **20, 21.**

Martin, B., Jr. (1964). *Delight in number.* New York: Holt, Rinehart, & Winston. Ages 6–8; **6, 21, 26.**

Martin, B., Jr. (1964). *Four threes are twelve.* New York: Holt, Rinehart, & Winston. Ages 6–8; **20, 21.**

Martin, B., Jr. (1964). *If you can count to ten.* New York: Holt, Rinehart, & Winston. Ages 6–8; **20, 21.**

Martin, B., Jr. (1971). *Number patterns make sense.* New York: Holt, Rinehart, & Winston. Ages 8–9; **22.**

McMillan, B. (1991). *Eating fractions.* Jefferson City, MO: Scholastic Book Services. Ages 6–9; **23.**

Merriam. E. (1993). *12 ways to get to 11.* New York: Aladdin; **19, 20, 21.**

Mollel, T. M. (1999). *My rows and piles of coins.* New York: Clarion Books; **26.**

Morgan, R. (1997). *In the next three seconds.* New York: Lodestar; **26.**

Morgan, S. (1994). *The world of shapes, squares, and cubes.* New York: Thomson Learning; **25.**

Morris, A. (1995). *Shoes, shoes, shoes.* New York: Lothrop, Lee & Shepard; **26.**

Murphy, S. J. (1997). *The best vacation ever.* New York: HarperCollins; **21.**

Murphy, S. J., & Remkiewicz, F. (2003). *Less than zero.* New York: HarperCollins; **21.**

Murphy, S.J. (2005). *Same old horse.* (6+) New York: HarperCollins. **25.**

Nagda, A. W., & Bickel, C. (2000). *Tiger math: Learning to graph from a baby tiger.* New York: Henry Holt; **25.**

Nagda, A. W., & Bickel, C. (2002). *Chimp math.* New York: Henry Holt; **21.**

Napoli, D. J., & Tchen, R. (2001). *How hungry are you?* New York: Simon & Schuster; **21.**

Nesbit, E. (1989). *Melisande.* San Diego, CA: Harcourt, Brace, Jovanovich. Ages 6–8; **26.**

Neuschwander, C. (1998). *Amanda Bean's amazing dream—a mathematical story.* New York: Scholastic; **21.**

O'Donnell, E. L., & Schmidt, K. L. (1991). *The twelve days of summer.* New York: William Morrow. Ages 6–8; **21.**

Older, J. (2000). *Telling time.* Watertown, MA: Charlesbridge; **26.**

Pilegad, V. W., & Debon, N. (2003). *The warlord's puppeteers.* Gretna, LA: Pelican Publishing Co.; **22, 25.**

Pinczes, E. J. (1993). *One hundred hungry ants.* New York: Scholastic; **24.**

Richards, K. (2006). *!Ya era hora, Max!* New York: Kane Press. **26.**

Schertle, A. (1987). *Jeremy Bean's St. Patrick's Day.* New York: Morrow. Ages 5–8; **15, 26.**

Schleim, M. (1972). *Moon months and sun days.* Reading, MA: Young Scott. Ages 6–8; **15, 26.**

Schwartz, D. M. (1985). *How much is a million.* New York: Scholastic; **24.**

Schwartz, D. M. (1989). *If you made a million.* New York: Scholastic; **24.**

Schwartz, D., & Kellogg, S. (2003). *Millions to measure.* New York: HarperCollins; **24.**

Scienszka, J., & Smith, L. (1995). *Math curse.* New York: Viking; **21.**

Sharman, L. (1994). *The amazing book of shapes.* New York: Dorling Kindersley; **25.**

Tang, G. (2002). *Mathematics strategies that multiply: The best of times.* New York: Scholastic; **21.**

Tompert, A. (1990). *Grandfather Tang's story.* New York: Crown; **25.**

Viorst, J. (1978). *Alexander who used to be rich last Sunday.* New York: Alladin; **21, 26.**

Viorst, J. (1992). *Sunday morning.* New York: Atheneum. Ages 6–8; **26.**

Weston, M. (1992). *Bea's four bears.* New York: Clarion Books. Ages 6–8; **21.**

Williams, S. (2001). *Dinnertime!* San Diego, CA: Harcourt; **21.**

Yates, P. (2005). *Ten little mummies: An Egyptian counting book.* Penguin Group. **24.**

Ye, T. (1998). *Weighing the elephant.* Buffalo, NY: Annick Press; **26.**

Children's Periodicals that Include Math Concepts

Barney Magazine and *Barney Family: Ideas for Parents* (magazine). P.O. Box 7402, Red Oak, IA 51591. Phone: 515-243-4543.

Beyond Counting. A quarterly newsletter. P.O. Box 218, Barrington, RI 02806.

Esplanade, Suite 304, Toronto, Ontario, Canada M5E 1A7. Ages 3–9.

Child Life. P.O. Box 10681, Des Moines, IA 50381. Ages 7–9.

Children's Playmate Magazine. Children's Better Health Institute, 1100 Waterway Blvd., P.O. Box 567, Indianapolis, IN 46206. Ages 4–8.

Math Power. Monthly magazine (eight issues) with activities for elementary grades. Scholastic, 2931 East McCarty Street, P.O. Box 3710, Jefferson City, MO 65102-3710. Phone: 800-631-1586; E-mail: mathpower@scholastic.com.

Sesame Street. Children's Television Workshop, P.O. Box 2896, Boulder, CO 80322. Ages 3–8.

3 2 1 Contact. P.O. Box 2933, Boulder, CO 80322. Ages 6–14.

Instructional Technology Publishers Used in this Text

AIMS Educational Foundation
P.O. Box 8120
Fresno, CA 93747-8120
888-733-2467
Fax: 559-255-6396

APTE
820 Davis Street, Suite 224
Evanston, IL 60201
847-866-1872

Baby Einstein Company LLC
1233 Flower Street
Glendale, CA 91201-2417
800-793-1454

Broderbund at Riverdeep
100 Pine Street, Suite 1900
San Francisco, CA 94111
415-247-3325

DLM Early Childhood Express
at SRA/McGraw-Hill
888-772-4543

Dositey Corporation
P.O. Box 49
Arlington, MA 02476
781-210-2324

Edmark (see Riverdeep)

Hulabee Entertainment
Oberon Media, Inc.
130 West 42nd Street, Suite 850
New York, NY 10036-7804
212-221-9240

Inspiration Software, Inc.
K–12 Software
8 West Broad Street, Suite 302
Hazelton, PA 18201
866-K12-SOFT
Fax: 866-539-6077

LCSI®
MicroWorlds JR
P.O. Box 162
Highgate Springs, VT 05460
800-321-5646
Fax: 514-331-1380

LeapFrog Enterprises, Inc.
Emeryville, CA 94608
800-701-5327

LEGO®MINDSTORMS™
800-835-4386

Lego Systems, Inc.
555 Taylor Road
P.O. Box 1600
Enfield, CA 06083-1600
Consumer Services 800-422-5346

Microsoft
1 Microsoft Way
Redmond, WA 98052
800-426-9400

Mindscape
28-32 High Street
Crawley, RH 10 1BW, UK

NASA
George C. Marshall Space Flight Center
4890 University Square, Suite 3F
Huntsville, AL 35816
256-544-0340

Neufeld Learning Systems, Inc.
7 Conifer Crescent
London, Ontario, Canada NGK 2V3
866-429-6284
Fax: 519-657-3220

Pearson Learning Group
Dale Seymour Publications
Customer Service Center
145 South Mt. Zion Road
P.O. Box 2500
Lebanon, IN 46052

800-321-3106
Fax: 800-393-3156

Riverdeep-Edmark

(see Broderbund for address)

415-659-2000

ROBOLAB
National Instruments Corporation
11500 N. Mopac Expressway, Building B
Austin, TX 78730
800-433-3488

Scholastic, Inc.
Scholastic Store
557 Broadway
Soho, New York, NY 10012

School Zone Publishing Company
P.O. Box 777
Grand Haven, MI 49417

Sunburst/Tenth Planet
1550 Executive Drive
Elgin, IL 60123-9979
800-321-7511
Fax: 888-800-3028

Tivola Publishing
Viva Media LLC
580 Broadway
New York, NY 10004-1613
212-431-4420

Tom Snyder Productions
80 Coolidge Hill Road
Watertown, MA 02172-2817
617-926-6000
800-342-0236

Visions Technology
P.O. Box 70479
Eugene, OR 97401

Wright Group
McGraw-Hill
19201 120th Avenue, N.E., Suite 100 Bothell,
WA 98011-9512
800-648-2970
Fax: 800-543-7323

Glossary

A

abstract symbolic activities—activities that involve the manipulation of groups using number symbols.

accommodation—when new information that does not fit into an existing scheme is modified or a new one is made.

action symbols—symbols that tell what action to take such as (add) or (multiply).

add—to join groups.

adult guided learning—learning in which the adult provdes the problem and/or materials and provides some direction and support for the child.

algebra—at the preoperational level algebraic thinking involves discovering and creating patterns.

algorithms—step-by-step procedures for solving problems.

almost whole—when a small part of something is removed, young children will view it as almost whole.

arbitrary units—the third stage of measurement where anything can be used as a unit of measure. Extends through the latter part of the preoperational period.

assess—the first step in instruction; where are the children now in their development?

assimilation—fitting information into an existing scheme.

association—one of the criteria that can be used as a common feature to form a group (i.e., things that do a job together, come from the same place, or belong to a special person).

autonomy—the aim of education is to achieve independent thinking.

awareness—the first stage in the learning cycle as adapted to early childhood education: a broad recognition of objects, people, events, and concepts that develops from experience.

axes—the names for the left side and bottom of a line graph.

B

balanced reading—a view that reading instruction should include a balance of phonics and whole language focus.

basic facts—number combinations that add up to one through 10.

bilateral symmetry—a line can be drawn through the middle of the shape or object and divided. Each side or part would be exactly like the other half.

bookmark—allows one to mark a Web site that one may want to visit again without having to conduct another search.

browser—enables searches on the World Wide Web.

C

cardinal meaning—the last number counted is the amount in the group.

cardinality—an understanding that the last number named is the amount in a group.

centration—the characteristic of preoperational children that causes them to focus on the most obvious aspects of what they perceive.

charts and tables—ways of visually depicting data.

checklist—a list of skills that can be dated as children accomplish them.

choose objectives—after assessment, decide what the child should learn next.

circle—a continuous curved line.

class inclusion—one class may be included in another (beagles and poodles are included in the class of dogs).

class name—one of the criteria that can be used as a common feature to form a group (i.e., animals, furniture, people).

classification—putting things into logical groups.

classifying—grouping or sorting according to properties such as size, shape, color, use, and so on.

cognitive structure—the grouping of closely related facts and phenomena related to a concept.

color—one criterion that can be used to place things in a logical group.

common features—one of the criteria that can be used to form a group (i.e., all have doors, handles, points).

communicating—recording ideas, directions, and descriptions orally or in written form such as pictures, maps, graphs, or journals so others can understand what you mean. One of the science process skills.

communication—oral, written, and pictorial language are used to explain problem-solving and reasoning processes.

comparing—finding a relationship between two items or groups of items based on a specific characteristic or attribute. One of the science process skills.

comparison stage—the second stage of measurement that extends through the preoperational period. Comparisons such as weight, length, and temperature are made.

compost—a mixture of decomposing vegetable refuse, manure, and the like for fertilizing soil.

computational fluency—computing with efficiency, accuracy, and flexibility.

concept application phase—after completing investigations and problem-solving experiences, taking the knowledge and applying it to a new situation. This phase expands the concept.

concept introduction phase—initial investigation and problem-solving experiences designed by the teacher and/or children to acquire knowledge of a topic. This phase provides opportunities to accommodate information.

concepts—the building blocks of knowledge; they allow for organizing and categorizing information.

conceptual subitizing—seeing number patterns within a group such as a large number of dots (usually more than five).

concrete operations—the third period identified by Piaget during which children attain conservation.

concrete whole number operations—solving simple addition, subtraction, division, and multiplication problems using concrete materials.

concreteness—the degree to which materials approach reality.

connections—the bridge between the informal mathematics learned out of school with the formalities of school mathematics. Concrete materials can serve this function.

conservation—the ability to retain the original picture in the mind when material has been changed in its arrangement in space. The care and protection of natural resources.

construction—making a space for some particular items to fit into.

contrived problems—problems devised by the teacher for which the teacher models a problem-solving procedure.

convergent questions and directions—having only one possible answer or activity.

cube—a three-dimensional figure with sides that are six equal-sized squares.

cultural time—the time that is fixed by clocks and calendars.

curiosity—a desire to learn or know.

curves—curved but not straight paths that connect two points.

cylinder—a three-dimensional figure with circular parallel bases.

D

data collection—recording information collected during observations.

design technology—an area of engineering where math, science, and technology become integrated as children apply their knowledge of spatial relations to building and construction projects.

development—changes that take place due to growth and experience.

direction—in spatial relations, indicates "which way" (i.e., up, down, across).

disequilibrium—when children realize that they do not understand something they previously thought they understood.

distance—in spatial relations, indicates relative distance (e.g., near or far).

divergent questions and directions—provide opportunities for guessing and experimenting.

divide—to separate a whole into parts.

dividend—the amount to be broken into equal parts in the division operation.

divisor—the number of parts that a group is divided into in the division operation.

download—loading information into a personal computer from the Internet.

dramatic role-play—taking on roles in pretend play.

duration—has to do with how long an event takes (e.g., minutes, days, etc.).

E

ECE—Early Childhood Education.

ECSE—Early Childhood Special Education

ELL—English Language Learner

English units—units of measure customarily used in the United States (such as inches, feet, and yards.) affecting the development of an organism or group of organisms.

equal—when groups have the same amount.

equality—a condition indicated by the ( ) action sign.

equals—an action term represented by the sign ( ).

equilibrium—when children have enough information to satisfy their curiosity and to create a new cognitive structure.

estimation—making a sensible and reasonable guess regarding how many or how much without counting or measuring.

ethnomathematics—mathematics learned outside of school.

evaluate—to find out if an objective has been reached through observation or questioning.

exploration—the second stage in the learning cycle as adapted to early childhood education: the construction of personal meaning.

F

factors—the numbers operated on in multiplication. **Curriculum Focal Points** break the standards areas down by grade levels.

formal operations—Piaget's final period that extends from about age 11 through adulthood.

fourths—the parts of a substance or a group when the substance or group is separated or divided into four equal parts.

fractions—an area of formal mathematics that grows out of an informal understanding of parts and wholes. During the primary grades children learn about halves, fourths, and thirds. They also use terms such as *pieces, whole,* and *almost whole.*

function—one of the criteria that can be used as a common feature to form a group (i.e., all used for the same thing such as eating, playing music).

G

general time words—words such as time and age.

geoboard—a square board with headed screws or pegs sticking up at equal intervals. Rubber bands are stretched between pegs to make a variety of shapes.

goals—broad statements that indicate what you want children to know and be able to do on completion of a certain unit of curriculum.

graphs—visual representations of two or more comparisons.

graphs, object graphs—the first stage in graphing using real objects such as cube blocks. Usually two items are compared.

graphs, picture graphs—the second stage of graphing where more than two categories may be compared and a more permanent record kept such as drawing pictures.

graphs, square paper graphs—the third stage of graphing where more than two categories may be compared and a more permanent record kept such as using paper squares.

graphs, squared paper—the fourth stage of graphing where data are recorded by shading in squares on squared paper.

grouping—the process of placing two or more smaller groups into a larger group.

H

half—a fraction term that can be used informally with young children. It indicates the division of a whole into two parts that are the same.

halves—the parts of a substance or a group when the substance or group is separated or divided into two equal parts.

heuristics—questions that children generate when solving problems.

hierarchical classification—there are classes within classes with a series developing larger and larger classes.

holistic evaluations—evaluation in which a rubric is used to place portfolios in groups such as strong, average, and weak.

hypotheses—devising a statement, based on observations, that can be tested by experiment. One of the science process skills.

I

IFSP—Individualized Family Service Plan

IEP—Individualized Educational Plan

informal learning—learning experiences initiated by the adult as children engage in their everyday natural activities.

informal measurement—measurement done by comparison or using nonstandard units (i.e., a shoe, a paper clip, a block).

inquiry—the third stage in the learning cycle. As adapted to early childhood education: learners compare their findings and is a major focus of science process skill.

integrated curriculum—curriculum that integrates math, science, social studies, language arts, music and movement, and visual arts, usually through projects and/or thematic units.

Internet—the worldwide computer connection.

L

learning cycle—phases of learning used for curriculum development and as teaching strategies: exploration, concept development, concept application.

Lego®/Logo—a combination of Lego® bricks and Logo programming that children can use to explore physics, technology, and mathematics.

length—in measurement denotes how long, wide, or deep.

less than ( )—a group or quantity comparison term and symbol.

lesson plan—a planned, sequenced series of steps to be implemented in order to accomplish a goal or objective. An educational activity plan.

line graphs—graphs made on squared paper grids connecting data points.

lines—connections between two points.

logical grouping—groups whose members have a logical connection (such as number, color, shape, or class).

logico-mathematical knowledge—knowledge that enables us to organize and make sense out of the world, such as classification and number concepts.

LOGO—a computer language that can be applied to many geometric experiences.

M

manipulative materials—materials that have parts and pieces that can be picked up and moved by the child in the process of problem solving.

material—one criterion that can be used to place items in a logical group (i.e., wood, plastic, glass).

mathematics learning disorder (MLD)—about 6% of school-age children cannot remember basic facts and/or cannot carry out basic procedures.

measurement—assigning a number to things so they can be compared on the same attributes.

measuring—quantitative descriptions made by an observer either directly through observation or indirectly with a unit of measure. One of the science process skills.

metric units—measurement units based on groups of 10.

more than ( )—a group or quantity comparison term and symbol.

multiple classification—requires classifying according to more than one criterion.

multiple intelligences—areas of strength identified by Howard Gardner.

N

naturalistic learning—learning that occurs as children go about their daily activities.

nonroutine problems—problems that involve more than one step and do not follow a predictable pattern.

notation—number and operations symbols.

number—one of the criteria that can be used to form a group (i.e., pairs or other groups of the same amount).

number sense—the concept or understanding of number.

number sentences—sentences that symbolize an operation such 3 4 7 or 8 6.

numerals—number symbols (i.e., 1, 2, 3, etc.)

O

object permanence—the realization that objects exist even when they are out of sight.

object recognition—the ability to identify objects using previously acquired information such as color, shape, and size.

objectives—state how you plan to achieve your goals.

observing—using the senses to gather information about objects and events. One of the science process skills.

one-to-one correspondence—the understanding that one group has as many members as another.

one more than—a concept basic to sequencing or ordering groups of amounts each one more than the other.

ordering—putting items in a logical sequence.

organization/pattern—arrangement of parts in a space so that they all fit.

P

parts—things have parts (e.g., legs, doors, handles) and groups have parts (e.g., each child gets two cookies).

pattern—one criterion that can be used to place items in a logical group (i.e., stripes, dots, plaid).

patterning—making or discovering auditory, visual, and motor regularities.

perceptual subitizing—being able to state how many are in a group without counting or grouping.

performance-based assessment—giving one or more students a task to do, which will indicate the student level of understanding of science concepts and thinking skills.

personal experience—the view of time held by young children (e.g., "When I was a baby. . .").

phonics—an approach to beginning reading that focuses on the elements of printed text such as letters and sounds.

pieces—a term used by young children to indicate their beginning knowledge of fractional parts.

place value—pertains to an understanding that the same numeral represents different amounts, depending on its position.

plan experiences—decide which strategies should be used to enable the child to accomplish instructional objectives.

play—the major medium through which children learn.

play stage—the first stage of measurement during which children imitate adults and/or older children using measurement tools such as rulers or measuring cups. This stage extends into the preoperational period.

points—introduced as small dots and later applied to making line graphs.

portfolio—a purposeful collection of student work.

position—in spatial relations, an indication of "where" (i.e., on, off, under, over).

preconcepts—incomplete concepts that develop before true concepts.

preoperational period—the second Piagetian developmental period that extends from about age two to age seven.

preprimary—the period before children enter first grade.

primary—grades one through three.

principles—basic rules that guide high-quality mathematics education.

problem solving—a major mathematics process standard.

process skills—label for fundamental mathematics concepts such as classifying, comparing, and measuring when applied to science.

product—the result of a multiplication operation.

Q

quantities above ten—when children understand the base quantity of ten they can move on to working with larger quantities.

quantity comparison—considering two groups of objects and deciding if they have the same amount or if one group has more.

quotient—the result of the division operation.

R

rational counting—attaching a number name to each object counted.

reasoning—the ability that enables children to draw logical conclusions, apply logical classification skills, justify problem solutions, and make sense out of mathematics and science.

record folder—a collection of anecdotal records and checklists.

rectangular prism—a three-dimensional figure with identical rectangular bases and four rectangular sides.

regrouping—moving groups from one column of numbers to another.

relational symbols—indicate that quantities are related, such as (equal), (greater than), and (less than).

relational time words—words such as soon, yesterday, early, etc.

remainder—in division the result may not come out with equal groups; there may be a remainder.

renaming—after a group has been moved using regrouping, the new number is renamed.

representation—demonstrating thought and understanding through oral and written language, physical gestures, drawings, and invented and conventional symbols.

representative thought—the ability to think through the solution to a problem before acting.

reversibility—when the arrangement of material is changed, the mind can reverse the process of change and visualize the original arrangement.

rote counting—reciting the names of the numerals in order from memory.

routine problems—problems that follow a predictable pattern.

rubrics—evaluation guides that show students' criteria for self-assessment.

S

scaffolding—assistance in learning from someone who is more mature.

select materials—decide which materials should be used in order to carry out an instructional plan.

self-correcting materials—materials that the child can use independently by trial and error to solve a problem with little or no adult assistance.

self-regulation—active mental process of forming concepts.

senses—sight, touch, smell, hearing, and taste.

sensorimotor period—first cognitive developmental period identified by Piaget. Extends from birth to about age two.

sequence—time as related to the order of events.

seriation—putting items in a logical sequence.

shape—one criterion that can be used to place items in a logical group (i.e., square, circular, triangular) and can be reproduced with geoboards or stencils.

signs—the tools of the mind, such as language, that we use for thinking.

size—a measurement term referring to volume, height, weight, and/or length.

skip counting—counting using quantities and number symbols other than ones such as "2-4-6-8 . . ." or "5-10-15 . . ."

social activity—time as viewed from the sequence of routine daily activities.

social knowledge—the knowledge created by people, such as rules of conduct.

sorting—the process of separating a larger group into two or more smaller groups.

spatial relations—a critical element in geometry.

special days time words—time as indicated by holidays and other special days.

specific duration time words—clock (minutes, hours) and calendar (days, weeks) words.

specific time words—words which refer to a specific time such as morning and night.

sphere—a three-dimensional circular figure.

square—a shape with four equal sides and four points or corners.

standard units—units of measurement that are standardized such as inches, centimeters, pounds, liters, and miles that everyone agrees on. Children begin to understand the need for standard units during the concrete operational period.

standards—provide guidance as to what children should know and be able to do at different ages and stages.

STEM—a current movement to encourage instuction in Science,Technology, Engineering, and Math.

subitizing—knowing instantly how many is in a group without counting.

subset—a smaller group within a larger group.

subtract—separate a group into two smaller groups.

sum—when groups are combined the result is referred to as the sum.

surf—a term referring to exploring the Internet.

symbolic behaviors—behaviors that appear during representational play when children use materials to represent something else, such as sand for food.

symbolic level—the stage at which children have connected sets and symbols and can record the solutions to concrete problems using number symbols.

symmetry—correspondence of two sides of a figure on each side of a line.

T

teach—do planned experiences with children.

teachable moment—a time when adults recognize that a child has selected to do an activity that provides a time to insert instruction.

temperature—in measurement, denotes how hot or cold.

texture—one of the criteria that can be used as a common feature to form a group (i.e., rough, smooth, hard, soft).

thematic units and projects—instructional methods that provide for the integration of math, science, and other content areas.

thirds—the parts of a substance or a group when the substance or group is separated or divided into three equal parts.

time as cultural time—the time that is fixed by clocks and calendars.

time as personal experience—young children have their own past, present, and future, such as "When I was a baby . . ."

time as social activity—the importance of daily routines in sequence is critical for young children.

time duration—how long an event takes.

time sequence—the order of events, such as daily routines.

time words—time-related vocabulary that is acquired gradually.

time words, general—words such as time and age.

time words, relational—words such as soon, tomorrow, now, etc.

time words, special days—Christmas, Kwanza, Ramadan, Passover, holiday, birthday, etc.

time words, specific—words such as parts of the day like morning and afternoon.

time words, specific duration—clock, watch, calendar words.

times—the action term for multiplication.

tortoise—a turtle that lives on land.

total—the resulting group amount when groups are combined.

trading—what happens when numbers are regrouped.

triangle—a shape with three straight sides and three points.

triangular prism—a three-dimensional figure with identical triangular bases and three rectangular sides.

turtle—the name for the cursor when using LOGO language to solve geometry problems.

U

understanding—the basic premise of the NCTM principles and standards that stands in opposition to just memorizing.

unit—measurements must be made with the same unit to be accurate and comparable.

URL—an Internet address.

utilization—the fourth stage in the learning cycle as adapted to early childhood education: learners can apply and use their understandings in new settings and situations.

V

volume—in measurement, denotes how much.

W

weather—the general condition of the atmosphere at a given time in regard to temperature, moisture, cloudiness, and so on.

webbing—strategy used to depict a variety of possible concepts and curricular experiences.

weight—in measurement, denotes how heavy.

whole language—an approach to beginning reading that focuses on developing reading naturally by beginning with good literature.

whole number operations—addition, subtraction, multiplication, and division.

wholes—all of some object or a group of objects.

World Wide Web (WWW)—contains Internet sites that enable students and teachers to connect with others around the world and to seek out a multitude of information.

Z

zone of proximal development (ZPD)—the area between where the child is now operating independently and where the child might be able to operate mentally with the assistance of an adult or a more mature peer.

Index